Charles Herbert Grinling

The History of the Great Northern Railway

Charles Herbert Grinling

The History of the Great Northern Railway

ISBN/EAN: 9783742810755

Manufactured in Europe, USA, Canada, Australia, Japa

Cover: Foto ©ninafisch / pixelio.de

Manufactured and distributed by brebook publishing software (www.brebook.com)

Charles Herbert Grinling

The History of the Great Northern Railway

THE HISTORY

OF

GREAT NORTHERN

RAILWAY

1845–1895

BY

CHARLES H. GRINLING

METHUEN & CO.
36, ESSEX STREET, W.C.
LONDON
1898

PREFACE

IN writing this book my prime object has been to give a complete account of the origin and development of the Great Northern Railway Company from its inception to the year 1895, a period, roughly speaking, of fifty years. In so doing, however, I have necessarily had to give much information with regard to other railways of Northern England and Scotland, and so I am not afraid to claim that the book forms a fifty years' record of the fortunes of all the great trunk systems connecting London and the North—a record hardly any part of which has previously been presented to the public. The style of presentation I have adopted will, I hope, at once satisfy by its accuracy and thoroughness readers already acquainted with the subject-matter, and attract "the general reader" by its continuous thread of narrative and strong dramatic interest.

As regards the facts given, I have spared no pains to insure correctness and comprehensiveness. Without seeking access to the private archives of the Great Northern Company, and so placing myself under obligations which could have been met only by a sacrifice of my impartiality, I have, nevertheless, been able to obtain information of the most intimate and authentic character with respect to all the chief events with which my History deals. Moreover, I have had most valuable assistance, which I acknowledge with great gratitude, from a number of the men mentioned most prominently in my narrative. To Lord Grimthorpe, Lord Colville of Culross, K.T., Sir Henry Oakley, Mr. Richard Johnson, and Mr. Archibald Sturrock—the five men now living whose connection with the

Great Northern undertaking has been longest and most valuable—I beg most respectfully to tender my special thanks, and I also take this opportunity of making grateful acknowledgment for the help rendered me by Mr. B. S. Brundell (whose very long connection with the Great Northern Railway has been terminated by death since I commenced this work), Mr. James Alexander, Mr. William Latta, Mr. Henry Walker, and my brother, Mr. W. J. Grinling. The numerous other officials of the Great Northern Company who have afforded me assistance will not, I hope, think that my appreciation of their kindnesses is less because I do not mention them by name.

It is very important that it should be clearly understood, however, that this work is not "official" in any sense of the word. For every fact given, and for every opinion expressed, I, the author, am alone responsible.

Finally, I dedicate what may be worthy in the work to the memory of my dear father, Mr. William Grinling, who served the Great Northern Company faithfully for over forty years.

CHARLES H. GRINLING.

LONDON.

CONTENTS

CHAPTER I.
IN THE REIGN OF KING HUDSON—ANCESTRY AND BIRTH OF THE HERO (1833-1844) 1

CHAPTER II.
HOW "FIVE KINGS" ISSUED AN EDICT TO "STRANGLE THE MONSTER INFANT AT ITS BIRTH" (1844-1845) 20

CHAPTER III.
WHO IS TO REAR THE INFANT?—THE MOTHERS BEFORE SOLOMON (1845) 33

CHAPTER IV.
THE INFANT IS CHRISTENED AND GIVEN LEAVE TO GROW (1845-1846) . 46

CHAPTER V.
THE HERO GROWS UP AMID STRAITENED CIRCUMSTANCES AND GETS TO WORK IN THE COUNTRY IN A VERY SMALL WAY (1846-48) . . 58

CHAPTER VI.
THE HERO COMES TO LONDON—END OF THE REIGN OF KING HUDSON (1848-1850) 74

CHAPTER VII.
THE FIGHT WITH "THE EUSTON SQUARE CONFEDERACY"—THE BATTLE OF THE EXHIBITION YEAR (1850-1851) 92

CHAPTER VIII.
"FINIS CORONAT OPUS" (1852) 113

CHAPTER IX.
THE SOUTH YORKSHIRE SPLIT—THE BREAKING-DOWN OF THE BARRIERS (1853-1855) 129

CHAPTER X.
"THE BATTLE OF THE RAILWAYS"—BREAK-UP OF THE "CONFEDERACY" (1855-1858) 151

CHAPTER XI.
AN ISOLATED INCIDENT:—THE FRAUDS OF LEOPOLD REDPATH (1856-1858) 166

CONTENTS

CHAPTER XII.
THE MIDLAND AGGRESSION (1858-1863) . . . **179**

CHAPTER XIII.
THE GREAT EASTERN ATTACK AND OTHER MATTERS (1863-1865) . . **198**

CHAPTER XIV.
GENERAL PROGRESS, INTERRUPTED BY A STARTLING ACCIDENT (1866-1867) **220**

CHAPTER XV.
THE "COAL WAR" AND THE C.O.A.L. LINE (1868-1871) . **236**

CHAPTER XVI.
THE INVASION OF THE MIDLANDS (1871-1872) . . **256**

CHAPTER XVII.
THE CAMPAIGN OF 1873, INCLUDING A PARLIAMENTARY FIGHT OF THIRTY DAYS (1872-1873) **276**

CHAPTER XVIII.
THE ZENITH OF PROSPERITY—THE SUBURBAN INCREMENT—THE ABBOTTS RIPTON ACCIDENT (1873-1876) **293**

CHAPTER XIX.
HARD TIMES—THE ARLESEY SIDING ACCIDENT—THE CHESHIRE LINES "LANE"—THE "GREAT EASTERN QUESTION" SETTLED AT LAST (1876-1878) **311**

CHAPTER XX.
GOING SLOW—THE FIFTY YEARS AGREEMENT AGAIN—THE SUBURBAN INCUBUS (1878-1881) **333**

CHAPTER XXI.
GENERAL PROGRESS (1881-1885) . . . **353**

CHAPTER XXII.
THE SUBURBAN INCUBUS STILL—THE RAILWAY RATES BILLS—THE EASTERN AND MIDLANDS—THE RACE TO EDINBURGH (1886-1888) . **373**

CHAPTER XXIII.
A GATHERING STORM—TWO BRIDGE-BUILDING ACHIEVEMENTS—THE CONVERSION OF STOCK (1889-1890) **389**

CHAPTER XXIV.
THE FIFTH LINE TO LONDON—THE SUBURBAN INCUBUS ONCE MORE—THE GREAT NORTHERN AND MIDLAND JOINT SYSTEM—THE RACE TO ABERDEEN (1890-1895) **403**

INDEX . . . **425**

THE HISTORY
OF THE
GREAT NORTHERN RAILWAY

CHAPTER I.

IN THE REIGN OF KING HUDSON—ANCESTRY AND BIRTH
OF THE HERO—1833-1844

THE Stockton and Darlington Railway, the pioneer of the public railways of the world, was opened, as every schoolboy should know, on 27 September, 1825, and about this same date, when the first short epidemic of "railway fever" prevailed, numerous surveys were made for similar undertakings in other parts of England. Amongst these was one made by the Messrs. Rennie for a line northwards from London, which they proposed should follow the valley of the Lea nearly as far as Ware, and thence pass by the valleys of the Rib and Quin and "the towns" of Braughing and Barkway to Cambridge. Here their original survey stopped, but in 1827 they extended it in a direct line northwards through Lincoln to York. By this time, however, the railway fever had quite subsided, having resulted in the incorporation of one important public company only—the Liverpool and Manchester, and it was not until the successful opening in September, 1830, of this, the first line constructed in England for the conveyance of passengers, that kindred projects again began to find favour. Then a proposal for a London and Birmingham Railway, also first made in 1825, was revived in the latter town, and, the services of George Stephenson and his son having been secured as engineers, a Bill for it was successfully passed through the House of Commons in the session of 1832. Being then thrown out in the Lords, it was revived in 1833, together with one for a Grand Junction Railway, which the Stephensons and Joseph Locke had in the meantime surveyed; and, these both passing into law in that year, a chain of railway communication became authorized from London, *via* Birmingham, to Manchester and Liverpool.

B

In 1833 also the London and Greenwich Railway was authorized, and schemes were set on foot for London and Essex, London and Dover, Grand Southern, London and Southampton, Great Western, and Grand Northern lines. The last-named was projected and surveyed by Mr. Nicholas Wilcox Cundy, and comprised a main line from London to York, *via* Bishop Stortford, Cambridge, Lincoln, Gainsborough and Selby, and branches to Norwich, Nottingham, Sheffield, Leeds, and Hull, the total length of the main line being 190 miles.

In York meanwhile a "Railway Committee" of the Corporation had been deliberating for twelve months already upon various plans for constructing a line from their city, and a young linen-draper, George Hudson by name, had produced considerable sensation by putting down his name for the greater part of the shares in a "York and West Riding" project. This he had favoured in preference to an alternative proposal for making a line from York to Doncaster, the advantages of which had been presented to the Committee by a deputation from the latter town consisting of Messrs. Edmund Denison and Robert Baxter.

In the neighbourhood of York a line from Leeds to Selby was already approaching completion, and in the Midlands, where the Leicester and Swannington coal line had been open since July, 1832, a project was making good progress for the construction of a Midland Counties Railway, "to connect the towns of Leicester, Nottingham, and Derby with each other and with London." Indeed, the Parliamentary notices for this were actually given in the autumn of 1833, but subsequently the Bill had to be withdrawn for lack of financial support. In the summer of 1834, however, the London and Southampton Railway, seventy-six miles in length, and several other smaller undertakings, were authorized, and this encouraged the promotion of a number of new schemes, several of which proposed to fill the blank still presented by the railway map on the eastern side of England.

In September, 1834, the prospectus was issued of the "Eastern Counties Railway—from London *via* Colchester to Norwich and Yarmouth," and about the same time Mr. James Walker (one of the engineers, it may be remembered, who had championed fixed engines against Stephenson's locomotives at the famous Rainhill trials, and who had since constructed the Leeds and Selby line) was employed by a party of gentlemen, headed by Mr. Handley, M.P. for Lincolnshire, to survey a Northern and Eastern Railway from London to York and Norwich. Early in 1835, too, Mr. Joseph Gibbs, a clever and sanguine engineer, who had made a considerable reputation in drainage works, projected a line to start from Whitechapel, London, and to run *via* Dunmow, Cambridge, Sleaford, and Lincoln to York, and this was submitted in the summer of 1835 to a Committee formed in London, to which the title of "Great Northern Railway Company" was provisionally given.

The second epidemic of railway fever was now raging, and all parts of the country were scenes of activity in railway projection. The London and Birmingham directors had made up their minds that it was desirable to extend the communication by their line north-eastwards as well as north-westwards, and so, on their behalf and that of local parties in the Midlands and in Yorkshire, George Stephenson was surveying lines from Birmingham to Derby, and Derby to Leeds, the former to be in connection not only with the London and Birmingham, but also with a projected line from Birmingham to Gloucester. At the same time, too, Mr. Vignoles was making a new survey for the Midland Counties line, which was also to connect with the London and Birmingham, viz., at Rugby; while the Railway Committee at York, with George Hudson as its leading spirit, having abandoned their projected West Riding line because of the difficult character of the country, were debating whether they should join with the Northern and Eastern or the Great Northern parties in promoting a direct line through the flats of Lincolnshire to the Metropolis.

It chanced, however, that Hudson paid a visit to Whitby during this summer of 1835, and there secured an introduction to George Stephenson, who happened also to be visiting that place. Then the York draper learnt something of the surveys which the engineer had already in hand for carrying a chain of railways from London to Leeds, and on his return to his native town he advised his Committee that before they pledged themselves either to Gibbs' or Walker's plans, the advice of Stephenson should be called in. The result was that they decided, instead of joining in the promotion of a new direct railway to London, to content themselves with the much smaller, and therefore much more easily practicable, scheme of a link line from York to connect with the Derby and Leeds at Normanton, and, as the latter had now been christened the North Midland Railway, the new project of the York Committee received the appropriate title of the York and North Midland. At the same time a Great North of England Railway Company was formed to carry on the chain of communication from York to Newcastle.

Bills for all the lines above mentioned came before Parliament in the session of 1836, when they all met with some measure of success, except that of Mr. Gibbs. He was a really able engineer, and his "report to the York and Norwich Committee of the Great Northern Railway Company," which is still extant, shows that he conceived his project in an enlightened and far-sighted spirit. But full of its national importance, he took no pains to conciliate private interests, and he had also to meet the hostility of the strong party who were supporting the rival Northern and Eastern scheme. The result was that his "Great Northern Railway Bill," being opposed by landowners on second reading in the House of Commons, was then summarily rejected by ninety-nine votes to eighty-five.

The Northern and Eastern Bill, on the other hand, was referred, without opposition, to a Committee, and before this Mr. Gibbs also was allowed to appear to explain the merits of his alternative project; but both parties found themselves strongly opposed by the London and Birmingham and Midland interests, the representatives of which claimed that their united undertakings would provide a route amply convenient for the through passenger to York and the North. This view, backed as it was by the great authority of George Stephenson, prevailed, with the result that the Midland Counties, Birmingham and Derby, North Midland and York, and North Midland Bills all passed; while the Northern and Eastern was cut down into a line from London to Cambridge only. The Eastern Counties Bill having no pretensions to provide a trunk line to the North, but proposing simply to connect London with Colchester, Norwich, Yarmouth, and the adjacent country, was allowed to pass in its complete form as promoted.

In 1837 the mania for railway construction gave way to panic—in modern slang, a "slump" followed the "boom"—and even the companies which had obtained powers found it hard to get their undertakings realized. In 1838, however, the London and Birmingham line was opened, and in the following year, by way of the Grand Junction and North Union, through communication north-westwards from the Metropolis was established as far as Preston; so that one night in September of that year Thomas and Jane Welsh Carlyle, returning home from Scotsbrig, were able to take a train at Preston, and, after "an excellent breakfast with deliberation to eat it" at Birmingham, were "safe landed at Euston Square soon after one o'clock." In the same year, too, the Midland and Counties, Birmingham and Derby, and York and North Midland lines were all opened, and the North Midland, though a line through very difficult country, was completed by the Stephensons in the spring of 1840. So, on the 1st of July in that year, Hudson, who in the meantime had become Lord Mayor of York, had the satisfaction to see the first passengers leave York Station for a through journey by rail to London, their route being by Normanton, Derby, and Rugby, at each of which places a change of train had to be made, and the total distance being 219 miles.

Meanwhile the question how best to carry the chain of communication further northwards into Scotland was being hotly discussed, and the terms "East Coast," "West Coast," and "Inland" routes had already become familiar. The Great North of England Railway Company had been compelled by financial difficulties to cut down its undertaking to a line from York to join the Stockton and Darlington at Croft Bridge, but George Hudson hoped that this, with the York and North Midland, would eventually become the trunk line from London to Newcastle and Edinburgh.

As things were, however, the Scotch traffic was leaving the York road to go by Birmingham to Preston, and thence by boat or coach *viâ* Kendal; moreover, a line was nearly completed from Preston to Lancaster, and several routes had been surveyed for carrying this on through Carlisle to Glasgow and Edinburgh. Railway projection elsewhere was now entirely at a standstill, but so keen was the interest in this subject of "communication with Scotland" that in August, 1839, a special Commission of the Board of Trade was appointed to consider it. The Commissioners were instructed not only to compare the merits of the routes north of York and Lancaster, but to include in their report "the relative merits of the two lines from London to York by Derby and Rotherham and by Cambridge and Lincoln." Thus the question of a "Great Northern Railway" once more came to the front.

Mr. James Walker had now ceased to be the Northern and Eastern engineer, but in reply to an invitation from the Commissioners he sent in plans showing the extension he had formerly proposed of that line northwards from Bishop Stortford through Peterborough and Lincoln to York. Mr. Gibbs, who had meantime been busy constructing the London and Croydon Line, also received an invitation to send plans, and this time he abandoned his "Dunmow route" and adopted what the Commissioners described as "a modification of the Barkway route," originally proposed by Rennie, as far as Cambridge, and thence by Sleaford and Lincoln to York as before. The total distance by Gibbs' route was 185 miles; by Walker's, 193 miles.

The Commissioners, however, did not find it necessary to weigh the respective merits of these two routes very carefully, because they came to the conclusion that neither of them should as yet be made.

"If this subject were now brought forward for the first time," they said in their report (which was not published till March, 1841), "and the relative merits of the existing line by Derby and Rotherham were to be weighed against the proposed route by Cambridge and Lincoln, we should have no hesitation after a full consideration of the properties of both in awarding the preference to the latter as a main trunk line; but as the former has been completed and has at this time by no means an overwhelming traffic, it does not appear to us it would be expedient to construct at the cost of probably more than four millions another line passing by Cambridge and Lincoln merely for the sake of shortening the distance for the through passenger to York and to the north of that city. Looking, however, to the highly productive district to the eastward of the Derby and Rotherham line wholly unprovided with railways, and the unusually favourable character of the country for their construction, we are of opinion that the period is not far distant when a new line will be formed, passing near Cambridge, Peterborough, and Lincoln, and that this line will in all probability be combined of parts selected from the different projects which have at various times been brought forward."

On the respective merits of the East Coast and West Coast routes between the north of England and Scotland the report of the Commissioners was of an equally non-committal character. In the belief that at present one line of railway only could be formed between the two countries they felt "bound to give the preference to that from Carlisle by Lockerbie, Beattock, Lanark, and Hamilton to Glasgow, with a branch from Thankerton, or Symington, to Edinburgh," but they noted so many points in favour of the rival East Coast route through Darlington, Newcastle, and Berwick, that George Hudson was not in the least afraid to refer to their report when (on 30 April, 1841) he presided over a meeting of representatives of six neighbouring railway companies, which he had summoned at Newcastle to consider what steps could be taken to carry on the Great North of England line. Thanks to the enterprise of Sir Hesketh Fleetwood in developing the port which bears his name, "West Coast" passengers could now leave Euston at daybreak, and, travelling by railway *viâ* Birmingham and Preston and by "a noble steamer" from Fleetwood to Ardrossan, could reach Glasgow by the Ayr railway, and even Edinburgh by coach, in time for breakfast the next morning. So the necessity for improving the rival "East Coast Route" had become urgent, unless it was to be deprived of the most profitable part of the through traffic with Scotland. The difficulty was, however, that except Hudson and the Stephensons, who were keenly interested in making a line to Edinburgh by Newcastle and Berwick, and Joseph Locke, whose mind was set on making the railway he had already more than once surveyed from Carlisle northwards, there were very few people at this time who really thought it worth while to establish through railway communication with Scotland at all. "What more can any reasonable man want?" asked the *Railway Times*, after pointing out the wonders of the new Fleetwood service. "If he were to travel the whole way by rail at the rate of twenty miles an hour, he could but arrive two or three hours earlier, before breakfast was ready or anyone up to bid him welcome."

When even the organ of the railway interest could talk in this strain, it will be inferred that in 1841 zeal for railway extension had sunk to a very low ebb. In the session of 1840 not a single railway Bill had been passed, and in 1841 one only, and that for a short branch line; and the general impression was that when the lines then in course of construction were completed the railway system of the country would

GREAT NORTH OF ENGLAND RAILWAY TIME TABLE.

The hours of Arrival and Departure are published monthly in Bradshaw's Railway Time Tables, No. 27 Brown-street, Manchester, price 6d

STATIONS	SOUTH TRAINS. (DARLINGTON TO YORK.)						STATIONS	NORTH TRAINS. (TIME TO DARLINGTON.)						
	1	2	3	4	5	6		1	2	3	4	5	6	7	8
Coaches leave NEWCASTLE...	....	5·15	7·15	10·45	1·30	10·45	Trains leave LONDON	9·0 a.m.	....	....	....	6·0	11·15	9·0
Trains leave DARLINGTON	6·15	....	....	....	11·30	11·30	BIRMINGHAM....	12·40	....	....	6·45	10·15	10	12·40
Croft	6·15	9·30	12·45	3·30	6·0	3·30	LEICESTER	1·24	....	....	7·45	10·35	1·45	1·24
Cowton	6·30	9·36	12·51	3·40	6·6	3·40	NOTTINGHAM ...	....	....	....	7·30	10·50	2·30	....
NORTHALLERTON.	6·48	9·51	1·0	3·52	6·21	3·52	DERBY	3·19	....	....	9·30	12·45	3·30	3·19
TRIMM	7·8	10·11	1·20	4·10	6·41	4·10	SHEFFIELD......	....	6·0	....	10·45	1·50	4·30	....
ALNE, &c	7·36	10·33	1·48	4·30	7·3	4·30	NORMANTON	5·44	7·26	....	12·20	3·14	6·0	5·44
Shipton	7·51	11·3	2·18	4·58	7·33	4·58	LEEDS..........	....	7·25	9·30	1·35	3·30	....	....
Arrive at YORK....	8·15	11·20	2·35	....	7·60	....	MANCHESTER ...	....	....	7·0	11·30	....	....	....
HULL	12·15	11·45	3·0	5·37	8·15	5·37	SOWERBY BRIDGE	....	6·20	....	....	....	....	....
MANCHESTER...	1·0	....	6·50	10·5	....	....	HULL	....	6·0	8·9	....	2·0	....	....
LEEDS..........	1·0	4·40	....	10·0	....	10·0	YORK	5·0	7·20	9·30	11·30	3·30	5·0	8·15	7·20
NORMANTON ...	0·55	2·30	5·0	8·30	....	8·30	Shipton	5·17	....	9·45	11·45	3·45	5·12	....
ECKINGTON	....	1·25	4·46	7·20	....	7·29	ALNE, &c	5·36	7·46	10·2	12·2	4·2	5·36	8·41	7·46
SHEFFIELD	....	2·55	....	....	....	....	TRIMM	6·10	8·14	10·33	12·33	4·33	5·54	9·9	8·14
DERBY	11·15	2·45	6·30	8·45	....	8·45	NORTHALLERTON	6·38	8·35	10·50	12·50	4·56	6·15	9·30	8·35
NOTTINGHAM ...	12·45	4·15	8·30	10·0	....	10·0	Cowton	7·0	8·54	11·17	1·17	5·17	6·34	9·49	8·54
LEICESTER.....	2·15	5·15	9·35	....	....	....	Croft	7·13	....	11·20	1·20	5·20	6·45	....	....
BIRMINGHAM ..	2·40	6·0	10·10	12·0	....	12·0	DARLINGTON.	7·30	9·20	11·43	1·45	5·45	7·0	10·15	9·20
LONDON . .	4·30	6·45	....	1·0	....	1·0	Trains by coach NEWCASTLE	....	1·20	3·30	5·30	9·30	11·0	....	1·20
	7·45	11·15	....	5·0	....	5·0									

First and Second Class Carriages are attached to all Trains; and Third Class Carriages to Nos. 1, 3, and 5, North Trains, and to Nos. 2 and 5, South Trains.
Time is allowed at York for the business of the Station.

Corrected to JULY 1st, 1841.
No Table of a previous date can be depended on.

not only be finished, but would even be in excess of profitable operation. Special objection was taken to the two parallel west and east lines, the Manchester and Leeds, and the Manchester and Sheffield, which had been sanctioned like nearly all the other larger schemes during the "mania" of 1836-7, and as the former was now open to a junction with the North Midland and York and North Midland at Normanton, many people were disposed to doubt whether it was worth while to finish the latter at all. Meanwhile, with the opening of the Great North of England from York to Croft Bridge, a considerable improvement was made in the communication north and south, and from 1 July, 1841, a time-table was published, of which we reproduce a part in facsimile, which showed a through communication between

London and Newcastle in seventeen hours, the route being by rail throughout from Euston Square to Darlington and thence northwards by coach.

Even this, however, was far from satisfying George Hudson, and in September, 1841, he called another conference of neighbouring railway directors at Newcastle, with the result that in the following month an arrangement was come to, by which six companies undertook to lease the Great North of England at a 6 per cent. guarantee, and to find the money for carrying the line northwards through Durham to Gateshead. A Bill for this was accordingly deposited under the title of the "Darlington and Newcastle Junction Railway" in November, 1841, and Hudson became chairman of the new company, when it was incorporated on the 18th of June of the following year. The terminus was to be at Gateshead, because a bridge over the Tyne was considered too onerous an undertaking at present. Indeed, it was not thought likely that either this or the completion of the West Coast route, for which Joseph Locke was now making a new survey, would ever be carried out, except by Government aid.

Not only were very few new companies formed at this time, but the existing ones were generally afraid or unable to make tributary branches. Thus the North Midland Company was urged by Robert Stephenson in 1842 to make a short line from Swinton or Wath to serve the South Yorkshire coal-field, and give a railway communication to Barnsley and Doncaster, but the directors could not make up their minds that such an extension would be profitable; and, when the London and Birmingham Company did venture to project a branch—from Blisworth to Northampton and Peterborough—so strong was the feeling of the landowners against it that it was carried through the House of Lords in 1843 by a majority of one vote only. Meanwhile moralists in search of an argument against excessive railway construction could point to the experience of the Midland Counties and Birmingham and Derby Companies, a rate-war between which for London traffic was being carried on with such vigour that the directors of the former had recourse, in the summer of 1843, to a *mandamus* from the Queen's Bench to compel the Birmingham and Derby Company to equalize its fares. In this, the first "war" of its kind in English railway history, Mr. James Allport, manager for the Birmingham and Gloucester Railway at Hampton Junction, played a leading part.

This was the condition of affairs between these two companies, when the directors of the North Midland—the line which carried the traffic of both northwards from Derby—suggested an amalgamation under one management of the three railways radiating from that town. The originator of the proposition was George Hudson, who had joined the North Midland directorate early in this year, 1843, after taking the leading part on a committee of inquiry into its affairs; and the reforms he had then introduced had so much enhanced his already great reputation, that he was now able easily to persuade the shareholders of the three companies to agree to this "Great Midland Amalgamation," a Bill for which was accordingly deposited for the session of 1844. The man who ten years before had been an obscure linen-draper at York, was now freely spoken of as "the Railway Napoleon."

During this autumn of 1843 the money market in London was in a remarkably easy state. The amount of bullion in the Bank, which two years before had been as low as four and a half millions, had trebled itself in amount. The rate of discount was $2\frac{1}{2}$ per cent., and Consols were above par. Money was very abundant, and the investments in foreign securities, in which it had until recently found full employment, had suddenly become extremely unpopular owing to "repudiations" on the part of several South American States. Hitherto the London brokers had left railway shares severely alone, and the lines so far constructed in England had been promoted not by financiers, but by solid commercial men—bankers, manufacturers, and merchants—who were interested in them, not as investments primarily, but as likely to improve trade in general, and their own businesses in particular. But, now that other fields of investment was proving unfruitful, the attention of "the City" began to turn to railway promotion; it was discovered to be a branch of speculative finance from which 10 per cent. dividends might be hopefully expected—for were not the London and Birmingham, Grand Junction and York, and North Midland paying this, and the Stockton and Darlington 15 per cent. ?—and so, all at once as it seemed, a condition of most intense apathy in regard to railway projection gave way to one of keen interest, rapidly passing through enthusiasm to a new and overpowering mania.

City men who studied the railway map of England in the autumn of 1843, could not fail to be struck by the fact that there was an immense blank as yet unreached by rails on the eastern side of England. The Eastern Counties line had now got as far as Colchester, and the Northern and Eastern to Bishop Stortford, but northwards of these places, throughout the counties of Huntingdonshire, Cambridgeshire, Norfolk, and Lincolnshire, there was not a yard of railway laid down from the Ouse to the Humber, and the only new line authorized to come near this district was the London and Birmingham branch, from Blisworth to Peterborough. On the map, therefore, there seemed ample room for a new trunk line between London and York, which would not only give the local accommodation, but form part of a through route to Darlington, Durham, Newcastle, and Scotland; and so it came about that in the later months of 1843 a committee was formed in London, of which Major William Amsinck and Mr. James Farquhar, of the firm of Messrs. Johnston, Farquhar, and Leech, solicitors, were the leading

MAP OF THE RAILWAY SYSTEM BETWEEN LONDON AND YORK IN 1843.
Reproduced from "Bradshaw's Guide," by permission of Messrs. Henry Blacklock & Co., Manchester.

spirits, to promote a "Direct Northern" railway, for which Sir John Rennie—who, as we know, had already plans for a line from London to York on his office shelves—and Mr. Gravatt were instructed to make a survey.

But the success of railways had not only changed the attitude of the City, it had changed that of the landed interest also; and so, during the winter of 1843-4, a strong desire arose among the landowners and farmers of the eastern counties to secure some of the benefits which other districts were enjoying from the new method of locomotion. One great want of this part of England—a want which was, of course, most keenly felt in the winter months—was that of cheaper fuel; for though there were collieries open at this time in Leicestershire, Nottinghamshire, and Derbyshire, the nearest pits with which the eastern counties had practicable transport communication were those of South Yorkshire and Durham, and this was of so circuitous a character, that even in places situated on navigable rivers or served by a canal, the price of coal often rose as high as 40s., or even 50s., a ton. In remoter places, to which it had to be carted ten, twenty, or even thirty miles along bad cross-roads, coal even for house-firing was a positive luxury quite unattainable by the poorer classes. Moreover, in the most severe weather when the canals were frozen, the whole system of supply became paralyzed, and even the wealthy had not seldom to retreat shivering to bed for lack of fuel.

This state of things was, of course, stoically borne, while there appeared no remedy for it; but in 1843, when the railway system was firmly established and praise of it began to be on every lip and in every newspaper, even the slow-moving inhabitants of Lincolnshire and the neighbouring counties began to take interest in railway promotion. Naturally enough, one of the first expedients which suggested itself was to seek assistance from "the Railway King," and so in February, 1844, Sir John Beckett, of Gainsborough, wrote formally to George Hudson, suggesting on behalf of himself and some of his neighbours that the North Midland Company should make a branch to their town. About the same time Sir Isaac Morley, an influential resident of Doncaster, came into communication for a similar object with Captain Laws, the energetic manager of the Manchester and Leeds Company; while a party of merchants trading in Sheffield, Worksop, and Retford projected yet a third west to east line to run to Gainsborough and Lincoln in connection with the Manchester and Sheffield Railway, which was now at last approaching completion. Meanwhile the larger landowners of Lincolnshire, the Earl of Winchilsea, the Earl of Yarborough, Earl Fitzwilliam, and Mr. Charles Chaplin of Blankney, were taking more interest in getting a north and south line through the county, and for this two projects were set on foot, the one suggested to Earl Fitzwilliam by an enterprising engineer named Rendel, and the other fathered by a committee, of which Mr. Chaplin was the leading spirit, and for which Mr. James Walker was persuaded rather reluctantly to re-survey his line of 1835. Moreover, Walker's former rival, Mr. Gibbs, also took the field again, and in this month of February, 1844, when all the above schemes seem first to have taken definite shape, he showed his "Great Northern" plans to a number of gentlemen, including Mr. Francis Mowatt, an East Indian director, and Mr. Edmund Denison, of Doncaster, M.P. for the West Riding of Yorkshire. The latter gentleman, as we have already noted, had twelve years before advocated a line from York to Doncaster as an instalment of a through route to London down the eastern side of England, and he now promised to support Mr. Gibbs' "Great Northern Railway," provided it was brought rather more to the west, so that his constituents in the West Riding and his neighbours at Doncaster might be better served by it.

In the year 1837, when England was suffering, as we have already noted, from the reaction from the first epidemic of "railway mania," stringent regulations against the promotion of bubble companies were adopted by Parliament. The chief of these were that a *bonâ fide* "subscription contract" must be proved by the promoters, and that one-tenth of the capital required must be deposited with Government authorities at the same time that the Bill for incorporation was presented to Parliament. This, of course, made it necessary for every new railway scheme to obtain very respectable support before its promoters could hope to pass the Standing Orders Committee, and indeed it had been one of the prime causes of the stagnation in railway promotion, which we have noted as prevailing in the years 1838 to 1843. Even in the spring of 1844—a "spring" when the fancy of investors all over the country was "lightly turning" to thoughts of railway speculation—the heavy deposit required was thought to press very heavily upon quite honest projectors. At any rate it compelled them to go to considerable expense in advertising their schemes in the newspapers and through the post, in order that they might obtain the signatures of intending shareholders, to whom "scrip," *i.e.*, the title deeds to shares when the company was incorporated—was issued in return for the 10 per cent. deposit preliminarily required.

Of the group of Lincolnshire projects just noticed the first to be put before the public was that fathered by Captain Laws and Sir Isaac Morley—the Wakefield and Lincoln, the prospectus of which appeared on 19 February, 1844. This was quickly followed on 22 February by that of Mr. Walker's resurrected line, now christened the Cambridge and York, the Provisional Committee of which included the Earl of Winchilsea, Mr. Chaplin, and Mr. George Hussey Packe, of Caythorpe, near Grantham. Proposing as it did to complete a second through route between London and the north in connection with the Northern and Eastern Railway, this project aroused instant opposition from the established companies, and in its issue of 2 March the *Railway Times* declared it to be its duty to them to "protest against and denounce this newest of reckless speculations and all concerned in its concoction." Immediately, also, the Midland directors woke up to the necessity of meeting actively the new competition which threatened them, and on 5 March the North Midland Board—the Amalgamation Bill was not yet passed, and so each of the three Derby companies still carried on its affairs separately—decided to promote a branch from their railway at Swinton to Doncaster, Gainsborough, and Lincoln, as proposed to Mr. Hudson by Sir John Beckett and other parties. Shortly afterwards the Midland Counties Board decided to make a branch in the same direction from Nottingham, passing through Newark to Lincoln, and these were advertised together as the "Lincolnshire Junction Railways," with Mr. Robert Stephenson as engineer.

Meantime, on 7 March, the prospectus of the Sheffield and Lincoln Railway had been published, and on the 13th of the same month the Northern and Eastern and Eastern Counties Boards, which, thanks mainly to the exertions of Mr. George Parker Bidder, were just on the verge of being amalgamated into one interest, decided to promote an extension to Lincoln "in such direction as would best serve the important towns and ports of Wisbeach, Spalding, and Boston." Next, on 4 April, Major Amsinck issued a map and prospectus of the "Direct Northern Railway," surveyed by Sir John Rennie and Mr. Gravatt—"a line to commence near King's Cross and pass through Chipping Barnet, Biggleswade, St. Neots, Huntingdon, and Peterborough to Lincoln, and thence by Gainsborough, Thorne, Snaith, and Selby to York," and this on 15 April obtained wide notoriety by being prominently referred to in the "money article" of the *Times*. Finally, on 17 April, the advertisement columns of the same newspaper contained the preliminary notice of Mr. Gibbs' revived and modified project, headed:

"GREAT NORTHERN RAILWAY.

"From London to York, through Hitchin, Biggleswade, Huntingdon, Stamford, Grantham, Newark, Gainsborough, and Doncaster, joining the Leeds and Selby and York and North Midland Railways near South Milford, with branch lines to Bedford and Lincoln, and a junction with the Manchester and Sheffield Railway."

The notice stated that "a detailed prospectus with names of the Provisional Committee" would be ready in a few days, and that in the meantime further information might be obtained on application to Messrs. Baxter, Rose, and Norton, solicitors, 50, Mark Lane, London.

Thus by the middle of April there were four north and south and three west and east lines in the field, every one of which proposed to enter Lincolnshire; and thus "threatened," as a contemporary writer put it, "with no less than seven different lines of railroad, with all the infernal machinery connected therewith," it was no wonder that the people of Lincoln became excited and full of party feeling on behalf of one or other of the projects. Probably because it had been first in the field, the Wakefield and Lincoln became the most popular line, securing a vote of the Town Council in its favour; and early in April its promoters still further improved their position by announcing their intention to extend their railway along the banks of the Witham to Boston, where they talked of making a junction with one of the Eastern Counties extension lines. Seeing that a large number of Lincoln people were shareholders in the Witham Navigation (which connects the city with the Wash, and was in 1844 by far its most important channel of conveyance), this proposal to construct a parallel, competitive railway would, if it had stood by itself, have been a most unpopular one; but the Wakefield promoters boldly disarmed opposition, and at the same time enlisted new support, by arranging a union of interests with the Navigation Company, under which the shareholders in the latter were guaranteed a permanent 6 per cent. dividend, while at the same time the public were promised a reduction of the water tolls. A similar arrangement was also made with Mr. Richard Ellison, the proprietor of the Fossdyke, another canal which connects Lincoln with the Trent at Gainsborough, while the canal interests, on their part, undertook to give land for the construction of the railway, which for the greater part of its course from Gainsborough was to be constructed along their banks.

Meanwhile the public announcement of the Direct Northern and Great Northern projects had had an immediate effect upon the councils of the Cambridge and York, and on 16 April—the day after the Direct Northern was noticed in the *Times*—they had passed a resolution intimating that a continuance of their line to London through Peterborough might become desirable. It was "urged" on them—so they explained afterwards—"by the northern interests that the public should not be subjected to the fifteen miles additional distance involved in the Cambridge route, when a more direct route through the centre of Hertfordshire, Bedfordshire, and Huntingdonshire could be obtained," and moreover, Mr. Whitbread of Bedford, who had now joined the Committee, had pointed out that local railway accommodation was badly needed in these counties. So on 23 April, Mr. Walker was definitely requested to continue his surveys right through to London. This important move soon became known to the Eastern Counties directors, with the result that they, having failed to effect a union with the Wakefield and Lincoln party, instructed Robert Stephenson, on 30 April, to continue his northward survey to Gainsborough and Doncaster. Thus there were now four schemes in the field for complete north and south trunk lines.

On 3 May, 1844, the first prospectus of the "London and York Railway" was issued. It stated that Mr. Walker had recommended that "the line of railway should commence at London, near King's Cross, and proceed in the direction of Barnet, Hatfield, Hitchin, Biggleswade, St. Neots, and Huntingdon to Peterborough, where it would join the line originally projected between Cambridge and York," and this new line, the prospectus added, had "the hearty concurrence and support" of the landowners affected. In evidence of this the Committee list now published included among many other new names those of Wm. Astell, M.P. for Beds, an East Indian director, his son Mr. John Harvey Astell, the Hon. O. Duncombe, of St. Neots, M.P. for the North Riding of Yorkshire, and Mr. Francis Pym, of the Hazells, Beds. This new and more formidable development of the scheme did not, of course, lessen in any degree the hostility already provoked towards it, and the duty it had imposed upon itself of denouncing the "wild project" was once more cheerfully taken in hand by the *Railway Times*. "Was it because the undertaking was not huge enough for public support," it asked, "that Cambridge as a starting point had been dropped—that seat of learned travellers deserted—the large traffic of taking students to and from the colleges removed from the table of estimates, and despised in comparison to proceeding direct to so celebrated and extensive a city as St. Neots." This addition to the original scheme of "fifty miles more of railway, with a new terminus into London through some 100 furlongs of house property, was," it declared, "a further sign of the extraordinary caution exercised" in bringing out the scheme, and the public might next expect to hear that York Minster had been "scheduled for removal to make room for a proper station" at the northern end.

Meanwhile the promised "detailed prospectus" of the "Great Northern" line did not appear, and the reason was that, almost immediately after its preliminary notice had been made public, the Cambridge and York—now London and York—Committee had appointed a deputation of their body to endeavour to arrange a union with the other parties of promoters who were occupying the same field. The result was that, on 17 May, a conference was held at the offices of the London and York solicitors in Parliament Street, Westminster, at which the Earl of Winchilsea, the Hon. O. Duncombe, Messrs. J. H. Astell, Chas. Chaplin, G. H. Packe and others represented the London and York Committee, and Messrs. Edmund Denison and Francis Mowatt the Great Northern. At this meeting a resolution was unanimously passed that the two committees should unite, and "that the efforts of all should be exerted to form a railway between London and York, to be called the 'London and York Railway,'" and at the next meeting of the London and York General Committee on 7 June, Messrs. Denison and Mowatt attended, and the former spoke "in highly laudatory terms" of the united undertaking. Thus the separate "Great Northern" project was dropped, and the name vanishes for a time from these pages. The Direct Northern party, however, still preferred to remain independent, claiming that their project had been first in the field, and on 18 May—the very day when the union of the London and York and Great Northern was announced in the press—Major Amsinck issued a counter advertisement announcing that Sir John Rennie and Mr. Gravatt had completed their surveys, and that a committee was being formed to carry out the railway they recommended, which would "form the most direct line between London and York."

Five days later—23 May—the titular "London and York" Committee sustained a loss by the resignation of their engineer, Mr. James Walker, who had found that the task of surveying and constructing a complete trunk line to the north was incompatible with his many other engagements. Thus the "Committee of Direction," which was now formed as a delegation from the General Committee, with Mr. William Astell, M.P., as chairman, and Messrs. Edmund Denison, M.P., and Francis Mowatt as vice-chairmen, had as its first duty to choose a new engineer for their combined and reconstituted undertaking. For this position the most obvious claimant was Mr. Gibbs; but the committee appear to have thought that for an undertaking of such magnitude a chief engineer of acknowledged eminence was required, and with this view a deputation was sent to Mr. Joseph Locke to ask him to undertake the work. The invitation was a tempting one to a man of ambition like Locke; but under ordinary circumstances he would probably have at least hesitated to accept it, because as engineer to the Grand Junction Company and projector of the just christened "Caledonian Railway," he had prior interests and engagements which it would obviously not be easy to reconcile with the position of engineer to the new eastern trunk line. But it happened that just at this time the Boards of the

Grand Junction and London and Birmingham Companies were at loggerheads, and so the former seem actually to have encouraged their engineer to take up the new enterprise, because it was likely to prove a formidable rival to Euston Square. However this may be, Mr. Joseph Locke did accept the invitation, and at once threw himself into the London and York plans with great energy.

On 11 June a new prospectus of the undertaking appeared, headed by a list of names "unequalled," according to *Herapath's Railway Journal*, "for extent and respectability," and it at once created an "extraordinary degree of sensation" (though at this time new railway prospectuses were appearing almost daily), for no new company, it was averred, had ever come out with such strength as this before. The prospectus stated that the two main objects of the undertaking were to shorten the distance between London and the northern parts of the kingdom, and to connect a population of one and a half million in Yorkshire with a population in London of about equal amount. The facilities to be provided for the transmission of corn, malt, flour, cattle, and wool were enlarged upon, and it was pointed out that Yorkshire, Derbyshire, and Nottinghamshire coals, Yorkshire manufactures and London goods would "find a ready market along the whole line." "The railway," said the prospectus further, "will give the farmers and graziers in the counties of Nottingham, Lincoln, Northampton, Bedford, and Hertford daily opportunities of sending their fat cattle to Smithfield in a few hours without the great loss now invariably sustained by travelling for days together on a turnpike road," and "the market gardeners of Biggleswade will be enabled to send their produce fresh to the London market in about two hours." A few days later an elaborate "first estimate of income" appeared in the newspapers, compiled by Mr. Robert Baxter, a solicitor of Doncaster, who, it may be remembered, had accompanied Mr. Denison on his deputation from that town to the York Railway Committee twelve years before; and this purported to prove that the traffic would from the first be sufficient to pay a dividend of "upwards of 9 per cent." on £4,500,000 —the amount of capital asked for. "In the language of Dominie Sampson," said the *Railway Times*, "and almost bursting with excitement, we can only say 'Prodigious!'"

Meanwhile, the Midland Amalgamation Bill had received the Royal assent, and at the first meeting of the united Boards, which was held early in June, Mr. Hudson had been, as a matter of course, elected chairman of the new "Midland Railway Company." This had extended the dominions of the York monarch southwards as far as Rugby; and, northwards, he had just become chairman of a newly-incorporated Leeds and Bradford Company, the practical object of which was to extend the Midland rails to the latter town. He was also on the Provisional Committee of the North British Railway, from Berwick to Edinburgh, the Bill for which had just passed the Commons after a hard fight; and, if this passed the Lords—as it was almost sure to do—only the link between Gateshead and Berwick would remain to be authorized to make the "East Coast Route" from York to Edinburgh complete. Meantime the works of the Newcastle and Darlington Junction Railway had been pressed on with extraordinary vigour, and by the middle of this June—a full fortnight before Hudson had promised—the twenty-seven miles of new line from Darlington to Washington, and the new terminus at Gateshead, were ready for opening. The occasion was made one of great ceremonial, and at 5.3 a.m. on 18 June a special train—precursor and prototype of many "racing trains" to the north—left Euston Station with George Stephenson and other eminent men on board, and reached Gateshead at 2.35 p.m., having covered the 303 miles in nine hours thirty-two minutes—"a feat unparalleled in the annals of railway travelling in the kingdom." Moreover, at the dinner which Hudson gave in the afternoon at Newcastle to a company of three hundred, the completion of the route through to Edinburgh, with bridges over the Tyne and Tweed, was spoken of as the matter of but a few more years.

Mr. Glyn, the London and Birmingham chairman, was to have attended this ceremony, but at the last moment he was detained in town to meet the chairman of the Grand Junction, so that the unfortunate differences between their two companies might be arranged. This was accomplished and a peace concluded, of which Hudson immediately took advantage to arrange a united plan of campaign against the London and York, "the Ishmael of railways," as Mr. Hutchinson, the Midland Quaker director, had just christened it. Hudson now recognized that Parliament could not be expected to resist the public demand for a new through route on the eastern side of England, and that the best policy for the established companies, therefore, was to combine to supply this themselves in such a way as would least damage their existing property. The Eastern Counties Company had just obtained powers for an extension to Peterborough, and its directors had, as we know, instructed Robert Stephenson to survey further extensions to Lincoln, Gainsborough, and Doncaster; but these towns Hudson regarded as belonging legitimately to his kingdom. Accordingly, he now proposed that his companies should fully occupy the district north of the Ouse by the York and North Midland making a branch to Doncaster, while the Midland extended its Swinton and Nottingham branches beyond Lincoln to Boston, Spalding and March, and that the Eastern Counties should come to March also by a deviation of its authorized Peterborough extension, thus making a through "East Coast" route by Cambridge, Ely, March, Boston, Lincoln, and Doncaster to the north. To this arrangement the Shoreditch Board was induced to agree by being promised a half share of the through traffic with York and places north of that city.

Further, in order to fill up the eastern side of the country more completely, and yet at the same time to avoid the making of any through route to the north more direct than the existing one *viâ* Rugby and Derby, the Railway King suggested that the Midland and Eastern Counties systems should be joined at Peterborough as well as at March, by the former making a new branch from its main line somewhere near Leicester through Oakham and Stamford; and in this he succeeded in securing the acquiescence of the London and Birmingham directors, though to some small extent it threatened the traffic of their Blisworth to Peterborough branch, already in course of construction. But Euston Square in return, it was arranged, should be allowed to embrace Bedford in its dominion by making a branch thither from Bletchley, while the Eastern Counties, which also had had designs on Bedford, was to stop short at Hertford and Biggleswade.

Such were the terms of the "great and valuable alliance" between the established companies which the *Railway Times* announced in its issue of 13 July, 1844, and which—in the language of that newspaper—"spread peace in the railway kingdom from Yarmouth to Holyhead." Thus the two projects for a main trunk railway on the eastern side of England—the London and York and Direct Northern —besides having to fight for supremacy between themselves, had now ranged against them the united forces of the existing companies, commanded by a leader whose ability and influence were everywhere acknowledged—George Hudson, the Railway King.

CHAPTER II.

HOW "FIVE KINGS" ISSUED AN EDICT TO "STRANGLE THE MONSTER INFANT AT ITS BIRTH"—1844-1845.

ALL through the month of June, 1844, application for "London and York" scrip flocked in to the office of the Committee at Lothbury from all sides. In the previous month of May, on the motion of Mr. W. E. Gladstone, the President of the Board of Trade, the amount of deposit required by Government had been reduced from 10 to 5 per cent. of the capital, on the ground that it was "undesirable to oppress speculation" at a time of commercial buoyancy, and this measure—a very ill-timed one as events proved—made the issue of the London and York scrip an easier task than it might otherwise have been. On the other hand, the Committee had to exercise all possible care to prevent persons subscribing to their share contract who might subsequently prove unable to pay the further calls on the shares.

Meantime, Mr. Locke and a deputation of the directors were out inspecting the country, with Messrs. Walker and Gibbs' plans in their hands, in order to decide finally upon the route of the line. The main point at issue was whether it should run across the fens, as proposed by Mr. Walker, or be brought more to the westwards in order to serve "the towns" (*i.e.*, Grantham, Newark, Retford, and Doncaster) as in the later plans which Mr. Gibbs had prepared at the instance of Mr. Denison; and on this question a rather sharp difference of opinion had arisen at the Committee, which it had been agreed Mr. Locke's arbitration should decide. Pending his decision the directors who accompanied the engineer found some difficulty in meeting the pressure which was brought to bear upon them in the various towns they visited; but, fortunately, in Mr. Denison, who by force of character had already made himself the leader of the party, the Committee had a representative who could be perfectly candid, and yet, at the same time, win not only respect but support. At a meeting held at Peterborough on 1 August, under the presidency of Earl Fitzwilliam, he did not hesitate to say bluntly that he would not consent to sacrifice the interests of the general public for the benefit of any town on the route. "Our main object," said he, "is to shorten the distance between London and Yorkshire. If a line through Peterborough is best for the general public, Peterborough shall have it, but, if not, it shall pass outside the town." Nevertheless, resolutions in favour of the London and York were passed both at the Peterborough meeting and at another held at Huntingdon on the following day.

A few days later Mr. Locke made his report, which was adopted by the direction, and on 22 August, 1844, an advertisement of the route of the proposed railway was published in the *Times*. It stated that the London terminus was to be "at King's Cross, near the New Road," and that the line was to pass "by Crouch End, Hornsey, Colney Hatch, between Whetstone and East Barnet, near to Potters Bar, west of Hatfield Park to Hatfield, by Welwyn, Hitchin, Henlow, Biggleswade, Sandy, with a branch to Bedford, by Tempsford, St. Neots, on the west side of Huntingdon, by Peterborough, east of Stamford, by Grantham and Stubton to Beckenham with a branch 4½ miles to Newark, by Doddington with a branch 4½ miles to the city of Lincoln, by the village of Lea to Gainsborough, by Misson, Tinningley, and Cantley to Doncaster, thence on to York." Thus the scrip-holders and the public learnt that Mr. Walker's "Fens" line, which, as we have seen, had been the basis of the original "London and York" undertaking, had practically been abandoned in favour of the "towns" line, which Mr. Gibbs had adopted at the instance of Mr. Denison.

North of Doncaster, however, the route was still, it will be seen, left very vague, and this was because the important question as to whether or not the new company should seek an independent access to York and to the West Riding had not yet been decided. Mr. Gibbs' plans, it may be remembered, had contemplated that the trunk line should terminate by "joining the York and North Midland and Leeds and Selby Railways at their junction near South Milford," and this undoubtedly was the most economical arrangement by which access to York and Leeds could be secured. On the other hand, there was much to be said in favour of making the new system independent throughout of existing railways and competitive interests. In this dilemma the London and York promoters came into communication, through Mr. Denison, with Captain Laws, the manager of the Manchester and Leeds Company, who was also, as we know, the leading promoter of the Wakefield, Lincoln, and Boston project; and as this line, as planned by its engineer, Mr. Cubitt, was to cross the route of the London and York at Doncaster, and so practically constitute branches from it to Wakefield on the one side, and to Lincoln and Boston on the other, Mr. Denison proposed that the two bodies of promoters should unite their interests, and that in that way the London and York should obtain access to the West Riding. Captain Laws, on his part, was feeling rather sore that his undertakings had been left out of account in the plans which King Hudson had laid, in conjunction with the London and Birmingham and Eastern Counties directors, for the occupation of Lincolnshire and the eastern side of England. The result was that on 30 August, at Normanton, he and Mr. Denison came to an arrangement under which it was agreed that the London and York plans should be enlarged to embrace the objects of the Wakefield and Boston Committee, and that the latter should be dissolved and five of its members placed on the London and York direction, its scrip being taken over by the latter so as to form an additional half a million of capital for the amalgamated undertaking. This important alliance, to which the Manchester and Leeds directors fully consented, was announced by an advertisement dated 10 September, 1844, and its immediate effect was to send up the London and York scrip, which had been a good deal depressed since the announcement of the Hudsonian combination, to a premium on the Exchange.

The question of access to the West Riding having been thus decided in favour of an independent branch from Doncaster to Wakefield, the Committee at once decided in favour of a through line to York also, and Mr. Locke was informed of this, and requested to continue his surveys accordingly on 4 September, just as he was about to start for Paris on business connected with the Paris and Rouen Railway. Since the adjustment of the disputes between the London and Birmingham and Grand Junction Companies, however, Locke had been subjected to a good deal of pressure to induce him to give up his connection with an undertaking so hostile to the interests of the existing companies, and the London and York Committee on their part had been warned that he would before long yield to that pressure. Nevertheless, they were hardly prepared for a letter which they received from him on 20 September, dated from Paris three days before, in which he summarily resigned his position as their engineer on the ground that he had not been properly consulted as to the alterations of the route which the new alliance with the Wakefield, Lincoln, and Boston involved. The Committee, in their reply (which bears unmistakable evidence of having been composed by Mr. Denison), did not hesitate to dismiss this reason as a mere excuse and to charge Locke with having designed his action in order to embarrass as much as possible the undertaking whose interests he had been engaged to serve, and it appears that they had good ground for this allegation, though Locke indignantly denied it.

However, whether it was the outcome of a plot or not, the secession of the eminent engineer did not, thanks to Mr. Denison's energy, embarrass the new undertaking at all seriously. The vice-chairman at once put himself into communication with Mr. William Cubitt, the engineer to the Wakefield, Lincoln, and Boston project, and in an advertisement dated "Monday morning, 23 September, 1844," the Committee was able to announce simultaneously the resignation of Locke and the appointment of Cubitt as engineer-in-chief to the undertaking. The late Mr. Brundell, of Doncaster, is my authority for a story that "Mr. Edmund Denison drove off post-haste very late at night to Cubitt's house at Clapham Common, roused the engineer out of bed, and there and then through the window—Cubitt being in his nightcap—arranged with him to undertake the engineership of the line."

There was need of all possible haste in completing the plans of new lines, because Parliament, alarmed at the prospect of being overwhelmed in its next session with railway bills, had already taken extraordinary measures to secure their preliminary examination "with a view to its information and assistance in forming a judgment" upon them. With this object the Board of Trade had been directed to institute an inquiry into the merits of competing projects, and accordingly on 20 August, 1844, a notice had been issued signed by Lord Dalhousie (who had just succeeded Mr. Gladstone as President of the Board), General Pasley, Captain O'Brien, and Messrs. G. R. Porter and S. Laing (afterwards Chairman of the Brighton Company). This announced that the Board had decided to examine, in the first instance, the London and York Railway projects, the projects for an east and west line between Lincolnshire and the West Riding, and the schemes for completing the railway communication between England and Scotland. So far, however, the London and York Committees had kept up well in the running. On the very day after the issue of this notice—21 August—Messrs. Astell, Denison, and Locke had formally laid the preliminary plans of their undertaking before the "Five Kings"—as the Board of Trade officials were soon nicknamed, and on 4 September Messrs. Denison and Locke had had another interview to announce the coalition with the Wakefield, Lincoln, and Boston—the very matter on which Locke afterwards complained he was not properly informed. Now, on 27 September, Messrs. Denison, Mowatt, and Baxter called upon Lord Dalhousie again, in order to inform him of the resignation of Locke, and of certain changes since made in the plans.

On 23 September, 1844—the same day that the appointment of Mr. Cubitt as engineer to the London and York Railway was announced—a new rival to that undertaking appeared in the field. The reader may remember being informed in the preceding chapter that at the time when Mr. Charles Chaplin was engaged in forming the "Cambridge and York" Committee with Mr. Walker as its engineer, another engineer, Mr. Rendel, was also surveying a north and south line through Lincolnshire, for which he had gained the powerful interest of Earl Fitzwilliam. But, as we have seen, Mr. Chaplin's party proved the stronger, developing, as has been described, into the London and York undertaking, and this Earl Fitzwilliam himself had supported at the meeting at Peterborough already noted. So nothing more had been said about Mr. Rendel's scheme until the end of August, when the route decided upon by Mr. Locke had been published, and it had been found that under the influence of Mr. Gibbs' Great Northern plans, the course through Lincolnshire, originally recommended by Mr. Walker, had been almost wholly abandoned in favour of a more westerly "towns line." Then grave dissatisfaction had arisen in the minds of some of the Lincolnshire gentlemen, particularly at the proposal to place Lincoln on a branch instead of on the main line, and the result had been that Mr. Handley, late M.P. for Lincolnshire, who, as the reader may perhaps remember, had promoted a north and south line, *viâ* Lincoln, as early as 1835, and one or two other members of the London and York Committee, had seceded from the party, and with the countenance and support of Earl Fitzwilliam had revived Mr. Rendel's "Cambridge and Lincoln" project. This was the new rival to the London and York, and a preliminary notice of it was issued, as just stated, on 23 September, 1844, the course proposed being *viâ* St. Ives, Ramsey, and Peterborough.

Almost simultaneously with the formation of this "cave" amongst their own party, the London and York Committee received a new and violent attack from their older rivals, the Direct Northern. This party came out at the end of September, 1844, for the first time with a full prospectus, wherein they charged the London and York Committee with having "appropriated seventy miles" of the Direct Northern line as laid out by Sir John Rennie and Mr. Gravatt and published in a map issued by Major Amsinck in April, 1844. Nevertheless they claimed that the railway now proposed by them from King's Cross to York, *viâ* Huntingdon, Stamford, Lincoln, Gainsborough, and Selby to York would be twenty miles shorter than the London and York line. Moreover they gave an "estimate of income," modelled on that prepared for the London and York by Mr. Baxter, which showed a dividend of $9\frac{1}{2}$ per cent. on a capital of four millions, *i.e.*, one-half per cent. more than that previously claimed for the rival undertaking. This, of course, called for a reply from the London and York, which Messrs. Denison and Baxter were able to make trenchant and lively reading; but the energetic Major Amsinck was not silenced, for on the very same day, 3 October, he issued a new manifesto, replying to the London and York reply.

Meantime Mr. Cubitt had been busy going over the country to see how he could best combine his own Wakefield, Lincoln, and Boston plans with the London and York line as laid out by Locke. The latter had suggested just before his retirement that the London and York should include a branch from Peterborough to Boston in its undertaking, and this was now adopted by his successor in conjunction with the Wakefield, Lincoln, and Boston project, which, it will be remembered, was to run along the banks of the Witham and Fossdyke from Boston to Gainsborough in accordance with the agreement with the canal interests. Beyond Gainsborough, however, Cubitt decided to alter the line which the smaller Committee had adopted by diverting the first part of it so as to make it rejoin the London and York "towns line" at Bawtry, and this enabled him to utilize some surveys which he had made for another small Committee—the Sheffield, Chesterfield, and Gainsborough—which was now persuaded to follow the example of the Wakefield party and abandon their independent project in favour of an alliance with the London and York. This necessitated the adoption by the latter of an additional branch from Bawtry to Sheffield, while from Doncaster to Wakefield the western section of the Wakefield, Lincoln, and Boston line formed another branch of about the same length. Thus amended and enlarged the complete undertaking of the London and York Committee became:

1. A main line from London to York . . . . 186 miles.
2. A "loop" line from Peterborough *via* Boston and Lincoln to Bawtry . . . . . . 86 ,,
3. A branch line from Bawtry to Sheffield . . . $20\frac{3}{4}$,,
4. A branch from Doncaster to Wakefield . . $20\frac{1}{4}$,,
5. Minor branches to Bedford, Stamford and "spurs," making a total of $327\frac{1}{2}$ miles—truly "a leviathan undertaking," beside which the 112 miles of the original London and Birmingham Railway or even the $171\frac{1}{2}$ miles of the Great Western system—then, as now, the longest English railway under one management—looked very small indeed. Mr. Cubitt's estimate for the construction of the whole was six and a half millions, and as five millions of London and York and Wakefield

scrip had now been taken up, the Committee decided not to issue any more, but to take over what little had been sent out by the Sheffield, Chesterfield, and Gainsborough party, and to rely for the rest upon the exercise of borrowing powers.

One great advantage of this enlargement of plans was that it enabled the Committee to make its peace with the people of Lincoln, many of whom had been alienated from its cause by the former decision to place their city upon a branch from Doddington. For now Lincoln was offered in one scheme a through north and south communication *viâ* Peterborough and Bawtry, and a good connection westwards with both Wakefield and Sheffield, and when Mr. Baxter explained this at a great meeting held in the city on 5 October, a resolution was passed in favour of the London and York by a large majority, despite an announcement by the Cambridge and Lincoln that they now had the support of King Hudson for their scheme. At this meeting the Doncaster solicitor was bold enough to denounce the great railway potentate in no measured terms, and Hudson, though he affected to despise Baxter as "a gentleman little known in the railway world," was roused to reply to him at great length at a Midland meeting a week later. On the same day as the Lincoln meeting, similar gatherings at Grantham and Huntingdon pronounced in favour of the London and York and against the Direct Northern, and on October 10th at Newark, and on the next day at Retford resolutions in the same sense were passed. Nevertheless, on 17 October Major Amsinck was able to announce through the press that all the Direct Northern scrip had been taken up.

The great epidemic of railway mania was now raging, and every day's newspapers brought new projects to light. Among those announced during this October, 1844, were the Great Grimsby and Sheffield Junction Railway, the Great Grimsby Extension Dock Company, the Wakefield, Pontefract, and Goole, and the Lincoln, York, and Leeds; and all these, together with the London and York, the Direct Northern, the Cambridge and Lincoln, the Sheffield and Lincoln, and the extensions of the Midland, York, and North Midland, and Eastern Counties systems, were duly deposited by 30 November. The result was that in a group headed, "Scheme for extending railway communicaiton between London and York, etc.," the Board of Trade officials had to place projects involving the construction of upwards of 1,200 miles of railway—"an amount not much less than that of the railways already in existence in the kingdom," and proposing a capital expenditure altogether of upwards of £20,000,000. Of course the London and York, with its 328 miles, was by far the largest single scheme. The Direct Northern simply proposed a main line only from London to York, 185 miles in length; the proposed Midland extension from Swinton *via* Lincoln and Boston to March, was no more than 124 miles, and the Cambridge and Lincoln 83. The latter was now definitely supported by Hudson, but it was freely stated that he was using it only as a weapon against his more formidable adversaries, and did not intend that it should be made even if the powers for it were obtained.

London 2 May 1844

My Dear Sir

I am obliged by your letter and am quite glad to hear so favorable an account of your proceedings — You may incur any reasonable or moderate expenses in printing &c. which yourself and Mr Seely may think necessary

Yours truly

Geo Hudson

AUTOGRAPH LETTER OF MR. GEORGE HUDSON, "THE RAILWAY KING," TO AN AGENT IN LINCOLN AUTHORIZING EXPENDITURE IN OPPOSITION TO THE PROPOSED "LONDON AND YORK RAILWAY."

Reproduced by permission of Mr. Edward Baker, Bookseller, 14 & 16, John Bright Street, Birmingham.

Full plans and sections of the various projects having been now deposited, the details of them were open for discussion, and a wordy warfare about gradients, earthwork, tunnels, bridges, etc., now commenced in the railway press and elsewhere. The works of the London and York were, as Mr. Cubitt afterwards said in the witness-box, "large but not difficult," involving about fourteen and a half million cubic yards of earthwork, fourteen tunnels, about 420 bridges, some of which, however, were very small affairs, a viaduct at Welwyn, 1490 feet long and 89 feet in greatest height, and forty-two stations, including the terminus at King's Cross. This was to cover ten acres for passenger accommodation and forty-nine acres for goods and coal, but Mr. Cubitt declared that he could build a thoroughly useful station for between £50,000 and £60,000—about the amount which the London and Birmingham had paid for its *archway* at Euston Square.

For the site of the passenger terminus which fronted on the old St. Pancras Road the Small-pox and Fever Hospitals and several streets of small houses had to be removed, but with this exception the carrying of the line out of London involved next to no destruction of house property, as it emerged into open and completely rural country within a mile of King's Cross. Nevertheless the first section of the line out of London promised to be by a good deal the most costly portion of the system. The prior occupation by the Eastern Counties Railway of the only level route by which a line could leave London for the north had compelled both the London and York and Direct Northern engineers to lay their routes through a country formed of a series of ridges and valleys, and Mr. Cubitt's sections for the first twenty-three miles showed an almost unbroken series of tunnels, cuttings, and embankments, no less than eight of the fourteen tunnels, the highest embankment and the deepest cutting on the system being all in this portion of the line. Indeed, had the new railway been laid out on the same principle which had governed Stephenson and Brunel in laying out the London and Birmingham and the Great Western lines, namely, that a practically level line must be secured, the amount of earthwork involved in getting through what are now called "The Northern Heights of London" would have been colossal. Fortunately, however, great advances had been made in the building of locomotives since the days when those two great lines had been built—even the short incline of 1 in 66 out of Euston, for which a stationary engine had long been used, was already being "negotiated" by a single locomotive, and so Mr. Cubitt was able to adopt 1 in 200 as the "characteristic" gradient of the new trunk line; that is to say, where a better gradient than this could not be secured without additional expense, he was content that the trains should have to face a rise of this degree. But even 1 in 200 was too stringent a ruling gradient to be adhered to in the neighbourhood of the London terminus. So, after the line had been carried beneath the Regent's Canal, a rise of 1 in 108 had to be tolerated for a distance of a mile and a quarter in order to reach the higher level at Holloway, from which again the line continued to rise with a very long stretch of 1 in 200 until its summit level was reached at Potters Bar, thirteen miles from King's Cross.

From Potters Bar Mr. Cubitt was able to keep on high ground

for another thirteen miles to Stevenage, where, however, a long fall of about six miles of 1 in 200 began; and, after that, from Arlesey to beyond Peterborough he was able to secure a practically level run of nearly fifty miles, save for a longish rise and longer fall (both 1 in 200) near Abbotts Ripton, sixty-three miles from King's Cross. Between Peterborough and Grantham the choice of the "towns" line in preference of that through the Fens had compelled the engineer to penetrate some heavy country, involving three miles of 1 in 176 north of Corby immediately succeeded by a tunnel, 1352 yards long, at Great Ponton—the longest tunnel on the line—and after that came a long fall of 1 in 200 down to Grantham; but thence to Doncaster the works were fairly easy, the most onerous being the bridge over the Trent at Newark. The loop, too, was very easy of construction except for bridges, and about half of it could be laid level without any serious earthwork at all.

Thus we see that except its largeness there was nothing about the London and York undertaking to daunt even the little-tested engineering skill of 1845, and so its opponents had only one really vulnerable point to attack. This was the great costliness of the undertaking, which, they alleged, must be largely in excess of the capital estimate, and at the Midland meeting on 20 January, 1845, George Hudson, with the assistance of figures furnished to him by Robert Stephenson, put the matter in the apparently conclusive form of a rule of three sum. "If," asked he, "the London and Birmingham Railway, with 14,000,000 cubic yards of earthwork, four and an eighth miles of tunnels, and no viaduct longer than 500 feet, cost £5,000,000, how much will the same length, namely, 112 miles, of the London and York cost from London to Grantham, with 13,000,000 cubic yards of earthwork, four and three-quarter miles of tunnels, and a viaduct at Welwyn, 1490 feet long and 89 feet high?" The answer, of course, was "not less than £5,000,000," whereupon Hudson, not knowing—for, indeed, it had not yet been publicly announced—that the capital estimate of the London and York had been increased by Cubitt from five millions to six and a half, declared triumphantly that "these juvenile promoters" would have "spent every shilling of their capital by the time they had arrived at Grantham," and that, in short, "if it were united with that humbug, the Atmospheric, the London and York would be the most complete thing in the world."

Allowing for Cubitt's addition, however, and for the advances in engineering science since the making of the London and Birmingham, this criticism of the London and York capital estimate was worth very little, as the sequel was to prove, and Hudson did his best to rob it of all effect on impartial minds by his reckless language with regard to the gradients and financing of the new railway. "I challenge them," he said, "to leave London with twenty carriages, and I will beat them to York" (*i.e.*, by the Midland route); "and what is more, I don't believe they will get there at all on a thick, foggy day, when the rails are greasy." Moreover, after the meeting, coming across Mr. Denison on the platform at Derby station, he went so far as to assert that the London and York would not have got capital to take them as far even as Grantham, "if they had got it honestly." This sneer had reference to the coalition with the Wakefield and Lincoln party, in which, as we know, Mr. Denison had been prime mover; but though reminded warningly of this latter fact, the Railway King repeated his charge of dishonesty. Thereupon Denison called him "a blackguard" to his face, and then turned his back upon him, and when Hudson endeavoured to explain that it was to the Committee he had referred and not Mr. Denison personally, the only reply he received was, "Hudson, I've done with you; go away!"

The Parliamentary session had now begun, and during February the Board of Trade presented its reports on several of the groups of railway schemes submitted to it; but that on the London and York group—which was unanimously admitted to be the most important—was still delayed. It was generally believed, however—even in the opposition camps—that when it came it would be in favour of the London and York line, and this belief prevailed until early in March, when all of a sudden the current rumour changed, and the Cambridge and Lincoln and Direct Northern parties showed unaccountable signs of confidence. On Saturday, 8 March, though no official announcement had yet been made, it was positively stated in the City that the London and York was to be reported against, so positively that large sales of London and York, and purchases of Direct Northern and Cambridge and Lincoln scrip were made, and on the following Monday, in response to some sort of official invitation, the precise nature of which was never disclosed, the Direct Northern party sent word to the "Five Kings" that they were willing to combine with the Cambridge and Lincoln by making the northern part of their line from Lincoln to York only. On the following day, Tuesday, 11 March, it was officially announced that the report of the Board was to be in favour of this combination and against the London and York *in toto*.

The excitement and surprise produced throughout the country was intense. Feverish sales or purchases of scrip were at once effected; the most extraordinary rumours as to the origin of the "Five Kings'" judgment were afloat; and the publication of the text of their report was awaited with intense anxiety. The London and York Bill had already passed its second reading unopposed, and on 12 March—the very next day after the Board of Trade's verdict was published—the Committee announced their intention of proceeding with it, "just as if no Board of Trade existed"—a decision for which they were loudly applauded by their supporters throughout the country and in the press. On the other hand, the *Railway Times* came out on 15 March with a flaming leader, which declared that "the monster bubble had burst; the mighty scheme which was to furnish the pockets of its supporters with the *spolia opima* of premiums to the tune of a million and a quarter has vanished into thin and unsubstantial air,

> "'And like the baseless fabric of a vision,
> Left not a wrack behind.'"

A day or two later, moreover, one of the Cambridge and Lincoln party, writing by Hudson's direction to Mr. Brogden, the latter's agent at Lincoln, declared that "the report from the Board of Trade must necessarily be so strong and powerful against this wild project, as will almost of itself be sufficient to strangle the monster infant in its birth."

Mr. Denison in the Commons and Lord Brougham in the Lords endeavoured to ascertain how it was that the Five Kings' verdict should have been known in the City, and sent by post and pigeon to the provinces four days before it was officially announced, and grave reflections on the conduct of the Five Kings were uttered, which gained general credence, amongst the London and York party at any rate, when on 20 March the full text of their report was published in the *Gazette*. An examination of this long and elaborate document—and probably no official report was ever examined more searchingly—showed that the *ex parte* criticism passed by Hudson at the Midland meeting on the London and York estimates had been accepted by the Board—and was in fact quoted by them almost *verbatim* in their report—although no opportunity had been given to Mr. Cubitt, or to any other representative of the London and York Committee, to explain or defend their figures; while, on the other hand, the estimates of the Direct Northern and Cambridge and Lincoln had been accepted without criticism. What was worse, many of the "facts" quoted by the Board in favour of their decision were found to be not only misleading, but absolutely inaccurate. Moreover, it appeared obvious that the officials had gone beyond their province in suggesting a new combination of routes instead of simply reporting on the merits of the various integral schemes which had been placed before them.

The fact was that—as Colonel Sibthorpe, the anti-railway member, said in the House of Commons—the Five Kings had undertaken a duty which "five angels could not have performed satisfactorily if they had come down from heaven and sat four hours a day as a Board." They had been instructed to report on matters of the greatest intricacy, involving numberless points of local detail, without any power to take evidence or hear advocates; in short, they had to do the work of a Parliamentary Committee without any of the facilities enjoyed by such a Committee; and, worst of all, they had to do what fortunately a Parliamentary Committee on a railway Bill never does—they had to give *reasons* for the decisions at which they arrived. Under these circumstances their prudent course should have been to have simply stated the arguments in favour and against the various projects in a colourless and non-committal manner; but, as we have seen, they were so indiscreet—to use the mildest term applied to them—as to adopt a precisely opposite course.

On 25 March—that is after a very short interval only for criticism—the London and York Committee issued an advertisement pointing out "a few of the most glaring mistakes upon the face of the report," and shortly afterwards the indefatigable Mr. Baxter completed a full answer to it, contesting its premises and arguments seriatim, and this was sent out from the London and York office, interleaved with the pages of the official document. Meanwhile the towns on the proposed London and York route line, most of which were left out in the cold by the approved Eastern Counties, Cambridge and Lincoln and Direct Northern combination, had risen in protest against the Five Kings' authority, and hardly a day passed without bringing with it intelligence that a new meeting had denounced the Board's report and exhorted the London and York Committee to persevere in the face of it. The inhabitants of Doncaster declared that they "assembled under the most alarming circumstances that ever menaced the prosperity of the town"; Bawtry accused the Board of "gross injustice"; Biggleswade learnt of its decision "with deep regret and disappointment"; Newark shared the "extreme disappointment and regret"; Wakefield heard of it with "deepest concern"; while at Lincoln feeling was now so sharply divided that a meeting of 6,000 people in the Beast Market broke up with stone-throwing, fighting, and general disorder upon the Mayor declaring that the resolution in favour of the London and York was passed. When the Cambridge and Lincoln partisans could no longer dispute this fact they declared that their opponents had hired "hordes of labourers at 2s. a head" to hold up their hands in favour of their line.

It was clear that the preliminary work done by Lord Dalhousie and his colleagues had increased rather than lightened the responsibility now impending upon Parliament.

CHAPTER III.

WHO IS TO REAR THE INFANT?—THE MOTHERS BEFORE SOLOMON—1845.

THE session of 1845 was to be pre-eminently a railway session, for at its opening there were no less than 224 Railway Bills awaiting consideration. Of these a few were voluntarily withdrawn by the parties promoting them in submission to the reports of the Board of Trade, but the work of clearing the ground which the Five Kings thus performed was small compared with that done by the numerous sub-committees appointed by the Commons to make a preliminary examination of the Bills to see if the Standing Orders of the House had been complied with. For as many of the projects had been conceived in the fever heat of the mania epidemic, and their plans, sections, and subscription contracts prepared in hot haste and by incompetent hands, the Standing Orders ordeal proved fatal to no less than thirty-nine of them, despite the fact that in numerous cases an agreement was come to amongst competing promoters not to oppose one another at this stage.

The London and York Bill, however, came through the Standing Orders most successfully, and, as we have before noted, it had already passed its second reading in the House of Commons before the adverse report of the Board of Trade was published. The Direct Northern, on the other hand, did not come before the Standing Orders Sub-Committee until April, by which time its promoters, in order to save expense, had prepared a No. 2 Bill for a line from Lincoln to York only, in accordance with their promise to the Board of Trade. But the Sub-Committee first decided that the notices given for the whole line were not applicable to the limited project, and afterwards on 29 April they announced that owing to some very serious errors in the engineers' sections the original Bill itself could not be allowed to proceed. Jobbers who after the publication of the Five Kings' report had sold London and York scrip and bought Direct Northern now began to regret their action.

Meanwhile the numerous Bills had been referred to the usual Private Bill Committees, but the way in which they had been "grouped" was causing much dissatisfaction to the London and York party. For while their own Bill, with the Direct Northern, the Cambridge and Lincoln, the Sheffield and Lincoln, the Midland extension from Swinton to March, the York and North Midland branch to Doncaster, the Eastern Counties extensions, and several other projects had been placed in Group X, the Syston and Peterborough was in Group T, the Nottingham, Newark, and Lincoln in Group V, the Great Grimsby and Sheffield Junction in Group U, and the Wakefield, Pontefract, and Goole in Group W. Yet all these were schemes the carrying out of which would seriously affect the position of the London and York undertaking. Particularly was this the case with the Syston and Peterborough, the line of which was actually planned to run from Peterborough to Walton, a distance of about three miles, practically over the same ground as the London and York. Yet the latter party, having as yet no legal status, found themselves refused a *locus standi* to appear against it, and had the chagrin of seeing it pass Committee stage in the Commons before the proceedings in Group X had so much as begun.

It was on 28 April that the Committee on the London and York group held its first sitting, Lord Courtenay (afterwards Lord Devon) being chairman, and the other members being Mr. Macgeachy, Mr. Baring Wall, Mr. C. Powlett Scrop, and Mr. Darby. It had fifteen Bills referred to it, and no less than thirty-two counsel were engaged for the various promoters. Great, therefore, was the disgust of these and of the small army of agents, solicitors, witnesses, and reporters—not to mention share-jobbers—who desired to be present, when it was found that it had been allotted one of the smallest of the wooden sheds in which, pending the completion of the new Houses of Parliament, Private Bill Committees were condemned to meet. Before the members of the Committee themselves arrived this room was completely filled, and upon its being cleared to enable them to discuss privately their order of proceedings, "counsel, solicitors, clerks, amateurs, and others were thrust into a narrow passage—a *rudis indigestaque moles*"—whereupon "some of the more merry of the persons ejected amused themselves"—according to the *Railway Times*' report—"by emptying buckets of water which hung against the walls" (being used for irrigating, and so cooling the tops of the sheds) "upon those who were immediately below them." When the doors were again opened a great crush ensued, and the reporters of the *Times* and other papers could not obtain admission. The consequence was some warm language in their columns on the following morning as to what they alleged was an attempt to fetter the liberty of the Press.

At the sitting on the next day (29 April) a larger shed was provided, but this was soon crowded with people as thick as they could stand; indeed, the largest of the committee-rooms subsequently built could not have held the throng which generally attended.* The result of the Committee's deliberations on the previous day had been that the London and York Bill was to be taken first, and so Serjeant Wrangham, who "led" for that party (Serjeant Kinglake, Mr. Paget, Mr. E. B. Denison—son of the vice-chairman and now Lord Grimthorpe—and Mr. Adams being with him), at once began to open his case. His argumenns, of course, were frequently directed against the statements and conclusions of the Five Kings' report, and with Mr. Baxter's detailed criticism of this in his hand—a criticism the publication of which had already done much to discredit the authority of the railway department of the Board, seeing that no attempt to reply to it had been made—he was able at once practically to spike this gun, so that it became useless to his opponents, if not even an incubus to them, practically from the commencement of the battle.

Owing to the magnitude of the London and York project and the mass of evidence which he had preliminarily to introduce, Serjeant Wrangham's speech lasted well on into the third day of the hearing—30 April. Then the local traffic evidence was commenced, which the London and York direction had decided to present with great fulness for the first sixty miles of the railway at any rate, seeing that it was a principal argument in their opponents' case that a new line northwards from London was not needed, but that the existing Eastern Counties Railway should be used as the base of a new trunk. So, passing over the first ten miles only, along which there was absolutely no population except a few farmers, country gentlemen, and rusticating "merchant princes," many of whom objected strongly to the proposed disturbance of their rural quiet, they commenced their case with witnesses from Chipping Barnet, where rural quiet was considered too dear an advantage seeing that it meant coals at 42s. to 45s. a ton, and the payment of 12s. for every 18 cwt. load of hay carted to the metropolitan market.

So, in the sarcastic language of the *Railway Times*, "Barnet with its grocers came upon the scene and looked as big as could be wished. One witness gave utterance to the astounding fact that he annually

---

* Mr. Mitchell, the veteran Committee clerk at the House of Commons, has told me that *the smell* of the London and York Committee-room will never be effaced from his memory.

received from London as much as fifty tons of goods, and that perhaps he went to London once a week. In fact, he thought he might say that he knew two others in the town who did as much. He would not go so far as to say that a superabundant supply of manure from London would augment his business, although he did not say it would not, as he had not considered the subject. He would, however, go this far and say that 'perhaps it would and perhaps it wouldn't.' This was his opinion, and nothing could shake it."

The evidence from Hertfordshire had not gone on for long before Mr. Macgeachy, who was a resident in that county, discovered that he had local interests which should have debarred him from being placed upon the Committee, and so he retired from it, being probably only too glad to be released from an inquiry which it was now certain would be abnormally long and tedious. On 7 May, for example, Committee and counsel were engaged for several hours in wrangling over a single point in the evidence of a professional "traffic-taker"—a personage of much importance in these early railway days—who was understood to declare that 16,500,000 sheep would come yearly by the new railway to the Metropolis, whereas the figure appearing in the official London and York estimate was 276,000 only. According to a newspaper report this apparent discrepancy was due to a misunderstanding "arising from the technical method of calculation traffic-takers adopt."

But the majority of the London and York traffic witnesses were men of higher calibre than professional calculators. They included the Chairman, Mr. Astell, who spoke as M.P. for Bedfordshire, Mr. G. H. Packe of Grantham, Mr. Charles Chaplin, the Right Hon. W. E. Gladstone, M.P., who appeared on 16 May to represent his constituents at Newark, Lord Worsley, and the Earl of Lincoln. On 22 May Mr. Edmund Denison came into the box, and he was followed on the following day by Mr. Joseph Pease, son of Edward Pease, "the father of railways," whose evidence as to the probable coal traffic on the line created a great impression. He gave an account of the efforts he had made since the completion of through railway communication to open up an overland trade for Durham coal in the West and South of England, but said that so far he had been baulked by his inability to obtain a low and trustworthy through rate and sufficiently rapid transit over a series of lines under numerous independent managements. He felt quite sure, however, that the opening of a direct route in one hand from York to London would produce "a perfect revolution in the coal trade throughout the whole length of the kingdom." Indeed, so certain was he of this, that he was willing himself to guarantee the £300,000 which the

London and York promoters had credited to themselves for coal traffic—to lease the coal business of the line for that sum in fact. But the London and York Committee did not intend to draw their coal traffic from the Durham field only. Mr. Baxter had already sketched out a scheme for bringing South Yorkshire coal, ready loaded in trucks, down the Dun Navigation to Doncaster, and so conveying it to London without a single break of bulk The rate per mile was to be $\frac{3}{4}d.$ a ton (a rate already in force to a small extent on the Midland Railway, but which the London and Birmingham directors had refused to adopt for the carriage of Derbyshire and Leicestershire coals to the London market), and on these terms it was reckoned that Durham and South Yorkshire coals would be saleable at King's Cross for 21s. a ton, thus giving the Metropolitan purchaser the benefit of a saving of no less than 8s. upon every ton he consumed.

This evidence as to coal traffic was not only irritating to the opponents of the London and York as tending greatly to strengthen the case for the Bill, but it also appeared to many of them to amount to a betrayal of the interests of railway proprietors generally. Directors and traffic managers protested loudly that a rate of $\frac{3}{4}d.$ a ton per mile was worse than unprofitable, and Mr. Robert Stephenson is said to have declared that if the London and York Bill was allowed to pass with its toll clauses unrevised, he would sell every railway share he had and never buy another. Nevertheless, the "Ishmaelites" proceeded steadily with their evidence, which was now generally acknowledged to have been very skilfully got up by Mr. Baxter, and by the end of May their spirits had risen to a very high pitch. In the opposition camps, on the other hand, the fear began to be frequently uttered: "Perhaps the monster bubble will not burst after all."

On 30 May Mr. Cubitt was called into the box to open the engineering evidence, and he soon showed that he was fully able to defend his estimates against the attacks which had been made upon them, albeit these had the authority of six "kings" at their back. Nor was his evidence less effective because it was not ostensibly framed to repel these attacks; indeed one of its best "hits" was the bluff declaration: "I have never read a line of the Board of Trade report." His cross-examination lasted through nearly two sittings, being carried on by a succession of counsel representing the opposing projects; and, as the same questions were repeated over and over again in different forms by men who, while affecting to go into minute details, displayed in many cases a complete ignorance of the elements of engineering, Mr. Cubitt, though of the most affable temper, had hard work to conceal his irritation, despite the fact that his opponents scored hardly a single effective point. Being asked for about the fourth time how he had bored a certain trial pit, he answered testily, "No, sir, I'll not tell you; you've bored *me* enough"; and more than once he was constrained to tell his learned badgerers to seek more intelligent instructions from the engineers on their own side.

The fact was that intelligence and argumentative effectiveness had now begun to be considered qualities of small consequence in the Hudsonian counsel compared with loquacity and resource in consuming time. King Hudson—as Brougham said in a speech before the House of Lords—was now "working with twelve-counsel-power" before the Group X Committee, with the main object of delay, so that its report—which he now seriously feared would be in favour of the London and York—might not be made that session; and though the daily expense of the proceedings was estimated at £3000 a day, he did not grudge the portion of this that had to come from the Midland exchequer, since he knew that he was dissipating the enemy's resources as well as effectually preventing, for a year, at any rate, the practical commencement of their undertaking. The London and York managers, on their part, could not afford to weaken their case by curtailment, and so upon the completion of the evidence and cross-examination of Messrs. Hawkshaw, Brunel, and Gibbs, engineers, and of Mr. Betts and his son, contractors—all of whom Mr. Baxter thought it wise to put into the box to confirm Mr. Cubitt's plans and estimates—no fewer than twenty-five days of the working session had been expended, and the cases for the Direct Northern project and for the Cambridge and Lincoln, Sheffield and Lincoln, and Midland and Eastern Counties Bills had yet to be heard.

Meanwhile the Syston and Peterborough Bill had received the Royal assent; the Nottingham, Newark, and Lincoln, and Wakefield, Pontefract, and Goole had both passed the Commons without reference to the proceeding in the London and York Committee, and Mr. Hudson had got his Newcastle and Berwick line—the last link in the East Coast Route north of York—through the Commons also, after a fierce contest with Brunel's rival "atmospheric" scheme. So all was going as the Railway King wished, except in Group X; but there on 10 June the Cambridge and Lincoln, like the Direct Northern before it, was reduced from a Bill to a "project" upon the discovery of some very serious errors in the levels. Nevertheless, the Cambridge and Lincoln party was able to consume nineteen precious days with evidence which *Herapath's Railway Journal* described as "tedious, unimportant, and insufferable nonsense," and, as June drew to an end, the Hudsonians became more and more assured that no report in favour of the London and York could be made that session.

They were not content, however, to rely upon obstruction simply, for on 30 June Mr. Hildyard, Q.C., before closing the Cambridge and Lincoln case, asked for the summary rejection of the London and York Bill. His plea was that Standing Orders had not been complied with, seeing that the Bill proposed to raise £6,500,000 capital, whereas £5,000,000 only was the figure appearing on the bulk of the scrip. To give time for the consideration of this point, the Committee adjourned until 12.30 the next day, when a great crowd assembled full of anxiety to hear a decision which might bring the whole contest to an end for the session. Another interval for a consultation with the Speaker increased the fears of the one party and the hopes of the other, and then Lord Courtenay announced that it would be competent for the London and York Company to raise seven millions under their Bill. Thereupon about forty people burst from the room, and the chairman was heard to remark in an undertone, "There goes share-jobbing."

The London and York party now determined—not a moment too soon—to make a push for a finish, and on the next day, 2 July, when the Direct Northern case was called on, Serjeant Wrangham gave notice that he should ask for a decision on his Bill so soon as the Committee should have been put in possession of all the evidence for the three competing north and south schemes. But the Direct Northern, naturally enough, took all the time they could over their evidence, and not content with this, on 9 July one of their counsel created a new "sensation" by declaring that he was in a position to prove that there were errors in the London and York plans similar to those which had proved fatal to the competing Bills. Serjeant Wrangham protested against the belated starting of such an objection; but the Committee, after taking a day to deliberate, decided that the allegation was too serious to be ignored. Thereupon messengers went off post-haste to the London Exchange, and pigeons were started from outside the House to provincial jobbers, for it was confidently reported that there was an error on one of the London and York branches of seventeen feet.

On 12 July particulars of the alleged errors were put in—about twenty in number, varying from seven to twenty feet—but upon examination of them, the London and York party found that they had been derived not from measurements upon the ground, but were merely discrepancies upon the plans themselves, *i.e.*, cases in which the scale measurements differed sensibly from the figures printed thereon. In such cases it was, and is, a recognized practice for the figures to prevail over the measures, but, not content with putting in this sufficient reply, the London and York counsel on 19 July produced the copper plates from which the plans had been printed, which showed that the latter had been drawn with perfect accuracy, and that the alleged errors were accounted for entirely by the shrinkage of the paper after it had been damped for printing. After this even the *Railway Times* was constrained to denounce the over-zealous partisans who had brought forward the objection, and Serjeant Wrangham characterized it as "destitute even of the semblance of honesty."

Meanwhile the Committee had acceded to the London and York request for an immediate decision, despite an energetic protest from Mr. Charles Austin, the "leader" for the Midland, who urged that the case for the Swinton to March line should first be heard; and on Monday, 21 July—the seventieth day of the hearing—Serjeant Wrangham was at last able to make his closing speech in reply. In an eloquent peroration he begged the Committee to sanction the London and York line, because it was calculated to confer abundance and improvement on a great district, "to bless the fields with increase, and to satisfy the poor with bread." Then Lord Courtenay, after rebuking the applause which had burst from the crowded room, announced that the proceedings would be adjourned until two o'clock on the following Wednesday, when he hoped to be able to announce the Committee's decision on the Bill. This adjournment for a day and a half was considered a bad omen for the success of the measure; and, as a matter of fact, there was actually a tie in the Committee—the chairman and Mr. Baring Wall being in its favour, while Mr. Powlett Scrope thought the Eastern Counties line should be used south of Peterborough, and Mr. Darby felt himself bound to vote against the Bill on a technicality, being one of those odd men who think the smallest technical difficulty of more consequence than the largest substantial interests of justice. So when two o'clock on Wednesday, 23 July, came, the fate of the Bill still hung in the balance, and the eager and excited crowd, which besieged all the avenues to the Committee-room and filled it almost to suffocation directly the doors were opened, was kept waiting until a quarter-past four before the members of the Committee came into the room. Then amid intense silence Lord Courtenay announced the decision as follows:—"I am instructed to state that the Committee have come to the resolution that the preamble of the London and York Bill is proved"—here he was interrupted for some moments by a triumphant shout and clapping of hands—"omitting the branches to Wakefield and Sheffield, which they have thought it right to postpone for future consideration in consequence of there being other lines before them which they consider as competing schemes with these." Hereupon a further cheer was raised, which the chairman instantly rebuked as "exceedingly indecent," and then the crowd poured helter-skelter from the room to bear to Stock Exchange, newspaper office, and railway headquarters the tidings in which so many were deeply concerned.

The seventy days' fight had thus ended in a brilliant victory for the "juvenile promoters" of the London and York undertaking, but their formidable foes, though discredited, were by no means disabled, and they at once prepared for a new attack. For this they found a ready weapon in the fact that the decision had been given without hearing the evidence for the Midland, York and North Midland and Eastern Counties extensions, although these had been included in Group X as competing projects with the London and York; so at the Midland half-yearly meeting on 25 July—only two days after the decision—Mr. Hudson announced amid "a hurricane of applause" that it was the intention of the Midland and York and North Midland directors to appeal on this ground to the House from the verdict of the Committee. "I feel it difficult," he said, "as an Englishman, to restrain my feelings when speaking of such proceedings. With breathless haste the Committee were resolved to pass the preamble of the Bill; with breathless haste they are resolved to report upon it; but I hope and believe that our appeal to the House will result in sending back the Bill to the Committee, so that its opponents may at least bring forward their case."

On the previous day, 24 July, Serjeant Wrangham had obtained permission from the Committee to divide his Bill into two parts, so that the trunk and loop lines, which had been sanctioned, might go on at once for third reading in the House, but on 26 July Mr. Charles Austin, Q.C., presented written protests from the Midland, York and North Midland and Eastern Counties Companies, urging again that their cases should first be heard. The Committee, however, declined to receive these documents, stating that they could be tendered with more propriety to the full House. Accordingly, on 1 August, when the report on the first part of the Bill came up for confirmation, Mr. Ward, M.P. for Sheffield, move for its recommittal, declaring that the refusal to hear the cases for the competing extensions formed "one of the strongest causes" for such a motion "ever brought before the House." Lord Courtenay and Mr. Darby replied, defending the course which the Committee had taken, and Mr. Ward's motion was ignominiously lost by seventy-nine votes to nineteen.

To get their Bill through third reading in the Commons and through all its stages in the Lords in the short time that now remained before the prorogation of Parliament, was a task which the London and York promoters would not have found easy if the opposition which had dogged their progress from the start had now been withdrawn. Instead of this it was to be conducted with more virulence than ever, and to be directed against a part of their Bill which had so far escaped criticism, namely, the subscription contract. These contracts had, as we know, been required by Parliament in order to check the promotion of bubble companies, but the futility of this device—now that mania was at fever-heat—had just been demonstrated during the proceedings in the House of Lords upon the Dublin and Galway Railway Bill, the subscription contract of which, it was discovered, had been allowed to pass the Standing Orders Committee, although it contained the names of paupers or fictitious persons to the extent of £500,000. Naturally enough, this gave rise to the suspicion that other contract signatures were similarly fraudulent; and thereupon the idea seems to have occurred to a Mr. Croucher, one of the numerous hangers-on of the Hudsonian party—at any rate it was put into effect mainly by him—that if the London and York contract, which had also been unopposed on Standing Orders, were now to be investigated, it might result in the bringing to light of a flaw, real and fatal, in the hitherto unimpeachable Bill.

With cool audacity Croucher and his assistants sent circulars to country postmasters, written on paper and in language which made them appear to have some authority from Parliament, asking them to send information as to the means or station of signatories to the deed whose addresses were in their neighbourhood, and they also employed emissaries to trace out others in London and its vicinity. By these means they in a short time compiled quite a long list of subscribers, responsible altogether for upwards of half a million of the London and York capital, who were alleged to be "needy persons, or paupers wholly unable to meet their respective engagements," or to appear on the contract by "fictitious names, descriptions, or places of abode." The next step was to embody these names and the allegations with regard to them in a petition, to which Mr. Henry Bruce, the deputy-chairman of the Cambridge and Lincoln Committee, was persuaded to put his signature; and this was presented on

4 August to both Houses of Parliament with the prayer that the
London and York Bill might not be allowed to proceed further
until a full inquiry into the financial *bona fides* of the undertaking
had been made.

The petition reached the Commons just in time to be heard when
the badgered Bill came up for third reading; but, thanks to the able
advocacy of Mr. Denison, it was not allowed to stop the measure at
that stage, though the House, fearful of being thought to cloak
practices by which many of its own members were deeply tainted,
would not refuse to appoint a Committee to investigate the allegations.
A similar Committee was also appointed by the Lords, and the two
tribunals carried on their inquiries simultaneously to the great disgust
of the scripholders named in the petition—who now found themselves
hauled up under fearful pains and penalties to prove their means of
credit or even their very existence in two separate Parliamentary committee-rooms. The Commons Committee, impressed with the urgency
of the matter, hurried on their proceedings in a manner which was
more zealous than dignified. On the afternoon of its first sitting, five
o'clock had long passed without sign of adjournment, and the scripholders in attendance, being strictly forbidden to depart without leave,
became almost beside themselves with rage. Says the *Times* report:

"Several resolute gentlemen were actually heading a march downstairs when it was announced that the Committee had adjourned.
'Pray, sir, is it till eleven or twelve to-morrow?' 'Why, they've only
risen to dine; they meet again at nine o'clock.' This was thought
to be a joke for a few moments till hon. members confirmed the sad
reality, and at nine o'clock the witnesses were again assembled in the
lobby in the worst possible humour. One old gentleman declared they
were more like a council of Red Indians than a Christian House of
Commons. Others enlarged upon the sufferings of their domestic
circles at such unexpected and unusual absence, and a country witness,
when it came to eleven o'clock, informed his sympathetic friends that
he had never been kept up to such an unearthly hour for the last
twenty years. When word was brought that the Committee would sit
till three or four in the morning, the elderly witnesses went off in
despair, and searching for soft spots on the tables and benches of an
empty committee-room, formed a kind of railway bivouac more novel
than picturesque. The more mercurial gentlemen amused themselves
with playing leap-frog, distorting other witnesses' names as they were
called in, wakening the policemen by alarms of fire and ringing the
division bell with great energy. It is said that such a scene was never
witnessed before in the House of Commons, and that the records may
be searched in vain for any similar instance of a Committee sitting
beyond midnight. It was hoped that the Committee would decide
upon the cases before three o'clock, but finding at one that a great

many witnesses remained to be examined, they gave in and adjourned at that hour until eleven. A number of refractory witnesses have been specially invited to attend by Speaker's warrant."

To many of those named in the petitions these inconveniences were the addition of injury to insult, seeing that their character and means to fulfil their engagements were unimpeachable except by reckless ignorance, but others, unfortunately, afforded examples of that unscrupulous speculation from the taint of which, at this time of mania, it was practically impossible to keep even sound enterprises exempt. Thus one name, which was down in the contract for no less than £12,000, was found to be that of a stockbroker's clerk—the son of a charwoman—who had been used as a tool by his masters; while another was Mr. Shakell, who was popularly known as "the great railway proprietor of the Charterhouse." This worthy admitted to the Committees that his sole sources of income were £26 per annum, which he received from an army pension—he was a retired cornet—and about £60 from the charity of the Charterhouse. He had, however, a rich brother living at Hockley Hall, Maidenhead, Berks, and on the strength of his brother's address he had obtained a large allotment of London and York scrip. But he did not keep any of it—"he knew better than that"—he sold it at a premium. "Did he make much money?" asked an honourable member. "Not half as much as he ought." "Had he any interest in the line?" "Not he, indeed." The examination of this witness is reported to have been "very facetious."

Meanwhile, after reporting in favour of the London and York main and loop lines, the Committee on Group X had continued its Herculean labours, taking on next the Bill of the Eastern Counties Company for an extension from Cambridge through St. Ives to Huntingdon. This was not only not opposed, but it was favoured by the London and York party, because it would give a good route to Cambridge for traffic coming over their lines from the north; and so it passed the Committee with little difficulty, making way for the London and York (Bawtry to Sheffield branch) Bill, and the rival Bill of the Sheffield and Lincolnshire Company. This contest resulted in a victory for the latter, whose main line from Sheffield to Gainsborough, there to join the Sheffield and Grimsby Junction Railway (which had just got through both Houses in another group) was sanctioned, while the Sheffield branch, promoted by the London and York, and a proposed branch of the Sheffield and Lincolnshire, from Retford to Lincoln, were both thrown out. Then on 5 August—on the eighty-third day, and in the fifteenth week of their sittings—this "record" Committee broke up with an important part of their task yet unaccomplished, for they reported to the House that the London and York (Wakefield branch) Bill, and the Bills for the Midland and York and North Midland extensions must be postponed for consideration in the following session.

It was not until four days later—9 August, 1845—when Parliament was on the eve of prorogation, and all hope of getting the London and York Bill through the Lords that session had been quite abandoned—that the reports of the Committees on the subscription contract reached the two Houses. The Commons report stated that the serious charges contained in Mr. Henry Bruce's petition had been made in many cases without taking the most ordinary means of inquiry; that it had been presented with the view of stopping the further progress of the London and York Bill, and to promote the interests of a rival company, and that the conduct of Henry Bruce was a gross breach of the right of petitioning. The Lords Committee also condemned the hasty and inconsiderate manner in which the petition had been drawn up. But the combined result of the two reports was to prove that £29,900 worth of London and York shares had been signed for by persons who could not be found, and £44,500 by persons stated to be without property, and the Lords report recommended that the Bill should not be read a second time in that House until a further investigation into the contract had been made. Thus the policy of the Hudsonian obstructionists was at last crowned with success, and so, with the London and York Bill hung up in a Parliamentary limbo between Lords and Commons, the great railway session of 1845 came to an end.

CHAPTER IV.

THE INFANT IS CHRISTENED AND GIVEN LEAVE TO GROW—
1845-1846.

IT was, of course, a severe disappointment to the London and York promoters that the decision of the House of Commons Committee which they had spent so much money and trouble to obtain had been stultified so far as the session of 1845 was concerned. Nevertheless, their partial victory was not only very encouraging for the future, but it also provided them with a most valuable new weapon in controversy. For Lord Courtenay, in his report on their Bill to the House, expressly refuted all the principal adverse arguments of the report of the Board of Trade, and therefore it was no longer possible for anyone to argue with effect either that a new trunk line all the way from London to York was not needed, or that the plans by which the London and York Company proposed to supply this need were not well laid out. Moreover, railway scrip continued to be the most popular form of investment, and so, despite the equivocal position of the Bill in Parliament, that of the London and York rose to a high premium on the Exchange.

Nevertheless, the authority of King Hudson, though far less absolute than it had been a year before, when Messrs. Denison and Baxter were gentlemen "little known in the railway world," still stood like a giant's stronghold right across the path of the new enterprise. The Railway King had had on the whole a very successful campaign in the session of 1845. He had carried through, in the teeth of formidable opposition, his Newcastle and Berwick Railway, thus completing, as far as Parliamentary powers went, the East Coast route to Scotland, the main part of which, from Rugby to Berwick, was under his practically absolute control. He had also secured for the Midland Company a good foothold on the eastern side of England, by obtaining for it powers for the Syston and Peterborough and Nottingham, Newark and Lincoln branches. Moreover, the Midland had risen from adversity to prosperity under his management, while the other company which was peculiarly his own—the York and North Midland—had continued its unbroken success. These facts and this greater one, that he—and he almost alone, as it appeared—had brought railway promotion out of stagnation and discredit into prosperity and popularity, were sufficient to explain, and in part to justify, the respect amounting almost to veneration in which he was now commonly held.

But even King Hudson was not strong enough to disregard the fact that a Committee of the House of Commons, after the fullest possible inquiry, had decided in favour of a new trunk line from London to the north; and so, recognizing that this had made his plan for appropriating Lincolnshire for the Midland Company a thing of the past, he set himself to work out a new, and even more Napoleonic, plan of campaign against his obstinate competitors. This was to become himself the projector and master of a complete eastern system of railways! Already, as we have seen, he had given a certain amount of support to the Cambridge and Lincoln project, but this was palpably insincere, and had the Cambridge and Lincoln been carried through in the session of 1845 and the London and York thrown out, he would almost certainly have taken steps either to secure its subsequent abandonment or else that it should be worked in such a way as not to compete seriously with the established Midland and York and North Midland route. This method of blocking the London and York enterprise, however, was now no longer available, and the only effective weapon against it which remained was a *bonâ fide* project for extending the Eastern Counties from Cambridge to York. Accordingly, as the best way of getting hold of this weapon, and at the same time preventing its use to the injury of Midland interests, Hudson secured the chairmanship of the Eastern Counties Company.

Ostensibly, the position was pressed upon him by a majority of the shareholders of this Company who were dissatisfied with the meagre results of the existing management. Ostensibly, the Railway King was reluctant to undertake this addition to his already too onerous responsibilities, and quite an effective little scene was played out at York, where Hudson was summoned from a festive gathering to receive a deputation from the Eastern Counties, and was apparently so unprepared for their offer that he had to ask for a night's sleep upon it before giving a final answer. But this is strategy of a kind to which men of the Napoleonic stamp have been ever prone, and there can be little doubt that had Hudson himself not set the ball in motion, this first of the many "revolutions" of which the Shoreditch Board-room was to be the scene would never have taken place.

It was on 13 October, 1845, that Hudson formally accepted the chairmanship of the Eastern Counties Company, and on 30 October he presided over a largely-attended meeting of its shareholders, who behaved, according to a newspaper report, "as if they were literally mad with joy" at his accession. The object of the meeting was to empower the directors to go to Parliament for an extension of their system from Cambridge, through Lincoln and Doncaster to a junction with the York and North Midland, and Leeds and Selby railways at South Milford; and Hudson announced that the Cambridge and Lincoln party had already agreed to exchange their scrip for shares in this new undertaking, and that he proposed to make a similar offer to the London and York scripholders, namely that they should accept £20 worth of Eastern Counties Extension Stock in lieu of every £50 worth of London and York Shares, to which they had subscribed. He admitted that the London and York had gained a partial victory in the House of Commons, but, as a great statesman had said, "Thank God there was a House of Lords," before which the Bill would have to come next session with an essential part of it—the subscription contract—already discredited, and he professed confidence that the holders of scrip would prefer the liberal terms of amalgamation he offered them to entering upon a new Parliamentary contest under such conditions. For the rest, he promised, amid wild cheering, to convert the hitherto unprofitable Eastern Counties within a year or two into a 10 per cent. line.

On the very same day, 30 October—probably as a counterblast to Hudson's rhodomontade—the London and York directors issued a circular from their office at Lothbury. They announced that, in accordance with the resolution of Parliament, "all Railway Bills should be resumed next session at the point where they had been left in the last," they proposed to proceed with their Bill in the House of Lords so soon as it should meet again, and that for this they had ample funds in hand from the original deposit. They proposed further to re-introduce the Wakefield Branch into the Commons in a separate Bill, together with an extension from Wakefield to Leeds, a cross-line from Stamford to Spalding, and new branches to Dunstable *via* St. Albans and Luton and to Hertford, and for these purposes they were about to issue scrip for an additional £100,000 of "extension stock." Finally, having in view the proved laws in their existing subscription contract, and the fact that the Standing Orders required that such contract should be entered into "subsequent to the commencement of the session previous to that in which application should be made for a Bill," they proposed to prepare an entirely new deed and to announce shortly the times and places at which it would be submitted for signature.

In this manifesto there was no hint of a desire for a compromise, and so Hudson appears to have thought that the time was not yet ripe for making his offer of amalgamation formally. At any rate, he said nothing further about the matter until 19 November, when an important public meeting to discuss the question of railway communication was held at Cambridge. At this the Railway King, who appeared in person for the Eastern Counties, urged—of course with the approval of the meeting—that Cambridge should be placed on a main line to the north, and he concluded his speech by an appeal to Mr. Pym, who represented his opponents, to bring about a conference with this object between the London and York and Eastern Counties directors. Mr. Pym undertook to report the proposal at the next meeting of his Board.

Meanwhile the London and York directors had issued another circular—dated 12 November—to announce that the new subscription contract would lie for signature in London and other places from 9 to 31 December, and to ask that all scrip should be sent in within the same dates for re-registry. This, however, became the occasion of long and inflammatory advertisements in the *Times* and elsewhere, signed "One of yourselves," which warned the scrip-holders against the new deed as a device for making them liable to take additional shares, and declared that it amounted to a confession that the whole Parliamentary contest would have to be fought over again *de novo*. These advertisements no doubt emanated from some hanger-on of the Hudsonian party, but they were well calculated to alarm the more timid of the London and York supporters. For, after reaching a climax in October, the railway mania had now given way to panic, and scrip-holders generally were as eager in November to "unload" as they had been in September to buy. Nevertheless, such was the character of the persons to whom the bulk of the London and York shares had been allotted, and such the confidence which the Committee of Direction had inspired, that by the middle of December nine-tenths of the scrip had been sent in for exchange, and the new contract had already received a long list of most respectable signatures.

It was under these encouraging circumstances that the London and York Board met on 16 December to deliberate upon the answer they should send to the amalgamation proposal which, as the result of Mr. Pym's action, they had received on 3 December from the Railway King. Hudson had then offered to allot £2,000,000 of Eastern Counties Extension Stock to the London and York scrip-holders if they would give up their independent undertaking, and he had suggested that a special Board meeting might fitly be held to consider this proposal.

E

But the London and York directors had wisely determined to take time to reply, and now in a letter adopted at their ordinary meeting—a letter which though signed "William Astell, Chairman," betrays the authorship of Edmund Denison in every sentence—they unhesitatingly declined the Eastern Counties offer, declaring that its acceptance would be "a gross breach of faith" with the public and their original subscribers, and that it was nothing more than "a bold effort" on Mr. Hudson's part "to raise the value of the Eastern Counties Stock, and, as Chairman of the Midland, to get rid of a rival."

"You surely cannot have calculated," the letter continued, "upon our giving your proposal our favourable consideration, and you will therefore not be surprised to learn that my colleagues unanimously decline to discuss with you so unreasonable a proposition, involving as it does a total abandonment of our whole scheme. . . . We shall ask leave to proceed with our Bill as rapidly as the forms of the House will permit, having without any further call ample funds in hand to meet all expenses. . . . Public opinion is decidedly in favour of a new line between London and York independent of existing interests and management. We therefore confidently expect that the merits of our scheme which obtained for us a verdict in the Commons will be equally appreciated in the Lords."

Two days later—18 December—the Cambridge and Lincoln Committee issued a circular announcing that their scrip must be exchanged at once for Eastern Counties Stock; but besides the London and York another party still remained outside Hudson's fold. This was the Direct Northern. Very soon after the prorogation of Parliament a meeting of the scrip-holders in this scheme had resolved to introduce a Bill next session for their integral project, and Mr. John Miller, engineer to the North British Company, had been instructed to prepare new plans, which were deposited at the Board of Trade on the historical "day of deposits," 30 November, 1845, as one of the 700 batches of similar documents which on that eventful Sunday were poured into the Government offices at Whitehall. A great many of these Bills were practically dead when they were deposited, but, contrary to general expectation, the Direct Northern managed to keep alive, owing mainly to the support it received from Scotland, and in January, 1846, when the worst of the reaction from the mania seemed over, it came out from its offices in Moorgate Street with a new and confident prospectus.

The Railway King displayed much pious sorrow that the London and York directors should have rejected what he termed "the olive-branch of peace," and his supporters in the Press did their utmost to frighten the scrip-holders into taking action on their own account by alleging that their deposit must now be exhausted, and that, because of the new deed, they would have to fight the Parliamentary battle over again in the Commons as well as in the Lords. Nevertheless, in face of calumny and gloomy forebodings—to both of which, indeed, they were now thoroughly inured—the London and York directors proceeded steadily in their course, and on 13 March, 1846, they had the satisfaction to see their Bill pass the House of Commons *pro formâ*, as their Parliamentary advisers had all along assured them that it would, while about the same time they received overtures of amalgamation from the Direct Northern party, whose Bill was still shivering on the brink of the Standing Orders ordeal. To these proposals, however, as to Hudson's, they replied that they could entertain no terms which involved the giving up of any part of their Parliamentary line.

On 6 April, 1846, the Bill came before the Standing Orders Committee of the Lords, and there the objection was raised by Lord Redesdale that the new contract deed was not legal. This check sent London and York scrip to a discount, while an appeal to the Attorney-General and Solicitor-General was made; but to the immense relief of the promoters the opinion of these authorities proved favourable, and so their Bill passed triumphantly the last of the dreaded Standing Orders ordeals. But meanwhile the Eastern Counties Bill had been withdrawn from the Commons and introduced into the Lords, and so a final pitched battle in Committee stage had yet to be fought.

"Hard work I don't mind; it's dirty work I abhor," Baxter had said aloud in the corridor at Westminster at the time when the proceedings in Henry Bruce's petition were in progress, and he had now occasion to repeat this remark. On 14 April, 1846, a circular was issued from the office of Mr. Henry Philipps, a solicitor, at 4, Sise Lane, E.C., purporting to emanate from a Committee formed with the concurrence of the holders of many thousand of London and York shares. These, it declared, were strongly in favour of making terms of amalgamation with the Eastern Counties Company on the ground that the passing of the London and York Bill would, in the existing state of the Money Market, be the greatest misfortune that could happen to the scrip-holders; and it exhorted other scrip-holders who endorsed these views to send in their names at once to Sise Lane. As the London and York directors, in a counter-circular issued on 17 April, warned the scrip-holders, this appeal "no doubt emanated from interested opponents," who were making their last effort to impede the Bill, and several large holders of scrip wrote to Sise Lane to rebuke the self-constituted Committee, one of them— Captain Hall, of the Indian Navy—declaring that he had sealed up his scrip when he had first received it, "like nailing the colours to the mast, determined to sink or conquer." Nevertheless the Committee, on

18 April, addressed a so-called offer of amalgamation to the Eastern Counties directors, and on the strength of this the latter, on 23 April, made a new offer to the London and York Board. This was that a joint Board should be constituted of twelve Eastern Counties and six London and York directors, to decide what lines should be made jointly and what abandoned.

This proposal practically amounted to placing the fate of the London and York plans in the hands of a majority of its inveterate opponents, and that it should have been made proves either that Hudson had grown reckless, or else that he greatly overrated the effect upon the position of his rivals of the proceedings of the Committee at Sise Lane. But the London and York directors knew by this time that they possessed the confidence of the great majority of their constituents, and, moreover, they had negotiations in hand with the Direct Northern which they now felt pretty sure would result in the addition of that party's funds and influence to their resources. Accordingly on 29 April they wrote to decline the Eastern Counties proposition, which they described as "an unworthy mode of attempting to dissolve the London and York Company"; and on the same day they issued another circular to their own party repeating that they had ample funds in hand to proceed with their line without a call till the next spring, and predicting the early conclusion of arrangements by which these funds would be greatly augmented. Six days later—on 5 May, 1846—an amalgamation contract was signed by Mr. Astell, on behalf of the London and York, and Mr. Capper, on behalf of the Direct Northern, under which it was agreed that the funds of the two undertakings should be amalgamated, in order to carry out the London and York scheme.

The details of this amalgamation were that the nominal value of the London and York shares was to be reduced by one half, and those of the Direct Northern by one third, and this was announced on 8 May by a circular issued from the London and York office, which requested that all scrip should be sent in at once to be endorsed according to the new arrangement. On the previous day the Sise Lane Committee had had the "extraordinary effrontery," as the London and York party termed it, to advertise the conclusion of terms of amalgamation with the Eastern Counties subject to the rejection of the London and York Bill, and to ask that scrip should be sent to *them* to be stamped to this effect, and "One of Yourselves" now again flooded the newspaper columns with appeals to the scrip-holders not to trust their directors, but to close with the Eastern Counties offer while it remained open to them. There is no doubt that Hudson countenanced—if he did not actually inspire—these tactics, and that he hoped by them to break up the London and York undertaking at a time when thousands of scrip-holders were eagerly availing themselves of the "Railway Relief resolutions" just adopted by Parliament to free themselves from liabilities into which in the previous summer they had maniacally rushed.

Nevertheless this, like Henry Bruce's petitions, the "olive-branch of peace" and other similar stratagems, failed of its purpose, and it was with a backing stronger than ever that the inexpugnable Bill came before the Lords Committee on 13 May. The Eastern Counties, the Sheffield and Lincoln, and more than a dozen other less important Bills were referred to the same Committee, but it soon became apparent that the chairman, the Earl of Lovelace, was in no mind to suffer a repetition of the procedure in the memorable Group X. He cut short the London and York traffic case with the assurance that the Committee were already convinced of the need of new lines south of Doncaster, and by 22 May the London and York evidence had been completed and the case for the Eastern Counties begun. Prior to this date the London and York directors had issued an advertisement calling the meeting of scrip-holders, required by Lord Wharncliffe's recently passed Act, before the Bill could come up for third reading, and this was to be held on Saturday, 30 May, by which time it was expected that the Bill would be almost, if not quite, out of Committee.

The fact was that the intrinsic superiority of the London and York scheme over the Eastern Counties extension was now practically admitted, and the only point which still remained at all in doubt was whether, in the existing state of the Money Market, and in view of the drain which railway construction was already making upon the resources of the country, it was politic to add this other huge undertaking to the numerous new lines already sanctioned in the sessions of 1845 and 1846. In his evidence on 19 May Mr. Cubitt had given £5,400,000 as his carefully-revised estimate for the construction of the London and York main and loop lines, but this was, of course, again challenged by the opponents of the enterprise, and both Hudson and Robert Stephenson, when they came into the box to give evidence for the Eastern Counties, declared that £10,000,000 was nearer the right figure. It was therefore still on the cards that the scrip-holders might even yet yield to fear, and to the importunity of the Sise Lane Committee, whose alarmist advertisements were still being scattered broadcast through the Press.

Under these circumstances the directors spared no efforts to obtain votes and proxies for the meeting on the 30th of May, which was held at the Hall of Commerce, Threadneedle Street, London, at the same time that the cross-examination of the Eastern Counties engineers was proceeding before the Committee at Westminster. Mr. Astell occupied the chair, supported by Mr. Denison, Mr. Charles Chaplin, Mr. Packe, Hon. O. Duncombe, and other directors, and he soon placed the issue of the proceedings beyond doubt by announcing that the directors held proxies for more than 60,000 shares, representing nearly two-thirds of the capital, whereas the approval of one-third only was sufficient under Lord Wharncliffe's Act to enable the Bill to be carried forward. The first resolution was, "That this meeting approves the Bill entitled, 'An Act for making a railway from London to York with branches therefrom providing for the counties of Hertford, Bedford, Huntingdon, Northampton, Rutland, Nottingham, and the three divisions of the county of Lincoln, to be called the Great Northern Railway,' and requests the directors to take all necessary steps for its prosecution," and this was submitted to the meeting in a short speech by Mr. Astell, and formally seconded by Mr. Denison. Then a scrip-holder—Major Richardson—rose from the body of the meeting and, upon being challenged to do so by Mr. Denison, moved an amendment in favour of an amalgamation with the Eastern Counties, the directors of which, he declared amid great uproar, would yet throw out the Bill, if it was persisted with, "whether by fair means or foul." In replying for the London and York Board Mr. Denison was not slow to take advantage of this confession as to the character and tactics of their opponents. No proposal for amalgamation with the Eastern Counties, he said, had yet been made which did not directly or indirectly involve the giving up of the London and York line; for, as for the proposition that a joint Board should be formed consisting of twelve Eastern Counties directors to six London and York, a boy of ten could predict their fate under such circumstances. "Our opponents are very cute," he continued amid laughter, "they are more cute than we are; they adopt tricks and devices which never would have occurred to us; we are unskilled and untutored in the railway world, and are shot at and hit in all sorts of ways. Why, these very parties who propose amalgamation are opposing us at this very hour, though not successfully, for I have to tell you that their engineer has completely broken down." Here he was interrupted by tremendous shouts of applause. "I tell you with confidence, and at the same time with pleasure, that the evidence which the engineer of the Eastern Counties gave in the course of yesterday has been scattered to the winds in cross-examination this morning, and that the statement that the London and York will cost £10,000,000 has been completely demolished." So forcible was Mr. Denison's speech that Major Richardson withdrew his amendment, and the resolution empowering the directors to proceed with the Bill was carried *nem. con.* "amid the most tremendous applause," says a report, "we ever heard." As for the Sise Lane Committee, not one of them ventured to raise either his voice or his head, and it came to light that they had proxies for 5796 shares only, although they had claimed at the outset to represent over 30,000.

The war was now virtually over as far as the Bill was concerned, and no one recognized this more quickly than Mr. Charles Austin, the eminent counsel who was "leading" for the Eastern Counties before the Lords Committee. He saw that he had a losing game to play, and he played it recklessly. During his concluding speech, which occupied the whole of the sitting on 4 June, he was more than once pulled up by the Committee for his mistakes, and more than once he allowed his simulated passion to outrun his discretion. "What are the public interests to me?" he is reported to have asked. "I am an advocate. I care not twopence whether the public interests are served or injured. I neither care nor hope to know anything about this line when my labours are at an end." Serjeant Wrangham replied in a manner which, if less animated, was more weighty and telling, and then the Earl of Lovelace announced that the Committee would give their decision on the following Monday, 8 June, at eleven o'clock.

Some time before the appointed hour the lobby of the Lords Committee Rooms was filled by counsel, agents, pressmen, and partisans, but the excited crowd was kept in suspense for more than an hour while their Lordships deliberated upon their decision in private. Then the counsel on both sides and Mr. Cubitt were sent for, and afterwards Messrs. Locke and Brunel, and the excitement increased when it was understood that the Committee were seeking independent engineering opinions, being still not fully satisfied as to the estimate of the London and York. Again the room was cleared, and then, a few minutes before one, counsel and agents were re-admitted at the Peers' door, and the public at the other, till the room—one of the largest in the new buildings—was filled in every part. As soon as quiet was obtained the chairman said, "It is my duty to announce to you, on the part of the Committee, that their decision is unanimous in favour of the London and York." Anything more that he may have intended to say was drowned by loud cheering which burst forth in the room, and was taken up far down the corridors outside.

Thus after "a contest unparalleled in railway annals"—to quote the subsequent words of the directors' report—the main Bill for the Great

Northern Railway was carried beyond the reach of opposition; but the Parliamentary battles of the promoters were by no means over, not even so far as the session of 1846 was concerned. As a small set-off to their great victory they had already suffered a small reverse by the defeat in the Commons of the South Yorkshire Railway, which Messrs. Denison and Baxter had promoted as an allied project to the Great Northern (to connect the South Yorkshire coal-field with the main system at Doncaster), and two similarly allied Bills—the East Lincolnshire (from Boston to Grimsby) and the Leicester and Bedford (which was to connect with the Great Northern at Hitchin), together with the Bills for the branches to Wakefield, Leeds, Stamford, Spalding, St. Albans, Luton, Dunstable, and Hertford, though they had been successful in the Commons, had still to face strenuous opposition in the Lords. This, during the ensuing two months, proved fatal to all of them except the Stamford and Spalding and the East Lincolnshire, while the Cambridge and Oxford, by which the Great Northern directors hoped to get access from Hitchin to Cambridge, was cut down by a Lords Committee into a line between Hitchin and Royston only. On the other hand, a Bill supported by the Manchester and Leeds Company for a line from Askern, near Doncaster, on the Great Northern to Methley, near Leeds on the Midland, with a junction with the Wakefield, Pontefract, and Goole between Knottingley and Pontefract, passed both Houses; and so also did the West Riding Union Bill which proposed to connect Bradford and Halifax directly with Leeds, the latter after a two-session contest with Hudson's established Leeds and Bradford Company—a contest which produced in miniature many of the features of the London and York war. Another two-session Bill, the Sheffield and Lincoln, also passed at last, together with the Sheffield and Lincolnshire Junction Bill for a line from Retford to a junction with the Great Northern loop line at Saxelby, while by another Act these, together with the Sheffield and Manchester and Great Grimsby and Sheffield Junction Railways, were amalgamated into the Manchester, Sheffield, and Lincolnshire system, to come under the management of a single directorate from 1 January, 1847.

Meanwhile the London and York Bill had received the Royal assent on 26 June, 1846—the same day as Sir Robert Peel's Corn Law Repeal Bill—and on 25 July, 1846, just within the month from the date of incorporation which the Act of Parliament allowed, the first general meeting of the Great Northern Railway Company was held at the Hall of Commerce, London, Mr. Astell occupying the chair. In their report the directors said that it had not yet been practicable to ascertain the liabilities of the amalgamated Company so as to prepare an exact balance sheet for presentation to the meeting, but that the directors thought it right to state "the general receipts and expenditure." This statement showed that the London and York Committee, after paying away no less than £251,144 during the two and a half years since the origin of the project, had a balance from the original and "extension" deposits of £115,358 "in cash," while the Direct Northern, whose disbursements so far had amounted to £89,945 only, had a balance "in cash and securities" of £334,125. This made a total balance in hand of £449,483, a sum amply sufficient to go on with without an immediate call on the shareholders; but the directors announced that they had power under their Act of Incorporation to pay 5 per cent. interest from 30 June, 1846, on all past payments and future calls, and the shareholders were invited to make payments in advance, on which this interest would be allowed, as soon and in such amount as they pleased.

To those among the shareholders who had funds at their immediate command this announcement was cheerful enough, but others who were suffering from the prevalent "tightness" of money looked forward with apprehension to the heavy calls which must come in the near future. The consequence was that the shares fell to a discount on the Exchange. The directors had a splendid record of victory behind them, but before them lay the task of carrying out the largest railway scheme ever sanctioned by Parliament. "The monster infant" had yet to be reared!

CHAPTER V.

THE HERO GROWS UP AMID STRAITENED CIRCUMSTANCES, AND GETS TO WORK IN THE COUNTRY IN A VERY SMALL WAY—1846-1848.

IT was no wonder that King Hudson opposed the London and York Bill with all the resources at his command, for its passing into law cut his kingdom in half and involved him in a conflict of duties and interests which even his ability and influence could not possibly reconcile. Even had the Eastern Counties Extension Bill been passed in preference to the London and York, Hudson would have had a hard task to combine the chairmanship of a trunk railway to the north from Shoreditch with the prior claims which the Midland shareholders had upon his interest, and to reconcile both with the positions which he held on the boards of the companies which were to complete the East Coast through route north of York. Now that a direct line from London to York was authorized with which it was the obvious interest of the East Coast lines to join hands, while to the Midland, York, and North Midland and Eastern Counties it was a dangerous rival, the position of the man who was attempting to hold the reins of all these undertakings in his single pair of hands became not honestly tenable.

Hudson's difficulties were further aggravated by two important developments which the session of 1846 had produced on the western side of England. These were the amalgamation of the London and Birmingham, Grand Junction, and other companies into the London and North Western systems, and the sanctioning after a tremendous contest of the Caledonian Railway. These two events meant that within a few years the West Coast route to Scotland would be completed, and that, when this came about, it would be the obvious interest of Euston Square to send all through passengers to the north *viâ* Crewe, Preston, and Carlisle, instead of sending a good proportion of them, as at present, by Rugby, Normanton, York, and Newcastle. Since the opening throughout from London to Gateshead in 1844 this latter had become the popular route to Scotland, and its position was shortly to be much improved by the opening of the North British line from Berwick to Edinburgh; but the gap between Newcastle and Berwick, involving very large bridges over the Tyne and Tweed, had yet to be filled up. So it was quite on the cards that the West Coast route might be completed throughout first, since the construction of the Caledonian was at once to be taken energetically in hand. At any rate, when the West Coast was finished, much of the present East Coast through traffic was certain to be diverted to it by Euston influence, unless the East Coast Companies had by that time secured for themselves an independent and more direct access to London. Therefore, though Hudson was still master of the lines from York to Berwick, and was also strong in the counsels of the North British, he had little chance of holding those companies back from their natural East Coast alliance with the Great Northern, although that alliance meant the practical extinction of the Midland and York and North Midland as far as through traffic was concerned, and the dooming of the Eastern Counties to an unprofitable life of agricultural drudgery within the limits of the district whose name it bore.

One position of vantage, however, the Railway King still held, and that was the footing which his companies had been able to secure in the London and York district before Parliament had definitely established the Great Northern in this territory. Hudson had determined—in his own words—to show that he "could provide Lincolnshire with a railway before other people had done talking about it," and so he had pushed on the construction of the Nottingham, Newark, and Lincoln line at "record" speed, with the result that it was opened for traffic on 1 August, 1846, barely more than a year, that is to say, after the Act for it had been obtained. In the following month the portion of the Syston and Peterborough line from Syston as far as Melton was brought into work, and in October, 1846, the easternmost section of the same line from Stamford to Peterborough; and from 1 January, 1847, this latter was worked in connection with the Eastern Counties extension to Peterborough from Ely and Cambridge, which was then opened throughout. After this the completion of the link between Stamford and Melton was all that was needed to establish a through connection between the Midland and Eastern Counties systems, cutting right through the centre of the Great Northern main-line territory.

But, through connection though it was, it was no good as a route for passenger traffic to and from the north—on both sides of Peterborough it was far too circuitous for that; and so Hudson, as the last chance of consolidating his kingdom, set himself to devise new connections better adapted for through service. In the session of 1846 he had promoted a line, called the South Midland, from Leicester to Hitchin, in rivalry with the similar "Leicester and Bedford" line which the London and York had supported; and now, in the autumn of 1846, after Parliament had rejected both these schemes, he forestalled the Great Northern directors by himself reviving the Leicester and Bedford Company, the scrip-holders in which he bought over by promising them the full value of their deposits in Midland Stock. This done, he invited Captain Laws, who had just left the Manchester and Leeds to become the Great Northern's "managing director," and Mr. Whitbread, the chief landowner in Bedfordshire, to a conference at Derby in October, 1846, and from this there resulted an agreement that the Great Northern should leave to the Midland the making of the line from Leicester to Hitchin, on the understanding that in conjunction with the Great Northern main line from Hitchin to King's Cross it was to form a route for London traffic to and from the Midlands alternative to the present route by Rugby to Euston Square. In order to ensure this, the agreement said that the line was to be from Leicester to Hitchin, "there to terminate"; but what Mr. Hudson's real object was became apparent when on behalf of the Eastern Counties he deposited a Bill to extend its just opened Hertford branch to Hitchin, and then inserted a clause in the Leicester, Hitchin, and Bedford Bill authorizing the Midland trains to cross the Great Northern at that place, in order to reach the Eastern Counties line. As a part of the same scheme, too, he deposited yet another Bill for an extension of the Eastern Counties from Cambridge to Bedford.

Thus, if this ruse was successful, another important slice of traffic would be abstracted from the Great Northern system, nor was this by any means the full extent of King Hudson's new plan of campaign. Another Bill which he deposited for this session of 1847, was for an extension of the Eastern Counties from Wisbeach (whither it had a line already authorized from March) to join the Midland's Nottingham and Lincoln branch at Newark; and yet another from Peterborough to join the authorized line of the "Ambergate, Nottingham, Boston, and Eastern Junction Company"—a company which had owed its incorporation in 1846 mainly to his royal support. Both these, as the reader sees, were to be cross-lines cutting right through the Great Northern's territory and joining the Eastern Counties and Midland systems into one interest.

One important result of this policy of the Railway King was to give a strategic importance, quite out of proportion to their business prospects, to such small companies as had been so fortunate as to acquire powers for cross-lines which would connect or intersect the territories of the great systems. Of this a striking-proof was the competition which now took place to buy up the line from Hitchin to Royston, powers for which had been obtained, as we have already noted, by a very typical product of the "mania," the Oxford and Cambridge Company; and at last, simply in self-defence—for it will be seen how valuable the possession of this line would have been as a new weapon in King Hudson's hands —the Great Northern was forced to acquire it at what even in those days was considered a high price, namely, a guarantee to its shareholders of a permanent dividend of 6 per cent. On the same terms —exorbitant though they afterwards proved—Mr. Denison and his colleagues were glad to obtain command of the Boston, Stamford, and Birmingham Company's authorized line from Stamford to Wisbeach, and of the East Lincolnshire Company's line from Boston to Great Grimsby; besides which they made an offer—also in the form of a guaranteed dividend—to the shareholders of the Ambergate, Nottingham, and Boston. But this Company, being also eagerly courted by the Midland and Eastern Counties, thought it would do better by maintaining its independence for a while.

Meanwhile King Hudson, in his truly royal style, had pledged the Midland to give a rent-charge guarantee of no less than 10 per cent. to the Leeds and Bradford Company in order to prevent its just opened railway from falling into the clutches either of the Manchester and Leeds, or the Great Northern; and upon the strength of this acquisition he was making a determined effort to block the Great Northern out of the West Riding of Yorkshire by promoting a direct line to be made by the Midland Company from Leeds to Wakefield. This, however, was even more of a forlorn hope than most of his other projects already named, seeing that a line from Askern, near Doncaster, to Methley, near Leeds, was already authorized to the Great Northern's ally, the Manchester and Leeds. Indeed, so confident were Mr. Denison and his colleagues of obtaining access to the capital of the West Riding by this route, that they deposited a Bill for the two short extensions necessary to make it serviceable not only to Leeds but also to Wakefield, and joined with the Leeds and Thirsk, the Manchester and Leeds, and the Leeds and Dewsbury Companies to deposit another for making a "central station" in the former town.

Thus the Company seemed at last to be in measurable distance of obtaining full powers for one of its main objects, namely, the provision of a direct line from Leeds—Mr. Denison's native town—to the

Metropolis; but meanwhile Mr. Baxter did not allow the directors to forget another object—which in his eyes at least had, from the first, appeared second to no other in importance—namely, provision for working coal traffic from the South Yorkshire pits. With this in view he set on foot in this autumn of 1846 a new scheme for a railway from Doncaster to the coal-field, for which he secured the support not only of Mr. Denison, but of Earl Fitzwilliam, Mr. Wentworth Vernon, and Lord Wharncliffe, all large coalowners; and to this South Yorkshire Railway Company, as it was called, the Great Northern directors were persuaded to subscribe one-third of the capital. On the other hand, the Midland and Manchester, Sheffield and Lincolnshire Companies both declined to give the project financial support, though its line was so laid out as to connect with their main systems also. They preferred to set on foot competing schemes of their own.

Thus hardly had the Great Northern emerged from the tremendous Parliamentary conflicts which gave it birth, before its directors were called upon to prepare for a new campaign, in which their undertaking was to be attacked at all points. This was the more burdensome to them because their natural desire, of course, was to concentrate all their resources upon the construction of their already authorized lines. They had charge—to quote from Mr. Denison's speech at one of the first half-yearly meetings—of "the largest project of the kind attempted by any company since railways had first been adopted in the country," and, moreover, by the end of 1846 they had expended over half a million of money in their undertaking, although not a single sod had been cut nor one brick put upon another for its works. They therefore felt it most unpleasant to have to look forward to a continuation of wasteful outlay in Parliamentary contests at a time when every pound was wanted to expedite the real work of the railway.

At the end of July, 1846, as already mentioned, they had told the shareholders that, after allowing for all disbursements to that date, they had a balance from the original deposits of just upon £450,000, but soon afterwards it was discovered that the expenditure both of the London and York and the Direct Northern preliminary to the passing of the Act had been very much under-estimated in this rough balance-sheet, and when an exact one was completed a few months later, it was found that the amount expended on both accounts up to the date of the passing of the Act, 26 June, 1846, instead of being about £300,000, came to the monstrous sum of £432,620 12s. 1d. Of this the London and York part—£309,206—was not excessive in view of the two tremendous Parliamentary fights they had waged, but that the Direct Northern should have expended £123,414, although their Bill in neither session had got beyond the Standing Orders, was proof of gross extravagance on the part of some of that party of promoters, and evoked some strong language from Mr. Denison, who had been assured at the time of the amalgamation that the Direct Northern expenses could not have exceeded £50,000. Moreover, when the time arrived for the final merging of accounts, about £50,000 of the Direct Northern balance was not forthcoming, and although in consequence of Mr. Denison's emphatic protests the deficiency was immediately covered by notes of hand from the directors, a breach in the ranks was thus created which by the end of the year widened into a final severance, all but one or two of the Direct Northern representatives being then balloted off the Board by the London and York majority in accordance with a resolution of the shareholders that the number of directors should be reduced from thirty to twenty-two.

On the other hand, however, the promise of immediate interest at 5 per cent. brought in many payments in advance of calls, and by the end of 1846 more than £100,000 was received on this account, which just about restored the balance in hand to the originally estimated figure. Meanwhile Mr. Cubitt had been busy with the permanent survey of the line, and in November, 1846, his finally revised schedules for the section of the line between London and Peterborough were handed to Mr. Thomas Brassey, already a railway contractor of eminence, who, to the great satisfaction of the directors, agreed in December to undertake the work at the prices therein named, accepting a penalty of £5000 per month if he did not complete the first fifty-nine miles from London to Huntingdon by 1 July, 1849, and the remaining seventeen miles to Peterborough by 1 November of the same year.

Immediately north of Peterborough a deviation of the Parliamentary route was necessary in order to bring it immediately alongside the just opened section of the Syston and Peterborough, in accordance with an undertaking given to the Lords Committee at the instance of Earl Fitzwilliam, who had pointed out the economy and advantages of joining the bridges, archways, and culverts of the two undertakings. Therefore it was impossible to proceed with the "towns line" from Peterborough to Doncaster until a Deviation Bill had passed formally through Parliament; so, partly for this reason and partly because of the much lighter character of the works, the directors decided to get the loop line open first. Accordingly, in January, 1847, they made an agreement with Mr. (afterwards Sir) Samuel Morton Peto—perhaps the most respected of the great contractors of the day—and his partner, Mr. Edward Ladd Betts (who, it may be remembered, had supported the Bill in the witness-box), to complete the works from Peterborough by Boston and Lincoln to Gainsborough by 28 February, 1848, it being a condition of their contract that they should receive £1000 or forfeit that sum per week for such time prior to or after that date as should be gained or lost in their undertaking.

The remainder of the loop beyond Gainsborough had, as we know, been authorized to rejoin the main line at Bawtry; but since the rejection of the branch from Bawtry to Sheffield the purpose of this particular course had been removed. Accordingly the directors decided on Mr. Cubitt's advice to remodel this portion of the system by carrying the loop farther northwards to join the main line at Rossington and by deviating the latter north of Rossington in order that it might pass Doncaster on the west instead of on the east. For this purpose a second Deviation Bill was deposited, and in the confident expectation that it would pass the directors made preparations already for letting the works from Gainsborough to Doncaster, and thence to York, "in the hope"—to quote the words of their report to the shareholders in February, 1847—"of having that portion of the line open for traffic simultaneously with the other parts of the loop, thereby completing the communication between Peterborough and York in the spring of 1848." Moreover, as the same date was named by Mr. John Fowler, the East Lincolnshire Company's engineer, for the completion of the forty-eight miles of that railway from Boston to Grimsby, the greater part of which lay over absolutely flat country, there was a good prospect of a through eastern line of communication being opened by that time not only to York, as just stated, but also to Great Grimsby (where extensive new docks were to be constructed by the Manchester, Sheffield, and Lincolnshire Company), and by this latter Company's line and the New Holland ferry to the important port of Hull.

The first half-yearly "ordinary meeting" of the Company was held at the Hall of Commerce, London, on 27 February, 1847, when, in the absence of Mr. Astell through illness, Mr. Denison occupied the chair. At the meeting an attempt was made to raise dissension by some of the Direct Northern representatives who had been balloted out of the directorate, but with this Mr. Denison was well able to cope. Right from the very beginning, as we have seen, the strong will and practical sagacity of this Yorkshireman had shaped the course of the undertaking; and when in April of this year death deprived the Company of the services and widespread influence of Mr. Astell, Mr. Denison became in name, as well as in fact, the head of the concern.

On 13 March, 1847, the first call was made, but only of 25*s*. per share on the 111,446 "London and York" shares, this being the sum necessary to equalize the amount paid, namely, £3 15*s*. on the whole of the 224,000 shares of £25, which, with 40,000 "extension" shares, now formed the capital of the Company. At the time of the meeting in February, 1846, 178,407 of the shares had been registered, and the register showed that they were held by "a highly respectable body of proprietors, numbering 3345," the great majority of whom held less than 100 apiece. This wide distribution amongst small holders who had bought for investment and not for speculation, had been the sheet-anchor of the undertaking in the tempest to which it had already been exposed, and now it was again to prove the source of safety throughout the more dangerous, because more prolonged, storm which was now gathering.

A serious reaction from the railway mania of 1845-6 had, of course, been bound to come when the money had to be found for the very many and costly schemes which in those years had been authorized, and equally, as a matter of course, it was precipitated by the enormous waste which had been involved in the process of picking out the sound projects from the foul heap of rotten ones which ignorance, by avarice, had brought forth. Just as much was it to be expected that, when the strain did come, popular enthusiasm would give way to panic, and that the very same people who a few months before had been speaking and acting as if the capacity of the country to make new railways was unlimited, would at once begin to speak and act as if even the established lines were going to cease to pay. All this was natural enough, and by itself it need not have affected greatly the Great Northern's fortunes. But, unfortunately, recklessness in one department of business had infected others; money had been spent lavishly not only in railway promotion, but also in sending goods to China and other Eastern countries, and in importing foodstuffs far in excess of the legitimate markets. In short, over-trading had been general, and so there began in 1847 a period of real scarcity of floating capital, when even men who had excellent records and unimpeachable security to offer found a great difficulty in raising cash. These were the conditions under which the funds for the largest joint-stock enterprise yet attempted had now to be raised.

Nevertheless, the first limited call brought in at once over £120,000, leaving £15,000 only in arrear upon it, and as payments in advance of calls still continued to be made, the prospects of the Company looked cheerful, until a new danger appeared in the

F

form of a proposal in Parliament that it should be made illegal for railway companies any longer to pay interest out of capital on calls. This proposal was coupled with another, namely, that all Bills for the new lines should be suspended for the session, and they both alarmed the Great Northern directors, who feared that their supplies would be cut short by the one, and their Deviation Bills by the other. The matter was referred to the consideration of a Select Committee, of which Hudson (now M.P. for Sunderland) and other chairmen of established Companies were members, whereupon it was commonly said that "the lambs" (*i.e.*, the young Companies) had been "handed over to the tender mercies of the wolves." But fortunately the recommendations of the Committee proved less trenchant than the original proposals, for they advised that the suspension of Bills should be made optional, and the prohibition of interest on calls confined to schemes at present unauthorized. But even this was embarrassing to the Great Northern, seeing that its "extension capital" was still before Parliament for sanction, and as the scrip for this had been signed eighteen months before on the faith of interest being paid on calls, Mr. Denison asked the House on June 7th to exempt it and other stock similarly circumstanced from the operation of the new resolution. This amendment, however, being opposed by Hudson, was lost on a division by seventy votes to twenty-seven. Thereupon the Great Northern Board promptly issued a notice that they would pay interest on the extension deposits to 30 June, before which date the resolutions did not come into force, and shortly afterwards they announced their intention of allowing the further interest to accrue until it could be paid out of the earnings of the railway.

Meanwhile the company had suffered a temporary reverse by the rejection of its Wakefield and Leeds extensions, a rejection which was the more irritating because the House of Commons Committee stated that but for a technical error in the levels they would have passed the Bill. As it was, they rejected the rival Bills of the Midland and Leeds and Dewsbury Companies—of the latter of which the London and North Western, which was just amalgamating with itself the Leeds and Dewsbury, was virtually the promoter—and passed the Leeds Central Station Bill in which, as before stated, the Great Northern was jointly concerned. To this, moreover, there was scheduled a contract under seal by which the Manchester and Leeds—now just being merged in the Lancashire and Yorkshire Company—gave power to the Great Northern to run its trains from Askern *via* Knottingley to Wakefield, and also as far as Methley on the way to Leeds.

The South Yorkshire Railway, from Doncaster as far as Barnsley, was also sanctioned after a stiff fight, and so were the leases of the East Lincolnshire and Stamford to Wisbeach lines, besides a number of small branches and all the more important deviations of the main line. But the most important deviation of all, that of the loop from Gainsborough to Rossington, was unexpectedly rejected in the Commons Committee on the opposition of the landowners, and, in addition to this, the company received another check this session by the rejection of the Royston and Hitchin Bill for the extension of that line to Cambridge. As, however, the lease of the Royston and Hitchin Company's line to the Great Northern was sanctioned and a proposed branch of the Eastern Counties to Royston thrown out, the directors had good hope of obtaining this important access to Cambridge in another year. The Eastern Counties, on its part, secured its Cambridge and Bedford Act, and also an Act for an extension from Wisbeach as far northwards as Spalding, where it was to join the Great Northern loop line; but the further extension from Spalding to Newark was also rejected, and also a York and North Midland extension from Selby to Gainsborough. The net result of the campaign was that the Great Northern repulsed all the new encroachments on its territory, though it was still unsuccessful in establishing itself securely either in the West Riding of Yorkshire or in Cambridge.

The Parliamentary campaign ended on 8 July, nine days before which—on 30 June, 1847—the second call of £2 5s. per share fell due. This was responded to in a most encouraging manner, the banking house of Messrs. Smith, Payne and Smith in London being literally besieged by shareholders, who paid in no less than £180,000 at that one place, and the total sum realized was over £340,000, making with the payments in advance considerably more than the whole amount called up. Nevertheless the directors, "owing to the state of the Money Market and studying the convenience of the shareholders to the utmost extent circumstances permit"—as their report to the half-yearly meeting in August put it—decided to abstain from letting the works from Doncaster to York. But at the end of July a further small contract was let to Messrs. Peto & Betts for the works from the east side of the Great North Road at Doncaster, northwards to Askern, with the object of forming an "end-on" junction there with the branch of the Lancashire and Yorkshire Company, over which, as already stated, the Great Northern had just obtained power to run its trains to Wakefield and to Methley on the way to Leeds.

Between the main line and Gainsborough matters, of course, were still at a standstill owing to the rejection of the Deviation Bill; but on the main portion of the loop substantial progress had already been made by Messrs. Peto and Betts, who had several thousands of men employed on their contract; and the directors were able to report this August that for some miles between Gainsborough and Boston the permanent way had already been formed and the rails laid ready for use. There were, however, several large bridges on this contract, notably one 729 yards long over the Witham at Bardney; and although this was to be constructed entirely of timber, it made it impossible that the line could be ready for traffic at any date earlier than the spring of 1848.

"We have no object in view," said Mr. Denison to the shareholders at their second half-yearly meeting on 13 August, 1847, "but to get the line made, and if you want the line made you must of course furnish the money"; so on 27 August notice of a third quarterly call of £2 per share was issued to fall due on 30 September. But just about this time, unfortunately, owing to the failure of the Irish potato crop and other calamities, the "tightness" of money greatly increased, and the result was that on this third call nearly £100,000 was for some time in arrear. During October the outlook became still more gloomy; in the language of *Herapath's Railway Journal* for 23 October, 1847, it became "most distressing to look down the railway share list." "New lines, no matter of what promise," said that paper, "are universally at a discount, £100 being worth about £50. Even those old and thoroughly established railways, whose highly remunerative qualities have been proved by the test of time and good dividends—they too are most heavily oppressed. One or two are just raising their heads with difficulty in the bright regions of premium, while many others are gasping on the verge of par or actually floundering in the slough of discount." Under these influences the Great Northern shares, which eighteen months before had commanded a £4 premium, fell to a discount of £5, those on which the full calls of £8 had been paid selling for £3 only.

This was almost entirely the result of the difficulties which holders, whose position a year ago had seemed quite secure, now found in raising ready cash; it did not spring from any real want of confidence in the future of the undertaking. Nevertheless it gave a new opportunity to persons, who, though Great Northern shareholders, were more interested in the Eastern Counties and Midland Companies, to bring pressure on the directors to abandon important parts of the new system. At the Eastern Counties meeting in August Hudson had predicted that his opponents would "stick fast in the treacherous

London clay," and now strenuous efforts were made to induce the directors to abandon the independent access into London at least, and to join the Eastern Counties either at Ware or better still at Peterborough. But this recommendation, though it was urged copiously through both post and press, had no effect upon Mr. Denison and his colleagues. They had long been convinced that the southern part of their system would in the end prove the most valuable, and they could now hardly have given it up, even if they had so wished, seeing that they had already paid nearly half a million on account of Mr. Brassey's contract. New liabilities however, they did endeavour to

ORIGINAL TIMBER VIADUCT OVER THE WITHAM AT BARDNEY.
From the "Illustrated London News."

avoid by making overtures to Mr. Hudson before again depositing a Bill for an independent line to Leeds; and on 16 October, 1847—considerably to their own surprise probably—they obtained their great opponent's signature to a contract which gave the Great Northern Company the right of running its own engines and carriages over the Midland from Methley into Leeds. Thus in a very unlooked for way did Mr. Denison realize one of his greatest wishes by obtaining power to give a new and much more direct railway service with London to his native town.

Meanwhile all idea of letting further contracts on the main line had been put aside, and it had been decided to "concentrate all efforts upon the loop line from Peterborough into Yorkshire, so as to open it and bring the capital expended into productive operation with the least possible delay." Of the hundred miles of line thus embraced seventy-six miles, namely from Peterborough by Boston and Lincoln to Gainsborough, would, it was calculated, be ready by September, 1848; but at Gainsborough there was a large bridge over the Trent to be built, which in any case would have delayed the opening of the line beyond that town even had the question of its course not been still in abeyance. In the meantime, however, access from the loop northwards would probably be obtainable over the Manchester, Sheffield, and Lincolnshire Companies' lines, which were already in course of construction, and so the directors decided not to return to the Bawtry route, but to deposit a new Deviation Bill for the line to Rossington, which was so obviously better, because it saved distance to the north. As for the main line between London and Peterborough, this, it was decided, must proceed at a slower rate, those works only being carried on which could not be postponed without ultimate loss.

All this time the Company's chief solicitors, Messrs. Baxter, Rose, and Norton—a firm which had been formed in the course of the London and York fight by the union of Mr. Baxter with Messrs. Barker, Rose, and Norton—had had their hands full of work in obtaining possession of the land required for the line. During the year 1847 nearly 1,200 contracts with landowners had to be arranged, and of some of these gentry Mr. Baxter was constrained to say, that "their acuteness as to the means of wringing out money from a railway company" was "beyond anything which he or any other individual could have conceived." Some of them even resorted to proceedings in Chancery, which the Company had to defend at great expense; and in cases where the contractors, letting zeal outrun discretion, commenced work on land the conveyance of which had not been duly carried out, they brought actions against the Company for unlawful possession and obtained heavy damages—which, however, the contractors paid.

"We have endeavoured as far as possible to avoid anything like a collision with any of the parties," said Mr. Denison at the third half-yearly meeting held on 24 February, 1848, "but there is an amount beyond which we were determined not to go; and therefore in Lincolnshire about a month ago we took our stand and said, 'We will not permit you to go further without the intervention of a jury.' Only last week some jury cases were tried at Lincoln and at Boston. The sums demanded amounted to £27,000; the sums offered by the Company amounted to £12,000; the sums awarded by the jury amounted to £11,800. (Loud cheering.) It is possible that some parties in the country may occupy their time in reading what falls from me; and I say to you, and I say to the public, that unless the parties with whom we have to treat will be more moderate in their demands, I shall advise my colleagues to go on continually making appeals to juries." At the same time he warned the shareholders that the cost of land would certainly exceed the original estimate.

In November, 1847, the directors issued notice of their fourth quarterly call, but for the convenience of hard-pressed shareholders they made it payable by two instalments, viz., 25s. on 1 December, 1847, and 25s. on 15 January, 1848. On the first instalment, however, a considerable amount remained in arrear, and in anticipation of the second the shares fell in December to £6 discount; but when it was found that the directors had powers under their original Act not only to withhold interest from shareholders in arrear, but to *charge interest* upon the amounts unpaid, and that these powers they were determined to use to the full, many of the defaulters found means to pay. So at the meeting in February, 1848, Mr. Denison was able to announce with satisfaction that, with what had been paid in advance, the cash received was only 7 per cent. less than the amount called up.

Meantime the works of the loop line had been carried on with all possible vigour, and Mr. Joseph Cubitt, who was acting as superintending-engineer of the line under his father, was able to report in February, 1848, that the permanent way between Peterborough and Spalding had already been ballasted for a distance of about eight miles, and that every exertion was being made to have a considerable length of way formed and completed ahead of the advancing ballast, so that this might now be laid down without intermission. Between Boston and Lincoln, also, about thirteen miles had been ballasted, and Mr. Cubitt expressed himself satisfied that the works generally between Peterborough and Gainsborough were in such a state that, with the necessary further expenditure, they could quite well be completed and opened in the following September, which, however, was six months after the date originally fixed. As for Mr. Brassey's contract, this, of course, had suffered from the limitation of expenditure, but considerable progress had been made with the earthwork in nearly all the principal cuttings; in five out of the seven tunnels the shafts had been sunk and the headings driven, the bridges and viaducts were in a forward state, and in all respects the contract was in Mr. Cubitt's opinion "in a perfectly satisfactory condition." On the third short contract of five miles from Doncaster to Askern, the earthwork was completed for more than half the distance.

In short, the directors had a report to make this February (1848) which practically disarmed criticism, and so the disappointment which the shareholders not unnaturally felt that greater progress had not been possible had to find vent in belated lamentations over the enormous amount of the preliminary expenses, and particularly over the amount of Messrs. Baxter, Rose, and Norton's bills.

"I am not at all surprised—I have not the slightest right to complain," said Mr. Baxter in reply, "that you should come here and say that the charges in the Parliamentary and law department are enormous. They are enormous—they are unprecedented—and it is an instance which will stand, I trust, without parallel to the end of the world, of the infirmity of that process and that constitution of Parliamentary Committees which renders it possible to entail upon a company half a million of money in preliminary expenses."

On 1 March, 1848, the Great Northern Railway Company began its first work as public carriers on a length of about thirty miles of railway, from Louth to New Holland on Humber (opposite Hull). Nearly half this route, namely, the fourteen miles from Louth to Great Grimsby, was completely under Great Northern control by lease from the East Lincolnshire Company, and the remainder was worked over by arrangement with its owners, the Manchester, Sheffield, and Lincolnshire, who, in return, worked over the East Lincolnshire to Louth. Thus half only of the rolling stock required for the line had to be supplied by the Great Northern.

The passenger stock, which was built for the Company by Mr. Williams, of Goswell Road, at once attracted attention from the excellence of the third-class accommodation, this being described as equal to second-class on most lines. The "seconds," also, were thought noteworthy for having "good glass windows and cushions on the seat," and the first-class were described as "as handsome and convenient as any man of the nicest taste or appreciation of comfort in travelling could wish." In the matter of engines the Company was well prepared, for about a year before the directors had appointed their chief engineer's brother, Mr. Benjamin Cubitt, to the position of locomotive-superintendent, and he had ordered from the well-known firm of Sharp Brothers and Company, of Manchester, fifty of their standard stock-pattern "single" locomotives, of a type already in use on many lines. Such of these "Sharpies"—as the men afterwards nicknamed them—as were delivered by 1 March, 1848, were well able to haul the light and slow trains on the level Lincolnshire line. Mr. Cubitt, however, had unfortunately died about six weeks before the traffic was commenced; so his place was hastily filled by the appointment of Mr. Edward Bury, who had recently retired from the position of locomotive-superintendent to the London and North Western Railway, having served that company—or rather the London and Birmingham—for twelve years. Under his superintendence and that of Mr. (now Sir) John Fowler, who was engineer both to the East Lincolnshire and to the Manchester, Sheffield, and Lincolnshire (eastern section), the traffic from Louth to New Holland was efficiently conducted. At the same time Mr. Bury set to work to increase the Company's locomotive

The Public are respectfully informed, that

On & after the 1st of April

The Times of the Departure of the Trains Will be as follows, viz.

From Louth to New Holland.

Week-day Trains.					Sunday Trains.	
1, 2, & 3. Parl. Train	1 and 2.	1 and 2.	1 and 2. Express	1 and 2.	1, 2, & 3. Parl. Train	1 & 2
7 0	8 30	11 15	3 45	5 45	8 0	5 0

From New Holland to Louth.

Week-day Trains.					Sunday Trains.	
1, 2, and 3. Parl. Train	1 and 2	1 and 2. Express	1 and 2.	1 and 2.	1, 2, and 3. Parl. Train	1 and 2.
8 30	11 0	1 15	3 45	7 0	8 0	5 0

ONE OF THE FIRST GREAT NORTHERN TIME TABLES (1848).

stock, both by hurrying on the completion of Messrs. Sharp's contract, and by giving new orders to Messrs. R. and W. Hawthorn, of Newcastle, and Messrs. Bury, Curtis, and Kennedy, of Liverpool. Of this latter firm he was himself the senior partner.

From 1 March to 30 June, 1848, the Great Northern Company received from traffic on the East Lincolnshire line the sum of £2,502 19s. Its total expenditure up to the latter date had been more than $2\frac{1}{2}$ millions.

CHAPTER VI.

THE HERO COMES TO LONDON—END OF THE REIGN OF KING HUDSON—1848-1850.

WHILE the Great Northern had thus succeeded in getting to work on a small Lincolnshire line only, the first great "race to the north"—the race to open the two great competing routes to Scotland—had reached a critical stage. The authorization of the North British Railway from Edinburgh to Berwick in 1844—a year before the Caledonian Bill passed—had given a decided start to the East Coast; but though the North British was completed and opened in June, 1846, the filling of the gap between Gateshead and Berwick had still to be waited for, and so it was not until October, 1847, that Mr. James Allport, the manager of the York, Newcastle, and Berwick Company, whom Hudson had brought from the Midlands about two years before specially to develop the East Coast traffic, was able to announce a through service from Euston *viâ* Rugby, Normanton, York, and Newcastle—timed to cover the distance between London and Edinburgh in thirteen hours and ten minutes.

This was a great advance on the Fleetwood service of twenty-seven hours, which, as the reader may remember, the *Railway Times* in 1843 had thought to be "all that any reasonable man could want." On the other hand, the route was not really a through railway one; for pending the completion of the great bridges which the Stephensons had in course of construction over the Tyne and the Tweed, passengers had to be conveyed by road from Gateshead to Newcastle and from Tweedmouth to Berwick. So, in point of comfort, the East Coast journey did not offer much, if any, advantage over that by the West Coast, by which a passenger could get a carriage right through to Preston, if not to Carlisle, and, if he left Euston at 10 a m., be landed at the end of his railway journey at 9.55 p.m., just in time to have supper and go to bed at Carlisle, with a prospect of an easy ride to Glasgow or Edinburgh by coach on the following morning. In this same autumn of 1847, moreover, the Caledonian got the first portion of its line open from Carlisle to Beattock, and thereupon the 10 a.m. from Euston was accelerated by forty minutes to Carlisle and a connection put on reaching Beattock at 11.16 p.m., whence the mails, and such passengers who might venture, were carried on by coaches timed to reach Glasgow at 5.4 a.m. and Edinburgh at 6.6 a.m.

This service remained in force until 15 February, 1848, when the Caledonian Railway was opened throughout to both the great Scotch cities, thus at last establishing a genuine through railway route between London and Scotland. Even then, however, the best times of arrival which were at first offered to travellers by the West Coast 10 a.m. express from Euston were: Edinburgh, 1.30 a.m.; Glasgow, 1.40 a.m. next morning; whereas the East Coast passenger leaving Euston at 9.30 a.m. was timed to reach Edinburgh at 10.35 p.m. By the summer of 1848, however, Captain Huish, the manager of the London and North Western, got the West Coast service into working order, and the result was that "Bradshaw" for July of that year showed a new train timed to leave Euston at 9 a.m. and to land passengers at Edinburgh at 9 p.m. and at Glasgow at 9.10 p.m. In response to this, the East Coast through connection with the 9.30 a.m. from Euston was accelerated to reach Edinburgh at 9.55 p.m.

Thus, on paper at any rate, the East Coast Companies held their own very well throughout the summer of 1848, and they had a prospect of doing even better in the autumn when the bridges across the Tyne and Tweed were to be ready for opening. Nevertheless they had to face the fact that so long as they were dependent for the eighty miles of their route from London to Rugby upon the co-operation of the London and North Western—the principal partner in the rival West Coast alliance—they could feel no real security as to receiving their fair share of the traffic. Their great desideratum, therefore, was independent access to the Metropolis, and it was largely, of course, with a view to this that Hudson had taken such pains to obtain in the previous year powers for the Midland to extend its main line southwards from Leicester to Hitchin. But the clauses to enable him to make a junction there with the Eastern Counties had by the vigilance of the Great Northern been thrown out of the Bill; and as the latter had so far resisted all attempts to prevent its system being made in its integrity, it seemed hardly worth while for the Midland to come to Hitchin—in the interests of the East Coast traffic certainly not—seeing that if a through route to London were thus formed, it would obviously be superseded so soon as the Great Northern got its main line at work throughout. In short, there could now be no doubt, as Mr. Denison said in his half-yearly speech in February, 1848, that the Great Northern "must form from

London to York the southern portion of the great eastern trunk line between London and Edinburgh." "I believe," he added, "that some of our most strenuous opponents are beginning to admit this; even Mr. Hudson will admit now that parties will go between London and Edinburgh by the shortest line."

But "shortest line" though the Great Northern undoubtedly was *in posse*, it was still a good way from being so *in esse*. On its main line between Peterborough and York not a sod had been cut except on the short length of five miles from Doncaster northwards to Askern, from which point, as we know, the Company had power to run over the Lancashire and Yorkshire (formerly Wakefield, Pontefract, and Goole) system to Wakefield and Leeds. As, however, the construction of a short link from Burton Salmon to Knottingley, which the York and North Midland Company had previously obtained powers to make, would, if Hudson did not prevent it, readily put the Great Northern in connection with York and the lines beyond, the delay in making the direct route from Askern to York did not greatly matter. But the postponement of the "towns line" between Peterborough and Doncaster, which the state of the Money Market still enforced, was a really serious affair from the point of view of the through connection with Scotland; and early in 1848 discontented shareholders began to ask whether the directors' policy of concentrating effort upon the loop was not going to prove a mistake.

These misgivings were increased by a serious disaster which befell the Company early in its Parliamentary campaign of this year. It happened that Lord Galway, one of the most violent of the fox-hunting opponents of railways,* whose family seat—Serlby Hall—is on the borders of Nottinghamshire and Yorkshire, had conceived a special antipathy to the Bill for deviating the northern part of the Great Northern loop. For this he had two reasons: the one that he was Master of the local fox-hounds, and the other that he was a son-in-law to Mr. Pemberton Milnes, of Bawtry Hall, who was very anxious that the original Act should be carried out, and Bawtry made the point of junction between the main and loop lines. Accordingly the Irish peer, who had a seat in the Commons, set to work to organize an opposition to the second reading of the obnoxious Deviation Bill, and this he did very effectively—and yet so secretly that the Hon. Octavius Duncombe, who was the only Great Northern director with a seat in Parliament this session, did not hear of it until about three

---

* Mr. Brundell, of Doncaster, relates that he was horsewhipped by this Lord Galway when surveying for the original London and York line between Blyth and Tickhill.

o'clock on 21 March, 1848, the very day when the second reading of the Bill was to come on. Having no time to rally a party of supporters, Mr. Duncombe thought that the best thing he could do was to move the postponement of the Bill for a couple of days, but to this Lord Galway proposed an amendment that it "be read a second time six months hence"—the regular Parliamentary form for rejection. This amendment was carried triumphantly by 176 votes to 32.

This was an alarming event for the Great Northern Board, for it threatened completely to upset the plans which had led them to make the loop before the towns line; but fortunately they found a fairly satisfactory makeshift in an alliance with the Manchester, Sheffield, and Lincolnshire. This Company, as we know, had powers for a branch from its main line at Clarborough, about five miles east of Retford, to join the Great Northern loop at Saxelby, from which point the Great Northern had granted it running rights into Lincoln in return for similar rights over the Manchester, Sheffield, and Lincolnshire from Retford to Sheffield; and, although the Sheffield directors—whose chairman, Lord Yarborough, was an old London and York Committee man—had intended postponing the construction of this branch to better times, they now acceded to the Great Northern proposal that the line should be made at once, so that the Great Northern might use it for through traffic in place of the just rejected Gainsborough to Rossington line. Accordingly Mr. John Fowler was instructed by the Sheffield Board to put the work immediately in hand, while at the same time, and with the same object, the Great Northern directors let a further contract to Messrs. Peto and Betts for the section of their main line from Retford to Doncaster.

Thus the Company got fairly well out of one difficulty created by Lord Galway's "surprise," but meanwhile they had been embarrassed by another, which arose from the fact that the rejected Deviation Bill had contained an important clause designed to relieve the "tightness" of the Company's finances. In the previous autumn some ingenious person—probably Mr. Baxter, the solicitor—had suggested that the option might well be given to shareholders to "split" their £25 shares into two of £12 10s. each, one of which should be guaranteed by the other a permanent 6 per cent. dividend upon the amount paid up, with the option of paying up the whole amount at once; while the other, or "deferred" half, should receive the balance of interest or dividend after the payment of the 6 per cent., and should be relieved from the pressure of calls. The main object of this was to enable shareholders who had a difficulty in meeting their calls to relieve themselves by disposing of half their shares to parties who would be willing — under the attraction of the 6 per cent. guarantee — to pay up upon them at once and in full; but, as Mr. Denison said, it had the further advantage of creating a stock paying 6 per cent.—if the whole capital earned enough—which would be "exceedingly valuable to quiet people in the country and in town," while on the other hand it held out an inducement to more speculative persons to come into the concern and take the chance of all dividends above 6 per cent.

Mr. Denison, however, did not urge the adoption of the scheme with any fervour—indeed, he told the shareholders at their meeting in February, 1848, that the directors did not wish it to be considered as "immediately recommended" by them, and Captain Hall—the naval shareholder, who, it may be remembered, had "sealed up his scrip in an envelope like nailing his colours to the mast"—objected to it entirely, on the ground that he liked "plain sailing, a good water-tight boat, and good ship room." Nevertheless, its inclusion in the Deviation Bill was approved unanimously by an "extraordinary general meeting"; and, when that Bill was rejected, Mr. Baxter was determined that if possible it should not be lost. He accordingly managed to re-insert the clause in the Company's "Isle of Axholme Extension Bill," which, after passing the Commons in the previous session, had been hung up in the Lords, and in this way it became law, though in a form slightly different from the original scheme. The chief alteration was that the "A" shares, as the deferred halves were called, were credited with the amount already paid up, so that the inducement of the 6 per cent. guarantee might operate to bring in the whole of the £12 10s. represented by each B share; but this did not prevent the latter from being greatly sought after, with the result that during the latter months of 1848, 360 shareholders availed themselves of the option of "splitting," the number of shares thus divided being 18,561.

For the rest, the Parliamentary campaign of 1848 was a comparatively small affair, its one other important result being that the Royston and Hitchin Company obtained powers to extend its line from Royston to Shepreth, a point on the authorized Cambridge to Bedford extension, with contingent powers for a further extension from Shepreth to Shelford on the Eastern Counties main line in case that Company should neglect to use its Cambridge and Bedford Act. This secured to the Great Northern access to Cambridge from the south, while from the north also there seemed good prospect of a through route being established *via* Huntingdon, seeing that the Eastern Counties extension from Cambridge to St. Ives and Huntingdon had already been at work for a year.

By the end of July, 1848, the works on Messrs. Peto and Betts' short contract in Yorkshire were so far advanced that the Lancashire and Yorkshire trains, which had been at work for some weeks on the Wakefield, Pontefract, and Goole system, could be allowed to run on from Askern over about three miles of Great Northern line to Arksey; and by the end of August the whole contract was so far completed that the trains could come two miles further to discharge and take up passengers at a temporary station at Doncaster, where for the first time, in September, 1848, visitors to the Races arrived by railway. About the same date—3 September, 1848—a further portion of the East Lincolnshire line from Louth to Firsby was opened; on 1 October

One of the First Great Northern Trains Passing over the Timber Bridge at Boston.
From "*The Illustrated London News.*"

the opening was completed to Boston, and on 17 October, 1848, the fifty-eight miles of the loop were opened from a junction with the Syston and Peterborough line at Walton (or Werrington), near Peterborough, to Lincoln, the day being observed as a general holiday in the locality and commemorated by "a sumptuous banquet," given by the Mayor and Corporation of Boston to the Great Northern directors and others, at which about 500 gentlemen sat down. Between Boston and Lincoln the competition between the new railway and the steam packets on the Witham Navigation was at first very keen; but by putting on *fourth-class* carriages at a halfpenny a mile the railway company soon drove the boats off the water.

The opening of the loop gave South Lincolnshire its first railway communication. Moreover, in conjunction with the London and North

Western or Eastern Counties lines from London to Peterborough, and the short section of Midland line from Peterborough to Walton, it opened up an entirely new route between the Metropolis and Lincoln; to which city a train service was immediately given more than an hour shorter from London than by the existing very circuitous route of the Midland Company. Another new service, more important than this, was put on by Boston, Grimsby, and New Holland to Hull, a route about forty miles shorter than the existing one *viâ* Normanton and Selby, and from 1 January, 1849, Her Majesty's mails were conveyed to Hull this way. Great Grimsby, too, where the works on the new docks were in active progress, was now for the first time brought into railway communication with the Metropolis.

Meanwhile between London and Peterborough the works on Mr. Brassey's great contract had been proceeding during the summer with full vigour under arrangements which, according to Mr. Joseph Cubitt's report in August, 1848, "warranted the expectation of their completion by the spring of 1850." Big though they were, the works had no terrors on that account to Mr. Brassey, whose various railway contracts in hand at this time in Great Britain and France represented a capital outlay of about £36,000,000, involving the payment of some £15,000 to £20,000 weekly in wages to an army of about 75,000 men. Of these between 5,000 and 6,000 were employed on the Great Northern, with the result that rapid progress was made in the very heavy earthwork in the "London clay district," while the brickwork and masonry also were generally kept well advanced.

What gave Brassey more anxiety than anything else was the formation of the permanent way over the soft undrained fens of Huntingdonshire, which for many miles were at this time little better than "a quaking bog," so that, as he himself said, "if you merely stood upon it, you shook an acre of it together." These were the words in which he is said to have described the state of things to a young engineer, named Stephen Ballard, to whom he was introduced on the Eastern Counties platform at Cambridge when returning one day from inspecting the Great Northern works. Ballard, who was employed at this time as resident engineer for the Middle Level main drain, which Messrs. Walker and Burges were constructing from the Ouse to Upwell, had already been mentioned to Brassey as a likely man to help him out of his difficulty; and now his conversation on the subject so impressed the great contractor that Brassey engaged him at once to become his agent in making the part of the line over the fens.

The first thing Stephen Ballard did was to go to the principal timber markets in the neighbourhood and buy up all the faggot wood there was for sale without giving the dealers time to raise the price against him by letting it be known that he wanted a large quantity. Then he had a number of rafts built of alternate layers of faggots and peat sods, and, having laid these on the swampy ground, he added weight to them little by little, so that the water was gradually forced out, while what solid matter there was beneath them was not displaced. In this way a comparatively firm foundation was secured, and on this was built not only the embankment of the line, but the brickwork for the bridges also, the same principle being observed in this work as in the other, namely, that the weight should be added very gradually so as to give plenty of time for the water to find its way out. Thus did Ballard lay the foundation of the Great Northern line over the fens, and of his own fame as an engineer.

Two years had now elapsed since the passing of the Great Northern Act, and with one hundred miles of line already at work, and the construction of seventy-six more—the most important and difficult part of the system—well forwarded under the able care of the Messrs. Cubitt, Mr. Brassey, and Mr. Ballard, the Great Northern directors had good reason to be satisfied with the progress they had made during a period of exceptional financial embarrassment. But now difficulties of a new kind "cropped up." At the fourth half-yearly meeting, held on 12 August, 1848—the very day and hour when "old George" Stephenson was dying at his residence, Tapton House, Chesterfield—Mr. Seneca Hughes, a considerable shareholder, proposed an amendment in favour of the exercise of greater economy, especially in the matter of the directors' allowances and the superintendent's and secretary's salaries, and this Mr. Denison met with the assurance that the subject of reduction had already been discussed at the Board, and should undergo further discussion in the future. Accordingly, in October, 1848, the matter was taken vigorously in hand, but it soon became apparent that in the cutting down of salaries Mr. Denison was anxious to go farther than the majority of his colleagues. The result was that on 24 November, 1848, he tendered his resignation of the chairmanship. About the same time Captain Laws, seeing that both directors and shareholders were indisposed to retain him as managing director at his existing salary of £2000 a year, accepted an invitation to return to the north as general manager of the Lancashire and Yorkshire at £1500.

Thus at the close of 1848 the prospects of the Company looked gloomy, but fortunately they had begun to brighten again before the shareholders met in February, 1849. Mr. Denison and Captain Laws both consented to remain on the directorate, and, though the

G

fifth half-yearly report was signed by Mr. Packe, the deputy-chairman, it stated that Mr. Denison "continued all the support in his power to the interests of the Company." So when the shareholders met at the London Tavern on February 23rd, they were not altogether surprised to see their old chairman again take his accustomed place. Mr. Denison at once stated that matters had been so arranged that he could with satisfaction continue to occupy the chair—a statement which was received with "loud and continued applause," and this was renewed even more heartily and unanimously when Mr. Seneca Hughes submitted a resolution testifying "unabated confidence in the zeal, ability, and judgment of Mr. Denison," and approving "his recent efforts to promote retrenchment and economy."

The report published prior to this meeting had stated that, "to avoid the immediate outlay of capital further northwards," an arrangement had been made with the York and North Midland Company "for the use of their line from Burton Salmon into York," and that a communication had been received recently from Mr. Hudson, M.P., the chairman of that Company, to the effect that the short connecting line from Knottingley to Burton Salmon was to be put in hand and completed without delay. This meant, not only that the Great Northern shareholders were to be saved from the necessity of finding money for their own line from Askern to York, but that through the York and North Midland they were to be admitted into the East Coast alliance. Consequently, the announcement of it immediately alarmed the Midland shareholders; and, on the other hand, it came too late to protect the Railway King from the distrust of his "York, Newcastle, and Berwick" subjects. On the contrary, at their meeting at York, held a few days before that of the Great Northern, they appointed a "committee of inquiry" into his conduct.

The inquiry did not proceed far before revelations were made seriously compromising the Railway King. Thereupon the Eastern Counties shareholders took alarm, and for *their* half-yearly meeting on 3 March, 1849, they assembled in a very rebellious spirit. The consequence was that Mr. Hudson's name was received with hisses and hoots (and his *fidus Achates*, Mr. Waddington, mobbed and jeered at) by the very same meeting which only three and a half years before had been "mad with joy" at his acceptance of their chairmanship. Nor was the end now far off. On 17 April, 1849, the Railway King resigned the chair of the Midland Company, and by the middle of May he had ceased to be at the head of every one of the railways whose fortunes he had so long controlled.

On 9 April, 1849—Easter Monday—a further portion of the

Great Northern loop line was opened from Lincoln to Gainsborough, making 125 miles of the Company's system open in all; but, as almost all of this was in the purely agricultural county of Lincolnshire, with no outlet northwards except by ferry across the Humber, and only a circuitous outlet southwards and westwards, the traffic remained almost entirely local and consequently of small amount. During the fifteen months from 1 March, 1848—the date of the first meeting—to 30 June, 1849, less than half a million passengers were carried in all, but the receipt from these—£40,184—was a large amount compared with that from goods and merchandise in the same period, which was £13,168 only. Altogether the gross receipts (including £4 for "fines for smoking in the Company's carriages") amounted

THE FIRST STATION AT SPALDING, LINCOLNSHIRE.
From "*The Illustrated London News.*"

to £61,682, and from this no less than 57½ per cent. for working expenses had to be deducted, so that the net revenue was not sufficient to pay the guarantees to the East Lincolnshire and Witham and Fossdyke Navigation lessors, much less to pay any interest on the two millions of capital, or thereabouts, which the Company had sunk in its opened lines.

This, of course, was, on the face of it, a very unsatisfactory result, but Messrs. Denison and Baxter were able to put rather a better complexion upon it in answer to shareholders' criticisms at the sixth half-yearly meeting held on 11 August, 1849.

"You must not expect," said the latter gentleman, "that the moment the line is opened the traffic will jump into your laps without an effort. There must be months to develop the traffic—do not judge of what it is to be by what it is when you have got a *cul de sac*, open only at one end. When you have got your trunk line opened—when you have got the entrance into Yorkshire from the Eastern

Counties and Lincolnshire opened—you will find to your full satisfaction that you have an ample return upon every sixpence of capital laid out."

"Then why have we not got our trunk line opened instead of this Lincolnshire line?" complained shareholders; and to this also Mr. Baxter had what he described as "a perfect answer." "The London end of the line," he said, "from the weight of the works could not be made in less than three or four years; the Lincolnshire line could be made in eighteen months. If the directors had laid out a million of capital on the towns line, and then had not got that towns line into London, the capital thus sunk would have been bringing in nothing for the next two years. They had therefore made the line into Lincolnshire first; and the Company was getting the traffic, such as it was, from that in the meantime."

All this time Mr. Brassey had been pressing on with his contract with full vigour; and to this meeting in August, 1849, Mr. Joseph Cubitt was able to report that, of the nine and three-quarter million cubic yards of earthwork, nearly three-fourths had been executed, and more than one-third of the total length—4503 yards—of the seven tunnels. These, however, did not include the two short tunnels immediately north of King's Cross, which had been reserved for separate contract; but in June, 1849, work on the more northern of the two, the Copenhagen tunnel—so called because it was to pass under the still open Copenhagen fields—was begun by Messrs. Pearce and Smith, of Manchester, and a few weeks later yet a third contractor, Mr. Jay, commenced operations between the southern end of this and the Regent's Canal. The proposed tunnel for passenger traffic under the canal had not yet been put in hand, nor had anything been done at this date towards clearing the ground for the passenger terminus between the canal and the old St. Pancras Road. But on these the opening of the line into London was not dependent, since it had been decided to erect a temporary passenger station at Maiden Lane on the north bank of the canal adjoining the goods station. Nevertheless it had been evident to Mr. Cubitt, since the beginning of 1849, that no opening at all would be possible till the autumn of 1850.

This accomplished, however, the Company, as Mr. Denison told the shareholders at this August meeting, would have a line to work over from London to York, which—" loop line" though it was—would be twelve and a half miles shorter than the established route *via* Rugby, Derby, and Normanton, with gradients which on the average would compare very favourably with those of the London-and-North-Western-cum-Midland. But, on the other hand, since the Trent

Valley line had been brought into use, the West Coast route between London and Edinburgh had become nearly thirty miles shorter than the East Coast; and so, if the Great Northern were content merely to supply a route to York equal to the present one *via* Derby, it could not hope to compete on an equality with the London and North Western for the Scotch traffic. But when the towns line was made from Peterborough to Retford, the distances from King's Cross to Edinburgh *via* Newcastle and from Euston to Edinburgh *via* Carlisle would be practically identical, viz., 400 miles; so for this and other reasons the directors decided to put the towns line in hand without further delay. Accordingly, in the early autumn of 1849 the section of fifteen miles from Corby to Grantham, which included the long "Stoke tunnel" and other heavy work, was let to Mr. Jackson, who commenced operations before the end of the year.

This, however, did not fully satisfy a party among the shareholders headed by Mr. Graham Hutchison, of Glasgow, These urged that the section from Askern to York also should be at once put in hand, their main argument being that this, with the towns line, would make the East Coast distance to Edinburgh about three miles shorter than the West Coast, and so secure to the former the carriage of the mails. On the other hand the directors pointed out that of the Company's potential capital, which with borrowing powers amounted to £8,284,800 in all, nearly 5½ millions had already been spent, while there was a further liability of 1½ million on existing contracts, so that about £1,200,000 only remained available, and of this a good part was already "ear-marked" for provision of additional working stock and other general expenses. Thus there could only be a small sum—less than half a million probably—left for making the forty-four miles of towns line still unlet, and, therefore, even if the Askern to York section were abandoned, new capital powers would almost certainly be required, while, if the independent line through to York were persisted with, as much as another million would probably be wanted, all of which would in all likelihood have to be raised by the issue of preference shares. Under these circumstances the shareholders at the meeting on 28 February, 1850, rejected Mr. Hutchison's resolution, though they debated the matter from 11 in the morning till 3.30 in the afternoon, when the landlord of the London Tavern sent up word that he had a large dinner at 4 o'clock and would be glad to be quit of them.

The revenue statement presented at this meeting was less unsatisfactory than the preceding one, thanks to the fact that during the last four months of 1849 the through communication between Lincolnshire and Yorkshire had been at work. As the result of great exertions on the part of both engineers and contractors, the two sections of line necessary to complete this, namely, the Great Northern line from Doncaster to Retford and the Manchester, Sheffield, and Lincoln line from Clarborough, near Retford, to Sykes Junction, near Lincoln, had been opened on 4 September, 1849, just in time for the Doncaster Race Meeting; and as the South Yorkshire Company's line from Swinton to Doncaster—over which the Midland had secured running powers—was opened at the same time great competition for the race-going passengers took place. The Great Northern provided special trains both from Peterborough and from Leeds, from which latter place, as we already know, it had running powers over the Midland to Methley and thence over the Lancashire and Yorkshire *via*

DONCASTER STATION ON ST. LEGER DAY, 1849.
From "The Illustrated London News."

Knottingley to Askern; but some over-zealous officers of the former Company took the high-handed action of pulling up the junction rails at Methley to prevent these trains from running, and it was only by producing their agreement with King Hudson and threatening legal proceedings that the Great Northern authorities got them replaced in time. This done, however, the Company was able to profit considerably by the race-going excursionists, and they and the passengers by the regular service now given daily between Peterborough and Leeds so far increased its revenue, that after the East Lincolnshire and Royston and Hitchin guarantees and the Witham and Fossdyke Navigations had been paid there remained a balance in hand of just over £10,000. This was the first profit earned by the Company, and by vote of the shareholders in February, 1850, it was appropriated to pay the interest on the preference stock created in lieu of the forfeited shares. At the same time the directors announced their intention of ceasing to pay interest on the ordinary shares out of capital after 30 June, 1850.

At the beginning of 1850 the Company was working 143 miles of its own and over more than fifty miles of "foreign" lines; but the traffic was still mainly of quite a local character, the coal business from South Yorkshire having hardly begun, the goods traffic between the West Riding and Lincolnshire being undeveloped, and the through passengers requiring one fast train only each way per day, which occupied $5\frac{1}{2}$ hours in covering the distance between Peterborough and

ONE OF THE "SHARPIES" STANDING IN GRANTHAM STATION.
From a photograph taken in 1858.

Leeds. For this traffic Mr. Bury, who since the resignation of Captain Laws had been chief executive officer of the Company, had a stock of about 100 engines, viz., the fifty standard passenger "singles" ordered by his predecessor, Mr. Cubitt, from Messrs. Sharp and Company, and commonly known as "Sharpies"; twenty other similar engines of the "single" class, but with driving-wheels 6 ft., instead of 5 ft. 6 in., in diameter, built by Messrs. R. and W. Hawthorn; fifteen four-wheel-coupled goods engines, and some also with six wheels coupled, from the same firm; five "extraordinary-looking saddle tanks" on four wheels with four-wheeled tenders, built by Mr. Bury's own firm, Messrs. Bury, Curtis, and Kennedy; and a few other goods engines of the "four-coupled" class, built by the Vulcan Foundry Company for Messrs.

Peto, Betts, and Company for use on their contracts, and subsequently sold to the Great Northern.

This stock did the work as yet required of it without difficulty (though the development of the coal traffic from South Yorkshire into Lincolnshire was beginning to put some strain upon it); but it was obvious that the condition of things would be altered altogether when the London to Peterborough section was brought into use. For this would mean not only the working of seventy-six miles of new line with gradients a good deal harder than any yet opened, but the necessity of putting on through services of trains from London to Yorkshire, Lincolnshire, and the North of England generally, to compete with the established and in some respects easier routes of the London and North Western and Midland Companies. Then, too, there was the opening into London of the heavy coal traffic to be thought of. In short, it would be equivalent to the opening throughout at one time of at least one hundred and fifty miles of line, and this was a thing the like of which no railway company had ever before attempted. All the existing lines had been opened piecemeal in short lengths. The shareholders, however, had been promised that the system should be open to London before they met again, and Mr. Denison and his colleagues were determined they should not be disappointed.

Obviously the principal *desiderata* were good engines and good men, and the directors soon saw that to obtain these they must begin at the top of their executive staff. Mr. Bury was a safe man, as his long tenure of office under the London and Birmingham had proved; but he was not an enterprising one; he commanded a very high salary, and his double position as their servant and head of a firm they dealt with was equivocal. So the directors decided to replace him by two younger men whom they found in a more "up-to-date" school—the school of Brunel and Gooch—namely, Mr. Seymour Clarke, who was London traffic manager of the Great Western Railway, and Mr. Archibald Sturrock, the same Company's works manager at Swindon. Accordingly, Mr. Clarke became "general manager" of the Great Northern, and Mr. Sturrock "locomotive superintendent," in place of Mr. Bury resigned.

These appointments were not made until April and May, 1850; so that the two men upon whom the main responsibility of working the new trunk line from London to Yorkshire was mainly to devolve, had barely three months in which to make preparations for their task. Mr. Clarke had to find competent staffs for seventeen new stations, including the London terminus, to organize such offices as were immediately necessary at King's Cross, to provide horses, carts, and omnibuses for "collection and delivery," and to attend to a thousand other details of traffic management. Mr. Sturrock, meanwhile, was overhauling the Company's rolling-stock as delivered or on order, supplementing it by new orders to Messrs. R. B. Longridge and Co. and E. B. Wilson and Co., endeavouring to obtain a sufficient number of men for drivers and stokers at a time when, owing to the rapid increase of the railway system, competent men of this class were at a premium, and at the same time planning a new type of engine in which the large heating surface and high steam pressure, which up to this date had given Gooch's broad-gauge "giants" the pre-eminence, might be obtained within the limits of the 4 ft. 8½ in. gauge without causing top-heaviness or making the weight of the engine too great for the then standard type of permanent way.

Meanwhile, the completion of the seventy-eight miles of line from Werrington, near Peterborough, to Maiden Lane, London, was being pushed forward with the utmost urgency by no less than four different firms of contractors. From the junction of the loop at Werrington to the south side of the River Nene at Peterborough the work had in the previous autumn been placed in the hands of Messrs. Peto and Betts, but during the winter it had been greatly hampered by floods; so that this contract, which included a considerable viaduct over the river and over the Eastern Counties and London and North Western lines, required even greater haste than the far larger undertaking of Mr. Brassey. On this latter the earthwork both in the London tunnels and in the cuttings was practically completed by May, 1850, but the great viaduct at Welwyn caused some anxiety, as during several weeks in the winter all work upon it had been stopped by frost, and the ballasting, too, was a source of difficulty especially at the London end, where eventually in the lack of better material simple burnt clay had to be used. The tunnel under Copenhagen fields was, as already stated, in the hands of Messrs. Pearce and Smith, who carried it through in good time, but the work of excavation between the south end of the tunnel and the temporary terminus, which Mr. Jay had in hand, was complicated by the fact that the North London Company was at the same time carrying its line from Willesden to the Docks over the same ground by a viaduct, and the sudden collapse of an arch of this caused a temporary "crisis" at this point. However, by the hearty co-operation of all concerned, this and all other difficulties were surmounted; by the beginning of August, as Messrs. Denison and Cubitt had promised in the preceding February, the line was ready for opening throughout for passenger traffic; and at seven o'clock on the morning of 8 August, 1850, the first public train—a "Parliamentary" one—started from the temporary station at Maiden Lane *en route* for Peterborough, at which place it arrived in about two and a half hours.

The directors, characteristically, decided not to put the Company to the expense of festivities to celebrate the opening, but they did

COLLAPSE OF THE NORTH LONDON VIADUCT NEAR KING'S CROSS.
From a rough sketch made on the spot.

not refuse an invitation which Mr. Brassey issued to them and to some four hundred others, to take a trial trip on the line on 5 August—three days before the public working began. The train, which consisted of two engines and seventeen carriages, left the temporary station at Maiden Lane about 9 a.m., and it arrived at Peterborough about 1.30 p.m., an intermediate stop of nearly an hour having been made at Welwyn to allow the party to descend to the valley and view the viaduct from below. Stops were also made at all the principal stations, at many of which cheers were raised by the assembled inhabitants. At Peterborough the invited guests "sat down to a very elegant repast" provided by Mr. Brassey, at which speeches were made by the host, Mr. Denison, Mr. Cubitt, and others. On the return journey the train, which Mr. Sturrock was driving, had a narrow escape of running into a ballast engine; whereupon Mr. Denison, who was on the engine, turned to Mr. Brassey, who was there also, and gave him—host though he was—a sharp reprimand for not having suspended all work during the trip.

Meantime the coal traffic from South Yorks to Lincolnshire had become fairly established (the Company having supplied 2000 waggons for the purpose); but the arrangements at King's Cross and other stations were not at first sufficiently complete to allow of either this or even the general goods traffic being extended to London, and even the passenger had during August to be confined to a small number of slow trains, the best of which occupied two and a half hours in covering the seventy-six miles of new line. Nevertheless, a goodly number of through passengers began to use the new route from the first, and on 17 August—only nine days after the opening—George Hudson was observed to take his seat in a first-class compartment at Maiden Lane as an ordinary traveller *en route* for Leeds. Here was Nemesis indeed! It was as if Jack's giant in the fairy story, instead of being killed outright, had shrunk to common size, and then used Jack's beanstalk to come down to live with men. The George Hudson who surveyed from the windows of that Great Northern carriage the monarchy that had been his, was now merely *magni nominis umbra*; and, as with a few words in praise of the excellence of the journey he left the station at Leeds, he passed also out of the history of British railways.

A VIEW OF THE "TRIAL TRIP," 5 AUGUST, 1850.
From "*The Illustrated London News.*"

CHAPTER VII.

THE FIGHT WITH THE CONFEDERACY—THE BATTLE OF THE EXHIBITION YEAR—1850-51.

THE opening of the Great Northern Railway from London completed two distinct through routes for traffic between the Metropolis and all the more important producing grounds, manufacturing districts, and ports of the kingdom, and so may be said to have inaugurated a new era in the history of British railways, by making the competition between companies, which prior to this date had found vent mainly in the Committee-rooms of Parliament, a principal factor in the actual working of the lines. That this should happen sooner or later was, of course, an inevitable result of the policy of Parliament, which, without declaring definitely in favour of a competitive system, had never taken any effectual measures to confine companies to separate territories; but prior to the opening of the Great Northern such competition in working had arisen on a small scale only, and so had been susceptible of speedy extinction. Thus, the first "rate war" in British railway history, that between the Midland Counties and Birmingham and Derby companies, had been put an end to, as we have seen, by the amalgamation of the two into the Midland in 1844; and a little later, when the Midland itself with the Manchester and Leeds had begun to compete with the Grand Junction for through traffic between Lancashire and London, it had been found readily possible to arrange a percentage division of the gross receipts—the first "pool," probably, in railway history—under which the development of business by both routes became the common interest of all three companies.

Though rendered precarious when the Manchester and Sheffield line had been opened throughout in November, 1845, this "pooling" arrangement had been maintained for four years after that date, a result which must be credited to the energy of Captain Huish, the very able general manager, first of the Grand Junction and afterwards of the whole London and North Western Company, who had succeeded in conjunction with the Midland and Lancashire and Yorkshire authorities in shutting out the Sheffield Company from all through traffic for that period. In 1849, however, the East Lancashire, North Staffordshire, and other new lines important as links in through routes had been completed, and early in the following year the Manchester, Sheffield, and Lincolnshire directors had engaged Mr. James Allport as general manager of their railway with the special view of his using the experience which he had gained on the York, Newcastle, and Berwick to break down the barriers which had been formed around it. Thus in 1850, a re-adjustment had become inevitable even before the great railway event of that year, the Great Northern opening from London, had actually taken place.

That such new arrangements, however, could not be securely based except on a recognition of the equality of King's Cross with Euston Square as a terminus for all North of England traffic, was too high a conception for the London and North Western authorities to rise to thus early. They saw only that the monopoly which they had enjoyed for more than a decade was in peril, but they still hoped that by diplomacy they might preserve a great part of it. The policy which they had entered upon for this purpose was to draw the principal provincial companies of northern England into a confederacy with them—a close confederacy, with Euston Square as its base, bound to promote each other's interests, and to block the Great Northern.

Two of the most important provincial companies, the Midland and Lancashire and Yorkshire, were already, as has just been said, in partial alliance with Euston Square, and, therefore, to make this alliance a closer one had not been a difficult task. Had the Midland carried out the powers it had obtained in 1847 for a southern extension from Leicester to Hitchin, King's Cross would have offered itself as at least an alternative London terminus for its traffic; but under the pressure of the financial crisis of 1848 these powers had been allowed to lapse. Originally, as we know, its main business had been to carry on the London and Birmingham traffic north-eastwards from Rugby, and now, bereft of the man whose genius had given its system for a time a wider power, and yet burdened with a most costly offspring of its union with him, the 10 per cent. Leeds and Bradford guarantee, it had been only too glad to return to the Euston Square protectorate, like a deserted wife returning to the parental roof. "Euston Square holds the strings; the Midland, I regret to say, has no independent existence"; this was the language in which Mr. Denison now described the position of the Company which only five years before—when George of York was king —had seemed to be the most powerful and prosperous in the kingdom.

Almost as striking as the fall of the Midland had been the rise—in political importance, *not* in financial prosperity—of the Manchester, Sheffield and Lincolnshire. To this Company, as we already know, the Great Northern directors had had to go, caps in hand, in 1848, to beg for the use of its Lincoln branch as a link in their through route to the north—a link all-important so long as the towns line was in abeyance; and now, in 1849-50, attention had been forcibly drawn to another fact, the recognition of which had at once exalted the Manchester, Sheffield, and Lincolnshire into first-class importance in inter-railway politics, namely, that if the Great Northern, when it opened from London, were to join hands with the Sheffield at Retford, a second route might be established between the Metropolis and Manchester, almost as short as the London and North Western main line. This had meant that the allegiance of the Sheffield Company was a *sine quâ non* of a combination to block the Great Northern in the interests of Euston Square, and so it had become necessary for Captain Huish to execute a complete *volte-face* in his attitude to this formerly despised Company, and to make every effort to convince its new manager, Mr. Allport, that the friendship of the London and North Western, Midland, and Lancashire and Yorkshire, would be of more value to his Company than any alliance with the Great Northern could be.

That in these efforts Captain Huish was successful must be attributed partly to his great skill in diplomacy—in which quality he probably excelled any English railway manager yet known except, perhaps, his pupil, Mr. (now Sir) Edward Watkin—and partly to the fact that he was in a position to confer immediate benefits upon the Sheffield, whereas the advantages of an alliance with the not yet established Great Northern were all in the future. In the light of subsequent events it is natural to wonder why the attractions of a partnership between the Sheffield and Great Northern companies for London and Lancashire traffic did not appeal more strongly to a manager so shrewd as Mr. Allport; but when we remember that such a partnership could not have been made properly effective till the Great Northern had got its London terminus and its towns line completed—which, as we shall see, was not accomplished until the end of 1852—and that it would have been at once exposed to the fiercest antagonism of the already firmly-established Euston Square confederates, we cease to marvel that Mr. Allport and his directors preferred to forego north and south traffic altogether in favour of the assistance which Captain Huish promised them towards the development of their undertaking in what seemed its more legitimate vocation as an east to west line. The execution of these promises involved some sacrifices on the part of the Midland and Lancashire and Yorkshire companies, which had to consent, for example, to the Manchester, Sheffield, and Lincolnshire being given a monopoly of the Hull traffic; but this consent was obtained under pressure from Euston Square. The result was that in the spring of 1850 Lord Yarborough, the Sheffield chairman, despite the fact that he had once been, as the reader may remember, a "London and York" man, was persuaded by Mr. Allport to sign a treaty which bound his Company as a member of "the Euston Square confederacy," as the anti-Great Northern alliance was soon nicknamed, for a term of seven years. Consequently, the Great Northern, while still a provincial Company only, found itself harassed by its late ally in a variety of ways. Thus, by Mr. Allport's instruction, the station authorities at Retford refused to continue to supply water there to the Great Northern engines, and so the through service between Peterborough and Leeds was hampered; while, at the same time, at Grimsby, blocks were placed across the rails so as to prevent the Great Northern from using the running powers which the Sheffield directors had granted it under the agreement of 1848, to carry on its through service to Holland, for Hull. Moreover, on one occasion at least, when the Great Northern passengers did at last reach the Humber ferry, they found that the last boat had been purposely sent away without them, and so had to spend the night in the railway carriages or on sofas at the station. Nor did a suit which the Great Northern instituted in the Court of Chancery have the effect of putting an end to these obstructive proceedings.

Meanwhile the Euston Square authorities pushed their "protectionist" policy so far as to endeavour to bring the North British Company into the "confederacy," so that the Great Northern might be shut out from Scotch traffic; and it therefore became of the utmost importance to the latter to make sure of its access to York and the places beyond. Fortunately its running powers over the Lancashire and Yorkshire line from Askern to Knottingley had been secured under a sealed agreement—had this not been so Euston Square influence might have brought about their discontinuance—and fortunately, too, the York and North Midland directors kept faith as to making the link line from Burton Salmon to Knottingley, which was completed in June, 1850. All, therefore, that now needed to be done was to convert into a formal compact the draft agreement which Captain Laws had made with King Hudson as to the Great Northern's access to York by this route. The Great Northern, of course, still had powers available for a line of its own from Askern to York, and a party of north-country shareholders now again came forward to urge that the Company should even yet make this section of its original plan, and so render itself independent as far as York. But, as Mr. Alderman Meek, of York, and other Great Northern directors pointed out, independence as far as York could be of small service unless it meant also connection with the line further northwards, and this line—the York, Newcastle, and Berwick—shared a station with the York and North Midland. It was far better to give up their independent powers if by so doing they could make the established York companies their friends. This argument prevailed, and the result was that a new treaty between the Great Northern and York and North Midland was signed in the summer of 1850, under which the latter gave the use of its line into, and station at, York on favourable terms, on the understanding that the Great Northern, so long as the agreement was faithfully observed, would not take any steps to make a line or station of its own. Thus it came about that an "end-on" junction at Askern—"in a ploughed field four miles north of Doncaster," to quote a phrase attributed to Mr. Denison—became the northern terminus of the railway which, as we know, was for three years fought over and talked about as "the London and York."

The objections to this arrangement, however, were chiefly sentimental, while its advantages were substantial; for by it, as its directors had hoped, the Great Northern secured the friendship not only of the York and North Midland, but of the York, Newcastle, and Berwick, and the North British, the latter of which had meanwhile resisted Captain Huish's wiles. The result was that in September, 1850—the first month in which the passenger services were properly organized from King's Cross—a through connection with Edinburgh was arranged by which first-class passengers were enabled to perform the whole journey in twelve hours, the same time as by the West Coast route, and about half an hour better than by the old—or, as it now came to be called, the "alternative"—East Coast route *via* Rugby and Derby.

But north of Edinburgh no through connections with King's Cross could be arranged in 1850, because the Edinburgh and Glasgow Company, which held the key not only to Glasgow, but to Perth and Aberdeen, had been sworn in to the Euston Square Confederacy. Similarly the Lancashire and Yorkshire and Midland companies refused all facilities for exchange of traffic at Leeds and Wakefield, although, as far as mileage went, the best route between the Metropolis and Bradford and other important places in West Yorkshire was over the Great Northern. In the same way the Manchester, Sheffield, and Lincolnshire Company declined to arrange any exchange at Retford of Sheffield, Huddersfield, or Manchester traffic, while at Grimsby it continued to obstruct, as much as it dared, the Great Northern traffic with Hull. Even the Eastern Counties Company—though it had little either to fear or gain from Euston Square—was induced to prefer, for such traffic as it had to send to or receive from the north, the old Midland route from Peterborough *via* Syston to the new and much more direct route of the Great Northern; and besides this, its directors, anxious to protect their own territory, delayed carrying out their undertaking to make the link line from Cambridge to join the Royston and Hitchin and Shepreth, so that the latter, which had been opened by the Great Northern in March, 1850, could be worked merely as an agricultural branch.

Thus during the first months of its operations as a London railway the Great Northern was restricted, except between York and Edinburgh, to traffic which it could carry throughout on its own trains; and moreover it was not until about Christmas, 1850, that the station arrangements were sufficiently complete to allow of goods trains being run on the Peterborough to London section. On the other hand, to all the important places except Edinburgh, to which it *could* book passengers, its route was considerably shorter than the routes from Euston or Shoreditch, the distance saved in the case of York, Newcastle, etc., being nine miles, and in the case of Lincoln and Peterborough no less than thirty miles; and this meant that, though the Great Northern charged its Parliamentary *maxima*, the established companies had to reduce their fares not only at the actually competitive points but at all intermediate places. Under the infection of the "mania," the London and York promoters had adopted, in their original Bill, a very low scale of *maxima*, but, fortunately for the old companies, they had just obtained, in the session of 1850, an Amendment Act empowering them to charge more, "in view," to quote its preamble, "of the generally acknowledged fact that the calculations of railway profits made in 1845-6 were erroneous." Nevertheless the reductions which had to be made on the old routes were considerable, and for making them the directors of the companies owning them took great credit to themselves. But, as Mr. Denison said, the Great Northern had not the slightest objection to other companies following its example of "charging its *maxima* and taking its chance"; and the credit (if any was due) belonged to the new comer, which might from the outset have employed the weapon of rate-reductions to break down the barriers which had been raised against the development of its legitimate through traffic.

As it was, however, an agreement to charge equal fares to points between which competition had already begun preserved a sort of peace until the end of 1850, and in the meantime negotiations were set on foot for a permanent settlement to prevent what was loosely called "ruinous competition." For this two alternative plans presented themselves, namely, division of territory, or division of gross receipts; but the former was obviously incompatible with the powers already granted by Parliament to the various companies, and so the latter — the "pooling" proposition, to give it its modern name — practically held the field from the first. The advantages claimed for it were that it would remove temptations to "rate-cutting"— to again make use of a convenient modern term—and obviate the necessity of running what were styled "duplicate trains," *i.e.*, trains working between the same points by different routes. These were consummations so devoutly wished for that, as an abstract principle, "pooling" was assented to on all sides.

But it was much easier to agree to the principle than to carry it into practice, and the negotiations for this did not get far before it became evident that there was still an essential difference of opinion between the two parties. The confederate companies argued that the Great Northern was entitled to share in that traffic only to carry which it had already effective arrangements, whereas the new comer asserted its right to a portion of all traffic for which its lines formed part of a reasonably good route. In other words, the Euston Square party wanted to stereotype the "protectionist" state of things which their treaties had brought about by arranging a division for a term of years on the basis of the traffic as then carried, whereas to the Great Northern, a not yet properly established Company, such a basis of division was obviously unjust.

In short, however much the Great Northern might favour "pooling" in theory, it could not in justice to itself assent to it in practice, except on condition that due credit was given to it for all reasonable routes available without regard to the barriers which, under Euston Square influence, certain of the provincial companies had raised against it; and that this was the only really sound position which his Company could take up, Mr. Denison—clear-sighted man that he was—seems to have grasped from the first. But the entire novelty and intricacy of the problem seems to have baffled some of his colleagues and Mr. Seymour Clarke, the general manager; and even Mr. Denison was not strong enough to hold to the right principle quite consistently in face of the tremendous pressure brought to bear to dislodge him from it. "Ruinous competition" was the bugbear of railway shareholders at this time; an agreement to divide traffic seemed the only safeguard available; and to withstand the drift of general opinion in such a matter was too hard a task for a single man. Thus it came about that, when in the autumn of 1850 a proposal was drawn up to divide the traffic between London and the places north of York between eight companies, viz., the London and North Western, Lancaster and Carlisle, Caledonian, North British, York, Newcastle and Berwick, York and North Midland, Midland, and Great Northern, Mr. Denison found himself practically obliged to assent to it, though it gave the Great Northern no share at all of the traffic with Glasgow, Perth, or Aberdeen, and what he considered a very inadequate share of the traffic with Edinburgh, Berwick, Newcastle, etc. "I am bound to say," he said in reporting this "Octuple Agreement" to his shareholders in March, 1851, "that unless I put very great value upon peace, harmony, and quietness, I should not have made such concessions—for concessions they are—because I am thoroughly convinced that unless there were great efforts made to divert the traffic from your line, your line would get a larger proportion of that traffic than I have consented should be taken. But I was apprehensive of the consequences of a severe contest, and therefore I made these concessions." The agreement, however, was limited, mainly by the Great Northern influence, to five years.

But "peace, harmony, and quietness" between the rival railway companies was specially wanted at the beginning of 1851 in view of the heavy excursion traffic which was expected in connection with the Great Exhibition to be opened in London on 1 May of that year; and so the Great Northern directors, after consenting to the "Octuple Agreement" for traffic north of York, made a further departure from the negative attitude towards "pooling," to which, as we have said, they ought in strict justice to have adhered, by themselves suggesting, in February, 1851, a similar agreement as to the traffic south of York. This, however, they thought it might be possible to limit to such traffic as both routes were already actively competing for, and accordingly they named six towns—York, Leeds, Wakefield, Sheffield, Doncaster, and Lincoln—the traffic between which and London they were willing to divide. At the same time they named the percentages to which in their opinion the Great Northern route was entitled. The confederates in reply objected to these percentages, naming others instead which were equally unacceptable to the Great Northern; and so, as a private settlement seemed unattainable, arbitration was suggested, and the Right Hon. W. E. Gladstone was chosen as arbitrator. "He has been at the head of the Board of Trade," said Mr. Denison, "and is as highly intelligent and as honourable a man as can be found."

In accepting this proposal and agreeing to the arbitration the confederate directors must have been fully aware that the Great Northern intended to limit it strictly to the six towns they had named. Nevertheless, the preparation of the reference to Mr. Gladstone had not proceeded far before their representatives took alarm at a casual remark which Mr. Seymour Clarke, the Great Northern general manager, let fall, that for Bradford and other towns not included in the reference the Great Northern still held itself free to charge what fare it liked. This, indeed, was consistent with the attitude which the Great Northern had taken up at first, when they had said that so long as for Bradford and similar places the confederates "blocked" their traffic, they must retain in self-defence full freedom of competition; but as we have said, their subsequent consent to "pool," if only to a limited extent, was a departure from this originally strict attitude; and so there was a good deal of force in the contention which the confederates now raised that if the Great Northern retained its freedom in the case of Bradford, the agreement not to compete for the six towns' traffic would be "futile and inoperative." This being repeated before Mr. Gladstone, he judiciously refused to proceed with the arbitration until both sides were agreed that a substantial result was to be expected from it. Thus the matter was brought to a standstill.

At the ninth half-yearly meeting, held at the London Tavern on 6 March, 1851, no dividend could yet be declared on the ordinary shares, but Mr. Denison was able to give a satisfactory report of the progress of business.

"The opening of the line from Peterborough to London," he said, "has not only added weekly receipts for that portion of the line, but (to my surprise, I confess) has increased materially the average weekly receipts of all the northern part. Whereas the northern end of the line which was first opened produced about £20 or £21 per mile per week, when the seventy-six miles of line were opened from Peterborough to London, it not only maintained its own £20 per mile per week, but had the effect of raising the average of the whole mileage to nearly £30, and from that to £34 or £36, showing that, although the London end has undoubtedly been very expensive to make—as you all knew and expected it would be—in five years from this time it will pay you better for the outlay than any other part of the railway. Therefore, I once more congratulate you that the gentlemen who divided the Committee in the House of Commons whether the London end should not have been struck off, were not successful."

The new through traffic developed by the opening into London, however, was not the only factor in this improvement of revenue. The coal traffic, although not yet open to the Metropolis, was already yielding about £1,200 a week, and it appeared "likely"—the directors reported—"to be a source of great and permanent income," provided that "economical" arrangements could be made in the principal coalfield—that of South Yorkshire. To this end it was necessary, they added, to "free it from the embarrassments occasioned by the interposition of an independent company."

The terms first arranged for the conduct of the coal traffic from South Yorkshire to the Great Northern system had been that the Great Northern should supply the waggons and engines, and that the South Yorkshire Company should receive the ordinary mileage toll for the use of its line, viz., two-thirds of the gross receipts, and these terms had been embodied with other matters in a "working agreement" between the two companies dated September, 1849. But it is rather difficult to understand why the South Yorkshire directors then agreed to this, for very soon afterwards they began to make it the subject of complaint. The Great Northern maximum toll for coal traffic, it will be remembered, had been fixed at $\frac{3}{4}d.$ per ton per mile; and so long as the joint traffic had yielded this, the South Yorkshire had really had no grievance, because the two-thirds of it which they got—$\frac{1}{2}d.$ per ton per mile—was the full amount they themselves were authorized to charge for the mere use of their line. But when the trade began to develop beyond Lincolnshire to more distant and more competitive markets, and particularly when the opening of it into London came to be considered, it became evident that less than the maximum of $\frac{3}{4}d.$ a mile must be charged—that, indeed, $\frac{1}{2}d.$ a mile or even less was all that "the traffic would bear," to use a modern phrase, if the competition of the sea-borne coal from Newcastle was to be fairly met. And, although to the Great Northern with its "long lead" of 154 miles from Doncaster to London, this $\frac{1}{2}d.$ per mile was expected to be a quite profitable rate, to the South Yorkshire, with its "short haul" of about sixteen miles only, it promised little margin for profit. Besides this, many of the directors and large shareholders of the South Yorkshire were coalowners also; and, when in this capacity they considered the London trade proposed by the Great Northern, they saw that it would mean a highly competitive and therefore low price for the coal—a price not so good perhaps as might be obtained in the nearer markets with which the Midland and Sheffield Companies could bring them in touch. There was a double reason, therefore, why the satisfaction of the South Yorkshiremen with their joint traffic with the Great Northern had begun to cool down, and why they now showed little zeal in seconding the latter's efforts to set going the London trade.

But on developing this London trade Mr. Baxter had set his

heart; and since his position as solicitor to both companies gave him unique influence, a remedy for the difficulties that had arisen was soon devised. This was that the Great Northern should take permanent possession of the South Yorkshire line by guaranteeing a certain fixed dividend to its shareholders. Of course, there was much haggling as to terms, but at last it was agreed that the dividend should begin at 3 per cent., for which the Great Northern was to be entitled to carry 200,000 tons of coal—the then extent of the traffic—and should be increased by ½ per cent. upon every additional 100,000 tons carried until 800,000 tons should be carried and 6 per cent. paid, after which any further quantity was to be carried without additional charge; when, however, the dividend had once reached 4½ per cent. it was not to recede therefrom. This agreement was signed by the chairmen of the two companies, Mr. Denison and Lord Wharncliffe, in February, 1851, and in the following month it was recommended to the shareholders of both for adoption at their half-yearly meetings.

Of course these terms were much more favourable to the South Yorkshire shareholders than was the working agreement of 1849. Nevertheless the shareholders of the little Company were not satisfied. As already explained, most of them had to consider not only their interest in the railway but their larger interest as coalowners, and they were shrewd enough to see that if they gave the Great Northern the power to force their coal—in the interests of its "long haul" from Doncaster into London—into a market which was not naturally a profitable one, they might lose a good deal more in this way than they would gain by the interest on their railway shares. Moreover, there was talk of their getting as good terms of amalgamation from the Midland or the Sheffield companies. So, while the Great Northern meeting approved the arrangement, the South Yorkshiremen, when called together for the purpose, showed a great reluctance in the matter; until at last Mr. Denison, who had never been properly converted to his friend Mr. Baxter's faith in the London coal trade, and held that the Great Northern was offering very generous terms for a by no means certain benefit, had some difficulty in controlling his temper. "I remember," he said afterwards, "that in consequence of some remarks being made to me, I used an expression not very classical, I am ready to admit. It was a very bad day, and like other people I had worn a bad hat. The hat was standing before me, and I said: 'I don't care that hat whether you accept the terms or not.'"

Meanwhile, however, a *modus vivendi* had been arranged between the general managers of the two companies by which the South Yorkshire was to receive 10*d.* per ton as its share of the through rate; and under this arrangement, in the spring of 1851, the coal traffic into London was, at last, actually commenced, four large groups of coal stores having been erected in the goods yard at King's Cross for its reception. About a year previously the London and North Western authorities had set up a coal depôt at Camden, to which they were bringing consignments from the Wigan field; but compared with the extensive arrangements at King's Cross this was a small affair; and so it may fairly be claimed for the Great Northern that it was the first railway company, not only to project, but to carry out the supply of coal to London on a large scale. Moreover, the Company acted at first not only as carrier, but as coal merchant also, buying the coal from the collieries, selling it to the public, and retaining the balance. As may be supposed, the competition with the sea-borne trade was at first very keen, and under its influence the price to the Metropolitan consumer, which a few years before had averaged 30*s.* per ton, soon fell as low as 17*s.*

Meanwhile, in the matter of the reference to Mr. Gladstone as to the "pooling" of competitive passenger and goods traffic, nothing was done up to the end of June, though on the 1st of July the cheap excursions for the Exhibition were to commence. For this, however, at the eleventh hour, a temporary agreement to charge equal fares was patched up, and for about a fortnight a crisis was staved off. But then the competition of very cheap fares by sea from Hull led to an unauthorized reduction by a local agent of one of the companies, and this was all that was needed to stir their long-smouldering rivalry into a blaze. Reduction followed reduction; the return fare from places in the West Riding of Yorkshire to London fell first to 15*s.*, then to 10*s.*, and then to 5*s.*, and it would probably not have stopped even at that figure had not the Great Northern excursion agent at Leeds put out a notice that whatever fare the London and North Western and Midland Companies might charge, the Great Northern would carry passengers for 6*d.* less. At Sheffield, too, the London return fare also fell to 5*s.*; but after a week or two the King's Cross authorities discovered that they were liable to pay more than this sum per passenger for the use of the Manchester, Sheffield, and Lincolnshire line between Sheffield and Retford, and so were actually losing money upon every person they carried. Thereupon they discreetly withdrew from the competition.

Severe as it was, however, the competition on the whole was not so "ruinous" financially as had been expected beforehand, because the greater number who travelled made up, to a large extent, for the very low fares they paid; but this addition to the traffic, which in any case would have been abnormally large, put a very serious strain upon the resources of the companies. In the matter of locomotive power, however, the Great Northern was, fortunately, well prepared.

We have already noted that Mr. Sturrock had commenced his tenure of office by giving orders for additional engines to two new firms not previously employed by the Company—Messrs. E. B. Wilson and Co., of Leeds, and Messrs. R. B. Longridge and Co. The former had almost immediately supplied two of their well-known "Jenny Lind" type of "singles," with driving-wheels six feet in diameter and inside cylinders 16 in. by 22 in., and now they were busy completing the delivery of fifteen others of a new class of four-wheel-coupled engines specially designed by Mr. Sturrock in accordance with his plan already mentioned of adopting upon the narrow gauge the large heating surface and consequent high steam pressure which he had seen introduced with so much success by Mr. Gooch upon the Great Western. Accordingly he had designed these new "four-wheel-coupleds" to have a grate area of 13·2 square feet, a fire-box heating surface of 102 square feet, and a steam pressure of 150. As to the ten express passenger engines delivered to the Company about this same time by Messrs. Longridge, they were built upon the patent which Mr. T. R. Crampton had designed in 1843 for obtaining a large driving-wheel with a low centre-line of boiler. Accordingly they had the largest "drivers" of any engines yet in use upon the Great Northern, viz., 6' 6" in diameter.

In the matter of signals the Great Northern was more fully equipped than other lines at this date—that is to say, it had fixed signals not only at the stations but in advance of them; but unfortunately its engineers had not yet found time to put up the electric telegraph; and this was a deficiency which even in these primitive days was severely felt. On the London and North Western the whole of the special exhibition traffic was organized by the aid of the telegraph, word being sent by it to Euston every morning as to what trains were to be despatched from each of the provincial termini, and a daily time-table was at once got out. But on the Great Northern, without the telegraph, nothing of this sort was possible; the officials at King's Cross were always uncertain as to how many trains might be on the road, and at Boston—where the locomotive headquarters had been temporarily located—Mr. Sturrock was often similarly in the dark. Under these conditions fixed signals could be of little service; the only effective safeguards were a good look-out ahead, steady but *not* fast running, and locomotives which could draw heavy loads without breaking down. It was, therefore, very fortunate that in this latter particular both the new class of "four-wheel-coupleds" and the "Cramptons" proved quite satisfactory.

Besides steady, punctual running and immunity from serious accidents, there was another good quality which speedily gave pre-eminence to the Great Northern passenger service. This was the great civility and attention which Mr. Seymour Clarke enforced amongst the members of the working staff. As Mr. Denison put it in one of his half-yearly speeches, "Formerly when the London and Birmingham and Midland lines were opened, people were almost obliged to go down on their knees to be allowed to enter a carriage. Now directors and managers have to make a most civil and respectful bow to parties to coax them to go"; and this civility and respect pleased the public. The result was that the Great Northern soon began to be talked of as "the favourite line to the north," despite the circuit which, pending the completion of the "towns line" (from Peterborough to Retford), the trains had to make *viâ* Boston and Lincoln, and in August, 1851, the Queen and Prince Albert set a seal upon its rapidly-acquired reputation by choosing it as their route to Scotland. By Her Majesty's special instructions a slow rate of travelling was maintained on this trip, but absolutely punctual time was kept, and upon reaching York the Queen expressed cordial satisfaction with her journey.

Following upon the Queen's departure from town came a great rush of country excursionists to return home, and on the next Saturday morning the temporary terminus at Maiden Lane was flooded with a crowd of no less than 3000 would-be travellers, only about one-third of whom could be put into the available trains. On this or another similar occasion—according to Mr. Vizier, the veteran station-master at King's Cross—a party of festive Yorkshiremen boarded a train intended for Lincolnshire, declaring that it must take them home; and Mr. Denison, who was on the platform, became so angry at their obstinacy that it was with difficulty he was restrained from attempting to dislodge them single-handed with his stick. In such emergencies as this cattle-trucks had not infrequently to be pressed into use for passenger service.

Meanwhile the arbitration by Mr. Gladstone had been at last set in motion—both parties being afraid of the responsibility of obstructing even a partial pacification—and during this August the referee was busily engaged in hearing the arguments in favour of the several routes, and awarding the percentages for the traffic of the six towns referred to him. But still the fares for the exhibition traffic remained unraised; and in the middle of August, when York races came on, the North

Western and Midland companies announced that they would take passengers from London and back again for 15*s.*, 10*s.*, and 5*s.*, for the three classes, though the Great Northern had previously announced that its fares would be 52*s.* 6*d.* first class, 40*s.* second class, and no third. Moreover at the North Western half-yearly meeting about the same time, Mr. Glyn, the chairman, impressed upon the shareholders the necessity of keeping up a large reserve fund, so as to fight the battle without reduction of dividend, a proceeding of which the *animus*, in Mr. Denison's opinion, was to drive the Great Northern into concessions at all costs. "But," said the latter at the Great Northern half-yearly meeting a few days later, "I at this time unreservedly tell you that as long as I am your chairman I will never give way. I am all for peace, but I will defend your interest, and I say at once—and I hope it will go to other companies with whom we compete—I will make no concession that I cannot conscientiously say ought to be made. The moment you compel me to make concessions against my honest conviction of what is right in principle and in your interest, I will make my bow." At this half-yearly meeting the Company declared its first dividend—at the rate of £1 10*s.* per cent. per annum on the original stock.

On the very same day, 26 August, 1851, Mr. Gladstone was engaged in completing his award for the six towns. Passenger and goods traffic had of course to be treated separately, so that there were twelve percentages to be fixed for each route. Six of these Mr. Gladstone made more than the Great Northern had asked, two the same, and only four less, the general result being to give the new route 63 per cent. of the whole traffic pooled. This was conclusive proof that the Great Northern's claims had on the whole been reasonable.

Being pleasing to the Great Northern, the award was, of course, just the reverse to the confederate companies, and a few days after its publication, when the Doncaster races came on, they gave vent to their feelings by charging for this the same low fares as to York races, although under the award they stood to receive 5 per cent. only of the passenger traffic between London and Doncaster, and even out of this they had to pay toll to the South Yorkshire Company for running over its line from Swinton. "It is abundantly clear," said Mr. Denison, "that they must have lost money by it, and I can come to no other conclusion than that they were under the influence of feelings which I hope I shall never entertain, and which I do not envy them the possession of." Worse than this, after the fares for the six towns were raised, the confederates still kept them much lower at Normanton and other intermediate points, with the result that passengers soon found it to be to their advantage to book thither and then re-book, and the receipts thus obtained were taken out of the operation of the pool. This course the confederates defended, when challenged, upon the ground that it was the inevitable outcome of the Great Northern's action in confining the pool to the six towns only, and they were very indignant when Mr. Denison described it bluntly as "nothing less than an evasion of the award." "I tell these gentlemen," replied the Great Northern chairman, "if they will do me the honour to read what I say, that I repeat it was an evasion, and an evasion of which they ought to be ashamed. I shall not be afraid of telling any man with whom I come in contact if I find him evading an agreement that he is doing so."

Meantime Mr. Denison, "first-class fighting man" that he was, had had to meet something like a revolt amongst his own shareholders, the cause of it being an agreement which the directors had made, through the medium of their ever-zealous agent, Mr. Baxter, to work a small system of lines in Norfolk called the East Anglian. To this agreement the objection of the Great Northern shareholders was two-fold, first, that it had been signed by Mr. Denison without authority from them, and second, that it involved a guarantee to the East Anglian Company of £15,000 a year, and this in face of the fact that the guarantees with which the Company was already saddled, viz., the 6 per cent. dividends to the East Lincolnshire and Royston and Hitchin companies, and the rentals of the Witham and Fossdyke navigations, had proved confessedly bad bargains. Moreover, guarantees, as we know, had been one of King Hudson's favourite weapons, and had fallen with him into bad repute.

"Mr. Chairman," said one angry Great Northern shareholder, a clergyman, "I happen to be a proprietor of shares in those unfortunate railways, the York and Newcastle and the York and North Midland. Why have they been unfortunate railways? Why have I lost more in them than I hold in the Great Northern? Simply because they hung those guarantees round our necks. But my dear brother shareholders, my dear brethren—(laughter)—you will excuse that slip—let us come to the real question. Are the directors of this Company to enter into agreements, and make leases, and hang things about our necks, without ever asking our leave?"

The lease of the East Anglian system was the less easy to defend because of the difficulties which the Great Northern authorities had already met with in their attempts to work traffic over it. It was, of course, much more in the Eastern Counties territory than their own, extending as it did from junctions with that Company's lines at

Wisbeach and Ely, to a junction with the "Norfolk" line at East Dereham; and the only access which the Great Northern had to it was by running powers over the Eastern Counties from Peterborough to Wisbeach, which running rights it had obtained in return for giving up the powers for a line of its own from Stamford to Wisbeach. But unfortunately between the Eastern Counties' station at Wisbeach and the commencement of the East Anglian line there was half a mile of line belonging to the former Company, over which its directors contended the Great Northern had no powers; and so, when in July, 1851, the latter had endeavoured to begin a through service *viâ* the East Anglian from Peterborough to Lynn, its officials had found the points at Wisbeach shut against them, and had had to get their passengers transferred by omnibus to East Anglian trains. Of course under these conditions neither passenger nor goods traffic could be properly developed.

Nor was this by any means the only bone of contention between the Great Northern and the Eastern Counties. The more important matter as to whether or not the Great Northern was to get access to Cambridge still remained in dispute. In the session of 1851 the Great Northern had promoted a Bill, for the second time, for making a line of its own into that town from the terminus of the Royston and Hitchin at Shepreth; and although this had been thrown out summarily on second reading by a combination of Eastern Counties and University opposition, the Great Northern—saddled as it was with the yearly liability of nearly £15,000 a year to the Royston and Hitchin shareholders—could not accept a decision as final which meant the shutting up of that line at its eastern end.

"We are bound in defence of our property," said Mr. Denison, "to say that we must by some means or other go from Royston to Cambridge.... The Eastern Counties (and I do not presume to find fault with them) are doing the best they can to protect *their* property, and they say to us, you shall not come into Cambridge.... Now, if there be any Eastern Counties shareholders here I will tell them with perfect respect that my duty will be to go to Cambridge. I will do it in the most amicable and harmonious way possible, if they will permit me, but go I must and undoubtedly I shall."

For once, however, the Great Northern chairman was hardly as good as his word, except in this sense, that he showed that with him the profession of a desire to settle a dispute, if possible, in a harmonious manner, was no empty form. In the autumn of 1851 negotiations with the Eastern Counties directors were resumed, and it was then strongly urged that in the comparatively small area under dispute with this Company a trial might be given to the principle of division of territory between rival railway systems. In the country at large, as we have seen, this had been rendered impracticable by the competitive powers already granted to the various companies by Parliament; but in the counties between the Wash and the Thames no directly competing lines had yet been laid out, nor had the Great Northern itself been granted any Parliamentary authority to invade this district. What competitive power it possessed there it had acquired, as we know, from companies separately formed, namely, the Royston and Hitchin, the Boston, Stamford, and Birmingham, and the East Anglian; and, though it was bound in justice to itself to use these powers so long as it was burdened with the liabilities attached to them, it could afford to forego them if the liabilities were taken over by another party.

This was precisely the arrangement that was now made. As the readiest means of at once securing, and paying for, freedom from Great Northern competition, the Eastern Counties directors offered to take over the latter's agreements with the Royston and Hitchin and East Anglian companies, and to become responsible in the one case for the 6 per cent. dividend, and in the other for the traffic guarantee. With this offer the Great Northern Board very willingly closed, with the single stipulation—insisted on by Mr. Denison—that the transfer of the Royston and Hitchin should be for fourteen years only; and at the same time they took advantage of the friendly feeling thus created to urge the Eastern Counties to exchange traffic at Peterborough, offering it a bonus of 20 per cent. on all competitive traffic, if it were consigned *viâ* Great Northern instead of being sent as heretofore by the Midland's Syston line. On these terms, accordingly, a general treaty between the two companies was concluded in the autumn of 1851; and from 1 April, 1852—as soon, that is to say, as the Eastern Counties had its link line from Cambridge to Shepreth ready for opening—the working of the Royston and Hitchin line was taken over by that Company.

Thus between the systems springing from King's Cross and Shoreditch, competition was almost entirely put an end to for a term of fourteen years; but in the much larger territory into which the Great Northern came into rivalry with the Euston Square confederacy, there still arose difficulties in completing even the partial pacification which was hoped for from Mr. Gladstone's award. In consequence of the "re-booking" artifice a second reference had to be made to Mr. Gladstone, as the result of which he altered the terms of his award so as expressly to prevent this evasion; but still the actual putting into operation of the pool was delayed, the reason being that neither party could be really satisfied with it so long as it was limited to the six towns. Yet so long as the confederacy continued to keep up its obstructive barriers against the Great Northern—so that, for instance, it was only by "bus"-ing and carting to and from Leeds that the latter could do any traffic with Bradford—Mr. Denison and his colleagues could not assent to a complete treaty of peace. In the end, however, the Great Northern gave way to the extent of undertaking not to disturb the rates and fares at places outside the "pool" during the five years for which it was to last, and on this condition it was at last brought into operation, being made retrospective from 1 January, 1851.

Thus the "protectionist" policy of Captain Huish gained a partial triumph, but it was a sort of triumph which in the nature of things could be but short-lived. As Mr. Denison said for the consolation of his party: "No fallacy could be so great as to suppose that the British public would travel circuitously if they could go directly; such a theory might do very well for railway makers, but not for the public; sooner or later traffic, like water, would find its own level." Indeed, in seeking to keep the Great Northern out of business for which naturally—if no artificial obstructions were raised—it offered the best facilities, the too astute politicians of Euston Square were simply repeating the mistake which King Hudson had made—and paid for—when he had endeavoured to prevent a direct line being made at all because it was contrary to the interests of the companies owning a circuitous route already established. "It is the character of the British public to improve," said Mr. Denison. "It is their spirit and genius to improve; and sooner or later the traffic must come to the shorter line."

Already, indeed, the Great Northern had established the truth of this by pushing its way into so many important towns and enforcing its right to the major part of their traffic under the Octuple and Gladstone awards; and already too in the case of the Bradford, Halifax, and other still "protected" traffic of the West Riding, the force of the natural law above stated had begun to assert itself in a way that no general manager's diplomacy could for long effectually resist. At the same time as the Great Northern had been struggling into being, a "West Riding Union Railway Company" had obtained powers, as the reader may remember, after an equally severe struggle, to remedy the deficiencies of the existing accommodation by making direct lines between all the more important towns of that district; but, unlike the Great Northern, this West Riding Union unfortunately had not succeeded in maintaining its independence, but had been absorbed in 1847 in the combination which had then given birth to the Lancashire and Yorkshire Company. Then had happened precisely what would have happened in the larger sphere had Hudson succeeded in his many attempts to absorb the Great Northern into *his* combinations: the owners of the old routes, having regained the ascendency, had found it to be to their interests not to carry out the new direct lines. Thus in the West Riding, at the time we have now reached, a fragment only of the Union scheme had been carried out, namely a sort of "loop" system connecting Halifax, Low Moor, and Bradford with each other and with the old circuitous Manchester and Leeds line at Sowerby Bridge and at Mirfield; while what was really the corner-stone of the whole project, the direct line from Bradford to Leeds, which was to furnish also a new direct route between Manchester and Leeds *viâ* Halifax, had been abandoned.

With this state of things, as may be supposed, the public was far from satisfied; still less was it pleased that the Great Northern, though it had forced its way into Wakefield and Leeds, should be hindered from extending the benefits of its direct route from London to Bradford and to Halifax. Therefore there existed in 1851 a double incentive to a new effort after improvement, and for such an effort to take shape it was only necessary for competent leaders to arise. These were now forthcoming in the persons of Messrs. Edward Akroyd and William Firth, two enterprising West Riding traders.

These gentlemen had been the most energetic of the original promoters of the West Riding Union, and they had joined the Lancashire and Yorkshire Board as representatives of that scheme, to retire from it subsequently in chagrin when they found that its execution was not earnestly carried on. But so soon as they had seen that public feeling was again with them, and the state of the money market favourable, they had returned to their original idea of accomplishing their purposes by means of an independent company, and accordingly they had taken counsel with Mr. Henry Nelson, an energetic solicitor of Leeds, and with Mr. (afterwards Sir) John Hawkshaw, the distinguished engineer. The result was that in the autumn of 1851 a Bill for a "Leeds, Bradford, and Halifax Junction Railway Company" was deposited, its immediate object being to complete the main part of the West Riding Union scheme by constructing the direct link still missing between Bowling, near Bradford, and Leeds.

Naturally enough, this attack upon the vested railway interests of the West Riding received all possible encouragement from the Great

Northern, and the result was that the relations between it and the Lancashire and Yorkshire, which the alliance of the latter to Euston Square had strained for some time, now for the first assumed a definitely hostile complexion. In November, 1851, Captain Laws, the manager of the Lancashire and Yorkshire, resigned the seat which, from the time of the Great Northern's incorporation, he had held upon its Board, and about a month later the Lancashire and Yorkshire directors sent a notice to King's Cross that the running powers which gave the Great Northern access to Wakefield and to Methley (for Leeds) would be withdrawn, unless in future full Parliamentary toll was paid. About this same time, too, the Sheffield Company gave similar notice that it should withdraw its leave for the Great Northern to run between Grimsby and the New Holland ferry; and thus the new year—1852—instead of inaugurating the term of "peace and quietness" for which the Great Northern authorities had hoped, found them with two Chancery suits on their hands, upon the issue of which depended their ability to continue some of their most valuable traffic. Fortunately, however, both suits were speedily decided in their favour, so that they had no serious reason to fear but that the policy to which Mr. Denison had pledged himself at the outset of this struggle with the Confederacy, namely, to go on "calmly and quietly asserting our rights," would be crowned with ultimate, if tardy, success.

CHAPTER VIII.

FINIS CORONAT OPUS—1852.

IT had not been until the year 1849 that any active steps had been taken towards the making of the sixty miles of "towns line" between Peterborough and Retford. At the end of that year, however, a commencement had been made at some of its heaviest points, under a contract let to Mr. Jackson, and so by the time of the opening from London in 1850 good progress could be reported on its heavier cuttings, its bridges, and its two tunnels—at Stoke and at Peascliffe. About this time, also, two further contracts had been let—to Messrs. Pearce and Smith and to Messrs. Oldham—and a little later the construction of the large bridge across the Trent navigation at Newark had been entrusted to Messrs. Rennie and Logan; so that during the autumn and winter of 1850 work had been going on throughout its whole length. In the spring of 1851 Mr. Joseph Cubitt had reported that completion by the end of that year might be looked for; but an almost continuous rainfall during the month of July had upset this calculation, and in August, 1851, there had been no prospect of the tunnels—which were the key to the whole—being completed before the following spring. Meanwhile, however, the station works had been commenced and rapid progress made with the Newark bridge, the span of which—262 feet—was to be longer than that of any other bridge yet built for the Company. The type of design which Mr. Cubitt had chosen for it was quite unique, being that known as the "Warren Truss," which has not been adopted elsewhere either before or since; nor was the engineer here content, as he had been at Bardney and other places on the loop line, with using timber wholly for the material. At Newark the floor of the bridge only was being made of timber. For the upper part, which may be described as a series of equilateral triangles, fastened at their apices by pins, cast and wrought iron was being employed.

The other principal work of construction which the Company had still in hand was the permanent passenger terminus at King's Cross. To obtain the site for this a Small-pox and Fever Hospital had had to be removed at a cost of about £60,000, and a good deal of excavation done, both which operations had caused much delay in the commencement of the station buildings. Since the beginning of 1851, however, the construction of these had been going steadily forward under the charge of the architect, Mr. Lewis Cubitt, and the contractor, Mr. Jay. The internal arrangements of the terminus were to be of a very simple character, consisting of two long platforms, one for departure and the other for arrival, separated from one another by fourteen tracks for the use of trains; and the building to enclose these was to be equally simple, for in laying his plans Mr. Lewis Cubitt had borne well in mind his uncle, Sir William Cubitt's,* dictum, that "a good station could be built at King's Cross for less than the cost of the ornamental archway at Euston Square." It was to consist—and its main outlines are still clearly traceable amid many additions and accretions—of two immense sheds, each 800 feet long, 105 feet wide, and 71 feet high, divided by a wall formed of piers and arches, and covered by an arched roof in two spans.

This roof, at the time of its construction, was probably the largest of its kind in the world, and the plan of it Mr. Lewis Cubitt borrowed from a riding-school which had been recently constructed at Moscow for the Czar of Russia. The girders which he was employing may be roughly described as bundles of planks so tied together that they overlapped one another lengthways, and thus each complete girder, when secured to the walls, became like a stretched bow. This, of course, necessitated great strength in the outer walls to resist the tendency of the planks to restraighten themselves, and on the west side the weight of a subsidiary building which was being erected there for the Company's offices promised to supply this want in a very satisfactory manner. But the eastern wall had to be built to abut immediately upon the Maiden Lane, now called York Road, where there was not sufficient room even for flying buttresses; and so from the first there were critics— Mr. E. B. Denison (now Lord Grimthorpe) was one at least—who predicted its subsequent failure to bear the strain put upon it. The facade which was to front direct upon the old St. Pancras Road— since diverted—was the only part of the building which was intended to be at all ornamental. Its appearance is too well known to need description. Of the whole building the architect himself said that it was to "depend for its effect on the largeness of some of its

* He had been knighted as one of the Commissioners for the Great Exhibition of 1851.

features, its fitness for its purpose, and its characteristic expression of that purpose." For material brick was being used almost exclusively except in the roof.

At the eleventh half-yearly meeting of the Company, held at the London Tavern on 27 February, 1852, a dividend was declared at the rate of £2 10s. on the original stock, making 2 per cent. for the year. Said the chairman on that occasion:

"The general receipts of the Company have greatly exceeded those of the previous six months, and during the first six weeks of the present year the traffic has increased about £3,000 a week as com-

THE ORIGINAL "WARREN TRUSS" BRIDGE OVER THE TRENT NAVIGATION NEAR NEWARK.

pared with the corresponding weeks of last year, the increase arising from each of the three chief sources of traffic—passengers, goods, and minerals. With respect to the working expenses they are undoubtedly large. In round numbers they are 50 per cent. One reason is that we run over 150 miles of foreign lines. Another way of accounting for it is that during the excursion period highly respectable persons—I am exceedingly sorry to say for your sakes—took advantage of the excursion trains, and our ordinary trains often went very nearly empty, so that at that particular period we were running double trains and receiving very low fares. With respect to the dividend, I think you will agree with me that under all the circumstances it is a fair and liberal dividend."

By this time the receipts from the coal traffic had increased to about £2,000 a week, and they might have risen a good deal higher than this but for the fact that the supply from the South Yorkshire field had been unequal to the demand. In so far as this could be met by the pit-owners increasing their gettings, it was a difficulty easily surmountable; but there was more than a suspicion that the owners were not fostering the London trade, but were preferring to send their output over the Midland and Sheffield systems to nearer markets where higher prices ruled. Now this, as we have already seen, was one of the contingencies to meet which the draft treaty of amalgamation between the South Yorkshire and Great Northern had been framed—"its value to us," Mr. Denison had said in regard to this treaty in March, 1851, "is the security of the whole of that coalfield to the Great Northern"; and so, notwithstanding the reluctance which some of the South Yorkshire shareholders had shown to ratify the action of their directors in the matter, the Great Northern directors had continued to urge the South Yorkshire Board to carry the amalgamation into effect. To this same end, also, all the influence of the common solicitor of the two companies, Mr. Baxter, had been directed, and the result had been that in the full confidence that the dissatisfied parties would in the end be persuaded or outvoted, the two directorates had deposited a Bill in the autumn of 1851 to authorize the amalgamation on the basis of the draft agreement.

Nor had this confidence proved ill-founded. Shortly afterwards the approval of the South Yorkshire shareholders had been obtained, and on 26 February, 1852—just one day before the Great Northern half-yearly meeting just referred to—the draft agreement had been converted by the two Boards into a formal sealed treaty. Then at an extraordinary general meeting held for the purpose immediately after their ordinary meeting, the Great Northern shareholders for the second time approved the terms—though not without protest from one or two of their number—and authorized their directors to join in prosecuting the Amalgamation Bill.

Meanwhile, simultaneously with this South Yorkshire business, the Great Northern directors had some other negotiations, also with the view to an amalgamation, in hand. These were with the Ambergate, Nottingham, Boston, and Eastern Junction—a Company of which the reader may remember to have already heard in this same connection; indeed, ever since its incorporation in 1846, the absorption of this cumbrously-named Company into one of the greater ones had appeared imminent. So far, however, it had obstinately retained its independence; but financial weakness—and the burden of a great deal of canal property forced upon it by Parliament—had prevented it from carrying out in its integrity the extensive undertaking foreshadowed by its name. As it was, all the railway it had made so far was a line twenty-two miles in length from a junction with the Midland's Nottingham and Lincoln line at the hamlet of Colwick —four miles east of Nottingham—to the town of Grantham; and having obtained permission from the Midland to run into, and use, its station at Nottingham, it had worked a local passenger and goods traffic, and also some coal traffic from the Nottinghamshire pits to Grantham since its opening in July, 1850.

Of this state of things the natural sequel seemed to be the absorption of the Ambergate—as it was still called—into the Midland, and this would almost certainly already have taken place but for the foresight and activity of Mr. Graham Hutchison, already known to us as a large Great Northern shareholder. This gentleman had become much impressed with the value which the Ambergate line would acquire if it could be worked from Grantham in conjunction with the Great Northern towns line. Accordingly he had "made a corner" in Ambergate shares—to use a modern phrase—and by his vote alone had succeeded in defeating a proposal for amalgamation with the Midland and London and North Western, though the terms offered were a permanent 4 per cent. guarantee. Now, therefore, in the spring of 1852, when the Great Northern came forward with a similar offer, Mr. Hutchison's influence was by itself sufficient to ensure its acceptance; and so in May, 1852—when the opening of the towns line was in very near prospect—a working agreement was signed by the two companies, under which the Great Northern thought to secure access to the important town of Nottingham, and also through Nottingham to the Nottinghamshire and Derbyshire coalfield, by a route no longer from London than the established one of the Midland and London and North Western.

But such an important advantage as this the confederate companies were not prepared to see handed to their great rival without a further struggle, and for this they found a weapon handy in the person of a recalcitrant Great Northern shareholder named Simpson, who was persuaded to bring a petition in Chancery against the Great Northern chairman to restrain him from carrying out the agreement with the Ambergate, on the ground that in signing it he had acted beyond his powers. Mr. Denison's case was defended by his son, Mr. E. B. Denison, already a barrister of eminence, but despite his able advocacy an injunction was granted restraining the Great Northern both from working the traffic of the Ambergate and from guaranteeing it a dividend. This decision was given on the 28th of June, 1852.

Meanwhile the South Yorkshire Amalgamation Bill had reached

Committee stage in the House of Commons, and had there been opposed most strenuously by the Midland Company, which naturally objected to the South Yorkshire coalfield being made the monopoly of its great rival. The Midland's representatives made out a strong case from the point of view, not only of their own rights, but of public interest, with the result that the Committee insisted upon the insertion in the Bill of a clause providing for free interchange of Midland traffic at Swinton Junction—"on the principle of a mileage rate." This meant, as Mr. Denison put it afterwards, that "if the Midland Company were to send twenty-five waggons to the junction, they could say to the South Yorkshire, 'take these waggons up to the coalpits, get them loaded, and bring them back again, and we shall pay you the mileage rate'"—a state of things obviously incompatible with the paramount object which the Great Northern had in view, namely, complete control of the traffic from the field. Under these circumstances Mr. Denison and his colleagues would probably have acted wisely if they had at once dropped the Bill. Instead of this, however, they sent it on under Mr. Baxter's charge to the House of Lords, and it passed into law on 21 June, 1852—a week, that is to say, before the decision in the Ambergate suit.

During this week the Great Northern Board received through the medium of Mr. Baxter a proposal from the South Yorkshire directors that meetings of the two companies should be convened at once in order to proceed with the amalgamation as authorized by the Bill just passed, on the terms agreed under the sealed contract of the previous February. It was accompanied, however, by a demand that at such South Yorkshire meeting and at future ones the Great Northern must waive the right of voting which it possessed in respect of its holding of South Yorkshire shares; and this demand Mr. Denison and his colleagues declined to accede to, or to act further in the matter of the amalgamation until it should be withdrawn. Thereupon the South Yorkshire responded with a reassertion of "the necessity and propriety" of their proviso, and this response reached the Great Northern directors on 6 July—eight days after the decision in the Ambergate case.

During these eight days the Great Northern chairman's thoughts had been very busy. He had been considering the effect of the injunction as to the Ambergate in all its bearings, and it had occurred to him that if the agreement with that Company was *ultra vires*, as the Vice-Chancellor had declared, the agreement with the South Yorkshire must have been also *ultra vires*—in which inference he found his common-sense reasoning confirmed by the expert opinion of his son.

Of course, as Mr. E. B. Denison pointed out, an agreement with the South Yorkshire could now be legally made seeing that an Act of Parliament for the purpose had been obtained; but liberty to make a new agreement and compulsion to carry out one already made were two different things, and, in view of the new aspect which the whole transaction has assumed since the clause in favour of the Midland Company had been inserted in the Act, the difference seemed to the Great Northern chairman a most important one. This opinion he communicated to his fellow-directors when the matter came up for discussion at their next Board meeting, and the result was that the question, from being merely whether or not the Great Northern should insist upon its view as to a minor point, became the much larger one as to whether or not it should proceed with the amalgamation at all.

Of course the suggestion of abandoning the amalgamation horrified Mr. Baxter, who strained every nerve to prevent such a collapse of his hopes and labours; and by his advice the South Yorkshire directors speedily brought the matter to a practical issue by sending in a claim under the agreement (which had been made to date from the beginning of the year) for the sum necessary to enable them to pay their guaranteed dividend for the half-year just expired. This put the Great Northern Board into a very delicate position. To refuse the money was to repudiate a sealed agreement; to pay it was to commit themselves for the future; moreover, Mr. Denison, particularly, was bound to be on his guard, for his son told him that if the agreement (which bore his signature) should be adjudged, like that with the Ambergate, to be *ultra vires*, he might be made liable to refund personally any sum paid under it. Under these circumstances the only safe plan seemed to be to pay the South Yorkshire a sum on account "without prejudice," and this accordingly the Great Northern Board decided to do; but upon receipt of it the South Yorkshire directors declared the full guaranteed dividend to which the agreement entitled them, ingeniously adjusting the accounts by withholding that due to the Great Northern on its shares.

This, of course, did not tend towards a settlement of the main question, and so the breach between the Great Northern chairman and its solicitor became daily wider—old friends though they were, and fellow-townsmen and comrades in many an honest fight. Mr. Denison could not forget that he had been "always lukewarm, to say the least," about the terms of the amalgamation—indeed, as we know, he had never cordially entertained the high hopes as to the London coal traffic from South Yorkshire upon which the whole transaction was based. Moreover, now that he had had time to realize fully the effect of the

Midland Company's facility clause, he had become firmly convinced that the price which the Great Northern Company had undertaken to pay on the understanding that it would obtain complete control of the coalfield would prove an unprofitable one now that the Midland had been admitted to it on terms almost as good. Mr. Baxter, on the other hand, still held that the Great Northern would benefit largely by the amalgamation; but, quite apart from this, he maintained that they had no option now but to go on with it, seeing that they had sealed an agreement to do so, and had co-operated with the South Yorkshire to obtain an Act for the purpose. But to this Mr. Denison replied that the agreement was invalid, and the Act permissive, not compulsory, and that therefore it was fairly open to him to advise his shareholders not to make a new agreement under the Act—nay, more, that it was his clear duty to do so, seeing that he now thought the amalgamation detrimental to their interests. This was the view that in the end prevailed. At a full meeting of the Great Northern Board, held on 25 August, 1852, a resolution in favour of a policy of masterly inactivity as to the amalgamation was proposed by Mr. Denison and unanimously adopted, notwithstanding some very outspoken protests from the solicitor.

Meantime a very important event in the history of the Great Northern undertaking proper had taken place—the opening for traffic of the sixty miles of "towns" line between Peterborough and Retford. From 15 July, 1852, goods and coal trains had been allowed to pass over it, and a fortnight later—from 1 August, 1852—its opening for passenger traffic had taken place, not only local trains, but the through expresses between London and Yorkshire being at once diverted to it from their original circuitous route over "the loop." This meant that the journey from King's Cross to York and to Leeds was shortened by about twenty miles, the distance to York becoming $190\frac{1}{2}$ miles and to Leeds $186\frac{1}{2}$ miles—about thirty miles shorter than by the London-and-North-Western-cum-Midland routes. The result was that the best Great Northern express trains now began to do the journey in each case in about five hours instead of in about six as at first, whereas the London and North Western and Midland, having accelerated their best services to about six hours in the case of London–Leeds, and six and a half hours London–York, in answer to the Great Northern's original challenge in 1850, were now obliged to submit to being more than an hour behind in both cases. For London–Edinburgh, too, the Great Northern's (East Coast) service, being now reduced in time from twelve to eleven hours, became an hour ahead of the West Coast, and practically extinguished the "alternative East Coast route" *viâ* Rugby and

Derby, though the latter continued to receive a percentage of traffic under the "Octuple Agreement."

Another important result of the opening of the towns line was that Nottingham was then for the first time brought into connection with the Great Northern system. This was effected by the junction at Grantham with the line of the Ambergate Company. For with that Company the Great Northern remained in potential alliance (pending the passing through Parliament in the next year of an Act to legalize their amalgamation); and accordingly in the Great Northern time-tables for August, 1852, the commencement of a service to and from Nottingham *via* Grantham was announced, by which passengers were to be landed in that town from London in a shorter time than by the established service of the London and North Western and Midland. This, of course, was resented by the confederates, who chose to regard it as a defiance of the Chancellor's injunction; and when on the opening day, 1 August, the passengers from King's Cross were actually drawn into the Midland station at Nottingham by a Great Northern engine, the officials there decided that the time had come to take active measures to defend their rights. Accordingly they got a *posse* of Midland engines together, and sent them, as on an elephant hunt, to hem in the Great Northern trespasser on all sides with its own kind; and although the driver of the latter—according to an eye-witness—made a desperate effort to charge through his captors, he was, of course, unsuccessful, and had to submit to see his locomotive borne away into imprisonment in a disused shed. The rails leading to this were then pulled up so as effectually to cut off escape; and although the Great Northern authorities defended the legality of their action by producing documents to prove that the Ambergate Company had *hired* the engine from them, it was not until seven months afterwards that the release of the captive could be obtained.

But as in any case the Ambergate had an indisputable right to run passenger trains with its own engines into Nottingham Station, the through connection between King's Cross could be maintained despite this high-handed capture; and even in goods traffic the new allies were able to do something by carting to or from the Ambergate terminus at Colwick. Such a state of things, however, could not be permanently submitted to, and, accordingly, it was proposed that the Ambergate, with the Great Northern's support, should obtain power to extend its line from Colwick to a new Nottingham station of its own. This, however, meant a heavy capital outlay, which might be avoided if only an amicable relationship with the Midland could by any means be brought about; and, improbable though this might seem in view of the recent action of the latter, there were other reasons which led Mr. Denison and his colleagues to think that an attempt to accomplish it was at least worth the making.

Of these reasons the chief was that the relations between the Midland and the London and North Western, after having become so intimate in the early part of 1852 that the terms of an amalgamation of the two companies had come within 2½ per cent. of settlement, had, on the failure of these negotiations, become decidedly less friendly. While the Euston authorities had turned their attention to an even more ambitious project—amalgamation with the Great Western, the Midland directors had taken steps to develop its undertaking in directions which pointed away from dependence on Euston Square. Thus in May 1852 they had entered into an agreement to lease for twenty-one years the line of the North Western Company—popularly called the "Little North Western" to distinguish it from its great namesake—a line which extended from Skipton, the northern terminus of the Midland's Leeds and Bradford line to Lancaster; and, more important still, under pressure from local landowners and others they had determined upon an attempt to revive in the next session of Parliament their lapsed powers for the southward extension to Hitchin. Taken together, these two moves obviously pointed to the development of a new Midland "Central" route between London and the north, and the revival of the Hitchin line was sufficient to show that for such a route King's Cross was looked to, temporarily at least, as the London terminus. More than this, the Midland Board had published the opinion at the time when their negotiations for amalgamation with Euston Square were in progress, that it was "essential" to their Company to be "permanently identified with some Company having a line to and terminus in London." Seeing, therefore, that those negotiations had come to nothing, it was at least not impossible that they might now listen to similar overtures from King's Cross.

It was under these circumstances that on 16 August, 1852, a fortnight only after the warfare in Nottingham Station, and a fortnight before the final decision not to proceed with the South Yorkshire guarantee, Mr. Denison wrote in his direct way to Mr. Ellis, the Midland chairman, to suggest that in his opinion "an earnest attempt ought to be made to unite the Great Northern and Midland railways upon the principle of a complete amalgamation." "They compete with one another," said he, "in the south and in the north, and they cross each other at two or three important points; there are double stations at several towns, and duplicate trains run where single ones would serve the public equally well. A very large annual expenditure would therefore be saved, and an amalgamation is so natural from peculiar circumstances, and (according to Mr. Glyn's published opinion upon the subject of competition and amalgamation) so inevitable that, I apprehend, no Parliamentary objection would be offered."

"Our Board," wrote Mr. Ellis in reply two days later, "is equally with yourself alive to the serious evils which are the inevitable result of competition between two lines which approach and intersect each other; they feel, moreover, the great importance, not only of putting an end to the needless expenditure of running double trains, but further and still more the imperative necessity of preventing a reckless outlay of capital in the construction of new lines. You are aware, however, that for many years the London and North Western and Midland companies have cultivated an intimate alliance, and that upon a recent occasion negotiations were on foot for a closer union of the interests of these companies. Candour requires me to inform you that, previously to the receipt of your letter, a proposal has been made to this Company to renew those negotiations."

This new proposal from Euston Square had, it appeared, been received at Derby two days only before Mr. Denison's letter; but even had the London and North Western not thus already renewed their overtures—to which step they were probably actuated by fear of what the "Little North Western" lease and Leicester and Hitchin revival might lead to—they would almost certainly have done so directly they had heard that a proposal for amalgamation had been received from King's Cross. As it was, they now pressed their own new proposals with such determination and liberality that the former difficulty as to agreeing to terms was soon removed, and with the consent of both their own and the Midland shareholders a Bill to authorize the amalgamation of the two companies was deposited for the session of 1853. With regard to the Leicester and Hitchin line, pledges had been given to the local people which could not now be withdrawn, so a Bill to revive the powers for that were also deposited. But the Great Northern directors foresaw that if this line was made and worked under the control of Euston Square, it would be blocked against traffic with King's Cross, and so they opposed it with a counter Bill for a branch of their own from Sandy to Bedford. At the same time other Bills were deposited for the amalgamation of the Ambergate with the Great Northern, and for the extension of its line into Nottingham, and thus there seemed every prospect of a new battle-royal in the coming session between the Great Northern and Ambergate on the one side, and the London and North Western and Midland on the other.

On 14 October, 1852, the permanent passenger terminus at King's Cross was opened for public traffic, the first train to use it being the 7 a.m. "Parliamentary" bound for York. The building was much admired; its outside was described as "wearing a magnificent appearance," and its inside as "presenting a vista of extraordinary effect"; and from shareholders a good many complaints reached the directors of their "extravagance in erecting so splendid a station." "I am authorized to state," said Mr. Denison in reply, "that it is the cheapest building for what it contains and will contain that can be pointed out in London; and I am told—I am not the architect, and I do not estimate it—that it will not have cost more than £123,500. If that is the case, I have no difficulty at all in saying that it is a very cheap station. Bear in mind, however, that we paid by arbitration and award, I think, about £65,000 for the two old buildings that stood there, and then we had to excavate the ground before the station was erected; so that I do not pretend to say that the whole cost is only about £123,000." Mr. Denison added that the Company had still in hand the erection of a hotel at King's Cross at an estimated cost of £30,000.

For the then passenger traffic of the Company, which consisted of three fast trains and ten slow ones out of London per day, and about as many into it, the accommodation thus provided at King's Cross was, of course, most ample, and the situation of the terminus at the junction of no less than five important thoroughfares at once proved itself a most convenient one for passengers. In respect of goods traffic, however, the directors had already reason for regret that they had not provided the Company with access and station accommodation nearer the heart of the Metropolis. There was no blame attaching to them for this, for had the undertaking been burdened with such an additional expense, it would almost certainly have failed to survive the fierce attacks made upon it; and, as things were, the Great Northern was at least no worse off in the matter of distance from central London than was the Great Western at Paddington or the Eastern Counties at Shoreditch. Indeed, the only railway terminus of this date which could really be described as in the heart of the Metropolis was that of the London and Blackwall Railway at Fenchurch Street.

Unfortunately for the Great Northern, however, into this one favoured station its great rival, the London and North Western, had obtained access by running powers over the North London *via* Bow, and, what was more serious, it had just set up a City goods station on ground of its own at Haydon Square, to which it obtained through railway access by this same route. Moreover, by another auxiliary line—the West London—it had access to Kensington, Chelsea, etc., and thus it had an advantage in competition which the Great Northern authorities had already begun to feel keenly. Therefore it was impossible for them to rest quite content, even with the spacious accommodation which they had now just completed at King's Cross.

But if railway directors themselves are discontented with the accommodation they are providing, it is a fairly safe inference that the public is still more discontented, though its reasons for dissatisfaction may not be the same. What the London public complained of in this

THE SMALL-POX HOSPITAL WHICH OCCUPIED THE SITE OF THE GREAT NORTHERN PASSENGER TERMINUS AT KING'S CROSS, LONDON.

case was not, of course, that one railway company had an advantage over the others, but that none of them gave, or could give, the direct "through" communication which, in its opinion, should be obtainable; and to remedy this it was proposed that a central station should be erected—say at Holborn, or the Haymarket—to which all the twelve companies should extend their lines. The leading advocate of this scheme was a very eloquent gentleman, Mr. Charles Pearson, who held the position of solicitor to the City Corporation, and he undertook the task of bringing it into favour with the investing public, or, failing that, with the Government.

Of course the concurrence, at least, of the existing railway powers was a *sine quâ non*, but when Mr. Pearson attempted to secure this he was met by many difficulties. The London and North Western having been at the expense already of floating the North and West

London companies, and by this means having obtained an advantage over its competitors, was not at all disposed to sacrifice this for the general good; the Eastern Counties was too much embarrassed financially even to second a new effort; and other companies had equally valid objections to raise. As for the Great Northern, its directors, as has just been said, were already alive to the desirability of getting better London accommodation for their goods traffic. Moreover they gave Mr.' Pearson a very respectful hearing, when he endeavoured to convince them that they would very soon obtain a large and profitable suburban traffic, if they could give to and from his proposed Central Station "a cheap, frequent, and rapid service" with such of their stations as lay (say) within fifteen miles of town. But, seeing that in 1852 there were four Great Northern stations only which fell in with this condition, viz., Hornsey, Southgate, Barnet and Potters Bar, and that a few "mansions, villas, and gardens of the aristocracy and merchant princes"—to quote from the just published *Itinerary of the Great Northern Railway*—were the only suburban residences within its district, it is not surprising that this remote prospect of inducing a large daily traffic to and from the City did not seem to the directors solid enough to justify them in undertaking a large liability to spend new capital. As for their City goods traffic, they thought they could do better by following the London and North Western example of utilizing the North London line, with which they had already a junction within their King's Cross goods terminus. Thus the only immediate outcome of Mr. Pearson's exertions was the deposit for the session of 1853, on behalf of an independent company, of a Bill for a "North Metropolitan Railway" to run beneath the "New Road" from Edgware Road to King's Cross—an instalment, merely, of a larger scheme which, it was still hoped, would eventually connect the Great Western, London and North Western, and Great Northern systems with one another and with the City.

With the completion and opening of the towns line and the King's Cross terminus, the objects of the original promoters of the Great Northern Railway may be said to have been pretty fully accomplished; but, as is almost always the case with great undertakings of this nature, they found that their actual outlay had far exceeded their first estimates. Up to the end of 1853 their expenditure on capital account had amounted to rather more than nine and a half millions, barely five millions of which had been provided by the original stock of the Company, the remainder having had to be raised by preference capital and by debentures; and now in 1852 they found it necessary to issue yet further preference capital to the amount of £750,000, in order to meet outstanding liabilities connected either with the general works of the undertaking, the enlargement of inadequate stations, or the provision of extra equipment and plant. Besides this, the East Lincolnshire guarantee, when capitalized, added another £800,000 to the total, and thus the whole sum which the 283 miles of lines now opened had cost amounted, in round figures, to eleven millions, whereas Mr. William Cubitt's final estimate for the 272 miles of the main and loop lines, as originally planned, had been, as the reader may remember, £5,400,000 only. Thus, even after allowing for the preliminary expenses and the interest paid out of capital during construction (neither of which were, of course, included in Mr. Cubitt's figures), the excess of actual cost over estimate was very large indeed.

With such an excess of cost over estimate it would not have been surprising if the Great Northern Railway had for many years been quite unremunerative to its original shareholders, but this, as we have already seen, was not the case. At the same half-yearly meeting—that on 26 February, 1853—at which Mr. Denison reckoned up the total expenditure on the line, and told the shareholders that it was "far beyond any calculation that was made originally," he also told them that twice £361,000—the amount earned for the six months just closed—gave "a larger sum of money, as earned already, than was calculated would be earned when the scheme came before Committee in Parliament, and," added he, "an immense number of persons, perfectly cognizant of these matters, prophesied we never could receive any such sum." Indeed, had it been possible to spread this revenue equally over the capital of the Company, large as that capital was, without the necessity of deducting a considerable amount first to make up the guarantees and the debenture and preference interest, the dividend that could thus have been distributed in 1852 would have amounted nearly to 4 per cent.

As it was, as we have seen, the holders of original undivided stock had been without dividend for six months only, viz., from 30 June, 1850, when the payment of interest out of capital had ceased until 1 January, 1851, from which the first dividend of 2 per cent. had dated; and now they were to get $2\frac{1}{4}$ per cent. for 1852 and over $3\frac{1}{4}$ for 1853. Thus from 1853—the first year during which the whole undertaking was at work—the "B" shareholders began to receive the whole of the 6 per cent. which they had been guaranteed by the "A," and even the "A" shareholders got something for the second half-year of 1853, viz., £1 8s. 3d. per cent. From that time onward, moreover, for a number of years, as we shall see, the return to these more speculative investors increased in a way which much more than repaid them for such loss and anxiety as they suffered during the first few years in which they had to go without remuneration.

Moreover, even if the Great Northern Railway had remained for many years entirely unremunerative as an investment, the exertions of those who had carried it into effect would still have been at once justified, in that it had already vastly increased the resources of the districts which it served. A single one of its achievements—the inland conveyance of coal to London—had alone produced an economy sufficient to pay a high interest upon the capital outlay, and the benefits already derived indirectly from this and other improvements which it had brought about, were not less real because they are incalculable.

CHAPTER IX.

THE SOUTH YORKSHIRE SPLIT—THE BREAKING DOWN OF THE BARRIERS—1853-1855.

MEANWHILE the breach between the Great Northern and South Yorks companies in general, and Mr. Denison and Mr. Baxter in particular, in reference to the abortive amalgamation, had been growing wider every day. The South Yorkshire shareholders complained that in order to amalgamate with the Great Northern they had refused better offers from the Midland and Sheffield—"Do you believe it?" jeered Mr. Denison; "I do not, or anything of the sort"—and they forwarded resolutions to King's Cross "containing accusations," to quote Mr. Denison again, "of repudiation, and appeals to moral feeling, and such slip-slop as that." "Yes," said the Great Northern chairman afterwards to his shareholders, "I unfortunately said, 'and such slip-slop as that.' The words 'slip-slop,' it was said, ought not to have fallen from the lips of a person who had the honour to hold two or three rather prominent situations. It was thought indecent, and I don't know what besides, and a gentleman belonging to the South Yorkshire read me a lecture; and I think his observation was that moral rectitude met with its own reward. I should have thought men of business, dealing with merchants, would have known better than to suppose that any such stuff would make any impression at all on a man at all fit to be at the head of a Railway Board."

In consequence of the remonstrances from the South Yorkshire, a second full meeting of the Great Northern Board was held on 1 November, 1852, to consider the matter further; but its only result was that the decision of 25 August was confirmed. Thereupon Mr. Baxter tendered the resignation of his firm from their post of joint solicitors to the Company, declaring that he could no longer be associated with "the dishonourable action" of its directors. These were strong words, but Mr. Baxter was bound to the Board by as strong ties of old friendship and past service; and these ties Mr.

Denison and his colleagues would certainly not have suffered to be cut through in a burst of temper. Unfortunately they had already been severed past mending by the sharp necessities of the situation. For that one man should continue the confidential agent of two Boards, which were in direct antagonism one with the other, was a state of things obviously unendurable, and, having to choose between the one service and the other, it was equally inevitable that a man of Mr. Baxter's strong will and conscientious character should go the way to which his convictions led.

Nevertheless to the solicitor himself, to Mr. Denison, and indeed to all personally concerned, the separation was a very painful one.

"Is it nothing," asked Mr. Baxter, with real feeling, "to be the legal adviser of the Great Northern Company? I am sure, gentlemen, you will bear with me when I say that I deem it an honour to any man to have such an office. I say nothing of the other fruits of the office, but it cannot be that the man, when discretion belongs to him and when haste has all gone by, will cast away the honour or the profits of such an office. . . . But as I cannot go any further with you on this matter let me retire. I have served, I hope faithfully, the Company by whom I have been employed. I have, with the utmost satisfaction, acted with the Board. Let us part as friends, and let there be no irritation or ill-feeling."

So, with mutual regret, the resignation was accepted, and the other joint solicitors to the Company—Messrs. Johnson, Farquhar, and Leach, who, it may be remembered, had come into the concern as solicitors to the Direct Northern—had now to take over the whole of the legal and Parliamentary business. In this difficult task they received very valuable assistance from Mr. E. B. Denison, who supplied—as he himself said—"in some degree, however inadequately, the place of Mr. Baxter in having a previous cognizance of all the affairs!" "I commenced my career," he told the Great Northern shareholders at their next meeting (February, 1853), "in 1845 under the instructions of Mr. Baxter. I was then in daily intercourse, and have been ever since, with the leading men in my profession, Mr. Austin, Mr. Talbot, and Mr. Serjeant Wrangham; and all those gentlemen have from the beginning to the end expressed their conviction that no Company ever had such a good legal adviser as Mr. Baxter. . . . I take leave to say most positively that no Company ever had a better adviser in legal matters—I am not sure that I might not say so good an adviser."

But now, alas!—and for a long time to come—the Great Northern directors were to have cause to wish that Mr. Baxter's acumen in legal and Parliamentary business was not so great, for the arts which he had mastered in their service were in the future to be turned against themselves. His resignation had barely taken effect before he obtained instructions from his South Yorkshire clients to lodge a petition in Chancery against the Great Northern to restrain it from paying any future dividend until the claims of the former under the disputed agreement of February had been met; and, when this was dismissed rather summarily by Vice-Chancellor Stuart, nothing daunted he carried an appeal to the Lords Justices, retaining for his counsel Sir Fitzroy Kelly, one of the most eminent common law barristers of the day. This, however, was also dismissed on 17 February, 1853; and then Mr. Baxter played his trump card: he sent a letter to Messrs. Johnson, Farquhar, and Leach, "couched," as Mr. Denison said, "in very gentlemanly professional terms," to the effect that if the amount owing to the South Yorkshire under the disputed agreement was not paid by the following Tuesday—22 February, 1853—the Great Northern's coal trains would be stopped!

The Great Northern directors had, in the meantime, decided that, on the assumption that the agreement of February, 1852, was invalid, they were entitled to fall back upon the prior arrangement under which, as will be remembered, they had been paying the South Yorkshire a mileage toll of 10*d*. per ton, but this, of course, was indignantly rejected by the smaller company; and so Mr. Denison, who, despite a bad attack of gout, was busying himself down at Doncaster in efforts after a peaceful settlement, had offered on his responsibility to give 1*s*. a ton. What happened next may be quoted from the racy narrative which the Great Northern chairman subsequently gave to his shareholders :—

I said, "I will give you one shilling provided you will allow that a ton of coal shall consist of twenty-one cwt.—twenty-one cwt. being the quantity which is delivered by the coalowners to those who buy the coal, but they said 'No!' and so we parted; and on the following morning, Sunday, at home, I got a copy of the letter which had been received by our solicitor, stating that if a certain sum was not paid on the following Tuesday (Monday alone intervening) they would stop all the coal trains. They must have known on the previous day what was coming and have thought it would distress me, being in the gout, to be told of all these horrors of the trains being stopped. Of course it threw me into a great state of consternation. . . . On the Monday night down comes one of our officers to Doncaster, well instructed by the gentlemen in London—' Go to-morrow and meet the general manager of the South Yorkshire and tender him anything that he asks, but with a reservation that it is tendered without prejudice and do not let the trains be stopped!'—indeed, I understand the direction to him in London under the advice of persons with tolerably good heads was, 'Pay 5s. per ton rather than let the trains be stopped!' However, they modestly said they must have 1s. 8d. per ton, 'but,' said their general manager, 'I will not accept it unless you pay it to me and take your chance; I will not take it under protest'; and then, drawing himself up, being three feet ten inches, and making himself nine feet six inches, he said, 'No, beyond my stop-signal you shall not go!' So the trains were stopped the whole of Tuesday, the whole of Wednesday, and part of Thursday.

"What happens in the meantime? The gentlemen in London, with the advice of their solicitors and counsel, applied to the court to prevent the stopping of our trains. The case again comes before this Vice-Chancellor Stuart, as they call him; and after poking his way a certain time at it he says, 'Well, I will grant an injunction to prevent the stopping of the trains on condition that the Great Northern Company pays 1s. 6d. a ton without prejudice, the difference to be paid back in case it shall be found to be too much.' If it had been 5s. it would have been paid, for our object was to set the trade free. There were 500 or 600 colliers out of work; the trains were all stopped; our engine-drivers were playing marbles or snowballs or something of that sort; the engines were standing idle; people were calling out for coals, but coals they could not get; and when I came up to London on Thursday I looked out of the window of the railway carriage, and there was not a single station with a coal on it, so that if the snowstorm had lasted I don't know where the people would have been. However, by the order of Vice-Chancellor Stuart, the stoppage of the trains ceased, and they began to run again exactly on the same terms which we had proposed to the general manager of the South Yorkshire, namely, that we should pay 1s. 6d. per ton without prejudice."

The object of Mr. Denison's journey to London was to attend the half-yearly meetings of the two companies—the Great Northern and the South Yorkshire—and at both of them, despite his gout, he defended his action in very vigorous speeches. There was, however, obviously nothing more to be done now but to fight out the question of the validity of the disputed agreement before the proper legal tribunal; and, with Mr. Baxter on the one side and Mr. Denison and his son on the other, the contest which ensued was destined, as we shall see later, to be a very stubborn one. Meanwhile, however, we must turn our attention to other matters even more important in their bearing upon the destiny of the Great Northern.

It may fairly be said that at the beginning of 1853 a crisis had been reached in the general policy of the British Government towards railway enterprise. As we have before noted, the completion of the Great Northern lines meant that there was now more than one serviceable route between London and every place of importance in the kingdom; and, so long as these routes remained under the control of rival companies, it was inevitable that competition should be a predominant factor in their working. But some of the forms which competition had taken, such as the blocking of junctions and the consequent stunting of some lines and unnatural development of others, were not only highly inconvenient to the travelling and trading public, but had become intolerable to the railway interest itself. Under these circumstances the amalgamation of rival interests had been fixed upon by directors and shareholders as their readiest — nay, their only available means of security; and the union of two of the largest companies — the London and North Western and Midland — had already got so far as the presentation of a Bill to Parliament, this being regarded by many as the preliminary to a general alliance. In other words, Parliament was now asked to sanction the initial step in a process which, if once set going, might bring the whole railway interest under one control; and the question was, would Parliament set it going, or, if not, what remedy of its own would it devise? For the one thing which all parties were agreed upon was that matters could not be allowed to remain as they were.

Obviously the subject was one requiring wider and more thorough consideration than was likely to be given it during the progress in their ordinary course of the North Western-cum-Midland and other minor Amalgamation Bills. It was accordingly agreed that the Bills should be "hung up" while a Select Committee of the House investigated the problem in all its bearings; and this Committee—of which Mr. Cardwell, President of the Board of Trade, was chairman, and Mr. Gladstone a leading member—recommended, in its turn, a further period of suspense and deliberation, during which amalgamations, or alliances of the nature of amalgamation, between railway companies should be altogether prohibited. Thus the union of the London and North Western with the Midland and of the Great Northern with the Ambergate were both put out of court for the session of 1853.

This decision of Parliament was not only beneficial in averting the very expensive contests which would inevitably have been waged had these Bills reached Committee stage, but, by showing the companies that Parliament was by no means so inclined as they had imagined to favour their sovereign remedy of amalgamation, it induced them to make new efforts to put an end to their skirmishes and blockades by other means. Accordingly, in the spring of 1853, the warfare at Nottingham was terminated by the confederate companies agreeing that the Great Northern and Ambergate should be given access to that town for London traffic under an extension of the Gladstone pool; and in like manner it was agreed that if the Great Northern withdrew its Bill for a Bedford branch and allowed the Leicester, Bedford, and Hitchin to pass without opposition, the Midland would undertake to make that line an open one to Great Northern traffic, that is to say, to run on it, when completed, a reasonable number of trains to fit in at Hitchin Junction with the Great Northern services, both passenger and goods. Thus the Great Northern, in addition to establishing its footing in Nottingham, secured access in the near future to two other Midland towns—Bedford and Leicester. In this same session of 1853, moreover, the Leeds, Bradford, and Halifax Junction Company—whose works were now in full progress—carried a "Further Powers" Act, under which the Great Northern secured running powers, not only over the new line from Leeds into Bradford, but also into Halifax over the portion of the West Riding Union scheme already constructed by the Lancashire and Yorkshire.

Thus the barriers originally raised against the Great Northern were gradually going down—as Mr. Denison had predicted they must—before its steadfast assertion of its rights; but there still remained two important districts, at least, from which it was altogether excluded—the district west of Sheffield and the district north of Edinburgh, although to both of these King's Cross should have been in the natural order of things as convenient a London terminus as Euston Square. The remedy, of course, was to convince the Manchester, Sheffield, and Lincolnshire in the one case, and the Edinburgh and Glasgow and Scottish Central companies in the other, that it was to their interest to arrange "through bookings and facilities" with the new route, and this was an object of which Mr. Denison and his colleagues never lost sight. On the other hand, to keep these companies bound to the old route exclusively was an equally ever-present object with Captain Huish and his directors; and great still was the potency of Euston Square. The result was that overtures from King's Cross were repeatedly rejected; with the Scotch companies practically nothing could be accomplished; and the negotiations with the Sheffield resulted in little more than the settlement on a somewhat firmer basis of the existing agreements under which the Great Northern obtained its access to Great Grimsby, to Hull, and to Sheffield.

We have already noted how, subsequent to the completion of the towns line and the London terminus, the Great Northern directors had been obliged to raise £750,000 of new capital, and this prepares us to find that even though the Company had now ceased to add to its mileage, its engineer, Mr. Joseph Cubitt, had still a considerable amount of constructive work on hand. This chiefly consisted of additions to stations, such as engine-houses, carriage-sheds, granaries, coal-depôts, warehouses, sidings, and stables for horses—for instead of depending, like the London and North Western, upon Messrs. Pickford and other established carriers, the Great Northern was doing street "collection and delivery" itself. When some of the shareholders were disposed to grumble that these "extras" were too expensive, Mr. Denison assured them that he was thoroughly convinced that they would pay for their cost better almost than any other portion of the undertaking.

"If you do not give your customers this accommodation," said he, "they will not send traffic by your line. If we had not built a very large corn warehouse in London the corn would not have been brought to us. Then, too, we have a very large potato trade—we bring potatoes up from Yorkshire as well as from Lincolnshire, which have hitherto been brought up by sea into the Thames, and the parties to whom they are sent must have places of deposit for their reception. The consequence has been that we have been driven to the necessity of building in the goods station at King's Cross a warehouse—not a very large warehouse, but one that will cost about £4,000—for the purpose of receiving the potatoes, and thereby setting the waggons at liberty. If you do not give all your customers the best means of accommodating their traffic when it comes upon the line you will lose the traffic."

Thus we see that the principle which was at the base of the Great Northern's coal business, that, namely, of "tapping new strata" of traffic by offering extra facilities, was being applied in other directions; and of this a fresh instance was given about this time by the Company joining with the Midland and Sheffield to start a traffic in fish from Grimsby by setting a small fleet of smacks afloat.

To Mr. Sturrock, their locomotive engineer, the instructions of the directors were—"Expend such a sum as will ensure efficiency without reference to cost per mile," and the result was that the working stock of the Great Northern soon became larger proportionately than that of any other company. Said Mr. Denison on this point: "When the manager applies to the Board for twenty-five or thirty engines, which cost £3,000 each, or for 1000 waggons, which cost about £75 each, it makes one stare; but then the question is whether it is prudent to say, 'No, we will not have these engines and waggons,' for that would at once stop the increase of traffic." One reason why the Great Northern needed more rolling-stock than other companies was because it alone supplied waggons for the coal traffic. "But," said Mr. Denison, "there is another reason—our carriages are so much preferred by the public that, although our line extends practically to York only, yet an immense number of our carriages run through to Edinburgh, York being only 200 miles, while Edinburgh is 400 miles. The traffic is a long traffic, and it requires us to have a large stock of carriages."

For the same reason, namely, that the Great Northern—in an apt phrase—is "fed from its extremities," the Company had from the first to have not only more locomotives, but those of better quality than were possessed generally by the other companies. We have already seen how Mr. Sturrock, to meet this want, had introduced on to the 4′ 8½″ gauge several of the features which in the "forties" had given an undoubted pre-eminence to the broad-gauge engines of the Great Western, and this process he now consummated by placing on the rails his well-known "No. 215," which was built from his designs by Messrs. Hawthorn and Company, of Newcastle-on-Tyne, and delivered for work on 6 August, 1853. The chief features of this engine were the large diameter of its driving-wheels and the great extent of its heating surface, the former being 7′ 6″ and the latter 1718·2 sq. ft. Its weight in working order was 37½ tons, and it stood on eight wheels, two pairs of "leaders," one of "drivers," and one small pair of "trailers." In short—in the words of Mr. Clement Stretton—it was "practically a narrow-gauge edition of 'the Great Western.'" Its designer claims that a speed of seventy-five miles an hour was frequently attained with it on favourable lengths of line, and that with engines of its class it would have been possible, had there been the demand, to run a train from King's Cross to Edinburgh in eight hours. The facts remain, however, that No. 215 was the only one of the class built, and that it was broken up in 1870. In 1853 Messrs. R. and W. Hawthorn also built for the Company from Mr. Sturrock's design twelve new "single" engines for express passenger traffic with driving-wheels 6′ 6″ in diameter—*i.e.*, the same diameter as the "Cramptons."

On 31 August, 1853, occurred the first serious accident upon the Company's system. On the afternoon of that day the five p.m. express from King's Cross bound for Yorkshire collided at Hornsey with a broken-down coal train, though the fixed signal in advance of the station had been set at danger. The driver, it appeared, had relied upon an ample "time-interval,' and had neglected to keep a proper look-out ahead. The accident was very alarming to the shareholders, because two very exalted personages—the Lord Mayor of London and the Bishop of Lincoln—happened to be on board the express, and since the passing of "Lord Campbell's" Act the liability of railway companies for compensation had been made proportionate to the income of the person injured. Fortunately, however, the rapping of two august heads together proved to be the extent of the injury in this case.

It was in this year, 1853, that the locomotive headquarters of the Company were removed from Boston, where, as we have seen, they

THE GREAT NORTHERN LOCOMOTIVE, "No. 215."

were at first temporarily located, to their present site at Doncaster, that place being considered better situated for obtaining a supply of labour, of coal, and of iron. The original building there erected consisted of a repairing establishment only, but this had hardly been completed when the directors decided to increase the accommodation so as to provide for the building, as well as of mending, of both engines and carriages; and by the end of 1853 the operations already carried on had reached such dimensions that 949 mechanics were employed. These, with the 536 women and 1026 children which formed their families, and the new tradespeople of various sorts necessary to supply their requirements, made an addition to the population of Doncaster in one year of more than 2500 souls.

Towards these people, in Mr. Denison's opinion, the responsibility

of the Company extended further than to the mere payment of their
weekly wages and the provision of cottages for such of them as could
not find accommodation in the existing town, and he accordingly
proposed that the Company should forthwith build a church and
schools at Doncaster at a cost which was estimated at £8000. This
proposition was endorsed by the Board and brought formally before the
shareholders at their fifteenth half-yearly meeting held on 25 February,
1854; but it became immediately evident that it was likely to arouse
much opposition and dissension. "I am not for stopping church
extension—God forbid!" said one speaker; "let us have as many
churches as you please, but they must not be paid for out of the
capital of a trading company." "Is it intended to alter the name
of this Company?" asked another. "Is it intended to be a railway
Company or a Church Extension Society?" And a third one wanted
to know where the end was to be if they were to become "first,
coal merchants, then hotel-keepers, and after that lay improprietors."
To this Mr. Denison answered, "with perfect respect," that he would
"not consent to live day by day," when he was at Doncaster, "seeing
the children of the great population brought there in the Company's
service running about the streets without having in the week a school
to go to or on Sundays a church for worship"; and in the matter
of the schools he carried his point, for £1000 was straightway voted
for their construction. But for the church an Act of Parliament had
to be obtained, and this gave time for the shareholders' opposition
to gather strength.

Meantime, the suit with the South Yorkshire Company as to the
validity of the agreement to absorb that undertaking had been dragging
along a slow and expensive course. Immediately after the temporary
stopping of the trains already described it had been carried before the
Court of Exchequer; but the members of that court had first deferred
judgment in order to have time for the fullest consideration, and then,
in June, 1853, given *seriatim* opinions which conflicted with one
another. As, however, one learned Baron only had held the agreement
to be *ultra vires*, while two had ruled in favour of its validity, the actual
judgment had gone in favour of the South Yorkshire Company, despite
the fact that the Lord Chief Baron, being unable to attend, had sent
word that "the inclination of his opinion" was on the other side.

Needless to say, the Great Northern authorities had not hesitated to
appeal, and accordingly, in November, 1853, the case had been re-
argued before the Court of Exchequer Chamber. It was not until
1 February, 1854, however, that judgment was given. It proved
confirmatory of the decision of the court below; but, as the Great

Northern's counsel still held that these decisions of the law judges were quite at variance with those given by the Courts of Equity in similar cases, the directors resolved to appeal to the House of Lords. "We have a painful duty to perform," said Mr. Denison, when making known this resolve to the Great Northern shareholders at their half-yearly meeting on 25 February, 1854—the same at which, as just related, the proposition for a church at Doncaster first came up for discussion. "We have a high respect for all the parties; we are doing a great deal of business with them; we take an immense quantity of coal from them. All we want to know is what are the rights of the respective parties. I only want to be assured what the law indisputably is, and then I will submit."

Since the opening in August, 1852, of the "towns line" between Peterborough and Retford, much trouble had been occasioned upon it by landslips, which on one occasion had buried a passing goods train, and on several others had necessitated the diversion of the through traffic for a day or more to its older course *viâ* the loop. In these same deep cuttings, too, trouble of a similar kind had been occasioned by snowdrifts. It was at the London end of the system, however, that renewal work of an expensive sort had first to be taken in hand. Here, it may be remembered, in the hurry to get the traffic running, burnt clay had been used for ballasting, and for this good clean gravel had now, in 1853-4, to be substituted; nor had this operation been thoroughly completed before it became necessary to commence re-ballasting generally. It was necessary also to renew at places the rails themselves, for it was found that, especially on the falling gradient between Potters Bar and the terminus, the traffic—and particularly the heavy coal traffic—had already, in 1854, inflicted serious injury upon the "up" road. The switches and crossings had also to be renewed at most of the principal stations.

The rails originally laid down throughout the system were "double-headed reversibles," in 18-feet lengths, weighing 72 lbs. to the yard, and resting in joint chairs, weighing 40 lbs. each, and intermediate chairs, 21 lbs., secured with two wooden trenails apiece to triangular sleepers. For the renewals, however, it was thought wise to use 82-lb. rails in 21-feet lengths, and to substitute "fish-joints"—which were just at this time coming into vogue—for the joint chairs. Even these heavier rails, however, had many of them to be re-renewed after a "life" of about three and a half years only, and for the first twelve years of its existence as a working railway the average annual charge which the Great Northern had to pay for renewals was £35,273—a sum which would have paid an additional 1 per cent. dividend upon its open stock.* In this way the coal traffic was responsible for an extra expense which its promoters had not reckoned upon beforehand.

Another operation which Mr. Joseph Cubitt took vigorously in hand in 1854 was "the establishment of the electric telegraph from and to every station between London and Hatfield for the purpose of regulating and controlling the passage of all trains and the intervals between them," with the object of "guarding against the possibility of one train being overtaken and run into by another." As we have already noted, the Great Northern had been, at the time of its first opening from London, entirely without the telegraph, which on other lines was already much valued as an aid to the "time-interval" system of traffic-working; but in 1852 six wires, erected by Messrs. Reid Brothers, had been opened from London to Peterborough, and very shortly afterwards all the "first-class stations" on the system had been brought by this means into instant communication. But that this was not sufficient for the safety of the trains—few and far between though they were in those days—had been demonstrated by the Hornsey accident. Hence the determination of the managers to endeavour to secure a "space-interval" by establishing the telegraph at every station. But—in Mr. Cubitt's own phrase—"the more extended application" of this tentative block system was dependent upon the result of the experiment of its working between London and Hatfield.

On 1 August, 1854, the line of the Leeds, Bradford, and Halifax Junction Company from Leeds to Bowling, near Bradford, was opened for traffic, and from that date the Great Northern trains began to run over it, and also over the Lancashire and Yorkshire line between Halifax and Bradford, thus affording those two important towns for the first time a direct communication with London without break of journey. This gave the Great Northern the right to call itself *par excellence* the London and West Riding Railway, an object at which, as we know, Mr. Denison and some others of its promoters had aimed from the first; and a still further improvement of its position in this important district was now promised from the passing of an Act in the session of 1854 for a direct line from Wakefield to Leeds, over which the Great Northern was empowered to work traffic. It was to be constructed, however, by an independent company promoted by the same party to whom the Leeds, Bradford, and Halifax owed its existence; and so, while the Great Northern's running powers in the West Riding were to be thus further extended, it was still to remain in the anomalous

* I take this figure and the details about the rails given above from a valuable statistical paper read by Mr. R. Price Williams before the Institution of Civil Engineers.

situation of not being able to call a single yard of railway there fully its own. It had bought from the Lancashire and Yorkshire a half-share in a viaduct at Leeds; it had set up goods stations in several towns, and it was joint owner of the passenger stations at Leeds, at Wakefield, and Knottingley. But its own rails—to recall Mr. Denison's phrase—still terminated "in a ploughed field four miles north of Doncaster," from which point to the West Riding, as well as to York, it was dependent on running powers over other companies' lines.

Meanwhile Parliament had been grappling strenuously with the general problems of railway politics; but, as was not surprising, considering the inconsistencies to which it was already committed, it had not succeeded in evolving—much less in acting upon—any uniform principles with regard to them. Between "protection" and "free trade" it still wavered —between the fear of impairing the privileges which it had granted to the old companies under their original charters, and the wish to give the public the full benefits of the enterprise of the new ones; and the result, as far as the session of 1854 was concerned, was the passing of a number of Acts, and the rejection of others, for reasons beneath which it is impossible to find any consistent reasoning whatever. The chief of these Acts, of course, was the first Railway and Canal Traffic Act, the "Cardwell Act" as it was, and is still sometimes, called, after the President of the Board of Trade who fathered it.

This Act, in motive and design at any rate, was a very decided step towards freer competition, and away from monopoly, for it invested the Court of Common Pleas with powers to compel any company to give "all reasonable facilities" at junctions, etc., to the through traffic of others. But, on the other hand, clauses which Mr. Cardwell originally embodied in it, making "through bookings" everywhere compulsory, had been withdrawn in deference to the protests of the established interests; and, even as it was, the Act would probably not have been allowed to pass had not the shrewdest of its opponents felt sure that it would be inoperative to secure the full objects which its authors had in view. Nor did it need a very keen eye to see that the opposite policy of protection to vested interests was still dear to Parliament, for in this very same session of 1854 an Act amalgamating the York, Newcastle, and Berwick, York and North Midland, and Leeds Northern into the "North Eastern" had been passed—an Act which placed the traffic of an important district in the hands of a single company.

On one point, however, there was no longer room for doubt. This was that the "protectionist" policy in its full development—the policy upon which Captain Huish had acted in forming the Euston Square confederacy originally and upon which his desire to absorb the Midland entirely was now based—would certainly not be furthered in any way by Parliamentary sanction. On the contrary it was against this policy, evidently, that the Cardwell Act, such as it was, was directed, and however inconsistent and wavering the action of the Legislature might have been, it was impossible to hope that it would stultify itself utterly by first passing a general Act to check practices for which two companies were mainly responsible, and then passing a special Act to strengthen those very companies' hands. Accordingly, when it had become evident that in some form or other the "facility clauses" of the Cardwell Act would pass, the London and North Western and Midland directors had found no course open to them but to withdraw their Amalgamation Bill. But this did not mean that they had determined to abandon the policy which Captain Huish had so long fostered. On the contrary, it meant that that very astute tactician, recognizing that he could not hope for success in flaunting a general law publicly, but at the same time recognizing that that general law was a futile one, had determined to pursue his aims by private treaty instead of by public act, and hoped to evade the disapproval of the Legislature by the simple expedient of not consulting it.

That this course was foredoomed to failure sooner or later even the London and North Western manager himself must have felt in his calmer moments, when he remembered the fate of so comparatively innocent a private treaty as that which the Great Northern two years before had made with the Ambergate, but from future risks of this kind Captain Huish appears to have deliberately averted his eyes, and to have fixed them only upon the immediate danger which he dreaded. This was that the Great Northern by way of its existing junction with the Manchester, Sheffield, and Lincolnshire at Retford and the new junction which the Midland was about to form with it at Hitchin, would, under the encouragement of the Cardwell Act, force its way into the whole Midland district and into Lancashire. This was the contingency to avert which, as we know, the confederacy had been formed originally; and, now that the same danger seriously threatened for the second time, the only weapon available against it was to strengthen the confederacy; if such strengthening were *ultra vires*, well there was nothing for it but to run the risk. These apparently were the considerations which led the London and North Western manager, in July, 1854, to make propositions to Mr. Allport, who in the previous year had left the Manchester, Sheffield, and Lincolnshire to become general manager of the Midland, and to Mr. Edward Watkin, who had gone from Euston Square to succeed Mr. Allport on the Sheffield, for new treaties between his company and theirs; and these propositions being accepted, a new confederacy was then formed on the old basis of working as one interest and preventing the Great Northern from getting any share in through traffic west of its existing system. It was no wonder that Mr. Denison complained afterwards to a House of Commons Committee that "the general managers laughed at the Cardwell Act."

Fortunately, however, in view of the new difficulties which thus threatened it, the Great Northern had just got rid of an old trouble. The law proceedings with the South Yorkshire Company had been terminated by mutual consent. As almost invariably happens in such cases, the agreement now arrived at was of the nature of a compromise. The Great Northern agreed to settle the South Yorkshire accounts up to 31 December, 1854, on the terms of the disputed agreement, upon the understanding that from that date matters should proceed upon an entirely new footing. This meant that the South Yorkshire Company was to give up for the future all claim to a guaranteed dividend and rest content with receiving a mileage toll, plus a reasonable terminal charge, upon the traffic actually carried. Under the circumstances this was probably as good an arrangement as could be arrived at; but, as we shall see, it left the door open to many future difficulties and disputes.

All this time, despite the disagreements we have been describing in regard to its principal field of supply, the Great Northern's revenue from coal traffic had been steadily increasing; and in the year 1854—the fourth year only in which the trade had been carried on in London—the gross receipts amounted to more than £300,000, the sum which had excited so much derision when included in the early estimate of the London and York promoters. This was a result of which all concerned had good reason to be proud, and especially was credit due to the general manager, Mr. Seymour Clarke, who from the commencement of his connection with the Company had been most zealous in developing this branch of its business, and to his brother, Mr. Herbert Clarke—a name destined to be widely known in the London coal trade—who had been installed at King's Cross almost from the beginning of the traffic as "sole agent for the sale of the coals carried by the Company." The method upon which these two energetic brothers, however, conducted the trade did not escape criticism, and at the half-yearly meeting in August, 1854, Mr. Plimsoll—a man whose name is now chiefly known for his efforts in the cause of seamen, but who at that time was endeavouring to establish himself as a dealer in South Yorkshire coals—made an attack upon what he rather intemperately described as "the pettifogging, contemptible, and wretched policy" which was "ruining the trade of the district."

"The coalowners," said he, "feel that great oppression is being exercised; that only one buyer can buy in the market—that is Mr. Clarke, and that the price is subject to his dictum—and I venture to say that if any five men with the ordinary capacity of barndoor fowls would investigate the subject they would perceive a very easy means of remedy. The plan I would suggest is, let any coalowner who pleases send his coal to London, paying you as much freight as you can get. The whole case lies in a nutshell. For the sake of some comparatively minor advantage, such as working the trucks more rapidly under the management of one person, you emasculate the whole thing and consequently cannot arrive at any proper development of the traffic."

In this complaint there was undoubtedly a good deal of truth as the sequel was to prove; but Mr. Denison in his reply showed that the matter was more complex than Mr. Plimsoll imagined. "The coalowners of the South Yorkshire field," complained he on his side, "will not meet the Great Northern Company upon fair and liberal terms. They will not supply us either with the quantity or with the regularity that we require; they have raised the price upon us at two or three different times; and we have been driven to the necessity of sending trucks into Durham, and of making arrangements with gentlemen who have coalfields at the back of Wakefield from whence a large quantity is now brought. In order to encourage the coal trade, we have bought a very large number of waggons, contrary to the practice adopted on other railways, but without which you would not have obtained anything like the coal traffic you now have. Mr. Plimsoll's proposition is to find waggons himself, and to send coal to London on his own account. He is perfectly entitled to do so, and we must take his waggons on certain terms; but I cannot consent that he should carry on his trade unfairly to the trade carried on by us."

But besides the lukewarm attitude of the South Yorkshire coalowners—an attitude which, as we have seen, they had maintained from the very first, and which had by this time cooled considerably the enthusiasm for the London coal trade with which Mr. Seymour Clarke and other Great Northern authorities had at its outset been infected by Mr. Baxter—another adverse influence was now being brought to bear upon this important branch of the Company's business. This arose, though the Great Northern did not know its primary cause at the time, from the new alliance between the London and North Western and Midland Companies, which, notwithstanding the decision in the Great Northern-Ambergate case, had, without a shadow of legal authority, secretly taken the form of a "common-purse agreement." Ten years before, as the reader may remember to have been informed incidentally already, the "London and Birmingham" directors had contemptuously refused to encourage a Metropolitan traffic from the Midland collieries on the ground that the rates it could pay were too small to be profitable; but gradually the influence of the Great Northern's example had made itself felt at Euston Square, and for some years the North Western had been doing a considerable coal trade, not only at a chief depôt at Camden, but at auxiliary stations in London, to which the lines of the North London and West London companies gave it access. Therefore, it only needed the stimulus of this common-purse agreement with the Midland—with its consequent removal of all difficulties as to settling proportions of through rates—to cause an increase in the "confederate" trade from the Derbyshire field, which almost brought it abreast, in 1854, of the Great Northern trade from South Yorkshire. In the following year, 1855, moreover, the Midland was actually able to send to Camden some of the South Yorkshire coal itself, the South Yorkshiremen being glad, one may be sure, to show that at a pinch they could be independent of the Great Northern even for the London trade. The Eastern Counties Company, too, had, since 1852, been bringing up a considerable quantity of Midland coal, *via* Peterborough. From these various competitive influences the Great Northern trade did not continue to develop at the same rate as at first.

Meanwhile, however, the Great Northern itself had obtained a very useful new weapon, both for defence and attack, in powers which it had at last obtained from Parliament in the session of 1854, "to work, lease, or purchase" the Ambergate line. In that same session, too, the Ambergate Company itself had obtained an Act for its extension to Nottingham, so that the Great Northern had now, potentially, established itself in that Midland town, despite all the efforts of the confederacy to prevent this. From April, 1855, it took over the working of the Ambergate line on the terms of paying that company 30 to 35 per cent. of the gross receipts of the traffic. In view of the growth of the coal trade the possession of this line by the Great Northern assumed a new and very great importance, because it enabled the Great Northern to "tap" the Derbyshire field, and so to prevent that growingly important district from becoming an exclusive monopoly of the Midland.

There was another barrier, too, which the Great Northern succeeded in breaking down in 1855—the barrier at Edinburgh. Strengthened by the amalgamation which in 1854 had given birth to the North Eastern,

L

the East Coast allies had renewed their efforts to get a share in the traffic of northern Scotland, and, through rates by the established route being still refused them, they had tried as a *pis aller* to open a new route through Fifeshire in conjunction with the Edinburgh, Perth, and Dundee Company, and by ferries across the Forth and Tay. In the autumn of 1854, however, a quarrel had arisen between the Caledonian and the Edinburgh and Glasgow companies, which at last gave the East Coast the opportunity it had so long waited for; and the result was that from 1 January, 1855, a through service and through bookings were arranged with the Edinburgh and Glasgow and Scottish Central as far as Perth, and shortly afterwards extended over the Scottish North Eastern to Aberdeen. But as in the case of the Eastern Counties traffic with the north, so in this case, the small companies were able to extort the "blackmail" of a bonus on the through receipts in addition to their legitimate mileage proportion, as their price for letting in the new route.

Since the winter of 1852-3 the Company had raised no new capital, and the result was that at 30 June, 1854, its liabilities for further expenditure on capital account were found to exceed by about £450,000 the small unexpended balance of the eleven millions odd which it had raised, as already noted, up to that date. These liabilities consisted of unsettled purchases of land, the completion of the Doncaster Locomotive Works, additional works on the line (including a new coal depôt at Holloway, and a "ticket station" there), the purchase from the Lancashire and Yorkshire Company of half the viaduct at Leeds already referred to, and contracts for engines and various kinds of rolling stock to meet the steadily increasing traffic and to provide for the working of the completed Leeds, Bradford, and Halifax, the authorized Bradford, Wakefield, and Leeds, and four new lines—from Kirkstead to Horncastle, from Barkstone to Sleaford, from Essendive to Stamford, and from Welwyn to Hertford—the construction of which also independent companies had in hand under agreements with the Great Northern to work them when completed. Accordingly, in August, 1854, the directors obtained the shareholders' authority to raise a million new capital, and having deposited a Bill to authorize this, they on 12 December, 1854, issued "scrip" for it rateably to the proprietors of the existing stocks—a similar course to that which they had taken in regard to their last increase of capital in 1852-3.

Then, however, it had been found quite easy to get the new stock taken up by the existing holders as £10 4½ per cent. preference shares, redeemable at six months' notice at 10 per cent. premium; but now in war time—for the Crimean War was in progress—it was not thought safe to attempt a repetition of this, albeit the position of the Company was stronger in 1854 than in 1852. What was now offered was 80,000 shares of £2 10s. each, bearing a 5 per cent. preference dividend and redeemable at 20 per cent.; and even on these terms, at the first call due on 13 January, 1855, scrip representing 14,000 of the new shares came back unaccepted. Nevertheless, seeing that the call paid on the 66,000 accepted shares, together with payments in advance of future calls, brought in at once £305,000—nearly one-third of the amount required—the directors were justified in reporting to the shareholders at their seventeenth half-yearly meeting held at the Albion Tavern on 28 February, 1855, that the operation might be considered a success.

THE ORIGINAL "TICKET STATION" AT HOLLOWAY, LONDON.

At this half-yearly meeting the dividend declared was at the rate of 5¾ per cent. on the original undivided stock, making the rate for the year 4¼ per cent.; and it would have been more but for the war, which had caused a rise in price in iron, in oil and tallow, in wages—"in point of fact"—to quote from Mr. Denison's speech, "in every item of railway expenditure." With the increase of gross receipts the ratio of working expenses to them had sunk from the 50 per cent. already noticed for 1851 to 45 per cent. in 1853; but in 1854 it had risen again nearly to 50 per cent.

The principal question discussed at this meeting in February, 1855, was the proposed church for the employees at Doncaster, for the construction and endowment of which the directors were promoting a Bill in Parliament this year. In the ordinary course this Bill would not have been discussed until the Wharncliffe meeting, necessary before it could become an Act; but so opposed were some of the shareholders to the project that they had determined, if possible, to put an end to it before it went further. Accordingly, no sooner had the chairman made his opening half-yearly speech than a shareholder, Mr. Billings, moved "that no money be spent by the Company for religious purposes until the dividend amounts to 8 per cent." Other amendments and motions similar in purpose were also proposed and strenuously supported; but in the chairman, with whom, as already stated, the church project had originated, and in Mr. E. B. Denison, now a Q.C., who was present as a shareholder to support his father, the opposition party found formidable antagonists.

"The object of the gentlemen who oppose this proceeding," said the younger Denison, "is to stop the Bill in the House of Commons. But no resolution of theirs *ipso facto* can stop the Bill in the House of Commons. The answer to that resolution will be that it was obtained at a small meeting by persons who came there for the express purpose of voting against the thing without any public notice to the shareholders. I state, therefore, distinctly, that if that resolution is passed to-day it will be stated distinctly and deliberately by the directors, if they do not omit their duty, that this was a packed meeting."

Naturally enough, this caused a tremendous uproar. Cries of "No! no!" "Shame! shame!" "He has insulted us," came from all sides, and one shareholder with stronger lungs than the rest made it heard that "for a father and son to call the meeting a packed one was more than he could stand."

"Some observations," said the chairman, rising amid confusion, "have been made by that young gentleman, who is my son. You are perfectly welcome to know that I am proud of him. He is in the habit of standing and arguing cases before quite as intelligent a community as is here. He is in the habit of making whatever observations occur to him, and he is answerable for them. You may deal with him as you think proper, but do not interrupt him."

In the end the resolutions against the Bill were withdrawn, but when —two days later—it came on for second reading in the House of Commons, it was there met with much the same objections as it had encountered amongst the shareholders. The object in view was approved almost unanimously; but that this method of carrying it out was a wrong one was a view so repeatedly and justly urged by people of so many different shades of opinion that Mr. Denison found the same conclusion practically irresistible. Accordingly, he consented to the withdrawal of the Bill. In January, 1855, however, the schools at Doncaster had been opened, their cost having exceeded by about £80 only the £1,000 voted for them in the previous February, and in them, in addition to valuable secular instruction, some religious teaching was already being given under the devoted superintendence of the Rev. J.

Campion, one of the clergy of the town. A church was subsequently erected by subscription amongst the shareholders and others, and opened in 1858.

Without question the most important event to which the Company had now to look forward was the termination of the "Gladstone" (or "Six Towns") and "Octuple" (or Anglo-Scotch) agreements, both of which were to expire by lapse of time at the end of the year 1855. We have already noted that in strict justice to itself the Great Northern ought not to have consented to either of these "pools," seeing that it was a corollary of them that it should be shut out from all share in the traffic of places beyond their scope; and in actual working they had entailed a further hardship upon the Great Northern. They had involved it in the doing of a great deal of extra work for little or no pay.

This state of things had arisen from the fact that to all the "six towns" and to all the places covered by the Octuple agreement (except Edinburgh, in which case, however, better gradients turned a mileage equality into an advantage for the East Coast) the Great Northern route from London had become a good deal the shorter since the opening of its "towns" line. Accordingly since that event, as we have seen, it had been able to give the quicker service to all these places, its advantage in most cases amounting to a full hour. At first the confederate companies seem to have resented this state of things as challenging them to extra exertions, and to have urged that it was contrary to the spirit of the pooling arrangements, which they seem to have regarded as intended to put an end to strenuous competition of any sort. In other words, they seem to have thought it the duty of the Great Northern to accommodate its better route to their worse ones.

The Great Northern authorities — anxious above all else to demonstrate the capacity of their route to the full in view of a new division of traffic after the five years—had refused to take any such view, and so the attitude of the confederates seems to have undergone a change. Recognizing that the proportion of revenue which each company was at liberty to appropriate remained the same, no matter whether it continued to carry the traffic or not, they seem now to have settled down very complacently to a state of things under which the Great Northern did the bulk of the work, in passenger traffic at least, while the pay continued to be pretty equally divided. Under the two agreements, it is true, an additional allowance was provided for in the case of any company working traffic in excess of the percentage allotted to it; but by arrangement between the general managers—

when making which Mr. Seymour Clarke does not seem to have been very wide awake — this extra allowance had been limited to twenty per cent., which by no means covered even the out-of-pocket cost of the extra work done. The result had been that the sums paid over by the Great Northern out of its actual takings under the two "pools" had amounted to £37,268 in 1853 and to £50,121 in 1854.

"There cannot be a more honourable or a more clever man than Mr. Gladstone," Mr. Denison had already said in the matter; "but I tell you that as a result of his award and of the Octuple agreement we are paying away £1000 a week. You will say they were injudicious bargains to make; I say I was forced into them."

It is not surprising that the Great Northern authorities now looked forward with relief and hope to the approaching revision, for from it they were entitled to expect to benefit in two ways: first, by getting a larger percentage of the traffic already divided; and second, by gaining admittance to other traffic from which they were, as things stood, excluded.

CHAPTER X.

"THE BATTLE OF THE RAILWAYS"—BREAK-UP OF THE CONFEDERACY—1855-1858.

THE clearer view we have now obtained of the *raison d'être* of the "pooling" arrangements under the Six Towns and Octuple agreements furnishes the key to a problem which in the last chapter must have seemed somewhat obscure to the reader. I refer to the persistency of the London and North Western Company, in 1854, in forming its new and closer alliances with the Midland and Sheffield companies, despite the knowledge that such alliances were distasteful to Parliament, contrary to the spirit, if not to the letter, of the Cardwell Act, and moreover that they might be upset at any time, as the Great Northern's private alliance with the Ambergate had been, by an injunction from the Court of Chancery. As we remarked at the time, the Euston manager, Captain Huish, appeared deliberately to avert his eyes from this last-mentioned risk, and to think only of the more immediate dangers which the new private treaties themselves prevented, namely, the opening of the junctions at Retford and Hitchin to the Great Northern; and now we see why the prevention of this in 1854 appeared to him so important as to justify almost any cost and any risk. It was in preparation for the renewal of the Gladstone "pool" in the following year.

For, as the reader now sees, the policy of the "pools" was linked hand in hand with the policy of the "junction barriers." The formation of the latter had been the preliminary in the first instance to the proposal of the former, and so it was to be again. If the whole railway system north of the Metropolis had in 1850-1 been as equally open to King's Cross as to Euston Square, Captain Huish would not then have been found insisting upon the pooling of competitive traffic as the only possible preventative of "ruinous competition"; on the contrary, he would soon have been persuaded, as he had since been in similar negotiations with the Great Western, that an agreement to charge equal rates and fares—the shorter distance ruling—was fully sufficient to meet this end. But, as we have already said, the necessity for preventing "ruinous competition" was only the ostensible argument for pooling; it was not the real argument—at any rate, it was not the whole argument. Ostensibly recommended solely as a device for preventing, in the interest of all parties, wasteful expenditure and loss of revenue, the real value of the "pooling" arrangements in the eyes of their inventors was an adjunct to his protectionist treaties. Unless he had first been able to renew his obstructive confederacy in 1854, Captain Huish would not have greatly cared whether the pools were renewed in the following year or whether they were dropped. But having renewed his treaties at great cost and risk for this special purpose, he was now most anxious to renew the pools also—and to extend them, as he had originally purposed that they should be extended, over the whole field of possible competition —because he hoped by that means to prolong, possibly to render permanent, that artificial restriction of traffic into his own channels, which it was the aim of his whole policy to promote.

Of course to the extent to which, as recorded in the last two chapters, the Great Northern had broken down the barriers originally raised against it, the London and North Western manager could not, in 1855, hope to accomplish all that he had hoped for in 1850. He could not, for instance, exclude the Great Northern from Bradford, Halifax, or Nottingham, seeing that its own trains were now running daily to and from those places, and he could not raise again the barrier which the East Coast companies had just broken down at Edinburgh. As a terminus for Anglo-Scotch traffic, indeed, King's Cross now stood irrevocably on an equal footing with Euston Square; and so, whether or not that traffic was again "pooled" might have been a matter of indifference to Captain Huish, if the only competition for it had been that of the two "coast" routes. This, however, was not the case. Since 1850, by way of the link line which the (little) North Western Company had provided between Skipton (Yorks) and Lancaster, a tentative third or "central" route had been in existence.

When the first "pool" had been made it had been possible to ignore this, simply because the "poor wretched little creature"—as Mr. E. B. Denison afterwards called the (little) North Western—could not make its voice heard in the councils of the larger companies. But now that the Midland, in its brief effort after independence in 1852, had acquired a lease of the North Western for twenty-one years it had become a factor of more importance. Accordingly by his common-purse agreement with the Midland in 1854, Captain Huish had taken pains to secure not only, as we already know, that the junction to be shortly formed at Hitchin should be closed against the Great Northern, but that all idea of developing the (little) North Western as a through route should henceforth be put aside. Having obtained this latter stipulation, he now regarded the renewal of the Octuple agreement as a matter of great moment, because, though he could no longer use that "pool," as he had done five years before, as the means of keeping the East Coast companies from getting beyond Edinburgh, he could use it in a precisely similar way to crush altogether the incipient development of a third—a central—route.

With his usual clearsightedness Mr. Denison very soon saw through this strategy, and he no sooner saw through it than he condemned it; but again, as in 1850-1, he found himself almost alone in this attitude. His general manager, Mr. Seymour Clarke—"the best of traffic managers but the worst of negotiators," to quote again a description from the future Lord Grimthorpe—seems never really to have grasped the drift of Captain Huish's tactics, either in 1850-1 or now. Accordingly, in this proposed new Anglo-Scotch alliance he saw only a proposal to divide the traffic, not only of Edinburgh as hitherto, but of Glasgow, Perth, etc., also on terms of practical equality between the two "coast" routes. Now equal terms with the West Coast was, as we know, an object for which Mr. Clarke, in common with the managers of the other East Coast companies, had been fighting for five years; and, now that it was at last within his grasp, he was not at all tempted to let it slip in order to clutch at other advantages, the most important of which seemed to him to be the very shadowy one of getting through to western Scotland over the (little) North Western route.

As for the injustice which the new agreement would inflict on the shareholders of the (little) North Western (whose main object both in building their line originally and in leasing it to the Midland had been to obtain through traffic with Scotland), this was a consideration which does not seem to have affected Mr. Clarke at all. So Mr. Denison, though himself keenly alive to that injustice and ready, as we shall see later, to make very great efforts to remove it when a more favourable opportunity offered, did not think it was his duty to refuse to sanction an arrangement warmly recommended by his general manager as a good one for their own shareholders simply because he knew that other shareholders, for whose welfare he had no responsibility, must suffer seriously from it.*

* With his usual frankness Mr. Denison afterwards told a House of Commons Committee, when cross-examined as to his action in this very matter, that a man was sometimes forced to do things as a railway chairman which as a private person he would shrink from.

"Some only of the managers met," wrote he in a subsequent account of the affair, "and from time to time discussed, and at last concocted, a new Octuple agreement into consent to which one or two dissatisfied companies were actually bullied by the majority. It was a semi-traffic and semi-territorial arrangement, and I never gave my cordial assent either to the principle upon which it was based or to the manner in which it had been accomplished. But when it was brought up before the Great Northern Board for confirmation I did not choose to take upon myself the responsibility of objecting to it."

This new "English and Scotch alliance" was practically concluded in July, 1855, though the Lancaster and Carlisle Company stood out from it for some months in the hope of getting better terms for the (little) North Western route; and immediately afterwards Captain Huish, Mr. Seymour Clarke, and Mr. Allport approached the even more difficult and critical problem—the renewal of the Gladstone treaty. This, in its existing form, embraced ten towns, for in addition to the six—York, Leeds, Sheffield, Wakefield, Doncaster, and Lincoln—which it had covered originally, four others—Nottingham, Newark, Stamford, and Peterborough—had subsequently been included in it; and both the confederate managers and Mr. Clarke now approached its renewal with the idea of extending it over a wider area, especially into "the district west of Sheffield." But the objects which the two parties had in view in wishing for such an extension were, it need hardly be said, very diverse.

Mr. Clarke seems to have thought that he would thus be able to secure to the Great Northern in western England the same benefit which under the English and Scotch alliance it had just obtained in Scotland, namely, such a share of the traffic as it was by its geographical position fairly entitled to; but Captain Huish's aim all along had been, as we know, *not* to divide traffic according to geographical position, but to keep it in defiance, one might almost say, of geography, from breaking away from the older channels. So, when *he* proposed an extension of the Gladstone agreement, *he* meant to use it, as he had used all the arrangements of the same kind from the first, simply to confirm for a further term of years the artificial barriers in favour of his own company which by his confederate treaties he had raised. "Certainly," said he now to Mr. Seymour Clarke, "let us make the new treaty to cover as much ground as possible. By all means let the district west of Sheffield be included in it"; but this did not, of course, mean that he was prepared to recognize the right of King's Cross to share the traffic of that district equally with Euston Square. On the contrary, it meant that having previously taken elaborate pains to prevent the Great Northern from obtaining any footing west of Sheffield, he was now anxious to divide that traffic for a term of fourteen years between the companies which had a footing there, in order that for that period he might stereotype the exclusion of the Great Northern from it, just as under the English and Scotch alliance it had just stereotyped the impotency of the (little) North Western as regards the London traffic with Scotland.

In carrying out this characteristic scheme Captain Huish had the warm support of both the other confederate managers—his familiar allies—Mr. Allport and Mr. Watkin; and so at every one of a series of general managers' conferences which were now held Mr. Seymour Clarke found himself confronted by this formidable triumvirate of opponents. As regards one part of his case, however, he stood on such firm ground that he could not be intimidated by superior numbers—namely, in insisting that, in view of the heavy payments which under the existing arrangements the Great Northern had to make out of its actual earnings, it was entitled to larger percentages of the traffic of the towns already "pooled." This all parties were obliged almost from the first to admit.

While they admitted it, however, the confederate managers were so niggardly in the increases they offered that Mr. Clarke found it necessary to claim a new reference to arbitration. To this the confederates assented, but claimed, as they had done five years before, that the reference should not be limited to the towns already covered, but should be extended over the whole area of possible competition. Moreover, in this connection they drew up certain "provisions and principles of division" to which they urged the arbitrator should be requested to "give due weight." The essence of these was to recognize the existing routes only (*i.e.*, those by which traffic was already travelling) as entitled to have percentages allotted to them; in short, they contained all that the confederates wanted to enable them to carry out what we have already seen to be their chief object in view, and as such the Great Northern general manager should have resisted them most strenuously. But Mr. Clarke had not, as we have already said, properly grasped from the first the design of his opponents, and so now he naturally failed to see the objectionable character of the machinery which they had framed for bringing it about — the more so as that machinery was connected with a most specious proposal for extending the division of traffic over an area from which the Great Northern had up to this time been excluded. Accordingly he allowed himself to be persuaded into signing the "principles and provisions" and recommending them as the basis of the new reference to arbitration. With this and a supplementary agreement that, between the lapsing of the existing arrangements and the conclusion of new ones, the *status quo* should in every respect be preserved, the general managers wound up their conferences on 17 December, 1855.

That this result gave the greatest possible satisfaction to Captain Huish goes without saying, and within three days he secured the confirmation of it both by his own and the Midland directors. There, however, his satisfaction was destined to cease. On 19 December, 1855, the Great Northern Board met, with Mr. Denison as usual in the chair, but in this case the general managers' conclusions, instead of being at once confirmed, were read and discussed in detail, and the more they were discussed, the stronger Mr. Denison's disapproval of them grew. Very soon he saw that Mr. Clarke had been out-manœuvred by his more astute coadjutors, and, disagreeable task though it was virtually to throw over his own general manager, he quickly made up his mind that this was the only course open to him, if his duty to the Great Northern shareholders was to be done. For the effect of the general managers' recommendations as he summarized them was to "preclude the Great Northern Railway Company for fourteen years from any participation in the traffic arising at and between London and any town on the Manchester and Sheffield Railway lying west of Sheffield, or from any new railway west of the Midland Railway, while the London and North Western and Midland companies would participate in the traffic arising at and between London and nearly every town lying east of Sheffield"; and this view being endorsed by a majority of the directors, they resolved that they were "not justified in adopting the recommendations," despite the fact that one of the four signatures to them was that of their own representative, Mr. Seymour Clarke.

When Mr. Denison and his colleagues decided upon this bold line of conduct, they probably knew pretty well what it would cost them. With their experience in the negotiations as to South Yorkshire amalgamation still fresh in their memories they could not have been unprepared for the cry of "repudiation!" which was now, as on that occasion, raised against them, nor could they have felt much hope that a new war in fares could now be averted, seeing that they had raised disagreement veritably at the eleventh hour. Nevertheless, what could be done to postpone the catastrophe they did. They agreed to a month's "armistice" on the basis of the old percentages—unfair though these admittedly were to the Great Northern—and in the meantime they neglected nothing that correspondence or interviews could suggest to promote a peaceful settlement on lines to which they could assent without sacrifice of essential principle.

The confederate directors, however, felt that they had the advantage, and they were determined to keep it. They would hear of no pooling arrangement except on the basis agreed on by the general managers; and they rejected unconditionally a Great Northern proposal to abandon pooling and to adopt "the principle of equal rates and fares instead," though this had already worked well for a year between the London and North Western and Great Western companies. Thus all negotiations failed, and at last, on 26 January, 1856—five days before the armistice expired—a letter reached Mr. Clarke at King's Cross, signed "Mark Huish, James Allport, and Edward Watkin," informing him that their companies were "forced to resume a competition for passenger traffic," though it was not their intention to make any change in the existing rates for goods and cattle.

Again, as at the time of the South Yorkshire crisis, Mr. Denison was confined to his house at Doncaster with a sharp attack of gout, but as soon as he heard that an actual declaration of war had been received at King's Cross, he summoned up his energies to write a letter to the confederate chairmen, Lord Chandos, Mr. Ellis, and Mr. Chapman. This he himself described as "a final appeal ere it becomes too late," but to write an appeal really worthy of the name was not at all in Mr. Denison's vein. So the letter, opening as a remonstrance, ended as a defiance. "Say if you like," it said, "'We decline to negotiate at all, or to refer the case for revision and settlement,' and I shall not in the least complain, but pray forgive me for saying that if negotiation or reference is to depend upon our confirmation of the four managers' minutes I must respectfully but irrevocably declare that I cannot consent."

This letter was sent to Lord Chandos on 29 January, 1856; on the following day Captain Huish sent to Mr. Clarke a notice of the new fast trains at greatly reduced fares which the confederates proposed to run from London to Yorkshire and Lincolnshire; and from 1 February, 1856, the trains and fares came into actual operation. Meanwhile, however, as the result of a chance meeting in the train between Mr. Clarke and Mr. Watkin, negotiations for peace had been once more set on foot, and on 6 February Mr. Denison, despite his gout, came to London by special arrangement to meet the directors of the other companies. Two long conferences, however, produced no settlement, and meanwhile all the Yorkshire and Lincolnshire passengers were being swept by the low fares into Euston Square; so on the 11th the Great Northern reduced its fares. Then what the newspapers began to call "the battle of the railways" began in earnest.

As in the exhibition year the first reductions were quickly followed by others. As then, so again, the people of Yorkshire and Lincolnshire flocked to the stations to take advantage of the cheap trips. "If this goes on," said Mr. Denison, "I should think the great majority of my West Riding constituents, washed and unwashed, will visit London in the course of next week." Meanwhile the Great Northern chairman, full of righteous indignation, had carried the dispute into the columns of the *Times*, and the readers of that paper enjoyed some fine examples of his epistolary style. "Such are the principles, moral and commercial," he ended his last letter, "on which this Euston Square confederacy is not ashamed to deal with smaller companies who have the audacity to make a stand against them. If railway business is to be carried on in this way it is of little use for Parliament to reject Amalgamation Bills. All the shareholders in the kingdom must sooner or later acknowledge the general managers at Euston Square as their masters."

As may be supposed this did not help to mend matters, and on 22 February, the day before the Great Northern half-yearly meeting, the morning papers announced further reductions on the part of the confederates; for instance, from London to York, first-class, 5s.; second-class, 3s. 6d.; and from London to Peterborough, first-class, 2s.; second-class, 1s. On the very same day, however, a proposal previously made by Mr. Denison and rejected, namely, that Mr. Gladstone should be asked to re-divide the traffic for which the Great Northern already competed without prejudice to the larger question as to whether or not its right to compete west of Sheffield should be allowed, was revived at Euston Square and assented to at King's Cross. The result was that the first thing the Great Northern shareholders heard, to their agreeable surprise, when they met next day was that a settlement had at last been arrived at, and that a circular was about to be issued by the four general managers withdrawing the low fares on and after the 1st of March.

This circular it had not been intended to publish until the last day of February, and premature disclosure of it at this Great Northern meeting on the 23rd had a curious effect. For the knowledge that there was one week—and one week only—during which the cheap fares were to remain in operation, greatly increased the rush of travellers to take advantage of them, and the Great Northern, being the shorter route to London from all the places in competition, was more than ever flooded with country people eager to avail themselves of a unique opportunity of visiting the Metropolis. During the last five days of February, according to a return published in the *Times* newspaper, 21,843½ passengers were booked to London by the Great Northern at the cheap fares, and the total receipt, £3756 15s., was more than double the ordinary earnings from the traffic in question. Under these circumstances, of course, the competition was far from being "ruinous" to the shareholders; but on the other hand, as in 1851, the increased cost of working and the strain upon the working-stock and staff of the system were very great. It was very creditable to the latter—as the directors testified in a special vote of thanks—that no accident of any kind occurred.

Meanwhile, a new attack had been levelled against the protectionist policy in the form of a Bill presented to Parliament by the (little) North Western Company, seeking running powers over the Midland and Lancaster and Carlisle lines, in order to enable it to carry Anglo-Scotch traffic in conjunction with the Great Northern. This Bill Mr. Denison supported in the witness-box, despite the fact that the new English and Scotch agreement was now in full operation. Of course, the whole force of the confederacy was against the Bill; but, nevertheless, with such champions as the two Denisons and Mr. Baxter (who was its solicitor), the (little) North Western—the adjective, said Mr. Hope Scott, Q.C., was now used "almost endearingly" by the Great Northern—was able to make a very plucky fight; and it was only because of a technical objection on the part of the Standing Orders Committee that it failed to obtain substantial redress. As it was, a nominal victory cost the confederacy £15,000 in expenses, and—what was even more serious to it—Mr. Denison, Q.C., was able to extract in cross-examination a full confession of what had up to this time been kept quite secret—the terms of the illegal common-purse agreement between the London and North Western and Midland.

This disclosure left the confederacy obviously at the mercy of a Chancery suit similar to that which had put an end to the working agreement between the Great Northern and the Ambergate four years before; but from some cause not apparent to the present writer—perhaps because the attention of the Great Northern directors became engrossed by a domestic calamity to be described in the next chapter, or perhaps only because of "the law's delay"—it was not until the spring of the following year—1857—that this gun could be brought to bear. Then, however, Mr. Isaac Burkill, of Leeds, a director both of the (little) North Western and of the Great Northern, took upon himself to file the necessary petition, whereupon the Euston Square authorities were informed by their legal advisers that it could not be defended. Accordingly on 12 May, 1857, their common-purse agreement with the Midland was declared to be at an end.

This, of course, meant practically the break-up of the confederacy, and the consequent collapse of the whole policy to carry out which it had been formed; but still Captain Huish struggled against the inevitable with that desperate courage and ingenuity which men of his type display to the full only when they have committed themselves beyond withdrawal to a hopelessly wrong course. Ever since the conclusion of the rate-war in February, 1856, he had been trying hard to take back the concession as to the limitation of the "pool," which he had then been forced to make, and, as in 1851, so now again, this had delayed the arbitration proceedings. The result was that it was not till quite late in the year that the hearings before Mr. Gladstone could be held.

Thus the award of that statesman as to the traffic referred to him was given almost simultaneously with the Chancery decision just mentioned, *i.e.*, in May, 1857, and so, before the actual putting of the pool into operation, Captain Huish was able to make yet one more attempt to extend its scope in such a way as, he hoped, might even yet save his "protectionist policy" from disintegration. Obviously, as he could no longer bind the Midland and Sheffield companies to his interests by private agreements, his object must now be to bring about a state of things under which such binding would be unnecessary; in other words, he had to aim at a hard and fast territorial division between the Great Northern traffic and his own. Accordingly, at an interview with Mr. Seymour Clarke at King's Cross, on 19 May, 1857, he offered to give to the Great Northern more liberal terms on the eastern side of England than even the Gladstone award assured to it, on condition that it should forego, for the fourteen years over which the new pool was to last, all share in London traffic west of Sheffield and the longitude thereof. This, said he, will "complete the good work Mr. Gladstone has commenced," and give to the pacification which his arbitration has brought about a stability which it must obviously lack so long as the Great Northern retains power to invade new districts.

By this time, however, Mr. Seymour Clarke had learnt to look for more in Captain Huish's proposals than they bore on the face of them, and so the real drift of this new scheme did not escape him. He saw what we have just pointed out—namely, that now the maintenance of private treaties was impossible, Captain Huish was seeking a new form of "protection" which would be independent of confederates; and he was tactician enough to see that Euston Square's extremity might be King's Cross's opportunity—that if the Sheffield and Midland found that the North Western was playing fast and loose with them, they might choose to outplay it at its own game. Accordingly, he turned a deaf ear to Captain Huish's proposals and took the first opportunity—it happened to be at a "fish dinner" given by the Earl of Yarborough at Grimsby on 1 June, 1857—to make them known to a gentleman upon whom he felt sure the news of them would have a decided effect—Mr. Edward Watkin, the Sheffield manager.

What effect Mr. Clarke expected from his communication may be judged from the fact that he took in his pocket down to Grimsby a copy of some proposals which he had had occasion to draw up—though without result—three years before for a complete interchange of traffic between his own and the Sheffield companies. Nor was he disappointed in his calculations. Mr. Watkin, as the reader already knows, had served a long apprenticeship at Euston Square; he had learnt his first lessons in railway diplomacy from Captain Huish himself; he knew every move in his late master's game. There was no need for Mr. Clarke to tell him at this time of day that a territorial division between the London and North Western and the Great Northern "meant annihilation" to the Sheffield Company, or to remind him that the abandonment of the Midland's common-purse agreement without a struggle meant that the existing treaties between his Company also and Euston Square were waste paper in the eyes of the law. These were considerations which Mr. Watkin had already taken into account. His recognition of them had led him already during the preceding six months to strain his relations with the North Western almost to breaking point; and now he could feel no doubt but that the time for decisive action had come. So, there and then, when the fish dinner was over, the two managers sat down at a table with Mr. Clarke's draft proposals between them, and they did not rise from it until they had laid the foundations of a most thoroughgoing alliance between their companies—an alliance based on the fullest and freest interchange of traffic between the two systems.

The work thus begun at the "fish dinner" was completed in an equally quiet way a week or so later in a window of the gallery of the House of Commons, and then in his bedroom at Eccleston Square—for he was again laid up with the gout—Mr. Denison gave his approval to what had been done. He stipulated, however, that the Sheffield—"the railway flirt" as it was afterwards not inaptly called—must prove itself to be quite "off with the old love" before being "on with the new," and further, that the new alliance should be an open one in every respect. So, when the former condition had been satisfied by Mr. Watkin producing a resolution of his Board which declared all agreements with the London and North Western at an end, the latter was provided for by the summoning of special general meetings of both

M

companies. The Great Northern meeting was held on 8 July, 1857, when the full terms of the agreement were read to it, and a resolution authorizing the directors to make application to legalize them in the next session of Parliament was put to a poll and carried by a majority of 13,597 votes and £1,443,501 of stock.

The part of the agreement which it was desirable, in view of past experience, to legalize by Act of Parliament was the giving to the Sheffield of a "bonus mileage" on the division of the joint London traffic and the guaranteeing to that company of a gross traffic of £10,000 a week—this being the price the Great Northern had agreed to pay for the Sheffield's *volte-face*. For the putting into effect of the alliance, so far as the actual interchange of traffic was concerned, no Act of Parliament was necessary, because not a yard of new railway had to be constructed, nor did either company wish any new running powers over the other's lines. The junction at Retford, as we know, had been in existence since 1849; since 1851 the Great Northern had been running to Sheffield; and since the opening of the towns line in 1852 the complete route between London and Manchester had been available. Whether it could be effective or not was wholly a matter of harmony or discord of train service.

Under the domination of Euston Square, the Sheffield managers had been forbidden to fit their Manchester trains even with the Great Northern *local* trains to and from Peterborough and Grantham, lest—as Serjeant Wrangham put it in a speech to which we shall presently refer—"a single through passenger should escape from the London and North Western net"; and now all that had to be done to bring the new policy into effect was to reverse completely the time-table arrangements. The result was that from 1 August, 1857—from which date the new arrangements came into vogue—passengers could travel to or from London Road Station, Manchester, from or to King's Cross in five hours twenty minutes—the same time as from or to Euston Square.

The putting of this through service into operation was, of course, an actual attack upon the London and North Western's long cherished monopoly, and it was all that was needed to kindle the latter's smouldering wrath into a blaze. Armed with the fullest sanction of warfare from an enraged half-yearly meeting, the Euston authorities proceeded to arrange their September time-table in the spirit of fiercest competition—to put on eleven trains each way instead of eight, to accelerate their "express" time to four hours forty minutes, and their "Parliamentary" time to seven hours,* to abolish "express" fares, and to offer numerous cheap excursions for the Manchester "Art Treasures

* It had been ten hours forty-five minutes.

Exhibition" which, like the Great London Exhibition of 1851, had come by coincidence to make the struggle hotter than it might otherwise have been. To these measures the new allies had, of course, to retaliate. They were handicapped, however, by a route fifteen miles longer, by harder gradients, especially west of Sheffield, and by the inferior condition into which, under the stress of constant poverty, the Manchester, Sheffield, and Lincolnshire permanent way and rolling stock had been allowed to fall.

It was, and is, 40 miles only by the Sheffield Company's route between Sheffield and Manchester, and yet Mr. Watkin, in 1857, could not, consistently with safety, get the distance covered in less than 80 minutes. So, upon the shoulders of the Great Northern, which was working the through trains between London and Sheffield, the full brunt of maintaining the competition fell. But again, as in 1851, Mr. Seymour Clarke, "the best of traffic managers," and Mr. Sturrock, most ready of locomotive engineers, proved equal to the emergency. Their 162 miles were covered daily in 220 minutes—44 miles per hour —and, though this meant five hours for the whole journey, *i.e.*, 20 minutes longer than what was now the best time of the North Western, the punctuality of the allies was so superior that very often the King's Cross passengers were landed first at the common station at Manchester —London Road. Moreover, as a concession to the Sheffield poverty, the allies' trains were made up almost entirely of Great Northern coaches, and these were admittedly superior to the North Western stock of that day.

We have said that the North Western and Sheffield companies had at Manchester a station in common, and here were seen the most exciting incidents of the fray. For not only was there a daily "race to Manchester," which anticipated the modern "race to Aberdeen" and made the junction outside London Road station a prototype of "Kinnaber," but there was actual physical strife between the joint owners which outdid even the engine-capture at Nottingham already described. According to a subsequent statement of Mr. Denison, Q.C.:

"The North Western authorities began to take people into custody for coming by the Sheffield trains into the Manchester station; they frightened an old lady out of her wits, and distracted several feeble people; but at last they got hold of a lawyer, who showed them they had 'caught a tartar'; and so after that no more passengers were apprehended. We" (*i.e.* the Manchester, Sheffield, and Lincolnshire, as whose counsel Mr. Denison was speaking) "had painted up our names over our shop, but they, being in possession, which is nine points of the law, swept them out with their brush. They kept a truck standing in front of the platform, and left timber trains in front of our express trains. They turned our clerks out of the booking-office"—indeed they nailed up the part which the Sheffield Company had been accustomed to use, and when one of the clerks, acting under instructions, made his way in through the window, they ejected him by the same way—"not, I hope," wrote their solicitor, "with unnecessary violence."

The lawyers could afford to treat the matter facetiously, for they —and they only—profited by it.

Not content with all this, the Euston authorities carried the war into the enemy's country. They reduced rates for traffic between Lancashire and Leeds, Lincoln, Peterborough, and other eastern places— a proceeding which, naturally enough, led the Midland, North Eastern, and other companies to cry out. Some abortive negotiations, however, served only to intensify the strife, and in February, 1858, both belligerents began to carry excursion passengers between London and Manchester for 5s., there and back, "giving them 15-inch seats, stuffed cushions and backs to lean against," to quote from the protest of an indignant Great Northern shareholder. But meanwhile a "Great Northern and Manchester, Sheffield and Lincolnshire Traffic Arrangements Bill" had been introduced into Parliament; and the conflict on the rails was overshadowed for a time by the greater importance of the issue to be decided in the House of Commons Committee-room.

It was in some respects like a repetition of the "London and York" fight, especially on the promoters' side, where Mr. Denison, Mr. Baxter —who, as Parliamentary agent to the Sheffield Company, was solicitor to the Bill—Serjeant Wrangham, and Mr. E. B. Denison once more fought side by side. The main issue, too, was the same—improvement *versus* vested interest; and King Hudson found a not unworthy successor in Captain Huish, fighting with his back to the wall for a sinking supremacy and a pre-condemned cause. Over twenty-one sittings the fight raged. Mr. Hope Scott made a most elaborate and ingenious speech for the opposition, and Serjeant Wrangham, during more than two hearings, poured out argument and rhetoric for the Bill. "A decision in favour of the petitioners," he concluded, "will tell the world that their obstructive agreements for locking up the traffic of a commercial country are looked upon with distinguished favour by a tribunal such as this, and that the sanction of the legislature has been given to that which legislation has previously sought to control. It is for you to say whether, yielding to the arguments of my learned friend, you shall denounce competition in the free passage of commerce between, perhaps, our largest emporium and the greatest and wealthiest of the world's capitals. With you it is to say, whether that route existing, constructed, in which untold millions are invested, shall be rendered available for the public, or shall be inflexibly closed against it. It is for you to choose between the two courses laid before you—to give to commerce that which is her life—freedom, or, if you please, to-make monopoly immortal."

At the conclusion of this speech the Committee deliberated for six hours. Then its chairman, Sir John Hanmer, announced a unanimous decision in favour of the Bill, at the same time declaring the private agreement of 1854 between the London and North Western and Sheffield companies to be *ultra vires* and contrary to public policy. Nevertheless, the opposition was renewed in the House of Lords, but with, if possible, less effect; and the Bill became an Act on 23 July, 1858. A month previously the London and North Western had agreed to adopt equal fares with the allies both for Manchester and Liverpool, so that the new route *viâ* Retford had now the recognition both of the rival interest and of Parliament.

Meanwhile the *volte-face* of the Manchester, Sheffield, and Lincoln had been imitated more slowly, but hardly less completely, by the Midland. Even as early as April, 1857, when the Leicester and Hitchin line had been first brought into work, some goods traffic had been sent through by it to and from King's Cross, and, when in the following month the common-purse agreement with the North Western was given up, there was no reason why this "surreptitious" interchange —that was the adjective which the Euston authorities had indignantly applied to it—should not become a free and open one. In the summer of 1857, moreover, Mr. Allport, who, as we have seen, had been all along Captain Huish's most zealous supporter in the "protectionist" policy, left the Midland to become partner in a shipbuilding firm, and this made *rapprochement* with King's Cross all the more easy. The result was that in the autumn of 1857 an agreement was included under which not only was the new junction at Hitchin made a fully open one, but running powers between it and King's Cross were given to the Midland on the usual terms, namely, two-thirds of the gross receipts. Thus on 1 February, 1858, Midland trains began to run in and out of the Great Northern's London terminus; and from 1 August, 1858, through bookings with King's Cross to and from Midland stations were brought into operation as fully as with Euston Square. Moreover, in July, 1858, the Gladstone Award was cancelled by notice from the London and North Western—a notice which, as before stated, it had been entitled to give directly the Great Northern went west of Sheffield; and so, except the English and Scotch agreement (which as we shall see remained in force for eleven years longer), nothing now remained of the elaborate edifice which Captain Huish during his twelve years *régime* had raised on behalf of the vested interests of Euston Square.

CHAPTER XI.

AN ISOLATED INCIDENT:—THE FRAUDS OF LEOPOLD REDPATH.
1856-1858.

"YOU have fought your way into a most respectable position; you are in a position which not one person in fifty in 1846 or 1847 believed you would obtain. Your property is perfectly sound; your prospects are in my opinion exceedingly good; you have nothing in the world to be afraid of. If you choose to take my assurance that everything is looked after as diligently as it can be, accept that assurance. If not differ from me, and propose a committee of investigation. I never laboured so hard in my life, either for myself or for anybody else, as I have done for the proprietors of the Great Northern Railway. I take no credit to myself; it was my duty to do it; and what I say of myself I say of my brother directors around me; I never saw men who looked more closely over their own accounts than they do after those of the Great Northern. I will say— and I say it with great pleasure—with respect to every officer who works under us, that I do not know any set of men whom I would sooner trust. The general manager stands here, and he is perfectly welcome to the admission that the line is worked in admirable order; and I will say of the other officers, from the secretary down to the humblest porter (and I do not believe we have a dishonest man in the whole lot), that I will turn my officers out against any officers in the kingdom. I will have men of honour and gentlemen about me if I am to be your chairman or one of your directors. The line shall be well worked."

So spake Mr. Denison in his characteristic downright fashion to the Great Northern shareholders at their twentieth half-yearly meeting on 23 August, 1856. . He spoke with perfect sincerity, and the greater part of what he said was strictly true; nevertheless, the utterance of it could not have been more unfortunately timed. Three months after this unqualified expression of their chairman's confidence in the Great Northern staff, the whole country was startled, and the shareholders thrown into consternation, by the announcement that frauds of the most wholesale character had been perpetrated upon the property of the Company, that by manipulation of the accounts of the share-registration department a sum exceeding £200,000 had been stolen, and that the head of the department, Mr. Leopold Redpath, had disappeared.

We have said that Mr. Denison had spoken the words just quoted with perfect sincerity, but it must be also said that he had spoken them rashly. For he had been personally informed in the preceding January that "a discrepancy" had been discovered between the books of the registration and accountant's departments, and he knew that an inquiry into the origin of the supposed "errors" was on foot. As long before as February, 1854, indeed, the then chief registrar, Mr. W. H. Clark, had been informed that there was a "comparatively trifling discrepancy" —on the side of excess—between the amount paid in dividends and the amount due to be paid on the stock registered, and, according to his own subsequent statement, he "had lost no time in taking steps to investigate the matter and to probe where the error lay." Unfortunately, however, he had been already under notice to retire from his position, to which he had been appointed immediately after the incorporation of the Company in 1846, as part of the agreement of amalgamation with the "Direct Northern" Committee to which he had been secretary—on the ground that "the Registration Office ought not to be loaded with the cost of its present staff," and so, when his notice had taken effect on 30 April, 1854, what he termed "the examinations for the adjustment of the accounts" had been uncompleted. It "has been resumed," he had written to Mr. Mowatt, the secretary—his official superior—on 25 April, 1854, "now that the pressure of current business has been disposed of, and in reference to it my successor will not experience any difficulty; in short, I feel confident that I shall leave everything in the department in a business-like condition."

Mr. Clark was quite right in thinking that his successor would "experience no difficulty" in reference to the discrepancies, for that successor was Leopold Redpath himself. He had received his first appointment in the registration office at the same time as Mr. Clark, and though a clerk only, while the latter was the departmental chief, he had had from the first the practical control of the office. For he had entered it with a knowledge of stock-registration work previously acquired in the service of the Brighton Railway Company, whereas Mr. Clark had been appointed, as has been already said, not for his capacity for this particular duty, but as compensation for displacement, and had, on his own subsequent admission, "no knowledge whatever of book-keeping or registration business." In his capacity of chief clerk, moreover, Redpath had conducted himself apparently "with regularity and propriety," and so upon Mr. Clark's retirement it had seemed quite natural that he should be promoted to be chief registrar; yet already, as was afterwards computed, he had stolen from the Company the sum of £120,537.

This being so, it was not surprising that the books showed "discrepancies," nor that, under Redpath's now absolute command there, they were not "probed" further in the registration office itself. In another department, however—that of the accountant—similar discrepancies very soon aroused uneasiness, particularly in the mind of the chief book-keeper, Mr. William Grinling; and he, in April, 1855, informed his friend, Mr. Henry Oakley, the chief clerk in the secretary's office, that he felt sure that the dividends were being regularly overpaid. Mr. Oakley reported the matter to the secretary, Mr. Mowatt, who immediately requested Redpath to furnish certain statements to clear up the matter, but the latter preferred to conduct an "inquiry" on lines of his own.

Meanwhile, Mr. Grinling himself had prepared a statement showing among other things that the dividend to 31 December, 1853, had been paid on a stock larger by £90,136 than the registered stock of the Company, and this he forwarded on 26 June, 1855, to the accountant—his chief—Mr. Reynolds, at the same time suggesting a course which in his opinion ought to "be adopted at once in order to ascertain the cause of the discrepancy. I am urged to do this," he wrote, "because the plan adopted by Mr. Redpath, although necessary in order to the ultimate settlement of the question, leaves untouched at present the most important point. . . . The excess on the A and B stock presents a very grave question and one that I submit demands immediate attention, and if not taken up before everything else may hereafter reflect upon those who have had charge of the matter." Mr. Reynolds, however, being on terms of personal intimacy with Redpath, and having perfect confidence in his integrity, did not feel called upon to substitute the course of inquiry suggested by Mr. Grinling for that which the registrar professed to have himself adopted for the same purpose.

So matters were allowed to slide until November, 1855, when the secretary again took up the matter, but it was not until 29 January, 1856, that he at last received Redpath's long promised statement, together with another from the accountant. These showed beyond doubt that dividends had been overpaid on some of the stocks, and they were passed on immediately by the secretary to the chairman, who upon his next attendance at the offices made some inquiries. He allowed himself to be satisfied, however, with the information that an investigation had been commenced by the registrar, which, it was hoped, would soon show where the "alleged errors" existed.

In September, 1856, Mr. Denison's attention was again directed to the matter by the secretary, who stated that the registrar did not pursue his inquiry "with anything like vigour." Thereupon Redpath was again pressed in regard to it, with the result that early in October he tendered his resignation. Then at last suspicion was fairly aroused, for the similar frauds committed by Robson in the transfer office of the Crystal Palace Company had just been revealed to the world, and on the 17th and 18th October returns were at last obtained which showed that stock to the amount of £137,000 was registered in excess in the books of the Company. This, moreover, was confirmed by a statement of the dividends paid, which the accountant had in the meantime furnished.

Redpath was now definitely called to account by the chairman; but he declared that "every discrepancy admitted of adjustment," and offered his "best assistance" to this end, while persisting in his desire to resign. But Mr. Denison, of course, told him that his resignation under the existing circumstances could not be accepted, and authorized the secretary to commence at once a full inquiry. The result was that a frightful system of fraud and forgery was brought to light; and upon the discoveries being reported to the chairman on 10 November, 1856, Leopold Redpath fled to Paris.

Apparently, however, he no sooner took this act of flight than he repented of it, for on the following day a telegraphic message was received from him, promising his return, and he actually passed *en route* the police officers who had been despatched in quest of him. He had named 4, Ulster Place, New Road, London, as his future address, and there on the morning of 14 November, 1856, he was found by Mr. Mowatt and a police officer, undisguised and apparently enjoying a hearty breakfast. Some days earlier a clerk in the registration office, named Kent, had also been arrested for complicity in the frauds, and on 15 November the two prisoners were charged at the Clerkenwell Police Court.

Immense public interest had been excited in the case, and at the first hearing the purlieus of the Court were densely crowded, but the details were at once too technical and too simple to hold the interest of any but those who were shareholders smarting under the sense of loss and wrong. Redpath had had, it appeared, practically unchecked control over the machinery of the registration department, and, though the cash transactions of that department were limited to the daily receipts of a few half-crowns for transfer fees, he had succeeded in robbing the Company of the huge sum of over £220,000. The very *a priori* impossibility of the thing had been his greatest assistance. Until the Robson frauds, which were brought to light a month only before those of Redpath, no one had dreamed that a joint-stock company—a comparatively new kind of institution, be it remembered—could to any large extent be robbed through its registration department; consequently, checks and counter-checks had not been thought of. In the Great Northern offices, as in the offices of all the other large companies in the kingdom, what appeared to be the simplest and most effective machinery of registration had been adopted without any special care to safeguard it against misuse. The result had been that an artful and audacious rogue, assisted partly by luck and partly by the remissness of his superiors, had been able to add to existing figures or to manufacture new entries in such a way as to create fictitious stock for almost any amount that he pleased; and this having been done, the conversion of the stock into hard cash, through the medium of brokers, had been a matter only of inventing a few names and forging the signatures of them on forms which were ready to his hand. About June, 1848, the first of these fraudulent sales had been carried out by Redpath, and the list, which for the purposes of the prosecution was obtained from his brokers, extended from that date to October, 1856—the very date of the revelations—and embraced 365 distinct sales of Great Northern stock to the amount of £206,047 10s., and 131 purchases amounting to £48,800.

Of course, directly the first revelations were made, a multitude of circumstances presented themselves which might have been expected to have aroused earlier suspicion. Redpath had left his first situation under a cloud; then becoming an insurance broker, or a wine and spirit merchant—or both—he had failed for £5000, and been sold up at his suburban residence in Dartmouth Terrace, Blackheath. He had entered the Great Northern service, it was true, with good credentials from the Brighton Company, and had lived quietly for some years afterwards, but at the time of his promotion to the chief registrarship in 1854 he had had a town mansion, No. 27, Chester Terrace, Regent's Park, and a "country place" at Weybridge, and yet he had been apparently eager to obtain an office, the salary of which was only £250 a year! That he paid £30 a year to his cook, had a courier to accompany him on his travels, and a fisherman and punt for angling excursions at Weybridge, kept a dozen other servants, gave splendid dinners, was intimate with peers, and as highly esteemed for taste by the rich as by the poor for benevolence—these and a hundred things like them were now excitedly gossiped over, and the wonder grew that they had not formed the ground of suspicious inference long before. But there is no place in which a man may live a double life with so little comment as in London. The reputation of being a successful speculator who, at the same time, clung to regular, respectable employment, had been sufficient for eight years to cover all the contradictions in Redpath's extraordinary career. Now, however, it was ended for ever, as far as his native country was concerned, for on 16 January, 1857, he was convicted at the Old Bailey and sentenced to transportation for life. Kent, his worst dupe, was acquitted of all criminal intent, and remained for years afterwards a respected servant of the Company.

After Redpath's conviction, however, the really serious part of the trouble created by his villainy still remained to be dealt with. To convict him, proof of a few specimen forgeries had been sufficient; the main tangle of his misdeeds had yet to be unravelled. Not feeling equal to the task themselves, the auditors of the Company called in the assistance of a professional accountant, who reported that it would be necessary to trace through all the transfers of stock from the birth of the Company in 1846, and for this purpose he brought a staff of about fifty clerks to King's Cross. The result was that in a few months an expense of £4700 had been incurred and only two out of seven stocks had been examined; while it was found that the practical effect of the operations was merely to reproduce certain results which Mr. Oakley, Mr. Grinling, and one or two others of the ordinary staff, working sometimes beyond midnight, had already arrived at. So, by general consent, the professional expert's services were forthwith dispensed with, and an immediate saving effected of about £100 a day.

Meanwhile, the question of how the heavy loss was to be dealt with had become pressing with a view to declare the dividend for the half-year ended 31 December, 1856. In order to ascertain their legal powers and responsibilities, the directors consulted the Attorney-General, Sir Richard Bethell (afterwards Lord Westbury), and Mr. Rochfort Clarke, Q.C., and these authorities stated that they considered the loss arising from the frauds "in the same light as any loss resulting to the Company from some great calamity, such as the falling of a tunnel or viaduct or an inundation, the cost of which would have to be defrayed before any profit capable of division could be considered to have accrued." They, therefore, recommended that before any dividend was declared by the Company "provision should be made for purchasing and extinguishing stock equal to the amount fraudulently created." As this had already been shown to amount to about £220,000 there did not, under these circumstances, seem much prospect of any dividend worth the name being paid for the half-year; and if there had been, another part of the legal gentlemen's opinion would have at once extinguished it, for they declared that as it was impossible to avoid paying on the fictitious stock equally with the stock legitimately issued, it followed "as a necessary consequence" that the Company could not "at present legally pay any dividend whatever." Under these circumstances, it was a decided aggravation of the shareholders' sufferings to be informed that the profit balance of £243,923 available would have enabled the directors, under ordinary circumstances, to have proposed a distribution which, added to that declared in the previous August, would have made the whole year's dividend—for the first time in the Company's history—amount to 5 per cent. upon the ordinary stock.

Of course, at the first shareholders' meeting after the discovery of the frauds—the twenty-first half-yearly meeting, held on 4 March, 1857—there was a great deal of pent-up indignation to be worked off, and Mr. Seneca Hughes gave the first vent to it by proposing a resolution that the directors should be made "personally responsible" for the loss. Common sense, however, soon showed the angry shareholders that it was one thing to pass such a resolution and quite another to enforce it. Accordingly Mr. Hughes' motion was negatived by a large majority, and another was passed appointing a "committee of inquiry," consisting of three shareholders and two directors, to inquire fully into "the accounts of the Company, including the registration," and to report to a special meeting to be convened for the purpose.

But an inquiry into the system of accounts, it was already evident, was a mere shutting of the stable door after the theft of the horse; the real matter to be fought now was how the loss was to be distributed amongst the various classes of shareholders. In the opinion already quoted from, the Attorney-General and Mr. Rochfort Clarke had suggested—somewhat inconsistently, it would seem, with their view as to the loss being one to be defrayed immediately out of profits—that the shareholders should agree to apply to Parliament for a Bill to legalize the fraudulent stock. This course accordingly the directors had recommended in their report to the meeting, with the proviso, however, that the Bill must not be one to "throw upon the preference stocks any portion of the loss in question, and thereby shake the confidence of the public in all such stocks." Moreover, without waiting for the meeting, they had had a Bill on these lines prepared; but when on 7 March, 1857—after the publication of the report, but before the meeting—it had come before the Standing Orders Committee of the House of Lords, Lord Redesdale, the chairman of that Committee, in the arbitrary manner for which he was dreaded, had absolutely refused to allow it even to be introduced, declaring that "no bad precedent must be set," because the loss was a large one, but that it "must be charged to the revenue and not to the capital of the Company." Moreover, on 12 March—one day before the meeting—a deputation of holders of open stock had waited upon the directors to urge practically the same course, namely, that the loss should be at once met out of the half-year's revenue; and the result was that at the meeting itself the directors consented to an amendment to the report being adopted to this effect. Accordingly for the Bill originally framed a new one was substituted to authorize the application of the net revenue of the Company available for dividend for the half-year to 31 December, 1856, to buying up and then cancelling stock of the Company to the extent of the forgeries and to paying all the expenses of Redpath's prosecution, etc.

Notwithstanding their previous declaration against "throwing any portion of the loss upon the preference stocks," the directors made no secret that the new Bill was intended to distribute it alike amongst all classes of shareholders; and when it was pointed out to them that its wording in this respect was ambiguous, they introduced an amendment to make it quite clear. This amendment was accepted by the Lords Committee, but opposed most virulently on third reading by two champions of the preference shareholders, Lord St. Leonards and Lord Wensleydale, both of them law lords, and the former an ex-Lord Chancellor, who abused the directors in unmeasured terms.*
Nevertheless the Bill passed intact through the Upper House, where it had been first introduced; but in the Commons a vigorous private canvass against it was organized, with the result that there the clarifying words were expunged. Thus the precise effect of the Bill was again made doubtful; but to drop it at this point would have meant deferring all declaration of dividend for another year, and so the directors had no option but to take it as it stood, with the chance that it might be held in law to carry out their intentions.

Accordingly it became an Act, and a scheme of dividend was prepared for the half-year to 30 June, 1857, under which the preference shareholders were made to suffer equally with the others.

* "Lord St. Leonards is a great authority," said Mr. Denison to the Great Northern shareholders, "but I must take the liberty of saying that no man living ever talked such a quantity of arrant stuff."

Against this, however, some of the former appealed to the Court of Chancery; and on 26 August, 1857—three days only before the half-yearly meeting—the Vice-Chancellor gave a decision that no dividend could be declared except on the footing of paying the preference shareholders their claims in full. The directors decided, in the interests of the ordinary shareholders, to appeal against this decision, and all declaration of dividend had again to be postponed.

The indignation of the shareholders had now reached fever-heat. To their original anger at the lax supervision which had allowed frauds of such magnitude to be carried on so long was added an almost universal dissatisfaction at the course which the directors had taken since their discovery. With the preference shareholders the Board was now at open war, while the ordinary proprietors distrusted them because they had at the outset sided with the other party. The result was that the twenty-second half-yearly meeting held at the London Tavern on 29 August, 1857, was perhaps the stormiest ever held in railway history. Hostilities commenced at the very outset by the shareholders objecting to allow the Chairman to affix the seal of the Company to the register of shareholders.

"There was a time," cried one indignant speaker, "when you could have affixed that seal to the register, and when you could have affixed your signature to any document, be it what it would, and the confidence of this proprietary would have gone with you. But the discussion which has occupied the last five minutes ought to serve to show you that their confidence in you has utterly gone" (loud applause) "deservedly, justly, irrevocably gone. And, sir, if any expression of opinion—if any description of question which this meeting can put should serve to relieve this Company of such a head as they are now ashamed of" (applause) "no time can be wasted, no consumption of time can be a loss of time if it serves to redeem, to rescue, and to save this vast property from a management which every man feels to have been the reverse of right, sound, and faithful."

The weight of this gentleman's eloquence, however, was somewhat discounted when it was found that he was the proprietor of barely more than £100 of stock.

Mr. Denison stated that he had never before in all his life been so abused, both in speech and by letter. He believed, in short, that many people were more enraged with him than they were with Redpath; and his son, Mr. E. B. Denison, Q.C., being present at the meeting to support his father, now came in for a share of the personalities. One speaker alluded to him as "the young May-moon on the chairman's right," whereupon the future Lord Grimthorpe rose to protest against his assailant "sitting at the end of the table squirting out his venomous observations" (hisses and confusion). Upon being appealed to to use his influence to restrain his son, the Chairman said: "If my son has had insulting language aimed at him he is not

Mr. Edmund Denison in 1856.
From a photograph by Maule & Fox, Piccadilly, W.

worthy of being my son if he does not repel it instanter" (loud applause). At last the elder Denison himself, goaded beyond all patience, aroused an uproar louder than all by declaring that he would "be damned if he would answer a question hypothetically."

The meeting was adjourned to await the result of the appeal against the Vice-Chancellor's judgment, but this, when received in the following November, 1857, proved an unqualified triumph for the preference shareholders. In a word, it placed them in the position of *guaranteed* proprietors, entitled to their full dividend and all arrears before anything could be distributed upon the open stock. As already stated, the whole profits for the half-year ended 31 December, 1856, had already been appropriated to making good the Redpath loss. Consequently, the dividend in arrear to the preference shareholders for that half-year had first of all to be paid out of the profits of the following half-year before any dividend could be distributed on the "original," the "B," or the "A." The result was, of course, that this section of the proprietary bore the whole loss from the frauds, receiving nothing at all in dividend for one half-year, and only a fractional amount, viz, 6s. per cent. original and 12s. per cent. B stock, the next. The directors could only plead in excuse that it was not their fault that the action of Parliament had thwarted their best endeavours to carry out the resolution of the March meeting, and remind the shareholders that no good could come of further complaints.

Meanwhile the Committee of Inquiry had concluded its investigations, and 7000 copies of the evidence it had taken, together with a report drawn up by the three shareholders' nominees, had been circulated at an expense of about £100 for postage alone. The inquiry had ranged, not only over the accounts and registration, but over all the affairs and traffic arrangements of the Company, and a number of matters had been selected for animadversion and suggested amendment. The vagueness and triviality of the charges, however, were in themselves proof that the laxness of supervision had been confined to the registration department, and that the general affairs of the Company were in a thoroughly sound state. But Mr. Denison was the last person to leave criticism of any kind unanswered, and accordingly the directors issued, with their report to the adjourned half-yearly meeting, a reply to the Committee, which was drawn up in the chairman's most vigorous and trenchant style.

"It is difficult," it concluded, "to see what good such a report as this can have done to anybody—except, indeed, that it must have convinced some persons who were not sufficiently sensible of it before, that the ability to declaim at meetings against an existing railway government and in favour of reform, is consistent with the smallest possible capacity for undertaking either the one or the other."

In the accompanying report the directors issued what may be fairly described as their "ultimatum." "If," they wrote, "the peaceful and rational majority of the proprietors think the character of the Company worth preserving, and that the time is come to make an end of the business which has caused so much ill-feeling, it is neither prudent for themselves, nor fair to those who have to fight their battle for them, to leave their opponents in even apparent command of the meeting. It is impossible to foresee what course may be taken at the approaching meeting by those who have created the disturbance at the last two. But the time is coming when no Company will get persons of character to serve them as directors if they are to be insulted by their constituents whenever they meet them publicly, and not even allowed to make the speeches necessary to conduct the business without interruptions. If the proprietors think their business would be better done by such persons as those who usually distinguish themselves by imputing the worst possible motives to the present directors in all their acts, it is easy for them to say so, and so soon as that opinion is deliberately expressed it shall be immediately acted on. But they must make their choice, and the proceedings of the ensuing meeting will probably be taken to indicate that choice in one way or the other."

This appeal produced the effect for which it was intended. Among the business announced for the adjourned half-yearly meeting which was held on 1 December, 1857, was a vote of censure on the directors for "their long mismanagement and neglect of the registration department." The resolution was moved, but its proposer was listened to with manifest impatience, and several of the subsequent speakers strongly appealed to the meeting to bury the history of the frauds in oblivion, and to leave their affairs with confidence in the hands of a directorate which, with this one exception, had done so well for them in the past. "You are perfectly welcome to know," declared Mr. Denison, amid repeated bursts of cheers, "that if I had not had a sincere respect for those whose property is embarked in this great undertaking, no consideration should have induced me to remain where I am. I know perfectly well that I lay myself open to observation when I repeat that, if I had not believed that under some particular circumstances if I had left the direction the property might have been damaged, I certainly should have made my bow to the board years ago. I have gained nothing by it. I ask for nothing. I have done my duty to the public; I have done my duty to you; and so long as I remain in the position in which I stand, no language that can be used will drive me from this position. I know perfectly well from conversation, from letters, and from my estimate of public opinion, that a very great majority of the shareholders in this concern *do* place the greatest confidence in the board with which I am connected." The result of the meeting proved that this estimate was a right one. When the resolution of censure was put about twenty hands only were held up in its favour, and the mover did not think it worth while to go to a poll.

It was not until the following August that a complete account could be submitted showing the exact amount of the loss to the Company from Redpath's frauds. The amount expended in the purchase of stock to extinguish that fraudulently created was £227,835; the loss by dividends paid on the fraudulent stock was £21,405; law charges, including the cost of the prosecution of Redpath, obtaining the Act of Parliament, and defending the suit in Chancery, had consumed no less a sum than £7575; £3937 had been paid to the professional accountant, and just over £3000 more had been spent by the Company itself in additional staff for adjusting the stock registers, stationery, and sundries. There was also a loss on income-tax of £7649, resulting from the profits for the half-year ended December, 1856, not having been divided; but this was nearly counterbalanced by a credit of £6702 for interest received from time to time on this money while in reserve. On the credit side also was the very considerable sum of £25,099 received from the proceeds of Redpath's estate. The net result was that out of the amount of £243,923 which had been set aside to meet the loss, only £4248 remained unexpended, and this was carried forward to the net revenue account of the current half-year. It is significant of the strong position which the Great Northern Railway Company had already attained, that so heavy a loss, occurring so early in the history of the undertaking, could thus be met out of a single half-year's profits.

CHAPTER XII.

THE MIDLAND AGGRESSION—1858-1863.

THE break-up of the Euston Square confederacy and the admission of the Great Northern in alliance with the Sheffield Company to the north-western parts of England meant that the third epoch in the history of the northern railways of England had definitely commenced. The first epoch, as we have seen, had extended from the opening of the London and Birmingham Railway in 1838 up to 1850, during which period the through traffic between London and the northern parts of the kingdom had all flowed to and from a single Metropolitan terminus—Euston Square. In 1850 a second terminus—King's Cross—had been opened, having physical connection with all parts of the North; but, as we have seen, from 1850 to 1858—the second epoch—traffic to and from King's Cross had been limited and hampered in the interests of the hard-dying monopoly of Euston Square. In 1858, however, the death-blow had at last been given to this monopoly by the verdict obtained from Parliament in favour of the establishment of the joint Great Northern and Manchester, Sheffield, and Lincolnshire route between London and Lancashire; and so, as has just been said, a third epoch had then commenced—the epoch of the dual control, if you like so to call it—the epoch during which there were two equal through routes for the northern traffic of the kingdom, the one starting from Euston Square, and the other from King's Cross.

Having thus fought its way to the proud position of equality with the London and North Western, it may be thought that the Great Northern has now put its fighting days behind it; but this is true in the sense only that in our subsequent pages it will not figure as the aggressor in great railway fights—that it has ceased to be the "Ishmael of railways," to recall the nickname given to it soon after its birth, when its official title was "the London and York." Having now won for itself recognition as a first-class power in the railway world, the Great Northern will not need in the future to wage offensive warfare; but the state of inter-railway politics, like that of international politics, is ever a state either of war or of "armed peace"; and the position which the Great Northern has acquired it will be found necessary for it to defend from attack with unceasing vigilance. One main trunk line between London and the North did not, as we have seen, satisfy the British public for long; and now that there are two routes these cannot give contentment to every interest. First a third, then a fourth, and then a fifth trunk railway are destined to be demanded, and against each of these in turn we shall find the Great Northern called upon to fight almost as stubbornly as we have seen that it was itself fought against in its early days.

To look back a little, then:—the sympathy with which we may so far have followed the progress of the Great Northern must not blind us to the fact that its success had already involved considerable hardship to other companies—more especially to the Midland and to the Eastern Counties. As laid out originally, as we know, by George Stephenson, the main trunk of the Midland system had been intended not only to connect a number of important provincial towns, but to form in connection with the southern part of the "London and Birmingham" line a main trunk route between London and Yorkshire; and, similarly, the Cambridge line of the Eastern Counties had been originally planned, as we saw at the time, as part of a "Northern and Eastern Railway" between London and York. True, the promoters of both these lines had made the serious mistake of supposing that the public would accommodate itself to the interests of the railway-makers by being content to travel circuitously, whereas the Great Northern promoters had clung with splendid perseverance to a truer faith—the faith which Mr. Denison expressed when he said, "traffic, like water, will find its own level; it will go by the shortest line." Still, when error on the one side and sagacity on the other are fully admitted, it cannot be denied that it was hard on the Midland and Eastern Counties shareholders that, having laid out their money largely with a view to getting "through" long-distance traffic, they should now find themselves deprived of almost the whole of it by the construction of a new route more direct than their own.

During what we have just called our second epoch—the epoch of "the confederacy"—the Midland, as we have seen, had been able to obtain some compensation for its losses in the form of "blackmail" extracted from the London and North Western by threats of allying itself with the Great Northern, and this had lasted until the collapse in 1857 of the illegal common-purse agreement between the two companies. But, all this time, the Midland, as we also noted, had been careful not to carry its subservience to Euston Square so far as to neglect to make its southern extension from Leicester to Hitchin; and the result of this wise policy had been that, as recorded in our last chapter but one, almost simultaneously with the collapse of the common-purse agreement, the long-threatened alliance with the Great Northern had been obtained. It had been obtained, moreover, on terms much more advantageous to the Midland than would have been forthcoming if a direct connection between the two systems had still been to seek.

The reason for this is very obvious. By coming so far south as Hitchin the Midland had put itself well on the road to follow up what since the opening of the Great Northern had become its only sound and safe policy—the development of itself as a through north and south system, independent both of London and North Western and Great Northern; and so, in addition to their natural desire to divert the Midland's London traffic from its original route *via* Rugby to the new route *via* Hitchin, the authorities at King's Cross had a second reason for giving the Midland liberal facilities. If they did not do so, it might at once follow up its Hitchin extension with a further extension into the Metropolis itself. The terms actually given under the agreement made between the two companies in 1858 were full running powers for the Midland trains between Hitchin and King's Cross and separate terminal accommodation for its goods traffic—a great concession, obviously, to a competing company; on the other hand, it meant immediately an increase of income to the Great Northern, seeing that the Midland undertook that the toll it was to pay for the running powers should amount to not less than £20,000 a year. Nevertheless, it may reasonably be doubted whether on the whole the treaty was a good move for the Great Northern. While it staved off an immediate application on the part of the Midland for a line of its own to London, it encouraged that Company in two other steps hardly less dangerous to Great Northern interests. These were the conversion of its working agreement with the (little) North Western into a complete amalgamation, so that Anglo-Scotch traffic by the "central route" might be developed in earnest, and a strenuous effort to establish a Midland route between London and Lancashire.

The latter effort was precipitated by certain arrangements which the London and North Western, Great Northern, and Manchester, Sheffield, and Lincolnshire companies sought to make in order to conclude permanently their Lancashire rate-war of 1857-8. That war, as we saw in our last chapter but one, had been put an end to in June, 1858, by a temporary agreement to charge equal rates and fares by both routes —rates and fares considerably lower than those which the London and North Western had charged before the Great-Northern-cum-Sheffield invasion; but, instead of being content with this, and recognizing what is now an axiom of English railway politics, that within the limits of equal rates, competition between rival routes is inevitable, the three companies, despite all past experience, started off again in pursuit of that will-o'-the-wisp which, as we have seen, had led Captain Huish into such disaster—in pursuit of arrangements to prevent competition of all kinds. For this purpose they made an agreement in November, 1858, to divide the whole of the London and Lancashire traffic amongst themselves in certain agreed proportions, and to work it for the common interest under the management of a Joint Committee. In a word they revived the "protectionist" policy with the alteration that instead of being directed against the Great Northern as before, it was directed by a combination, which included the Great Northern, against the Midland.

There was another important respect, however, in which this "Triple Alliance," as it was called, differed from the similar alliances contracted under the *régime* of Captain Huish. It was made quite publicly—nay more, the three companies parties to it, acting apparently under the force of a reaction caused by the bad odour into which Captain Huish's ultra-legal methods had fallen, deposited a Bill in Parliament for the purpose of obtaining legal sanction for the arrangements. The sequel, however, demonstrated the much greater shrewdness which Captain Huish had shown in preserving strict secrecy in regard to all traffic agreements of this character. For no sooner were the terms of the "Three Companies Bill"—as it was called—made public, than the Midland, North Staffordshire, and other companies whose lines formed parts of alternative routes between London and Lancashire, entered most energetic protests against it on the ground that it would act most prejudicially upon the development of their alternative routes; and the Midland especially was able to make out a strong case on this ground, because already it was doing a small amount of London and Manchester traffic by carrying it on its own trains from King's Cross, *via* Hitchin and Leicester into North Derbyshire, and thence forwarding it by the London and North Western lines *via* Stockport. The result was that in consequence of the opposition of the Midland Company, the "Three Companies Bill," after passing the Commons, was thrown out by the Lords.

There could be no doubt as to the reason why the Lords Committee rejected the Bill, for they accompanied their decision with a rider to the effect that no arrangements of the kind contemplated could be regarded as satisfactory unless the Midland was included in them. Accordingly, for the session of 1860, a new Bill was framed in which provision was made for the inclusion of the Midland; but at the same time a new "Three Companies Bill" was also deposited, in the hope, apparently, that if the one failed the other might pass. The latter, however, was again thrown out on the opposition of the Midland, and the "Four Companies Bill" on that of the North Staffordshire; and then the members of the Triple Alliance realized that if other companies were to be kept out of the through traffic with Lancashire, it must be done not publicly but privately, after the manner of Captain Huish. Accordingly, after the rejection of the Bills, the London and North Western and Sheffield Companies, going back to their old policy of "laughing at the Cardwell Act," refused to take on traffic which the Midland wished to forward into Lancashire from London and other competitive places. In a word, they "blocked" their junctions at Stockport and Beighton against the Midland just as in the days of the confederacy they had blocked the junction at Retford against the Great Northern.

In this way the development of the Midland's route to Lancashire was entirely arrested, and about the same time, *i.e.*, in the spring of 1860, steps of a rather more complicated character were taken to arrest the development of its "central route" to Scotland. It will be remembered that under the English and Scotch Alliance of 1856, as well as under the Octuple Treaty of 1851, the existence of this central route had been practically ignored, as far, at least, as London traffic was concerned. The Midland, in return for considerations which it had received under its "confederate" alliances with the London and North Western, had been content to claim such proportions only of the through traffic with Scotland as it was entitled to as part owner of the "alternative East Coast route" *viâ* Derby and Normanton. But upon the collapse in 1857 of its common-purse agreement with the London and North Western, the advantages which had made it worth the Midland's while thus to minimize its powers as regards Anglo-Scotch traffic had of course ceased. Thereupon, as we have just seen, on the strength of the running powers it had secured in 1858 over the Great Northern, it had at once made new arrangements with the (little) North Western, whereby, instead of starving that "poor wretched little creature" as heretofore, it had absorbed it and begun to send its Scotch traffic over it, instead of by the East Coast lines *viâ* Normanton and York.

If the traffic thus sent, however, had been thrown into the English and Scotch "pool," obviously the Midland would have gained no benefit from its change of route; and, recognizing this, its representatives had so managed matters so far that the "central route" receipts were not "pooled," but were divided between the several companies over whose lines the traffic passed in the more ordinary way according to mileage. But this, as obviously, was a questionable proceeding; accordingly, early in 1860, it was brought officially to the notice of the other members of the alliance. Thereupon the Midland urged that, as it was sent *via* Hitchin—*i.e.*, by a route which had come into operation since the formation of the alliance—the "central" traffic might legitimately be kept out of the "pool"; but the majority of the companies refused to accept this view, and so, pending the settlement of the dispute, the Railway Clearing House was directed to collect the whole receipts of the central route in future, and to hold them in suspense. Thus the Midland appeared for the time to be rather neatly "hoist with its own petard"; for, but for its own former subservience to Euston Square and indifference to the injustice which its acceptance of bribery from that quarter had entailed upon the (little) North Western, a proper status might have been given to the central route at the time the English and Scotch Alliance had been made. Nevertheless, that the construction now put upon the terms of that alliance by the West and East Coast companies involved great injustice to the Midland cannot be denied, especially in view of the fact that the opening of the long-projected link between Ingleton and Tebay was in a few months' time considerably to improve the central route.

It was under these circumstances that Mr. Allport was invited to give up his shipbuilding business and return to the general managership of the Midland to strengthen that Company and to break down the barriers which had been formed against it, just as in 1850 he had broken down similar barriers formed against the Sheffield. He accepted the invitation, and the first step he took was to cultivate an alliance with the Lancashire and Yorkshire. This, of course, was directed against the Triple Alliance of the London and North Western, Great Northern, and Sheffield—in fact, it at once opened up Lancashire, circuitously, to Midland traffic; and its announcement, coupled with a rumour that a complete amalgamation of the Midland and Lancashire and Yorkshire was in course of arrangement, led the Joint Committee of the Triple Alliance, at one of its meetings in the autumn of 1860, to take into serious consideration a far-reaching proposition which had been hinted at several times before. This was that the London and North Western and Great Northern should jointly absorb the Manchester, Sheffield, and Lincolnshire.

This, indeed, seems to have been the end which the ever-scheming manager of the Sheffield, Mr. Watkin, had had in view from the beginning of the friendly relations between the three companies; but Mr. Denison had, as he said afterwards in evidence before a Parliamentary Committee, "turned a deaf ear—a cold shoulder—to it; he did not care about the matter at all." Indeed, one can well believe that this was the attitude of the Great Northern chairman to the whole of the Triple Alliance proceedings. One can hardly believe that he can have entered with any zest into a policy so similar to that against which he had fought with all his might when it was directed against his own Company. Probably he acquiesced in the Triple Alliance, as we saw he acquiesced in 1855 in the English and Scotch Alliance, simply because he would not take upon himself the responsibility of standing in the way of arrangements which, however objectionable they might be from the point of view of true railway statesmanship, were from the point of view of the traffic returns and the next half-year's dividend very highly recommendable.

However this may be, the fact remains that towards the close of 1860, despite Mr. Denison's "cold shoulder," a strong disposition showed itself amongst the directors of the three companies to pursue the policy which had dictated their alliance a step farther by converting the Manchester, Sheffield, and Lincolnshire from an independent company into the joint property of the London and North Western and Great Northern.

The first measure taken was to depute the three general managers to meet and discuss terms, and, as usually happened when Mr. Watkin met other managers, Mr. Watkin did not come off second best. On this occasion he persuaded Mr. Seymour Clarke and Mr. Cawkwell (the latter had succeeded Captain Huish at Euston) to agree that the Sheffield Company should be guaranteed a dividend to begin at $1\frac{1}{2}$ per cent. in 1861, and to rise by $\frac{1}{4}$ per cent. stages until it reached a permanent $3\frac{1}{2}$ per cent. in 1866; and, though the former figure and not the latter had been, and proved in the future to be, the normal dividend of the Sheffield open shareholders, these terms of amalgamation were, on their general manager's recommendation, adopted by the London and North Western directors by a majority of twenty-five to one. This minority of one consisted of none other than the chairman of the company, Lord Chandos, who thereupon resigned his position and wrote a private letter to Mr. Denison explaining his reasons for so doing.

The Great Northern chairman received the letter—as we have already seen him receiving other important communications—when he was in bed with the gout at Doncaster. It being Christmas time, however, he had a competent counsellor at hand in the person of his son, Mr. E. B. Denison, Q.C., and the father and son were not slow in coming to the conclusion that the bargain which Messrs. Clarke and Cawkwell had made with Mr. Watkin was a most improvident one, in spite of the contrary opinion of the London and North Western Board. As usual, Mr. Denison was able to carry his own Board with him. The result was that on 23 January, 1861, the Sheffield Company was informed that the Great Northern Company declined to proceed further with the proposed joint amalgamation, at any rate on the basis suggested by the general managers.

Mr. Watkin was, of course, greatly chagrined at this upset to his schemes. On the very next day, 24 January, 1861, he spent several hours closeted with Mr. Robert Baxter at the latter's office at Westminster, and the same evening he dined, according to previous engagement, with Mr. Seymour Clarke at the Great Northern manager's residence at Hatfield. Walking to the station after dinner, Watkin said, "I have been doing a thing to-day which will make the ears of you Great Northern tingle." A few days later it was announced that an agreement had been concluded between the Manchester, Sheffield, and Lincolnshire and South Yorkshire directors under which the former undertook to absorb the undertaking of the latter on the terms of a dividend-guarantee.

In a speech which he made to the House of Commons Committee, before which this South Yorkshire transfer came up for sanction, Mr. Denison, Q.C., did not hesitate to charge Mr. Watkin with making the arrangement simply to spite the Great Northern. "Do you not see," he said, "by the mere juxtaposition of those two days, that Mr. Watkin went, red-hot from the disappointment at losing his own guarantee, to go and buy up the South Yorkshire? Nothing more than the two dates is necessary to explain the motive of the Manchester, Sheffield, and Lincolnshire Company in making this agreement." On the other hand, however, it must be remembered that absorption of the South Yorkshire by the Sheffield had been within the range of practical railway politics since 1851, that more recently the two companies had entered into intimate relations in order to carry on jointly a coal traffic to the port of Grimsby, and that at this very time they were engaged together in promoting new railways in North Lincolnshire with a view of providing a direct route from Yorkshire and Lancashire to Grimsby, and also of opening up the newly-discovered Keadby ironfield. But at a Sheffield half-yearly meeting a year or two later Mr. Watkin himself declared that "the South Yorkshire agreement was entered into for *political* as well as for commercial purposes," and on this occasion and many others he complained that the terms of the agreement between the Sheffield and Great Northern to do London and Lancashire traffic jointly was working unfairly to his Company. It seems pretty certain, therefore, that his predominant motive in securing the South Yorkshire was the calculation that if the Sheffield system was thus enlarged so as to comprise the Great Northern's means of access not only to Lancashire but to the coalfield, the King's Cross Board would be compelled by sheer political necessity to give better terms to the Sheffield Company, if not, sooner or later, to buy it up, South Yorkshire and all.

For it was a fact, plain for every railway politician to see, that no matter how strong a justification Mr. Denison had had for going back upon the South Yorkshire amalgamation agreement in 1852, the failure of the Great Northern to secure control of the coalfield railway, either in that way or some other, had seriously arrested the development of its coal traffic to London. Since its commencement in 1851, the coal traffic from South Yorkshire to King's Cross, as we have already seen, had grown continuously, and was now far in excess of the original estimate; but it had almost certainly not grown at anything like the rate at which it might have grown, had the Great Northern had the working of it entirely in its own hands. The Great Northern, as we have seen, had been the pioneer of the railway coal traffic to London, and for a year it had carried a tonnage far in excess of that of other companies; but it was rapidly losing its supremacy in this respect.

This supremacy had been first threatened, as we have already seen, in 1854, when the Midland and London and North Western, under their "common-purse" agreement, had commenced to develop traffic vigorously from the Derbyshire, Leicestershire, and Nottinghamshire fields; and now that by virtue of its running powers from Hitchin the Midland was for all practical purposes a London company, the competition between it and the Derbyshire coalfield on the one hand, and the Great Northern and the South Yorkshire coalfield on the other, had entered upon a new and critical stage.

In such competition the Midland field had the great natural advantage that now the route *viâ* Hitchin was open, it was, broadly speaking, thirty miles nearer to London than the South Yorkshire. On the other hand, in the latter district the seams of coal were proving generally thicker and the roofs stronger, making working less expensive. More important still, the quality of the coal was better when got. Under these circumstances there was *primâ facie* little reason why the two coalfields should not be on an equality as regards the London market.

What seemed likely to turn the scale in favour of the Midland trade, however, was, that the Midland Railway Company, when it had completed a new depôt for coal which it was building on land of its own adjoining King's Cross, would be in a position to carry it on "in one hand" from the pits to the Metropolis; and that—more important still—Mr. Allport and his directors, as their purchase of this land showed, were determined to develop quite a new coal-producing industry in Derbyshire with a single eye to the London market. On the other hand, the cultivation of the South Yorkshire trade was in three hands, the coalowners (who had originally established themselves, be it remembered, by the help of water carriage), the South Yorkshire Railway Company, and the Great Northern; and the aims and interests of these three had never properly been harmonized. It was not only that the South Yorkshire Company, under the agreement substituted for the abortive amalgamation, insisted on having 1d. per mile, and sometimes more, for the passage of the coal over the sixteen miles "average distance" of its line between the pits and Doncaster, and so prevented the total rate to London from being a really low one, though the Great Northern contented itself with half that amount for each mile of its longer haul. What was more serious was that the coalowners—and in a sense the small railway company also—had never resolutely set themselves to cultivate the London market. On the contrary, as we have already seen, they often starved that market when it suited them to send a larger proportion of their output to their older markets nearer at hand.

That this was the prime cause of the stunted development of the Great Northern coal traffic had been proved by the failure of prescriptions to remedy that complaint, which had been based upon other diagnoses. Thus, some of the chief buyers of South Yorkshire coal in London, and the coalowners themselves also, had persistently declared, as we have already seen Mr. Samuel Plimsoll declaring, that the root of the evil was that one buyer only had been allowed to deal at first-hand—that, in short, the Company itself had acted as coal-merchant through the agency of Mr. Herbert Clarke; and, the drawbacks to this system having been proved to outweigh its advantages, the directors had, in the summer of 1859, modified it to the extent of allowing other men besides Mr. Clarke to act as agents to the coalowners. Moreover, from July, 1860, as the result of a Chancery suit, the Company had been compelled to desist altogether from selling the coals on its own account, and Mr. Herbert Clarke's connection with it, other than as a "freighter," had ceased. These changes, however, had not, so far, materially improved the trade, and the reason for this clearly was that the prime difficulty remained untouched. Not through many agents any more than through one would the South Yorkshire coalowners properly cultivate the London market. It was by fits and starts only that they were really in earnest about it, when from exceptional causes their trade nearer at home was slack.

That this state of things was remediable by any measures which the Great Northern Company could have taken seems, in the light of after events, highly problematical; but this much is certain, that the move which, as just recorded, Mr. Watkin made so dramatically in January, 1861, of buying up the South Yorkshire Railway for the Sheffield Company threatened, if not met by some counter-move, not only to deprive the Great Northern of all remaining chance of remedying it, but to aggravate it in a considerable degree. For, if the "embarrassment occasioned by the interposition of an independent company in their principal coalfield"—to quote the phrase used prophetically by the Great Northern directors just before the commencement of their London coal trade in 1851—had been one of the prime causes why that trade had not developed satisfactorily, it was obviously likely to become a more potent cause of evil when the "independent company" which interposed was converted from a small affair into a much larger and more powerful one, with interests which, as far as the coal trade was concerned, might conflict diametrically with the interests of the Great Northern. It was, as we said, the competition of nearer markets mainly which was preventing the London trade from South Yorkshire from increasing more rapidly. Now it was over the system of the Sheffield Company—the new lessors of the South Yorkshire Railway—that these nearer markets were mainly reached.

Thus in calculating—to adopt a colloquialism often used afterwards to describe the transaction—that he would "get at" the Great Northern by his acquirement of the South Yorkshire, Mr. Watkin showed his usual shrewdness; and when he had heard of Mr. Denison's surprise and wrath at the news, and how with his usual bluntness the Great Northern chairman had characterized the proceeding as "a dirty trick," he probably chuckled and said to himself that the shaft had gone home. For, however angry he might be, Mr. Denison could not shut his eyes to the fact that Mr. Watkin's move had made his former attitude of "deaf ear—cold shoulder" to a more intimate relationship with the Sheffield no longer tenable. So when, as the second move in his game, Mr. Watkin offered a half-share in the South Yorkshire lease to the Great Northern, Mr. Denison could do nothing else but agree that

Mr. Seymour Clarke should meet the Sheffield manager and see if they could arrange "equal terms."

But equal terms could not be arranged, though the two managers had many meetings over the business. It was not only that Mr. Watkin had so far let his "political" motives outweigh his "commercial" instincts—not an uncommon thing with him—in the bargain he had made with Mr. Baxter as to have pledged himself to give exorbitant terms to the South Yorkshire Company. There was a difficulty much more fundamental, namely, that the purposes for which the Great Northern wished to obtain control of the coalfield system were, as the reader will readily see, quite incompatible with the sharing of that control with the Sheffield Company upon equal terms. The result was that the Great Northern directors came to the conclusion that they could gain nothing, and might lose a good deal, by involving themselves in a half-share in the improvident bargain which Mr. Baxter had extorted from Mr. Watkin.

But, as has been said already, there can be little doubt that Mr. Watkin had all along calculated that sooner or later the Sheffield shareholders would be relieved of this and of all their other burdens by the amalgamation of their whole property either by the London and North Western and Great Northern jointly (as he had already so nearly accomplished), or by the Great Northern alone; but unfortunately for this, as for most of the schemes in which he embarked in the course of his remarkable career, his energy and ambition were too abundant for him to concentrate his attention on one object at a time. In this instance, instead of settling down to follow out the difficult line of policy which he had marked out for the Sheffield Company, he undertook in July, 1861—not instead of the Sheffield general managership, but merely as a piece of extra work—a mission to Canada to investigate the embarrassed affairs of the Grand Trunk Railway Company; and in his absence the men who were left in charge of the Sheffield took a step which upset completely his long-cherished schemes.

In his book on the Midland Railway, Mr. F. S. Williams* has already told the story of how in the autumn of 1861 Messrs. Beale, Hutchinson, and Allport, of the Midland Company, were out examining the country between Buxton and Manchester—surveying it, in fact, in connection with a new through line into Manchester which the Midland had all but resolved to promote as a weapon against the Triple Alliance—when unexpectedly in a by-lane they came upon a dog-cart in which a director and two officers of the Sheffield Company were riding. The

* *The Midland Railway*, pp. 116-17 (popular edition).

representatives of the two companies spent the rest of the day very amicably together, and shortly afterwards Mr. Allport entered into negotiations with Mr. Chapman, the Sheffield chairman. The result was the conclusion of an agreement under which the whole policy of the Triple Alliance was reversed by the Sheffield Company undertaking to admit the Midland traffic to Lancashire, instead of excluding it therefrom. Temporarily the route was to be by the existing junction between the two systems at Beighton, but for the session of 1862 the Midland was to deposit a Bill to make, not a new through line as it had proposed, but a link line only from Buxton to join at New Mills a branch of the Sheffield's system, over which into Manchester it was to have perpetual running powers. This agreement, in Mr. Watkins' view, robbed the Sheffield property of half that value in the eyes of the Great Northern and London and North Western which he had schemed so long to give to it, and his anger was such that he at once resigned the general managership of the Company.

Nor was Mr. Watkin the only person who thought he ought to have been consulted before the agreement between the Midland and Sheffield was made; the Great Northern directors also thought they should have had a say in the matter. For it was for London and Lancashire traffic primarily, as we know, that the prior agreement between the Great Northern and Sheffield—the "Fifty Years Agreement," as it was now and afterwards called—had been made in 1857, and of this agreement one of the clauses (which the reader will do well to bear carefully in mind) was: "Neither Company party to this agreement shall make any bargain, treaty, agreement, or arrangement with any other Company, or do any act which can in any way directly or indirectly affect the traffic of the other Company, or prejudice this agreement, without the consent of the other Company party thereto." Moreover, the agreement—this clause and all—had, in accordance with a general Act recently passed, been approved by the Board of Trade as recently as 10 April of this very year, 1861. Yet here was the Sheffield Company making an agreement which would have the effect of setting up a new Midland route between London and Manchester without so much as giving its Great Northern partners notice of the matter.

Under these circumstances the Great Northern directors applied in December, 1861, to the Court of Chancery for an injunction to prevent the Sheffield and Midland companies from carrying out their new treaty. Both this application, however, and an appeal were dismissed; nor did Parliament, in the session of 1862, listen to the Great Northern plea that on account of the Sheffield's breach of faith the Midland's Bill for its extension line to New Mills should be thrown out.

Thus the Midland was put on the road to become a "first-class power," as far as traffic between London and Lancashire was concerned; and meantime Mr. Allport was working hard to raise it to a similar position in regard to traffic between England and Scotland. In September, 1861, the "short cut" line from Ingleton to Tebay was opened, and at the same time a still more important contribution to the formation of a really effective "central route" was being provided by the North British Company, which was on the point of reaching Carlisle by an extension of its Hawick line. Thus there was every encouragement to the Midland to develop an Anglo-Scotch traffic independently of the East and West Coast routes, had it not been for the construction which the companies owning those routes were seeking to put upon the English and Scotch Alliance of 1856. For, as we have already seen, if that construction was the correct one, no matter how hard the Midland might work to develop a new through service, it could earn no more from Anglo-Scotch traffic than the very meagre proportion it was already receiving.

Accordingly, it had become a great object of policy with Mr. Allport, either to upset the alliance altogether, or to secure a revision of it in favour of more liberal treatment of the central route, and looking about for a lever which he might use for this purpose, he found what he wanted in a conference which was held towards the close of 1861 between the managers of the principal companies, with the view of agreeing upon a scale of excursion fares to be charged for the special traffic in connection with the International Exhibition to be held in London in 1862. With the experience of the 1851 Exhibition traffic still fresh in their memories, the representatives of the railway interest were naturally anxious to avoid the recurrence of "ruinous competition"; but just as in 1851 the measures proposed to this end were objected to by the Great Northern on the ground that they were prejudicial to its larger interests, so now, in 1862, the Midland manager took a precisely similar stand. He declared that he would make no agreement to charge equal fares for the Exhibition traffic until a more adequate share of the traffic between England and Scotland was assured to his Company.

Had the decision rested with the Great Northern alone, this claim of the Midland would probably have been fairly met—at any rate, Mr. Denison told a Parliamentary Committee in 1863 that he was quite prepared to revise the English and Scotch Alliance in order to do more justice to the central route; but of course the Great Northern was one only of nearly a dozen companies interested. Moreover, the company most opposed to revision was the North

Eastern, which had a good deal to lose if the Midland's Scotch traffic definitely left its old route, *via* Normanton and York, in order to go by the new route *via* Skipton, Ingleton, and Carlisle; and with the North Eastern and the North British the Great Northern had, in 1860, succeeded in making arrangements for the formation of an "East Coast joint stock," *i.e.*, carriages belonging jointly to the three companies to run daily between King's Cross and Edinburgh—a partnership too valuable to be imperilled by a difference of policy with regard to the rival interest of the Midland. Against the central route, too, both the Great Northern and North Eastern had a special bond of opposition in the fact that its further development would be a temptation to the North British to become less zealous for the East Coast partnership in the interest of its new line to Carlisle. The result was that the Midland's claim to a revision of the English and Scotch Alliance was refused, and in retaliation the Midland commenced a competition in fares for the Exhibition traffic, which, though not so severe as that of 1851 and 1856, brought the return fare from Yorkshire to London down to 15*s*. first class, and 8*s*. second; moreover, it had an element of real warfare which the earlier battles had lacked, inasmuch as both Midland and Great Northern trains ran into, and out of, the same terminus—King's Cross.

As to the working of the Exhibition trains *en route*, this in 1862 was greatly facilitated by the electric telegraph (which the reader may remember had not yet been installed on the Great Northern in 1851). For this was not only very useful for keeping the officials all over the line well informed as to what "specials" were running, but by its aid some progress had been made, as we have already seen, in working traffic upon the "block system," *i.e.*, in keeping an interval of space as well as an interval of time between following trains. Only in the case of the four longer tunnels, it is true, was this new system as yet worked "absolutely"; on the lines generally a cross between working by time-interval and working by space-interval had been evolved which, according to a high authority, was "probably properly understood only by the Great Northern managers themselves.* Nevertheless there can be no doubt that the danger of one train catching up and running into another had been greatly minimized and the risks of running a heavy special excursion traffic considerably diminished since 1851. Still the responsibility resting personally upon the managers and men was much heavier than in our era of almost perfected safety appliances, and it is not at all surprising that under

* Mr. Preece, the eminent electrician, *vide* a paper he read before the Institution of Civil Engineers in 1863.

O

the strain Mr. Seymour Clarke's health temporarily broke down. When all was safely over, the directors expressed their relief and thankfulness by voting a sum of £4000 to be distributed in bonuses amongst the working staff in consideration of the fact that "280,943 additional passengers had been conveyed with safety and regularity."

Meanwhile the Midland had been pushing on with the construction of its separate coal depôt adjoining King's Cross—the nucleus of the St. Pancras of the future,—and by the summer of 1862 the work was so far advanced that the Great Northern managers, being badly in want of more siding room for the Exhibition trains, thought there was no injustice in giving the Midland notice that by 30 June, 1862, it must give up the accommodation for coal traffic in the Great Northern's own premises which it had enjoyed since 1858. Unfortunately, however, the Midland was not able to make it convenient to quit so hurriedly; and thereupon the Great Northern officials, in their anxiety to clear the sidings, took certain summary action which by the aggrieved Midlanders was described as an "eviction in the night." Added to the ill feeling which the competition for the Exhibition traffic had aroused, this proved "the last straw" in breaking down the patience of the Midland with the equivocal position it occupied in London. Already the project had been set on foot by some independent promoters for making a new line from London to join the Midland at Hitchin; now, under the leadership of Mr. Allport, the Midland decided to take up this scheme —to promote, in short, an extension to the Metropolis.

Prior to taking this decision finally, however, the Midland directors applied to the Great Northern for running powers between Hitchin and King's Cross in perpetuity, the existing powers being terminable on either side at seven years' notice. But this the Great Northern directors could not see their way to grant. As Mr. Denison put the matter to his shareholders, "giving a right in perpetuity would practically be giving a share in the freehold; you could not eject them afterwards." So instead of it the Great Northern offered to give more permanent running powers, and to undertake to double their line between Hitchin and London (for which, they pointed out, they already had the land), provided that the guarantee of traffic on the part of the Midland was raised from £20,000 to £60,000 a year. In the enlightened belief, however, that even four lines between Hitchin and London would not for long prove sufficient for the traffic of the two companies, Mr. Allport and his directors refused to be turned from their original purpose, and in October, 1862, they decided definitely to promote an Extension to London Bill in the next session of Parliament. The proposed line was to start from a junction with their Leicester and Hitchin line at Bedford, and to run through Luton, St. Albans, and Mill Hill (all places which the Great Northern was already tapping by branches) to a London terminus at St. Pancras, a terminus the nucleus of which, as we have said, they already possessed in their newly-opened coal depôt at Agar Town.

It was avowedly the coal traffic from the Derbyshire field to which the Midland authorities looked chiefly to make this extension to London profitable—a hope in which they were encouraged, not only by the rate at which that traffic had increased in recent years, but by the fact that, with a view specially to the London market, a great many new pits were being opened in the district. These same facts, however, had not escaped the attention of the Great Northern directors. On the contrary, when considered in connection with the Sheffield's acquirement of the South Yorkshire Railway, they had convinced the Board at King's Cross that their Company must obtain a footing in the Midland Counties coalfield. Accordingly in the summer of 1861 —immediately after the Sheffield purchase of the South Yorkshire— they had obtained permanent possession of the Nottingham and Grantham line at a guarantee to its shareholders of a £4 2s. 6d. dividend (with the right to purchase the whole property on the repayment of the capital at par value); and now, in this autumn of 1862, they followed up this step, and met the new aggression of the Midland, by depositing a Bill to extend the Grantham and Nottingham line from Colwick up the valley of the Erewash into the very heart of the Derbyshire and Nottinghamshire coal district, side by side with the existing line of the Midland.

This new "Codnor Park line"—as it was called after the place in the Erewash Valley at which it proposed to terminate—was not necessary, however, for the making of physical connection between the Great Northern system and the coalfield. There was a through route already *viâ* a junction at Nottingham between the Nottingham and Grantham and Midland lines, and over this Derbyshire coal had passed on to the Great Northern ever since it had first made connection with the Grantham and Nottingham in 1852. This, however, was "local" coal chiefly; anything like a proper traffic through to London *viâ* Grantham could not be developed because the Midland Company had persistently refused to make through rates. From Clay Cross— the centre of the Derbyshire field—to Nottingham Junction they exacted the high toll of 2s. 2d. per ton, and this had proved fatal— as they meant it should—to competition with their own routes to London *viâ* Hitchin and Rugby.

In going to Parliament, therefore, for a line of their own, the Great

Northern directors had in view, not so much actually making such a line as forcing the Midland by the threat of one to give through rates. Accordingly, when the Midland authorities showed a disposition to accede to this without forcing a contest in Parliament, they on their part were quite ready to withdraw their Bill. But, while recognizing that the recognition of the Great Northern as a carrier to London from the Derbyshire coalfield was now inevitable, Mr. Allport and his directors were not inclined to concede this without obtaining some *quid pro quo.* The Midland itself had a grievance in the matter of through rates. This was that, to protect its South Yorkshire coal traffic, the Great Northern, when giving the running powers in 1858, had stipulated for a minimum toll of 1s. 9d. per ton for its thirty-two miles of line between Hitchin and London, which compelled the Midland still to send the bulk of its coal traffic *viâ* Rugby. Accordingly they on their part insisted that any agreement which gave the Great Northern free access to Derbyshire for coal traffic must give the Midland also free access (without any minimum toll) to its new St. Pancras depôt.

They insisted further that it must provide for stability of rates to competitive points, and—most important of all—must provide that "the rates from the Yorkshire, Derbyshire, Nottinghamshire, and Leicestershire collieries, carried by either or both companies to London" should "be equitably adjusted to each other," so that "as far as possible the through charge from the various collieries" should "be made fair one with the other." Accordingly these principles were embodied in a "Coal Traffic Agreement," which the reader will do well to bear carefully in mind, for it will become of great importance at a later stage in this history, and this Mr. Allport and Mr. Walter Leith (the latter acting as deputy for Mr. Seymour Clarke) signed on behalf of their respective companies on 23 January, 1863. In accordance with this agreement the Great Northern withdrew its Codnor Park Bill.

But its Extension to London Bill the Midland on its part could not be persuaded to withdraw, nor could the Great Northern directors see their way clear to allow it to pass unopposed, so a Parliamentary contest could not be avoided. In this the Great Northern expected to have the powerful support of the London and North Western Company, but at the eleventh hour Euston Square withdrew its opposition to the Bill, and Mr. Denison and Mr. Walter Leith had to appear alone as railway witnesses against it. But with a strong case for, public interest at its back and an exceptionally powerful array of counsel to the fore, the Midland Bill would probably have borne down the strongest opposition. As it was, it passed through Committee stage with comparative ease. The "London and York" Bill to make a second trunk line to the North had been, the reader remembers, seventy days before a Commons Committee, and then the decision had not been conclusive. This Midland Bill, to complete a third trunk line, was disposed of by a similar tribunal within ten days. On the basis of the tolls paid to it by the Midland in 1862, the Great Northern had to expect a loss of £90,000 a year when the new line was made, and all the consolation Mr. Denison and his colleagues had was that under the agreement of 1858 the Midland had had to give seven years' notice, until the expiration of which, in February, 1870, it must pay its minimum traffic guarantee of £20,000 a year.

CHAPTER XIII.

THE GREAT EASTERN ATTACK AND OTHER MATTERS—1863-1865.

WE have already noted the anomalous nature of the position which for a number of years after its opening to London the Great Northern Railway occupied in the West Riding of Yorkshire. To provide a direct route between the West Riding and London was, as we have more than once seen, one of the main objects for which the Company was promoted, and since the completion of its towns line in 1852—nay, even for two years before this, when its main route northwards had been *via* Boston and Lincoln—it had given by far the best service between London and two of the most important West Riding towns, Leeds and Wakefield; yet for access to these towns it had been at first entirely dependent upon running powers over Lancashire and Yorkshire and Midland rails. In 1854, as already noted, these running powers had been extended into Bradford and Halifax by the opening of the main line of the Leeds, Bradford, and Halifax Junction Company, and in 1857 they had been still further extended by the opening of the Wakefield, Leeds, and Bradford—afterwards called for greater clearness the West Yorkshire—Company's line, providing a direct route between Wakefield and Leeds, on to which the Great Northern through traffic was at once diverted from its original route to Leeds *via* Methley. In 1859, moreover, a Great Northern through service between London and Huddersfield had been commenced under joint arrangements with the Manchester, Sheffield, and Lincolnshire Company, the route being *via* Retford and Penistone, whence to Huddersfield the Sheffield Company had running powers over a line belonging to the Lancashire and Yorkshire; and in Parliament that same year full facilities by this route had been secured to the allied companies by the insertion of "through booking and forwarding clauses" in the Lancashire and Yorkshire and East Lancashire Amalgamation Act. Thus, to all the more important towns of West Yorkshire the Great Northern had, by the end of the fifties, obtained an access which from London was more direct than that of other companies, and in all these towns it had provided itself with station accommodation—separate for goods and joint for passengers. Yet in every case between these station holdings and its own rails the lines of two or more "foreign" companies intervened.

This was a state of things which could no more be completely satisfactory to the Great Northern than as we have just seen a similar position of dependence with regard to access to London was satisfactory to the Midland. Accordingly, efforts to improve their footing in the West Riding had already been made by the King's Cross Board. Thus, in 1860 they had revived the project for a direct line from Doncaster to Wakefield which, it will be remembered, had formed part of the original "London and York" undertaking: but this had been strenuously opposed by the Lancashire and Yorkshire Company on the ground that it was a breach of the agreement under which access to the West Riding over its lines had been secured to the Great Northern, and after a severe contest the Bill had been thrown out, though by a bare majority only of the House of Commons Committee. In the following session of 1861 it had been revived again with the warm support of important West Riding commercial bodies, but again on the opposition of the Lancashire and Yorkshire it had been rejected. Yet, strange to say, in the next year, 1862, powers for practically the same lines were obtained with the addition only of a fork to join the South Yorkshire system at Stainforth.

The reason why Parliament had thus authorized in 1862 a line which it had refused to authorize, not only in the two preceding years, but on two other previous occasions, must be sought in the different circumstances under which the last Bill for the purpose was promoted. In the first place, the applicants this time were not the Great Northern, but independent promoters, nor could these be accused of being Great Northern "jackals," as had been the case once before in 1857, when the line had been promoted by a separate company; on the contrary, they were actually opposed in Parliament by the Great Northern because they sought compulsory running powers over the West Yorkshire and Leeds, Bradford, and Halifax lines. Secondly—and more important still—they promoted the line, not as before under the title of the Doncaster and Wakefield, but under a brand new one, "The West Riding and Grimsby"; and the object they put in the forefront was, not to provide a new route for the Great Northern's West Riding traffic, but, in conjunction with the South Yorkshire system and certain new lines which, as already noted, the South Yorkshire and Sheffield companies were promoting jointly through North Lincolnshire to provide a new direct route whereby the manufactures of the West Riding could reach the sea. Thus it came about that this West Riding and Grimsby

Company obtained powers in 1862 to make the direct line which the Great Northern had so long wanted between Doncaster and Wakefield.

Turning now from Yorkshire to Lancashire we find that by means of its alliance with the Manchester, Sheffield, and Lincolnshire Company, the Great Northern had, by the date we have now reached, obtained a footing not only in Manchester, but also in Liverpool. Free access for their traffic to Liverpool, indeed, had been a concession on the part of Euston Square upon which the allied companies had insisted as one of the conditions upon which the Lancashire rate-war of 1857–8 should be permanently concluded, and it had eventually been made one of the principal bases of the "Triple Alliance" that by buying up the undertaking of the St. Helens Company and making a new line from its terminus at Garston to Liverpool, the London and North Western should provide a second route between Manchester and Liverpool—in addition to George Stephenson's original line—principally to accommodate the Sheffield and Great Northern traffic. Owing to the rejection by Parliament of the Triple Alliance Bill, however, this arrangement had been interfered with; and then, after the failure of the proposals for the absorption of the Sheffield system by the two larger companies, Mr. Watkin had persuaded the Great Northern to join with his company in making the line from Garston to Liverpool jointly, and at the same time to seek running powers between Garston and Manchester. A Bill for this purpose accordingly had been obtained in the session of 1861.

But this was not all. In this same session of 1861 Bills had been promoted by local parties for lines from Stockport to Timperley and from Northwich to Helsby—the latter under the title of the West Cheshire Railway; and as these lines, together with others under construction, promised to provide a direct route from the Manchester, Sheffield, and Lincolnshire system not only to Liverpool (without going through Manchester), but also to the important salt district of Cheshire and to the port of Birkenhead, both the Sheffield and the Great Northern companies had at the instigation of Mr. Watkin subscribed to this capitals, the Great Northern's share being £50,000 to the Stockport and Timperley, and £65,000 to the West Cheshire. In the following session of 1862, moreover, a further subscription of £8000 to the West Cheshire was authorized; and now, in 1863, seeing that for lack of funds the construction of the new through route to Liverpool and Cheshire still lagged, the allied companies obtained power to subscribe a further £220,000 each to be divided between the Stockport and Woodley, the Stockport and Timperley, the Cheshire Midland, and the West Cheshire. Thus, by degrees and under pressure from their Lancashire allies, the Great Northern directors were sliding into an expenditure on lines altogether remote from their own system, and for purposes which had not for one moment been contemplated at the time of the original promotion of the Company.

This was the more curious and difficult to justify, inasmuch as at the base of their own system—in London itself—they had shown a quite contrary disposition with regard to subsidizing new undertakings. Thus, they had been pressed most strongly to subscribe to the Metropolitan Railway Company when this had been incorporated in 1854 to take over the powers given in 1853 to the North Metropolitan Company and to extend its Paddington to King's Cross line into the City; but Mr. Denison had said that, though he sincerely wished the "underground" line to be made, he could not make up his mind that it would be wise for the Great Northern to risk money in it. The result had been that, though the Great Northern had taken powers to subscribe £175,000, the money had never actually been found, and the Metropolitan had almost collapsed for lack of support. Meanwhile, in 1859, another scheme, called the "Great Northern, Holborn, and City," had been set on foot, and this again the King's Cross Board had refused to support, though their own solicitors, Messrs. Johnson, Farquhar, and Leech, had been amongst its principal promoters.

In the light of after events there can be little doubt that the Great Northern would have benefited greatly, in the long run, if not immediately, by having an extension of its own into the City of London. Nevertheless, there were good reasons why the directors allowed this Holborn scheme to drop. In the first place, they had already, after some trouble, established their right to have their traffic forwarded between King's Cross and the City over the North London line, had set up a City goods depôt at Royal Mint Street, approachable by this North London route *via* Bow, and had just obtained powers (in 1859) to make a new junction with the North London at Maiden Lane to supersede the one originally constructed there, which was on a very bad gradient.* In the second place, the Metropolitan Railway was to be made, notwithstanding their refusal to subscribe, and their Company was to have running powers over it from King's Cross to Farringdon Street. In the third place, it seemed very doubtful whether, having already authorized the Metropolitan, Parliament would subsequently authorize a Great Northern extension. Under these

---

* Nevertheless, it had been used on occasion for through traffic, the Queen having travelled that way more than once between Windsor and the Great Northern system.

circumstances the refusal of the Great Northern Board to commit itself to support the "Great Northern, Holborn, and City Bill" seems to have been very reasonable.

The result was that the Metropolitan Company was left in the posesssion of the field, and, having obtained the right man for engineer in Mr. John Fowler, it pressed on at last with the construction of its line. But the bursting of the Fleet Ditch and other difficulties had still had to be surmounted, and so it was not until January, 1863, that the first section from Paddington *via* King's Cross to Farringdon Street was ready for opening. Nor was it until August of the year that the Great Northern trains came first upon the line.

The occasion for their first coming was rather dramatic. The Metropolitan was laid originally as a "mixed gauge" line—*i.e.* its rails were laid on both broad and narrow gauge—and it was worked at the outset by the Great Western Company. Towards the close of July, 1863, however, a dispute between the Great Western and Metropolitan Boards culminated in a summary notice from the former to the latter that after 9 August, 1863, they should withdraw their rolling stock. Thus Mr. (afterwards Sir Myles) Fenton, the manager of the Metropolitan, found himself in the position of having to find within ten days sufficient engines and carriages to work at least a quarter-of-an-hour service over his line. In this emergency he threw himself upon the generosity of the Great Northern and London and North Western, and from both these companies he obtained the loan of carriages; but engines were not so easy to find, seeing that under the Metropolitan Company's Acts those emitting steam and smoke in the ordinary way could not be used. Fortunately, however, Mr. Sturrock had already prepared at the shops at Doncaster a few smoke-condensing engines for the Great Northern's own "underground" traffic—the commencement of which had been arranged for 1 September, 1863—and some others he now adapted within the time available by fitting them with a pipe and flexible tube leading from the exhaust pipe of the engine to the tender.

When the rolling stock was thus provided, however, a new difficulty presented itself. This was that the "middle rail" for narrow-gauge working was found to be defective. Consequently the first few days of the new arrangements were a time of great anxiety to all concerned. However, all difficulties were successfully surmounted, and on 1 October, 1863, the Great Northern's "suburban and city" service was commenced. The passengers by the first through train to Farringdon Street are said to have expressed their delight by swooping down in force upon a refreshment buffet, newly opened at the station, and consuming all it contained.

Being still confined to a few stations on the main line, the suburban traffic was as yet quite a small affair. The through connection with the City, however, was expected at once to increase it; moreover, in the session of 1862 an Act had been obtained by an independent company for branches to Highgate, Finchley, and Edgware, primarily for suburban residential traffic. Near the crossing over the Seven Sisters Road, at which point the new branch was to leave the main line, a couple of

---

GREAT NORTHERN RAILWAY.

On and after the 1st July,
A NEW STATION
WILL BE
OPENED
AT
SEVEN SISTERS' ROAD,
HOLLOWAY,

At which Passenger Trains will call as under:

DOWN.	WEEK DAYS.	SUNDAYS.
King's Cross...dep.	6.30, 9.35, 11.20, 3.0, 5.10, 6.5, 7.0, 9.20	7.30, 9.0, 5.20, 6.0
UP. Seven Sisters' Road ..dep.	8.20, 9.18, 11.25, 1.20, 5.20, 7.15, 8.41	9.35, 8.28, 8.55

Fares between King's Cross and Seven Sisters' Road Stations.

SINGLE.			RETURN.	
1st Class.	2nd Class.	3rd Class.	1st Class.	2nd Class.
7d.	4d.	2½d.	10d.	6d.

SEASON TICKETS.

1st Class ...	£2 9 0	£3 3 0	£3 16 0	£4 7 6	£4 14	£5 7 6	£5 15 6	£6 9 6	£6 11 6	£7 10
2nd Class ...	1 11 6	2 0 6	2 8 9	2 16 3	3 3	3 9 0	3 14 3	3 15 9	4 4 6	4 10

No Goods or Coal business will be conducted at Seven Sisters' Station.

By order,   SEYMOUR CLARKE,
London, King's Cross Station, 26th June, 1861.   General Manager.

Waterlow and Sons, Printers, Carpenters' Hall, London Wall.

---

wooden platforms, hardly deserving the name of a station, had been opened from 1 July, 1861, for the accommodation of the few residents in that rural neighbourhood. This was the very humble beginning of the important station now known as Finsbury Park.

The new junction with the North London at Maiden Lane, which was opened in 1862, proved at once very useful not only for traffic to and from the Royal Mint Street Depôt, but also for traffic with the London Docks; but the Company had not had to wait for this before commencing a through London dock traffic. Since March, 1858, it had enjoyed a very serviceable through route to the docks by way of the Welwyn and Hertford Railway. As early as 1853 an independent company had been formed to construct this line, seven miles in length, with the object principally of connecting the Great Northern and Eastern Counties systems at their southern ends; and, in accordance with this object, arrangements had been made under which the line, when opened, had been worked over by both those companies. At the same time a system of "through booking" to and from Great Northern stations and Victoria Docks, Blackwall, and other Eastern Counties stations near London had been brought into force. These arrangements had lasted until 1860, when an extension of the Hertford and Welwyn line on the western side of the Great Northern to Luton and Dunstable had been completed, giving the centre of the straw plait industry its first railway communication. Thereupon the Great Northern directors had entered into negotiations with the small Company—now called the Hertford, Luton, and Dunstable—which had ended in its being permanently absorbed into the Great Northern in 1861 at a guaranteed dividend.

Though continuing the through bookings to and from the London Docks, the Eastern Counties directors showed a disposition to regard the presence of the Great Northern with its own line at Hertford as a breach of the territorial division of 1852; nor was this the only act of the sort of which they found cause to complain about this time. For the session of 1862 the King's Cross Board joined in promoting a Bill to enable their Company to acquire the undertaking of the "Norwich and Spalding Company," the part of whose line already opened, from Spalding to Holbeach, the Great Northern was already working, and as the whole undertaking, despite its title, extended as far as Sutton Bridge only, they at the same time entered into negotiations with another small company which had just obtained powers to continue the through route to Norwich from Sutton as far as Lynn. Under these circumstances it is not surprising that the Eastern Counties directors took alarm. It looked as if the Great Northern, not content with having thrust the Eastern Counties aside from sharing in all the best of the "through" traffic, was now going to make its own route from the North to Norwich, and thus divert from the established route *via* Peterborough some more of such scanty long-distance traffic which the Eastern Counties Company still possessed. As matters turned out, however, the alarm proved groundless. The Great Northern and Norwich and Spalding Amalgamation Bill was withdrawn before reaching Parliament, the latter Company preferring to await the completion of a line which another small company had just projected from Spalding to Bourn in the hope that together with the Bourn and Essendine and Essendine and Stamford Railways they might in time make up a trunk route between the Midlands and the east coast.*

Nevertheless, the peace which, since the territorial division of 1852, had reigned between the Great Northern and Eastern Counties companies, was not destined to last much longer. Under the treaty of 1852, as the reader may remember, the country east of the Great Northern main line, between the Wash and the Thames, had been given over, so far as London traffic was concerned, to the Eastern Counties Company for a term of fourteen years—the Hitchin and Shepreth line having been physically transferred under the arrangement,—and at the same time it had been arranged that the latter should receive a bonus of 20 per cent. on all through traffic to the north which it handed over to the Great Northern at Peterborough. As to through traffic *from* the north, however, there had been no arrangement, and thus the Eastern Counties Company had not been able to obtain any adequate share in the traffic to London from the coalfields and manufacturing districts of Yorkshire. From Derbyshire, by way of the Midland's Syston and Peterborough line, it was able to obtain some coal, not only for its country stations but for a Metropolitan depôt which it had opened at Whitechapel; but the route over the "sigmoid flexure" (as Charles Austin had once called the Syston and Peterborough line), and thence from Peterborough *via* March and Ely, was very circuitous, and the traffic consequently was not very profitable.

This state of things nothing but sheer weakness had compelled the Eastern Counties Company to put up with so long, and so matters had assumed a different aspect when, in 1862, the amalgamation which produced the Great Eastern Railway had at last been successfully carried through. Prior to this the Board at Shoreditch had been obliged to devote what little spare strength it had to keeping peace between the numerous small companies which occupied the northern parts of its district. Now their combined energies could be directed to a revival of the policy of King Hudson and his predecessors— the policy of converting the line from Shoreditch to Cambridge into a through route between London and the north.

Indeed, if the Great Eastern was to be made to pay, this policy was

* Meantime the Norwich and Spalding (which from 1 July, 1862, was opened throughout to Sutton Bridge), the Bourn and Essendine (opened June, 1860), and the Stamford and Essendine (opened October, 1856) were all worked by the Great Northern as branches.

practically the only one available. In the existing state of things, as Mr. Hope Scott put the matter to a Parliamentary Committee, the Company was "in the painful position of having a great deal of railway which had cost a great sum of money, but very little traffic." True, it had now had the monopoly of a large district; but, as Mr. George Parker Bidder —the man who had done more than any other to bring about the Great Eastern amalgamation—said on the same occasion, "land has its limits of production. It can only grow a certain quantity of wheat and grain, and feed a certain quantity of cattle. We are therefore driven to go out of our district for traffic." "What you want," retorted Mr. Hope Scott, "is to take some of the fat off the Great Northern dividend and apply it in the form of lard to your more meagre system. You have gone to the sea for fish, you have gone to Holland for Dutchmen" —this was in allusion to the steamboat service which the Great Eastern had just started from Harwich—"and now you want to invade the Great Northern district for coals."

It was, indeed, a coal traffic from the Yorkshire field after which the newly-formed Great Eastern Company specially hankered; for, as things were, a few thousand tons only was all of South Yorkshire coal which found its way to the Whitechapel depôt. For this, of course, the reasons were obvious: first, that the best route available —*via* Peterborough—was circuitous; and, second, that it did not suit the Great Northern directors to make favourable through rates by this route, inasmuch as traffic over it would in all likelihood be diverted from their own route to King's Cross. Accordingly, to improve their position effectually, the Great Eastern had to do two things—first, to shorten their route, and, second, to obtain a power to fix through rates; and with this view its directors promoted a Bill in the session of 1863 for a new line from March to Spalding, whence to Doncaster they had asked for running powers over the Great Northern's loop and main lines. In opposition to this the Great Northern directors themselves promoted a line from Spalding to March, and over this they offered to the Great Eastern, not running powers, but full facilities for exchange of traffic at March.

'Between these two conflicting proposals it was found impossible to effect a peaceful compromise. Accordingly, a Parliamentary contest resulted. In the Commons the Great Northern secured a complete victory, their Bill being passed and that of the Great Eastern thrown out; but in the Lords the Great Eastern secured running powers over the new line to Spalding. By another Act the Great Northern obtained power to flatten the gradients of its loop line between Spalding and Gainsborough; but the attempt which it revived again this session to get powers to make the loop really what its name implied, by extending it to a second junction with the main line near Doncaster (and so superseding the circuitous run over the Manchester, Sheffield, and Lincolnshire line to Retford), proved fruitless. The district south-east of Doncaster is a great hunting country, and again, as in 1848 (if the reader has not forgotten the rejection of the same line then), "horse-flesh proved stronger than iron."

However, in view of the designs of the Great Eastern Company, the Great Northern directors realized that they must make new exertions if they were to retain their hold upon the South Yorkshire coal traffic and upon Lincolnshire. So, for the session of 1864, they deposited a Bill for the fifth time for the completion of the loop from Gainsborough to Doncaster, while in a second Bill for the same session they sought powers to make a new line, about eighteen miles in length, from Honington to Lincoln, in order to shorten the distance between London and Lincoln, by making a new route *via* Grantham. In connection with this latter scheme, they proposed to absorb the undertaking of the Boston, Sleaford, and Midland Counties Railway Company—from Barkstone, near Grantham, through Honington and Sleaford to Boston—the working of which they had already in hand.* They further proposed to make a new line from Sleaford southwards to Bourn, also about eighteen miles in length, and to absorb the undertaking of the Bourn and Essendine Company, thus providing themselves with a new loop line. By these measures they reckoned to block the advance of hostile lines by the Great Eastern.

These precautions were the more necessary because the Great Eastern was far from being satisfied with the running powers it had obtained to Spalding (which, indeed, were of little use to it), and so was coming to the session of 1864 with a really bold and far-reaching plan of campaign. In this the prime mover was none other than Mr. Robert Baxter, who had been called in by the Great Eastern Board as their Parliamentary adviser, and he had brought to the business not only ripe experience and an intimate knowledge of railway promotion in the district, but a personal enthusiasm for the principal object which the Great Eastern authorities had in view. As we have already noted, what Mr. Bidder and his colleagues wanted above all things was to develop a coal traffic from South Yorkshire to their London terminus, and the reader does not need to be told that there was no man who believed more strongly in the possibilities of such a traffic than Mr. Baxter. It was he who had startled the railway world by first proposing it in 1845; now he startled the railway world

* Opened, Barkstone to Sleaford, June 1857; Sleaford to Boston, April 1859.

again by declaring that, notwithstanding the large traffic which the Great Northern was already doing from South Yorkshire, and notwithstanding the certainty that with the completion of the Midland system to London the competition of Derbyshire coal would become keener even than it already was, there was room for the construction of a new line, the primary object of which was to be the supply to the Metropolis of South Yorkshire coal.

The idea of constructing a trunk line to London for coal traffic only was not itself a novel one. No less an authority than "old George Stephenson" is said to have favoured it in earlier days, and a line of the sort from the Durham coalfield to the Metropolis had been actually projected by a Mr. Thomas Wood of Durham. Later Mr. (afterwards Sir John) Hawkshaw had taken up with the notion, and now this eminent engineer was persuaded by Mr. Baxter to join with Mr. John Fowler, who was just fresh from his triumph over the Fleet Ditch and other "Metropolitan" obstacles, in laying out a "coal line" to run from South Yorkshire to the Great Eastern system. It was christened the "Great Eastern Northern Junction Railway," promoted by a new company, half the capital of which was guaranteed by the Great Eastern and half by the "General Credit and Finance Association," and supported in Parliament, not only by the Great Eastern, but by the West Riding and Grimsby and South Yorkshire companies.

The line which Messrs. Fowler and Hawkshaw produced was planned to run from Long Stanton, a place on the Great Eastern system between Cambridge and St. Ives, *viâ* Peterborough, Bourn, Sleaford, Lincoln, and Gainsborough, to a junction with the West Riding and Grimsby Company's system at Askern, a distance of 108 miles; in other words, it proposed to occupy the country between the main and loop lines of the Great Northern, following much the same course as Hudson's Cambridge and Lincoln line of 1845. But, though it professed to serve the towns just named, it was laid out to pass, not *through* them as an ordinary line would have done, but *outside* them, making connection with them by branches. These made up its total length of 134 miles in all. By thus avoiding town property it was hoped to ensure cheapness in the cost of construction, despite the fact that to ensure cheapness of working no gradient on it was to exceed 1 in 400; that, in fact, the line was to be on a dead level throughout its whole course.

It was upon this proposed levelness that the main argument for the new line was based. On such a line, it was contended, the maximum train-load of coal for one engine might be increased from 240 tons—the then limit on the Great Northern—to 400 tons; in short, the line

MAP OF RAILWAYS IN LINCOLNSHIRE, &c.

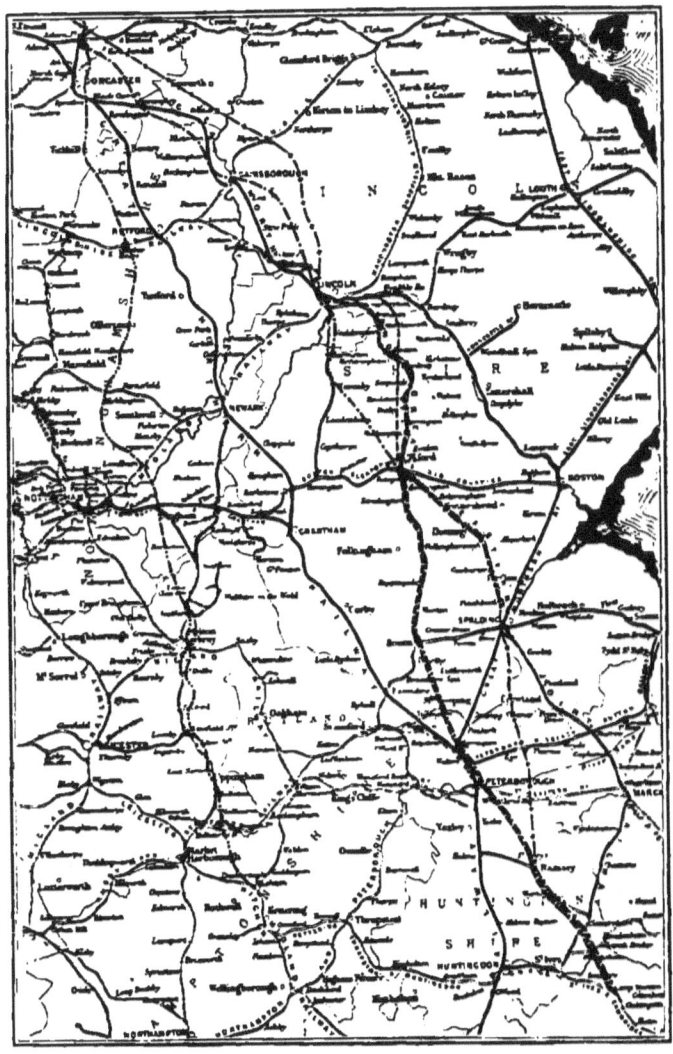

REFERENCE

Great Northern Railway (Main & Loop Lines)   shown thus _____
Great Eastern Northern Junction Railway, proposed 1864 _ _ _ _ _ _
Coal Owners Associated London Railway   1871 _ _ _ _ _ _ _
Midland & Manchester, Sheffield & Lincolnshire Rly. 1873 _ _ _ _ _
Great Eastern Northern Extension Railway, proposed 1878 _ . _ . _ .

was put forward as "incomparably the finest in the kingdom" for coal traffic, and "equivalent to the invention of a new machine to do the same work as the old at two-thirds of the cost." Moreover, the Great Eastern authorities, under Mr. Baxter's advice, gave practical proof of their belief in its possibilities by offering to carry long-distance coal over it at the unprecedentedly low rate of $\frac{1}{4}$d. a mile—"the fascinating farthing," a facetious counsel called it—provided the coal was handed to them in full train-loads.

These were the principal features of the "Great Eastern Northern Junction Railway," as it was first prepared for presentation to Parliament in 1864 by Messrs. Baxter, Bidder, and Bartholomew (the reader remembers the latter as manager of the South Yorkshire Railway in 1852); but when the counter-plans of the Great Northern became known to them, the three "busy B's, bent on bettering themselves," as the promoters were nicknamed, found it necessary to alter their project a little. For, while for coal traffic the Great Northern loop line, when its gradients were flattened, and it was completed to Doncaster, promised to afford almost, if not quite, as efficient a "machine" as their own, the Great Northern's other proposed extensions offered what in its original form their "rude coal line" had no pretensions to, namely, substantial improvements to the general accommodation of the locality. Consequently, despite the fact that as a main line their scheme was to give Lincoln, Peterborough, and the other towns the go-by, and to neglect small consignments in search of full train-loads, Mr. Baxter and his associates had to endeavour to prove that for general local requirements—for Lincoln passengers, Haxey potatoes, and Ancaster stone, for example —they could give as efficient a service as the Great Northern.

The result was that "the Busy B's" modified their plans. As eventually presented to Parliament, their scheme was described not as a coal line simply, but as a line "perfect in all respects, with a special adaptation to the carrying of coal." "Mr. Fowler," said Mr. Hope Scott, when on behalf of the Great Northern he came to criticise the engineering evidence, "adopts the French *spécialité*, and just as a French tailor would put up *spécialité de pantalons*, when he wanted you to buy coats and waistcoats quite as much as nether garments, so Mr. Fowler, laying out his line for the general merchant tailor business, makes a *spécialité* of this particular adaptation."

The fight before the House of Commons Committee was the longest since the historic fight over the "London and York." It lasted through twenty-five sittings, and the chairman, Sir John Hamner, being in bad health to start with, became so knocked up before the end that on some days he had to be carried between the committee-room and his bed. For the promoters and against the Great Northern Mr. Baxter worked as hard and as zealously as nineteen years before he had worked for the Great Northern and against a line almost identical with the one he now championed. According to Mr. Hope Scott, who with Mr. E. B. Denison conducted the opposition, "Mr. Baxter drew Mr. Burke's brief; Mr. Baxter drew the greater part of Mr. Bidder's evidence, and Mr. Baxter was called himself." The Committee had "Baxter *à la* Burke, Baxter *à la* Bidder, and Baxter *au naturel*." Nevertheless, in spite of all this, and in spite of the weighty engineering evidence of Messrs. Fowler, Hawkshaw, and Daniel Gooch, the Great Eastern Northern Junction Bill was rejected, and every one of the Great Northern proposals was authorized, except the Sleaford and Bourn line, which, however, got through in the following session.

The "Busy B's," however, were not yet beaten, and in the House of Lords they renewed the contest with a view to securing running powers for the Great Eastern. All they obtained, however, was "facility clauses" providing for the passage of Great Eastern traffic over the Great Northern loop line at rates to be mutually agreed, with an appeal in case of disagreement to an arbitrator—clauses which the Great Northern had offered before the Parliamentary fight and the fairness of which was now confirmed by both Houses. In this same session, in view of the lapsing in 1866 of the agreement under which the Great Eastern was working the Shepreth and Hitchin line, the Great Northern renewed its application for admission to Cambridge; and, by threatening to make a line of its own into the town, obtained running powers from Shepreth over the Great Eastern, the latter promising to double its line between Shepreth and Shelford for the purpose.

In this great fight of 1864 the historian has missed—and the reader too, perhaps—the inspiring presence and "swashing blows" of Mr. Edmund Denison. The fact is that the old chairman's fighting days were nearly over. At the age of 77 gout and other ailments could not as in the old days be shaken off at the call to battle; and not only was Mr. Denison not in the committee-room, but he could not occupy his place at either of the Great Northern half-yearly meetings in 1864. He was a remarkably robust man, and he had ten more years yet to live; nevertheless, and in spite of the unanimous resolution of his colleagues to the contrary, he resigned in December, 1864, not only the chairmanship but his seat on the Board, on the ground that he was no longer strong enough to perform the duties adequately. He had been the leader of the undertaking, as we know, almost from its first origination twenty-one years before, and from 1847 he had been its titular as wel as its real head. "From the beginning," said his successor, Colonel Packe, who also had been associated with the Company since its origin, "his whole mind has been devoted to one object, namely, to bring the Company to perfection, and to work it for the benefit of the shareholders."

In this, as the reader knows, he had encountered continuous and extraordinary opposition, but in the end he had been singularly successful. For the half-year to 31 December, 1864, the dividend declared by the directors was at the rate of £8 15s. on the original stock, making the rate for the year £7 2s. 6d.—the highest yet reached; while for the two preceding years it had been £6 10s. In short, to quote again from Colonel Packe, there was "no other undertaking so large and having overcome so many difficulties which was paying a better dividend." Mr. Denison had "succeeded in getting and working one of the best railways of the country." He had shown himself at times, perhaps, unduly combative, and in return he had been, as we have seen, the recipient of a very large amount of public, and even personal, abuse. But the feeling cherished with regard to him by the vast majority of those with whom he came in contact cannot be better demonstrated than by a quotation from a speech delivered at the time of his retirement by Mr. Seneca Hughes—a Great Northern shareholder who, like Mr. Denison, had been associated with the undertaking from its beginning, and who at the time of the Redpath frauds, as we have seen, and at many others had been a constant assailant of the policy of the Board. "Mr. Denison," said Mr. Hughes, "was an example of what a chairman ought to be at a public meeting. He displayed remarkably good temper, though he had every opportunity given him of displaying irascibility. Throughout he manifested so good a disposition that I believe he won the hearts of all who attended these meetings." He was succeeded on the Great Northern Board by his son, Mr. Christopher Denison.

Before leaving behind the Parliamentary session of 1864, we must note that in it had been settled the very vexed question of the destiny of the South Yorkshire Railway. So long before as June, 1861—to refresh the reader's memory—the Manchester, Sheffield, and Lincolnshire Company had formally agreed to lease this line; but in the spring of 1862 the negotiations for making the lease a joint one with the Great Northern had been revived informally by the chairmen of the two companies, Messrs. Denison and Chapman, and then, for the second time, the Great Northern had come very near to getting a control of the coalfield system. On the first occasion, in 1852, it will be remembered, it had been Mr. Denison's "lukewarmness" chiefly which had broken off the matter, but in these second negotiations the course of events had been the reverse of this. After Mr. Denison had agreed with Mr. Chapman to take the half lease (on the condition that the exorbitant terms extracted by Mr. Baxter from Mr. Watkin should be reduced to a fixed 5 per cent. guarantee to the South Yorkshire), a majority of the Great Northern Board had refused to ratify the bargain. The result had been that in the session of 1863 the Sheffield Company had promoted a Bill to authorize it to take the lease alone.

This Bill the Great Northern had opposed on the ground that its access to the coalfield had not been properly secured under it, and the fight before the House of Commons Committee had proved a very fierce one. Nominally the victory had gone to the Great Northern, for the Committee had reduced in its favour the tolls chargeable on coal exchanged at Doncaster; but really the triumph had proved an empty one, for the Sheffield directors had declined to proceed with the Bill on these terms. In the session of 1864, however, they had introduced another, and before this had reached committee stage the parties, wearied of conflict, had come to an agreement as to the tolls, which, while it fell short of the Committee's decision in 1863, gave security and some relief to the Great Northern traffic. On these terms the Bill had been allowed to pass, and thus the Manchester, Sheffield, and Lincolnshire Company had obtained possession of the South Yorkshire Railway, albeit at a cost which was to prove very oppressive to itself. To what extent Mr. Watkin (who had returned to the Sheffield in 1863, and in January, 1864, had become its chairman) was able to compensate the shareholders for the "commercial" badness of the bargain by using it as a "political" weapon against the Great Northern, we shall see as this history proceeds.

Meantime the destinies of three other small Yorkshire railways in which the Great Northern was interested—the Leeds, Bradford, and Halifax, the West Yorkshire, and the West Riding and Grimsby—remained to be settled. The latter was not yet ready for traffic, but the two former, as the reader knows, had now been worked over by the Great Northern for a good number of years. They had been worked over since their first opening also by the Lancashire and Yorkshire Company, in whose direct route between Lancashire and the West Riding, indeed, they formed links almost, if not quite, as important as in the Great Northern's route between the West Riding and London. It had therefore been for some time pretty obvious that either the Great Northern or the Lancashire and Yorkshire, or the two companies jointly, would sooner or later acquire full possession of the two small systems; but the fact that there were thus two would-be purchasers in the field was making the sale of them a more complex and tedious operation than it might otherwise have been.

The Leeds, Bradford, and Halifax Company (which in 1856-7 had added to its original Leeds to Bowling line an extension through Gildersome to join the West Yorkshire at Ardsley) was the first to be brought to terms, it being arranged in 1863 that it should be leased permanently by the Great Northern for the guarantee of 7 per cent. dividend for every 5 per cent. the Great Northern earned. But when sanction for this arrangement was sought from Parliament in the session of 1864 the opposition of the Lancashire and Yorkshire brought about its refusal. In the meantime, however, the Great Northern had come to terms with the West Yorkshire Company also, having agreed to lease its undertaking—a main line from Wakefield to Leeds, branches to Batley and to Ossett, and a third share in a joint line to Methley—at a guarantee of a minimum dividend of 6 per cent.; and, as this arrangement strengthened their claim to secure the Leeds, Bradford, and Halifax, the King's Cross Board decided to prosecute Bills for both in the session of 1865. As for the Lancashire and Yorkshire, to it they were willing to give full facilities for the passage of its through trains over the lines, but with this, they contended, it ought to be satisfied. Twenty years before it might have made the direct lines between the West Riding towns itself, but instead of that—as we noted in an earlier part of this book—it had first opposed, and then acquired only to abandon, the "West Riding Union" undertaking, leaving the objects of this to be subsequently carried out by the Leeds, Bradford, and West Yorkshire companies. In short—in the language of Mr. Hope Scott—the Lancashire and Yorkshire had "endeavoured to keep out the tide of railway improvement in the West Riding by arguments little better than Mrs. Partington's, which was a mop, you know"; whereas the Great Northern had come in with, and moved with, the tide. Was it not about time, then, that Mrs. Partington should step aside?

But Mrs. Partington would not step aside. On the contrary, that "most wealthy, most respectable, and most conservative company"—to quote a description of the Lancashire and Yorkshire given by Mr. Baxter in 1864 to a House of Commons Committee—was roused by a sense of injury to unprecedented exertions. That it had lost its chance of buying up the two Leeds lines was not the only grievance it had at this time. A second grievance was that by a subterfuge the direct route from Doncaster to Wakefield had been obtained, on to which the Great Northern's through traffic was about to be diverted from the old

Knottingley route; and yet a third, that the North Eastern Company had just obtained powers for a direct line from York to Doncaster, to follow the same course as the abandoned Askern and York section of the "London and York," and that by this, too, the use of the Lancashire

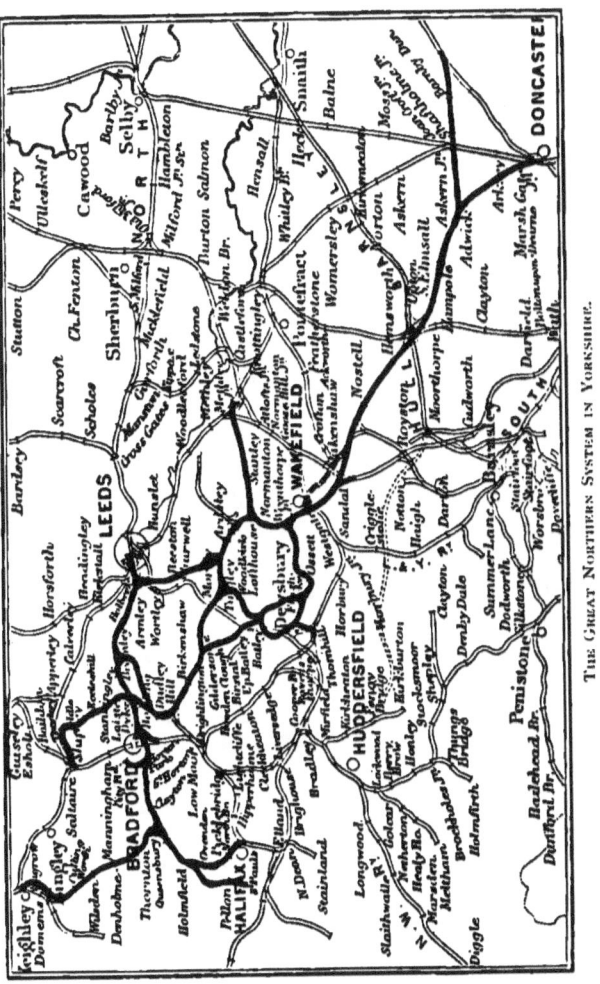

THE GREAT NORTHERN SYSTEM IN YORKSHIRE.

and Yorkshire's Askern to Knottingley line was to be superseded. That these substitutions of direct for circuitous lines were inevitable results of the rise of the tide of improvement Mrs. Partington refused to recognize. She felt only that she was being hardly used.

The result of this feeling was a violent reaction, under stress of which the Lancashire and Yorkshire passed at one bound from being the most conservative to being the most revolutionary of railway companies. In the autumn of 1864 its directors joined hands with the directors of the Great Eastern with no less an object than to revive the just rejected Long Stanton to Doncaster project. But this time it was not to be put forward as a coal line primarily. It was to be a main connection between the Great Eastern and the Lancashire and Yorkshire systems — a new fourth trunk line, in short, between London and the North.

The effect of this proposal was felt in every railway boardroom in England; but the companies which it concerned most were the Great Northern and Manchester, Sheffield, and Lincolnshire. It threatened them together as joint carriers between London and Lancashire, and it threatened them separately, the one as the London and West Riding railway and the other as the main railway between Lancashire and Lincolnshire. They were bound, therefore, to draw together for defensive action; and that that action should be thoroughgoing became Mr. Watkin's peculiar care. His policy of forcing the Great Northern to buy up the Sheffield for "political" reasons had by this time recovered from the shock administered to it by the inopportune admission of the Midland to Manchester. He still calculated that amalgamation was sure to come sooner or later, and that the more intimate he could make the relationship of the two companies the quicker and better terms he would get for his shareholders.

From this point of view he felt it to be extremely fortunate that the direct line from Doncaster to Wakefield—a line more important than ever to the Great Northern now that the Lancashire and Yorkshire had turned hostile—was in the hands of the West Riding and Grimsby Company. For, as the reader knows, this undertaking, besides being a direct railway between Wakefield and Doncaster, was also, as its name expressed, a link in a through route between the West Riding and Grimsby; and, because it was this, the Sheffield Company, in the interest of its docks at Grimsby, had subscribed to its capital. For these reasons Mr. Watkin had a considerable hold on the small company; and so when, in the autumn of 1864, the Great Northern wanted to buy it up so as to prevent it from falling into the hands of the Lancashire and Yorkshire and Great Eastern combination, he was able to urge, very reasonably, that, if it was bought up at all, not the Great Northern, but the Great Northern and Sheffield jointly must be the purchaser. Thus, without appearing to have any ulterior motives, he was able to put the Sheffield on the way to becoming half-owners of the Great Northern's future means of access to the West Riding.

Thus one new partnership between the Great Northern and Sheffield was set on foot; but Mr. Watkin had a much larger enterprise of the same kind in view, to understand which we must turn aside for a moment to see how matters have been progressing in Lancashire. Of the four "Cheshire lines," in financial support to which the Sheffield and Great Northern companies were already, as we know, jointly involved, two—the Stockport and Woodley and Cheshire Midland—had been opened in 1863, and the Garston and Liverpool—also a joint Sheffield and Great Northern affair—had at the time we have now reached just been opened, completing, in conjunction with a series of London and North Western lines, over which, it may be remembered, the Great Northern and Sheffield had obtained running powers, a new route between Manchester and Liverpool. Since the authorization of these arrangements, however, the Midland, as we know, had obtained access over the Sheffield system into Manchester, and it naturally wanted to get to Liverpool also. Accordingly, it was now proposed that the Midland should be admitted to a third share in the Garston and Liverpool line, and that the Cheshire lines should at the same time be wholly bought up and vested in the same tripartite ownership. This, with the running powers they possessed from Manchester to Garston, promised to secure to the three companies access to Liverpool and the territory west of Manchester generally, no matter what competition the Lancashire and Yorkshire or London and North Western might set up.

These arrangements were agreed to, and embodied in a Bill, but they did not fully satisfy Mr. Watkin. With one of those bold and sudden strokes with which he was wont to disconcert, not only his opponents, but his allies, he deposited at the same time another Bill for a new direct line from Manchester to Garston on the ground that the "running-power route" was not adequate for the three companies' traffic. The Bill was deposited in the name of the Sheffield Company only, but obviously Mr. Watkin calculated upon receiving support in Parliament, and financial aid afterwards, from the Great Northern and Midland; nor was he disappointed. In view of the proposed combination between the Lancashire and Yorkshire and the Great Eastern, the Great Northern and Midland had special reasons for wishing to strengthen their positions in Lancashire; they were also both quite dependent there upon alliance with the Manchester, Sheffield, and Lincolnshire. They thus found themselves compelled by "political" more than by commercial considerations to back Mr. Watkin's new

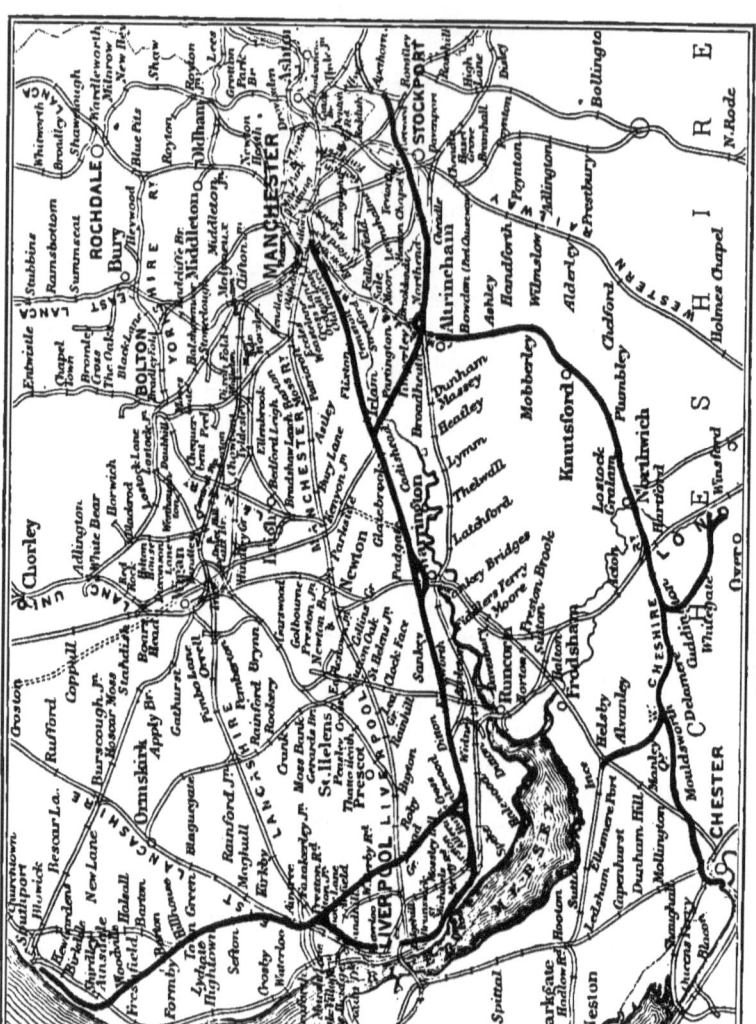

"The Cheshire Lines" Joint System.

direct line against the opposition of the London and North Western and Lancashire and Yorkshire.

Thus to the fighting session of 1864 succeeded a fighting session of 1865; but one of the most important battles in it—the battle with the "Great Eastern and Lancashire and Yorkshire Junction Bill"— was easily decided. The Bill was not allowed to reach Committee stage; it was thrown out on second reading in the Commons on 14 March, 1865. In vain did Mr. John Bright and other Radical members—practically ignorant of the merits of the question—plead in favour of "free trade in railways," and protest that the Great Eastern was being excluded from the north because its line would be so much the best—so much more efficient a "machine," to recall Mr. Baxter's word—that it would ruin the existing ones. The Great Northern was not trying to exclude the Great Eastern from the north; it had offered full facilities for interchange at March, and it had even gone so far in October, 1864, as to offer running powers for coal traffic from March to Doncaster at rates to be mutually agreed or settled by arbitration. Seeing that this was more even than a Parliamentary Committee after the fullest consideration had considered the Great Eastern entitled to, the House rightly decided that the Great Northern should not be put to the expense of fighting the battle in Committee over again.

There were contests in Committee, however, over the Leeds, Bradford, and Halifax and West Yorkshire Amalgamation Bills, and over the Bill for the new direct line between Manchester and Liverpool; but in all of them the Great Northern was on the winning side. The two Leeds lines were secured without great difficulty (though Mr. Vernon Harcourt worked hard for the Lancashire and Yorkshire); but the Manchester and Liverpool Bill evoked a battle-royal. However, with Mr. Watkin as chief witness and Mr. Denison, Q.C., as leading counsel (an unusual spectacle this Watkin-cum-Denison combination!), the Sheffield and its allies bore down all opposition, and the "fifth line" between Manchester and Liverpool received the sanction of Parliament.

Thus as the outcome of two fighting sessions the Great Northern repulsed the aggression of the Great Eastern, and consolidated its position as a trunk line to the West Riding of Yorkshire, to Lincolnshire, and to Lancashire. These were great things to do, but as we shall see later they were not done without cost. Mr. Denison was very fortunate in leaving the Company when he did. Its status among the established lines had been secured, and the effect of new competition had not yet been greatly felt.

CHAPTER XIV.

GENERAL PROGRESS, INTERRUPTED BY A STARTLING ACCIDENT.
1866-1867.

IN following up the part played by the Great Northern Company in the development of traffic between England and Scotland, it is important to distinguish between the East Coast route and the East Coast joint service. The title "East Coast Route," though now often applied to the whole line of railway from King's Cross *viâ* York, Newcastle, and Berwick to Edinburgh, properly belongs only to the part of this line north of York; and that part, as we saw in an earlier section of this book, was carried through by Hudson and the Stephensons prior to the construction of the Great Northern between York and London, and without any regard for Great Northern interests. It was in the interest of the old route between York and London—the Midland route *viâ* Derby and Rugby—that the Railway King worked so hard to connect York with Edinburgh; but, by the irony of fate, it was decreed that the Midland should enjoy the through traffic for a very few years only. Almost from its first opening into London, as we have seen, the Great Northern—Hudson's *bête-noir*—superseded the Midland as the channel for "East Coast" traffic to and from the Metropolis.

But, whilst the East Coast route itself was thus to the Great Northern a fortunate inheritance bequeathed to it in spite of himself by its great opponent, the East Coast joint service, so far as it was established at the date we have now reached, was to a very large extent the Great Northern's creation. It had been the Great Northern which, by running (as soon as its towns line was opened in 1852) its 191 miles between London and York in five hours, had enabled the whole 402 miles between London and Edinburgh to be covered by the East Coast in eleven hours, an hour less than by the rival West Coast route; and it had been the Great Northern which, despite shareholders' grumblings as to increased working expenses, had supplied the carriages which had run through between King's Cross and Edinburgh almost from the first. Moreover, it had been at the suggestion of the Great Northern that a special stock of carriages had been provided for this purpose from 1860—the common property of the Great Northern, North Eastern, and North British companies, and known from that date as the East Coast Joint Stock.

This event marked the definite admission of the Great Northern as London partner in the East Coast alliance. The "alternative East Coast route," *viâ* Normanton and Derby, had, as we know, been given some prominence in the English and Scotch "pool" of 1856, but by 1860 it had become a mere shadow. The Great Northern, North Eastern, and North British companies were recognized from that date onwards as *the three* "East Coast Companies," and as such they began, as we shall now see, to work together to protect their interests in northern Scotland.

Under the agreement of 1856, as the reader already knows, the East Coast route had been admitted to a half-share of the traffic beyond Edinburgh; nevertheless, its position in Glasgow, Perth, Aberdeen, etc., had by no means been secured. The North British rails ended at Edinburgh; for access westwards and northwards of that capital it was dependent upon facilities given it by the Edinburgh and Glasgow and Scottish Central companies, and these companies were "West Coast" by traditional sympathy; so much so, indeed, that but for the opposition in Parliament of the East Coast companies they would have become definitely "West Coast" in 1860 by amalgamation into the Caledonian. Accordingly if, when the agreement of 1856 expired and a new division of the Anglo-Scotch traffic had to be made, the East Coast companies were to be in a position to enforce their claim to as large or a larger share than they already had, it seemed necessary that their status beyond Edinburgh should be improved.

It had been under these circumstances that Mr. Richard Hodgson, the very able and ambitious chairman of the North British Company, had conceived the idea of bridging the estuaries of the Forth and the Tay, acquiring the system of the Edinburgh, Perth, and Dundee Company (over whose route through Fife, it will be remembered, the East Coast companies had made an attempt to work in connection with ferries across the Forth and Tay in 1854, when the Edinburgh and Glasgow and Scottish Central had held the door to the north shut fast against them), and so making an East Coast route proper not only to Perth, but also to Dundee, for Aberdeen. The plan, of course, had seemed a startlingly bold one from an engineering point of view; but it had been at once taken up in earnest by the North British engineer, Mr. (afterwards Sir) Thomas Bouch, and he had prepared designs for Forth and Tay bridges. The former was to consist of a number of large spans of 500 feet each, with approach viaducts in shorter spans at either end.

The next step of the North British Company had been to seek powers to absorb the Edinburgh, Perth, and Dundee system, and this it had accomplished by an Act of 1862. Then a great deal of plotting and counter-plotting had taken place between the North British and its allies, on the one hand, and the Caledonian and its allies on the other; and the outcome of it all was the signing on 12 May, 1865, of a "Scotch Territorial Agreement." Under this Mr. Hodgson secured the withdrawal of Caledonian opposition to his company's bills for bridges across the Forth and Tay, and to the amalgamation of the Edinburgh and Glasgow with the North British. But, as the price of it, he had himself to consent to the Caledonian acquiring the Scottish Central.

Thus, by the exertions of their Scotch partner, the East Coast companies secured the ownership of a route to Glasgow, and the prospect of a route of their own to Perth and Dundee; but, having regard to the magnitude of the works involved, the latter prospect was rather a remote one; and, meanwhile, by the amalgamation of the Scottish Central with the Caledonian, the existing route was to be given over to definite West Coast ownership. This to the North Eastern and Great Northern did not seem to be a state of things in which it was safe to acquiesce. Accordingly, notwithstanding the agreement which their ally had made, they vigorously opposed the Scottish Central Amalgamation Bill in Parliament in 1865. They were not successful in throwing out the Bill, but they secured the insertion in it of very stringent clauses in favour of East Coast traffic.

In the following session of 1866, however, practically the same contest had to be fought over again. Then, the Caledonian came to Parliament for power to acquire the Scottish North Eastern Company's system extending from Perth to Aberdeen, and a long-drawn out and very expensive fight resulted. Again the Caledonian Company carried its Bill, but again the East Coast companies obtained clauses in their favour—the most stringent clauses which their lawyers could devise—which went so far as to say that the Caledonian must treat the East Coast traffic "as if it were its own proper traffic or traffic it was desirous of cultivating to the utmost."

Thus the long Parliamentary warfare between the two coast routes ended in leaving them on a practical equality; and meantime, as we have already seen, they had been making common cause to check the development of a central route. This, indeed, as we noticed at the time, had been the prime object with which the English and Scotch Alliance had been formed in 1856; but we have already seen how the Midland, from the time when the payment to it of "blackmail" from Euston Square had been declared *ultra vires*, had joined hands with that "poor, wretched little creature," the (little) North Western, to upset the alliance; and when in July, 1862, the North British Company had completed its extension from Hawick to Carlisle, it also, despite its prior East Coast attachment, had begun to agitate on behalf of the central route. In the following year, moreover, had come the passing of the Midland's Extension to London Act, and this of course had made the case for a revision of the Anglo-Scotch arrangement very much stronger than before.

Still, however, no general agreement to revision could be obtained; and at last, to bring matters to a head, the Great Northern had given notice (12 August, 1863) that until the matter was settled, it should object to any further division under the agreement of any receipts whatever. Already, since April, 1860, as the reader may remember, the Railway Clearing House had been directed to collect all the "central" receipts and to hold them in suspense; and now, owing to the Great Northern's action, it had to treat all the divisible "coast" receipts in the same way. Nevertheless another year passed without an amicable settlement having been arrived at, and so the Midland, on 22 July, 1864, filed a Bill in Chancery against the other members of the alliance, praying that the rights and interests of themselves and the several other railway companies might "be ascertained and declared" by that "honourable court," or "in such manner as the honourable court shall think fit to direct."

For reasons not clear to the present historian (perhaps because he is no lawyer) this Chancery suit did not come on for hearing until 17 July, 1866, all but two years after its filing; and in the meantime the Midland, under Mr. Allport's bold leadership, took a decisive step to establish the central route. It obtained powers from Parliament in 1866 for an access on its own rails all the way to Carlisle. Against such a new fact as this no ten-years-old agreement could possibly have prevailed, even if it had had all the power of the law behind it, and when on 28 July, 1866, Vice-Chancellor Kindersley condemned altogether the construction which the West and East Coast companies had sought to put upon the alliance, and declared that if it had been intended to bear such a construction it was *ultra vires*, it became obvious, even to the most confirmed "protectionists" amongst the coast companies' managers, that any further attempts to check the natural development of the central route were foredoomed to failure. Until the Bedford and London and Settle and Carlisle lines were completed its full power to compete with the coast routes would not, of course, be established; but after that it *must* so compete, and in anticipation of this event, the Great Northern and North Eastern companies had good reason to congratulate themselves that they had secured running powers from Berwick to Edinburgh for their joint traffic, and also facilities beyond Edinburgh independent of the North British. For there was good reason to fear that the latter might now be tempted to neglect East Coast interests in order to develop its new "Waverley route" to Carlisle.

Thus by the summer of 1866 the Midland had fully asserted, and partly realized, itself as a third trunk route between London and the North. Meanwhile, however, the attempt to develop a fourth trunk route *via* Cambridge and Lincoln had utterly failed, and the Great Eastern had fallen back, in apparent hopelessness, into the seclusion of the Eastern Counties. This, however, had not been due to any unreasonableness on the part of the Great Northern. "The moment the Bill" (*i.e.*, the Great Eastern and Lancashire and Yorkshire Junction Bill of 1865) "was thrown out," Colonel Packe had said to the Great Northern shareholders, "in coming out of the lobby, I said to one or two of the Great Eastern directors, 'Now I am quite as ready to make an arrangement with you as I was twenty-four hours ago'"; and the result had been that negotiations between the two companies had been once more set on foot. The Great Northern had already offered running powers over the loop line for coal traffic, with power to the Great Eastern to fix its own rates for coal, and this offer it now renewed.

But though this might have satisfied the Great Eastern a year before, when its eyes had been fixed upon the South Yorkshire coalfield only, it did not satisfy it now that the greater ambition of reaching the West Riding of Yorkshire, and Lancashire also, had been aroused. What its directors now wanted was a line of their own to the North; and, obviously, the chief reason why they had not got this from Parliament was that the Great Northern already occupied the district through which their advance had to be made with its "loop" and other lines. Accordingly what now came to be proposed was that the Great Eastern should become half-owners of the part of the existing "loop" between Spalding and Gainsborough at a price to be agreed or settled by arbitration, and should pay half the cost of construction of the extensions which the Great Northern was making from Spalding to March and from Gainsborough to Doncaster; and to this the Great Northern agreed.

The arrangements, however, did not end there. Having been put on the road to become half-owners of a through route from its existing system at March to Doncaster, the Great Eastern, it was agreed further, was to have running powers to Wakefield over the West Riding and Grimsby line, the joint purchase of which the Great Northern and Sheffield companies undertook at once to complete; while for Lancashire traffic it was to obtain facilities by arranging to exchange with the Sheffield Company at Lincoln. "By these arrangements" the Great Northern directors said in their report of August, 1865, "the Great Eastern will obtain access to Lancashire, Yorkshire, and the North, an unnecessary outlay in the construction of new lines will be saved, the existing railways of the Great Northern and Manchester, Sheffield, and Lincolnshire companies will be utilized, and the convenience of the public secured."

The arrangements, of course, involved a considerable outlay on the part of the Great Eastern Company, but so far, apparently, were its directors from thinking this beyond their strength that they strongly pressed the Great Northern, after the first treaty had been made, to enlarge it so as to include the joint construction of a new direct line from Spalding to Lincoln. This was somewhat reluctantly agreed to, and the King's Cross Board joined with the Great Eastern and Sheffield in promoting the necessary Bills for the session of 1866, in the full expectation that a very troublesome question had been at last disposed of and a most costly contest terminated. This confidence, however, was very soon rudely shattered.

In the middle of February, 1866—after the publication of the Great Northern report announcing the completion of the arrangements, but before the half-yearly meeting of the Company—Mr. Oakley, the Great Northern secretary, received a curt letter from the Great Eastern secretary enclosing a resolution of his Board to the effect that "in the present position of the Company" it was "undesirable to proceed with" the Arrangements Bill. Mr. Oakley was instructed to reply immediately expressing "surprise and regret" on the part of the Great Northern directors, and demanding "the honourable fulfilment" of the Great Eastern "obligations"; but the case was one in which honour, perforce, had to be left out of the question. There had been a "revolution" at Shoreditch—one of a series which followed one another there in the second half of the sixties; a committee of investigation had sat, and the result of its report had been that the leaders of the Board which had made the agreement with the Great Northern had received their *congé*. Their successors, no doubt, had every wish in the world to fulfil honourably the obligations handed over to them. But their predominant obligation, of course, was to the shareholders who had elected them, and this obligation seemed to them to overrule the other. A company which was not only paying no dividend, but was under the urgent necessity—so the committee of investigation had reported—of raising 1½ million of new capital as the least sum which would enable it to put its existing undertaking properly into repair, was in their opinion not in a position to incur such extensive new liabilities as the half-purchase of the Great Northern loop and the joint construction of the new Spalding and Lincoln line involved. There was nothing for it, they insisted, but for both companies to accept the situation and to withdraw the Arrangements Bill from Parliament.

Nor was this the full extent of the inconvenience which the financial embarrassments of the Great Eastern inflicted on the Great Northern in 1866. The reader has already been told that in anticipation of the re-transfer of the Royston and Hitchin, and as the price of the withdrawal of a Great Northern extension to Cambridge, the Great Eastern had agreed before a Parliamentary Committee in 1864 to give running powers over its existing line between Shepreth and Cambridge, to double the part of it between Shepreth and Shelford, and to provide additional station accommodation in the University town. But when at the end of March, 1866, the agreement of 1852 expired, and the Hitchin and Shepreth line had to be handed back to the Great Northern, the work for these purposes had not even been begun. Consequently the Great Northern's Cambridge traffic was conducted at first at a great disadvantage.

Nevertheless, the Great Northern was, from 1 April, 1866, established at Cambridge, and in this same year it succeeded in gaining a footing in another not unimportant Eastern Counties' stronghold, Lynn. For some years, as the reader has been already informed, it had been working the so-called Norwich and Spalding line, from Spalding nearly due eastwards to Sutton Bridge, but we have seen how an attempt made in 1862 to absorb this and the Sutton and Lynn Company into the Great Northern had been unsuccessful, the reason being that a third small company obtained powers in that year to carry on the east-and-west line of communication from Spalding to Bourn. Now—in the session of 1866—the Sutton and Lynn and the Spalding and Bourn promoted a Bill to amalgamate themselves under the title of the Midland and Eastern Company, to acquire a lease of the Sutton and Spalding line, and to construct a further extension of their system due westwards from Bourn to join the Midland at Saxby.

This Bill was supported by the Midland Company and opposed by the Great Northern, and a Parliamentary contest resulted. In the course of it, the Great Northern made an offer that, if the new Bourn to Saxby line were given up, it would give running powers over an existing route from Bourn to the Midland system *via* Essendine (a place just north of Peterborough on the Great Northern main line) and Stamford—a route constructed by two small companies but now absorbed into the Great Northern. This offer the Midland and Eastern Company thought it worth while to accept, while, to pacify the Midland, the further arrangement was made that the new route should be worked jointly by it and the Great Northern, the Midland and Eastern Company being guaranteed a minimum rental of £15,000 a year. The result was that from 1 August, 1866, a connecting service of trains was put on which brought the Great Northern's main line at Essendine and its loop line at Spalding into direct communication with Leicester (*via* Stamford and Syston) and with Lynn (*via* Sutton Bridge).

Meanwhile, despite the collapse of the Great Eastern, the Great Northern and Sheffield companies had proceeded with their Bill for becoming joint owners of the West Riding and Grimsby Railway, and in the session of 1866 it passed into law—the terms, as far as the Great Northern was concerned, being that it should give £210,000 of its ordinary stock for a like amount of West Riding and Grimsby stock. Already, from 1 February, 1866, the line from Doncaster to Wakefield had been open, and at once the Great Northern's trains to and from the West Riding had been diverted to it from the old route *via* Knottingley, thus saving twenty minutes on the through journey. The Great Northern's express time between London and Leeds, a distance of $186\frac{1}{4}$ miles, had thus become 4 hours 35 minutes. Yet another important opening in 1866 was that of the link line of the Chatham and Dover Company from a junction with the Metropolitan at Farringdon Street to Blackfriars. This enabled the Great Northern to commence a through traffic in coal and goods to the south of the Thames, in consideration of which advantage the Company had contributed £300,000 to the construction of the link line at $3\frac{1}{2}$ per cent. interest secured as a rent charge on the Chatham and Dover undertaking.

The Great Northern Railway had now been open from London for sixteen years, and all that time it had worked passenger trains at a high rate of speed; yet, during a period throughout which, owing to the imperfection of appliances, fatal railway accidents had been lamentably frequent, it had enjoyed an enviable immunity in this respect. In 1853, as already recorded, there had been a collision at Hornsey; in

1857, one of the then new Manchester expresses, which even then covered the seventy-six miles from London to Peterborough in ninety-five minutes, had been thrown off the rails at Carlton (between Newark and Tuxford), owing to a large piece of the line having been washed away by flood-water;* in 1859, a mistake on the part of a signalman and the absence of interlocking, had caused a collision between a Great Northern and Midland train at Hitchin junction; and in 1860, owing to the neglect of a drunken guard to apply his hand-brakes, a Manchester excursion train had run into the "dead-end" of King's Cross Station.† In none of these accidents, however, had fatal injuries been received by passengers. Indeed, it seems that the one and only passenger killed outright on the system up to this time was, curiously enough, the eldest son of one of the original promoters and directors of the Company, Mr. Francis Pym, of Biggleswade, who had met his sad death in April, 1860, by the wrecking of an express—again one of the Manchester "fliers"—when it was passing through Hatfield station, the cause being the displacement of a rail, which flew up and killed a platelayer at the same time. Unfortunately for the Company, Mr. Pym died intestate, leaving a widow and nine children, and, as the property was all entailed to the eldest son, the others were legally unprovided for. Under these circumstances a jury awarded £1000 compensation to the widow, and £1500 to each child—£13,000 in all, and the Company, after appeal, had actually to pay £9000 and about £2000 costs besides.

This Pym case, as may be supposed, had troubled the shareholders a good deal, but it had not affected the reputation which the Great Northern had gradually acquired in the minds of the general public of being an exceedingly safe line to travel upon. Consequently the sensation created was very great, when on the morning of Monday, 11 June, 1866, the newspapers announced that an accident of the most alarming and unprecedented kind had occurred on the system—that three trains had come into collision in the middle of a tunnel, that the *débris* had been converted into a huge bonfire, and that it was still unextinguished. The details of this sensational "Welwyn Tunnel accident" are briefly as follows:—

* Being unable to prove negligence, as required by Lord Campbell's Act, the unfortunate sufferers by this accident did not obtain a penny of compensation, though they brought a whole series of actions for the purpose. At the last of these Lord Campbell himself was the judge, and, when the jury could not agree, he is reported to have told them, by way of a stimulus, that in days gone by they would have been liable to be "taken in a cart to the confines of the county and thrown into a ditch."

† This accident nearly terminated the career of Charles Bradlaugh, whose life Mr. Vizer, the stationmaster, claims to have saved by prompt action.

Half an hour after midnight, between Saturday and Sunday, 9 and 10 June, 1866, a train of empty coal waggons on its way from King's Cross northwards broke down in the centre of the long tunnel just north of Welwyn, owing to the bursting of a boiler tube of the engine. Very shortly afterwards its rear was collided with by a Midland goods train on its way to Hitchin Junction, the impetus being such that some of the Midland trucks were thrown over so as to foul the "up" line. Hardly had this occurred when a meat train from the north bringing the supply of Scotch beef for London's Monday market, and travelling at a good speed, dashed into the *débris*, producing a mingled ruin of nearly one hundred trucks, which in places was piled up almost to reach the "soffit" of the tunnel.

The engine of the meat train was overturned and the coal scattered from its furnace, and, as luck would have it, some casks of oil, which some of the waggons of the Midland train had contained, were also strewn upon the ground. The result, of course, was that a roaring fire was ignited, and fanned from an air-shaft, which happened to be immediately overhead, it soon spread throughout the whole *débris*. This was the state of affairs when Mr. Seymour Clarke, who had been called up from his bed at Hatfield, Mr. Johnson, the chief engineer, who came from Barnet, and such other officers and men as could be hastily collected, arrived about dawn at the south end of the tunnel. The situation that confronted them was an appalling one. From the mouth of the tunnel suffocating clouds of smoke and waves of intense heat were issuing, and the sound which came from within was like the roar of a mighty cataract. At intervals, too, came the terrifying reports of explosions. Finding it impossible to effect an entrance at this end, Messrs. Clarke and Johnson led their men over the fields to where the rails again issued near Knebworth, and as they scaled the high ground beneath which the tunnel passes they saw flames every now and then emerge from the top of the air-shaft. This, they knew, was more than eighty feet above the level of the rails! From the Knebworth end it was found possible to enter with a gang of men and remove the rear waggons of the "Scotch meat"; but as the men neared the seat of the fire the intense heat drove them back. Nothing more could be done until the fire had to some extent expended its fierceness.

By this time the column of flame issuing from the air-shaft had aroused the countryside, and the only fire-engine available—a small one belonging to the Marquis of Salisbury's Hatfield estate—had been despatched to the scene. This was brought to play on the conflagration from the south end of the tunnel, water being brought to it by locomotives in tenderfuls; and, meanwhile, the country people gathered from all parts to see the sight. Fortunately, being Sunday, the ordinary traffic of the line was sparse, and what there was Mr. Clarke soon arranged to be diverted on to the Hertford and Cambridge branches, between the termini of which a circuitous connection was available over the Great Eastern Railway. At the same time urgent messages were sent to King's Cross, Doncaster, and elsewhere, that as large a force of men as possible might be mustered, in order to renew the attack on the *débris* as soon as its fiery defence had been broken down.

It was not until six o'clock on the Sunday evening—seventeen hours after the collisions—that an entry could be effected from the south end of the tunnel. Then Mr. Johnson and Mr. Budge of the locomotive department led in a gang of about 450 navvies and mechanics, and soon sufficient of the outlying *débris* was cleared away to allow the fire-engine to be brought to bear upon the centre of the fire—a smouldering and still sometimes flaming mass beneath the air-shaft. When this was at last deadened two powerful cranes were brought in to assist in the removal of the heavier wreckage; but so great was the accumulation that it was not until nine o'clock on the Monday morning that even goods trains could be allowed to pass, and not till the Tuesday that the passenger service could be resumed. Fortunately the tunnel itself was but slightly damaged.

Among the *débris* were found the charred bodies of two men, whose tragic fate had in it an element of retribution. Neither of them had any business to have been where they met their deaths. One of them was identified as a fireman in the employ of the Metropolitan Company, and it became clear that he had been attempting to make a free and illicit journey north in the brake-van of his friend, the guard of the coal train. The other was this guard himself, whose place of death convicted him of neglecting his elementary duty of going back when the breakdown had first occurred, to give warning to any following train.

Inquiry showed, however, that it was the system of signalling which was most at fault, and this was the more alarming because the accident had occurred in a long tunnel, *i.e.*, on one of the few sections of the line where, as already noted, an attempt had been made to introduce properly the newly-invented and much bepraised "block system." "We have had the block telegraph system in operation for a considerable number of years, and find it very beneficial," Colonel Packe had said at the half-yearly meeting in the preceding February; yet it seems more than likely that had there been no block working on the line at all, this particular accident would not have occurred. For it was, no doubt, reliance upon the new system which caused the guard of the coal train to neglect to carry back the danger-signal himself, and, indeed, though it was his duty according to rule to do so, no ill consequence would have occurred from his neglect, had not the telegraph signalling completely failed.

The moral, of course, was not that the principle of the block system was wrong, but that, if worked at all, it must be worked with appliances which could be depended upon. Accordingly Mr. Johnson was instructed to provide new telegraphic stations between London and Hitchin, while Mr. F. P. Cockshott, the newly appointed "superintendent of the line," was set to work to revise the code of communications. These precautions were all the more necessary because of the rapid rate at which, thanks to a general expansion of trade throughout the country, the traffic of the line had increased, and was still increasing, especially at the London end. True, the withdrawal of the Midland traffic between Hitchin and London was shortly expected; but already since the passing of the Midland's Extension to London Act in 1863 the Great Northern's own general traffic had so increased as to promise more than to make up for this loss when it should come; and besides this, there was the new traffic of the Luton and Dunstable, Hertford and St. Albans[*] branches—all of which join the main line in the neighbourhood of Hatfield—and, above all, the largely increasing suburban traffic to be provided for. Consequently for some years the question of widening between London and Hatfield had been before the directors.

In regard to this question the great difficulty was, and still is, that there are no less than seven tunnels within the first thirteen miles of the Great Northern line out of London. On this account the directors had shrunk from proposing an actual duplication of this section of the line; so, instead of this, they followed up a suggestion which Mr. Denison had made just before his retirement. They proposed to make a loop line to leave the main line near Hornsey, to pass through the promising residential district around Enfield, and to join the main line again at Welwyn by way of a junction at Hertingfordbury with the Welwyn and Hertford branch. This, they thought, would have the double advantage of relieving the main line and opening up a new suburban district, and despite the opposition of the Great Eastern Company, which also wanted to tap the locality of Enfield, they obtained Parliamentary powers for it in 1865 under the title of "the Hornsey and Hertford Railway."

[*] This had been constructed by a separate "Hatfield and St. Albans Railway Company," incorporated in 1862.

Still, however, the problem of congestion between Hornsey and King's Cross remained, and it became intensified as the completion of the Edgware and Highgate line drew near. Moreover, in addition to the increasing "City and suburban" traffic, an entirely new traffic

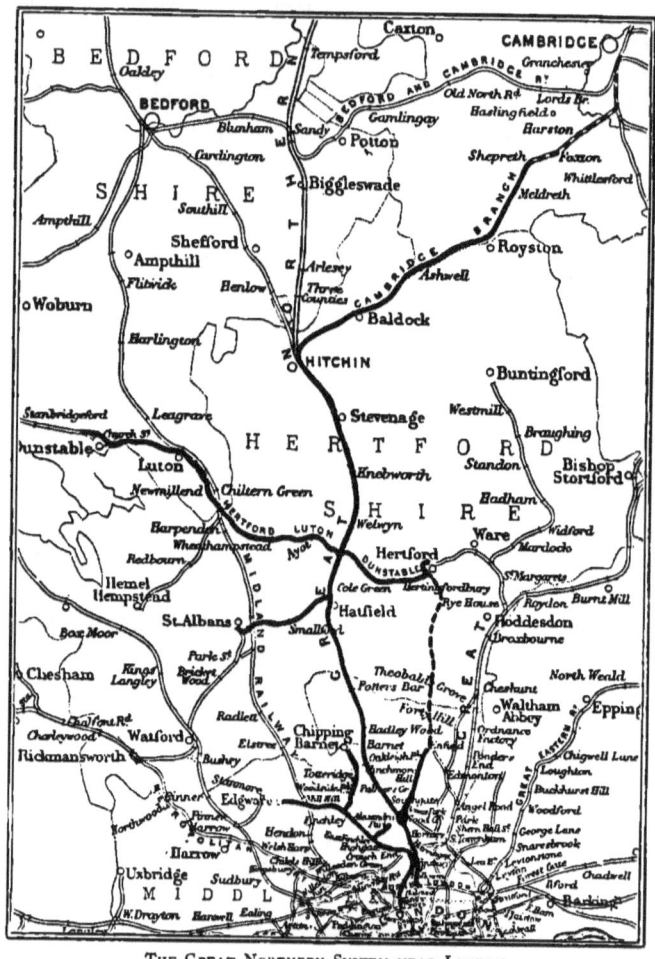

THE GREAT NORTHERN SYSTEM NEAR LONDON.
(Showing the abortive "Hornsey and Hertford" scheme.)

was expected in connection with the "Alexandra Palace" in course of erection on Muswell Hill, to which the Edgware Company (with the support of the Great Northern) had obtained powers in 1865 to make a branch from Highgate. As things were, passenger trains—express and slow—goods trains and coal trains had all to use the same two tracks; and although in the immediate vicinity of King's Cross a separation was effected from the fact that the goods and coal trains (except the few bound to and from the south of the Thames) issued from, and branched off into, their depôts without passing through the Maiden Lane tunnel, yet, on the other hand, this made the congestion between the Maiden Lane and the Copenhagen tunnels especially bad, because "up" goods and coal trains in order to reach their destination had to cross the "down" line on the level. This, clearly, was a state of affairs most dangerous to a frequent traffic, and so in the session of 1866 the directors applied to Parliament for powers to make a second Copenhagen tunnel as a separate channel for goods and coal traffic, while about the same time they instructed Mr. Johnson to lay down additional lines between Seven Sisters Road and the north end of this tunnel. Between Seven Sisters and Holloway they had already acquired a large piece of land for new sidings for goods and coal traffic, in addition to the forty-five acres bought originally for the King's Cross goods station.

Meanwhile the construction of the three new Lincolnshire lines was being rapidly pushed forward, and before the August half-yearly meeting in 1867 they were all opened: the March and Spalding, nineteen miles, on 1 April; the Lincoln and Honington, eighteen miles, on 15 April; and the Doncaster and Gainsborough, eighteen miles, on 15 July. The completion of the latter would no doubt have been deferred had it been necessary to construct a new bridge over the Trent, as contemplated when the Act for it was obtained; but, as it was, arrangements were made to use the existing Trent Bridge of the Sheffield Company. At the same time the Sheffield made a claim for traffic diverted from its line between Sykes Junction and Retford, which, of course, was now superseded by the new route *via* Gainsborough. The whole matter was referred to the arbitration of Mr. T. E. Harrison, the eminent engineer, and he awarded the Sheffield Company a sum of £25,450 as compensation for diversion, and a toll for the use of their bridge equal to one mile's receipts on all traffic passing over it.

A through route from the Great Eastern system at March *via* Spalding, Boston, and Lincoln to Doncaster being thus complete, both the Great Northern and Great Eastern Boards were anxious that it should be used in the manner most profitable and fair to the two companies. With this view, accordingly, new negotiations had been set on foot, with the result that a fresh agreement had been drawn up and signed by the two chairmen, Colonel Packe and Mr. C. H. Turner, on 12 March, 1867, after an interview of ten hours. Under this it was arranged that the Great Eastern should have running powers from March to Doncaster immediately, on the condition that within seven years it purchased half of the through route between those points. In return the Great Northern was to obtain access *via* Cambridge to Newmarket, and also to the Great Eastern station at Lynn. After all, however, this agreement came to nothing, for the Great Eastern claimed a right under it to exchange traffic with the Lancashire and Yorkshire Company at Doncaster, which the Great Northern in its own interest and in that of its ally, the Sheffield, felt obliged to refuse. Moreover, a second modified agreement signed on 7 August, 1867, also came to grief, because Mr. Turner was soon afterwards thrown out of office by another "revolution" in the Great Eastern directorate. It seemed as if this "Great Eastern Question" never was, but "always to be," settled.

On 22 September, 1867, the Edgware and Highgate line was opened for traffic. As already noted this consisted of a branch, eight miles in length, from a junction with the Great Northern main line near Seven Sisters Road Station, through Crouch End, Highgate, and Finchley to Edgware; and the powers for it had been obtained in 1862 by an independent company, to whose original capital, however, the Great Northern had subscribed one-third. In the session of 1866 this company had promoted an extension from Finchley to High Barnet, and this had been authorized despite the opposition of the Great Northern, which had taken up with a rival scheme from Finchley to Potters Bar, hoping again to combine suburban development with "loop" relief. This event had led the Great Northern Board to determine they had better obtain complete control of the too independent little company, and accordingly they had made an agreement in June, 1866, under which the Edgware and Highgate undertaking, including the Barnet branch, was taken over at a guaranteed dividend beginning at 2 per cent., rising by stages to 5 per cent., and then giving way to the conversion of Edgware and Highgate into Great Northern stock, in the proportion of £78 10s. of the latter to £100 of the former.

The Edgware and Highgate was the last completed of a series of extensions and amalgamations which within seven years nearly doubled the original Great Northern undertaking both in mileage and in capital. Up to the end of 1860 the mileage owned by the Company had remained at its original figure, 283 miles (though the miles worked over had increased from 130 to 194), and little more than another million had been added to the eleven millions (in round figures) which we saw the original system cost. From that date, however, as we have seen, a period of rapid extension and accretion had commenced. In 1861 the Nottingham and Grantham, and Hertford, Luton, and Dunstable lines were permanently acquired, and the expenditure on the Cheshire lines commenced; in 1863 and 1864 powers for the Lincolnshire extensions were obtained, and the Boston and Sleaford and Bourn and Essendine companies absorbed; and in 1865 the amalgamations of the Leeds, Bradford, and Halifax, and West Yorkshire were carried out. In 1866 the Royston and Shepreth line reverted; the half-purchase of the West Riding and Grimsby was carried out; the Edgware and Highgate was absorbed; and, a fact not yet fully noted, the whole system of railways in Cheshire and Lancashire, extending from Godley to Chester, and from Manchester to Liverpool, and including Mr. Watkin's new direct line between the two latter towns and a new "central station" in Liverpool, were vested in the Manchester, Sheffield, and Lincolnshire, Great Northern, and Midland companies jointly, a separate managing body being created by delegations from the three Boards, entitled "The Cheshire Lines Joint Committee." The result was that by the end of 1867 no fewer than 200 miles had been added to the system originally owned by the Great Northern, making its total mileage 487, and its total capital cost, including fixed charges, quite twenty millions.

Those who are wont in season and out of season to denounce additions to a railway company's capital account will do well to note that this rapid expansion was accompanied by a substantial rise of dividend. At the end of the fifties, as the reader knows, the Company had only just begun to pay 5 per cent.; at the time our history has now reached it was regarded, with good reason, as a safe 7 per cent. concern. Moreover, it had passed almost unscathed through the financial crisis of 1866—a crisis fatal to several ambitious railway administrations.

CHAPTER XV.

THE COAL WAR AND THE C.O.A.L. LINE—1868-1871.

TOWARDS the close of Chapter XII. of this history the reader was warned of the importance likely to be assumed in the future by a certain "Coal Traffic Agreement," which we then saw made by Mr. Allport on behalf of the Midland Company, and Mr. Walter Leith on behalf of the Great Northern (23 January, 1863). The occasion of this agreement, it will be remembered, was the admission of the Great Northern *viâ* Nottingham into the Derbyshire coalfield, and its main principle was that the two companies, now that they were both to be carriers from the two coalfields from which the rail-borne supply of the Metropolis was principally drawn, should not only charge equal rates from the same collieries to all competitive points, but should so regulate these rates that the charge from one colliery should be "equitably adjusted" to the charge from another. The rates, it was further agreed, were to be based, as far as their calculation by mileage went, on the shortest railway route from each colliery; but the provision as to "equitable adjustment" meant that the strict mileage principle was not to be pushed so far as to exclude the more distant pits, or the more distant coalfield, entirely from a market. On the other hand, it meant also—in the view of Mr. Allport at least—that geographical superiority was to be given an "equitable" value—that it was to be taken into consideration along with other natural advantages which the various collieries might possess.

The great difficulty of putting a principle of this kind into actual practice—of giving considerations of geographical and other natural advantages a fair value in the shillings and pence of rates—is very obvious *primâ facie*, but in this particular instance there was a special difficulty. This was, that as regards the South Yorkshire field neither the Great Northern nor the Midland had a free hand. Between both of them and the pits was the South Yorkshire Railway, and this company—which was before Parliament in 1863, it will be remembered, for power to transfer its undertaking to the Sheffield Company—

though invited to come into the agreement, had declined to do so. The fact was that in this transition stage of its existence, the South Yorkshire's attitude towards the London coal trade was even more undecided and confused than it had been before. What it was chiefly concerned with in 1863 was to preserve its power to take its $1d.$ per ton per mile out of the whole London rate, and so all it was able to promise was that, when its charging powers were adjusted under its Transfer Act, it would treat both Great Northern and Midland alike.

It was with the ground to this small extent cleared before them that Mr. Swarbrick, the accountant of the Midland, Mr. James Grinling, the accountant of the Great Northern, and three other officers met at King's Cross on 12 February, 1863, to decide what the rates from the various collieries were for the future to be. The crucial point was, how much value was to be given to the thirty miles geographical advantage as regards the London market which, on the average, the Derbyshire pits possessed over the South Yorkshire pits, and this was ultimately decided by agreeing to fix the rates from Doncaster and Swinton to London so that, with the addition of the South Yorkshire Company's toll, whatever it might be, the South Yorkshire rate to London should always be $1s.\ 4d.$ more than the rate from Clay Cross, the most central of the Derbyshire collieries. When the actual rates fixed on this principle were worked out on the mileage of the shortest routes, this was found to mean that South Yorkshire coal was to be carried by the Great Northern from Doncaster to King's Cross at $\cdot 39d.$ per ton per mile, whereas on Derbyshire traffic from Clay Cross to St. Pancras the Midland was to receive $\cdot 45d.$ only; and from this point of view, therefore, it looked as if South Yorkshire coal was being rated on a lower scale per mile than Derbyshire by way of "equitable adjustment" of its greater distance from the market. Moreover, the "gross differential" of $1s.\ 4d.$ fixed under the agreement was $3d.$ less than the actual difference between the South Yorkshire and Clay Cross rates at the time the agreement was made. Nevertheless, if the Great Northern officials thought they were acting generously towards South Yorkshire they deceived themselves. When to the $\cdot 39d.$ per ton per mile which the Great Northern agreed to put up with on its "long lead" of 156 miles from Doncaster to London, was added the $1d.$ per ton per mile which the South Yorkshire Company demanded for its "short haul" of sixteen miles "group distance" from the pits to Doncaster, the rate to be charged on South Yorkshire coal throughout became $\cdot 46d.$ per ton per mile—a fraction more, that is to say, than the rate charged throughout on Derbyshire coal from Clay Cross. In other words, the fixed "differential" meant that Derbyshire was to have the whole benefit of its geographical superiority, notwithstanding all the talk about "equitable adjustment."

This was a curious and, as events proved, a very unfortunate outcome of the Coal Traffic Agreement; but while the advantage which Derbyshire gained under it may be fairly credited to the diplomatic ability of Mr. Allport, the disadvantage to South Yorkshire cannot so fairly be placed upon the shoulders of the Great Northern. For, as the figures just quoted show, the Great Northern, in the interests of South Yorkshire, agreed to accept a lower rate per mile from Doncaster than the Midland was to have from Clay Cross; and, though in view of the Great Northern's longer "lead" this could hardly be called a serious sacrifice, yet, on the other hand, it must be remembered that to make serious sacrifices for South Yorkshire was not a thing which at this time of day the Great Northern could be reasonably expected to do. The whole *raison d'être* of this agreement of 1863 was that in the future, as regards the London coal traffic, the Great Northern was to be a Derbyshire Company as well as a South Yorkshire Company. It was really only natural that Derbyshire should get the better of South Yorkshire under the agreement, seeing that, of the two companies making it, one—the Midland—was already, and the other—the Great Northern—wished to be, closely identified with Derbyshire's interests, whereas the company which was taking South Yorkshire's interests into its keeping—the Manchester, Sheffield, and Lincolnshire—held aloof from the whole affair.

Thus it came about that, at this early stage in the contest for the possession of the Metropolitan coal market, Derbyshire was able to enter the lists with its full geographical advantage secured to it in terms of shillings and pence—an average advantage of 1s. 4d. in its rates to London fixed for "five years certain," and unalterable except after reference to arbitration—and under these circumstances what under other conditions might have proved a fierce fight between the two coalfields became simply a "walk over" for the nearer one. True that, as already said, the South Yorkshire had in the years before the agreement of 1863 contended with some success, thanks to the better quality of its coal and other advantages, against a higher "differential" than 1s. 4d.—at one time, indeed, it had been as high as 2s. 2d.; but in those years the Derbyshire field had been comparatively undeveloped, the Midland's facilities for sending the coal to London had been much less than they had since become, and there had been periodical outbreaks of "rate cutting" which had made the higher differential not a thing to be depended upon. From 1863 onwards all this was changed. The differential was fixed; the

Midland had its own coal depôt in London; there was an alternative Great Northern route available *via* Nottingham, and there was the stimulating prospect of the speedy opening of the Midland's own Bedford to London line. Under these circumstances it was not surprising that in the years immediately following 1863 very many new pits were sunk in the Derbyshire district with the special view of supplying the London market.

As often happens in such cases, several exceptional circumstances contributed to "fill up the cup" of South Yorkshire's misfortunes. It was harassed by labour troubles, from which Derbyshire remained happily exempt; a more than usually terrible accident occurred at one of the principal pits, the financial crisis of 1866 was followed by general depression of trade, and then, on the top of all, came the exceptionally mild winter of 1867-8, followed by an exceptionally hot spring and summer, in consequence of which the house-coal trade became very slack. Trade depression and slackness, it is true, were influences which affected all coalfields alike; but whereas Derbyshire could console itself that, when a revival came, the opening of the Midland's line to London (which took place in 1868) would place it in a specially favourable position to take advantage of it, South Yorkshire had no such consolation. It saw in the Midland's new line, on the contrary, an additional "handicap" to competition. As regards the London market, the position of South Yorkshire had become desperate, and Mr. Seymour Clarke voiced a very general sentiment when in writing on 1 September, 1868, to Mr. Underdown, the general manager of the Sheffield, he said: "Something must be done if the South Yorkshire trade is to be kept together."

Of course, the obvious "something" to be done was to make a reduction in the South Yorkshire rate, and this, in fact, was what Mr. Clarke suggested to Mr. Underdown. "If," wrote he, "we will undertake to carry South Yorkshire coal at a rate that will give us no more than we get for Durham coal, say $\frac{1}{4}d.$ per ton per mile, will your Company take 1s. toll (instead of 1s. 4d.) from all collieries to Doncaster? This matter will come up for discussion at the London Conference on Monday. Please reply as early as you can."

The London Conference mentioned in this letter was an association of directors and general managers which had been formed a few months before, with a view to the amicable settlement of questions affecting the interests of railways generally, and before this tribunal the general question of "equitable adjustment" of coal rates to collieries had already been raised by Mr. Clarke, with the view of re-opening the specific problem of South Yorkshire *v.* Derbyshire.

Before carrying the matter further, however, he naturally wished to know what attitude the Sheffield Company would take up. Would it repeat its aloofness of 1863, or was it ready to second an effort on behalf of the declining trade of South Yorkshire?

This question, however, the Sheffield could not answer off-hand. Mr. Underdown, in the first place, had to consult his chairman, and Mr. Watkin was too busy with a hundred other matters—South Eastern, Grand Trunk, Great Eastern, Humber Ironworks, and receiving the honour of knigthood from the Queen—to give the subject attention at once. In the second place, when he did give it attention, there was the old question of the "commercial" use of the South Yorkshire lease as against its "political" use to be carefully weighed. Commercially, the Sheffield Company had suffered a heavy loss from the lease; even the large coal traffic which it had developed from South Yorkshire to Grimsby had not made up for this, because it was "hard coal" chiefly that was wanted at Grimsby, while for the soft coal —the house coal—which had to be mined at the same time, the Sheffield had been able to open up no sufficiently large markets on its own system. Commercially, therefore, an improvement in the South Yorkshire trade to London was very desirable in the Sheffield's interest, but Sir Edward Watkin was not disposed to purchase that improvement at the cost of too great a "political" concession to the Great Northern.

Consequently, before Mr. Seymour Clarke got his answer, a lot of discussion had to take place, and possibly he would not have received a favourable answer at all, had not a new influence in the meantime been brought to bear. This took the shape of a memorial from the South Yorkshire coalowners—the "culmination" of complaints they had been making during the previous few years. In this they represented that their trade was "seriously suffering from the very heavy and unequal rates imposed on South Yorkshire coal compared with the rates between London and the Derbyshire and Durham coalfields," and they assured the directors of the Sheffield and Great Northern companies that unless a remedy could be applied they would be "compelled to take steps permanently to curtail the get of coal" at their collieries. This memorial was signed by Earl Fitzwilliam, Lord Wharncliffe, and all the principal coalowners of the district; but the leader of the movement, the reader will not be surprised to hear, was Mr. Robert Baxter, who, moreover, acted as spokesman to a deputation which presented the memorial to the Great Northern Board on 5 January, 1869.

The Great Northern directors, of course, answered that they were already bringing pressure on the Sheffield Company for the relief of

South Yorkshire, and recommended the coalowners to concentrate their influence upon that quarter. The result was that about a month later, 9 February, 1869, the basis of a combined effort on behalf of the South Yorkshire coalfield was arranged between Sir Edward Watkin and Colonel Packe. Under the agreement then made the Great Northern obtained, for the first time in its history, the power to fix a through rate on a uniform scale per mile from the South Yorkshire collieries to London, the Sheffield agreeing to exchange its fixed toll of 1s. 4d. for a proportion of this new through rate equal to thirty miles—its actual distance, it will be remembered, was sixteen miles—with a minimum of 1s. "If, however," the memorandum significantly added, "the rate, in competition with the Midland, is reduced so low as ¼d. per ton per mile, then the Sheffield Company's minimum shall be 10d."

That they made this last proviso shows that the allied companies fully anticipated a fight with the Midland; nevertheless, the Great Northern directors did their utmost to avert hostilities. On the very next day after the signing of the agreement between Colonel Packe and Sir Edward Watkin, Mr. Oakley, the Great Northern secretary, was instructed to write to the Midland Board inviting it to appoint a deputation to confer with a deputation from the Great Northern Board "with a view to a re-arrangement of the rates for the coal traffic of the two Companies to London on a more equitable basis than at present exists," as a preliminary to the general discussion of the question of coal rates which had been fixed to take place at the London Conference in the following April. "I am further explicitly to state," wrote Mr. Oakley, "that this invitation is given in the most friendly spirit and with a sincere desire to meet the present difficulties by a fair and businesslike settlement."

But Mr. Allport and his directors, on their part, were conscious of no "present difficulties," nor had they any desire to re-arrange the rates either in a friendly spirit or otherwise. In their opinion "a fair and businesslike settlement" already existed under the agreement of 1863. If the new points which the Great Northern wished to raise affected the railway interest in general, then they might be discussed, as arranged, at the London Conference. But if a revision of the agreement of 1863 was what the Great Northern really wanted, then it ought to take the steps to this end which were provided by that agreement itself. The agreement provided for a reference to arbitration in case of any difference arising in regard to the matters dealt with under it. Why, then, did the Great Northern not go to arbitration? This, in substance, was the answer which the Great Northern got to the above letter and also at the April meeting of the London Conference. Thereupon Mr. Seymour Clarke announced that his directors accepted the situation, and would go to arbitration.

The effect of this decision, of course, was that, pending the arbitration, no effect could be given to the agreement made between Colonel Packe and Sir Edward Watkin, and this gave the latter an opening of which he was not slow to make use. At the next meeting of the Great Northern and Manchester, Sheffield, and Lincolnshire Joint Committee, held on 12 May, 1869, he told the Great Northern representatives bluntly that if the existing state of things in South Yorkshire was not shortly remedied the Sheffield Company would be "compelled to liberate the coalfield" by the construction of a new line to connect with the Great Eastern.

This threat was the more serious because Sir Edward Watkin, besides being the Sheffield chairman, was now also a director of the Great Eastern, having been elected to a seat on its Board as the result of the second "Shoreditch revolution"—the "change of ministry" which, the reader remembers, upset the agreement made with the Great Northern in August, 1867. Sir Edward was not supreme at Shoreditch, it was true; for the shareholders, having been so fortunate as to secure the services of Lord Cranborne (who almost immediately became, and still is, Marquis of Salisbury) had preferred to elect *him*, and not Mr. Watkin, as their chairman. But, on the other hand, the Marquis of Salisbury was in favour of a forward policy. "We are poor at present," he said in reference to a temporary traffic arrangement made with the Great Northern in June, 1868, "and so must put up with what other people give us, but we mean some time to have a line of our own to the North." And so, with Sir Edward Watkin on its Board and the possibility of an alliance with the Sheffield to stimulate it, there was no knowing what the Great Eastern might not do. However, the Great Northern was now committed to the arbitration, and had to go through with it. If it could convince the arbitrator that the obnoxious differential must be reduced and so make its peace with the South Yorkshire coalowners, all might yet be well.

Meantime, while the preliminaries of the arbitration were being settled by the lawyers, another very important question pressed for attention at the Great Northern and other Boards. At the end of this year, 1869, the English and Scotch Alliance was to expire by lapse of time—what, if anything, was to take its place? Since the decision in the Midland's favour of the Chancery suit of 1866, the "pooling" provided for under the alliance had been confined to the traffic of the two coast routes, whilst the traffic of the central route had been divided by mileage between the companies carrying it. Should a new agreement now be made to include all three routes in a pool, or should pooling and percentage division be in the future dispensed with and the companies owning the several routes be allowed to compete freely for the traffic and retain all that they got according to mileage, subject to an agreement to charge equal rates and fares? This was the new question which for the time being superseded that of coal rates in interest for the Great Northern and other Boards.

Amid much that was uncertain, as to one thing at least there could be no two opinions at King's Cross—that, in view of either contingency, the East Coast companies must show that they could hold their own. A serious difficulty in regard to this, however, was the position of the North British. The financial storm of 1866 had worked havoc upon

Express Passenger Engine "7' 0" Single."
Built from Mr. Stirling's designs in 1868.

many railway companies, but the North British had felt its effect most of all. Its ambitious chairman, Mr. Richard Hodgson—"the Scotch Hudson"—had fallen; the Forth Bridge had gone under financially even before its engineer, Mr. Bouch, had been able to sink an experimental pier; and then, in a violent reaction from its former aggressive policy, the North British had actually entered into "a common-purse agreement" with the Caledonian. Fortunately, however, as we already know, the Great Northern and North Eastern had foreseen and provided against such a contingency as this, and now at this critical juncture in the Anglo-Scotch traffic arrangements they brought the remedy they had provided into play. From the beginning of June, 1869, the North Eastern began to use its running powers between Berwick and Edinburgh for the joint traffic, and, together with the Great Northern, it enforced the independent facilities which the two companies had obtained in 1865-6 as regards the lines beyond the Scotch capital. The result was that the public got a ten-hour service between London and Edinburgh, a new train being put on—the Aberdeen racing train of the future—which left King's Cross at 8 p.m., and was timed to reach York at 12.40, Edinburgh at 6.5, Perth at 8.59, and Aberdeen at 12.20.

Hardly had these arrangements been made when it became evident that no renewal of the English and Scotch Alliance would be carried out. The fact was that as a preventative of competition "pooling" had proved a complete failure. Unable by competition to increase immediately their share of the "pooled" traffic, the companies, nevertheless, had been afraid to cease to compete, lest they should be unable to enforce their claim to a proper share when a revision of the pool had to be made. It is true that equality and stability of rates and fares had throughout been secured, but this had been obtained just as well in regard to other competitive traffic by a simple agreement to charge equally. Under these circumstances the prevention of "ruinous competition" could no longer be put forward with any show of reason as necessitating "pooling"; and, on the other hand, the policy which, as we have several times before pointed out, had been the real basis upon which the Gladstone, Octuple and English and Scotch pools were all formed—the "protectionist" policy invented by Captain Huish—was by this time utterly discredited. It is not surprising, therefore, to find that, from 30 June, 1869, the last of these cumbrous arrangements—the English and Scotch Alliance—was put an end to "by mutual consent," and its place taken by a simple agreement to charge equal rates and fares between competitive points. The Great Northern benefited immediately by this change, because the traffic it had actually carried had throughout been in excess of the percentages allotted to it under the agreements.

In July, 1869, the arbitration upon the Coal Traffic Agreement of 1863 commenced, the arbitrator being Sir John Karslake, the Attorney-General of the day. The appointment of a lawyer instead of a practical railway man for an arbitration of this character was subsequently condemned in strong terms by Mr. Denison, Q.C., lawyer though he was himself, and the choice of Sir John Karslake for the work certainly had this drawback, that, being a man much engaged with other matters, he was able only at long intervals to give days for the hearing. Two meetings were held before him in July, 1869, two more in October, one in January, 1870, one in February, and one in May, when the evidence of the railway managers, coalowners, and others was at last concluded, but even then the parties had to wait three months longer for the award.

During this period of thirteen months, of course, a great many things happened; but the only one which it is important for us to note here is the resignation of Mr. Seymour Clarke. About the time of the commencement of the arbitration his health had again broken down, and after waiting for nearly twelve months, in the hope that it might recover, the directors were reluctantly obliged to accept his resignation and to fill the vacant general managership by the appointment of Mr. Oakley, who had been in the service of the Company since 1849, and its secretary since 1858. As we have already noted, it is to Mr. Seymour Clarke, next to Mr. Denison, that credit must be given for the very notable success which the Great Northern Railway had achieved since it began its career as a carrier from London in 1850. Throughout the whole of these twenty years Mr. Clarke had been its general manager, and he had done his work in such a way as not only to satisfy the shareholders, but to serve the travelling public in no ordinary degree.

On 22 August, 1870—two days after the Great Northern half-yearly meeting, at which Mr. Seymour Clarke's resignation was announced—Sir John Karslake's award was published. It proved to be as short as the proceedings incident to it had been long. After rehearsing the circumstances under which the reference to him had been made, the Attorney-General said: "I award that no alteration be made in the rates for coals in the said agreement or submission to arbitration mentioned and referred to."

MR. SEYMOUR CLARKE,
GENERAL MANAGER OF THE
GREAT NORTHERN RAILWAY, 1850-1870.

Being a wise man he did not name his reasons for this decision, but it appeared that the argument that had most weight with him was that, as already pointed out, the Great Northern was charging less per mile on South Yorkshire coals from Doncaster to London than the Midland was charging on Derbyshire coals from Clay Cross to St. Pancras, and this being so he did not think that it would be an "equitable adjustment" for the Great Northern's rate to be further reduced. The fact that the Sheffield Company's high toll for its "short haul" made the throughout rate per mile on the South Yorkshire coal actually higher than the Derbyshire throughout rate despite the longer distance of the former from the market, Sir John Karslake seems to have thought it right to leave out of account, seeing that the Sheffield Company was not a party to the arbitration. In other words, he interpreted the phrase "equitable adjustment" as having reference only to the charges made by the Great Northern and Midland companies. He ignored the action of the Sheffield Company, and by so doing failed to give any weight to the larger meaning of "equitable adjustment"—the putting of the two coalfields on a fair footing to compete in the London market.

Thus the net result of the proceedings, which from first to last had consumed sixteen months, was *nil* as far as relief to the South Yorkshire coalfield was concerned; and, needless to say, such a result could not be the end of the matter. Mr. Allport, of course, was thoroughly satisfied to let it rest where it was, and so also might the Great Northern have been—for were they not also in the Derbyshire field? But there were two other parties—the South Yorkshire coalowners and the Sheffield Company—to be reckoned with, parties represented by such formidable champions as Mr. Baxter and Sir Edward Watkin, and the latter took immediate action. "The untoward award of Sir John Karslake," he wrote to Colonel Packe on 3 September, 1870, "compels me to ask what your Board have to propose in reference to the South Yorkshire coalfield, which cannot be allowed to be closed as respects the London market"; and when no reply came in time for the Sheffield Board meeting, he telegraphed for one to be sent back by wire. "Subject referred to a committee" was the answer he received from King's Cross (9 September, 1870).

At a Cheshire Lines Committee on 21 September, when Sheffield, Great Northern, and Midland representatives all met, Colonel Packe and Sir Edward Watkin arranged that the latter should attend a conference at King's Cross at the end of the month; but before that meeting took place the South Yorkshire coalowners had taken the field. At a meeting at Barnsley on 27 September a deputation consisting of Messrs. Baxter, Bartholomew, and eight others was appointed to take immediate steps to contest the right of railway companies to act on the principles confirmed by the award, and the prompt remedy was resolved upon of negotiating with the Sheffield Company for a specially low rate to the port of Grimsby, so that by steamers (which it was proposed, if necessary, to charter for the purpose) South Yorkshire coal might be sent to London by sea. At the same time "some astute coalowner"—perhaps Mr. Baxter—suggested that, having regard to the fact that the rates agreed between the Great Northern and Midland in 1863 included one from Retford to London (fixed for the benefit of a few collieries near the former place) which was 7*d.* less than the much-abused rate from Doncaster, some advantage might be gained if the Sheffield could be persuaded to make Retford instead of

Doncaster in future its chief place of delivery of coal to the Great Northern. But an objection to this, of course, was that the route from South Yorkshire to Retford was very circuitous.

On the following day (28 September, 1870) the deputation of coal-owners headed by Mr. Baxter waited upon Sir Edward Watkin, when the Grimsby and Retford suggestions were then both discussed. To the former Sir Edward willingly acceded, agreeing to make a special rate of 1s. 2d. per ton from South Yorkshire to Grimsby plus a proportion of the profit, if any, on the sale of the coal in London; and, with regard to the suggested delivery to the Great Northern at Retford, he mentioned that his company would be shortly opening a new piece of line at Mexborough which would shorten the distance for them. He added, however, that he doubted whether the plan would be of any real service.

Meanwhile the Retford suggestion had reached the directors at King's Cross and had been rather eagerly caught at by them as a means of extricating themselves from the "mess"—the word is Colonel Packe's—in which they felt themselves to be. So when on 29 September Sir Edward Watkin arrived to keep his engagement to meet them, one of the first things he was asked was: "Can you deliver the coal to us at Retford? because, if so, we feel ourselves fully at liberty to take it on at the lower Retford rate." Upon Sir Edward Watkin answering that, though the thing would be awkward until the new Mexborough line was opened, nevertheless it might be done from some of the nearer South Yorkshire pits at any rate, the matter was clinched there and then. Accordingly next day Mr. Underdown wrote to the coalowners* announcing this, and stating the readiness of the Sheffield Company to perform the carriage to Retford for 1s.—a reduction of 4d. on its Doncaster toll, which, added to the 7d. difference between the Great Northern's Retford and Doncaster rates, would make a total reduction of 11d. in the through rate,—provided that the coalowners would agree to reduce their prices for the London market by 2s. per ton—*i.e.*, to make an additional sacrifice themselves of 1s. 1d. On 4 October, 1870, the coalowners again met at Barnsley and decided to accept this proposal.

One day during this first week of October, 1870, it chanced that Mr. Allport and Mr. Oakley drove together in a cab to attend a meeting at the Great Eastern offices at Shoreditch. The conversation, naturally enough, turned upon Sir John Karslake's award, and Mr. Allport,

* Afterwards, when the wrath of the Midland broke, Sir E. Watkin tried hard to prove that this Retford artifice was first suggested by the Great Northern at his meeting with them on 29 September, but that it had been previously discussed between the Sheffield and the coalowners is conclusively proved by Mr. Underdown writing to the latter about it on 30 September as of a thing already known to them.

as Mr. Oakley thought, began to "crow" about the result of the arbitration. "I flatter myself," said he, "that I know more about the coal traffic than any of the managers; even Clarke himself, I think, never understood it properly." Thereupon the desire arose in Mr. Oakley's mind to "disturb," as he afterwards said, such "amiable self-satisfaction"; and, knowing as he did that by the diversion to Retford the differential in favour of Derbyshire was to be reduced from 1s. 4d. to 5d. without any breach of the agreement of 1863, he retorted: "Wait a bit! We may circumvent you yet." The remark struck the Midland manager at the time as "foreshadowing some action," but he afterwards dismissed it as "a mere playful expression, not to be taken seriously."

It recurred to his mind, however, on the morning of Monday, 8 October, when he found in that day's *Leeds Mercury* a report of the coalowners' meeting at Barnsley, already referred to, which stated that in accordance with Mr. Underdown's letter, promising a reduction in the rate, it had been decided to reduce the price of coal sent *via* Retford by 2s. a ton, "to enable the South Yorkshire owners to meet the competition of the Derbyshire and North of England collieries in the London market." Mr. Allport's immediate action was to write a peremptory letter to Mr. Oakley. "We cannot assent," said he, "to the terms of our agreement being evaded in this way. The present rate for South Yorkshire coal to London is 8s. 2d. a ton, and it will be necessary for you to charge from Retford whatever rate will, with the reduced charge of the Manchester, Sheffield, and Lincolnshire Company, bring the rate to that amount. I shall be glad to hear from you by return that you will do this, and that it is not the intention of your Company to assist the South Yorkshire colliery owners or the Manchester, Sheffield, and Lincolnshire Company in evading our agreement with you."

Needless to say, the Great Northern authorities did not admit either that the agreement was being "evaded," or that they were under obligation to raise the agreed Retford rate, and, as Mr. Oakley had gone away for a short holiday, Mr. Allport got no answer whatever to his letter. He waited for a fortnight, and then upon pressure from Derbyshire coalowners who represented that the report of a reduction in the South Yorkshire rate was already stopping their trade, he wrote again, on 24 October, 1870, both to Mr. Oakley and to Sir Edward Watkin, threatening reprisals if the request made in his former letter was not promptly attended to. The Great Northern manager now replied that the matter had not seemed to him to be pressing, as very little coal had yet passed by Retford, but that he would be pleased to see Mr. Allport on the subject at King's Cross on the following Friday, before the meeting of the Great Northern Board.

The position of the newly-made Great Northern manager was undoubtedly a trying one. He was between two fires—fires directed by two of the most experienced and adroit campaigners who have ever borne arms in railway warfare.

On Friday, 28 October, Mr. Allport came to King's Cross more peremptory than ever in his demands, and, hardly had he strode out of Mr. Oakley's room, indignant at the "meagre answers" he had received, and declaring that he should strongly advise his Board to reduce at once their rates for Derbyshire coal to London, than there came an equally peremptory telegram from Sir Edward Watkin :—

"As your Board is sitting, please answer the following question specifically: If we lower the South Yorkshire toll, will you become bound to keep the rates from Doncaster and Retford at their present amount without augmentation?"

"Promise to increase the Retford rate!" Mr. Allport thundered. "Promise not to increase it!" demanded Sir Edward Watkin. We will do "nothing contrary to the agreement with the Midland," was all the Great Northern Board could reply to Sir Edward Watkin. "We will go again to Sir John Karslake, if you like, and ask him if under the circumstances we are bound to raise the Retford rate," was the utmost concession they could make to Mr. Allport.

And, as if Mr. Allport and Sir Edward Watkin were not enough, there were Messrs. Baxter and Bartholomew also to be reckoned with —the Busy B's who were proving more than ever worthy of their nickname. They had carried through the Retford artifice, and had arranged also for a service of boats from Grimsby, but these were temporary measures only. Something more was needed to "liberate" the South Yorkshire coalfield permanently, and in their own minds Messrs. Baxter and Bartholomew had already decided what that something was to be. The "coal line" of 1864 was to be revived, and revived, too, in the next session of Parliament. Some men would have thought it impossible to deposit in November the plans of a line the promotion of which they had not resolved upon until October. Not so the Busy B's. If the Sheffield and Great Eastern companies would assist, the thing could be done, and they had already broached the subject to Sir Edward Watkin. The result was that, when on 1 November, 1870, Mr. Allport wrote again to Mr. Oakley complaining of the "nonchalance" with which, in his opinion, the Great Northern was treating the coal question, the Great Northern manager could retort that it was not he, but Mr. Allport who did not appreciate the "only really serious" point. "This," he added, "you will probably admit, when you know that Messrs. Watkin, Baxter, and Bartholomew met at Doncaster on Saturday last, and decided to apply for a new line on the east of our own. Mr. Johnson, our engineer, tells me to-day" (2 November) "that he met one of their surveyors measuring near Sleaford yesterday. I forbear from further words lest I should aggravate the position."

Mr. Allport, however, refused to swerve in the least from the position which he had all along taken up. In his view the maintenance of the difference of 1s. 4d. in the rates was absolutely necessary for the protection of the Derbyshire coal traffic, and this difference the Great Northern had, he said, agreed to preserve under all circumstances. The justice of this agreement, moreover, had been confirmed after prolonged arbitration proceedings. Yet by the diversion of the traffic to Retford the spirit of it was being broken—and not only the spirit but the letter, for was there not a clause in the agreement directed against "booking short," which "expressly provided against the very mode of evasion which was now being attempted?" What, under such circumstances, could the Midland do but retaliate? So on 9 November, 1870, its Board decided, on Mr. Allport's advice, to reduce its Derbyshire rates by the same amount by which the South Yorkshire rate had been reduced by the Retford artifice, viz., 11d., so as to bring back the differential again to 1s. 4d.

This meant the commencement of a rate war, and it filled the Board-room of every northern railway with excitement. A special meeting of the Great Northern directors was hastily summoned, but before it could meet Sir Edward Watkin had time to write to Colonel Packe to know whether the Doncaster and Retford rates would be reduced to meet the Midland reduction, and the day of the Great Northern meeting he twice telegraphed the same inquiry. The Great Northern Board replied that they were forwarding a resolution to the Midland expressing their willingness to return to the *status quo* before the Retford diversion, if the Midland would consent to a new arbitration. "Do you mean that you are going back to the 1s. 4d. differential?" responded Sir Edward at once. "We mean what our resolution says," replied Mr. Oakley.

But after all it was impossible for the Great Northern to avoid following up the fight. The Midland would hear of no new arbitration, and so before November was out not only was the Great Northern obliged to reduce its Derbyshire rates, but the London and North Western, Great Western, and Great Eastern also found it necessary to make reductions in their coal charges. Lord Salisbury, on behalf of the Great Eastern, Mr. H. S. Thompson of the North Eastern, and Sir Edward Watkin, all pressed for a reference to a "practical umpire," but in vain. On 7 December, 1870, the Midland Board passed a resolution "respectfully but firmly declining any arbitration or mediation which directly or indirectly reopens Sir J. Karslake's award," and declaring that the agreement of 1863 had been made void by the Great Northern's evasion of it, and on 20 December the Great Northern retorted with a counter resolution accepting this position so far as the termination of the agreement was concerned.

Up to this time, despite all Sir Edward Watkin's hustling, the Great Northern had made no reduction in its rate from South Yorkshire beyond the $7d.$ which the diversion to Retford had brought about; but now that the agreement of 1863 was formally at an end, its directors felt quite free to alter the rate as they liked. They lost no time, therefore, in making their new freedom known to the South Yorkshire coalowners and to the Sheffield Company, with the view, if possible, of making their peace with these parties. The matter was the more urgent because amongst the deposit of new Bills for the session of 1871 appeared one for a line from the Great Eastern system at Long Stanton—the same point whence, it may be remembered, the line of 1864 had been planned to start—to a junction with the Manchester, Sheffield, and Lincolnshire system near Market Rasen in Lincolnshire, and there could be no doubt that this was the outcome of some sort of agreement between Mr. Baxter, Sir Edward Watkin, and the Great Eastern.

But though the Great Northern was now free to fix what rates from South Yorkshire it liked, nevertheless the crucial point remained as before—what relation was the South Yorkshire rate to bear to the Derbyshire rate—and, as before also, this depended largely upon what share in the through South Yorkshire rate the Sheffield Company intended to exact. Two years before, it will be remembered, prior to the arbitration proceedings, and when the Great Northern had hoped to get a re-adjustment of the rates through the medium of the London Conference, Sir Edward Watkin had agreed that the Sheffield should commute its $1d.$ per mile toll for a proportion equal to thirty miles —nearly double its actual mileage—of whatever through rate the Great Northern might fix. This agreement, accordingly, the latter now proposed to enforce, but with the proviso that, in view of the lowness of the existing rates and the likelihood of further competitive reductions on the part of the Midland, the minimum of $10d.$ for which Sir Edward Watkin had stipulated in 1869 should be reduced to $8d.$ If the Sheffield Company will agree to this, said the

Great Northern to the coalowners, we will undertake to make the differential between the South Yorkshire rate and the Midland rate from Clay Cross 8*d.* only, instead of the 1*s.* 4*d.* of which you have so much complained.

These proposals were discussed at meetings held between representatives of the Great Northern, the Sheffield, and the coalowners at Leeds on 29 and 30 December, 1870. The outcome was that, upon the Sheffield agreeing to accept the 8*d.* minimum "for a trial period of three months," the Great Northern from the beginning of the new year reduced the South Yorkshire rate so as to bring the differential down to 8*d.* as agreed. The Midland Company promptly responded on 5 January, 1871, with a reduction of its Derbyshire rates to bring it back again to 1*s.* 4*d.*, and so on 16 January the Great Northern had to take a further 8*d.* off South Yorkshire, besides, of course, reducing for Derbyshire also. Not to be daunted, the Midland on 2 February took off yet another 8*d.* off Derbyshire, making a total reduction of 2*s.* 3*d.* per ton since the beginning of the "war."

This was "ruinous competition" indeed, and the Great Northern felt bound to pause before continuing. In the first place, every new reduction meant simply a fresh present to the coalowners and coalmerchants—for, owing to a very exceptional demand for coal at this time, the consumer was obtaining little, if any benefit. In the second place, the effort which the Great Northern had already made on behalf of South Yorkshire had not apparently had the smallest effect in improving the attitude towards it of Mr. Baxter and Sir E. Watkin. Mr. Baxter had gone away hurriedly from the meeting at Leeds, had taken no notice of a letter Mr. Oakley had sent after him asking for his co-operation in the campaign upon which the Great Northern was about to enter, and was apparently as bent as ever on prosecuting his new coal line. Sir Edward Watkin had given a very grudging assent to the Sheffield's minimum being reduced to 8*d.*, and when writing on 30 December, 1870, to give this, he had told Colonel Packe that the Great Northern must give "some guarantee and security for the future freedom" of the South Yorkshire traffic if they wished to "obviate the necessity" of the Sheffield "energetically promoting an independent means of communication." What he meant by this he had revealed explicitly in a second letter (9 January, 1871), in which he expressed "no doubt that the directors of the Sheffield Company would recommend their proprietors to be satisfied for the present with full running powers for mineral traffic over the Great Northern lines south of Doncaster and Lincoln," and in a third letter, written three days later, he had asked for "a frank and specific answer" to this, "yes or no," on the following Friday. If you refuse such obviously needful and just safeguards," he wrote, "we have no alternative left but independent access to our market over another railway."

"Another railway" obviously meant Mr. Baxter's new coal line, but the Great Northern directors did not allow themselves to be frightened by the threat. They were conscious that they had done, and were doing, their full duty by the South Yorkshire coalfield; they remembered that they had met and beaten Mr. Baxter's coal line already in 1864; and, as for an alliance between the Sheffield and the Great Eastern, it seemed hardly possible that Parliament could sanction such a proceeding in view of the clause in their own "Fifty Years Agreement" with the Sheffield—an agreement Parliament had most formally ratified—by which each of the two companies had bound itself not to do any act to the injury of the traffic of the other. Therefore, not only did they not send back an immediate "yes" to Sir Edward Watkin's modest request for running powers to King's Cross, but they kept him waiting two months for his answer, and then told him on 12 March, 1870, that they had "failed to discover any reason" for granting what he had asked. On the same day they decided to make yet one more reduction in their South Yorkshire rate to meet the Midland reduction of 2 February, and so bring the differential again to the 8$d.$, to which they had pledged themselves with the coalowners.

Thus the Great Northern was still between the two fires—the Midland on the one side, Mr. Baxter and Sir Edward Watkin on the other, and the Midland now brought a new battery into play. At their next Board meeting on 24 March its directors decided not only to reduce their Derbyshire rates by yet another 8$d.$ to bring back the differential to 1$s.$ 4$d.$, making the total Clay Cross rate 3$s.$ 2$d.$ per ton only, but to withdraw from the Great Northern the through rates into the Derbyshire field which it had enjoyed since 1863. Accordingly on Friday, 30 March, 1871, they sent their mineral manager to Doncaster to inform the Great Northern mineral manager that from the following Monday, 2 April, coal forwarded from Derbyshire to London *viâ* Nottingham and Grantham would have to pay the higher local rate from the pits to Nottingham, which meant that "for all purposes of healthy trade"—to quote Mr. Oakley—the Great Northern was to be excluded from the Derbyshire field. Nor was this a slight loss which its championship of South Yorkshire had brought upon the Great Northern. It meant the cutting off of a trade which had brought in recently quite £50,000 a year!

Having thus re-secured its monopoly in Derbyshire the Midland was in a position to raise its rates by degrees; and, as each raising of the Derbyshire rate was thus made, the Great Northern (after making a final reduction of 8*d*. on 2 April* to meet the Midland reduction of 24 March) followed suit by raising the South Yorkshire rate, being careful, however, that the differential should be kept at 8*d*. as it had promised. Meanwhile, the Bill for the new line from Long Stanton to Market Rasen—the Coalowners' Associated (London) Railway Bill Mr. Baxter had called it, for no reason, apparently, except that the initials spelt C. O. A. L.—had been formally introduced into Parliament, and on 26 April, 1871, it came before a Committee of the House of Commons.

The contest lasted for nearly a month, and it was chiefly remarkable for the "strange bedfellows" it made. The chief witnesses for the Bill were Mr. Baxter—who had also advanced the deposit money and vouched for half the preliminary expenses—Sir Edward Watkin, the Marquis of Salisbury, and Mr. Samuel Swarbrick (lately Midland accountant, but now Great Eastern general manager), and the chief witnesses against it were Mr. Oakley and Mr. Allport! The new line proved to be so badly laid out that probably under no circumstances would Parliament have sanctioned it; and when the Great Northern offered to give power to the Sheffield and Great Eastern companies jointly to make a through rate for coal from South Yorkshire to Shoreditch over the existing route *via* the Great Northern loop line, it was obvious that the construction of a new route could serve no public interest. But Sir Edward Watkin, as Mr. Denison, Q.C., said in his most telling speech for the Great Northern, was "equal to the emergency." He was forced to admit that the Great Northern had fought the Midland on behalf of South Yorkshire, and so brought about its own exclusion from the Derbyshire field; nevertheless, he refused to admit that South Yorkshire interests could be safe so long as they were wholly or partly under Great Northern control. "I cannot trust you. I tell you frankly," he said to Mr. Horace Lloyd, the Great Northern counsel (meaning by "you," of course, the Great Northern Company), and upon this text Mr. Denison based the most destructive part of his speech in reply. "I have not invited this issue," he said, "of the confidence in the Manchester, Sheffield Company, or in Sir Edward Watkin personally; but if Sir Edward Watkin chooses to come here and tell a body of gentlemen such as the Great Northern Board that he cannot trust them, he invites inquiry into his own antecedents. I

---

* This final reduction brought the South Yorkshire rate down to 3*s*. 10*d*. per ton for a distance of 172 miles.

am merely dealing with him in his railway character—in any other character I have nothing to say to him—but I should like to know if any company in England has done such things as the Manchester, Sheffield have done — hawked itself about as buyer, as seller, as guarantor and guarantee; bribed to shut up their traffic, bribed to open their traffic. There is not a conceivable bargain to which they have not been parties, and here they come to ask to have justice. I only wish it to be administered to them."

"And now, sir," continued the Great Northern counsel, "what is it that they want? You know from the best authority, that of Sir Edward Watkin himself, what he wants, namely, power to fix Great Northern rates, or power to run over the Great Northern line, with, as you know, a nuisance to sell. When people come to have *bonâ fide* use of a thing they content themselves with facility clauses, but when they ask for absolute running powers they are very often for the purpose of being sold to the persons over whom they are got, as a nuisance. The next time the Manchester, Sheffield, and Lincolnshire Company goes into the market there will be this excellent property to sell—running powers over the Great Northern, valued at I don't know what. The time may come when it may be worth the while of somebody to guarantee them $3\frac{1}{2}$ per cent., not with the view of getting that out of it, but for indirect purposes, and that is why he wants the Bill." In short, apart from Mr. Baxter's almost religious enthusiasm for the South Yorkshire coalfield—an enthusiasm which had not been thoroughly well founded even when enlisted in the promotion of the Great Northern itself, and which in a subsequent chapter we shall see openly discounted as "fanaticism"—the case for the Bill rested solely upon the "political" designs of Sir Edward Watkin. Therefore it is not surprising that the Committee declared "the preamble not proved" (23 May, 1871).

Thus the Watkin-cum-Baxter battery was silenced for a time, and the Great Northern was free to turn square to face the fire directed by Mr. Allport.

CHAPTER XVI.

THE INVASION OF THE MIDLANDS—1871-2.

WE have noted that the Great Northern, unlike many British railway companies, had passed unscathed through the financial crisis of 1866. Nevertheless, like other companies, it had felt the effect of the timidity and "tightness" which had characterized the money market during the two following years. Accordingly, prior to the half-yearly meeting in February, 1868, the directors — to quote the language of their report—"had felt it their duty to revise carefully the Company's position with the view to reduce the liability for further capital expenditure." Fortunately the more important of the extensions upon which the Company had embarked during the earlier sixties— extensions which between 1860 and 1867, as we noted two chapters ago, had increased its capital from about twelve to about twenty millions—had by this time been completed, but still a further liability of over three millions remained unfulfilled. This the directors proposed to reduce by about one-third by obtaining from the Board of Trade, under a Railways Relief Act just passed, power to abandon several authorized extensions not yet begun.

The more important of these were the Sleaford and Bourn line, and the northern part of the Hornsey and Hertford — the part between Enfield and the junction with the Hertford branch at Hertingfordbury,—but in the case of the Sleaford and Bourn the Board of Trade refused the application on the ground that it was unjust to the locality that the Company should thus abandon powers for which it had twice petitioned Parliament. In the other case, however, a warrant of abandonment was duly obtained. Thus the Hornsey and Hertford was made more than ever at variance with its name by being cut down from a loop line to a short suburban branch ending at Enfield.

The abandonment of the section between Enfield and Hertingfordbury, however, was sanctioned only upon the condition that the southern part of the scheme should be carried out within the time prescribed by the original Act. Accordingly, early in 1869 the works of this, 4½ miles in length, were let to Mr. Joseph Firbank. The new branch was to leave the main trunk at Wood Green, a mile north of Hornsey (there had been a small station at Wood Green since 1860), and the contract included also the laying of a duplicate pair of tracks from Wood Green southwards as far as Seven Sisters Road. These, with the duplicate lines already laid south of Seven Sisters Road in connection with the Edgware and Highgate branch, were to make four tracks all the way from Wood Green to the mouth of Copenhagen Tunnel.

The widening of this tunnel itself, however, was, like the "loop" duplication between Hornsey and Welwyn, postponed for a time, but it had become obvious, despite the now complete withdrawal of the Midland traffic, that not only this, but the Maiden Lane tunnel also, would have sooner or later to be doubled to provide for the rapid increase of "City and suburban" business. Since 1 March, 1868, the Great Northern's suburban trains had been working over "the widened lines" between King's Cross and Farringdon Street—lines which the Metropolitan Company had constructed specially for the use of the Great Northern, Midland, and London, Chatham, and Dover, and in joint possession of which those three companies had been confirmed upon their guaranteeing a minimum traffic; and from 1 June, 1869, the Great Northern began to work its trains beyond Farringdon Street to and from Moorgate Street—a section of which station it rented from that date as a City terminus. Moreover, from about the same time, by arrangement with the London, Chatham, and Dover Company, it began to run to and from a West-end terminus, Victoria, *via* Farringdon Street and Blackfriars.

Quite a feature in the internal history of the Company at this time was the sudden rise into importance of the "Seven Sisters Road Station." In February, 1868, the directors decided to add "a foot-bridge and waiting-shed" to the original wooden platforms opened there in 1861; and when they followed this up a year later by proposing an expenditure of £1146 on "waiting-room and covering of platform," some of the shareholders began to protest. "That Seven Sisters Road has become an incubus,' Mr. Seneca Hughes declared. "It is like the weird sisters, or like the daughters of the horse-leech crying, 'Give, give!'" On the other hand, another shareholder—who had stated that he had "some friends at Colney Hatch" (loud laughter)—protested that if they did not supply a "covering at Seven Sisters suitable for human beings to be protected" it was "rather inhuman to have the station at all." "Why all this fuss about granting £1146 for keeping in repair and adorning the Seven Sisters?" a third speaker put in, "I have known two sisters cost double the money." In August, 1869, the new public park adjoining this station was opened, whereupon its name was changed from Seven Sisters Road to Finsbury Park.

In this same year, 1869, an exceptional expenditure had to be incurred at the passenger terminus, King's Cross. The reader may remember that the roof of this structure had been originally constructed with wooden girders—bundles of planks stretched like the wood of a bow,—and that, when describing this peculiarity, we noted the great strain which it put upon the outside walls, especially on the eastern side, where there was no support from subsidiary buildings, nor room for sufficient flying buttresses. The result was that in 1869 it had become obvious that this side of the station was "shaky"; and, the strengthening of the wall being for the reason we have just named a matter of great difficulty, it was decided to adopt the other alternative of renewing the roof by the substitution of iron girders for the wooden ones. The operation, obviously, was not an easy one, seeing that it had to be carried out without interfering with the traffic of the station; but, by the construction of a large travelling stage which could be moved on wheels along the platforms, the difficulty was successfully got over, and during 1869 and 1870, the whole of the thirty-three "bays" of the roof over the eastern or "arrival" half of the station were one by one reconstructed in the more solid material. In view of the fact that the western wall, being supported by the Company's offices, had shown no signs of shakiness, it was not felt necessary to proceed at once with the renewal of the "departure" side of the roof, but in the belief that this, too, would have to be done sooner or later, the timbers of the stage were carefully numbered and preserved. The cost of the work done in 1869-70 was about £13,000, and the whole of it was charged to revenue account.

Meanwhile the time of rest for capital account, which the state of the money market had enforced, had been brought to an end both by a financial recovery, and by the fact that it was necessary to proceed at once with outstanding extensions, even in those cases where extension of time had been obtained. Accordingly at the beginning of 1870 active measures were taken to obtain the land for the Bourn and Sleaford and Finchley and Barnet lines.* About the same time, too, the Cheshire Lines Joint Committee let the contract for the

---

* The powers for this, it may be remembered, were taken over with the Edgware and Highgate undertaking. Powers similarly acquired for an Edgware and Watford line the Great Northern succeeded in getting leave to abandon.

new direct Manchester and Liverpool line, and commenced to acquire the land for its Liverpool Central Station. We have already noted that up to the end of 1867 the Great Northern, as third owner in the Cheshire lines, had contributed nearly a million to railway undertakings west of Manchester, and in 1870 it had not only not received anything in the shape of interest on this expenditure, but, ever since the opening of the first completed of these undertakings in 1863, had had to pay some thousands every half-year as its share of the "loss on working" them. The last to be completed—the West Cheshire—was not opened until 1870, and so the through traffic to Birkenhead, which, it may be remembered, was one of the main objects of the construction of the lines, could not be commenced in that year. But even when this was accomplished any return of profit still seemed remote; and so the Joint Committee decided to press on at once with the construction of the Manchester and Liverpool line and of the new Liverpool station, in the hope that the remunerative results of these undertakings might compensate their shareholders for the unprofitableness of those already carried out.

In this same year, 1870, a new joint liability into which the Great Northern had entered in partnership with the Lancashire and Yorkshire Company forced itself prominently forward. As long before as 1863 a local company had been set on foot under the leadership of Mr. Edward Akroyd (whom the reader may remember as the chief promoter of the Leeds, Bradford, and Halifax Railway) to make a line northwards from Halifax up the Thornton Valley to Keighley; but, as the country is a very difficult one for railway construction, the project, as ultimately sanctioned by Parliament in 1864, had amounted to no more than a line 2½ miles in length from the Lancashire and Yorkshire's low-level station at Halifax (into which the Great Northern also was working) to the populous township of Ovenden. To the capital of this the Great Northern and Lancashire and Yorkshire had each promised to subscribe one-third (£60,000).

Subsequently some deviations in the original line had been found necessary, and for these a new Act had had to be obtained, which had not passed through Parliament until 1867; and then the state of the money market had prevented the commencement of the works. The result was that in 1870 the company had to come before Parliament once more for an "extension of time." For preliminary expenses, however, the Great Northern and Lancashire and Yorkshire had already advanced a sum of £24,000, and so, while the Extension of Time Bill was pending, their directors came to the conclusion that if they were to safeguard the money already spent and ensure the carrying out of the undertaking they had better obtain jointly complete control. Accordingly, with the consent of Mr. Akroyd and his friends, they had clauses inserted in the Extension of Time Bill to vest the Halifax and Ovenden Railway in the joint ownership of their two companies, and in this form it became law in the session of 1870. Soon afterwards the works of the line were put in under the engineering superintendence of Mr. John Fraser, of Leeds.

This Mr. Fraser should properly have been mentioned before this in these pages, for he had been associated, either as assistant or as chief engineer, with all the lines which the Great Northern Company had acquired up to this time in the West Riding of Yorkshire. In these various undertakings—the Leeds, Bradford, and Halifax, the West Yorkshire, the West Riding and Grimsby, and this just mentioned Halifax and Ovenden—he had worked in double harness with a solicitor of Leeds, Mr. Henry Nelson, head of the firm of Nelson, Barr, and Nelson, whom we did note in an earlier chapter as helping Messrs. Akroyd and Firth to promote the Leeds, Bradford, and Halifax. Now we have to become acquainted with two further Yorkshire extensions which these "jackals"—as their class is sometimes profanely called—provided for the Great Northern "lion." These were the Bradford, Eccleshill, and Idle, and Idle and Shipley railways.

The former of these lines was to be three and a half miles and the latter two and a half miles in length; the Acts for them had been obtained in 1866 and 1867 respectively; and, as they were both laid out to act as "feeders" to the Great Northern system by bringing it into direct connection with busy manufacturing townships in the neighbourhood of Bradford, the Great Northern Board had consented to the insertion of clauses in those Acts empowering it to subscribe to their capital. At the same time it had undertaken to work them when made. However, as in the case of the Halifax and Ovenden, the state of the money market had delayed operations, and now, in 1870, in the flush of revived national prosperity, the Great Northern directors were persuaded to take over the undertakings *in toto*, subject to the sanction of Parliament in the following session. At the same time, also on the advice of Messrs. Nelson and Fraser, they decided to promote other tributary branches from their existing system to Dewsbury, Pudsey, and Crofton—all in the West Riding of Yorkshire.

Nor does this exhaust the list of extensions in the West Riding to which the Great Northern Company became committed during the years 1870-1. Yet another undertaking, called the Bradford and Thornton, has yet to be mentioned. This line was first projected, like the Halifax and Ovenden, as part of a through route through the

Thornton Valley to Keighley; but it was subsequently modified, owing to the costly engineering features which Mr. Fraser's plans for the through line had presented, into a branch from Bradford to Queensbury and Thornton only. For this Mr. Nelson deposited a Bill for the session of 1871 in the name of an independent company of which the Messrs. Foster, of Queensbury, were the chief supporters. During its progress through Parliament, however, the Great Northern directors were induced to make an agreement to take it over—for, if they did not do so, it seemed quite likely that the Midland would,—and so a bargain was struck, the local promoters, on their part, agreeing to subscribe half the capital and to receive for it 80 per cent. of Great Northern original stock. In this same session of 1871 the Bill for the transfer of the Bradford, Eccleshill, and Idle, and Idle and Shipley undertakings to the Company, and for the construction of the Dewsbury, Pudsey, and Crofton branches, passed into law.

By this time the Wood Green and Enfield line had been completed and opened (April, 1871) and the Bourn and Sleaford and Finchley and Barnet lines were approaching completion, so that these new liabilities in Yorkshire did not raise the Company's prospective capital expenditure on new lines to more than a million sterling. On the other hand, there were not wanting indications that in the future the construction or acquirement of new lines was not to be the only serious charge which capital account was to be called upon to bear. At the time of the financial panic in 1866, when the accounts of railway companies had come to be much more closely scrutinized than before, no charge of overloading the capital account had been brought home to the Great Northern directorate; indeed, in distributing expenses between revenue and capital it had been and continued to be the policy of the Board to err, if anything, on the side of overburdening revenue. Thus the whole cost of renewing the line with 84-lb. instead of 72-lb. rails had been charged to revenue, and the greater part, too, of the cost of replacing the timber bridges at Bardney, Bawtry, and a number of other places with more solid structures of iron and brickwork—an operation which had become necessary throughout the system within fifteen years of its first opening. More recently too we have seen an example of the same practice in the charging to revenue of the whole cost of the renewal of the King's Cross roof. It is true that, when in 1867 the advisability of gradually replacing iron rails by steel and 6-ton or 7-ton waggons by 9-ton had brought the question of capital *v.* revenue account definitely into notice, the shareholders had decided on the advice of the Board that a proportion of the expense thus incurred should in the future be regularly charged to capital, to prevent injustice being done to holders of deferred or "A" stock; but in 1870 this resolution had again, on the advice of the directors, been rescinded, and it had been resolved that revenue should again bear the whole cost of rail and waggon renewals, these having in the meantime, it is fair to add, become less burdensome than before. In spite of all this, however, the fact remains that now, from 1871, the demands on capital account for works connected with the existing undertaking—as distinguished from works of extension—threatened to become much larger than they had formerly been.

This seeming contradiction is explained by the fact that the lines, stations, and general equipment with which the Company had provided itself from the outset first began about 1871 to show themselves seriously inadequate for the requirements of the increased traffic. Reaction from an abnormal depression of trade made the increase of railway business very rapid from 1870 onward, and during the period of depression the Company had opened a number of new lines which now for the first time began to pour a full tribute of traffic into the main channel. The result of these two influences was that demands for increased siding accommodation, for enlargement of stations and warehouses, and for a larger supply of rolling-stock rose up from all parts of the system. On the lines themselves, too, the working of the trains became much more difficult, and as a remedy for this it became necessary largely to extend the block system and the interlocking of signals and switches, involving the erection of costly signal boxes quite separate from the station buildings. All these were "additions to estate" which had to be paid for out of capital, and in 1871—the first year in which the demands for them became clamorous—the shareholders had to be asked to sanction £102,309 at their February meeting, and £79,742 in August for expenditure on capital account apart from the current outlay on new lines. Nor were these to prove exceptional charges. In February, 1872, the directors reported that "the increase of traffic and efficient working of the railway" necessitated the expenditure of a further sum of £208,997, and in August, 1872, an additional £170,487 had to be sanctioned under the same head.

Thus, what with liabilities in Lancashire, liabilities in Yorkshire, and liabilities for equipment generally, the Great Northern directors had a good deal on hand in 1871. Nevertheless, they found themselves constrained in that year to initiate new movements involving other liabilities compared with which those which we have just enumerated were small affairs. In so doing they were impelled to some extent by a general feeling in favour of new enterprises—a feeling which pervaded every railway Board-room at this time, and was the natural reaction from the extreme timidity of the preceding three years. In short, they fell victims to a periodic wave of railway mania; but, even if no such general feeling had existed, they would still have been obliged to have embarked on one, at least, of the new undertakings now to be mentioned. Not to have done so would have been to have allowed the Midland Company to deprive them permanently of one of the most valuable branches of their trade.

From 1 April, 1871, as recorded in our last chapter, the Great Northern had been excluded from the Derbyshire coalfield "for all purposes of healthy trade" by the action of the Midland Company in withdrawing from the agreement it had made in 1863 to give through rates from the pits to the Great Northern *viâ* Nottingham. Now, since 1863 the Derbyshire field had definitely superseded the South Yorkshire as the principal source whence the rail-borne coal supply of London was drawn. Therefore, it was quite impossible for the Great Northern to acquiesce in being thus excluded, and to return to the position of depending principally upon South Yorkshire for its coal traffic. Under the new state of things which the development of the Derbyshire field had brought about, the Great Northern had either to secure re-admission to that district on equal terms with the Midland, or else to lose irrevocably, not supremacy in the London coal traffic—that it had lost already—but status of any valuable kind as a London coal carrier. Under these circumstances the very least which the Board at King's Cross could do was to revive its Codnor Park line of 1863.

As it happened, however, the "Derbyshire extension" railways, which the Great Northern directors promoted for the session of 1872, were a good deal more than a mere revival of the Codnor Park project. For this there were various justifications. The starting-point chosen was the same as before—Colwick, three miles east of Nottingham, the terminus of the original Ambergate line—but instead of branching off to the south-west as the Codnor Park line had done, the line which the Great Northern engineer, Mr. Johnson, was instructed to lay out took a northerly direction for a few miles. The purpose of this was to tap some 4000 acres of coal-producing land belonging to the Duke of St. Albans' Bestwood estate, which had not yet been worked for lack of railway communication. Thence turning westward through Bulwell and crossing (on a viaduct over 100 yards long) the Leen Valley and the Midland's Mansfield line, the new railway was planned to run to Kimberley, a course which had the double justification that the inhabitants of this place, about 4000 in number, had petitioned the Great

Northern to come to them, and that Kimberley lay on the direct route from the Bestwood estate to the mouth of the Erewash Valley. For to reach the Erewash Valley, the heart of the coal-producing district, was in 1871, as in 1862, the Great Northern's prime object.

Up the Erewash Valley, then past Codnor Park to Pinxton, Mr. Johnson carried his line, and so far it was a reproduction of the Codnor Park scheme, with the addition of the *détour* to tap the Bestwood estate; but a terminus at Pinxton was not the end of the scheme. Instead of forming the main project, as in 1862, the line up the Erewash Valley was made this time a branch only of a larger undertaking, an undertaking which had two other objects—to reach Derby and to connect with the system of the North Staffordshire Company. South-west from Kimberley is Ilkeston, the inhabitants of which, numbering about 10,000 in 1871, were just adding the uncongenial trade of iron blasting to their original industry in hosiery and lace; and here the Great Northern was warmly welcomed, for the Midland's "Ilkeston Station" was $1\frac{1}{2}$ miles out of the parish, and the accommodation it gave was so poor that people said they preferred to walk wherever possible rather than to use it. Moreover, the Great Northern proposed to go on in a direct line, nine miles only in length, to Derby, whereas the Midland's route to Derby was not only much longer than this, but involved a "change," and often much delay, at Trent Junction.

At Derby the Great Northern scheme recommended itself by proposing a station nearer the centre of the town than the Midland, and by offering the benefits of competition in a place which since King Hudson's first amalgamation of railways in 1844 had been almost monopolized by the Midland Company. Nor was it proposed that the new route should come to a "dead-end" in Derby. Still continuing in a north-westerly direction through Mickleover and Etwall, it found its final goal at last in a double junction with the North Staffordshire system at Egginton, near Burton-on-Trent, into which important town the latter company undertook to give the Great Northern running powers. The Erewash Valley—Derby—Burton—here was an invasion of the Midlands indeed!

To sum up this Derbyshire and Staffordshire Extensions Bill, the Great Northern proposed under it to construct new railways $40\frac{1}{2}$ miles in length at an estimated total cost of £1,097,467—a pretty considerable new liability to add to those to which it was already committed. Nevertheless, its new projects for the session of 1872 could not be allowed to end even there. For, imperative as was the necessity to enforce re-admission into the Derbyshire coalfield,

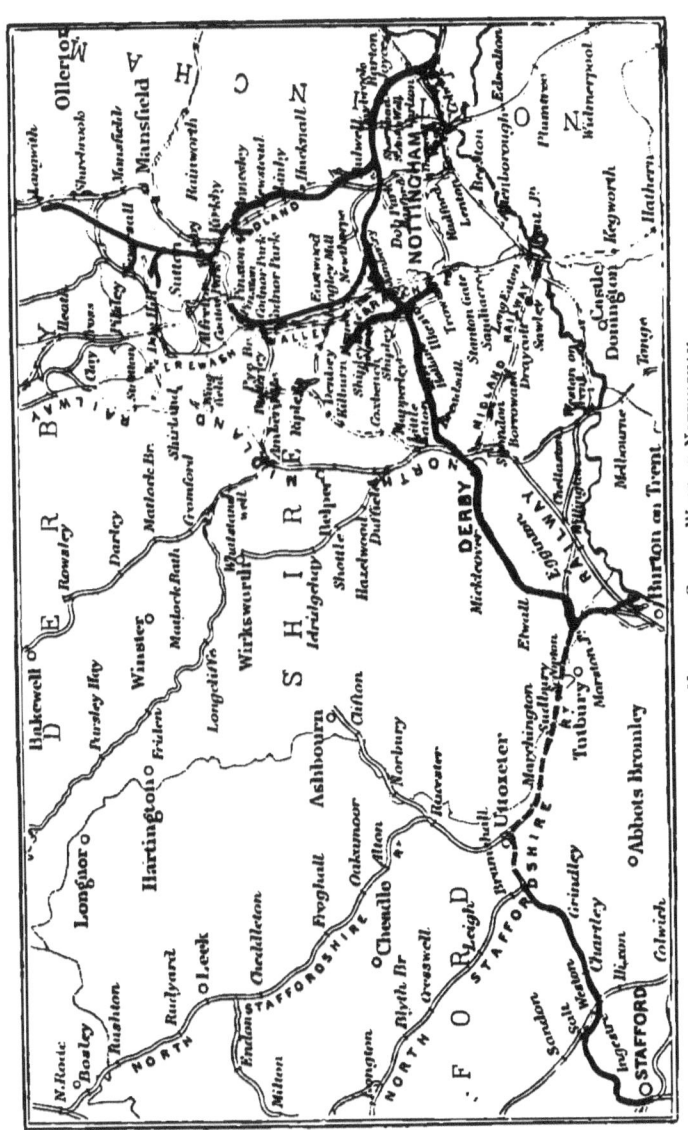

there was another demand upon the Company hardly less imperative—the demand to relieve the congestion of traffic in the neighbourhood of King's Cross. This was, as we know, a necessity which had been recognized as long before as 1866, when powers had been obtained to double the Copenhagen tunnel, and so provide a separate channel for goods traffic between Holloway and the terminus; but depression of trade and the withdrawal of the Midland's London traffic had combined, as we have seen, to postpone the execution of this work; and now, in 1871, the directors decided to seek the same object by another road. They proposed to construct a link line from Finsbury Park to the North London system at Canonbury.

The Bill embodying this proposal was what is known as a "Various Powers Bill," and it covered also the transfer to the Great Northern of the already authorized Bradford and Thornton undertaking, and the making of a new short line at Dewsbury to connect the authorized branches from Batley and from Ossett. The estimate of capital to be expended under it was £706,715.

Meantime, while Mr. Leech and Mr. Johnson, the Great Northern official solicitor and engineer, were putting these important and onerous projects into shape, another solicitor and engineer—Messrs. Nelson and Fraser—no less keen to protect Great Northern interests and to extend its powers because their connection with the Company was unofficial—had yet another ambitious extension of its system in hand. Readers, perhaps, remember Mr. William Firth, of Leeds, comrade with Mr. Akroyd in promoting the Leeds, Bradford, and Halifax line, and chief promoter also of the West Yorkshire Company, and they should have been informed before this that, after those two undertakings had been amalgamated with the Great Northern, a seat had been found for Mr. Firth on the Great Northern Board. Thus seated, he had become by force of character a leader in the Company's counsels. He had just taken a principal part, for example, in the "coal war," and now in another direction his active mind was to influence the policy of the Company.

As chairman of the West Yorkshire Iron and Coal Company, Mr. Firth's attention had just been drawn to the fact that there were fields of ironstone undeveloped in Leicestershire. When he had mentioned this to some friends of his in the West Riding—Mr. Clayton of Bradford, Mr. Illingworth of Leeds, and others—he found that they, too, were interested in Leicestershire, because, as woollen manufacturers, they did a large trade with that county, first obtaining some of their wool in its raw state from thence, and then, after turning it into yarn in their Yorkshire works, sending it back again to Leicester to be made up into hosiery. As things were, this traffic, together with a not inconsiderable traffic in leather and shoes in connection with the newly-established shoe trade of Leicester, and in machinery from the Yorkshire shops, was carried almost entirely by the Midland Company. A competitive Great Northern route seemed, therefore, very desirable.

Prominent director of the Great Northern though Mr. Firth was, he and his friends did not think it politic to propose point blank to the Board at King's Cross that it should seek powers to make a new connection between Yorkshire and Leicestershire. They preferred to adopt again the course taken in regard to the Leeds, Bradford, and Halifax, West Yorkshire, West Riding and Grimsby, and other undertakings—to initiate them under the auspices of a new company; and, naturally enough, they put the work in the same hands as before—the very capable hands of Messrs. Nelson and Fraser. The latter surveyed the country, and laid out a line to leave the Great Northern main line at Newark, to cross the Grantham and Nottingham branch near Bottesford, pass through Melton Mowbray, and thence, after continuing due southwards to a place called Tilton, to turn round at right angles, and run due westwards into Leicester. This "quadrangular elbow" at Tilton—as a Parliamentary counsel afterwards called it—was dictated partly by the physical conformation of the country between Melton and Leicester—which, as hunting-men well know, consists of a series of hills and deep valleys—but it had the additional advantage that it passed through a district which gave indication of being rich in ironstone. In this district Mr. Firth, developing apparently a sudden desire to become a gentleman farmer, was just negotiating for the purchase of a large farm.

To form, provisionally, "a Newark and Leicester Railway Company" was an easy task in Mr. Nelson's skilful hands—the support of Messrs. Firth, Clayton, and Illingworth was sufficient of itself to float the thing,—but what seemed likely to be not so easy, seeing that the line was to run through a country famous for its hunting, was to conciliate the landowners. By far the greatest of these is the Duke of Rutland, and it was well known to have been the then Duke's opposition which had more than once before stood in the way of the district getting long before this the north and south communication which it admittedly wanted. It was, therefore, with some misgiving that Messrs. Nelson and Fraser approached the Duke's agent, Mr. Green, on the subject of their line, and with much delight that they received towards the end of October, 1871, a cordial invitation to come to Cheadley to interview his Grace himself on the subject.

The fact was that the Duke of Rutland's attitude towards railways had, during the previous year, undergone a complete change. He had not gone so far, perhaps, as his neighbour, the Marquis of Exeter, who had confessed himself "a damned fool" for keeping railways out of Stamford; but, in the light of a discovery of ironstone on his estate near Waltham, he *had* gone the length of writing through Mr. Green to the Great Northern Company to say that his "scruples" as to the making of a branch from Grantham to Melton (which had several times been suggested) had been "removed by a consideration that it would be beneficial to the district." The Great Northern not having responded to this invitation, Mr. Green had applied next to the Midland, and after some delay Mr. Allport had actually shown the agent plans for a line from Nottingham to Saxby (the next station east of Melton on the Syston and Peterborough line) with a branch from Melton to Waltham. This, however, the Duke had characterized as "not the kind of accommodation that the district required."

This unsatisfactory proposal had come from the Midland a few weeks only before Messrs. Fraser and Nelson arrived to put their plans before the Duke. Consequently he was the more disposed to give those gentlemen a favourable hearing. At the interview itself they got no conclusive answer, but a few days later, on 2 November, 1871, Mr. Nelson received a telegram from Mr. Green: "The Duke gives his consent conditionally, viz., to be proceeded with this session, the Great Northern taking up the line and making it."

Perhaps on the same day—certainly within the same week—as Messrs. Nelson and Fraser were explaining their plans to the Duke of Rutland at Cheadley, an interview as to the construction of a very similar line to theirs through the same district was taking place in London. The parties to it were Mr. Blenkinsopp, solicitor to the London and North Western Company, and Sir Edward Watkin. Sir Edward was still eager to "liberate the South Yorkshire coalfield," and the design he had now formed for the purpose was to make a new route, not on the eastern side of the Great Northern—that had failed too recently to be repeated—but on its western side through Nottingham and Leicestershire. This route, he had persuaded himself, the London and North Western authorities had had in mind twenty years before, when he had been Captain Huish's trusty henchman at Euston Square. Accordingly, having had the necessary connecting line surveyed—from Doncaster through Worksop to join the North Western at Market Harborough—he had gone in his dashing way to Mr.

Blenkinsopp and asked him if he thought his Company would be disposed to go into it with the Sheffield as a joint scheme.

The London and North Western, however, had "other fish to fry." It had just concluded an agreement of amalgamation, subject, of course, to the sanction of Parliament, with the Lancashire and Yorkshire; and with this in view it had little to gain and much, in the light of past experience, to risk by entering into a new alliance with the Sheffield. Nor does Mr. Blenkinsopp appear to have thought Sir Edward Watkin really serious in his proposition. In a private letter written to Mr. Oakley a day or two after the interview—a letter which turned up rather awkwardly afterwards for the Sheffield chairman—he characterized the proposed Doncaster to Market Harborough line as "a wonderful scheme!!" However, he reported the matter to his Board, and at the end of October they curtly declined the offered partnership.

But, "wonderful scheme!!" or not, the Doncaster and Market Harborough line was put into a Bill, which in this busy autumn of 1871 the Sheffield Company deposited, and in this form Sir Edward Watkin was able, with characteristic adroitness, to turn it to considerable account. The Midland, as we have already incidentally noted, had also been laying plans for new lines in Yorkshire, Nottinghamshire, and Leicestershire, and these, as now put into Bills, had taken the form of a line from Shireoaks (near Worksop) to Doncaster; another— the one which Mr. Allport had shown to Mr. Green—from Nottingham to Saxby; and another, to continue the same route southwards, from Manton to Rushton. Thus the Midland, too, was proposing to occupy the district which the Duke of Rutland's influence had so long kept closed.*

One day, late in November, after the publication of the Bill deposits, Sir Edward Watkin had occasion to meet the Midland chairman, Mr. Price, on other matters. After these had been disposed of he took a pencil and a map and sketched in the Midland projects together with his own "wonderful scheme" and the lines which the Great Northern and its "jackals" were promoting. He then boldly suggested that the three companies might mutually agree to abandon their projects pending the issue of the London and North Western and Lancashire and Yorkshire Amalgamation Bill. The Midland chairman at once expressed his willingness to give up all his company's lines except the Nottingham and Saxby; but the Great Northern directors, on being applied to, rejected the proposal entirely. Nevertheless Sir Edward Watkin succeeded in holding Mr. Price to his part of the bargain, and so, in return for the Sheffield's sacrifice of its "wonderful

* This district is shown on map at p. 209.

scheme," which without the North Western's support had not a chance of passing, the Midland's Shireoaks and Doncaster and Manton and Rushton projects were withdrawn from Parliament.

Meantime, in accordance with the Duke of Rutland's stipulation, Mr. Nelson—without feeling the smallest reluctance, one may imagine—had deposited a Bill for the Newark and Leicester line in such a shape that it could at any time during its progress be taken over by the Great Northern, and he succeeded on 2 December, 1871, in bringing the matter before the Board at King's Cross. The Great Northern directors had to consider the question from two points of view—commercially, in relation to the traffic the new route might be expected to obtain, and "politically," in view of what Mr. Oakley called "the disturbed state of the district in a railway sense"—and from both points of view they found, after careful inquiry, that the undertaking had much to recommend it. It does not appear that they considered it so carefully from a third point of view—the view as to whether they were justified in adding a new liability to the onerous ones to which they were already committed. Whether they did so or not, however, the fact remains that in February, 1872, they decided to take over the Bill as a Great Northern undertaking. The Erewash Valley—Derby—Burton—Leicester—Mr. Allport's fire was being returned with interest!

Meanwhile the twin questions of the toll to be paid by the Great Northern to the Sheffield on South Yorkshire coal to London, and of the differential to be maintained between South Yorkshire and Derbyshire were once more causing trouble between the parties. The Sheffield, it will be remembered, had agreed in December, 1870, to commute its fixed 1s. 4d. toll for a proportion of the through rate equal to thirty miles, subject to a minimum which was to be 10d. normally, but 8d. while the fierce competition with the Midland lasted; and in accordance with this agreement it had received 8d. only from January, 1871, to the following July. Then, however, a raising of their total rates on the part of both Midland and Great Northern had brought the thirty miles proportion up to 10d., and in November a further raising increased it again to 11½d.; but still the Sheffield Company were dissatisfied, the more so in view of the fact that the demand for coal in London and the price paid for it there had more than kept pace with the raising of the rates. The result was that in January, 1872, Mr. Underdown, the Sheffield manager, wrote to inform Mr. Oakley that "from and after 1 February next the proportion accruing to" his Company, "temporarily arranged during the severe competition," would have to be "increased to 1s 2d. per ton."

In replying to this letter Mr. Oakley expressed extreme surprise that the arrangement as to the thirty miles proportion should be called a temporary one. The only part of it which the Great Northern had regarded as temporary, said he, was the 8*d*. minimum. Except on the faith of a permanent reduction on the part of the Sheffield, the Great Northern would not have bound itself to the coalowners to keep the differential so low as 8*d*. "The rates now in force," he added, "are 1*s*. 7*d*. less than those charged prior to this arrangement, and it is manifestly absurd for your Company to expect us to bear the loss of 1*s*. 5*d*. out of that amount."

We certainly had no intention, retorted Mr. Underdown in effect, of giving up permanently our right to charge the toll you agreed to when you withdrew your opposition to our taking over the South Yorkshire in 1864. We must, therefore, insist upon our share being now brought back more nearly to that—its normal amount. Very well, then, the differential must be increased, replied Mr. Oakley. So on 1 February he sent a circular to the coalowners stating that as the Sheffield had failed to fulfil their part of the bargain, and now insisted on having 3*d*. more than its thirty miles proportion, the total rate must be increased by 3*d*., and the differential as against Derbyshire from 8*d*. to 11*d*. Mr. Baxter, naturally enough, at once wrote to protest, on behalf of the coalowners, against the Great Northern having departed from its agreement to keep the differential at 8*d*. Mr. Oakley, however, sent him copies of the whole correspondence with the Sheffield, and received no further complaint.

In the light of these events the Great Northern directors had the more reason to congratulate themselves that, if their Bill now before Parliament passed, they would be able to make Derbyshire and not South Yorkshire the principal source of their future coal traffic, and when at the half-yearly meeting on 20 February, 1872, the Bill was submitted to the shareholders for their approval, it was obvious that they, too, were of the same opinion. "The thing is forced upon us inevitably," said one speaker, Mr. Wilkinson of Nottingham. "It would have been well for us if we had spent our money in this way earlier; but it is never too late to do right. I agree that it is very undesirable to increase our capital except under urgent circumstances; but there are circumstances in which, if you do not take off your coat, someone will rob you of your coat and waistcoat by cutting them off your back." "I believe, and I sincerely believe," said another speaker —Mr. Shirley of Doncaster—"that it is for the benefit of the Great Northern proprietary that you should make these lines."

But, of course, the question still had to be answered — would Parliament sanction a new line into Derbyshire? and the answer was doubtful enough to make Mr. Leech and Mr. Oakley extremely anxious to present a strong case for public interest. As to this, of course, a great deal depended upon the attitude which the Derbyshire coalowners themselves might take up, and it soon became clear to the Great Northern authorities that the fact that their Company had been hitherto regarded as the champion of the South Yorkshire field against the Midland's championship of Derbyshire was being skilfully used by the agents of the latter company to prejudice local opinion against the new line. The Great Northern is coming here not to help Derbyshire, but to "bully" it in the interest of South Yorkshire, was the doctrine which Mr. Allport and his assistants sedulously circulated. Mr. Oakley found it extremely difficult to argue down this damaging impression.

Under these circumstances he decided to put his reply in a form which would speak for itself. With the approval of his directors he went to Euston Square and arranged to give the London and North Western running powers over the new line from Burton-on-Trent to the coalfield. This done, he called a meeting of the Erewash Valley coalowners, and by demonstrating to them that he proposed to bring not only the Great Northern trains to their service, but those of the London and North Western also, which company certainly had no South Yorkshire bias, he turned their hitherto lukewarm attitude into one of hearty support.

The Great Northern's two invading schemes—the Derbyshire and Staffordshire and the Newark and Leicester—together with the Midland's Nottingham and Saxby project, and its proposed branch from Melton to the Duke of Rutland's ironstone, were referred to a single Committee of the House of Commons, over which Mr. Myles William O'Reilly, a noted chairman of that day, presided. The Derbyshire and Staffordshire, or Great Northern (No. 2) Bill—as it was officially called to distinguish it from the Various Powers Bill already mentioned—was taken on first on 2 May, 1872; and Mr. Denison, who, of course, "led" for the Great Northern, devoted the greater part of his opening speech to a characteristically "breezy" history of the events which had led up to the promotion of the line. "We did not propose to upset the agreement," he said, when he came to the crucial point—the conduct of the various parties after Sir John Karslake's award—"but we came to this conclusion, that inasmuch as the Midland had suggested to the arbitrator to take a highly technical view of it, we would see whether we could not find a technical view. We began to look at the agreement and see whether we could drive our coach and six through it; we found a hole, and that was Retford."

"You may take it," he repeated a few minutes later, in answer to a question from the chairman, "that the sending by Retford was the beginning of the war."

This looked like a rash admission, and naturally enough the Midland caught it up and made play with it till the phrase "coach and six" became a by-word. But Mr. Denison had carefully weighed his words beforehand, and with the instinct of a great advocate he had foreseen which way they would tell. He had admitted at the outset the worst charge which could be brought against his clients. Mr. Venables, the Midland's counsel, was, of course, fully primed to expose the Retford "circumvention," and nothing would have pleased him better than to have been able to bring it out at a critical period of the case with all the force of a revelation. But, after Mr. Denison's coach and six had passed, in what style could he take the road? As it was, he declaimed against the "deliberate violation of an agreement" and the "repudiation of an honourable debt"; but to this Mr. Denison replied with a scorn which recalled his father's ridicule of "moral slipslop" in the first South Yorkshire transactions. "This is a case in which there is really a great deal of morals," said he, "but the Midland Company are the last people who ought to come here to use the language they have used. On the contrary, they ought to be ashamed of themselves, to shrink into their shell, to say the least that can be said about faith, arbitrations, agreements, or anything of the kind, and to leave the Bill as, I will not say, an unopposed Bill, but as a Bill which ought to have been fought on any grounds than those on which they have fought it." At the conclusion of this speech on 3 June, 1872, Mr. O'Reilly gave the Committee's decision in favour of the new line in its entirety. It was a signal triumph for the Great Northern—a signal humiliation for the Midland.

Three days later—6 June, 1872—the hearing of the competing Leicestershire Bills was commenced, and as the Great Northern was not opposing the Nottingham and Saxby, whereas the Midland was opposing the Newark and Leicester, the case for the latter was taken first. Here there was no question of morals or agreements; the matters to be decided were simply whether the traffic of the towns of Leicester and Melton and the ironstone deposits at Tilton and Waltham were of sufficient value to justify the construction of a new line. The Great Northern brought representative and expert evidence to prove the affirmative; the Midland negative rested almost entirely on the evidence of Mr. Allport. "Just remember," said Mr. Denison in reply, "the number of people that must be wrong and who must be almost idiots in this case if Mr. Allport is right. Mr. Oakley

T

cannot measure traffic; Mr. Green knows nothing of the country between Grantham and Melton; Professor Ansted knows nothing about geology; people at Leicester know nothing about their own complaints; and, finally, when somebody from Leicester gives you a matter of fact and not an opinion, all Mr. Allport says is, it is not true. . . . When Mr. Allport comes in contact with mankind at large, mankind at large is generally wrong—all kinds of mankind, geological professors, tradesmen of every description, ironstonemen and everything else—there is one man and one man only that knows everything, and that is Mr. Allport." Unfortunately for Mr. Allport, however, Mr.

BRIDGE OVER FRIAR GATE, DERBY.

O'Reilly and his Committee proved as wrongheaded as the rest of mankind, for on 14 June, 1872, they approved the Great Northern Bill and threw out the Midland branch to Waltham. The latter's Nottingham and Saxby line passed unopposed.

But the campaign of 1872 was not yet over. "Thank God," said the Midland Company, "there's a House of Lords," and at the beginning of July they renewed their opposition to the two Great Northern Bills before a Committee presided over by Viscount Hardinge. The Derbyshire and Staffordshire got through unscathed, despite some rather strong residential opposition from Derby; but the Newark and Leicester was not so fortunate, chiefly because the Great Northern authorities, confident in the favour of the Duke of Rutland, underrated the strength of the opposition of other landowners. "I could almost fancy that I was on my first Bill," said Mr. Denison, "that I was fighting the old battle of the London and York, to hear these old topics of traffic tables and alternative lines, the difficulties of gradients, that minerals cannot pay, that local traffic is worth nothing. . . . There is no kind of public case against this line, and as for the two landowners' cases I am afraid I must offend them again by laughing at them. I can only call them ridiculous." The laugh, however, was destined to be on the other side. The opposition of the sporting landowners—one of whom was Mr. Hartopp, a well-known master of foxhounds—though ridiculous in the eyes of the railway people, apparently had weight with the noble lords who formed the Committee. At any rate, they sanctioned the line from Newark as far as Melton Mowbray only and threw out the portion between Melton and Leicester.

Thus at last the invasion of the Midlands received a check. The coalfield, Derby, and Burton had been carried triumphantly; but the attack on Leicester was brought to a stand at Melton, and the West Riding men who had fostered this scheme found that all they had got so far was powers to make a line which would be practically useless except for the carriage of Melton pies to the north. Nevertheless, in view of the rival schemes—dropped for the year, it was true, but far from being dead—for carrying a new north and south line through Leicestershire, the Great Northern had done well, as we shall see, to secure a footing in that county, though so far as Melton only.

CHAPTER XVII.

THE CAMPAIGN OF 1873, INCLUDING A PARLIAMENTARY FIGHT OF THIRTY DAYS—1872-1873.

AS we have already noted, the Great Northern "won its spurs" as a passenger line in 1851, when despite the handicap of an incomplete equipment and with a route to the North no shorter as yet than the established one, it more than held its own in the Exhibition traffic. As we afterwards saw, however, it was the services put on after the opening of the towns line in 1852 which definitely stamped the Great Northern as "the premier line for speed."

To cover the 191 miles from King's Cross *viâ* Knottingley to York in four hours fifty minutes—practically forty miles an hour—was a performance unequalled in the fifties, not even on the exceptionally flat road of the Great Western; but this was not the best the Great Northern did in that decade. In 1857, as we have seen, the "Manchester fliers" were put on, and although the forty-four miles an hour between King's Cross and Sheffield, which we have already noted as the first performance of these trains as far as the Great Northern was concerned, was a *tour de force*, modified when the original fierceness of the competition abated, yet the timing as subsequently fixed—three hours fifteen minutes for the 138 miles between King's Cross and Retford (the Manchester, Sheffield, and Lincolnshire engine now came on at Retford instead of Sheffield as at first), meant a "journey-speed" of forty-two miles an hour; quite the best thing done in Great Britain up to the date we have now reached, albeit with a light train. The next best run of this epoch, furthermore, the Great Northern also furnished—London to Leeds in four hours twenty-seven minutes, a journey-speed of $41\frac{3}{8}$ miles an hour. The London and North Western and Midland's best rates in 1871 were barely over forty miles an hour.

Moreover, if we take a more general view (accepting the standard of an express train to be not less than thirty-six miles an hour), we find that the Great Northern in 1871 ran an average of 13·2 daily express journeys over each mile of its line, while the average of such journeys on the London and North Western was 10·9 per mile, and on the Midland 10·2—the rest being nowhere. Thus under the management of Mr. Oakley, Mr. Cockshott, and Mr. Patrick Stirling, as under that of Mr. Seymour Clarke, Mr. Leith, and Mr. Sturrock, the Great Northern was still "leading the world" in railway speed.*

As every schoolboy should know, it was the general custom on British railways prior to 1872 to confine the advantages of high speed to first-class and second-class passengers. Nevertheless it is a mistake to suppose that the "third-class by all trains" reform which the Midland Company introduced in April of this year was altogether an abrupt innovation. Not only had competition—first of the Great Northern

"No. 260."
ONE OF THE LAST GREAT NORTHERN LOCOMOTIVES DESIGNED BY MR. STURROCK.
From a photograph kindly lent for reproduction by the builders of the engine, Messrs. John Fowler & Co., of Leeds.

against the London and North Western and then of the Midland against both—already led to the abolition on the northern lines of the special "express fares" which had been charged generally during the forties and earlier fifties, so that 3d. per mile had become the limit charge for first-class travelling and 2d. for second; it had also produced a marked improvement already in the accommodation given to third-class, penny-a-mile, passengers. Throughout the fifties and earlier sixties, except on excursion trains—freely run, as we have seen, on special occasions—the accommodation given to the third class had gone little beyond the one "Parliamentary train," stopping at every station, which since 1844 every company had been compelled to run

* For a general survey of railway speeds in 1871, see "The Proceedings of the Statistical Society, April, 1884," for an able and very industrious paper on the subject by Lieut. WILLOCK, R.E., to which I am much indebted.

each way every day throughout its system. But when from October, 1868, the Midland had got its own London line at work for passenger traffic, it had initiated the practice of extending the Parliamentary penny-a-mile fare to some of its second-best fast trains, and in this innovation it had been liberally followed, under stress of competition, by the Great Northern. Thus from 1869 the latter had begun to carry third-class passengers at penny-a-mile fares by such trains as the 9 a.m., the 12 noon, and the 9.15 p.m. from King's Cross, thus enabling that class to travel from London to Nottingham in three hours ten minutes, from London to Leeds in four hours fifty minutes, from London to York in five hours, and from London to Edinburgh (by night) in eleven hours—as good a service, in short, to most important towns, and a better in some cases, than the service which had been hailed as so wonderful an improvement when introduced for the higher classes in 1852. Nevertheless there was a big gap between this service even and the admission of third-class, penny-a-mile, passengers to all trains, the announcement of which "on and after 1 April, 1872," was made by the Midland directors with startling suddenness at the end of March.

The Great Northern, on its part, immediately followed suit by throwing open all its expresses, with one exception, to third-class passengers; and that exception—the 10 a.m. Scotchman—was rather a nominal than a real one, because it was accompanied by the putting on of a new train—10.10 a.m. from King's Cross—open to all three classes, which was timed to do the journey to Edinburgh in as short a time as the ten o'clock train had taken hitherto, viz., ten and a half hours. But "to maintain the special character of the express service by the East Coast route to Scotland"—to quote the Great Northern directors' report of August, 1872—the 10 a.m. train itself was accelerated to reach Edinburgh in nine and a half hours.

In 1869, as the reader may remember, the night train then put on to leave King's Cross at 8 p.m. had been timed to cover the whole distance to Edinburgh in ten hours, and subsequently this had been accelerated to nine hours forty-five minutes—the North Eastern's new direct line from York to Doncaster having in the meantime been opened (January, 1871). Nevertheless, the nine and a half hours day service now put on was a great improvement, so far as the Great Northern was concerned, upon anything of the same kind attempted up to this date. For out of the time of the day train, it must be remembered, twenty-five minutes had to be allowed for luncheon at York; moreover, the difficulties of the North British line from Berwick to Edinburgh and certain other things prevented the acceleration being equally distributed throughout the whole journey. Consequently to make this new "Flying Scotchman" possible, it fell to the Great Northern to cover its distance from King's Cross to York—188 miles by the new route *viâ* Selby—in four hours fifteen minutes—that is to say, to make a journey-speed of forty-four miles an hour. This, however, proved quite within the capacity of the new type of locomotive with outside cylinders and 8-ft. driving-wheels, which Mr. Patrick Stirling had recently turned out from the Doncaster works.

This year, 1872, was a very exceptional one for railway business in Great Britain. Thanks to great national prosperity, traffic receipts increased — as Colonel Packe put it—"almost hourly," but at the same time the cost of almost everything used on a railway increased also—iron, wood, grease, and especially coals; and the cost of labour, too, rose much higher than ever before. In response to memorials received from their workmen, the Great Northern directors were obliged, for fear of a strike, to introduce from the beginning of the year a nine hours' day in their locomotive workshops and also, as far as possible, amongst the men employed on the permanent way; and at the same time similar memorials had to be dealt with from guards, shunters, porters,

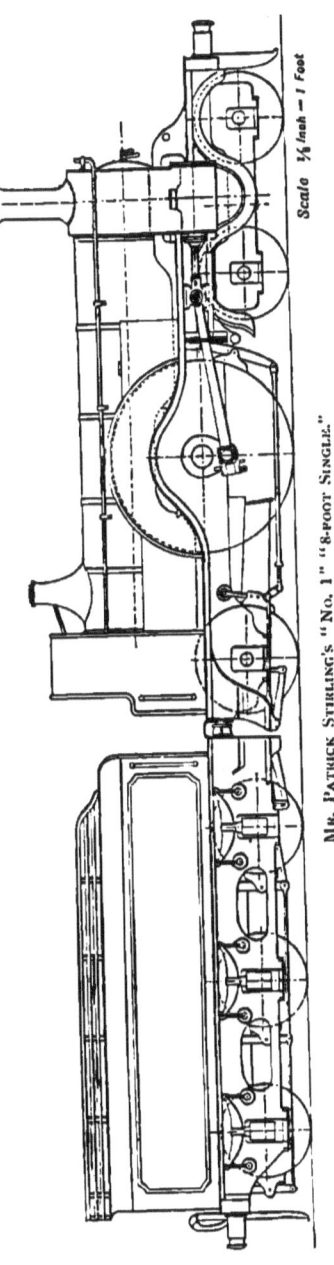

Mr. Patrick Stirling's "No. 1" "8-Foot Single." Scale ⅛ inch = 1 Foot

Reproduced from "The Railways of England," by W. M. Acworth, by kind permission of Mr. John Murray.

and others engaged in the traffic. The result was that the rate of pay had to be increased, and the hours of labour reduced, generally throughout the whole staff, involving an addition to working expenses of about £20,000 in the year. Considerable difficulty and greater expense also were incurred in providing labour for the necessary relaying of the line. Nevertheless, thanks to an increase of about £180,000 in traffic receipts during the year—an increase which, though the largest on the Company's records, would probably have been a good deal larger but for its exclusion from the Derbyshire coalfield—the rate of dividend paid again reached its high-water mark —£7 2s. 6d. per cent. per annum.

This was the more satisfactory because a considerable amount of new capital had already been sunk, as yet unproductively, on some of the numerous new works to which, as we have seen, the Company had committed itself since the revival of railway enterprise in 1870. True, the Bourn and Sleaford and Finchley and Barnet lines were now carrying traffic, the former having been opened on 2 January, and the latter on 1 April, 1872; but in Yorkshire the works of the Eccleshill and Idle, Idle and Shipley, and Dewsbury branch railways were all absorbing considerable sums without return, whilst the two new joint undertakings under construction, the Manchester and Liverpool, and the Halifax and Ovenden, were also responsible for serious drafts upon capital account. Moreover, in view of the fact that the Alexandra Palace on Muswell Hill, after having stood incomplete for ten years, was at last to be finished and opened, the directors found it necessary in the autumn of 1872 to put under construction the branch from Highgate to Muswell Hill, for which the Edgware and Highgate Company,. it may be remembered, had obtained powers in 1865. Besides all this, there was, as already noted, an exceptionally heavy current expenditure of capital for station enlargements, new sidings, new rolling-stock, extension of the block system, and interlocking apparatus.

With such liabilities as these on hand, and a very large additional outlay in immediate prospect, the Great Northern directors had good reasons for abstaining from further aggressive enterprises. But unfortunately, in the existing state of inter-railway politics, to abstain from aggression meant practically to abstain from self-defence. The fact that two schemes for completing a new north and south route through Leicestershire and Nottinghamshire had been deposited for the session of 1872—the one by the Sheffield Company, and the other by a mysterious "jackal," a solicitor of Bury, in Lancashire, named Harper—left little doubt that in the following session, now approaching, a renewed attempt would be made by other companies to fill this district; and it was in this light, quite as much as in that of the commercial advantages to be derived from occupying the locality

CALDER BRIDGE, DEWSBURY.

themselves, that the Great Northern directors had to consider what course they should take with regard to their mutilated Newark and Leicester undertaking. The Great Northern wanted to get to Leicester and the people of Leicester wanted the Great Northern—they had held an "indignation meeting" after the Lords' mutilation of the Bill—

moreover, Mr. Firth, Mr. Clayton, and the other Yorkshiremen who had originally promoted the scheme were naturally anxious to make it complete; but, as we have just said, the prime considerations with regard to the matter were not commercial but "political."

Before the Commons Committee in the session just passed a suggestive dialogue had taken place between Mr. Bidder, one of the Midland counsel—son of the George Parker Bidder we have already heard of—and Mr. John Fowler, consulting engineer to the Great Northern. It related to the "rectangular elbow," which, as we have said, the Newark and Leicester line had been planned to form near Tilton. Mr. Fowler had explained that the object of this was to avoid engineering difficulties and to serve Mr. Firth's ironstone field, but Mr. Bidder had suspected a deeper design. "Is there not another point of view," he had asked, "in which that elbow would be advantageous—if you want to come in a future session for a line to Market Harborough?" "Well," said Mr. Fowler, turning round to look at the map, the idea apparently striking him for the first time, "I think that is a very good suggestion. Now that you call attention to it, it really would enable a very good line to be made."

Thus out of the mouth of an opposing counsel the Great Northern authorities took an idea which bore fruit now that, with the possibility of a revival of Sir Edward Watkin's "wonderful scheme" before them, they had to lay their plans for the session of 1873. They decided not only to re-introduce the rejected Melton to Leicester line, but to promote also a second fork to go due southwards from Tilton to Market Harborough. But whilst thus enlarging the original Newark and Leicester project, they did not greatly enlarge the outlay of capital involved. For, before definitely deciding upon the extension to Market Harborough, they succeeded in persuading the London and North Western Company to become equal partners with them in what now came to be the main part of the scheme—the through line from Market Harborough to Newark, leaving the fork from Tilton to Leicester only to be made by the Great Northern Company alone.

Of course, this formed a scheme which promised, if authorized, effectually to block the way to any anti-Great Northern route through the same country, and, therefore, its advantages in the eyes of the King's Cross Board were obvious. Nevertheless, the price which they agreed to pay for the London and North Western's co-operation in it was undoubtedly high. It amounted to placing that company in the Derbyshire and South Yorkshire coalfields on terms of practical equality with themselves and the Midland. For South Yorkshire traffic the North Western was to be given running powers between

Newark and Doncaster, and to Derbyshire it was to be given access *viâ* Nottingham—a much better access than that which it had already been given *viâ* Burton, under the Derbyshire Extensions Act of 1872. For the purposes of this new North Western route into Derbyshire, and also, of course, for such purposes as the Great Northern could put it to, a junction line was to be made between the new joint line and the Grantham and Nottingham branch, a line to leave the former at Stathern and to join the latter near Bingham. This, of course, was to have the further effect of placing the North Western advantageously in the town of Nottingham.

In return for such important concessions as these, the advantages which the Great Northern on its part obtained, beyond the North Western's initial consent to the partnership, were, it must be confessed, somewhat meagre. They amounted to two sets of running powers—from Market Harborough southward to Northampton, and from the same neighbourhood eastward to Peterborough. For the purposes of the latter run the London and North Western undertook to construct a missing link between Seaton and Wansford, while the Great Northern, on its part, agreed to fill up a second much shorter gap between its own and the North Western station at Peterborough.

Thus *per se*—commercially—this partnership with Euston Square—an event, by the way, which showed how fast things had moved since the days of the "confederacy"—was not a very good bargain for the Great Northern; but that the grounds of policy upon which it was based were solid ones was shown by an event which took place in this same autumn of 1872. This was nothing else than an alliance between the Midland and Sheffield companies to carry out Sir Edward Watkin's "wonderful scheme." It was initiated by Mr. Price, the Midland chairman, who on 10 October, 1872, wrote to Sir Edward Watkin to suggest that, as the time for new deposits was approaching, it might be well for them too to try again, as in the previous year, to "harmonize" the projects of their companies. Sir Edward, of course, readily responded; and the result was that the joint Bill of the Great Northern and London and North Western, when deposited in November, 1872, found a counterpart in a joint Bill of the Midland and Sheffield—a Bill for a new through line from Rushton (a place on the Midland's main line, a few miles south of Market Harborough) *viâ* Tilton and Melton (where a junction was to be made with the newly-authorized Midland line from Nottingham), to a junction with the Sheffield main line at Worksop, and thence to join the North Eastern at Askern, and the South Yorkshire at Hexthorp and Conisborough. Obviously this was a project which threatened Great Northern interests in all sorts of ways, and obviously, also, the fact that they had a counter scheme ready for occupying the same route greatly improved the Great Northern's chance of averting the danger.*

On 29 October, 1872—about three weeks after his letter to Sir Edward Watkin, just referred to—Mr. Price, the Midland chairman, wrote another letter, which was also destined to have an important bearing upon the interests of the Great Northern. The addressee this time was Mr. John Crossley, of Halifax, and its subject a projected new through line from Huddersfield through Halifax to Keighley—a project for which Mr. Crossley and other leading men of Huddersfield and Halifax had been working ever since 1863. In 1864 a Commons Committee had rejected their line—the same Committee which had passed the smaller Halifax and Ovenden undertaking,—but the fact that a part of the route had thus been occupied had not prevented another Committee in 1867 from sanctioning the Huddersfield, Halifax, and Keighley line as well. Then, however, the Midland directors, overburdened just then with liabilities, had brought the enterprise to a standstill by withdrawing in the Lords the support they had given in the Commons.

So nothing more had been done until the date we have now reached —1872—when Mr. Crossley and his friends had "warmed up again" —to quote a phrase of Mr. Denison's—and were preparing to go to Parliament once more. Great was their chagrin, therefore, to learn from Mr. Price on the date mentioned above that the Midland was again too occupied with other matters—its joint line with the Sheffield being the chief of these—to take up their project.

"I have made this announcement at the earliest possible moment," wrote Mr. Price—as a matter of fact Mr. Crossley had been waiting some weeks for his answer—"so as to set you and your friends free to prosecute your own scheme if you think fit"; and, despite the lateness of the season, the promoters of the Huddersfield, Halifax, and Keighley line acted upon this suggestion in a way which caused Mr. Price subsequently to regret that he had made it. For not only did they give the Parliamentary notices for their line, but, tired of waiting upon the Midland, they put themselves into communication with the Great Northern. The Board at King's Cross, however, though prepared to fill up the district between Halifax and Keighley —for that, as we have already noted, had been the full object originally of both the Halifax and Ovenden and Bradford and Thornton undertakings—were not prepared to go southwards from Halifax to Huddersfield, much less were they prepared to adopt the

* For Map see p. 209.

further suggestion which some of the local promoters now made to carry the new line beyond Huddersfield to Manchester. The result was that the Huddersfield, Halifax, and Keighley line was after all dropped as far as the session of 1873 was concerned.

Before it was dropped, however, the Great Northern was led definitely to pledge itself at a meeting at Leeds to an important forward movement in the district, namely, to join the Halifax and Ovenden and Bradford and Thornton lines, and to continue them in one route northwards to Keighley — provided that people in the district would find half the capital in the same way as was already being done for the Bradford and Thornton. This had the effect of arousing Colonel Akroyd, the Messrs. Foster, of Queensbury, and other former advocates of a through line up the Thornton valley, to immediate activity. The month of November being already well advanced, it would under ordinary circumstances have been impossible to have given notices and deposited plans for the session of 1873; but, fortunately, in Messrs. Nelson and Fraser, a solicitor and engineer were available who, in connection with the promotion both of the Halifax and Ovenden and the Bradford and Thornton, had already made preparations for the through scheme now talked of. Mr. Fraser, too, happened to be well acquainted with the plans prepared for the Huddersfield, Halifax, and Keighley project. Under these circumstances it was found possible to deposit a Thornton and Keighley Bill just in time for the next session, and this was done in the name of a "provisional committee," of which the Messrs. Foster, Colonel Akroyd, and Mr. John Crossley (who, now that the connection with Huddersfield seemed unattainable, had thrown himself into the new movement) were the leading members.

Meantime Mr. Nelson, in his familiar character of "jackal," had placed this new "feeder"—snatched, as it were, from the jaws of the Midland—before the "lions" at King's Cross, and both its taste and its savour—its commercial advantages and its "political" value—had given satisfaction at the Great Northern Board. Besides this, they were already committed to fill up the district, provided that the local people found half the capital; and so, when at a meeting at Leeds on 23 December, 1872, the provisional committee gave an undertaking to do this on the same terms as for the Bradford and Thornton, viz., to be exchanged for 80 per cent. of Great Northern original stock, the deputation from King's Cross at once gave an undertaking in return that the Great Northern would on those terms take over the Bill and make the line, if authorized. Thus the Company became committed to a further capital expenditure of £640,000.

Meanwhile the burning question of the hour, in railway boardrooms, in factories, and at every hearth, was the extraordinary state of the coal trade. Whether from greatly increased demand or from artificially restricted supply, or, as seems most probable, from a combination of both causes, there was a veritable coal famine in the land, especially in London, where the price—45*s*. a ton or thereabouts—was higher even than in the pre-railway days. Besieged with orders from all directions, the coalowners were masters of the situation, and the railway companies, while suffering severely as coal consumers, were unable to recoup themselves to any appreciable extent as carriers, because, even at normal rates, they were unable to obtain a sufficient supply for the markets on their lines. Especially was the Great Northern in bad case, being dependent almost entirely upon one field—the South Yorkshire. The coalowners of that district had never been, as we know, really zealous for the London trade; and now they were literally starving it in order to feed more profitable provincial markets. Moreover, from October, 1872, the Sheffield Company insisted once more upon having its full 1*s*. 4*d*. per ton out of the through rate. Consequently, to keep the differential as compared with Derbyshire at 10*d*.—to have allowed it to be higher than this would have been fatal to what South Yorkshire trade was still left—the Great Northern had to be content with a rate of 4*d*. per ton per mile, the lowest rate charged at this time by any company for coal.

Even at this rate, however, the Great Northern could not get a sufficient supply of coal for its London market; and so, on 8 November, 1872, Mr. Oakley sent out a circular calling "the serious and earnest attention of the South Yorkshire colliery owners to the subject." "Clearly," said he, "the decrease in the South Yorkshire trade to London cannot be attributed to this Company's charge for carriage, our rate for 156 miles being actually 6*d*. per ton less than that paid from the nearer Clay Cross pits"—about 124 miles. "It is not the province of this Company to interfere between the coalowners and their customers on the question of price; but if, as alleged, the decrease in the South Yorkshire trade has been caused by the high prices demanded by the coalowners, it is our duty, in the interest of our proprietors, to direct attention to the permanent loss of trade which will probably ensue." This circular, however, produced no good result, and at the end of the year the Great Northern directors seriously considered whether they ought not to adopt the extreme remedy of forcing their way into the Derbyshire field again, without waiting for the construction of their new line, by putting on an extremely low rate from Nottingham to London—a rate low enough to counterbalance the Midland's high charge between Nottingham and the pits. Eventually, however, they decided to make a second appeal to the South Yorkshire coalowners (7 January, 1873).

The *causa causans* of this decision undoubtedly was that the Great Northern was once more between two fires. In view of the attitude of the coalowners and of the Sheffield Company, it had the strongest possible temptation—nay, justification even—to throw up the ungrateful rôle of devoted servants to the South Yorkshire field; but, just as in 1871, so again, its directors felt that, if they did not resist this temptation, they would be playing straight into the hands of Sir Edward Watkin and Mr. Baxter. For it was upon Sir Edward's old plea—we "cannot trust" the Great Northern, therefore we must have a new access to London for our South Yorkshire coal traffic—that the Sheffield Company was making out a case for its new partnership with the Midland, and Mr. Baxter, on his part, would certainly have thrown himself heart and soul into that "wonderful scheme," had the Great Northern at this crisis favoured Derbyshire and so, practically, thrown over South Yorkshire.

As things were, however, Mr. Baxter hesitated. Enthusiast as he had always been, and "fanatic" as he had now become, on the subject of the South Yorkshire trade to London, he had not the slightest difficulty in persuading himself that a new route to London from that coalfield was wanted, notwithstanding the fact that by its existing route the Great Northern had never been able to get a full traffic, not even at the time of keenest "war," when it had reduced the rate to 3*s*. 2*d*.—·24*d*. per mile—per ton. On the other hand, the could not blind himself to the obvious danger arising from the partnership in the new route of the Midland Company—the creator and sworn champion of the rival Derbyshire to London trade. True, that under the agreement made between Sir Edward Watkin and Mr. Price, the Sheffield Company was to have running powers into St. Pancras —the running powers into London which had been so long the object of Sir Edward's ambition; but with regard to the coal traffic Mr. Baxter found that these powers were not unrestricted. At the instance of Mr. Allport a very significant proviso had been attached to them —that for the run between Rushton and St. Pancras the Midland was to have the power of insisting on a rate per mile being charged equal to the rate it was charging for Derbyshire coal over the same route. It was obvious to Mr. Baxter that this would have the same effect as the famous agreement of 1863; it would revive the obnoxious fixed differential between the rates from the two coalfields.

Accordingly Mr. Baxter insisted that, as a condition of the South

Yorkshire coalowners supporting the new line in Parliament, the proviso as to the rates must be expunged; and this demand was conveyed by Sir Edward Watkin—not unwillingly, one may imagine—to the Midland Company. But, as may also be readily imagined, Mr. Allport, the champion of the 1s. 4d. differential, met the demand with the most strenuous opposition; and the question was still at issue between the parties when, on 21 March, 1873, a Commons Committee, presided over by Sir Hedworth Williamson—the same chairman who had sat on the C. O. A. L. line of 1871—commenced the hearing of the Great Northern and London and North Western's Joint Bill. Then, however, it was definitely announced in the witness-box by Mr. Oakley that the Great Northern intended to give running powers to the North Western between Newark and Doncaster without restriction as to the rates to be charged for coal. Upon this Mr. Price and Mr. Allport gave way before "the eloquence and importunity" of Sir Edward Watkin. The obnoxious proviso was withdrawn from their joint Bill, and the result was that at a meeting on 19 April the South Yorkshire coalowners, under Mr. Baxter's leadership, decided to support the Rushton line.

Meanwhile in Parliament the case for the Great Northern and North Western line had closed, and that for the Sheffield and Midland had commenced before the same committee. The latter lasted from 3 April to 7 May, 1873, and then there was landowners' opposition to be heard, so that it was not until 13 May—the twenty-seventh day of the whole hearing—that Mr. Venables, the leader for the Rushton Bill, could begin his reply on the whole case. As far as the Midland Company was concerned, he maintained that it had made out "an overwhelming case" for the new line on the double ground of improving its connection with the North Eastern, and of relieving its existing main line. As for the Sheffield, it had for years wanted a new route for South Yorkshire coal to London; it meant to keep its Fifty Years Agreement with the Great Northern so far as Lancashire traffic was concerned, but it was perfectly at liberty to send the South Yorkshire coal by whatever route it liked, seeing that it had acquired the South Yorkshire Railway since the making of the Fifty Years Agreement. As for the question of South Yorkshire *versus* Derbyshire, Mr. Allport, it was true, said counsel, "holds, and still holds, and will hold to the end of his days, that 1s. 4d. is exactly the differential that ought to exist between the two coalfields," but he had been obliged to "put his convictions in his pocket." The Midland Company, as it "confessed with great shame, but for this particular purpose of argument with some satisfaction," had been "completely beaten in the conflict with the Great Northern about South Yorkshire coal." The South Yorkshire would "always compete at a very great advantage in respect to rates with the Derbyshire."

A case which needed to be supported by such very double-edged arguments as these did not need much refutation, but what was wanted Mr. Denison administered next day. The Midland wanted a relief line! said he. Why only a year ago, in reply to the Great Northern's Derbyshire Bill, they had said they could carry any amount of additional traffic. The Sheffield had always wanted a new outlet to London for South Yorkshire coal! No, it was not Sir Edward Watkin but Mr. Baxter who had originated the C. O. A. L. line of 1871, and the Sheffield was not *bonâ fide* promoting the present line for coal traffic, but for the purpose of "getting its claws into the Midland" with the view to a dividend guarantee. The Sheffield had been the worst enemy of the South Yorkshire coal.

"They said—We have that bit of line; we will neither let other people run over it at a reasonable rate, nor carry ourselves at a reasonable rate; and the Great Northern has to suffer for it— unhappy Great Northern, whatever anybody else does, it has always to raise or lower its rates to make things square. . . . The Great Northern are to do everything anyone wants and always to be abused for breaking agreements and oppressing the public if they do not do it. But we can live under it. We have not been frightened hitherto. Whenever we have gone to Parliament we have succeeded, and we are not afraid of not succeeding still."

At half-past three on the following day, 15 May, 1873, amid a scene of great excitement, the Committee gave its decisions. They proved to be entirely satisfactory to neither party. The joint arrangements between the Great Northern and London and North Western were rejected altogether. The line from Melton, *viâ* Tilton, to Leicester was given to the Great Northern alone, thus completing its original Newark to Leicester project, as far as Parliamentary powers went; and lines from Conisborough, on the South Yorkshire Railway, to Shireoaks, near Worksop, and from Melton to Rushton, were given to the Midland and Sheffield jointly. At once Sir Edward Watkin persuaded the Midland to alter the agreement between the two companies so as to give the Sheffield running powers from Shireoaks to Melton *viâ* Nottingham, and this alteration he attempted to get embodied in their Bill when the Committee met again next day. Mr. Denison, however, frustrated this design, and the new running powers were left dependent upon private agreement merely. But the Committee refused assent to a further petition of the Great Northern's counsel that they should strike out the Sheffield

U

from partnership between Melton and Rushton and give that line to the Midland alone.

Meanwhile, during the progress of this "thirty days' fight"—the longest the House of Commons Committee-rooms had seen since the seventy days' fight over the London and York—another contest had been waged before another Committee, presided over by Major O'Reilly. This was over the Bradford, Thornton, and Keighley Bill. This Bill had been petitioned against by a number of interests—by the Midland, by the Lancashire and Yorkshire, by a small company called the Keighley and Worth Valley, whose directors were disappointed that Mr. Fraser had not been able to join his new line with theirs, and by the Corporation of Bradford, which was anxious for the safety of its reservoirs at Doe Park and Manywells. It had been supported, on the other hand, by many petitions from the locality, and with regard to one of the most important of these a rather curious train of events had occurred.

The petition was from the Halifax Chamber of Commerce, signed by Mr. William Morris, its president, and it had happened at the end of March, more than a month before the Bill had come on for hearing, that this Mr. Morris had fallen in with Mr. Allport—quite accidentally in the lobby of the House of Commons. Owing to a curious mistake made by Sir Edward Baines, who had introduced Mr. Allport to Mr. Morris as "the manager of the Great Northern," the conversation had turned upon the Thornton and Keighley Bill, but it had not gone on long when the misunderstanding had, with much laughter, been put right. Then Mr. Morris had confessed that the Halifax Chamber of Commerce, though it had petitioned in favour of the Great Northern Bill, would greatly have preferred the Huddersfield, Halifax, and Keighley scheme, which it had been hoped the Midland would have taken up; whereupon Mr. Allport on his part had avowed that the Midland, though it had petitioned against the Great Northern Bill on the ground that the district was already sufficiently accommodated, was in reality anxious to come to Parliament in a future session with a scheme of its own. Full of this information, Mr. Morris returned to Halifax, with the Easter holidays to work in. He consulted with other leading men there upon the new aspect which Mr. Allport's avowal had given to affairs, and eventually opened formal negotiation with the Midland through the medium of Mr. Matthew William Thompson, a Midland director, who happened to be Mayor of Bradford for the year. The result was that on 23 April, 1873—still before the Bill had reached Committee stage—the Midland Board sent a resolution to Halifax pledging themselves, if the Thornton and Keighley

Bill were rejected, to apply in the session of 1874 for the larger Huddersfield, Halifax, and Keighley scheme.

The next step of Mr. Morris and his associates was to issue large posters throughout the neighbourhood calling a public meeting in the Town Hall on the next market day—Saturday, 3 May, 1873. This proved one of the largest and most exciting ever held in Halifax. There could be no doubt but that a line in the hands of the Midland to start from Huddersfield (to which place that Company already had running powers) to pass through Halifax and to join the Midland main system again at Keighley would be the best possible line for the town, but, on the other hand, there were many who, as Mr. Crossley expressed it, were "tired of being bandied from pillar to post" by the Midland, and who suspected that its latest move was simply "a ruse" to block the Great Northern Bill. So when the meeting "divided" (as it did literally, the two parties going to opposite sides of the hall) the numbers on each side were almost equal; however, the resolution in favour of waiting to the following session was declared carried. In the following week, accordingly, the Mayor of Halifax gave evidence before the Commons Committee *against* the Great Northern Bill, though his "proof" had actually been prepared *in its favour*. Nevertheless, the Bill passed the Commons on 12 May, 1873, three days before the decision, already recorded, on the Leicestershire and South Yorkshire projects.

But in neither case was the battle over. The House of Lords had yet to be reckoned with; and with regard to the Leicestershire Bill, it looked as if the thirty days' fight might have to be fought all over again. True that the "wonderful scheme"—"this great through scheme from everywhere to everywhere" Mr. Denison had termed it—had come out of the Commons as a head and tail without a body; but it was still quite alive, thanks to Sir Edward Watkin's prompt surgery; and with the addition of the new agreement as to running powers it was to be put before the Lords as much a through scheme as before. Moreover there was a danger that, now the rival joint line from Market Harborough to Tilton had been rejected, the landowners of that district, who had in the Commons strongly opposed the Midland and Sheffield, might now turn round and support that line as a *pis aller;* and so Messrs. Nelson and Fraser took care to be present at a landowners' meeting which was held at East Norton on 4 June, 1873. It was then arranged that, on condition that the North Western and Great Northern pledged themselves to revive their line in the following session, the landowners would renew their opposition to the Rushton and Melton line in the Lords.

A month later—7 July, 1873—the opposing Bills in their mutilated shapes came before a Committee presided over by Lord Camoys. The Great Northern had no landowners' opposition this time to its Melton and Leicester line; it had satisfied Mr. Hartopp, the master of foxhounds, by a deviation, and so, in Mr. Denison's phrase, it did not "encounter his pack this year." But the Midland and Sheffield, as we have just said, had a strong combination of landowners against them; and whilst cutting short the case on other points, the noble Lords gave the landed interest full weight. The result was that the Great Northern Bill passed as it was, while the rival Bill was still further mutilated by the excision of the portion between Rushton and Melton. The "wonderful scheme from everywhere to everywhere" was thus reduced to a local coal line from Shireoaks to Conisborough. It was not surprising that under these circumstances its promoters decided to withdraw it altogether.

This decision was given on 11 July, 1873, and so Mr. Denison was set free to take his place as Great Northern "leader" in the Bradford and Thornton Bill when that reached Committee stage in the Lords on 14 July. The Midland again appeared in opposition, and its advisers went the length of placing a map on the wall showing the line it intended to promote in the following session. But this Mr. Denison immediately attacked as "a totally imaginary line which had no earthly business to be there, being in no sense before the Committee"; and at the conclusion of his speech the Committee not only ruled out the map, but refused the Midland a *locus standi* to oppose on the ground that its sole objection to the new line was the competition it threatened. After this the only opposition which remained, that of the little Keighley and Worth Valley Company, was soon disposed of, and on 15 July, 1873, the Great Northern Bill passed the Lords.

Thus as the net result of its prolonged Parliamentary campaign of 1873, the Great Northern got powers of access to Leicester and to Keighley, and by obtaining powers to connect the Bradford and Thornton and Halifax and Ovenden lines secured a route of its own all the way between Bradford and Halifax.

CHAPTER XVIII.

THE ZENITH OF PROSPERITY—THE SUBURBAN INCREMENT—
THE ABBOTTS RIPTON ACCIDENT—1873-1876.

OF the new lines which we noted as under construction by the Great Northern Company in 1872, one had by this time been opened for traffic. This was the branch from Highgate to Muswell Hill to serve the Alexandra Palace. As the portion of this line within the Palace grounds was constructed at the expense of the Palace Company, all the Great Northern had to make was a connecting link between this and Highgate, one mile eleven chains in length; but as this involved a considerable viaduct over the valley between Highgate and Muswell Hills it was a heavy work, costing a sum of over £50,000. Yet, though not put in hand until the autumn of 1872, the line was completed in good time for the opening of the Palace to the public, which took place on 24 May, 1873.

The day proved a beautifully fine one, and the rush of passengers to the Palace is still remembered at the booking-offices at King's Cross as one of the greatest ever experienced there. "Even the first-class carriages," says the *Times* report, "were crammed to the windows with rough and eager holiday makers."

The new Palace was a great success. On Whit-Monday, 2 June, 1873, it was visited by about 60,000 people, and even as early as noon on the following Monday, 9 June, a goodly number of people had congregated. Then, all on a sudden a cry of "Fire!" was raised. Those visitors who were in the Palace itself rushed out of it as soon as the alarm reached them; and then, turning, they saw that the dome was in flames. Travelling downwards from the roof the fire attacked the main body of the building, gaining in fury as it reached more combustible materials, and in less than an hour the whole structure was on fire, sending up dense volumes of black smoke interspersed with lurid flames into the clear summer sky, and creating the greatest excitement for many miles around.

In answer to an urgent telegram, Mr. Oakley sent down from King's

Cross to Wood Green the two fire-engines kept at the Great Northern terminus, and they arrived just after the local engine had been got out and before any of the six engines despatched by the Metropolitan Fire Brigade arrived by road. But already the destruction of the Palace was almost complete; and, even if the engines had arrived earlier, they would have been of little service, because the Palace Company had neglected to make any arrangements for obtaining water in any quantity, though there were reservoirs at the foot of the hill, near Wood Green. The result was that the carelessness of some workmen, who had gone to their dinner, leaving a lighted brazier in the dome, had the effect of depriving the Great Northern Company within a couple of hours of a most promising source of new income, for during the sixteen days of the Palace's brief career about 99,000 passengers had been conveyed to it over the Great Northern line. By opening a suburban station, however, just outside the grounds at Muswell Hill, the Company was able to earn some small return on its expenditure on the new line pending the rebuilding of the Palace, which was immediately taken in hand.

The only other "openings" in 1873 in which the Great Northern participated were the extension to Skegness, from 28 July, 1873, of the Wainfleet and Firsby Company's* line (worked by the Great Northern), and the partial opening of Sir Edward Watkin's new Manchester and Liverpool line in the autumn of the year. This latter, the reader will remember, had been granted by Parliament in 1865 to the Sheffield Company alone; but it had afterwards been vested with the Cheshire lines in the tripartite ownership of the Sheffield, Great Northern, and Midland, and to the works of it and of the Central Station in Liverpool the Great Northern had by this time contributed as its third share about half a million of money, in addition to the million or thereabouts which it had previously contributed to the Cheshire lines proper. As we have seen, moreover, it was to this new direct line that the Cheshire Lines Committee had for some time been looking to stop the dead loss of some thousands a year to each of the partners, which had up to this time resulted from the working of their other lines. Pending the completion of the Liverpool Central Station little use could be made of the new line for passenger traffic; but, notwithstanding this, Colonel Packe was able to point out to the Great Northern shareholders, at their half-yearly meeting in February, 1874, that, for the first time on record, the item in the net revenue account for working the Cheshire lines was on the side of profit instead of loss.

Nevertheless, a profit of £2,206 for the half-year on an expenditure

* Incorporated 1869. Line opened from Firsby to Wainfleet, November, 1871.

of a million and a half was a small figure—"I think I may say it is a miserable figure," said Colonel Packe frankly;—and a still more gloomy feature of the situation was that, notwithstanding the completion of the direct line, there seemed little prospect of "these hungry Cheshire lines," as a Great Northern shareholder called them, being satisfied in the near future with much less than the £100,000 per half-year which had for some time past been a standing charge on their account to Great Northern capital expenditure. True, the Liverpool Central Station was nearing completion—it was partially opened in March, 1874,—but in 1872 the Joint Committee had thought it necessary to go to Parliament for powers to construct a Central Station in Manchester also, and the works of this had yet to be taken in hand. Moreover, even now that they had a direct through route entirely in their own hands both from Manchester to Liverpool, and from the Sheffield system to Liverpool without going through Manchester, the Great Northern and Midland authorities found that they could not compete on equal terms with the London and North Western for the very important shipping traffic of Liverpool, because the Cheshire lines goods station at Brunswick Dock was disadvantageously situated at the southern extremity of the port. Accordingly the Joint Committee now decided to promote a Bill in the session of 1874 for a new line, eight miles in length, to Huskisson Dock at the north end of Liverpool, and this involved the Great Northern in a further capital liability of £266,000.

Meantime the new branches in Yorkshire—the Bradford, Eccleshill, and Idle, the Idle and Shipley, and the Ossett and Dewsbury—had all, since their commencement in 1872, been absorbing considerable sums of capital each half-year without return, and early in 1873 a yet more serious drain upon capital account had been begun by the letting of the contracts for the section of the Derbyshire extension from Colwick to Pinxton and for the North London junction line from Finsbury Park to Canonbury. The former, about eighteen miles in length, was let to Messrs. Benton and Woodiwiss, and the latter, one mile thirty-one chains, to Mr. Joseph Firbank, and they both involved heavy works. But, as we have already said, the objects they were to serve were so urgent that, notwithstanding the continued high prices of all materials and of labour, it seemed essential that they should be prosecuted at the highest possible speed.

One of the main objects of the line from Finsbury to Canonbury was to divert goods traffic from the existing junction with the North London at Maiden Lane, and so relieve congestion in the King's Cross goods station, and between it and Holloway; but, since this measure had been decided upon in 1871, the increase of the Company's London traffic had been so large that now, in 1873, it became absolutely necessary to devise some additional and more thorough plan of relief. For this two alternatives presented themselves : an enlargement of the existing goods terminus at King's Cross, or the construction of an entirely new goods station nearer the heart of London. Already, since about 1860, as the reader may remember, the Company had had a City goods station at Royal Mint Street; but the site of this not being central and the railway route to it *viâ* Bow being circuitous, the greater part of the freight which the Great Northern carried to and from the City had, nevertheless, to be carted to and from King's Cross. This necessitated a large stock of road vans and horses; for, unlike the London and North Western and other companies (who employed Messrs. Pickford and other pre-railway carriers as their agents), the Great Northern had from the first been its own street carrier in London. In Yorkshire too, after employing an agent up to 1869, it had since that date acquired its own carting stock. The result was that, at the date we have now reached, its carts numbered over 900, and its draught horses about 1,500.

To maintain and renew these was, of course, an important branch of current expenditure, and at this time of high prices it had become specially onerous. Indeed, the scarcity and consequent great costliness of horses was almost as much a matter of public complaint in 1873 as the scarcity and high price of coal. Consequently to diminish street cartage was an important object with the Company. This, then, was one reason why it seemed better to make the new provision for goods terminals in the City instead of at King's Cross.

There were other reasons equally cogent. The London and North Western at Broad Street and the Great Western at Smithfield had central City depôts already, and had so obtained important advantages in competition; and most conclusive argument of all—the "widened lines" of the Metropolitan Company offered a channel from King's Cross to the City which could very well accommodate a good deal more traffic than was at present put upon it. Lastly, the Metropolitan Company had a piece of most suitable land about four acres in extent to let adjoining its station at Farringdon Street. So the Great Northern directors decided in 1873 to lease this land and construct a new goods terminus upon it.

We have just said that the "widened lines" of the Metropolitan from King's Cross to Farringdon Street could readily accommodate additional traffic, but this was not the case with the Great Northern's own tunnel beneath the Regent's Canal. This tunnel had been constructed originally, the reader will remember, simply to give access to and from the passenger terminus; but since the opening of the connection with the Metropolitan, "City and suburban" trains, through goods and coal trains to and from the south of the Thames, and other new traffic had been using it; and now, if Farringdon Street was to be made a principal terminus for London goods, the use of it would be far larger than ever. Under these circumstances the directors decided to apply to Parliament in 1874 for powers to double this "Maiden Lane tunnel." At the same time they decided that they must spend a sum of £50,000 in erecting new departure platforms and sidings at the passenger terminus, King's Cross. Besides all this, it was very evident that the long-contemplated doubling of the Copenhagen tunnel could not be much longer postponed.

Meanwhile, at other principal stations on the main system—Peterborough, Grantham, Retford, Doncaster, Lincoln, Leeds, Bradford, &c.—heavy demands on capital account had to be met for station enlargements, new warehouses, sidings, &c. On the main lines generally, too, the outlay for facilitating traffic working, which we noticed as first becoming serious about 1870, had since that date increased in every half-year. When in August, 1871, the directors had reported that by the close of that year the block system would be completely installed between London and Yorkshire, they had probably thought that that would be the end of serious outlay for signalling apparatus; but, with the block stations in many cases three or even four miles apart, it had since been found that the new system of space intervals between trains not only did not increase the capacity of the main line, but actually diminished it. So it had become necessary to set to work at once to shorten the block sections, while at the same time an auxiliary remedy had had to be sought in the provision of "passing places," *i.e.*, duplicate lengths of line between block stations on to which slow trains could be shunted while the faster ones went by. By the end of 1873 about half a dozen of these had been provided alongside the main lines in various parts, and by the same date the original instalment of the block system had been largely extended. The result was that on its 162 miles of main line between London and Askern the Great Northern had by this time 109 block stations. Indeed, this part of its system was probably better equipped in this respect than any other British railway company at the same date.

This meant, of course, not only a considerable outlay of capital but a serious increase of working expenses for wages of signalmen, &c., and in this year, 1873, also, as in the previous year, the cost of labour and the price of coal, iron, and other railway requisites continued abnormally high, so that the ratio of working expenses to receipts reached the highest figure on record—53 per cent. Moreover, a heavy sum had to be paid in compensation for an accident at Retford, which occurred on the very same day as the shareholders' meeting, 23 August, 1873. On the other hand, 1873, like 1872, was a year of very great expansion of gross receipts, the total increase over the previous year being about £200,000, though 1872 itself, as we saw, had achieved a "record" increase of £180,000 over 1871. The result was that the dividend paid on the original stock was 2s. 6d. higher than ever before—£7 5s. per cent. for the year.

This was not only the highest dividend that the Great Northern Company had paid up to that time, but is higher than any it has paid since; in a word, it marks the zenith of the Company's prosperity, and there was a peculiar appropriateness in this being reached at this date. It coincided most opportunely with the closing of the lives of three men who had been linked with the undertaking since its inception— Edmund Denison, Colonel Packe, and Major Amsinck, the last-named of whom died in 1873, and the two former in 1874. Colonel Packe was succeeded in the chairmanship by Colonel the Honourable Octavius Duncombe, but he, though also an original director of the Company, had retired from the Board in 1850, and had not been re-elected until 1857. The "old order" was changing, "yielding place to new." Mr. John Harvey Astell, director, Mr. Joseph Leech, the Company's solicitor, and Mr. E. B. Denison, Q.C., who, under the title of Sir Edmund Beckett, now succeeded to a baronetcy which his father had held for a few months only, were now the sole survivors of those who from the first and throughout had fought the Great Northern's battles.

Compared with the session of 1871, 1872, and 1873, the Parliamentary session of 1874 was a quiet one for the Great Northern; nevertheless, it produced some important results. The Cheshire Lines Committee's Bill for its new Liverpool line was passed, and also a "Great Northern Further Powers" Bill for the new Maiden Lane tunnel and other works; but again the chief interest centred round projects for new lines in the Midlands. In fulfilment of their pledge to the landowners, the Great Northern and London and North Western re-introduced their Bill for extending the Newark and Leicester line from Tilton to Market Harborough, and for vesting the part of it between Bottesford and Tilton (the London and North Western did not seek again to share in the portion between Bottesford and Newark) in their joint ownership; but the Midland and Sheffield joint project for occupying the same ground was not revived, the Midland preferring to promote again the line from Manton to Rushton, which Sir Edward Watkin, it may be remembered, had persuaded Mr. Price to withdraw in the autumn of 1871. In further evidence that the Sheffield's "flirtation" with the Midland—as Sir Mordaunt Wells, Q.C., had described the alliance of 1872-3—was completely "off," these two companies had antagonistic schemes on foot in Yorkshire this session, the Midland joining with the North Eastern Company in promoting a line from Swinton to Knottingley, while the Sheffield had a scheme of its own to cover practically the same ground. It being, of course, undesirable in Great Northern interests that the Midland and North Eastern should come into closer relationship, the Great Northern supported the Sheffield scheme.

Notwithstanding Midland opposition, the Tilton and Market Harborough Bill got through both Houses successfully. So at the price of admitting the London and North Western to Nottingham and to Doncaster, the Great Northern relieved itself of half its liability for making the already authorized line from Bottesford to Tilton, and got powers of access, at half liability also, to Market Harborough with running powers to Northampton. But the Midland, nevertheless, got its Manton to Rushton line. On the other hand, both the Swinton and Knottingley, and the Leeds, Pontefract, and Sheffield Junction—as the Sheffield Company's project was called— were thrown out in the Commons; but, this decision being regarded with some reason as a practical joke on the part of the Committee, the North Eastern and Midland companies subsequently obtained leave for their Bill to be re-committed, buying off Sheffield and Great Northern opposition to this by undertaking to give those companies running powers over the new line when made. In this form the Swinton and Knottingley Bill eventually passed into law.

In this same summer of 1874 Mr. Fraser got the Great Northern's new branch, $6\frac{1}{2}$ miles in length, from Laister Dyke, near Bradford, to Eccleshill, Idle, and Shipley, the connecting line from Ossett *viâ* Dewsbury to Batley, four miles, and the Halifax and Ovenden, $2\frac{1}{2}$ miles, open for goods and mineral traffic. Meanwhile Mr. Johnson reported that the North London Junction line would be ready before the end of the year, and that every exertion was being made to get the first twenty miles of the Derbyshire extension open for traffic by the following April. The fact that owing to the continued high price of coal and to strikes in South Yorkshire and Durham the coal traffic of the Company had fallen off in the half-year to 30 June, 1874, by £29,000, made this latter work even more urgent than before. A new work which Mr. Johnson had to take in hand in 1874 was the extension of the block system to the loop line and branches, and in this same year, too, all the principal stations were resignalled, interlocking apparatus extended to every junction of any importance, and lock-bars attached to all facing switches. Thus the Great Northern set an example to other companies in the prompt adoption of the most approved safety appliances.

On 7 October, 1874, the Midland directors announced that on and after 1 January, 1875, they intended to abolish second-class carriages throughout their system, to reduce their first-class fares to the existing second-class level ($1\frac{1}{2}d$. per mile), and to cease to give a reduction on return fares. This produced in the railway world a sensation greater even than that caused by the "third-class by all trains" edict of March, 1872; and as the new change was not, like the other, to be put into force simultaneously with its announcement, there arose, naturally enough, a strenuous agitation to induce Mr. Allport and his Board to reconsider their decision. The Great Northern directors joined with the Boards of all the other leading northern railways in an appeal to the Midland at least to postpone so far-reaching an alteration until a general conference had discussed the whole subject; but Mr. Ellis (who had succeeded Mr. Price in the Midland chairmanship upon the latter's appointment as one of the Railway Commissioners created under the Traffic Act of 1873) boldly upheld both the wisdom of the change and his company's right to independent action. Consequently the Great Northern, London and North Western, and other companies who competed with the Midland had, very reluctantly, to take in hand a revision of their fares also. Particularly were they loath to reduce their charges to first-class passengers—who, said Colonel Duncombe, had "never made any complaints," and, as things were, could "travel from London to York or to Edinburgh at a fare which in the old posting days they would almost have had to pay for turnpikes";—but, to quote Colonel Duncombe again, they were in "the somewhat humiliating position of not being their own masters." Accordingly, at the end of the year, Mr. Oakley issued a notice to the effect that, while second-class carriages would still be retained on the Great Northern, in no case would its fares be higher than by any other route.

A chief reason, no doubt, why the Great Northern directors decided not to follow the Midland's example of abolishing "second-class" was the rapidly growing importance of the suburban traffic on their line—a kind of traffic which more than any other demands a threefold classification. Throughout the sixties building operations had been carried on in the neighbourhood of Holloway and Finsbury Park with the utmost vigour, so that it was not until after the latter station was passed that the

Times reporter, on his way to the opening of the Alexandra Palace in May, 1873, found that "bricks and mortar began to give way to fields and hedges." Moreover, the Company's suburban collecting-ground had been largely extended by the opening of the branches to Edgware, Barnet, and Enfield. The result was that whereas for the half-year ended June, 1867—before the opening of the first of these suburban branches—the number of holders of season-tickets on the Great Northern was 2,457, for the half-year ended December, 1874—the date our history has now reached—it was 6,480.

Under these circumstances it is not surprising that in this winter of 1874-5 what we may call "the problem of the neck of the bottle"—the problem that, whilst separated to a great extent elsewhere, all classes of London traffic on the Great Northern had to use a single "up" and a single "down" track through the Copenhapen tunnel—clamoured once more, and this time very literally, for solution. As we have said, the congestion thus occasioned was intensified by the fact that the "up" goods traffic after passing through the tunnel had to cross the down line on the level to reach the goods terminus. True that, by the opening of the new depôt at Farringdon Street which took place on 2 November, 1874—exactly a year after the commencement of the works—this evil was to some extent lessened, because some of the goods trains could now be sent straight on through the Maiden Lane tunnel into the City without entering the King's Cross depôt at all. Nevertheless, on the whole, the new state of things produced by the opening of the City goods terminus was worse than the old, seeing that the congestion was now extended into the Maiden Lane tunnel also. The result was that suburban passengers were often delayed half an hour or more in traversing the one and a half miles of railway between Holloway and the Metropolitan Junction.

To relieve this state of things, as we have said, powers for the new junction line from Finsbury Park to Canonbury had been obtained in 1872, and, though the works of this were very heavy, including a tunnel three-quarters of a mile long near Canonbury, the carrying of the "down" track of the junction line beneath the four tracks of the main line by a subway "on the skew," and the entire reconstruction, with four platforms, of Finsbury Park Station, it was opened for goods traffic on 14 December, 1874. By this means traffic between Finsbury Park and the Docks and the Royal Mint Street Depôt was diverted from the "congested area" near King's Cross; nevertheless, the relief to the suburban passengers was so unappreciable that early in January, 1875, under the additional provocation of some changes in the season-ticket rates introduced in connection with the general revision of passenger fares, a number of them went the length of assembling at an "indignation meeting" at the City Terminus Hotel. The chairman of this meeting was Mr. Waddy, Q.C., M.P., and another speaker was Mr. Littler, also subsequently a Queen's Counsel—in which capacity, indeed, we shall meet him in a later chapter—and now Chairman of the Middlesex County Council. The upshot of the meeting was the appointment of a deputation to wait upon the directors at King's Cross.

There could be no doubt that this movement on the part of the suburban season-ticket holders was to a large extent justifiable, for the Great Northern directors were not by any means blameless in the matter. As long ago as 1866, as the reader may remember, they had gone to Parliament for powers to double the Copenhagen tunnel, and though the financial crisis of 1867, and the withdrawal of the Midland traffic in 1868, had no doubt justified the postponement of that work, it ought certainly to have been one of the first operations taken in hand at the time of recovery in 1870. Of course, the excuse of the Board was that they had then taken up the alternative North London Junction scheme. Unfortunately, their subsequent action in opening a new central City goods depôt to be reached, not by the North London, but by the Metropolitan, had to a large extent deprived the Canonbury line, even before it was opened, of usefulness as a channel for goods traffic. Under these circumstances it was imperative that they should now realize without delay the second object for which as we saw at the time they had planned the North London Junction—the object of obtaining an alternative route for passenger traffic from Finsbury Park to the City *viâ* the North London's Broad Street extension.

The Act of 1872 authorized the Great Northern "to enter into agreements for the use of and access to Broad Street Station," and ever since its passing negotiations with this object had been on foot; but the difficulty was that not the North London Company only, but the London and North Western also, had to be brought to terms. Both in the original North London line and that "happy afterthought," the branch from it to the City, the North Western had taken a large financial interest; moreover, in the agreement under which the Broad Street terminus had been constructed it was expressly provided that no other company should be admitted to it without consent from Euston Square. The result was that the Great Northern's utmost endeavours to secure running powers from Canonbury to Broad Street proved futile, and so under pressure of the season-ticket holders' agitation the King's Cross Board had to agree to an alternative arrangement. This was that the North London Company should send *its* trains to the Great Northern's suburban stations—not, however, under running powers, but under special terms; viz., the running company to be paid, in addition to its mileage proportion of all through fares, a fixed sum per train-mile for haulage over the Great Northern, for the use of its rolling stock, and for the services of its train staffs. For goods traffic, however, to the Docks and Bow (for Royal Mint Street) the Great Northern had running powers already, and these it now began to exercise in lieu of the arrangements under which up to this time the North London had taken forward the Great Northern waggons with its own engines. For passenger terminal accommodation the Great Northern agreed to rent a section of Broad Street Station.

These new arrangements with the North London Company were brought into force from 1 February, 1875. Since that date, accordingly, passengers to and from Finsbury Park, and all the suburban stations on the Great Northern north of that junction, have had the advantage of an alternative City service to and from Broad Street, about seven minutes shorter than the Moorgate Street service *viâ* the Metropolitan. Moreover, the North London's has the additional attraction of being a "daylight route," whereas the other is largely underground. Thus the complaints of the Great Northern's suburban passengers were completely silenced for a while, and for a time also the Company's capital account was relieved from the somewhat heavy demands which had been made upon it during the previous few years for new carriages for the suburban service. On the other hand, the new arrangements meant that what may be called "the suburban increment"—the new revenue from residential traffic which had formed no small part of the very large expansion of the Company's passenger traffic since 1870—had in the future to be divided with the North London as well as with the Metropolitan.

Of course, now that this suburban increment had come and seemed certain to go on coming, it was easy to lament that the Great Northern was not in a position to cater for it without "foreign" help, and to see how profitable a City extension of its own might now have become; and, indeed, without blaming the Board for not having exercised a foresight almost more than human, a candid historian can hardly avoid making the criticism that in this matter of London accommodation it seems at a critical time to have pursued no very definite policy. Thus it now came about that after spending nearly half a million of money to make a new connection with the North London, much of the benefit of which had to be surrendered to that Company, the Great Northern had still not solved, nor even postponed for a time, its "neck of the bottle" problem. On the contrary, owing largely to its inconsistency in making the Metropolitan and not the North London its principal route for City goods traffic, it was now obliged to spend almost as much money in widening its approach to King's Cross and to the Metropolitan as if its new North London Junction had not been made. In the summer of 1875 the directors found—in the language of their August report—that it was "imperative that the doubling of the Maiden Lane and Copenhagen tunnels should now be proceeded with," and forthwith they let the contract for the new Copenhagen tunnel to Mr. Firbank, who by the time of the August meeting had the works "fairly commenced." The location of the new tunnel was on the west or "down" side of the original one, and it was to be devoted to goods traffic only, forming indeed a separate channel from Holloway into the King's Cross goods station. A bridge or "flying junction" was to be constructed at its north end to carry the "up" track over the main lines, and so the old level crossing at the south end of the existing tunnel was to be done away with and that tunnel left free for traffic to and from the passenger terminus and the Metropolitan.

Meanwhile the works had also been put in hand of a link line, four miles in length, from Sedgebrook on the Grantham and Nottingham branch to Barkstone—a line for which the Company had obtained powers in 1873 to form a through route for Derbyshire coal to Lincolnshire; in Yorkshire Mr. Fraser had made a start with the Bradford and Thornton, and Halifax, Thornton, and Keighley undertakings, and in Derbyshire Mr. Firbank had been called in to reinforce Messrs. Benton and Woodiwiss in getting the Erewash Valley line open for coal. Bad weather and other hindrances, however, prevented Mr. Johnson from enforcing the same punctuality in this case as on the Canonbury line and the Farringdon Street works, and even when the rest of the line between the coalfield and Colwick was ready, the great cutting at Kimberley—$2\frac{3}{4}$ miles long through hard magnesian limestone—was far from being complete. Mr. Johnson, however, had a temporary line run up at the side of the cutting on a gradient of 1 in 35, and so the Company at the end of August (1875) was put once more into communication with the Derbyshire coalfield for London traffic after an exclusion of $4\frac{1}{2}$ years. This had the immediate effect of increasing its mineral traffic receipts by £32,000 in the half-year.

During this same summer of 1875 the Alexandra Palace was reopened, and this event and the general reduction of fares enforced by the *coup d'état* of the Midland combined to produce an increase of nearly four millions—about seventy per cent.—in the number of passengers carried over the system. The increase in receipts, however, was by no means proportionate, and the directors estimated that on account of the reduction of fares the passenger revenue for the year was about £50,000 less than it would otherwise have been. Moreover, the period of great national prosperity was now at an end. Consequently, the general increase of goods traffic was small compared with what it had been in the preceding years of great expansion. Further, the grain and potato harvests both proved deficient.

Since the beginning of the period of expansion in 1870, however, the merchandise tonnage carried by the Company had increased by thirty-five per cent., the mineral tonnage by eighteen per cent., and the

KIMBERLEY CUTTING WHEN IN COURSE OF CONSTRUCTION, SHOWING BOTH TEMPORARY AND PERMANENT LINES.

number of passengers by about 100 per cent. It was not surprising, therefore, that large outlay had been, and continued to be, necessary for enlarging the capacity of the main system. The most important operations to this end were the improvement of the signalling apparatus, the laying down of "passing places" at favourable lengths of line, and the extension of station buildings, and it was estimated that from the beginning of 1870 to the end of the year 1875 the Company spent £203,000 on the extension of the block system and interlocking, £200,000 on passing places, £310,000 on improvement and enlargement of stations, and £221,000 on new sidings and goods sheds, making a total capital outlay in five years, if the cost of the Farringdon Depôt and other works in London was also included, of £1,270,000 for facilitating and safeguarding the traffic on the main system. Moreover, the block system involved a heavy additional charge to revenue for maintenance and for the wages of signalmen, for it was estimated that when in 1876 the system was extended throughout the whole of the Company's lines, the number of additional signalmen required had reached 462. Altogether, it was estimated that with interest on outlay, maintenance and wages, the cost of the block system had become equal to one per cent. dividend on the Company's open stock.

Naturally enough, these years of abnormal expansion of traffic had produced some of the worst railway accidents known to British railway history; but, as a reward for the enlightened outlay just specified, the Great Northern still enjoyed the reputation, which we saw it acquired early in its career, of being a very safe as well as a very fast line to travel upon. True that in 1870 there had been two very grave disasters on its main line—the one on 21 June, near Newark, in which no less than sixteen excursionists returning to Yorkshire from a day in London had met at midnight a shockingly sudden death, and the other on the day after Christmas at Hatfield.

The cause of the first of these, however, had been the breaking of an axle belonging to a Midland, Sheffield, and Lincolnshire waggon (which had thrown part of an "up" goods train across the path of the "down" passenger), and of the second the breaking of a carriage tyre; and as for neither of these occurrences could the Great Northern be held blameworthy, it did not suffer seriously from them either in prestige or in pocket. Since the Welwyn Tunnel accident in 1866 the only serious blot on the Company's record for safety had been the accident at Retford already incidentally mentioned, and in this case the shareholders had had to suffer from one of those failures of human agency against which no complete safeguards can be provided. In direct defiance of signals a "goods" driver had driven his train through Retford Station into collision with an excursion train on its way from Manchester to Grimsby.

But, while with this exception the Great Northern's record as a safe line had remained unblemished, it had nevertheless suffered, not only in the case of the Retford accident, but in many other instances, from the stringency of the law as regards a railway company's liability for damage to the passengers and goods it carries. In 1867 a Royal Commission had recommended the limitation of this liability to a fixed amount in cases of personal injury to passengers, and in the sessions of 1868 and 1869 a movement in Parliament to carry this into effect had been headed by Mr. Christopher Denison, who, in so doing, had laid much stress upon a most remarkable case of hardship to the Great Northern

—the case of Miss Warren at Spalding Station. This lady, a dancing mistress, had tripped over a hole in the carpet of the station waiting-room, sustaining thereby an injury to her spine, and although the Company brought evidence to show that there had been no hole in the carpet in the early morning, but that it had been probably kicked open on the same day by "some gentleman with thick boots"—"it is a farming district," explained Mr. Oakley—she had obtained compensation to the amount of £1500. The recital of this case by Mr. Denison made a considerable impression on the House of Commons, and as the result a Select Committee was appointed to investigate the subject of compensation. Nevertheless no amendment of the law had resulted.

However, despite such cases as Miss Warren's and such human fallibility as that exhibited at Retford, the Great Northern had up to this time undoubtedly profited by its outlay on safety appliances, and now that the block system and interlocking had been so largely extended and the whole line resignalled, the directors had every right to entertain the expectation that such profit would display itself in a marked degree. This expectation, alas! as we shall now see, was destined to bitter disappointment.

At a few minutes before six on the evening of Friday, 21 January, 1876, a coal train, consisting of thirty-three waggons, drawn by a powerful six-wheel-coupled engine, left the New England coal sidings, just north of Peterborough, *en route* for London. The day had been one of a pouring rain with the wind in the south-east, but about dusk it had suddenly veered to the north, and brought on, without warning, an unusually heavy fall of snow. Through this storm the coal train, which had been late in starting from Peterborough, ran without incident about seven miles to Holme; but here the signalman, knowing that the Scotch express, timed to leave Peterborough at 6.28, was due, pulled over his lever to set the signal to danger in order to direct the coal train to shunt into a siding. Frozen snow, however, as it was discovered afterwards, clogged the signal connections; consequently the semaphore arm remained in the "safety" position, and the signalman was astonished to see the coal train pursue its journey.

The next signal-box was at Abbotts Ripton, and with this the Holme man at once communicated by telegraph. The result was that when the coal train arrived there it was stopped by the waving of a hand-lamp from the box. The Scotch express being by this time a good deal overdue, the coal driver was immediately directed to shunt into the station siding to allow it to pass, and the signalman at the same time, of course, pulled over his lever to set the northwards signal to "danger" during the operation. But again, owing to the frozen snow, the semaphore did not rise. The result was that while the last four trucks of the coal train yet remained foul of the main track, the Scotch express dashed into them at full speed.

The engine fell across the down line, dragging after it its tender, the guard's van, and several North Eastern carriages, and the contents of its fire-box were strewn over the ground. But its driver, Cattley by name, very soon picked himself up, and, despite the fact that one of his hands was crushed and a finger completely torn from it, most pluckily exerted himself to prevent a general conflagration. Meanwhile Lord Colville of Culross, deputy-chairman of the Company, who with another director, Mr. Robert Tennant, had been returning in the "Scotchman" from a railway meeting at Doncaster, had after the crash of the collision found himself standing unhurt in the snow; and, being joined by other passengers and by some platelayers who had hurried to the spot from their cottages near by, he made his way to the signal-box.*

The signalman, in answer to eager inquiries, declared that he had already set his signals to "danger," and telegraphed warning of the disaster to the signal-boxes on either side of his own; but as he appeared to be in a mazed state, a "relief clerk," who happened to be among the uninjured passengers, mounted the engine of the coal train, and started off southwards to give warning and fetch assistance, while, as an additional precaution, platelayers with fog-signals were sent in both directions along the line. Then, in the glare of the flames from the scattered contents of the fire-box, the work was commenced of rescuing the injured and imprisoned passengers, whose moans and cries for help had by this time become very piteous.

A young girl had just been taken out from the *débris*, and two women were being extricated, when a loud whistling was heard, followed by the "bang! bang!" of fog-signals and the roar of a train approaching from the south. The rescuing party had barely time to rush aside on to the slope of the cutting before the powerful engine of a passenger train cut its way through the tender of the Scotch express, and then, glancing off and dragging its tender after it, fell over on its side on the very slope where they were standing, while the guard's van and leading coaches, breaking off on the other side towards the "up" line, mounted upon the already shattered carriages of the "Scotchman." No wonder that this second horror piled upon

* There was no station at this date at Abbotts Ripton.

the first deprived even those who were unhurt of the use of their senses for a while. "Do we change here?" one passenger was heard to shout.

The new train, it appeared, was the 5.30 from King's Cross bound for Leeds. It had passed the preceding signal-cabin just at the very moment when the signalman there was receiving the "line blocked" signal from Abbotts Ripton, and had met the coal engine about 800 yards from the scene of the accident, from the whistle of which it had received its first warning that anything was wrong. But as it was equipped with hand-brakes only, and was coming down a bank of 1 in 200 on rails rendered greasy by the snow, it had been impossible for the driver of its engine (one of Mr. Stirling's "eight-foot singles," which had been exhibited at the "Railway Jubilee" in the previous year) to slacken speed to any appreciable extent. Consequently, it had been running at a rate of at least thirty miles an hour when it had caused the second collision.

Meanwhile, however, the coal engine had hurried on to Huntingdon, and the telegraph there had been set to work, with the result that not only were other following trains stopped, but a large force, headed by Mr. Oakley, Mr. Johnson, and Mr. Cockshott was soon brought upon the scene. Fires were lighted, ambulances and cranes brought up, and all through the bitter winter's night the work of clearance was carried on.

Meantime reports of the accident became circulated in London, and before midnight King's Cross was visited by many anxious inquirers—some of them persons of note—who had relatives in one or other of the trains. But particulars of identification came slowly, and the task of pacifying the anxious ones and restraining their eagerness to be conveyed at once to the scene of the accident, proved an extremely painful one for Mr. Forbes, the secretary, and other officials in charge at headquarters. Among those who were killed, or who afterwards died of their injuries, were the eldest son of Mr. Dion Boucicault, the actor and dramatist, the only surviving son of Mr. Matthew Noble, the sculptor, the brother and two nieces of Dr. Burdon Sanderson, the scientist, and another gentleman, also named Sanderson, who was agent to the Marquis of Exeter. Amongst passengers who escaped injury were Count Schouvaloff, the Russian Ambassador, and no less than three railway directors—Lord Colville, Mr. Tennant, and Mr. Cleghorn of the North Eastern. Two youths travelling in the same compartment as Lord Colville were killed. The total number of killed was thirteen, and no less than fifty-three others were wounded.

It was under the shadow of this awful disaster that the Great Northern shareholders met for their fifty-ninth half-yearly meeting on 19 February, 1876. Nor were the prospects of the Company in other respects very cheerful. Owing to a comparatively small increase of gross receipts, and a large unproductive outlay of new capital, the dividend for the year had sunk to £6 10s. per cent.; and, after the raising of a million of new capital in the year just passed, the creation of a further amount of £2,500,000 had to be faced—so the directors reported—in the near future. It was evident that the period of exceptional prosperity was over, and that hard times for the Company had begun.

CHAPTER XIX.

HARD TIMES—THE ARLESEY SIDING ACCIDENT—THE CHESHIRE LINES "LANE"—THE "GREAT EASTERN" QUESTION SETTLED AT LAST—1876-1878.

BY the end of 1867—which date we noted as marking the close of the Great Northern Company's first period of extension—we found that its mileage had increased from the original 283 to 487 miles, and its capital cost (including fixed charges) from about twelve millions to about twenty millions. At 487 the mileage remained stationary until 1871, when, as we have seen, the Wood Green and Enfield branch was brought into use. In 1872 the Bourn and Sleaford and Finchley and Barnet lines were opened, in 1873 the Alexandra Park, in 1874 the Ossett and Dewsbury, and in 1875 the Finsbury Park and Canonbury, the Bradford, Idle, and Shipley, and the Sedgebrook and Barkstone. In the autumn of 1875, also, the reader will remember, the Erewash Valley line was opened for coal traffic; but the full opening of the first section of the Derbyshire extension—twenty miles in length—did not take place till 1 August, 1876. However, if we include this twenty miles—as we are justified in doing, seeing that coal was the main object of the line—we find that by the date we have now reached—February, 1876—the mileage of the system had reached 540—an increase of fifty-three miles since 1867. In the same period its capital cost had been increased by no less than seven and a half millions, the total raised by shares, or represented by fixed charges, being now twenty-seven and a half millions.

These facts clearly reveal why it was that less prosperous times had now set in for the Company's shareholders. "The increase of capital—the disastrous increase—for a quarter of a century I have harped upon this same string," cried Mr. Seneca Hughes; and shareholders who had been impatient at his harping in 1872 and 1873 now applauded it. Nevertheless, the theory of a closed capital account remained as great a fallacy as ever. That it was not addition to capital merely that was depressing the Company's dividend, was proved by the fact that the highest rate of capital increase had been, not in the years just passed, but in the period from 1860 to 1867, and that then it had been accompanied and followed (except in the years of universal trade depression) by most satisfactory dividend returns. The difference was that, whereas in the first period of extension capital and mileage had been increased concurrently, in this second period, as the figures just quoted show, a rate of new outlay almost as great as before had been accompanied so far by a much smaller relative addition to mileage. In short, it was not increase to capital *per se* which—in the exaggerated language of Mr. Seneca Hughes—was threatening "ultimately to prostrate" the shareholders; it was increase of capital unaccompanied by a proportionate increase of earning power.

To a certain extent, it is true, the seven and a half millions of new capital spent since 1867 had increased earning power out of proportion to the addition to mileage to be shown for it. Thus nothing, of course, had been added to mileage by the more than a million which, as we have seen, had been spent on improvements of the main system; yet this outlay had not only increased the capacity of that system, but had been absolutely demanded if traffic was not to be turned away. Further, the figure of 540 miles given above does not include the Great Northern's share in the two new joint undertakings, the Manchester and Liverpool and the Halifax and Ovenden; yet these lines (which had absorbed about one and a half millions between them since 1870) were already remunerative to some extent. Thirdly, the opening of the Erewash Valley line was really a more important addition to earning power than was denoted by its mileage *per se*, because it meant the recommencement over the whole system of the most important traffic in Derbyshire coal. These facts have to be taken in qualification of the bare statement than an outlay of seven and a half millions had given fifty-three new miles only.

But, while in these quarters development of new revenue was to be immediately expected, in others, unfortunately, a continued process of unproductive outlay had still for some years to be faced. The second and third contracts on the Derbyshire and Staffordshire extension, from Kimberley to Derby, and from Derby to Egginton, had only quite recently been let; of the Leicestershire lines one section only—from Market Harborough to Bottesford—had so far been put in hand; and on the heavy works of the Yorkshire extensions —the Bradford and Thornton, and the Halifax, Thornton, and Keighley—so little had been done that it was necessary to go to

Parliament in this year, 1876, for an "extension of time." The Manchester Central Station, too, was still a long way off completion, and the line to the north end of Liverpool still further: whilst in London the new Copenhagen tunnel was not far advanced, and the

VIADUCT AT ILKESTON, DERBYSHIRE.

contract for the new Maiden Lane tunnel not yet let. Finally, to provide for the increased traffic and for the working of the new lines, the directors had felt it to be necessary in August, 1875, to recommend the construction of seventy-two new engines and a large number of new carriages and waggons at a capital cost of over a quarter of a million. To sum up, there was a further addition to capital of at least three millions to be faced without prospect of its producing any immediate increase of earning power.

On the top of all this had come the Abbotts Ripton accident, disagreeable enough as entailing a drain on revenue for compensation, but still more disagreeable in the "moral" which it enforced. For the coroner's jury appended to its verdict of "Accidental death" a rider censuring the directors for "endeavouring to conduct so heavy a mineral traffic without providing a special line of rails for its transit"; and without attaching much weight to this crude and hasty expression of opinion, the directors themselves could not but share in the view which, as the result of their own and other similar disasters, had now become generally accepted—the view that the time had come for passenger and goods traffic to be separated on all main lines. If the block system had not "broken down," as the newspaper writers of this date were fond of saying it had, it had certainly failed to avert a series of very terrible accidents. Moreover, the mechanical appliances by which it had to be put into effect were, the Abbotts Ripton disaster showed, liable to failure under stress of weather; and that accident had also shown that in the absence of better brake-power a fast and heavy passenger train might run past a danger signal with terrible results. The Great Northern, it was true, had already adopted experimentally a continuous brake known as "Smith's vacuum," with fairly good results, and a Royal Commission had recently held trials of this and others. The mechanism of signalling, too, was obviously open to improvement to avert the special dangers which the Abbotts Ripton accident had disclosed.* Nevertheless, while consoling themselves that by improvements such as these an immediate repetition of such a terrible diaster might be averted, the Great Northern directors were still forced to the conclusion that in the near future it would be necessary to provide a complete system of relief lines, so as to separate the goods traffic almost entirely from the passenger.

Nor was it increase of gross traffic merely that threatened to necessitate this drastic measure. There were a number of auxiliary influences at work, all springing directly or indirectly from the new competition of the Midland Company. We have already seen how that company had signalized its independent establishment in London

---

* Two improvements introduced on the Great Northern as results of the accident were a new type of semaphore arm which works clear of the post, and so is unlikely to get clogged with snow, and the alteration of the *normal* position of the arm from "safety" to "danger." Either of them probably, but certainly the latter, would, if adopted earlier, have prevented the accident altogether.

by two important innovations involving a general reduction of passenger fares. The result of this was that more passengers had now to be carried to earn the same revenue, which meant heavier and more frequent trains. Indirectly also, as we have seen, owing to the desire of the Great Northern and other companies still to give extra benefits to the two higher classes, a general acceleration of speed had resulted. Further, since 1874 the Midland had introduced "Pullman cars" on its principal passenger services, and this had compelled the Great Northern and North Western to provide improved, and therefore heavier, first-class carriages and to give sleeping accommodation on their night "Scotchmen."

Similarly, as regards goods traffic, the new competition had caused the work to be done at higher pressure than before. For instance, it had become the rule for goods consigned from Yorkshire, Lancashire, or the Midlands to London or *vice versa* to be delivered within twelve hours. This, of course, meant a much faster rate of running for goods trains than in former easier-going days. Moreover, with the opening of the Settle and Carlisle line, which was fixed for 1 May of this year, 1876, the new competition was to be extended more fully to the Scotch traffic. So it was out of the question for the Great Northern to look for relief, as it might under other circumstances have done, in a reduction of speed, frequency, or weight of trains. On the contrary, it had to prepare for additions in these respects in order to maintain its position as the "premier line" to the North.

Such was the somewhat critical condition of Great Northern affairs, when, in April, 1876, information reached King's Cross that the Great Eastern directors desired to reopen negotiations with a view to a new exchange of traffic facilities between the two companies. Since June, 1868, as the reader was informed incidentally in a previous chapter, there had been in force an agreement, made at that date between Colonel Packe and Lord Salisbury, under which the Great Eastern had obtained powers to have its own agents in the principal northern towns to be reached *viâ* its connections with the Great Northern and Sheffield systems, and to book through traffic between those towns and all places (including London) on its own system at rates to be mutually agreed and divided by mileage. But, as we have already noted, this arrangement had been accepted by Lord Salisbury and his colleagues merely as a *pis aller*. To have a line of its own into Yorkshire had been, as we know, the goal of "Eastern Counties" policy in King Hudson's time. As soon as "Eastern Counties" had been superseded by "Great Eastern," this policy, the reader remembers, had been revived by Mr. George Parker Bidder. It had been again revived, as we also saw, in connection with the C. O. A. L. of 1871.

Nor was it because of Great Northern obstruction that the traffic arrangement just mentioned had been all that the Great Eastern had so far been able to obtain. Ever since 1865 the King's Cross Board had been willing, as we have seen, to place the Great Eastern in Yorksire on rails of its own by admitting it to half-ownership of its loop line from March to Doncaster. No less than three times in the sixties, the reader may remember, an arrangement of this character had been on the verge of completion, when it had been upset by the poverty of the Great Eastern Company and consequent want of stability in its directorate; and again so recently as 1873 this poor Cinderella among railways might have emerged from her seclusion by means of running powers to Doncaster. Unfortunately, the utmost guarantee of traffic which her guardians could see their way to offer, had been less by £5,000 than that which the Great Northern had been willing to accept.

It was obvious, however, that so small a difference as this ought not to form a permanent obstacle to a new agreement. So after some preliminary overtures between Mr. Oakley and Mr. Swarbrick in the autumn of 1875, the matter came up again, as we have just said, in April, 1876. At the beginning of May the Great Eastern directors sent a written statement of the terms they now proposed, but the Great Northern found "the pith in the matter"—the phrase was Mr. Oakley's—not in the detailed suggestions thus made (which were to a large extent a repetition of what had been so nearly arranged so many times before), but in the final clause of the statement. This referred to the desirability of some "more intimate relations" being established between the two companies.

Obviously this pointed to a willingness on the part of the Great Eastern to consider proposals for a complete amalgamation, and in their anxiety for relief lines the Great Northern directors caught rather eagerly at the suggestion. Amalgamation with the Great Eastern, thought they, might mean obtaining on easy terms that duplicate route from the North to London which their traffic appeared imperatively to demand. Certainly it would mean the acquirement of another long-felt Great Northern want,—a genuine City terminus,—seeing that the Great Eastern had recently completed its splendid new London station at Liverpool Street. Accordingly, Colonel Duncombe and Lord Colville were appointed as a delegation from the Great Northern Board to carry on negotiations on this new basis.

Meantime, from 1 May, 1876, the Midland's Settle and Carlisle line was opened for passenger traffic. This meant that the central route between London and Scotland was at last full-grown, and so it became necessary, as we have already foreseen it would, for the companies owning the two rival coast routes to exert themselves to meet the new competition. The Great Northern and North Eastern companies decided upon a general acceleration of their joint service. Accordingly from 1 June, 1876, the time taken by the 10 a.m. Edinburgh (first and second-class only) train from King's Cross to Edinburgh was reduced from $9\frac{1}{2}$ hours to 9 hours, that of the following third-class train from $10\frac{1}{2}$ hours to 10, and of the night express from $9\frac{3}{4}$ hours to $9\frac{1}{4}$. This meant that by the first-named of these trains the Great Northern had to cover the 188 miles between London and York in four hours—a journey-speed of exactly forty-seven miles an hour; and this made it necessary for Mr. Stirling to provide some of his "eight-footers" with improved and larger tenders, so that they might cover the first $105\frac{1}{2}$ miles from London to Grantham without a stop—quite the longest continuous run at this date. The general result was that for Edinburgh the East Coast service (with the advantage of a few miles shorter route) remained as far ahead as ever of the two others. Even for Glasgow it remained quicker than the Midland's, though it was beaten, thanks to a very decided advantage in mileage, by the West Coast.

Though it did not join in promoting these accelerations of the East Coast service, the North British Company, notwithstanding the large interest it now had in the central route, did not interpose any obstacle to their being carried out. The same compliance, however, was not shown by the Caledonian Company when it was pressed to extend the benefit of them to Perth and Aberdeen. On the contrary, it appealed to the Railway Commission against the requirements which the Great Northern and North Eastern sought to enforce under their "facility clauses." The Commissioners, however, gave a judgment favourable to the East Coast companies on all the more important points of the case (July 1876). Consequently the Caledonian was compelled *inter alia* to carry on passengers who left King's Cross by the night express —8.30 p.m.—so that they reached Perth at 8.40 a.m., and Aberdeen at 12.40. This made practically a "dead heat" with the West Coast night service, the "Special Scotch Mail"—8.40 from Euston—being "booked" to reach Aberdeen at the same time, *i.e.*, 12.40 p.m., and Perth at 9 a.m. Prior to this the West Coast had enjoyed a superiority of nearly four hours as regards the northern parts of Scotland.

There was, however, one unsatisfactory feature in the business. This was that the harder work entailed by these accelerations had to be done for less money than before, seeing that the Midland was now able to enforce the extension of its reduction of fares over the whole of the Anglo-Scotch passenger traffic. Thus the first-class fare between London and Edinburgh—to give a single example—had to be reduced from £3 10s. 0d. to £2 17s. 6d. The Midland authorities, it is true, insisted that, as far as their Company was concerned, the general effect of their reclassification and revision of fares had been profitable; but the Great Northern and London and North Western held quite a contrary opinion, and at the half-yearly meeting of the former in August, 1876, Colonel Duncombe supported this view by the statement that during the half-year the Company had carried 681,017 more passengers, and yet the increase in its receipts was £4859 only, *i.e.*, little more than 1½d. per additional passenger.

By this time nearly half of the 593 yards of new Copenhagen tunnel had been mined by the contractor, Mr. Firbank, and he had also got the new Maiden Lane tunnel well in hand. At Doncaster, too, an important enlargement of the existing accommodation was in progress, including a reconstruction of the passenger station and a new engine shed on the Carr to accommodate one hundred engines. At the same time the new Great Northern and London and North Western joint line from Market Harborough to Bottesford was in course of formation, and the contract was about to be let for the section from Bottesford to Newark, to be made by the Great Northern alone. On 1 August, 1876, as already noted, the first section of the Derbyshire extension, from Colwick to Pinxton, was opened fully; but it took time for any considerable amount of passenger traffic to be developed upon it. Of coals, however, 115,000 tons had passed over it during the half-year to 30 June, 1876. This, however, was rather less than was needed to balance the falling-off from South Yorkshire, where strikes had cut off a good part of what was left of the London trade.

Meanwhile no progress had yet been made with the negotiations with the Great Eastern. Yet another "revolution" seemed imminent in the directorate of that unfortunate company. Mr. M. T. Bass had put himself at the head of a movement to place Sir Edward Watkin at the head of its affairs, notwithstanding the fact that that gentleman had already the South Eastern and Metropolitan besides the Sheffield to manage, not to speak of a number of minor concerns; and it looked as if the negotiations between the Great Northern and Mr. Parkes and his colleagues would prove as futile as so many similar negotiations had been in the past. Again, however, as in 1868, when Lord Salisbury had been preferred to him, Sir E. Watkin failed to secure the Great Eastern chair, and on 29 October, 1876, Colonel Duncombe was able to report at the Great Northern Board that he had arranged with Mr. Parkes that Mr. Oakley and Mr. Swarbrick should confer together to see whether the principles of an amalgamation could be arrived at.

The outcome was that early in November each Board made a proposal of terms. Assuming the Great Northern average dividend to be 6 per cent., the Great Eastern proposed that the Great Eastern ordinary stock should be guaranteed 25 per cent. of this (*i.e.*, £1 10s. 0d.) in 1878, and that this proportion should be increased by 5 per cent. (*i.e.*, 6s. every year) until it reached 55 per cent. (*i.e.*, £3 6s. 0d.) in 1884, in which year permanent fusion was to take place at that ratio. But having regard to the fact that the Great Eastern dividend during the previous seven years had averaged 11s. 9d. only, whereas their own average had been nearer 7 per cent. than 6, the Great Northern directors thought this price too high. Accordingly they submitted a counter proposition. This was that the Great Eastern dividend should be £1 5s. 0d. only to commence with in 1878, should rise by 5s. instead of 6s. stages, and that the ultimate fusion in 1884 should be at 50 per cent. instead of at 55. In other words, they were willing to buy up the Great Eastern at half-price, but at no higher. These terms, however, proved 5 per cent. too low for the Great Eastern directors to accept, and, the Great Northern Board on its part being convinced that it could not in justice offer more, the negotiations fell to the ground.

But the problem of relief lines still remained, and the Great Northern directors now felt that they must face this without reference to any arrangement with the Great Eastern. They therefore returned to a plan which they seem to have had before in their minds. This was to make a new link line from Shepreth—which, the reader may remember, is the terminus of the Hitchin and Cambridge branch so far as Great Northern ownership is concerned—to March, where Great Northern ownership begins again in the line which we saw opened from Spalding in 1867, to give a direct connection with the Great Eastern system. Thus this new link would have the effect of extending the loop line southwards to Hitchin, and so practically duplicating the main line between Hitchin and Peterborough; and from Hitchin southwards a couple more links—say from Stevenage to Hertford, and from Hertingfordbury to Enfield—would, with the new tunnels under construction near King's Cross, complete the doubling right into London. This was the plan which now commended itself to the Board at King's Cross; and, knowing that in the position of their capital account they must take it by piecemeal, they instructed their solicitor, Mr. Leech, to deposit a Bill for the session of 1877 for the Shepreth to March line as the first instalment.

Mr. Leech was making haste with this work (for November had been well advanced before the rupture of the negotiations), when rumours reached King's Cross that the Great Eastern Company meant to deposit a Bill for a direct line from Spalding, through Sleaford, to Lincoln. Such a line, as we know, had been often projected before, and the Great Northern Board was fully aware that it would be to their Company's interest to make it some day, as an alternative to the existing circuit by Boston. But, if the Great Eastern meant to enter the field again, the matter had become urgent; and so Mr. Leech's instructions were hastily enlarged to include the deposit of a Spalding to Lincoln line also. Post-haste, he despatched one of his staff to Lincoln to give the necessary notices, but the only way to accomplish this in the time was by persuading the publisher of the local paper to issue a special edition, for the sole purpose of the railway advertisement.

Hardly had these arrangements been completed when two serious calamities befell the Great Northern Company. One of them was the sudden death, on 26 December, 1876, of Mr. Leech, who up to a few days before had been, as we have seen, actively engaged in the Parliamentary affairs of the Company. An able, conscientious, but thoroughly unostentatious man, Mr. Leech's name has, perhaps, not appeared in these pages so often as his great services to the Company warrant; for he had been connected with the undertaking since its very commencement, and at its sixtieth half-yearly meeting, held in August of this year, he had reminded Colonel Duncombe that he had not missed attendance at a single one of those gatherings since the first one in 1846. Now he had died in harness, and the directors had to look for a new chief legal adviser at a time when most important Parliamentary business was in hand. Fortunately, in Mr. Henry Nelson, of Leeds, a successor to Mr. Leech was available who was already, as we know, devoted to the Company's interests. Indeed, he was now its fully-recognized agent in Yorkshire and the midland counties. Accordingly, the firm of Nelson, Barr, and Nelson was appointed to succeed Johnson, Farquhar, and Leech as Great Northern solicitors-in-chief.

But Mr. Leech's death had been preceded, three days before, by a still more serious calamity—an accident on its main line almost as distressing in its consequences as that which had occurred at Abbotts Ripton only eleven months previously. It was the afternoon before

Christmas Eve, a time when, of course, traffic was unusually heavy; consequently the Manchester express—the 2.45 from King's Cross—had to be run in duplicate. The first section left punctually under the charge of a most experienced driver, Thomas Pepper by name, with whom Mr. Cockshott exchanged a few words on the platform relative to the special need for caution at the Christmas season; and it had performed in safety nearly half of its run-without-stop to Peterborough, and was descending at a speed of at least fifty-five miles an hour the long bank of about 1 in 230, which begins just north of Hitchin, when its driver saw the Arlesey Siding "distant signal" at danger about 150 yards ahead. He immediately shut off steam, applied what brake-power he had under his control, and whistled to the guards to do the same. Nevertheless, speed had not slackened to any considerable extent when about 500 yards further on the "home signal," also at danger, came into view. Just beyond it Pepper and his fireman descried to their horror some derailed trucks of a shunting "goods."

Seeing in a flash that a collision was inevitable, the two men threw themselves from the foot-plate. The driver alighted on his head in the garden of the Arlesey Siding station-master's house,* in full view of the station-master's wife; and next moment, with a terrific crash, his engine collided with the goods trucks, cut its way through them, and became embedded in the ballast beyond. The tender was torn from the engine, and became entangled with the trucks. The six front carriages were completely smashed, the framework of one of them coming to rest upon the top of a truck with its wheels inverted.

With most commendable promptitude—probably with the recollection of what had happened at Abbotts Ripton in his mind—a policeman in the Company's service named Monk, having escaped unhurt from the wreck, made his way to the signal-box, and assisted the terrified signalman to send warning to all following and approaching traffic. The result was that for many miles in both directions a long stationary procession of trains collected. Meanwhile, by the same telegraphic agency, breakdown gangs were brought to the scene, and the work of clearance was commenced. Almost miraculously—as now appeared—several passengers who had been travelling in the carriages totally wrecked had escaped with slight or no injuries, and to the surprise of all it was found that in addition to the driver and fireman, both of whom had been killed on the spot, three others only had sustained fatal hurt. Thirty passengers, however, were injured, some of them very seriously.

This accident revealed very clearly the weaknesses of the then

* The station has since been rechristened "Three Counties."

available appliances for safeguarding traffic and the great danger of continuing with such appliances to intermingle a very fast passenger traffic with a heavy business in goods and coal. The beginning of the disaster had been the derailment of four trucks of an "up" goods train as it was being shunted across the "down" track into the siding; but this was the *occasion* only of the accident; its *cause* was the inadequacy of the appliances put into use for stopping the express. Of course it is possible that it was not the appliances, but the man, that failed—that Pepper and his fireman both neglected to notice the advance signal; and in the absence of any but circumstantial evidence —for both driver and fireman were dead—this, indeed, was the view which the coroner's jury was led to take. But by experts their verdict was severely criticized. Having regard to Pepper's long experience, the special caution he had received from Mr. Cockshott, and some other facts too minute to be here mentioned, it is much more probable— almost certain, in fact—that, as the narrative just given assumes, he tried his best to obey the distant signal, but that against the combination of high speed, a falling gradient, and greasy rails, the hand-brake power proved as ineffective as in the case of the second collision at Abbotts Ripton. Nor is this, indeed, in the least surprising. At the official inquiry into the accident Mr. Stirling stated that at the brake-trials held at Newark before the Royal Commission about eighteen months before a train of about the same weight as this Manchester express, and similarly equipped with non-continuous brakes, had run on after steam had been shut off, and the brake-power applied, no less a distance than 1200 yards along a level track!

Seeing, therefore, that the distant signal at Arlesey Siding was 898 yards only ahead of the scene of the derailment, and the gradient there a falling one, the disaster was one which, given the combination of circumstances, had been bound to happen under the then conditions of working. Nevertheless it is not easy to see what safeguard against such a contingency had been available to the Great Northern authorities, short of restricting very considerably the speed of all the express trains on their system. A continuous brake, it is true, would almost certainly have pulled up the express in time; but the blame in this respect rested not with the railway company, but with the Royal Commission on Railway Accidents. For this body, though it had held its brake-trials as long before as June, 1875, had not yet published its report; and pending this (which was reasonably expected to settle decisively the question as to whether or not continuous brakes were trustworthy, and perhaps to recommend a type of brake for universal adoption) the railway companies were practically powerless to act vigorously in the matter, except at the risk of involving themselves in a large premature outlay. As for the other precaution which, obviously enough, might have prevented this accident—the working of the block system with greater stringency, so that not one, but two sections, should be kept between trains on the same rails,—that was a remedy which, unless carried out quite regardless of expense in the matter of signal-boxes and men, would have hampered the traffic to such a degree as to have necessitated its discontinuance after a week's trial. It is noteworthy, however, that the Great Northern engineer, Mr. Johnson, had foreseen that, without better brake-power, the block system did not properly provide against the very contingency which occurred at Arlesey Siding, viz., the breakdown of a train just beyond a block station. It is on record, indeed, that he raised the point at a discussion at the Institution of Civil Engineers in 1874, to be answered by Mr. Allport that the distance signal ought to be sufficient protection in such a case.

The above analysis reveals the fact that in the absence of continuous brakes the Great Northern authorities at this date were practically compelled to work their traffic under conditions which made the occurrence of such an accident as the one at Arlesey Siding quite calculable beforehand. This being so, it is not at all surprising that in their report to the shareholders in February, 1877, the directors stated that "with the experience of this lamentable accident before them" it was "impossible to resist the conviction that the greatest measure of safe and efficient working" could "not be secured without further accommodation for the traffic." Accordingly they strongly urged the approval of the plan of relief lines which, as we have seen, they had already adopted "with the view of providing a second direct and serviceable line from the North to London."

Needless to say, this was an unpleasant announcement for the shareholders, the more so as the report at the same time stated that a revision of the original estimates for the new lines already in hand, in the light of what had already been spent upon them, had swollen their existing capital liability to $4\frac{1}{2}$ millions. What seemed the inevitable conclusion, however, was voiced by a speaker at the meeting—Mr. Robert White—when he said: "We are absolutely bound by circumstances to provide some other means of transit for our goods traffic; we must have relief lines." So, in spite of the customary opposition of Mr. Seneca Hughes, the sanction of the meeting was given to the Shepreth and March and Spalding and Lincoln Bill, and also to a Further Powers Bill, the chief object of which was to raise new capital for the works already in hand.

In the case of the former Bill, however, what Mr. Hughes' opposition had not achieved, was soon afterwards accomplished by the House of Commons Committee on Standing Orders. For upon being informed by the Great Eastern counsel that every copy of the Lincoln newspaper containing the notices of the proposed line from Spalding had been purchased by Mr. Leech's enterprising emissary, this tribunal summarily threw out the Bill. At the same time, however, the Great Northern Board received a semi-official invitation to deposit a new Bill; but when it was deliberating as to whether it would accept this — on the very day, 1 March, 1877, indeed, when the directors were sitting to decide this point — Lord Claud Hamilton, the deputy-chairman of the Great Eastern, arrived at King's Cross with new proposals for amalgamation from that Company. This at once decided the Great Northern Board not to proceed with their relief lines that session. At the same time they sent back a favourable answer to the Great Eastern's proposition, which was that a modification of the terms previously offered should be discussed.

Actuated, however, by some revelations contained in the just published report of the Railway Accidents Commission, the Great Northern appended a proviso to their answer. This was that their engineers should be allowed first to make a more detailed examination of the Great Eastern's plant and permanent way. The request was acceded to, and so it was not until 17 May, 1877, that a formal meeting between delegations of the two Boards took place. It was then decided to fix the terms of amalgamation, if possible, first, and to make the question of what renewals were to be carried out prior to fusion a secondary consideration; accordingly, the proposals previously made on both sides were reviewed. The result was that the Great Eastern agreed to accept the Great Northern's former terms subject to the alteration that the fusion at 50 per cent. was to take place a year earlier than therein proposed, *i.e.*, in 1883. Subsequently, upon the subject of renewals, a good deal of difference of opinion was displayed, and nothing could be agreed except a reference, the terms of which were but vaguely defined, to Mr. T. E. Harrison, the engineer of the North Eastern. But, on the whole, the meeting proceeded and broke up so amicably that Colonel Duncombe, for one, thought the amalgamation as good as settled.

A new development, however, was a proposal, which came from the Great Eastern before the end of May, that the amount to be expended by the Great Eastern for renewals should be fixed, prior to the reference to Mr. Harrison, "at some moderate outside sum";

and when the Great Northern Board sent back a curt refusal of this, together with a rather peremptory demand that "a definite answer" as to the terms already arrived at should be received by them "on or before Tuesday next, the 5th of June," relations became once more strained. Determined not to be "hustled," the Great Eastern Board delayed its answer till 7 June. Then it sent a resolution to the effect that it would recommend its shareholders to accept the terms already agreed upon, provided that the 6 per cent. which had been assumed from the first as the average Great Northern dividend should be absolutely guaranteed for ten years as the minimum which the Great Eastern proportion of stock was to receive.

The Great Eastern authorities can hardly have expected this new proviso to be accepted, but, as a retort, it was decidedly telling, for since the 6 per cent. assumption had been adopted, the Great Northern dividend had actually sunk $\frac{1}{2}$ per cent. below that figure. Nevertheless, for the Great Northern directors to have assented to the proviso would have been, as they subsequently pointed out to their constituents, to have guaranteed a preferential dividend to the Great Eastern ordinary shareholders for ten years after the date of fusion, and this was an entirely different thing from simply taking over the latter's stock at 50 per cent. Accordingly they "unhesitatingly declined" the new proposals. The result was an abrupt rupture of the negotiations.

Meanwhile continuous and rapid progress had been made on all the various new works to which the Great Northern Company was already committed. Indeed the amount expended on capital account during the six months to 30 June, 1877, exceeded a million pounds —a "record" outlay for a single half-year. Fortunately, however, some portion of the extensions, albeit only small ones, could now be brought into remunerative working. Thus the first section of the Bradford and Thornton line from Bradford to Great Horton and Clayton, nearly four miles, was brought into use for merchandise and coal this summer, and so also was the branch, two and a half miles, from Stanningley, near Leeds, to Pudsey Greenside. In August, too, the new Copenhagen tunnel was opened, thus completing the separation of the goods from the passenger traffic from the King's Cross terminus as far north as Wood Green. From the beginning of this same year the Company took over the working (at 50 per cent. of the gross receipts) of the just opened Louth and Lincoln Railway, 20 miles in length, to construct which a separate company had been incorporated so long before as 1866.

Perhaps the most important opening in 1877, however, was that of the Manchester Central Station, which took place on 2 July. This meant that the direct "Cheshire line" from Manchester to Liverpool could at last be utilized to the full for passenger traffic; and at once, thanks to the enthusiasm of Sir Edward Watkin, a service was put on between these two towns greatly superior to that in operation on the two existing direct lines—an express train being run each way every hour to cover the distance, thirty-five miles, in forty-five minutes with one intermediate stop only, at Warrington. As a result the Cheshire receipts went up £10,000 in six weeks, and Lord Colville, acting as deputy to Colonel Duncombe at the Great Northern meeting in August, 1877, declared that they had got "pretty nearly to the end of the Cheshire Lines lane." He forgot, probably, that Colonel Duncombe had made precisely the same prediction when the direct line had first been opened four years before

These openings, of course, relieved to a very welcome extent the amount of capital sunk unproductively. On the other hand, a new outlay of nearly £45,000 for station enlargement had now to be sanctioned; a further sum of £20,000 for the block system and interlocking; and about £12,000—an instalment of an important new item—for continuous brakes. Moreover, with the view of developing an export coal traffic from Derbyshire to the east coast after the model of the Sheffield Company's traffic from South Yorkshire to Great Grimsby, the directors decided, with the shareholders' approval, to subscribe £20,000 to the construction of a new port at Sutton Bridge, for which a local company, headed by the Messrs. English, of Wisbeach, had obtained powers in the sessions of 1875 and 1876.

Meanwhile, the Great Eastern Company, after breaking off the negotiations for an amalgamation, had sent on 3 July, 1877, a new proposal for a traffic arrangement on the old basis of joint ownership and running powers, and at the same time they had invited the Great Northern Board to say in return what Great Eastern lines they were disposed to take joint ownership in for the purpose of utilizing them as a relief route. Accordingly, on 19 July a proposal was sent from King's Cross to Liverpool Street that the whole of the existing lines belonging to the two companies between Shepreth and Doncaster *viâ* Cambridge, Ely, March, Spalding, Boston, Lincoln, and Gainsborough should be converted into joint property, so that the two companies could at once begin to work traffic over it in both directions, and that at the same time powers should be obtained for shorter routes between Shepreth and March and Spalding and Lincoln, to be made so soon as they should mutually be thought desirable. Further, in return for thus placing the Great Eastern at Doncaster

—the key to the whole of the North,—the Great Northern asked for running powers from Huntingdon to Cambridge and Newmarket, and from Ely to Norwich and Yarmouth. This proposal, however, the Great Eastern indignantly declined, on the ground that it was an attempt "to obtain a complete control of the Great Eastern system without securing to the latter company the advantages of amalgamation," and at the same time (31 July, 1877) they announced their intention of having a line of their own from Spalding to Lincoln immediately surveyed.

This meant, of course, that the Great Northern must deposit a Spalding to Lincoln Bill again also, and that a fight in Parliament must decide between them. In short, it was a declaration of war, and the King's Cross Board made arrangements accordingly. Meanwhile, however, a new and equally important *crux* of policy forced itself upon their immediate attention. This was nothing less than a proposal which seems to have originated with their own chairman, Colonel Duncombe, that the Great Northern and Midland jointly should lease the Manchester, Sheffield, and Lincolnshire.

The reader knows very well already that a lease of the Sheffield to one or more of the three first-class north-and-south powers had for years been "within the range of practical politics." Nor is it difficult to see why the Great Northern chairman brought forward the suggestion again at this particular time. To put the matter briefly: a "turning" in "the Cheshire Lines lane" had actually been reached, as Lord Colville had predicted; but round the corner such an unsatisfactory prospect had come into view that Colonel Duncombe had decided that buying out the Sheffield was the only hope of better things. For now that the worst of the huge capital outlay seemed to be at an end—though this was by no means certain, seeing that the line to the north end of Liverpool was still in hand, and that the two "central stations," though opened, were neither of them completed—Sir Edward Watkin, as we have partially seen already, had begun to increase working expenses at a rate which left small hope of much of the new revenue of the direct line remaining over as profit. Not content with an hourly service of expresses between Manchester and Liverpool, he was urging the Great Northern and Midland to allow him to run them half-hourly, and complaining to the Sheffield shareholders that he was not allowed to work the joint system with sufficient "steam" and "go." To recall Sir Edmund Beckett's phrase, the Sheffield had fairly "got its claws into" both the Great Northern and Midland, and, if the two latter companies wanted freedom, they had got to pay for it.

Accordingly, in consultation with Mr. Ellis, the chairman of the

Midland, Colonel Duncombe drew up a proposal for a joint lease of the Sheffield, the pith of which was an ultimate guarantee of a 4 per cent. dividend to the latter; and on 16 October, 1877, at a meeting at Sandy, he submitted this to Sir Edward Watkin. Seeing that the dividend actually paid by the Sheffield during the previous ten years had averaged £2 3s. 6d. only, the offer was an extremely liberal one, and even Sir Edward could not on the spur of the moment find any objection of importance to make to it. So four days later—20 October, 1877—it was authoritatively announced in the newspapers, to the intense surprise of the Stock Exchange and of shareholders, that negotiations were fairly in train. No terms were as yet announced; but it did not need a prophet's vision to foresee that Sir Edward Watkin would make a good bargain for his company. Accordingly, the Sheffield stock rose rapidly in the market.

But on this and other occasions it was the fate of Sir Edward Watkin that he could not let a good thing alone—that he must be trying to better it. Thus it was that on this same day, 20 October, he wrote to the Great Northern chairman to say that his company must have "a dry four per cent." under a guarantee which had "the full nature of a rent-charge," or else—poor Spenlow!—he could "not carry the lease with his colleagues." Colonel Duncombe replied that his Board wished to give the best security that Parliament would allow, but that its precise nature was "for the lawyers to settle"; whereupon Sir Edward answered that if a full rent-charge could not be given the ultimate dividend for the Sheffield stock must be $4\frac{1}{2}$ per cent., and that his shareholders also must be given the full benefit of their "prudent nest-eggs of reserves." After this several amended statements of terms passed between the parties; but Sir Edward Watkin would not budge from either of his alternatives, namely, 4 per cent. on "gilt-edged" security to take precedence even of debenture interest, or $4\frac{1}{2}$ per cent. if the guarantee was to be an ordinary one. So after a final meeting in the Board-room at King's Cross in November the negotiations "went off." According to a circular thereupon issued by their chairman to the Sheffield proprietors, this failure of his efforts caused him extreme regret.

By this time the deposit of the new Bills for the session of 1878 had been made, and the Great Northern had learnt the full scope of the hostile intentions of the Great Eastern Company. These, they found, amounted to nothing less than a revival of Mr. Bidder's Northern Extension scheme of 1864. Moreover, the promotion of the Bill was in the same hands as before—the all too capable hands of Mr. Robert Baxter; while the engineer whom the Great Eastern had employed was

Sir John Hawkshaw—also, as the reader may remember, one of the combination which had fathered "Bidder's line." The result was a second "Great Eastern Northern Extension" scheme, which not only reproduced the name and many of the engineering features of the former project, but revived another old acquaintance of ours, "the fascinating farthing"—the ¼*d*. per ton rate for coal carried from South Yorkshire to London in 400 ton loads. Moreover, a very peculiar "Baxterian" rider was subsequently added to this farthing-a-ton clause —a rider intended to secure to the coalowners that the reduction on the existing through charge should be 9*d*. per ton at least.

And, as if not enough in themselves to arouse the most strenuous opposition from the Great Northern and Midland companies, these old heresies of Mr. Baxter's were supplemented by a new and original one invented by Mr. Parkes. The object of this was to win the support of the Chambers of Commerce and other commercial bodies in the West Riding of Yorkshire, and it amounted to an undertaking that the rates for certain articles of staple traffic between that district and London should be reduced by as much as 5*s*. per ton—or rather, as Mr. Parkes preferred to put it, that they should be put on the same scale as the rates which severer competition had secured for traffic between London and Lancashire. Thus the Great Eastern deliberately challenged a fight with all the established north and south powers.

The Great Northern directors on their part had deposited a Spalding and Lincoln Bill—in the depressed state of its finances they dared not revive the Shepreth and March line also; but, before accepting a Parliamentary contest as inevitable, they made, in February, 1878, a final effort to bring about a peaceful settlement. To this end they modified the proposal at which the Great Eastern had taken such umbrage in the previous July to the extent of withdrawing their demand for running powers to Norwich and Yarmouth, and of suggesting that Huntingdon instead of Shepreth should be the southern commencement of a joint system—provided that the Great Eastern would at once double its existing single line between Huntingdon and St. Ives. However, the utmost concession which this modified proposal evoked from the Great Eastern Board was that, if their Bill was allowed to pass unopposed, they would be prepared to meet the Great Northern to see how the new through line thus authorized could "be made available to afford the utmost accommodation to both companies"; and, it being impossible for the Great Northern to go *that* length in its desire for peace, there was "no alternative," as Colonel Duncombe told his shareholders at their February meeting, "but to submit the whole thing to the consideration of Parliament."

Accordingly, on 7 March, 1878, the hearing of the competing Bills began before a Commons Committee. The Chairman once again was Major O'Reilly, and many old friends and enemies met to engage in what for some of them was to prove their last great Parliamentary battle. Except in the case of Mr. Baxter, however, whose enthusiasm for a new line for South Yorkshire coal to London now amounted to sheer fanaticism, there was an obvious lack of sincerity about the proceedings. Both sides knew at heart that the matter must end in a compromise on the lines of those so nearly concluded many times before. Mr. Parkes and Mr. Swarbrick, when cross-examined by Sir Edmund Beckett, could give no substantial reasons why the Great Eastern had refused the Great Northern's last proposal. So the directors of the latter, on their counsel's advice, renewed this offer in a more precise form on 19 March, and on 4 April, when Mr. Oakley went into the box, he stated that he should "not only have no objection, but should be very glad," to have a clause inserted in his Company's Bill, binding it to carry out the scheme of joint ownership therein suggested.

After this Sir Edmund Beckett had an easy task when, on the following day, he rose to reply on the whole case. "What will this new independent line to the North do?" he asked. "Will it break up any existing monopoly? Not a bit of it. It is not pretended that the Great Northern has not competition already for every pound—every ounce of the traffic which it carries. If the Great Eastern had been advised by anybody except a fanatic, they would have said, not all this about their farthing a ton, but that, instead of their 5500 square miles remaining a close monopoly, they would give running powers, they would give through rates—they would give anything. But is that what they say? No, not a bit of it—not even Newmarket. So this line, as I say, makes all these mistakes, accomplishes none of the usual objects, serves nobody, breaks up no monopoly, introduces no new competition which could not be had without it. And what does it do? It pretends to reduce some rates. So in order to gratify that person, whoever he is, who has put up this scheme for the benefit of the South Yorkshire coalfield, the Great Eastern ask a Committee of Parliament arbitrarily to reduce all the rates in England. They do not care what they do, evidently. They have got into this scrape and they do not see their way out of it. Rather than pay their share for lines which were made in comparatively cheap times, they want to make a new railway, 130 miles long, in the dearest times that were ever known. They say that unless you let them do that they cannot carry for a farthing a ton. What they mean I do not know, except in the curious whim I have adverted to already, that unless you let them ruin themselves a little more they will not ruin themselves at all. They will ruin themselves a great deal by leaving themselves no profit, or hardly any, by carrying coal at a farthing a ton; but they will condescend to do that only if you will let them muddle away three millions of money, or four millions, or whatever it may be. That is their logic; I cannot help it; that is what they say. Why? Because they have an ambitious and reckless adviser. But it is perfectly plain that Mr. Parkes is not that gentleman. There is somebody else behind. The people who are now advising the Great Eastern seem to be quite satisfied if they can pull down other people's houses with their own. The Great Eastern shareholders will suffer if you do not protect them." And then finally—not as a peroration, for this great advocate never made perorations—came the renewed offer in detail of joint ownership with the Great Northern, the "proper solution of the question" which was to save the Great Eastern from itself and "avoid sacrificing all the railway shareholders in England" to "the mere reckless wilfulness" of a "fanatic."

In reply for the Great Eastern, Mr. Cripps made an exceedingly adroit speech. But he must have felt before he began it that the battle was already lost, for the compromise which Sir Edmund Beckett had just offered had been actually proposed by the Great Eastern itself barely a year before, and no advocate probably ever essayed a more hopeless task than that of persuading a Committee of Englishmen, sitting in that product and factory of compromise, the British House of Parliament, to deliberately turn aside from a *via media* in favour of an extreme and revolutionary course. Therefore, Mr. Cripps' speech amounted to no more than a display of dialectics; and at its conclusion on the afternoon of 8 April, 1878, the Committee was able to declare almost at once the substance of its decision. "We are not prepared," said Major O'Reilly, "to pass the line of the Great Eastern Company. At the same time we are of opinion that the Great Eastern Company ought to have free access to the North. This, we are of opinion, can be done on the basis of giving them joint ownership of the lines from March to the junction south of Doncaster—Rossington or Black Carr Junction—with completely free access to the other companies north and south of Doncaster. . . . We are prepared with this view to pass the Great Northern Bill with clauses to ensure its being made suitable for a through line for the purpose of the Great Eastern Company, to enable the Great Eastern Company to obtain a free access to the North."

In order that all the expense incurred in the long hearing might not be thrown away, Major O'Reilly was anxious to settle the matter at once by amending the Great Northern Bill, but after much discussion this was found impossible. Accordingly, that Bill was passed for the construction of the Spalding and Lincoln line, and the Great Eastern Bill as a money Bill, with clauses binding the two companies to carry out the terms of the compromise in the following year; and in the session of 1879—to anticipate a little in order to complete the matter—a joint Bill was brought in and passed. This authorized the vesting in the two companies, under joint ownership, of the whole of the system of railways from Huntingdon by St. Ives, March, Spalding, Sleaford, Lincoln, and Gainsborough to Black Carr Junction near Doncaster. It enacted that the new joint line from Spalding to Lincoln should be constructed with gradients not exceeding one in 400, and that improved junctions should be put in at Huntingdon and St. Ives, the former to facilitate Great Eastern and the latter Great Northern through traffic. It also provided for the management of the joint undertaking by a Joint Committee consisting of five directors of each company. Thus, after thirty years of constant controversy, the "Great Eastern question" was settled at last.

CHAPTER XX.

GOING SLOW—THE FIFTY YEARS AGREEMENT AGAIN—THE
SUBURBAN INCUBUS—1878-1881.

THUS once more, thanks to the brilliant advocacy of Sir Edmund Beckett, Mr. Oakley's great talent as a witness, and above all, to the straightforward honesty of its policy, the Great Northern had gained a notable victory in Parliament. Such successes, however, prove often of doubtful advantage, and certainly the shareholders by this time had reasons for wishing that the Company's many applications to Parliament in the earlier seventies had not been quite so favourably received. For it was no longer possible to disguise the fact that in the flush of exceptional prosperity and under the pressure from outside of many powerful influences, some "political," others local, the Company had then committed itself to a greater number of extensions than it could possibly carry out simultaneously without decline of dividend. Even if they had been its only liabilities, and could have been carried out under continuously favourable conditions, these extensions must have involved some loss of profit. Accompanied as they had been by other unforeseen, but very large, liabilities for the maintenance and improvement of the existing system, and needing to be completed, as they now did, at a time of depressed trade, they had become a burden which was grievous to be borne.

Fortunately, however, the victory over the Great Eastern, accompanied though it was by a new joint liability for the direct Spalding to Lincoln line, did not involve much additional burden to capital account, having regard to the greater extent of existing mileage which was to be thrown into the joint ownership by the Great Northern. Moreover, in the same month as this Parliamentary success—April, 1878—works hitherto entirely or largely unproductive were more fully opened in four different parts of the Company's system. The Derbyshire and Staffordshire extension was opened throughout *viâ* Derby to Egginton for all kinds of traffic; the section of the Newark and Leicester line between Bottesford and Newark (providing a shortened route between Derbyshire and Nottingham and the northern part of the system) was opened for goods and coal; the Pudsey branch in Yorkshire was fully opened, and the new Maiden Lane tunnel, King's Cross, was brought into use. Moreover, Mr. Fraser had by this time nearly completed the great tunnel, 2500 yards long, at Queensbury, albeit no less than eight shafts had had to be sunk for it, the deepest 413 feet, and considerable trouble had been encountered owing to water-bearing strata. Thus there was good prospect of the portion of the Bradford and Thornton line already opened being very soon linked with the Halifax and Ovenden joint line, thus completing the new route between Bradford and Halifax.

On the other hand, in the joint line from Market Harborough to Bottesford, in the "Cheshire line" to the north end of Liverpool, in the extension of the Ossett and Dewsbury line to Batley and other minor works, the Company had sunk unproductively at the end of the half-year a capital sum of nearly two millions, which was certain to absorb quite a million more before it became remunerative; and the Tilton and Leicester, and Thornton and Keighley lines, involving another million at least, had not yet been begun. Thus the prospect of being able to give rest to the capital account was an extremely remote one; and as, under the depressed conditions of trade generally, there was little prospect of another such expansion of revenue as had occurred in 1872 and 1873, it was well nigh impossible that the rate of dividend could improve within the next few years. On the contrary, there was a likelihood that it might decline further, and already it had dropped from the high-water point of £7 5s. per cent. per annum for 1873 to £5 5s. per cent. for 1877. Under these circumstances it was not surprising that in the summer of 1878 the administration of the Board was subjected to severe scrutiny and some bitter criticism.

Of course the very large increase of capital in recent years, the consequent decline of dividend, and the heavy future liabilities, were the points to which critics specially drew attention; but one of them, at least, did not confine himself to such obvious instruments of attack. This gentleman, Mr. J. P. Lythgoe, appears to have been to some extent a professional assailant of railway administrations. Some ten years before he had headed an attack upon the North British directorate, and, more recently, he had assisted Mr. Bass in his endeavour to place Sir Edward Watkin in the Great Eastern chair *vice* Mr. Parkes. Whether his aim now was to enthrone Sir Edward at King's Cross, or whether he wished simply to "bear" Great Northern stock, cannot be stated with certainty. It is certain only that, on 19 June, 1878, he issued a pamphlet which accused the Great Northern Board, *inter alia*, of having charged a million pounds too much to capital account for expenditure on rolling stock—of having, in short, paid dividends during the last two or three years which, reduced though they were, had not been fairly earned. Against a Board like the Great Northern's, whose policy had always been, as we have seen, to err, if at all, on the side of burdening revenue unduly, this charge was so misdirected that it seemed

Strines Cutting and Queensbury Tunnel, Ovenden, near Halifax, when in course of construction.

to some neither necessary nor dignified for the directors to reply to it, especially as Mr. Lythgoe was not himself a shareholder. But, upon facts coming to their knowledge which pointed to hasty sacrifices of stock by ignorant and therefore panic-stricken shareholders, Colonel Duncombe and Lord Colville thought it best to issue, on 28 June, a circular emphatically contradicting the accusation. Moreover, the Board immediately commissioned Mr. Ramsbottom, ex-locomotive engineer of the London and North Western, and Messrs. Fletcher and Company, public accountants, to make an independent investigation for the satisfaction of the shareholders.

This action proved very wise and well-timed. The reports from the independent experts refuted completely the pamphleteer's allegations; and the gist of them, being embodied in the directors' half-yearly report together with a fuller statement than usual of the financial position of the Company, relieved to a large extent the anxiety of the shareholders. The result was that the half-yearly meeting held on 23 August, 1878, instead of being a stormy one, was characterized by a feeling of the utmost confidence in the directors — "a feeling," said Colonel Duncombe very gratefully, "which has been unexampled as far as I can recollect in the annals of the Company." "It will be an inducement to us," he added, "not to rest upon our oars, but to do the utmost we possibly can to improve the splendid property which exists in the Great Northern Railway, and which it will take even now a great many years to develop."

Nevertheless, it was obviously necessary to "go slow" as regards capital expenditure. So, notwithstanding much local grumbling, the letting of the contract for the Tilton and Leicester line was again postponed, whilst, in the case of the Thornton and Keighley, the directors contented themselves with making arrangements for the "headings" of the four tunnels, so that delay might be avoided when the rest of the works were put in hand. Meanwhile, however, earning-power was receiving some very welcome reinforcements. From 1 July, 1878, the Newark and Bottesford line was brought into use for passengers in addition to goods, and on 14 October the opening of the Bradford and Thornton was extended from Clayton to Queensbury (though, unfortunately, owing to the non-completion of the big "Strines cutting," 1033 yards long and fifty-nine feet deep, between that place and Ovenden, the new route between Bradford and Halifax could not yet be opened). Moreover, the development (thanks to the Wainfleet and Firsby Company's line, which, as already noted, the Great Northern had worked since its opening in 1873) of a new watering-place at Skegness on the Lincolnshire coast was now producing a considerable revenue from excursion traffic, about 220,000 such passengers being conveyed thither from Nottingham, Yorkshire, and London in 1878. Further, since October, 1877, the Company had been working the Louth and East Coast Company's line, twelve miles in length, from Louth to another new watering-place, Mablethorpe.

The opening too, from 1 June, 1878, of the bridge across the Tay in Scotland, and the consequent improvement of the North British route northwards *via* Fifeshire, was of some benefit to the Great Northern; and it promised to be of much more benefit when Sir Thomas Bouch had completed his similar, but of course much longer, bridge over the Forth, the foundation stone of which was laid with much ceremony on 30 September, 1878. The Forth Bridge Company, incorporated in 1873, had been promoted jointly by the North British, the Midland, the North Eastern, and Great Northern; but their liability in the matter was limited to a guarantee of a minimum revenue, and in this the Great Northern was responsible to the extent of one-sixth only.

The next year, 1879, was the culmination of a period of trade

STRINES CUTTING, OVENDEN, NEAR HALIFAX, WHEN IN COURSE OF CONSTRUCTION.

depression, and, of course, the railway companies suffered greatly therefrom. Nevertheless, in the first half of the year, thanks mainly to its new Derbyshire coal traffic, the development of which received a very opportune stimulus from strikes at the north of England collieries, the Great Northern was able to report an increase in gross receipts of over £66,000. One-third of this, however, was absorbed in increased working expenses owing to the opening of new lines, &c. In the second half of the year minerals again showed a satisfactory increase, proving beyond doubt that the 1½ million of capital spent upon the Derbyshire extension had been well laid out; but the passenger traffic in the later summer and autumn was spoiled by most miserable weather, and from the same cause the grain and potato crops failed almost completely in Lincolnshire and the south-east of Yorkshire, producing a diminution of about 80,000 tons in agricultural produce alone. The result was that the net increase of revenue was not sufficient to meet the new capital outlay, and the rate of dividend for the year fell from £5 5s. 0d. to £5 2s. 6d.

A contributory cause of this decline, no doubt, was that, also owing to the bad weather, it was not until quite the end of the year that any considerable extent of new line could be brought into use. From 30 June, 1879, it is true, a portion of the joint line through Leicestershire was opened; but the opening southwards was as far as Melton Mowbray only, and it was not until 15 December that the remaining portion between Melton and Market Harborough could be brought into use. This, however, completed the through route between Newark and Market Harborough and enabled the Great Northern to commence its running powers to Northampton. On the other hand, it enabled the London and North Western to become a much more formidable competitor than before in the Derbyshire coalfield and in the town of Nottingham. On 1 December, 1879, the link between Queensbury and Ovenden was at last completed, and the new Great Northern route opened between Bradford and Halifax.

The sixty-seventh half-yearly meeting of the Company, held on 20 February, 1880, was a gloomy occasion. Shadows were cast over it not only by the decline of dividend, but by the deaths, within the preceding three months, of two men, the loss of whom was felt greatly—Colonel Duncombe and the highly-respected secretary of the Company, Mr. Alexander Forbes. Colonel Duncombe died on 3 December, 1879, and by his decease the Company lost a chairman of the highest character; "as conscientious, straightforward, and honourable a man as ever lived," to quote the eulogy pronounced by his successor. Mr. John Harvey Astell was now the sole survivor of the original directors of the Company; Lord Colville of Culross, K.T., who succeeded to the chairmanship, had been a director since 1863 only.

At the beginning of 1880 the contract for the Tilton and Leicester line was at last let, to the great satisfaction of the people of Leicester, who had begun to think they were not going to get their new line after all; and about the same time the Great Northern and Great Eastern Joint Committee let the contract for the first section of their Spalding and Lincoln line from Spalding to Sleaford. On the other hand, the outlay on the so-called Cheshire lines seemed at last to be nearly approaching an end, for the line to the north end of Liverpool, terminating in a new goods station at Huskisson Docks, was reported to be far advanced towards completion. The Great Northern had by this time expended just about three millions as its third-share to the Cheshire lines joint system, and the return it was getting from this expenditure was utterly inadequate, even when full allowance was made for the extent to which the lines acted as "feeders" to the main system. However, the opening of the new Liverpool extension placing the Great Northern at the most important docks in Liverpool, was now looked forward to by the more sanguine as "the turning in the lane."

With the exception of the joint Bill, already referred to, for confirming its arrangements with the Great Eastern Company and an unimportant "Omnibus Bill," the Great Northern directors had wisely abstained from new promotions in the session of 1879, and the only other measure in the passing of which they had then participated had been a Bill promoted by the Stafford and Uttoxeter Company (incorporated 1862), which had given the Great Northern running powers from Egginton Junction to Stafford. From Yorkshire the Board had been much pressed to apply for powers for a new line up the Spen Valley from Batley to Heckmondwike, Liversedge, and Cleckheaton—indeed, a deputation from this district had been, in Mr. Oakley's phrase, "an annual festival at King's Cross since 1876. But in 1879, and again when making their deposits for 1880, the Great Northern directors turned a deaf ear to these petitions, having decided that this project, though a good one, must be postponed till easier times. On the other hand, the claims of another valley—the Leen Valley in Derbyshire—appeared too strong to be resisted. This district was now rivalling the valley of the Erewash in coal production, and yet as things were, it was practically a monopoly of the Midland Company, though the new Great Northern line passed by its very mouth. Accordingly in the session of 1880 the King's Cross Board promoted and passed a Bill for a branch, eight miles in length, from their existing line at Bulwell, up the Leen Valley to Newstead, to make connection *en route* with the Bestwood and other important collieries.

Besides this, in this session of 1880, the Great Northern committed itself to lend on mortgage, in addition to its £20,000 it had already contributed, a sum not exceeding £35,000 to the Sutton Bridge Dock Company, to rescue that concern from great financial straits. In this same session, too, an event happened in yet another Parliamentary committee-room which was fraught with somewhat momentous consequences for the Great Northern Company. Some influential Huddersfield people were promoting a Bill, with Messrs.

Fraser and Fowler as their engineers, for a line from their town to a junction with the West Riding and Grimsby Railway at Nostell, with the object of providing a connection between Huddersfield and the Great Northern more direct than the existing Lancashire and Yorkshire and Manchester, Sheffield, and Lincolnshire route *via* Penistone and Retford; and having failed to persuade the King's Cross Board to support their scheme, they were asking for compulsory running powers from Nostell to Doncaster. This demand the Great Northern, as joint owner of the West Riding and Grimsby line, felt obliged actively to oppose; but its partner in that line—the Sheffield Company—though it also petitioned against the Bill, did not think it necessary to instruct counsel to appear against it. The Sheffield authorities thought—so they explained afterwards—that, with not only the Great Northern but the London and North Western and Lancashire and Yorkshire as its opponents, the Bill could not possibly pass.

The Great Northern, however, though strongly opposing the compulsory running powers, had, as may be readily imagined, no objection to the main object of the Bill. Accordingly Sir Edmund Beckett's cross-examination of the promoters was directed, not against their case in itself, but rather to ascertaining whether a compromise with them could not be effected. The result was a proposal which proved acceptable to both parties. This was that, in return for withdrawing its opposition to the running powers to Doncaster, the Great Northern should be given running powers over the new line into Huddersfield; and in the temporary absence of Mr. Oakley in the country, Mr. Fowler was put into the witness-box, that through him in his double capacity of co-engineer for the Bill and consulting engineer to the Great Northern, the terms of an agreement to this effect might be conveyed to the Committee. At the conclusion of Mr. Fowler's evidence Sir Edmund Beckett announced that the Great Northern's opposition was withdrawn.

It chanced, however, that while Mr. Fowler was under examination, Mr. Underdown, the Sheffield manager, came in casually from another room just to see how the proceedings were going on. When he heard questions being asked as to "an agreement of reciprocity" with the Great Northern, he was astounded. It was as great a surprise, he said afterwards, as any incident he ever met with in his railway experience. Happening to be standing just behind Mr. Nelson, he asked that gentleman to let him see a rough copy of the agreement which he was holding in his hand. Having seen it and realized what it meant, he went straight off to his company's solicitor—the matter was so pressing, he said, that there was not time even to consult Sir Edward Watkin—

and begged him to lose no time in instructing counsel to appear for them. The result was that on the following morning Mr. Underdown was able himself to go into the box and, in examination by Mr. Littler, Q.C., to protest most strongly on behalf of the Sheffield against the agreement between the promoters and the Great Northern being embodied, as was proposed, in the Bill.

In one of the lines of objection which he thus took Mr. Underdown was on firm ground, viz., in maintaining that running powers must not be given over a line of which his company was joint owner without its being at least consulted in the matter. But when he went further than this and declared that for the Great Northern to encourage in any way a new route between Huddersfield and London was to commit a breach of its Fifty Years Agreement with the Sheffield, he took up a very vulnerable position. For though on the face of it Clause 14 of that agreement—the clause forbidding injury on the part of the one company to the traffic of the other—seemed to cover a case which might involve the diversion of an important branch of their joint traffic to a new route, yet, in giving evidence in favour of the C. O. A. L. line in 1871, and again in supporting the Rushton line in 1873, Sir Edward Watkin had expressly denied this comprehensive interpretation of the clause, declaring that "the traffic of the other company" which each of the parties had bound itself not to injure in any way without the other's consent, meant only the traffic to promote which the agreement had originally been formed. Nevertheless, Mr. Underdown insisted that in his opinion the Great Northern was bound under the agreement not to divert *any* traffic, and after his evidence to this effect and a speech from Mr. Littler, the Huddersfield Bill, "reciprocity clauses" and all, was rejected by the Committee (15 June, 1880).

This rejection, as we shall see presently, entailed grave consequences to the Great Northern; but in its immediate result, probably, it was a matter rather of relief than regret at King's Cross. For had the local company obtained its powers, there can be no doubt that the Great Northern would have had to take them over as it had taken over so many of Mr. Fraser's lines before, and, excellent "feeder" though it might have proved when developed, the Great Northern was, as we have seen, not at all in a position to supply any more such feeders with the expensive preliminary nourishment which in most cases they had been found to require. Upon the Tilton and Leicester, the Bradford and Thornton, the Spalding and Lincoln, its latest enterprise in the Leen Valley, and other minor works, it had a further capital expenditure still in prospect of quite two million pounds. Nor was this by any means the sum of its pressing liability for capital outlay. The accommodation for goods terminal at King's Cross, supplemented though it had been by the City depôt at Farringdon and by about forty acres of siding ground acquired at various times between Holloway and Finsbury Park, was once more showing signs of inadequacy, and in August of this year 1880 the directors had to recommend the purchase of twenty-one more acres for sidings between Finsbury Park and Hornsey at a cost of £21,000. The suburban traffic, too, was increasing at such a rate as to demand the recommendation at the same time of two new stations, now known as Stroud Green and Bowes Park; and there could be no doubt that in the near future a further much heavier expenditure would be involved on its account.

Nor were revenue prospects encouraging. The general trade of the country had improved, it was true, and the harvest promised to be better than the deplorable one of 1879; but, meanwhile, the distressed agriculturists of Lincolnshire and other counties were tiding over by cutting down expenditure wherever possible. The result was that they travelled very little, used about 40,000 tons of coal less than usual in the half-year to 30 June, 1880, and imported about 10,000 tons less of general merchandise. Nor, after all, did the harvest prove better than in 1879, for in the latter part of the summer most abnormal rains set in. Then, on the top of all, the drainage arrangements—always a great problem in the flat districts of eastern England—broke down. The rivers Trent, Don, Welland, Nene, and Witham all became unmanageable, and the Glen completely burst its banks near Bourn, and flooded no less than 8000 acres of arable land.

The result was most deplorable. During the later autumn and winter Lincolnshire, in which the Great Northern had 104 stations, was little better than a waste of waters, and the line between Spalding and Bourn, being flooded for a length of two miles to the depth of four or five feet, had to be wholly closed for traffic from 9 October, 1880, to 1 February, 1881. It made matters worse that this, as the reader may remember, was not a Great Northern line proper, but formed part of the Midland and Eastern leased system which the Great Northern and Midland worked jointly under the agreement of 1866. Consequently these two companies had to pay the minimum rent of £15,000 to which they had pledged themselves, notwithstanding the complete stoppage of the through traffic. Nevertheless, rather to the disconcertion of the Stock Exchanges, the Great Northern directors were able to avert a further decline of dividend.

This satisfactory result was mainly due to a substantial increase in the passenger and goods traffic between London and Yorkshire; and this, while attributable primarily to a revival of trade, was very creditably stimulated by the extraordinary exertions which the Great Northern authorities made in 1880 to develop their London and West Riding service. During the seventies, as we have seen, the place which the Great Northern had won for itself originally of "pioneer line" had been usurped by the Midland Company by virtue of its startling series of innovations—third-class by all trains, revision of classes and fares, and introduction of Pullman cars. But at the very end of the decade—November, 1879—the experimental running of a dining-car between London and Leeds—the first car of the kind seen in England—reasserted the enterprise of King's Cross, and from February, 1880, this novelty was placed regularly on the London and Leeds service. Under the arrangements then made the car made

GREAT NORTHERN FOUR-WHEEL-COUPLED PASSENGER LOCOMOTIVE.

two journeys daily, viz., Leeds 10 a.m., King's Cross 2 p.m., and King's Cross 5.30 p.m., Leeds 10.10 p.m. Compared with the four hours twenty-seven minutes service which, as we noted in an earlier chapter, the Company gave London to Leeds passengers as early as 1871, this was not very fast running. Moreover, the Company's best West Riding train at this date—the 10.10 a.m. from King's Cross, Leeds 2.30 p.m.—showed a seven minutes advance only on the 1871 performance. But when on 1 June, 1880, Mr. John Noble, Mr. Allport's successor in the Midland general managership, inaugurated a new series of expresses from St. Pancras to the West Riding viâ Nottingham, Mr. Oakley, Mr. Cockshott, and Mr. Stirling made a sensational answer. On 4 June, 1880, a circular was put out from King's Cross that from Monday the 14th instant three new trains would be put on to cover the 186 miles between the Metropolis and the capital of the West Riding in three and three-quarter hours, and from 1 July to the end of September the same timing was given to two other trains—the trains to which was attached the heavy dining-car. This meant a journey-speed of forty-nine and a half miles per hour—

a long way the best thing yet done on a regular service. Moreover, on 31 August, 1880, the Company brought the Lord Mayor and his suite from York to King's Cross in three hours thirty-seven minutes, with a ten minutes stop at Grantham—a journey-speed of fifty-two miles an hour.

Meanwhile the Huddersfield promoters had been meditating upon, and discussing in their Chamber of Commerce and elsewhere, the rejection of their junction line, and they had come to the conclusion that they were the victims of an unholy conspiracy between the Great Northern and Sheffield companies. "If there is such an agreement as Mr. Underdown suggests," their counsel, Mr. Venables, had said— "and I do not believe he would invent an agreement, though he may have put an exaggerated interpretation upon one—could the power of Parliament be better exercised than in disregarding it?" And, though Parliament, presumably, had not so exercised its power, nevertheless the Huddersfield people conceived hopes of upsetting the supposed conspiracy in another way. For, most fortunately for their designs, it happened that in this very year, 1880, the Fifty Years Treaty between the Great Northern and Sheffield came up for decennial revision before the Railway Commissioners. Accordingly the Huddersfield promoters seized the opportunity to appear by counsel before the Commission, in the names of their Corporation and Chamber of Commerce, to demand that the obnoxious Clause 14 should be expunged from the agreement.

The two railway companies—the Sheffield taking the lead—endeavoured to evade this attack on the plea that the Commissioners had not jurisdiction to do what was asked. On 2 December, 1880, however, this point was decided against them; nor were they any more successful in an appeal which they made, in April, 1881, to the High Court. Consequently the case was to come up again before the Commission in the following July.

In addition to this Huddersfield case the Great Northern authorities had some not unimportant Parliamentary business in hand in 1881. This took the shape of a "Various Powers Bill," the most important enterprise included in it being the purchase of the undertaking of the Stafford and Uttoxeter Company, a line about twelve miles in length, extending from a junction with the North Staffordshire Railway near Uttoxeter to a junction with the London and North Western near Stafford. Running powers over this line *viâ* the North Staffordshire, the Great Northern had acquired, as already mentioned, in the session of 1879; but the directors had subsequently found that the permanent way was in very bad repair, and, as the financial position of the

Company owning it precluded hope of remedy for this otherwise, they entered into negotiations to purchase it outright. After a good deal of haggling they made an agreement to give £100,000—considerably less than the vendors had already spent—for the complete ownership of the undertaking and its right of access to the London and North Western station at Stafford; and thus they expected to get a good share of the traffic of the Potteries district, and, particularly, to be able to open a profitable market there for Derbyshire coal. On the other hand, to put the new acquisition into proper repair, a capital outlay of about £40,000 had to be provided for. Nor was this the only new liability which the Great Northern incurred this session. Their Various Powers Bill included also the construction, at an estimated cost of £125,000, of two short lines (in all five miles in length) between Beeston and Batley in the West Riding of Yorkshire, the enlargement of Nottingham station, and other minor works. On the other hand, it reduced the liability on the Thornton and Keighley line by empowering the Company to utilize a small portion of the existing Worth Valley line, and to make arrangements with the Midland for a joint station at Keighley.

Meantime, under the sanction of the Sutton Bridge Dock Company's Act of the previous session, the further sum of £35,000 had been lent to that undertaking, making the Great Northern's interest in it £55,000 in all, and this had enabled the contractors to push on rapidly with the works. The result was that by the middle of May, 1881, the docks were ready for opening. In addition to the Great Northern's contributions, about £180,000 had been spent upon the works. About thirteen acres of water had been enclosed, and extensive warehouses with the most approved hydraulic machinery provided; and the opening was looked forward to with great anticipations. It was "confidently believed," in the language of a contemporary newspaper, "that the development of a populous seaport had been inaugurated at the mouth of the River Nene." On the eventful day—14 May, 1881—the first ship, *The Garland*, owned by the Messrs. English, of Wisbeach, entered the docks with a cargo of 1,150 tons of pitchpine from Norway, and this she at once proceeded to unload, preparatory to taking on board a return cargo of Derbyshire coal which the Great Northern had brought to the dock-side *viâ* the Midland and Eastern system. In a word, the first day of the working career of the new port passed off with much *éclat*.

On the second day, however, it became evident that something was wrong. While the tide was coming in, there was too much water in the docks; while it was going out, there was not enough. In short, it was clear that the lock at the entrance was not watertight. So business operations had to be suspended, and an examination taken in hand by the engineers. But the precise cause of the leakage could not be discovered, much less a speedy remedy for it, so it was decided to take further and more eminent engineering advice. Meanwhile, instead of getting a large new traffic, as they had expected, in coal from Derbyshire to Sutton Bridge, and in merchandise from Sutton Bridge all over the kingdom, the Great Northern directors found themselves in the position of having sunk £55,000 in docks which refused to work.

By this time the Great Northern's access to another dock—the Huskisson Dock, Liverpool—had been at last secured by the completion of the "Cheshire Line" to the north end of that city; but the results so far had not been satisfactory. With characteristic thought for the future rather than for the present, the Cheshire Lines Committee had provided a very large goods station at Huskisson, and this, while the traffic was in its infancy, was proving extremely costly to work; moreover, a disagreement had arisen between the three partners as to what traffic should be handled there. On the top of this came a heavy compensation bill for injuries to passengers caused by a train being driven too fast into Manchester station. The result was that the Great Northern's share of the profit on the Cheshire lines working fell to £16,000 for the half-year to 30 June, 1881. Nevertheless the Joint Committee, with "the turning in the lane" always in view, committed itself in the session of 1881 to work a new line from Liverpool to Southport, powers to construct which were obtained by a local company.

In July, 1881, the application of the Huddersfield people for a modification of the Fifty Years Agreement between the Great Northern and Sheffield companies duly came on before the Railway Commission. The Great Northern was represented by Mr. Pope, Q.C., and the Sheffield by Mr. Littler, Q.C., and both counsel strongly urged the importance to their clients of the maintenance of the agreement as it stood. It had "worked splendidly well for the public," Mr. Littler said, and it ought not to be abrogated "simply because the Corporation of Huddersfield thought something had been decided by a committee of the House of Commons on an issue wholly different from that upon which it was quite certain the committee did decide." However, the judgment given by the Chief Commissioner, Sir F. Peel, was practically against the companies. He said that "in the uncertainty that a route convenient at one time would always continue to be so, it seemed inexpedient that a railway company if occasion should arise should not be free to accommodate the use of its line to what might be advantageous to the public"; and upon this ground the Commission refused sanction to the continuance of the agreement, unless the companies would assent either to the omission of Clause 14, or the addition to it of a proviso to exempt from its operation any route opened since October, 1860, the date of its original ratification. During the hearing both companies threatened that if Clause 14 were expunged they would drop the agreement altogether; but now they decided to accept it without that clause, in preference to being burdened by the Commission's comprehensive proviso. Accordingly the treaty was sanctioned for another decennial period from 1 November, 1881, and under its provisions, which still included an obligation on both com-

BRIDGE NEAR NEWSTEAD ABBEY, DERBYSHIRE.

panies to send all through traffic, not otherwise consigned, by the route of the other, a bonus mileage in favour of the Sheffield, and the remedy of "arbitration running powers" in case of breach, the joint working between London and Lancashire *viâ* Retford went on as before.

Meantime the Great Northern's outlay of new capital had again become very large. In addition to pushing on more vigorously than before with the Bradford and Thornton and Tilton and Leicester lines, and contributing their half-share to the Spalding and Lincoln, the directors had put the works of the Leen Valley branch in hand. Fortunately, however, this last-named undertaking began very soon to make a return. As early as July, 1881, coal trains began to run over it from the Bestwood Colliery, and from 18 October the mineral traffic of the branch was commenced in earnest. The result was an increase for the half-year to 31 December, 1881, of over a quarter of a million tons of coal carried over the system, making the tonnage carried from the Derbyshire and Nottinghamshire fields more than a million in the year. The directors had now more than ever cause for congratulation that they had carried out their extension into that district.

In this summer of 1881 the "Spen Valley annual festival" (to recall Mr. Oakley's phrase) recurred three times over. In other words, the inhabitants of Cleckheaton, Liversedge, and Heckmondwike came in three separate deputations to urge the claims of their district; and the Great Northern Board, seeing that they were now at last in sight of the end of their long-standing liabilities in other localities, and seeing also that, except in Lincolnshire, trade and traffic had much improved, did not feel justified in repeating their former *non possumus*. Accordingly they instructed Mr. Fraser to go over the ground and report. Then they themselves went down to the district, and finding it, in Mr. Oakley's words, "full of chimneys and smoke and people, the most cheerful sights a railway manager can see," they at last decided to promote the long-wished-for extension. So for the session of 1882 they deposited a Bill for a line from a junction with their Batley and Dewsbury line up the Spen Valley to Cleckheaton. In the preparations for this, unfortunately, Mr. Nelson missed the co-operation of his old ally, Mr. Fraser, who died before completing the surveys, and the Company thus lost the services of a most able and successful engineer. But an efficient substitute was available in the person of Mr. Fraser's son-in-law, Mr. William Beswick (now Mr. W. B. Myers-Beswick).

All this time no proper effect had been given to the joint arrangements with the Great Eastern—for it had been agreed that the completion of the direct Spalding and Lincoln line should be awaited before the other lines were placed under the joint control—and yet, albeit that with better times traffic was once more increasing at a rapid rate, the problem of relief to the Great Northern's main system had ceased to demand attention. The fact was that the problem had been solved by the successful adoption of continuous brakes. In accordance with the unanimous recommendation of the locomotive engineers of the twelve largest railways in England, the Great Northern had continued to favour the simple vacuum brake in preference to the Westinghouse automatic, and as early as January, 1878, the type which Mr. Stirling had adopted—"Smith's Vacuum"—showed its efficacy in a collision at Hatfield between the night "Scotchman" and a broken-down goods train. The circumstances were very similar to those at Arlesey Siding, yet, thanks to the promptness with which the speed of the express was checked, no passenger was seriously injured. This, of course, encouraged the directors to a generous expenditure on brake-power, and at the half-yearly meeting in February, 1881, Lord Colville was able to report that continuous brakes had been fitted to 90 per cent. of the Company's passenger engines, 88 per cent. of its tenders, and 85 per cent. of its carriages—a better record in this respect probably than any other company could show at this date. It is significant that at the same meeting Lord Colville reported the lowest half-yearly payment on record for compensation for personal injuries, £899; albeit in that half-year, as we have seen, the exceptionally fast running was done between London and Leeds.

But whilst continuous brakes, combined with a further shortening of the block sections, had removed the urgent necessity for relief lines, the "neck of the bottle" problem had become more pressing than ever. In this the prime factor was the continued rapid growth of the suburban traffic. In 1873 the *Times* reporter, going to the opening of the first Alexandra Palace, had found the aspect north of Finsbury Park "thoroughly rural"; but now, in Lord Colville's words (January, 1882), "towns" were "springing up within two or three miles of King's Cross as fast as people" could "build them." The number of season-ticket holders (most of whom on the Great Northern are daily City and suburban travellers) had increased from 11,350 in 1879 to 14,420 in 1881, and notwithstanding the arrangements with the North London and the duplicate tunnels at King's Cross, the suburban residents on the line had begun to complain of delays almost as loudly as before. Having regard, therefore, to the rate at which London was spreading northwards, and also to the great expansion of general traffic which had now set in, the directors considered that they must lose no more time in making a thorough-going provision for the future.

Had Mr. Denison's Hornsey and Hertford scheme of 1865 not been abandoned such provision would already to a large extent have been made. As things were, the alternative lay between reviving that scheme and making an actual duplication of the main line throughout the eight miles between Wood Green and Potters Bar, despite the existence of five tunnels within that area. After mature consideration the Board decided that they must seek powers not only to double all these tunnels and the lengths of line between them (where this latter had not already been done), but also to treble the Copenhagen and Maiden Lane tunnels and carry out other additional widenings between King's Cross and Finsbury Park. Accordingly for this they made their Bill for the session of 1882 a "Various Powers Bill," covering these important suburban improvements as well as the Spen Valley undertaking, already mentioned.

Hardly had this decision been come to when an event occurred which forcibly illustrated the arguments in its favour. On a snowy morning—10 December, 1881—the 8.25 train from High Barnet, bound for Broad Street, after leaving Finsbury Park about 8.25, was stopped by signals at the south end of the Canonbury tunnel, which, as the reader may remember, forms part of the Great Northern link line from Finsbury Park to North London. After standing there about six minutes the train was knocked ahead about a yard and a half by a blow in the rear; whereupon some dozen of the passengers alighted on to the ballast—to find that another train had run into theirs. They were immediately ordered to get in again by their engine-driver, who had just been signalled forward by a green flag from the North London junction signal-box, and the train arrived at Canonbury Station about 9.15 without damage.

Meanwhile the second train—the 8.58 from Finsbury Park to Broad Street, crowded like the first with suburban passengers, remained in the tunnel at the place where the slight collision had occurred. The driver went to the outside of the tunnel, but could hear nothing, and so decided to draw slowly ahead after the first train towards Canonbury. Just then a "down" train passed, and hardly had the noise of it subsided when a third "up" train ran into the rear of the second, which was now moving slowly forward out of the tunnel.

Just before this new collision the rear-guard of the second train, Henry Catherall, had alighted from his van with a red lamp in his hand with the intention of following the down train out of the tunnel. He heard the crash, but continued to go back till he collided in the darkness with an open door of the third train, which the collision had of course brought to a standstill. Being in complete darkness the numerous passengers in this—the 8.43 from Enfield, which had left Finsbury Park at 9.6—were greatly frightened, and seeing Catherall's lamp some of them cried to him for help. He told them to get out of the carriages, to go beyond the "down" line, and to stand as close as they could against the wall of the tunnel in case a second "down" train might be coming. Many of them obeyed his order, huddling together against the cold wall of the tunnel in terror and darkness. Catherall continued to go back, and had got about three carriage-lengths past the brake van of the third train, when he became aware that yet a fourth "up" train had entered the tunnel—indeed, he saw its wheels approaching through the smoke. His hand was already in his pocket to take out a fog-signal, and he immediately placed this on one of the "up" rails; but directly he had done so he caught his foot in a sleeper and fell at length in the "four-foot" in front of the approaching locomotive. With wonderful presence of mind he rolled himself over on to a "six-foot"—the space between the two tracks—to hear in quick succession the explosion of the fog-signal and the crash of a third collision.

The fourth train, which had left Finsbury Park at 9.13, was running at about twenty miles an hour when the collision occurred. So great, therefore, was its impetus that its engine rose on to the rear van of the third train and seemed to the horrified crowd of passengers hugging the tunnel wall to stand for a moment poised in mid-air, as if hesitating whether it should fall and crush them. To their intense relief it heeled over away from them and fell with a new crash against the other wall of the tunnel; but the groans and screams that now arose, chiefly from their own train, told them that those who had remained in the carriages had not been so fortunate as themselves.

Meanwhile the guard Catherall had picked himself up, and, though his lamp was now out, had groped his way to the north end of the tunnel, nearly 500 yards beyond which was the Great Northern No. 1 signal-box. Immediately on emerging into the open he threw up his arms to attract the signalman's attention, still keeping on running as he did so (for he could hear another train approaching from Finsbury Park), and as he drew nearer he saw to his horror that both the "home" and "distant" signals were "clear." On the signalman coming to the cabin window, Catherall shouted wildly to him to stop the coming train; but it was not till the guard was close under the box that the signalman, William Hovey, understood, and pulled over his lever. The result was that the fifth train from Finsbury Park —which but for Catherall's prompt and plucky action might have added yet another to the awful series of collisions—pulled up under Hovey's window almost at the same moment as the breathless guard arrived there from the other direction.

This man, William Hovey, who had thus been calmly employed for twenty minutes in sending train after train into the tunnel to their destruction, had been eleven years a signalman in the Great Northern service, had received many half-yearly bonuses for good conduct, and held a certificate that he was competent to take charge of any signal-box in the London district. He was neither ill, nor the worse for drink, nor had he been on duty for many hours. He had simply put a wrong interpretation upon a telegraphic signal which he received from the North London box at the Canonbury junction. The signalman there, having (as he declared, but Hovey denied) sent the ordinary "block" signal, "six beats" in answer to Hovey's signal for leave to send on the train which had made the first collision, had supplemented it by "seven beats," which, according to the North London code, was also a "block" signal, the extra beat indicating that the block would not be for long. But the "seven beats" signal, not being in the Great Northern code, was a strange signal to Hovey, and, looking it up hastily in the North London rules posted in his box, he found it described as "permissive block." Now "permissive block" in the Great Northern code meant that a train might be sent forward, but with caution; and accordingly Hovey (though he knew that under his Company's rules "permissive block" working was not allowed at all for passenger traffic) sent on the train, displaying a green "caution" flag (which does not appear to have been observed) at his window at the same time. Each time after this, when he asked permission to send on the following trains, the signal "seven beats" was repeated from Canonbury, and each time he followed the same course as at first. So the three successive collisions occurred, killing five passengers and a guard, seriously injuring ten others, bruising and shaking 117 more, and giving fifty-four others the opportunity to put in claims for very slight damage or for lost hats, umbrellas, and other property.

CHAPTER XXI.

GENERAL PROGRESS—1882-1885.

ON the evening of 25 January, 1882—about six weeks, that is to say, after the accident in the Canonbury tunnel—a dense bank of fog arose, it is impossible to say where, and approached London from the north. Until about 5.10 that evening the atmosphere at Hornsey Station was perfectly clear, but then all on a sudden the fog-bank arrived there, with the result that people on the "down" platform could not see the lamps on the "up" side, though a moment before they had been shining brightly enough. Travelling slowly southwards along the course of the Great Northern line, the fog encountered about 5.20, not far beyond Hornsey Station, the 4.23 train from Victoria (London) to Enfield, the passengers in which were thereupon astonished to find the perfectly clear atmosphere in which up to this point they had performed their journey become changed to the thickest blackness. Owing to the breakdown of a "goods" at Wood Green, their train, as luck would have it, was detained in Hornsey Station by signal. Meanwhile the following train—the 4.59 from Moorgate Street also bound for Enfield—left Finsbury Park, and pursued its journey in absolutely clear weather, up to and past the Finsbury Park No. 5 signal-box.

The signalman in charge there had, of course, not yet received "line clear" from Hornsey, so he was holding his signal at danger against the following train. But this signal being some distance north of his box, he was not at all surprised to see the train go past him, nor did it occur to him, though he was looking out of the window, to shout to the driver that there was danger ahead. Hardly, however, had the train passed, when he found his signal-box completely enveloped in fog. Looking ahead now he could not see his signal, nor could he tell for certain whether the train had stopped under it as he had expected; so, with a presentiment that it had not, he at once sent his boy to the spot to see. The boy quickly returned with the news that there was no train there, and the horrified signalman rushed to the conversing telegraph to send the alarm to Hornsey.

But the wire was already engaged in the transmission of a long message between more distant points, and, do what he could, he was unable to obtain command of it for several minutes.

Meanwhile the train from Moorgate Street had passed the danger-signal just a moment after it had been completely obscured by the fog; and the driver, never dreaming of danger inasmuch as the signalman had seen him go by without comment, had pursued his course towards Hornsey. Despite the dense fog which now enveloped him, he very foolishly did not slacken speed, and, worse than this, he miscalculated the distance in the darkness. The result was that he was still driving at a rate of at least twenty miles an hour when at the same moment the pale glimmer of the Hornsey platform lights and the redder glare of the rear lamp of the train still standing there forced themselves upon his vision through the now thinning darkness. The next moment his engine was ploughing its way through the shattered rear coaches of the other train.

The first man to run to give help was a fog-signalman, who at the time of the collision had been making his way down the platform to take up his post under the very signal which had been disregarded; and other assistance, of course, was soon forthcoming. Moreover, inasmuch as the Finsbury Park signalman was already alive to what had happened, there was no danger of a further catastrophe. As it was, however, two passengers were killed and twenty others injured. Naturally enough, such another catastrophe to suburban trains occurring so soon after the one at Canonbury caused the utmost alarm throughout the whole district. As for the Great Northern shareholders, a combination of pure accident with what at worst was failure of judgment only on the part of experienced servants, had involved them for a second time within two months in a heavy bill for compensation.

At an extraordinary meeting of the Company held on 6 January, 1882, Lord Colville had already warned the shareholders that "ere long" they would be asked to sanction "a very large additional capital expenditure near London," and, albeit the *Times* newspaper had called him sharply to account for "almost boasting" as to the enlargement of the capital account, at the ordinary meeting on 10 February he justified and maintained his tone. "The matter," he said, "can be delayed no longer. We are now carrying a traffic which produces £3,400,000 a year on the same rails near London as twenty years ago, when there was a traffic producing £1,300,000 only; besides which we are influenced by the enormous suburban traffic which is now coming upon our line, and by a desire to obtain additional security in working that traffic. To show you what that traffic has become between the years 1867 and 1881, I may mention that the money receipts have increased from £39,000 a year to £195,000 a year, or 395 per cent., and the passengers have increased from 1,700,000 to 12,900,000. The expense of the widening work must necessarily be heavy, and I tell you fairly that I think it will cost

Lord Colville of Culross, K.T.

in one way and another a million of money. But it is not intended that the whole outlay shall be made at once. We ask for power to carry out the project as necessity arises."

In face of these facts the shareholders could not do other than approve the Bill placed before them so far as it was concerned with suburban widenings, and that part of it subsequently passed through

Parliament without difficulty. But upon the portion dealing with the Spen Valley line a contest had to be fought with the Lancashire and Yorkshire Company. It commenced before a House of Commons Committee on 2nd May, 1882, the Great Northern being represented by Mr. Bidder—for Sir Edmund Beckett, to the great loss of the Company, had retired from the Bar in the previous year—and the Lancashire and Yorkshire by Mr. Littler.

The Lancashire and Yorkshire directors objected to the Bill not only for what it actually proposed to do, but because they feared, not without reason, that if the Great Northern was allowed to make a line to Cleckheaton, it would not stop there, but would go on at some future time by this route to Halifax in direct competition with their own main line. They soon realized, however, that to conduct their case in Committee on these uncompromising lines would be to court defeat. They could not deny that, as things were, the population of the Spen Valley was very badly off for getting to London. It could not get a through train to the south without going eastwards to Wakefield or northwards to Bradford, and that part of the journey, owing to the numerous "changes" involved, often took half as long as the whole of the rest. "But," said Mr. Littler, "this is not a population that travels for travel's sake. These hard-working, industrious, hard-headed Yorkshire manufacturers know a good deal too well what to do with their time to go 'gadding about,' to use one of their own expressions, to London, whenever they have the chance. When they travel it is for the pocket's sake, and if the pocket's sake is not worth a quarter of an hour's deviation, you may depend upon it they will not go, and not a single human being will go by reason of your shortening the route by making this new line. One gentleman said, 'You know I live three miles away, and I drive to Batley.' I would not mind making a little investment that he would do the same when this alteration is made—put his portmanteau into his dogcart and drive to Batley. And yet this new line would have been made at £70,000 a mile. If the communication with Wakefield is so bad, it is very easy to remedy; the Great Northern have only just to ask to put through carriages on our trains. They have not asked us for through carriages, still less for running powers on our line Surely it would be better to put on a few extra trains than to make a new railway, which, as they admit, would be for more than a third of its distance within half a mile of existing and most costly railways."

This argument persuaded the Committee to throw out the Great Northern Bill, but it also virtually pledged the Lancashire and Yorkshire to give the Great Northern increased facilities for serving the Spen Valley district. Therefore, immediately after the conclusion of the Parliamentary contest, Mr. Oakley opened negotiations with Mr. Thorley, the Lancashire and Yorkshire manager, which speedily resulted in an agreement between the two companies. Under this the Great Northern acquired running powers over the Lancashire and Yorkshire Calder Valley line between Wakefield and Halifax and over its Cleckheaton and Heckmondwike branch; while the Lancashire and Yorkshire received in return what they had long hankered after, namely, running powers over the Great Northern and Manchester, Sheffield, and Lincoln joint line from Wakefield to Doncaster. Moreover, in order to carry out this arrangement effectually, it was agreed to make several new junctions between the two systems, a joint Bill for which was accordingly deposited for the session of 1883.

Seeing that the cost of these junctions was estimated at £150,000, whereas the new line would have cost at least £500,000, this arrangement was quite as welcome to the Great Northern as the approval of its own line would have been.

In this same session of 1882, the Great Northern Company became definitely committed to join in an undertaking which both from an engineering point of view and financially has proved, so far, one of the most notable successes of British railway enterprises—the Forth Bridge. We have already noticed incidentally in these pages the rise of two projects for bridging the Firth of Forth. We have seen how the first of these, fathered by "the Scotch Hudson"—Mr. Hodgson, chairman of the North British — went down in the financial storm of 1866, before the physical storms had been allowed to try the strength even of an experimental pier; and how after twelve years' interval the foundation stone of a newly-designed structure was actually laid. Fifteen months after this, however—in December, 1879—the similarly designed Tay Bridge fell, bringing down with it a train and its living freight, and so once more a *force majeure* stopped the bridging of the Forth. Indeed, so hopeless had the task seemed, in face of the Tay Bridge disaster, that in the session of 1881 the Forth Bridge Company had promoted a Bill to abandon their existing works, without proposing any substitute for Sir Thomas Bouch's now discredited design.

The Great Northern and North Eastern companies had, as we know, the fullest facilities for their through traffic to and from the northern parts of Scotland over the established route *via* Larbert Junction, and so the fall of the Tay Bridge and the proposed abandonment of the Forth Bridge undertaking did not cause them any very grave concern. But the other "East Coast" partner, the North British, was affected much more seriously, because without the bridges the part of its system in Fifeshire was isolated from the rest. Moreover, in conjunction with the Midland, the North British wanted the new route to the north of Scotland, because the "central-route" traffic had no special facilities over the Caledonian lines. The Tay Bridge it was strong enough to revive by itself, but the larger undertaking was quite beyond its unaided strength. So, at the eleventh hour—after the deposit of the Abandonment Bill—its directors opened negotiations for the reconstitution of the Forth Bridge Company. Three eminent engineers, Mr. T. E. Harrison, Mr. Fowler, and Mr. Barlow gave their opinion that, the Tay Bridge disaster notwithstanding, a durable structure could be built, whereupon the withdrawal of the Abandonment Bill was agreed upon Then a design for a new bridge on the cantilever principle was prepared by Mr. Fowler, and approved by Messrs. Harrison and Barlow. The next step was to form a new Forth Bridge Company to carry the new design into effect, and to this the same four railway companies as before undertook to guarantee a dividend at the rate of 4 per cent. The guarantee was in the proportion of 30 per cent. by the North British (which also undertook some other obligations), $32\frac{1}{2}$ per cent. by the Midland, and $37\frac{1}{2}$ per cent. by the Great Northern and North Eastern jointly and equally. These arrangements were embodied in a new Bill which successfully passed through Parliament in the session of 1882. The North British had carried its new Tay Bridge Bill in the previous session.

In the session of 1882, also, the Great Northern obtained powers for the purchase of the undertaking of the Louth and Lincoln Company, a line about twenty miles long, extending from Bardney to Louth, which, as already noted, the Great Northern had been working since December, 1876. The price paid was £200,000, but as much as £380,000 had already been spent upon the line. This session, too, the Great Northern directors acquiesced in the passing of a Bill to authorize the Sutton Bridge Dock Company to raise £160,000 of extra capital for the purpose of reconstructing their unfortunate works; but the view taken of the practicability of this by the eminent engineers consulted—Sir John Coode and Mr. Fowler—had not been very encouraging; indeed, there was by this time more than a suspicion that their location on a sandy, shifting soil had been a fatal mistake. Under these circumstances, Mr. Christopher Denison, who represented the Great Northern on the Dock Company's Board, was not able to advise his colleagues at King's Cross to increase their Company's already too large interest in the misadventure. Nor could the Great Northern directors persuade themselves that after this unhappy experience they were justified in recommending a contribution to the construction of docks at Boston on the same coast, for which purpose a company had been incorporated in the session of 1881.

The August Bank holiday in this year, 1882, was remarkable for the rush of excursion traffic to the newly-developed watering-places on the Lincolnshire coast—Skegness and Mablethorpe. To Skegness alone the Great Northern carried 20,000 people on that day, and it would have carried more had not Mr. Cockshott been obliged to refuse two applications for special trains owing to lack of rolling stock.

"We were overtaken by the traffic upon that day," admitted Lord Colville at the half-yearly meeting in the same month, "and, though we got the people to Skegness all right, we could not get them away like clock-work. It is single line part of the way. But I am happy to say that that enormous traffic was conducted without any accident. Some people, no doubt, were rather later in getting to bed than usual; but it was a beautiful day, and no doubt they all enjoyed themselves very much."

This was in answer to a shareholder, who had complained that some of the return excursion trains had been six or seven hours late, and that—"not through the strength of the beer, but from irregularity and combination of arrangements on the railway"—a man he knew who had wanted to return to Leeds had found himself at about three in the morning at Nottingham.

Meanwhile, from 6 March, 1882, more than half of the new Spalding and Lincoln line—from Spalding to Ruskington, nearly twenty-four miles—had been opened for traffic, and from 1 August the remainder—from Ruskington to Pyewipe Junction, near Lincoln, nineteen miles—was brought into use. More important still, from this latter date the pre-existing Great Northern lines between March and Spalding and between Pyewipe and Black Carr Junction, Doncaster, fifty-one miles in all, and the Great Eastern line from March to Huntingdon, twenty-three miles, were placed, together with the new Spalding to Lincoln line, under the control of a Joint Committee of the two companies' Boards as the joint and equal property of both. This diminished Great Northern mileage proper by twenty-eight miles, and it also diminished the Company's capital outlay by the sum of £415,000, that being the amount which the Great Eastern Company paid as the difference in value between the sections of pre-existing lines now vested in joint ownership. The Great Northern's half-share of the cost of the new Spalding to Lincoln, however, was quite £100,000 more than this.

But the essence of the arrangement was, as we know, that the Great Eastern Company had now at last realized its long-thwarted ambition and had become a main trunk line—the fourth trunk line—between London and all the northern parts of England. For many years, as we have seen, it had done a certain amount of long-distance north-and-south traffic by way of its junctions with the Great Northern at Peterborough, March, and Huntingdon, and since 1868 it had been allowed to have its own canvassing agents at Great Northern and Manchester, Sheffield, and Lincolnshire stations in Yorkshire and Lancashire. Now it was actually at Doncaster on its own rails, with full facilities to make direct contact there with the Lancashire and Yorkshire and North Eastern companies.

Of course, if it had achieved this by a line entirely its own, as we have seen it more than once had tried to do, it would have been in a position to inflict a more serious loss upon the Great Northern than the scheme of joint ownership permitted; but, as things were, the injury which the Great Northern suffered was considerable. Firstly, the pre-existent stream of through Great Eastern traffic was diverted from the old channels *via* Peterborough, March, and Huntingdon to the new joint line, and this meant that the Great Northern got very much less mileage out of it than before. In the second place, the Great Eastern became an almost equal competitor in Lincoln, Gainsborough, and Doncaster—places which up to this time had been practically Great Northern preserves so far as traffic with London was concerned. In the third place, it was stimulated to canvass much more vigorously in Yorkshire and Lancashire. The result was that the Great Northern not only did not get any immediate increase of revenue in return for its £100,000 net increase in capital outlay and the addition to working expenses which the new Spalding to Lincoln involved, but, on the contrary, lost about £50,000 within the first five months of the new arrangements. All the consolation which Lord Colville could offer to his shareholders was, that it was better to have half the receipts of a joint line than to have another through competing line entirely against them. The same remark applied to the joint arrangements with the London and North Western in Leicestershire.

On 2 October, 1882, just about a year after its opening for coal, the Leen Valley line was opened for passengers. The Tilton and Leicester and Thornton and Keighley undertakings, however, were still a good way off completion, though on the former some goods traffic had been running since May. With a foresight which may yet prove to have been enlightened, the directors, under Mr. Fraser's advice, had acquired no less than thirty-six acres of station ground at Leicester, and upon this the commodious buildings which the deceased engineer had planned had yet to be erected under the superintendence of his successors, Mr. Beswick and Mr. Henry John Fraser. However, now that the line, with this exception, was practically finished, the directors decided to postpone its opening for passengers no longer than was necessary to allow its numerous cuttings and embankments proper time to consolidate. Accordingly, temporary terminal arrangements were made at Leicester, and on 1 January, 1883, the passenger opening took place.

LEICESTER STATION, G. N. R.

On the Thornton and Keighley line, on the other hand, there was still, as it proved, another year's work to be done before any traffic at all could be set running. We have already noted that this line contains four tunnels within its nine miles, and the longest of these, the Lees Moor tunnel, is no less than 1534 yards. A still greater work is the Hewenden Viaduct, which is 376 yards long, and 123 feet in greatest height. Its foundations, moreover, had to be sunk exceptionally deep, the greatest depth being no less than $62\frac{1}{2}$ feet. It contains 17 arches of 50 feet span, and these are constructed of brick, the rest of the material being stone. Besides this there is another great viaduct, 150 yards long and 45 feet in greatest height, at Cullingworth. At Denholme, moreover, on account of the heavy slips in the cuttings, inverted arching with very strong side walls had to be constructed. From Denholme to Keighley, a distance of over five miles, the line falls continuously at gradients averaging one in fifty.

The reader remembers that the five hours service between London and Manchester put on by the Great Northern and Sheffield companies jointly in 1857 was, as far at least as the part of it worked by Great Northern engines was concerned, the best piece of locomotive work at that date, involving, as was pointed out, a speed of forty-four miles an hour all the way between London and Sheffield; and that, even when the best time for the whole journey was extended to five hours and ten minutes, the Great Northern's forty-two miles an hour throughout between London and Retford remained the best performance in England up to 1871. Subsequently, owing to the competition of the

EXPRESS PASSENGER ENGINE.
7 feet 6 inches "Single" Driving-Wheel.

new Midland route, the Great Northern and Manchester, Sheffield, and Lincolnshire time had been accelerated to four hours fifty-five minutes, which had brought the Great Northern's King's Cross and Retford speed to forty-four miles an hour again. Still, thanks to its fifteen miles shorter route and its easier gradients as compared with the Sheffield's line, the London and North Western had retained a ten minutes' advantage, on paper at least; and the Midland, too, with a route only three miles longer than the North Western's (though its gradients are much harder) had shown the same time—four hours forty-five minutes—as its booked running. Now, in 1883, however, by a magnificent spurt, the Great Northern and Sheffield got ahead of both their rivals by reducing their time to four and a half hours. To accomplish this without putting too heavy a burden upon its gradient-handicapped partner, the Great Northern had to cover its $105\frac{1}{2}$ miles between London and Grantham (to save a stop the change of engines was now made there instead of at Retford) in 125 minutes—a journey-speed of $50\frac{3}{5}$ miles per hour.

Thus the Great Northern once more, in 1883, beat its own, and *a fortiori* all other, records for high speed on a regular daily service. In the previous year, moreover, it had established another remark-

HEWENDEN VIADUCT, NEAR KEIGHLEY.

able record for speed on special trips. On 24 June, 1882, it had brought the Prince of Wales from Bradford to London in three hours forty-eight minutes, including a five minutes' stop at Grantham, a journey-speed of fifty and a half miles an hour. This performance, it is true, does not equal on paper the fifty-two miles an hour journey-speed of the York and London run of 31 August, 1880; but having regard to the fact that the route from Bradford to Doncaster is hilly, whereas that from York to Doncaster is almost flat, the 1882 performance was in actual locomotive work quite as good, if not better, than the other. Moreover, on 21 December, 1883, the Lord Mayor's run of 1880 was almost exactly repeated with a heavier train, the Prince of Wales being brought from York to King's Cross in three hours thirty-seven minutes in a "special" of seven vehicles.

To sum up for the second time the Great Northern's position in the matter of speed: it was running on the average in 1883 twenty-three express journeys daily over each mile of its system, as compared with seventeen run in the case of the London and North Western and twelve in the case of the Midland. Moreover, it showed the largest increase of express mileage in the period from 1871 to 1883—an increase of no less than 92 per cent., notwithstanding a simultaneous increase in the weight of trains of at least 50 per cent. To put the matter in another way, its sixty-seven daily expresses ran 6,780 miles (500 of which were on very stiff gradients north of Wakefield) at a running average* of forty-six and a half miles per hour. It was computed that this was a greater amount of express running than the whole of the rest of the world outside England could show at this date.

On 1 January, 1884, the section of the Thornton and Keighley line from Thornton to Denholme was opened for both goods and passengers; and as the opening throughout to Keighley, for goods at least, was expected to take place on 1 April, Lord Colville was justified in announcing at the half-yearly meeting in February, 1884, that the Company had at last arrived at the end of its great extensions—"liabilities undertaken in the days of prosperity and having to be paid for in the days of adversity." "No enterprising or speculative engineers," he added, "need pay any visits now to our general manager, for Mr. Oakley is always 'not at home' to such visitors. What capital we shall expend henceforth will be in the improvement of our existing property."

As a matter of fact, the Keighley line was not fully opened until

* Readers familiar with the literature of express trains will know that "running-average" (in the phraseology invented by Mr. Foxwell) differs from "journey-speed" in being exclusive of time consumed by stops. For nearly all the figures given as to this part of my subject, I must again express my great indebtedness to the writings of Mr. Foxwell and Lieutenant Willock (vide *Proceedings of Statistical Society* for 1883 and 1884, and *Express Trains, English and Foreign*, by FOXWELL and FARRER.)

1 November, 1884, but it will be convenient and not unjust nevertheless to accept this statement of Lord Colville literally, and to treat the beginning of the year 1884 as the end of the second period of extension in the Company's history—a period which may be said to have commenced in 1870. 1867, it will be remembered, we treated

THE PRINCE OF WALES' SALOON.

as the close of the Company's first period of extension, during which its original 283 miles were increased to 487, and its capital cost from about twelve millions to about twenty; and we have also noted already how by the beginning of 1876—about midway in the second period of extension—mileage had reached 540 and capital about twenty-seven and a half millions. Neither of these mileage totals, however, included the Great Northern's share in joint undertakings, these not being then reckoned in the official returns. Inclusive of these, the 1867 total becomes 537 miles, and the total at the beginning of 1876 603 miles.

Between the beginning of 1876 and the date we have now reached Great Northern mileage proper had been increased, as we have seen, to a considerable extent both by the construction of new lines and by the purchase of existing ones. But still more rapid had been the growth of joint undertakings, and in the case of the arrangements with the Great Eastern, as we have seen, this latter process had been at the expense of the former. Thus, inclusive of the Thornton and Keighley and the Hatfield and St. Albans lines (the latter of which had been purchased by Act of Parliament in 1883), the Company's total mileage in 1884 was 784 miles—an increase of 181 miles upon its total in 1876; and of this increase about half was represented by the Company's shares in new joint undertakings. Its total joint line mileage in 1884 (*i.e.*, one-half of the West Riding and Grimsby, the Halifax and Ovenden, the Great Northern and Great Eastern Joint, the Great Northern and London and North Western Joint, and the Bourn and Lynn leased lines, and one-third of the Cheshire lines and the Methley) amounted to no less than 157 miles.

Meanwhile the capital of the Company, raised by shares or represented by fixed charges, had risen to just upon thirty-seven millions. This meant that in its second period of great extension from 1870 to 1884 it had added about seventeen millions to its capital outlay, while adding 247 miles to its system, *i.e.*, that it had raised its outlay per mile from about £40,000 to nearly £50,000—a very heavy average for a system a good part of which is through agricultural country. Under these circumstances a watering down of profits was naturally to be expected, especially as the Leicester and Keighley lines were as yet undeveloped. Nevertheless, the decline in dividend which had actually taken place—a drop from a safe 7 per cent. to an uncertain 5 per cent.—was too large to be accounted for simply, or even mainly, by the increased capitalization.

Moreover, such part of the loss in profit as was due to the new capital expenditure seems attributable rather to misdirection of outlay than to excess. The Company had spent capital fast, but not faster than it might have done with comparative impunity, had the objects of its outlay been more happily chosen. The extension into Derbyshire and the numerous short branches in the West Riding of Yorkshire had already proved very provident enterprises; but if, say, two out of the three millions squandered under Sheffield influence upon the Cheshire lines had been spent upon a Great Northern extension into central London, it is impossible to doubt but that a much better result would have been achieved. And not only in the case of the Cheshire lines, but in Leicestershire and Lincolnshire also, the policy of joint lines was turning out an unfortunate one. The Leicestershire joint system had established the London and North Western, and the Lincolnshire the Great Eastern, as formidable competitors in Great Northern districts, and to have paid half the cost of introducing new competition was a considerable qualification of the advantage derived from having prevented that competition from being entirely hostile. The Great Northern would probably have done better to have kept its money for the improvement of its own main system and to have let the promoters of competing north-and-south lines do the worst, if direct opposition to them had not been successful.

The fact is that the Great Northern's attitude towards competitors seems to have been, from the year 1858 onwards, a good deal too pacific. Up to 1858 it had been, as we saw, essentially a fighting line; but when in that year its position as a first-class railway power had become established, its policy had changed. The explanation seems to be that its directors had become so imbued with the futility of the obstructive tactics of George Hudson and of Captain Huish that they went to the other extreme of neglecting a proper assertion of their vested interests. That the Midland and Great Eastern should become first-class railway powers also had been, it is true, inevitable sooner or later. But clearly to postpone the inevitable, not to hasten it, should have been the object of Great Northern policy. Yet it was with the help of the Great Northern that the Midland had first reached London in 1858, and it was with the help of the Great Northern that the Great Eastern had just reached Yorkshire.

Thus we have arrived at the main clue to the decline in Great Northern prosperity between 1873 and 1883—competition. It was in that decade that the Midland had taken its great revenge for the loss which it had itself suffered upon the first opening of the Great Northern from London. Already, in the sixties, it had cut the Great Northern out as a coal carrier, but this was small damage compared with the injury which, in the seventies, the latter's passenger business received at the hands of Mr. Allport. Between 1850 and 1872 the Great Northern, thanks to the directness of its line and the enterprise of its management, had developed a passenger business as profitable probably as any railway traffic the world has seen. It was a long-distance traffic, a high-class traffic, and a regular traffic. It was exactly the traffic, in short, to which a comparatively high scale of fares was suited. It was not of a class quickly to make up in quantity what it lost in quality. Yet, by the action of the Midland Company, this sacrifice of quality—profitable, on the whole, under the wider Midland conditions—had been forced willy-nilly upon the Great Northern. The Great Northern had got more passengers, no doubt, owing to the reduction of fares, but the net result had been to increase working expenses quite out of proportion to any increase of revenue. These seem to have been the main reasons why the Company had fallen, in 1884, into comparative adversity.

With regard to the future, however, a very hopeful tone prevailed at the seventy-fifth half-yearly meeting, held on 15 February, 1884. A large shareholder—Mr. Green—spoke of the directors' report as "one of the most satisfactory reports we have listened to for a great many half-years," and Mr. Robert White prophesied that with the rest to the capital account—a sort of rest which, he said, the Company required as much as an overworked man needs physical and mental rest— profits, and consequently dividends, would increase. Lord Colville replied that he quite concurred, and that the directors had every intention of giving the undertaking the rest of which Mr. White had spoken.

Nevertheless, the outlay for the completion of the Keighley line and the Leicester terminus had to be continued throughout 1884; and a start had to be made, too, with the suburban widenings. With regard to the latter, Lord Colville had said in August, 1883, "For the present we have given that up; we cannot afford to do it, and we must get on as best we can without doing it"; but the continued increase of the suburban traffic absolutely forbade a long postponement, and in April, 1884, the contract was let to Mr. Lovatt for the triplicate Copenhagen tunnel. This was regarded as the most pressing of the widening works, because the second Copenhagen tunnel, as we know, had been appropriated entirely to goods traffic to and from the King's Cross terminal yards. Consequently the whole of the London passenger traffic and the goods to and from Farringdon Street and the south of the Thames had to use the single pair of tracks in the original tunnel. But, having to be carried under some very heavy buildings, the new eastern tunnel threatened to be more difficult and costly to construct than any other one of the four similar works already carried out between King's Cross and Holloway. About the same time the erection of two new suburban stations was taken in hand--at Haringay (between Finsbury Park and Hornsey) and at Hadley Wood (between Barnet and Potters Bar).

The Various Powers Act obtained by the Company in 1884 was an unimportant measure, providing only for minor works and for an extension of time for the Beeston and Batley link line. But it had to oppose at some expense a Lincoln and Skegness Railway Bill, which after passing the Commons was withdrawn from the Lords. Moreover, its interests, in common with those of other companies, were seriously threatened by a Bill for the Further Regulation of Railways, which Mr. Chamberlain, the President of the Board of Trade, introduced this session as a Government measure. Ostensibly framed to carry out the recommendations of a Select Committee of the House of Commons which had sat during 1881 and 1882, this Railways Regu-

COPENHAGEN TUNNELS, KING'S CROSS (NORTH END).

lation Bill was very objectionable to the companies on account of the greatly enlarged powers which it proposed to confer upon the Railway Commissioners. Accordingly a Railway Companies' Association was formed to oppose it, Mr. Oakley accepting the position of honorary secretary. However, Parliament could not find time to discuss the subject in the session of 1884. The result was that Mr. Chamberlain's Bill came to nothing; and for the session of 1885 the larger companies, acting in concert, deposited Bills of their own for the purpose of consolidating and simplifying their charging powers in accordance with the report of the Select Committee.

On 30 October, 1884, the Company suffered a severe loss by the sudden and premature death of its deputy chairman, Mr. Christopher Denison, after twenty years' very able service on the Board. Thus, after forty years' unbroken association with the undertaking, the name of Denison ceased to appear amongst the list of its directorate. Of the original members of the Board, however, Mr. John Harvey Astell still survived, and of the executive officers, Mr. Oakley, Mr. Johnson, and Mr. William Grinling had been in the service almost from the first. But amongst the younger members of the staff death had been lamentably busy. The decease of Mr. Alexander Forbes had been followed by that of the goods manager, Mr. John Ashley, and of his successor, Mr. R. Dymant, both very able officers from whom much had been expected in the future.

The publication of the Rates Bills deposited by the railway companies produced a great public outcry, it being alleged that their object was to increase merchandise rates generally and to legalize preferential rates for foreign produce; and as both these charges were based on complete misconceptions, the Railway Companies' Association instructed Mr. Oakley to address a letter to the *Times* in reply. "The companies disclaim emphatically," wrote Mr. Oakley, "any intention of acting adversely to the general interests of trade and agriculture. They recognize that their own well-being is dependent upon the national prosperity, and they claim from Parliament and from their opponents a counter-recognition of the public advantage of settling on a fair and equitable basis the conditions upon which the railway service of the country may best be conducted."

This letter, which appeared in the *Times* of 31 January, 1885, checked the public clamour to throw out the railway companies' bills summarily on second reading. But they suffered the same fate as Mr. Chamberlain's measure; Parliament was not able to find time to discuss them.

In this session of 1885 the Company obtained an Act empowering it to extend its Woolsthorpe ironstone branch in Leicestershire (which had been opened since July, 1883) to reach another field of ironstone at Harston, to extend its Pudsey branch so as to form a junction with the Gildersome branch near Bradford, and to construct a new colliery branch to Heanor in Derbyshire. The total length of new line thus authorized was about nine miles, and the new capital liability about £200,000.

In this same session, too, the Cheshire Lines Committee obtained Parliamentary confirmation of its agreement to work the line, thirteen miles in length, of the Southport and Cheshire Lines Extension Company. This line had been partially opened from 1 September, 1884, and was fully opened on 1 June, 1885. It gave the Great Northern and its partners access to an important Lancashire seaside resort; but the increase of revenue thus produced was at first more than swallowed up by increased working expenses.

From 1 May, 1885, the Great Northern followed the Midland's lead of ten years before to the extent of discontinuing the use of second-class carriages in the Lincolnshire, Nottinghamshire, and Derbyshire districts. Notwithstanding the admission of third-class passengers to all trains in 1872 and the reduction of first-class fares in 1875, the Great Northern receipts from second-class had continued for some years to show a satisfactory gross increase, and this was still the case as regards suburban traffic. But proportionately the use of the intermediate class had declined on the system as a whole from 25 per cent. in 1872 to 6½ per cent. in 1884. Moreover, the proportion of first-class passengers had declined in the same period from 7 per cent. to 3½ per cent. Under these circumstances it was pretty evidently a waste of locomotive power to haul two superior classes of carriages except in the neighbourhood of London and other large towns, but the directors decided to try the effect of abolishing the intermediate class on the confines of their system before making the change on the main line. The result of the first two months' working was that of 15,842 passengers, who, it was estimated, would have used the second-class had it been retained, 4,386 went into the first-class and the rest into the third. For some years already, it should be added, the Great Northern had furnished its third-class carriages with stuffed seats and backs. In fact, the accommodation now provided at 1d. a mile was practically as good as the first-class accommodation of the fifties, for which between 2d. and 3d. a mile had been charged.

During the second half of 1884 and the first half of 1885 the traffic of the Company was seriously diminished by depression of trade, which was particularly severe in the West Riding of Yorkshire. Moreover, in the spring of 1885 a strike occurred in the South Yorkshire coalfield, but for which, thanks to the continued increase of its Derbyshire trade, the Company's mineral traffic would have been very satisfactory. As things were, gross receipts remained practically stationary.

Under these circumstances "rest," as regards capital outlay, was imperatively called for; and, except the new Copenhagen tunnel, about 65 per cent. of which was completed by the summer of 1885, the suburban widenings had still to be postponed. In the previous year the works at Leicester had been completed, and the new joint station with the Midland at Keighley was finished in the spring of 1885; so that during the greater part of that year the Beeston and Batley extension was the only new line in hand. But a considerable outlay of capital on enlargements and improvements could not be avoided. The timber bridge over the River Witham near Boston, for instance, had to be reconstructed in iron*; a new goods shed and coal sidings had to be provided at Laister Dyke, near Bradford; a large warehouse had to be provided at Holloway for storing and preparing provender for the 1723 horses which the Company now kept for cartage purposes; a carriage-cleaning shed for the suburban stock had to be erected near Finsbury Park; and a new granary at Burton-on-Trent. To meet such charges as these, and to provide new rolling stock, an addition to capital account of about £100,000 a half-year had become normal.

* Half the cost of this, however, was charged to revenue.

CHAPTER XXII.

THE SUBURBAN INCUBUS STILL—THE RAILWAY RATES BILLS—THE EASTERN AND MIDLANDS—THE RACE TO EDINBURGH.
1886-1888.

THE position of the Great Northern Railway Company at the beginning of 1886 was more satisfactory and promising than for some time past. Depression of trade, it is true, still hung over the manufacturing districts; but there was good prospect of a revival in the near future. Meanwhile a better harvest in both grain and potatoes, and the removal of the restrictions which had in the previous year been placed on the transport of cattle, had produced improved conditions already in the agricultural parts of the system. Under the stimulus of severe weather the coal trade was unusually brisk, nor were there any signs of such another calamity as the South Yorkshire colliers' strike of 1885. With continued rest to the capital account there was good hope that the dividend, which had sunk to £4 10s. per cent. in 1884 and 1885, would at last begin a course of recovery.

Unfortunately very early in the year this hope sustained a serious setback. About 8.30 on the morning of 10 February, 1886, when a dense fog prevailed, an "up" train crowded to the doors with suburban passengers was standing in Finsbury Park Station under the protection of a signal worked from Finsbury Park north box. The signalman in charge there bore an excellent character, having received no less than eighteen bonuses for good conduct, and he had been on duty two hours only. Yet, being unable to see the standing train on account of the fog, he forgot that it was there and let in another upon it. Fortunately the second train was travelling very slowly, and so the immediate results of the collision were not disastrous. But from experience in regard to the Canonbury and Hornsey accidents the Great Northern authorities well knew by this time the high prices which suburban passengers, travelling at exceptionally low fares, can exact not only for broken limbs and shattered nerves, but for battered hats and lost umbrellas. Consequently they could not but anticipate another very serious bill for compensation.

Lord Colville went too far when at the half-yearly meeting in August, 1886, he said that this accident had occurred notwithstanding the adoption of "every possible precautionary invention"; for to meet this very class of contingency Mr. W. R. Sykes had already devised and fitted up to some extent on the London, Chatham, and Dover system his electric "lock and block" apparatus. Nevertheless, the Great Northern chairman was justified in laying special stress upon "the anxiety which must necessarily attend the working of a large and constantly increasing suburban traffic." Moreover, seeing that by such an accident as this at Finsbury Park the profit on that traffic for a long period was liable to be suddenly swallowed up, the directors had good reasons for not making any special exertions to develop it further. Nevertheless, if the whole traffic of the system was not to be paralyzed at its London end, it was absolutely necessary that the programme of suburban widening, authorized in 1882, should be further proceeded with. So, now that the new Copenhagen tunnel was approaching completion, contracts were let for a new single-line tunnel between Wood Green and Southgate on the eastern side of the existing double-line one and for the widening of the line (involving the construction of large retaining walls) between Finsbury Park and Hornsey. Outside the suburban area the construction of duplicate lines at certain points between Potters Bar and Biggleswade, involving the widening of two bridges at Knebworth, had been put in hand in the previous year.

On 3 April, 1886, a large meeting of the Great Northern shareholders was held at Willis's Rooms, London, to protest against a new Railway and Canal Traffic Bill which Mr. Mundella, Mr. Chamberlain's successor as President of the Board of Trade, had just introduced into Parliament. In answer to a circular sent out only four days before by Mr. Fitch, the secretary of the Company, no less than 6400 shareholders wrote approving of opposition to the Bill, and under the presidency of Lord Colville the meeting proved a very successful one. The chief speaker was Lord Grimthorpe (under which title Sir Edmund Beckett had just been raised to the peerage), and thus this loyal champion of the Company made his reappearance at a Great Northern meeting after an absence extending from the time of the Redpath frauds—the time, as the reader may remember, when he had sat by his father's side and received the nickname of "the young Maymoon." Notwithstanding his seventy years he made a long, racy, and yet exceedingly weighty speech, containing an extraordinarily accurate forecast of the subsequent development of the railway rates question.

For the first time in its history the Company had no Bill of its own in Parliament in 1886, but it was interested in a number of Bills promoted by other parties. Thus it obtained powers in this session to work the traffic of the Nottingham Suburban Railway, a line a little over three and a half miles in length, which a local company was authorized to construct between Nottingham and Daybrook (a station on the Great Northern Derbyshire extension). But a similar arrange-

LORD GRIMTHORPE.

ment made with the East and West Yorkshire Union Company for working their line, about five miles, between Leeds and Lofthouse was withdrawn in consequence of alterations insisted on by the Commons Committee. Two years before a local company had obtained powers to make a high-level station at Halifax, with a connecting line to join the Great Northern's existing line at Holmfield, and now in 1886 it promoted a Bill to enable the Great Northern and Lancashire and Yorkshire companies to work its line, when made, under a guarantee to it of a 3½ per cent. dividend. With the approval of the two larger companies this Halifax High Level Bill passed through some of its stages, but owing to the dissolution of Parliament it had to be hung up for a year. From the same cause Mr. Mundella's Railway and Canal Traffic Bill fell to the ground.

On 20 June, 1886, the new triplicate Copenhagen tunnel was brought into use. This afforded instant and most welcome relief to the congestion of suburban traffic (which since the passing of the "Cheap Trains" Act of 1883 had been intensified by the large number of London workmen who had come to live in the Great Northern's district) by providing a clear run on the "up" side from Holloway to York Road, King's Cross, separate from the long-distance trains. The construction of the tunnel by the contractor, Mr. Lovatt, under Mr. Johnson's superintendence, had proved most successful, very little damage having been done to the heavy buildings overhead, though these had not been underpinned. The subsidence of the surface varied from a maximum of 3½ in. to a minimum of 1 in. Thus the cost of the work was materially lessened, the amount of compensation exacted by overhead property-owners being very small. About the same time also the first section of the Heanor branch in Derbyshire, from Ilkeston to Nutbrook Colliery, was brought into use.

During the second half of 1886 the bright outlook of the beginning of the year became quite obscured. The harvest of 1886 proved in Lincolnshire the worst of a bad series to which that of 1885 had formed a solitary exception. Consequently the Company's grain and potato traffic fell off during the half-year by 45,000 tons, while its coal traffic was also slightly reduced by the same cause. Nor could there be much doubt now that, apart from the quality of its harvests, the value of Lincolnshire to the Great Northern had been permanently depreciated, partly by the admission to it of the Great Eastern, but more seriously by the competition of foreign agricultural produce under the stimulus of improved ocean transport.*

But the most serious of the adverse circumstances against which the Company had to struggle in 1886 was the heavy compensation bill for the Finsbury Park accident, the amount of which exceeded the worst anticipations. No less than 347 claims had to be met, and although not a single bone of any of the claimants had been

* From this point of view it is curious to remember that the Great Northern's original Act and the Corn Laws Repeal Act received the Royal Assent on the same day.

broken, the total sum which the Company had to pay in compensation was £33,000—a sum equal, it was estimated, to the whole profit on the suburban traffic for six months. In this same year, too, a passenger, who had been injured several years before in a slight collision in Doncaster Station, having gone to law and obtained a verdict of £800, went for a new trial and obtained a second verdict for no less a sum than £3,750. In addition to this the Company had to pay about £1,000 in law costs for this one case.

Revenue suffered a further exceptional tax in the second half of the

COPENHAGEN TUNNELS, KING'S CROSS (SOUTH END).

year from an expenditure of about £6,000, which Mr. Johnson found it necessary to make after the hard winter of 1885 for extra repairs to tunnels and bridges, and under these circumstances it was decided to postpone until quite late in the year the renewal of the western half of the roof over the King's Cross passenger terminus, though the necessity for this had been announced by Lord Colville at the February meeting. The reader remembers that the eastern or "arrival" half of the original timber roof was renewed in iron during 1869-70, and now, at the end of 1886, the timbers of the huge travelling stage which, as we noted, was used for this purpose, were taken from their place of storage, and the same operation repeated on the "departure" side. It was not until the end of 1887 that the work was completed, and the whole cost of it was charged as before to revenue, though with some assistance from a "contingent fund" which the directors had been able to lay by for such purposes, notwithstanding their obligations to the "A" shareholders.

Under its Act of 1882, which authorized its suburban widenings and other works, the Company had taken powers to raise two millions of new capital; but since then it had not gone to Parliament for capital powers. Consequently, though a portion only of the work near London had been done, it was now in need of authority to raise more money. Accordingly, in a Bill which it was found necessary to deposit for the session of 1887 for a number of deviations and minor works, the authorization of a million additional capital was incorporated. "The more the directors go over the line," said Lord Colville in regard to this, "the more they are convinced that the expenditure of capital for increasing and bettering the accommodation on the existing system is absolutely necessary. With the exceptions of some short mineral lines and some short lines and junctions in Yorkshire, our expenditure of late has been on this principle. We are widening the main line for the first five or six miles out of London; a very large outlay is going on in doubling the line near Leeds, including a new station at Holbeck, and also at Laister Dyke, near Bradford; we are building a new goods warehouse at Bread Street, in the City of London, very large new stables at Clerkenwell, and other important works. The Derbyshire lines have involved the construction of a very large sorting sidings for coal waggons at Colwick, near Nottingham. We have constructed there about twenty miles of sorting sidings, and have already purchased 150 acres of land. We have up to this time spent there £92,000, and we have a further estimated liability of £70,000, for the place is not large enough. It is for the purpose of carrying out such works as these, which are quite indispensable for the safety and the working of the traffic, that we now ask for further capital."

On 17 January, 1887, Mr. J. H. Astell, the senior director of the Company, and son of its first chairman, Mr. William Astell, died, after no less than forty years of active and valuable service on the Board. He was succeeded by Mr. William Beckett, M.P., third son of Mr. Edmund Denison, who thus restored the connection between the Company and the Beckett-Denison family, which had been temporarily severed, as already noted, by the death of Mr. Christopher Denison in 1884.

During the first half of 1887 the effects of the deficient harvest of the previous year were seen, as usual, in a falling off of the export and import traffic of the agricultural districts. The week of the Queen's Jubilee celebrations also entailed a serious temporary loss, the merchandise and coal traffic being diminished thereby by about £16,000, which was modified to the extent of about £2000 only by an increase of passenger traffic. During the half-year new duplicate lines for goods traffic were brought into use at three parts of the main line, and the bridge carrying over the North Western line at Batley was reconstructed. The new docks constructed by an independent company at Boston were opened this half-year, too, and a satisfactory increase of 16,000 tons to the Great Northern's coal traffic resulted. But in regard to the Sutton Bridge Docks, Mr. W. L. Jackson, the Great Northern director who had taken Mr. Christopher Denison's place on that Dock Company's Board, had to report in August, 1887, that no satisfactory plan had yet been devised for resuscitating their undertaking.

WIDENING THE LINE AT ARMLEY, NEAR LEEDS.
Showing the removing of "spail" earth.

From 1 November, 1887, a change of a minor character was made in the working of the East Coast traffic with Scotland, which was destined, as we shall see presently, to lead to momentous results. Third-class passengers were admitted to the two "special nine-hour expresses" leaving King's Cross and Edinburgh respectively at 10 a.m. In 1872, it will be remembered, when the Midland's "third-class by all trains" lead had had to be followed, a special exception had been made in the case of these 10 o'clock trains; but, after adopting a similar course originally, the West Coast companies had for some years past admitted the third-class to their best day trains. The result had been that, while first and second-class passengers between London and Edinburgh continued to gain a full hour by using the East Coast route instead of the West Coast, for third-class there was nothing to choose between the two. The admission of third-class to the two nine-hour trains, however, made the East Coast service again an hour better for all three classes.

On the other hand, the nine-hour service between King's Cross and Edinburgh had ceased to be what it had been when first put on in 1876—the best locomotive performance in which the Great Northern was concerned. Eclipsed temporarily by the forty-nine and a half miles per hour journey-speed of the $3\frac{1}{2}$ hours Leeds trains of

"Down Scotchman" passing Sandy Station (1 August, 1887).
From a photograph by Cameron Swan, Esq.

1880, the forty-seven miles per hour between London and York of the two "Flying Scotchmen" had been permanently surpassed so soon as the $4\frac{1}{2}$ hours service between London and Manchester had been put on, its journey-speed between London and Grantham being, as already noted, $50\frac{2}{3}$. Moreover, from 1 July, 1884, the Manchester service had been further accelerated to $4\frac{1}{4}$ hours. The result was that the "Manchester Fliers" daily covered the $105\frac{1}{2}$ miles between King's Cross and Grantham in 119 minutes—$53\frac{3}{8}$ miles per hour,—whereas the "Flying Scotchman" from King's Cross was allowed 135 minutes for the same distance. But the latter was the heavier train.

Early in March, 1888, the new single-line tunnel between Wood

Green and Southgate was brought into use for "up" goods traffic, and soon afterwards a new line for down goods was completed between Finsbury Park and Hornsey. In connection with the widening between these two places, the land on the Haringay estate, which we noted as acquired in 1881, was laid out as reception and sorting sidings for goods and coal traffic, and these also were brought into work at the beginning of 1888. The Leeds widenings and improvements, too, were finished about the same time, and the Beeston and Batley line was opened for coal traffic from Batley to Soothill Colliery. Still,

"UP" EXPRESS PASSING SANDY STATION (1 AUGUST, 1887).
From a photograph by Cameron Swan, Esq.

however, much of the suburban widening programme remained to be carried out, and already a further instalment of it had been put in hand. This was the widening of the cutting in which stands Southgate Station, the erection of large retaining walls there, and the reconstruction of the station with duplicate lines.

We have said that by the end of 1880 the Company had fitted nearly the whole of its passenger rolling stock with continuous brake-power, and by the time we have now reached this operation had been long completed. But, unfortunately, the preference which Mr. Stirling and other eminent locomotive engineers had shown for the simple vacuum brake over the automatic vacuum had proved not to have been well founded. Several accidents, it had appeared, might have been averted, or greatly minimized in their effects, by automatic action on the part of the brake apparatus; so, at the beginning of 1888, the directors decided to convert the whole of the stock. The cost was estimated at £48,000, and it was decided to charge half to capital and half to revenue, the latter charge to be spread over four years.

Meantime, since the beginning of 1883, the works on the great Forth Bridge had been making steady progress; but, as almost invariably happens in the case of great engineering works, both the time and capital originally estimated for the work were proving insufficient. Accordingly, in the session of 1888, the Forth Bridge Company promoted a Bill for the raising of an additional half million of money, the four railway companies agreeing to extend thereto their guarantee of interest at 4 per cent. Fortunately, however, thanks to the character of the guarantors, it had been possible to raise all the capital so far expended at a premium, which premium had sufficed to pay interest during construction; and so the railway companies had not yet had to pay anything directly either out of revenue or capital towards this most costly undertaking. The completion of the bridge was now expected about October, 1889.

In 1888, as in 1886, the Great Northern had no Bill of its own in Parliament; but, in addition to the Forth Bridge Bill, a number of others in which the Company was interested were before the Legislature. The most important of these was a revival by Lord Stanley of Preston, the President of the Board of Trade in the Conservative Ministry, of the Railway and Canal Traffic Bill, which his Liberal predecessors, Mr. Mundella and Mr. Chamberlain, had, as we have seen, failed to pass into law in 1884 and in 1886.

Being fathered this time by a Peer, the Rates Bill was introduced first into the Upper House, and in that assembly the champions of the railway interest succeeded in obtaining a clause providing that the new schedule of rates which the Board of Trade was to be empowered to prepare should be "on the whole equivalent" to the existing powers. This basis of revision, however, was rejected in the House of Commons, and, despite all the efforts of the companies, the Bill ultimately passed into law in a form which left the discretion of the Board of Trade in the matter practically uncontrolled. But the initiative in the process of revision was left to the railway companies, who were given six months' grace under the Act to prepare, and submit to the Board, a new classification of freight and revised schedules of rates. So Lord Colville was able to give the Great Northern shareholders the assurance at their meeting in August, 1888, that no reduction of their revenue could be enforced for another year at least.

Another important Parliamentary contest in which the representatives of the Great Northern were called upon to play a part in the session of 1888 arose out of a Bill deposited by the Eastern and Midlands Railway Company. This was a company formed in 1882 by an amalgamation of the Midland and Eastern (which itself, as the reader may remember, had been an amalgamation of the Sutton and Lynn, the Spalding and Bourn, and the Spalding and Sutton*), the Peterborough, Wisbeach and Sutton, the Lynn and Fakenham, the Yarmouth and North Norfolk, and the Yarmouth Union —in short, it was a union of all the small companies in the eastern counties which had not entered either the Great Eastern or the Great Northern fold. It had occupied ever since its formation, however, a peculiar and anomalous position. For its system was divided into two sections, and while it worked the "eastern section" quite independently, the "western section" was worked for it by other companies —the Peterborough, Wisbeach, and Sutton by the Midland, and the Bourn and Lynn (or Midland and Eastern), as the reader may remember to have been already informed, by the Midland and Great Northern jointly. The Midland had obtained the working of the Peterborough, Wisbeach, and Sutton at 50 per cent. of the gross receipts; but the terms upon which the Bourn and Lynn was worked jointly by it and the Great Northern included, as we have

* Otherwise called the Norwich and Spalding.

more than once noticed, a minimum guarantee to the owning company of £15,000 a year. Accordingly, the Midland was exposed to the temptation—and according to the Eastern and Midland authorities had succumbed to it—to "starve" the Peterborough, Wisbeach, and Sutton, in order to make up its share of the Bourn and Lynn guarantee.

This grievance was carried by the Eastern and Midlands Company before the Railway Commission; but facts then given in evidence went to prove that the through traffic between the Midland system and the eastern counties was travelling neither by the Bourn and Lynn nor by the Peterborough, Wisbeach, and Sutton—that, in short, it was not going by the Eastern and Midlands system at all, but was being exchanged with the Great Eastern at Peterborough. The Midland's explanation of this was twofold—first, that it had a prior agreement with the Great Eastern, and second, that its junctions with the Eastern and Midlands were not efficiently workable for through trains; and, as the result of this, the Eastern and Midlands Company had become convinced that the only effective way to mend matters was for them to make a really serviceable and direct connection between their system and the Midland. Accordingly they revived for the session of 1888 the project for a direct link line from Bourn to join the Midland's system and Peterborough line at Saxby—a project which, the reader may remember, had been promoted by the Midlands and Eastern as long ago as 1866, to be dropped when the Great Northern had offered running powers—"a pig in a poke" the bargain now appeared to have been for the Midland—*via* Essendine and Stamford.

But the Bill as presented to Parliament in 1888 was not limited to a revival of this extension project. In addition to this the Eastern and Midlands Board made an arrangement with the Midland that the latter should, in the near future, absorb the whole "western section" of their system, and in connection with this the two companies entered into a very intimate traffic agreement with regard to the "eastern section" also. Of course, if the part of the western section between Bourn and Lynn was absorbed by the Midland, the Great Northern was still to retain its powers as joint lessee. Nevertheless, the change of ownership was pretty certain to be felt adversely at King's Cross. Worse than this, when Mr. Oakley and Mr. Nelson examined the traffic agreement, they found that it meant that the traffic between the eastern section and every important competitive place in the kingdom, except London, was to be "hypothecated" to the Midland route. Under these circumstances the Great Northern authorities had no option but to oppose the Bill, and, though not successful in throwing it out altogether, they succeeded in preventing the obnoxious traffic agreement from being scheduled to it.

Towards the end of May, 1888, the London and North Western and Caledonian companies gave notice that from 1 June their best day trains by the West Coast route between London and Edinburgh would be accelerated from about ten hours each way to nine hours—the same time as the corresponding East Coast trains. This was obviously a reply to the change which, as already noted, the East Coast companies had made in the previous November, of admitting third-class passengers to their nine-hours day service. But, as will be seen, it amounted to a good deal more than a return, in the matter of the relative positions of the two routes, to the *status quo* prior to November. It not only restored the equality as regards third-class traffic, but it gave the West Coast what it had not had since the ante-Great Northern days, when both services started from Euston—equality for first and second-class Edinburgh traffic also.

To support their claim to this all-round equality, notwithstanding the physical superiority of the East Coast route, the West Coast companies could argue from the analogy of the London and Manchester service, in which case, as we have seen, the Great Northern and Manchester and Sheffield companies had by hard running overcome a similar superiority of long standing. And, indeed, the advantage of seven miles in distance, by virtue of which the East Coast companies had maintained their supremacy in the London-Edinburgh traffic, was half only of the mileage advantage which the London and North Western possessed in the case of London-Manchester. As for gradients, if those of the Caledonian handicapped the West Coast, those of the Sheffield line handicapped the joint service to Manchester still more. But to this argument East Coast advocates could reply, that whereas the four and a quarter hours' run between London and Manchester involved, apparently, the highest rate of speed to which the London and North Western could, or cared to, rise, the nine-hour service to Edinburgh, as we have seen, by no means gave the Great Northern the hardest locomotive work of which it had shown itself capable. On the contrary, to knock off a quarter of an hour from its time between London and York was a thing which Mr. Cockshott and Mr. Stirling could arrange without a moment's misgiving. Moreover, the North Eastern authorities, on their part, were equally ready to make the same acceleration between York and Edinburgh, and so there was no difficulty at all in reducing the East Coast time to eight and a half hours. This change was announced in the middle of June, and brought into force from 1 July, 1888.

With the East Coast thus ahead again by half an hour the month of July was wearing peacefully to a close, when, quite unexpectedly, on Friday, 27 July, notices were posted at Euston Square that from the following Wednesday, 1 August, 1888, the West Coast time between London and Edinburgh would be eight and a half hours also. This meant that in the busiest week of the whole railway year, and when the Anglo-Scotch holiday traffic was just about to reach its height, the West Coast companies had deliberately sprung a surprise upon their rivals. Very fortunately, however, it happened that the Great Northern and North Eastern Boards both met on this Friday—the one at King's Cross and the other at York,—and thus they were able at once to open telegraphic communication with one another. Three working days only remained before the West Coast acceleration was to come into force, but those days sufficed for every necessary arrangement for a second East Coast acceleration to be made. Another quarter of an hour was knocked off the "booked time" of each section of the journey—nor did this involve making the Great Northern's time between London and York faster than the Lord Mayor's "special" had run in 1880, and the Prince of Wales's "special" in 1883—and on the eventful "first" the West Coast's eight and a half hours was capped by eight hours by the East Coast. Both trains arrived at Edinburgh before time.

The "race to Edinburgh" had now begun in earnest, and the newspapers and the public began to get excited. On 3 August the West Coast companies announced a third acceleration to eight hours, to begin on the following Monday, the 6th, and not only were they as good as their word, but their train ran into the Caledonian Station at Edinburgh on that day at 5.52 p.m., *i.e.*, eight minutes before time. But it had evidently been "stripped" for the work, for it consisted of four carriages only, and weighed no more than eighty tons. The East Coast, on the other hand, continued to work their ordinary train of seven, eight, or nine coaches—six-wheelers, it is true, as compared with the West Coast's eight-wheelers—but of a weight of 100 tons at least. The engines employed on the Great Northern throughout the "race" all belonged to Mr. Stirling's "8-foot single" class—outside cylinders, 18×28 in. stroke, heating surface 1250 square feet, weight 40 tons.

Having regard to their longer distance and harder gradients, the West Coast trains, notwithstanding their lightness, probably did the best work while eight hours remained the booked time on both routes. But it remained so only just as long a time as the East Coast authorities needed to get the rush of "grouse" tourists out of the way. Then, on 13 August, they once more accelerated their booked time—to seven hours forty-five minutes. The greater part of the quarter of an hour thus knocked off was obtained by taking out the stop at Berwick and otherwise quickening up between York and Edinburgh; but the Great Northern's allowance for King's Cross to York, which had been reduced from three hours thirty-five minutes to three hours thirty-two minutes on 6 August, was now again reduced—to three and a half hours exactly, a journey-speed of $53\frac{3}{7}$. The West Coast reply was to run on the very same day in seven hours thirty-eight minutes. To this, on the following day, 14 August, the East Coast responded with seven hours thirty-two minutes. On that day, however, a conference of representatives of the companies was held, and a truce was patched up. Under this the times to be booked, until the end of the month, were fixed at seven and three-quarter hours for the East Coast and eight hours for the West.

In accordance with this truce the Great Northern authorities loyally kept their booked time from King's Cross to York at three and a half hours, though they felt that their capabilities had not by any means been fully "extended"; but, with the racing spirit now fairly aroused in the engine-drivers, it was impossible to restrain "running ahead of time." The result was that on every day from 15 to 31 August, except three, the Scotchman arrived at York with some minutes to spare, its best performance being three hours twenty-two minutes, and its worst (the three exceptions just mentioned) exactly booked time. Moreover, on the last day of the month, with the connivance of the authorities, the drivers set deliberately to show what *could* be done. Unfortunately, a check a little outside Doncaster, a slow-down at Shaftholme junction, and a two minutes stop at Selby for the drawbridge, made the time to York one minute worse than the previous "record," and north of York, too, there was more than one check. Nevertheless the train entered the Waverley Station, Edinburgh at $5.26\frac{3}{4}$, having thus beat the previous record for the whole journey—the seven hours thirty-two minutes of 14 August—by five and a quarter minutes. Four consecutive miles had been covered at 76·6 miles per hour.

Thus with three hours twenty-two minutes for the 188 miles between London and York—a journey-speed of $55\frac{1}{2}$ miles per hour—the Great Northern beat all its previous records for individual runs. Nor had its life-long supremacy for high speed generally yet been overcome, though the Midland and the London and North Western were pressing it in this respect much harder than ever before. The Great Northern's total express mileage in 1888 amounted to 9,544 miles daily at a "running average" of forty-seven miles per hour, while the Midland on a system 25 per cent. larger showed at the same date an express mileage of 11,381, with a "running average" of 46¼. Having regard to its harder gradients this Midland record was extremely good on paper. Unfortunately, it was greatly marred by unpunctuality in practice, whereas the Great Northern maintained the habit of keeping time, which it had acquired very early in its

GREAT NORTHERN SIX-WHEEL-COUPLED GOODS LOCOMOTIVE.

career under the rigid discipline of Mr. Denison and Mr. Seymour Clarke. As regards comparison with the lines south of London, the best goods trains on the Great Northern showed journey-speeds of thirty miles an hour and more—a speed which at this date was about the average of the best fast passenger trains of the South of England companies.* In connection with the Great Northern's fast running, it may be mentioned that practically the whole of its system had been by this time laid with steel rails.

* For the facts and figures as to speed given in this chapter I must again acknowledge my indebtedness to Mr. Foxwell's *Express Trains;* also to *Great Northern Speeds*, by the Rev. W. J. Scott. Mr. Foxwell works out a comparison between the companies in 1888 by dividing their daily express mileage into the lengths of their systems over which the express trains actually ran. The largest "resulting multiplies" are Great Northern, 33; Midland, 16½.

CHAPTER XXIII.

A GATHERING STORM—TWO BRIDGE-BUILDING ACHIEVEMENTS —THE CONVERSION OF STOCK—1889-1890.

FROM 1884 (when we saw the Great Northern second period of great extension closed with the completion of the Thornton and Keighley line) until the date we have now reached—the autumn of 1888 —the mileage of the Company had increased no more than from 784 to 791. But an arrangement had now to be recorded which had the effect of adding immediately thirteen miles to the system, and which led, as we shall see, to a much larger addition afterwards. This was the acquirement jointly with the Midland Company of the "western section" of the Eastern and Midlands system.

This step was practically forced upon the Great Northern directors by the passing of the Saxby and Bourn Bill in the session of 1888. For although, as already recorded, the clause "hypothecating" Eastern and Midlands traffic to the Midland Company was expunged from that Bill in deference to Great Northern protests, yet the sanctioning of the direct line from Bourn to the Midland system and the powers given to the Midland to absorb the Bourn and Lynn and Peterborough, Wisbeach, and Sutton lines at any time in the future, remained as a serious menace to Great Northern interests. Accordingly when, soon after the passage of the Bill, the Midland and Eastern and Midlands authorities showed a willingness to allow the powers which the Great Northern already possessed as joint lessee of the Bourn and Lynn to be converted into joint ownership not only of that line, but of the Peterborough, Wisbeach, and Sutton also, the Board at King's Cross was fain to step aside from the course of non-extension to which Lord Colville, as we have seen, had lately pledged it, and to join in prosecuting for the session of 1889 a new Bill to authorize this joint ownership. Half of the thirty-four miles of the Bourn and Lynn the Great Northern was already reckoning as part of its system, so the addition to its mileage was, as already stated, thirteen miles only, *i.e.*, half of the Peterborough, Wisbeach, and Sutton. To Wisbeach the

Company had almost from its origin, as the reader may remember, possessed runnings from Peterborough over the Great Eastern lines *viâ* March, and the abortive attempt it made in 1851 to invade the eastern counties by that route in connection with its temporary lease of the "East Anglican" has been recorded in an earlier chapter. The advantages which the new route now offered lay in its being quite direct from Peterborough to Wisbeach, and in its extending beyond that place to connect with the rest of the Eastern and Midlands system at Sutton Bridge. This gave the Great Northern a good chance of competing with the Great Eastern for the London traffic of the whole of northern Norfolk (including the important seaside resort Cromer), and even to some extent for the London traffic of Norwich and Yarmouth.

Including the obligations entailed by this new acquisition, the capital of the Great Northern Company, raised by shares or represented by fixed charges, became about 39½ millions in 1889, as against thirty-seven millions in 1884. This meant that the desire of the directors to give "rest" to the capital account had been so far successful that, whereas from 1861 to 1884 the rate of increase had averaged quite a million a year, from 1885 to 1889 it had averaged half that amount only. Moreover, there was good hope that this reduced rate would be the normal one in the future, for as regards liabilities for new lines the Company was exceptionally free. The only works of this kind on hand were the Beeston and Batley link line, the Heanor branch, and the new junctions with the Lancashire and Yorkshire, and the two former of these, as we know, were partially open already. On the suburban widenings, it was true, a further expenditure, estimated at £400,000, was impending, but this was not a great deal more than had been spent within the previous two or three years upon the same account; nor did other works for the improvement of the existing system threaten to be heavier than they had been during the past five years. Therefore, when in the first half of 1889 the depression of trade at last definitely lifted, and passenger, goods, and mineral traffic all showed satisfactory increase, the directors and officers had good reason to hope that the ebb-tide of adversity which had brought the Company's dividend down to £4 7*s.* 6*d.* per cent. in 1886, 1887, and 1888, was at last on the turn.

On the otherwise clear horizon, however, an ominous cloud had already gathered. It was a cloud no bigger than a man's hand, but the man was Sir Edward Watkin. Although Sir Edward's name has been absent from this history since we noticed his rejection in 1877 of a guarantee dividend for the Sheffield larger than that company has ever been able to earn either before or since, his activity in the railway world in 1889 was as great as ever. He whom we saw emerge from a subordinate position at Euston Square to become in 1853 general manager of the Sheffield was now chairman, not only of that company, but of the Metropolitan, the East London, and the South Eastern. Moreover, for five years or more he had been carrying on a vigorous campaign with military experts and with successive Parliaments with the object of obtaining powers to make a tunnel beneath the English Channel, and it was commonly believed that he had resolved to crown his career by linking this with the other undertakings over which he presided, so as to establish a through route in one hand from Liverpool *via* London to the coast of France—"a sort of backbone," to quote the cant phrase he himself used later, "to the railway system of the country."

What made this more than idle talk was that slowly but surely the Metropolitan system was being pushed northwards. Early in the eighties extensions as far as Aylesbury had been authorized, and in this year, 1889, there was a Bill before Parliament, with Sir Edward Watkin as its chief promoter, which, under the misleading title of the "Worcester and Broom Railway Bill," sought to give the Metropolitan running powers more than twenty miles further northwards to Moreton Pinkney, and thence westwards right away to Worcester. The Bill proposed that the Metropolitan Company should be empowered to subscribe £100,000 to the construction of a link line which was needed between Quainton Road (near Aylesbury) and Moreton Pinkney, and to work a through service between London and Worcester.

For this same session the Sheffield Company had deposited a Bill for an extension from its existing main line at Beighton, near Sheffield, southwards to Annesley, there to make an "end-on junction" with the Great Northern's Leen Valley line. The obvious and professed object of this was to give the Sheffield Company access to the North Derbyshire coalfield, and coming as it did from the north to meet the Great Northern branch from the south, it was not in this respect at all obnoxious to Great Northern interests. But when looked at in connection with the simultaneous desire of the Metropolitan Company to come further northwards in precisely the same longitude, it had a larger significance which did not escape the notice of the authorities at King's Cross.

In March, 1889, before either the Beighton to Annesley or the so-called Worcester and Broom Bills had reached Committee stage, Mr. Oakley received a letter from Mr. William Pollitt, successor to Mr. Underdown in the general managership of the Sheffield Company. This stated that the Sheffield directors were desirous that the new line they were seeking to make from Beighton to Annesley should be "an open road to give the district the greatest possible increased accommodation," and that with this object they proposed an exchange of running powers with the Great Northern, viz., the Sheffield to be allowed to run to Nottingham by way of the Great Northern's Leen Valley line, in return for the Great Northern being allowed to run to Sheffield *viâ* Beighton. "My directors are quite willing," Mr. Pollitt added, "that an agreement should be entered into and scheduled to the Bill that nothing in it shall prejudice the rights of either of our companies under the agreement of 1 October, 1860" (*i.e.* the Fifty Years Treaty).

But the Great Northern authorities were not to be misled by talk about "an open road" and "district accommodation." They felt that they must consider the designs of Sir Edward Watkin's companies collectively and fully, and that until this had been done no answer could be given to the Sheffield well-seeming offer. Accordingly a special committee of their Board was appointed to discuss the matter in all its bearings.

To those of this committee, of course, who had been connected with the Company for any length of time the threatening danger appeared in its main aspect as an old acquaintance. A little more than a year before, at a Sheffield half-yearly meeting, Sir Edward Watkin, in the course of a review of the various efforts, all futile, which he had made to improve that company's undertaking, had referred to the Rushton to Askerne joint scheme of 1873. This, he said, had been suggested to him by the Midland chairman, Mr. Price, and he now described it as "the most masterly proposition ever made by an enlightened railway chairman." Nor did the Great Northern authorities need this hint to show them that the proposed junction between the Sheffield and the Metropolitan, the first steps towards which were so ill-concealed in the Bills now before Parliament, was in its main features a revival of the Rushton scheme.

Nevertheless, in the long interval which had elapsed between the two "conspiracies," the Great Northern had been thrown to some extent off its guard. At its half-yearly meeting in February, 1884, in answer to a shareholder who had brought Sir Edward Watkin's rumoured new ambitions to his notice, Lord Colville had said, speaking without book, that the Great Northern, "*having running powers to Manchester,*" would not, he thought, suffer very much even if a new trunk route to Sheffield *viâ* Aylesbury was eventually constructed. As a matter of fact, however—and this the committee of the Board now realized as the most serious factor in the situation—the Great Northern had not "running powers to Manchester" in the ordinary acceptation of the words. All it had under the Fifty Years Agreement was "contingent running powers," the contingency being its ability to prove to the satisfaction of an arbitrator that the Sheffield Company was not working the joint traffic properly. Worse than this, the terms upon which such running powers would have to be exercised according to the agreement of 1860—80 per cent. of the gross receipts to the owning company—were such as would make the Great Northern's working quite unprofitable, if the Sheffield were at the same time working a route to London of its own.

These facts furnish the clue to the reply which on 4 May, 1889, Mr. Oakley sent to Mr. Pollitt's letter of the previous March. With his usual frankness Mr. Oakley expressed his directors' apprehension that the line from Beighton through Nottingham might eventually "form part of a new competing line from the North to London in connection with existing and projected railways," and he stated that in view of such a possibility his Board anticipated that the Sheffield Company would be "willing and indeed desirous to give the Great Northern Company such reasonable protection as they were fairly entitled to." He therefore proposed that, in addition to providing for the exchange of running powers already suggested, the new agreement proposed should give the Great Northern running powers from Retford to Manchester, and that the Sheffield Company should bind itself therein not to promote or assist any other company or person in promoting "any extension of their railway south of the town of Nottingham."

In his reply, dated 7 May, 1889, Mr. Pollitt told Mr. Oakley that he "must know" that his suggestions were "neither reasonable nor such as the Sheffield Company could accept." "What you are asking," he wrote, "is, in effect, to re-enact the very clause which was included in our agreement of 1 October, 1860, but which was struck out by the Railway Commissioners in 1881 at the instigation of the Huddersfield Chamber of Commerce, as in their opinion opposed to the interest of the public. Your company is already entitled to run over our line if the Sheffield Company throw any difficulties in the way of through traffic, and my directors would be willing to amend this clause in the agreement of 1860 so as to make it clear that the running powers should come into effect, if it can at any time be shown to the satisfaction of the Railway Commissioners that the Sheffield Company are actively diverting from your system by means of the lines to be authorized by this Bill any traffic your company is entitled to under that agreement." He further offered to modify the percentage to be paid under the contingent running powers to the Sheffield as owners from 80 to $66\frac{2}{3}$ per cent. of the gross receipts. To this Mr. Oakley curtly replied on the following day that his directors were "unable to accept as satisfactory the proposed slight modification of the agreement of 1860"; they therefore declined the exchange of running powers, unless the Sheffield Company would give an obligation that the "proposed line, if granted by Parliament, should not be used for the purposes of extension south of Nottingham."

The negotiations having thus failed, the Great Northern lodged a petition against the Sheffield Bill, and instructed Messrs. Pope and Balfour Browne to appear for them against it when it came before a Commons Committee a few days later, viz., on 14 May, 1889.

"We have practically nothing to say against this line as a line to the north," said Mr. Balfour Browne in his speech, "and I do not wish to be supposed to be saying anything against it; but I have a strong interest for the Great Northern in saying, 'Do not let this company have the means of getting further south at any rate during the time that their agreement with us lasts.' We say, 'We will let you into Nottingham if you will not go south.' Mr. Pollitt says, 'I will not agree to that.' Why? Because they *are* going south. But if they have that intention, then I ask you to say that you have not the whole scheme before you, and that you will wait till you see the whole scheme before you pass it. I think they are getting perilously far south, if you let them have this Bill at all."

The Sheffield authorities, however, had skilfully repeated the tactics which the Great Northern had employed, it may be remembered, in the case of its extensions into Derbyshire. It had secured the support of the London and North Western by giving running powers—the very running powers which the Great Northern had refused. So the strong local case which Mr. Pollitt and Mr. Findlay, successor to Mr. Cawkwell at Euston Square, were able to make out, carried the Bill through the Commons in spite of the opposition of the Great Northern and the still keener opposition of the Midland.

The defeated companies decided to renew the fight in the Lords; but before the Sheffield Bill got there, Sir Edward Watkin's other project—the so-called Worcester and Broom—came before another Commons Committee, presided over by Mr. Woodall. On behalf of this Sir Edward himself went into the box. But though he admitted, under cross-examination, that the proposed railway from Quainton Road to Moreton Pinkney might not pay as "a distinct piece of line," but would need to be worked "in connection with a good through line," the Great Northern was unable to put its case against this further attempt to get a new through line by piecemeal for lack of *locus standi* before the Committee. But, very characteristically, Sir

Edward Watkin was not limiting his ambition to linking the Metropolitan with the south-eastern part of the Sheffield system. He very evidently had an alternative, or duplicate, project in mind for carrying on his projected London and Worcester route through Wales (where he was busy forming a "Welsh Union") to a north-western junction with the Sheffield in Lancashire, and against this the London and North Western and the Great Western companies were able to appear. On behalf of the Buckinghamshire landowners, too, Mr. Bidder protested against their district being cut up, not for any public interest, but to favour Sir Edward Watkin's "predatory excursions." The result was that the Bill was thrown out (27 June, 1889).

Meanwhile the Great Northern had presented a petition to the House of Lords against the Sheffield's Beighton to Annesley Bill praying that, if that line were sanctioned, a proviso might be inserted in the Bill to forbid its being used "as a means or reason for further extensions by the Sheffield Company in breach of the agreement of 1860." This petition, accordingly, Mr. Littler, the Sheffield counsel, had to meet when he opened his case for that Bill before Lord Camperdown's Committee on 10 July, 1889. "Your lordships will be rather amused to hear," said he, "that there was a clause in the agreement of 1860 which had some such meaning as is put forward in the Great Northern petition; but on opposition before the Railway Commissioners to the renewal of the agreement that clause was struck out on the ground that it was contrary to public policy, and the assurance they now ask for is an assurance which we venture to think your lordships will not allow us to give as being contrary to public policy. At some future time Parliament might think it necessary that a line should be constructed further south. We have no intention of making any such extension, but I submit that Parliament would not allow us to bind ourselves to any such condition as that."

The outcome, as usual, was that a compromise was effected. The Sheffield authorities wanted the running powers to Nottingham *bonâ fide* for local traffic, and so they offered to bind their company not to use those powers as a means of going further south, while still maintaining that with regard to the use of the new line they must be left quite free. Seeing that the Bill seemed to be in a fair way to pass in any case, the Great Northern had nothing to lose by accepting this offer, while it gained by so doing running powers over the new line into Sheffield. Accordingly the bargain was signed, the Great Northern opposition was withdrawn, and the Bill passed.

But if in accepting this compromise the Great Northern allowed themselves to be influenced at all by Mr. Littler's declaration on behalf of the Sheffield Company that it had "no intention of making any such extension," they soon realized that they had not gauged correctly the parties they were dealing with. Immediately after the rejection of the Worcester and Broom Bill, Sir Edward Watkin seems to have resolved to throw off all disguises and to go openly for a direct line to connect the Sheffield and Metropolitan systems; and, apparently, nothing but the hope that the Great Northern might be willing to share the expense of the enterprise—a sufficiently bold hope even in view of what the Great Northern had already done in the way of joint undertakings—prevented him from immediately preparing a scheme for the session of 1890.

That there was no repetition of "the race to Edinburgh" in 1889 must be attributed solely to the forbearance of the East Coast companies. The truce under which, as already stated, the booked times by the two routes had been fixed at seven and three-quarter hours East Coast, and eight hours West Coast, until the end of August, 1888, had been succeeded by an "informal understanding" that after that month the best time should not be less than eight and a half hours. This, while half an hour only better than the East Coast's best time before the "race," was no less than one and a half hours better than the best pre-racing running on the West Coast; yet the West Coast company took advantage of the "understanding" to make a "dead heat" with their rivals for Edinburgh throughout the summer of 1889. More than this, they quickened up very considerably their best times to Perth and Aberdeen.

Now since 1876, when the East Coast companies it may be remembered had compelled the Caledonian to co-operate with them in accelerations, the best times to Perth and Aberdeen had remained the same * by both routes, having been reduced concurrently from twelve hours (Perth) and sixteen hours (Aberdeen) in 1876 to eleven hours and fourteen hours respectively in 1887. Yet now, in 1889, the West Coast acceleration—"London to Perth in ten hours fifteen minutes, London to Aberdeen in twelve hours fifty minutes"—was replied to by a quickening by fifteen minutes only of the previous times by the rival route, leaving the East Coast half an hour behind to both places. The explanation of this was two-fold. In the first place, unlike the West, the East Coast route to the north of Scotland is through Edinburgh, and so the Great Northern and its allies were reluctant to do anything which might be, or seem to be, a breach of the eight and a half hours truce as regards that place. In the second place, the East Coast companies were waiting for the opening of the Forth Bridge.

* Not precisely the same to Aberdeen at first, but practically so.

Nevertheless, Mr. Stirling's engines had one opportunity to "make a record" in 1889, viz., in the course of a journey which the Shah of Persia took on 26 July from Bradford, *via* London, to Brighton. His special train left Leeds at 4.55 p.m., and, notwithstanding a fifteen minutes' stop at Grantham, it reached York Road Station, King's Cross, at 8.37. Reducing the Grantham stop to five minutes, which was the utmost required for changing engines (the additional ten minutes being for the purpose of preparing dinner for the Shah), this was equivalent to 185 miles in three hours thirty-two minutes—a journey-speed of over fifty-two miles an hour; and considering the greater weight of the train (which contained a dining-car in addition to the Shah's saloon) it was probably even a better piece of work than the run of the "Prince of Wales's special," Bradford to London in three hours forty-eight minutes, which we have already recorded as taking place in 1882. Moreover, from 1 November, 1888, the best daily time between London and Leeds was reduced to three hours fifty minutes—very fine running, albeit five minutes worse than the exceptional speed between those points in the summer of 1880.

During 1889, as already noted, British trade at last completely shook off the depression which had so long hung over it, and the general improvement was fully shared in by the Great Northern, its traffic receipts for the second half of the year showing an increase of over £133,000. As usually happens, however, in such times of expansion, a great advance in the price of coal and other materials and in the cost of labour absorbed a large share of this additional revenue. Nevertheless, the dividend rose by $\frac{1}{2}$ per cent.—to £4 17s. 6d., and it might perhaps have got up to 5 per cent., but for an exceptional charge of £20,000 upon revenue for the year for the reconstruction of the bridge over the Trent Navigation, at Newark.

The original bridge at this place (opened for traffic in 1852) was, as the reader may remember, of the form known as the "Warren Truss," and was not only unique in this respect, but was the largest span of its kind in the country, it being 257 feet from centre to centre of its bearings. As early as 1879, however, it had shown signs of wear, and it had been found upon examination that the inner links of the diagonals in the centre of the bridge had elongated $\frac{5}{18}$ of an inch, thereby putting all the stress upon the outer links. Accordingly, under Mr. Johnson's instructions, the method of laying the floor had been altered so that all the members might do the work required of them. In 1888, however, fresh signs of weakness had appeared, and then Mr. Johnson had decided upon an entire reconstruction. The new bridge, as designed by Mr. E. Duncan, one of the Company's assistant engineers, is of the class of truss known as the "Whipple-Murphy," and is made entirely of steel. The chief difficulty in its construction lay in the fact that it could not, for obvious reasons, be built *in situ;* but the fact that the old structures consisted of two separate single-line sections, and that the same plan could be adopted in the case of the new bridge, made the process of transposition a good deal easier than it might otherwise have been.

The *modus operandi* was briefly as follows. A building site was chosen alongside the railway embankment on the north side of the river, and here the two sections of the new bridge were put together separately by the contractors, Messrs. Handyside of Derby, the process taking about ten months. Meanwhile, parallel to the bridge itself, a staging was formed on piles upon which two railway tracks were laid side by side. Upon the outer of these each section of the old structure was, in turn, "shunted" on trollies by means of hydraulic jacks, while first one and then the other of the new sections was propelled by similar means, first on to the innermost track upon the staging, and thence into its place over the river. Thus the operation of transposition was completed within fourteen days, and, as single-line working was kept open throughout, the traffic of the line was not at all seriously interrupted.

This remarkable undertaking was brought to a successful termination on 29 January, 1890; but the fame of it was quite overshadowed by the completion within the same month of the greatest bridge-building achievement the world has yet seen—the great viaduct over the Forth. On 21 January, 1890, two trains were driven upon this bridge side by side from the south end, their total weight upon the bridge being 1800 tons, and the engineers had the great satisfaction of finding that, even when placed in the most unfavourable conditions of loading, this huge weight had no effect upon the stability of the structure. The official opening of the bridge took place on 4 March, 1890.

Meantime, besides the Newark bridge, Mr. Johnson had had important engineering works in hand during 1889 in connection with the suburban widenings between Barnet and King's Cross. In February of that year the directors had announced that the continuous increase in the London suburban traffic required the immediate completion of the duplicate "up" and "down" lines all the way between those points. Accordingly, contracts were immediately let for three new single-line tunnels, two of them to form a duplication of the original double-line tunnel between Southgate and Barnet, and the other to complete the duplication between Southgate and Wood Green, where, it will be remembered, a new single-line tunnel had already been constructed and opened in 1887. These works had to be carried on simultaneously with the widening at Southgate Station which was still far from complete, and with similar widening operations at Wood Green. Moreover, both at Southgate and at Barnet subways for foot

THE NEWARK DYKE BRIDGE WHEN IN COURSE OF RECONSTRUCTION.

passengers—to replace level crossings—were about this same time taken in hand, operations difficult of execution while fast and heavy trains were continually passing overhead.

The new stations at Wood Green and Southgate and the new western tunnel between those places were all brought into use within the first half of 1890, but now yet another important suburban work had to be taken in hand. This was the provision of a triplicate "Maiden Lane tunnel" to separate the passenger trains starting from the terminus from the passenger and goods trains coming off the Metropolitan in the same complete way as, since the provision of the second Maiden Lane tunnel, the "up" traffic had been separated within the same area. Like its two predecessors, this third or western tunnel had to be carried beneath the Regent's Canal; but this was not the part of the work which threatened to be most difficult. A much more onerous portion of the undertaking was on the north side of the canal, for there the tunnel had to be constructed, at a very small depth below the surface, beneath ground occupied by the Company's goods terminals, consisting of heavy goods sheds, sidings upon which trucks were constantly moving, and roads used by many vans.

For these suburban works and other purposes the Company obtained powers in the session of 1890 to raise a new million of capital. In the same Bill it obtained authority to purchase the line, four miles in length, of the Spilsby and Firsby Railway Company (which it had been working for about twenty years already), the price agreed being £20,000 in cash and the taking over from the little company of £8,333 of debentures. Nor did this one Bill cover the whole of the new powers secured by the Company this session. In a second Bill authority was obtained for the "conversion" of the whole of its ordinary capital.

This step did not originate with the directors, but was pressed upon them pertinaciously by some of the largest shareholders in the concern. Its main object was to extend over the whole of the ordinary stock the "splitting" process which, the reader may remember, was devised in 1847 to meet the great financial difficulties under which the original undertaking of the Company had to be carried out. The essence of the 1847 plan from the point of view of its originators was, as we have already noted, to accelerate the paying of calls by giving an immediate 6 per cent. upon the "B" or "preferred" halves of the shares if these were immediately paid up in full; but, as Mr. Denison, it may be remembered, had predicted at the time, the splitting had produced a further and permanent advantage. It had divided the stock into two classes—a 6 per cent. stock, "exceedingly valuable to quiet people in the country," and a speculative stock which might get nothing at all, or might, as it had in the days of great prosperity in the early "seventies," get 8 per cent. or even more, while the other was getting its 6 per cent. only. In short, as Mr. Grinling, the Company's accountant, now put the matter in 1890, "the one half-stock held out peculiar advantages to the investor, and the other held out peculiar advantages to the speculator," and that these advantages had been appreciated was proved by the fact that the two halves, if taken together, had for a great many years shown a price from 12 to 15 per cent. better than the undivided ordinary stock.

Under the clauses originally obtained for the purpose in its Act of 1848 the Company possessed powers for extending the division to stock subsequently created; but it was not considered expedient to use them now for two reasons. The first of these was that since 1851 the powers had been allowed to fall into abeyance, and the second, that it was not desirable to carry out the new "splitting" on precisely the same lines as before. To get the full benefit of the measure it was necessary—to quote Mr. Grinling again—"to adapt the old principle to the modern value of money"; in other words, it was necessary to fix the preferred dividend at a point a good deal lower than 6 per cent. Already, under the authority of Acts obtained during the "eighties," the Company's preference stocks proper had been consolidated and "watered down" from their original $4\frac{1}{2}$ or 5 per cent. to a uniform 4 per cent., and this had had the effect of sending up their price as much as 8 or 10 per cent. Thus, in proposing as they now did to convert each £100 of ordinary undivided stock into £75 of 4 per cent. "preferred" and £50 of "deferred," the directors calculated upon the improvement of its marketable position in two distinct ways:—first by its division into investment stock and speculative stock, and, second, by the special adaptation of the former to the modern value of money. It was an adaptation, too, of course, to the modern dividend of the Company.

On the other hand—from the point of view, at any rate, of those "quiet people in the country" who form so large a proportion of railway shareholders—the scheme of conversion had one serious drawback. It threatened to make the constitution of the Company's capital, and the calculation of what dividend some of the classes of stock would actually yield, exceedingly complicated affairs. The dividend being necessarily declared as upon the original undivided stock, the fact that they received quite different rates from this was already a matter of perplexity to simple-minded holders of "B's" and "A's." But this was as nothing compared with the intricacy which was to be introduced by the combination of "splitting" and "watering" now proposed. To simplify matters as far as possible, the directors insisted that the new "splitting" must not be optional, as the old had been, but compulsory; but while by this step they provoked opposition from amongst that large class of Englishmen who object on principle to this kind of compulsion, all that they gained by it was the reduction of the future ordinary stocks from a possible five to a possible four—and this by the elimination of the only one which would have been quite simple. For, while Parliament could be asked to make compulsory the "conversion" of all stock as yet undivided, it could not justly be asked to compel all holders of the "B's" and "A's" to "re-divide" and "convert," for the reason that the "B's" possessed a right as against the "A's" to a cumulative dividend (in case the profits of any year did not yield their 6 per cent.), and this right "conversion" would destroy. The only thing to be done with regard to the "A's" and "B's" was to provide that they should be converted whenever equal amounts of each were voluntarily brought in for the purpose.

Thus the "conversion" scheme, when placed before the shareholders at two meetings specially held for the purpose on 25 April and 27 June, 1890, excited opposition from two classes of persons: persons who, to recall the phrase used by Captain Hall, R.N., in regard to the original splitting, "liked plain sailing, a good water-tight boat, and good ship-room," and the persons of the class already alluded to by whom compulsion as regards their private property is always resented. Nevertheless the advantages of the proposal were undeniable. So upon a show of hands at the first meeting a large majority declared in its favour, and at the second—the "Wharncliffe meeting"—held according to statute after the Bill had passed the Commons, its further prosecution was formally approved. In the Upper House some modifications were made in the proposals as to the capital and income of the guaranteed and leased lines, but with that exception its provisions were sanctioned. During the following autumn and winter the process of "conversion" was laboriously carried out.

CHAPTER XXIV.

THE FIFTH LINE TO LONDON—THE SUBURBAN INCUBUS ONCE MORE—THE GREAT NORTHERN AND MIDLAND JOINT SYSTEM—THE RACE TO ABERDEEN—1890-1895.

AS noted in our last chapter, the official opening of the Forth Bridge took place on 4 March, 1890. It was not until 1 June, however, that passenger trains began regularly to use the bridge. From the latter date the East Coast through traffic to and from the northern parts of Scotland was diverted on to it, the trains being now carried on throughout beyond Edinburgh by the North British Company's engines — through Fifeshire and down the beautiful Glen Farg to Perth, and across the Tay Bridge, and thence by Dundee and Montrose, hugging the coast, to Aberdeen. Prior to this date, as the reader knows, the East Coast route had become merged in the West Coast at Larbert Junction, and its through coaches had been hauled by the Caledonian Company over the 100 miles and more between there and Aberdeen under stringent "facility clauses." Now, by the completion of the two great bridges, the East Coast companies had a separate route of their own as far north as Kinnaber Junction, thirty-nine miles only from Aberdeen. Between Kinnaber and Aberdeen, moreover, they had obtained running powers over the Caledonian line.

Thus the Forth Bridge meant two improvements in East Coast conditions — a through run with their own engines all the way both to Perth and to Aberdeen, and the increase of their former small advantage in mileage to nine miles in the case of London–Perth, and $16\frac{1}{2}$ between the Metropolis and the "Granite City." The result was that they were able at once to accelerate their best train—the eight p.m. from King's Cross—to reach Perth in nine hours fifty-five minutes instead of in ten hours forty-five minutes, and to reach Aberdeen in twelve hours fifteen minutes instead of in thirteen hours twenty minutes. The whole distance from King's Cross to Aberdeen being now $523\frac{1}{2}$ miles, this meant the very creditable journey-speed of just under forty-three miles per hour throughout. But unfortunately the North British "Waverley Station" at Edinburgh proved unequal to the new traffic brought into it, and the result was that the acceleration in "booked" time north of Edinburgh was throughout the summer of 1890 often turned into a "deceleration" in actual practice, while south of Edinburgh the North Eastern and Great Northern refrained from increasing their pace because of the "8½ hours truce" of 1888. On the other hand, the West Coast companies, having a route to the North which did not touch Edinburgh, were able to exert themselves to meet the new competition of the Forth Bridge without regard to that truce; and with an accelerated service only a few minutes longer in "booked" time than their rivals, they quite carried off the palm in actual running.

On 25 July, 1890, the Great Northern directors received from the Board of Trade a draft classification of merchandise traffic, and a schedule of maximum rates and charges applicable thereto, which, in accordance with the provisions of the Railway and Canal Traffic Act of 1888, the Board of Trade proposed to embody in a "Provisional Order" to be submitted to Parliament for sanction in the following session, along with other similar "Orders" applicable to each of the other railway companies. This was the outcome of a most complicated and tedious process of revision of classifications and schedules in which representatives of the Board and of the companies had been engaged ever since the passing of the new Act. The first step, as already noted, had been for the companies themselves to submit a uniform classification and new individual schedules; then, early in 1889, these had been made public by the Board of Trade, and criticisms invited from traders. Needless to say, such criticisms had come in very freely, whereupon it had been decided that the best way to deal with them was to open a public inquiry at which the parties might be represented by counsel and all the *pros* and *cons* fully discussed. At this inquiry, which had commenced on 15 October, 1889, and lasted in all over eighty-five sittings, Mr. Oakley, in his double capacity as Great Northern general manager and hon. secretary of the Railway Companies' Association, Mr. Twelvetrees, the Company's goods manager, and Mr. Barrs, of its solicitors' department, had been unremitting in their attendance and in their exertions to secure a settlement favourable to the companies. Therefore both they and their directors were the more disappointed now to find that, as far as they could judge, the new schedule which the Board of Trade had adopted was not such as would "afford an adequate or fair return upon the large capital invested in the Great Northern undertaking." It looked as if the battle would have to be fought all over again before Parliament in the session of 1891.

Nor was this, momentous though it was, the most important Parliamentary contest to which the Great Northern authorities had to look forward for that session. It was now evident that a pitched battle with the Manchester, Sheffield, and Lincolnshire would be inevitable—a battle in which the stakes on the Great Northern side would be a joint traffic worth about £125,000 a year to it alone, and proper access to joint lines, to which it had contributed nearly three and a half millions. For, under Sir Edward Watkin's influence, the Manchester, Sheffield, and Lincolnshire directors had by this time fully convinced themselves that a new access to London was what was wanted to lift their undertaking out of its lifelong impecuniosity; and a so-called "amicable arrangement" which Sir Edward had suggested to Lord Colville—the construction of a new trunk line jointly—was one which the Great Northern Board could not for one moment entertain. Therefore, when in the autumn of 1890 the Sheffield directors deposited a Bill for a line, ninety-two miles in length, to start from the end of its new North Derbyshire branch at Annesley (the branch which, the reader remembers, it had had "no intention of extending" in 1889) and to run *via* Nottingham and Leicester to join the Metropolitan Extension at Quainton Road, the Great Northern directors, officers, and shareholders realized that they had to face a Parliamentary contest which would rank amongst the greatest in their Company's history. "Gentlemen," said Lord Colville at the half-yearly meeting on 13 February, 1891, "your directors consider it their duty to resist by every means in their power the passing of a measure so subversive of all good faith towards a friendly company, and they trust that in the course they are compelled to take they will meet with the hearty concurrence and support of every shareholder."

Meantime two small additions had to be made to Great Northern mileage in work. From 1 August, 1890, the Beeston and Batley link line, a little over four miles in length, the works of which, as we know, had been long in hand, was at last opened fully, and from 1 January, 1891, the Firsby and Spilsby line, also about four miles, was taken over by purchase. Moreover, from September, 1890, the line of the Halifax High Level Company from Holmfield to Halifax was opened, and worked jointly by the Great Northern and the Lancashire and Yorkshire, and thus the Great Northern obtained access to a new terminal station at King's Cross, Halifax, no less than 325 feet above the level of its existing passenger terminus in that town. To understand fully the advantage of this one must be familiar with the extraordinary physical conformation of the district. Nor were the Company's improvements in the West Riding of Yorkshire yet completed. The junction lines between Pudsey and Low Moor, Bradford, which it had agreed with the Lancashire and Yorkshire Company to make as long before as 1882, had not been put in hand until 1890, and they contained some heavy works. Moreover, at Laister Dyke, in the same neighbourhood, a site for an enlarged station had to be excavated out of solid rock.

Throughout 1890 Mr. Johnson had been making good progress with the London suburban widenings, and in February, 1891, he was able to report that the "up" single-line tunnel north of Southgate had been opened since 15 October, 1890, that the "down" tunnel at the same place was well advanced, and that about one-third had been completed of the new double-line tunnel just outside King's Cross. The engineering difficulties of this latter work had, at the suggestion of the contractor, Mr. Lovatt, been ingeniously surmounted by the use of an invention known as "Jennings' patent needles," with the aid of which it had been found possible to "drive" the tunnel all the way from the north side of the Regent's Canal to the north face. Owing to its nearness to the surface this would not have been possible had the ordinary process of roofing with timber been the only one available, and consequently the "cut and cover" process would have had to have been adopted, to the great disturbance of work in the goods terminus overhead. But by the use of the patent steel bars in place of timber, and by lowering the section of the tunnel about three feet at the crown, the margin left below the surface was increased by five feet six inches. Thus it was possible to carry the work beneath the rails, warehouses, and van-roads of the goods station without opening out to the surface at all.

Thus the Company was in a fair way to the speedy completion of duplicate, and in places triplicate, tracks throughout the whole of its suburban area between Barnet and King's Cross. Nevertheless, it was no nearer getting rid of the "suburban incubus" than it had been at any time within the previous twenty years. "I have from time to time explained to you," Lord Colville had said to the shareholders in February, 1890, "the enormous difficulties which we have to encounter in getting our suburban traffic into London; and we cannot shut our eyes to the impending certainty that ere long we shall be compelled to find means of taking that traffic more thoroughly into the heart of London than we now do." The fact was—though Lord Colville did not put it into so many words—that the extreme limit was fast being reached of the capacity of both the Metropolitan and North London companies to carry Great Northern passengers to and from the City in the busy hours of the day. Mr. John Bell, the Metropolitan manager, would have it, it is true, that the fault lay with the Great Northern time-table arrangements, and that there was ample accommodation still available on his company's "widened lines." But in October, 1890, Mr. Oakley had pointed out to him that between 8.28 a.m. and 10 a.m. daily twenty-eight "up" trains in all passed over those lines, and between 5.1 p.m. and 7.11 p.m. forty-two "down" trains, the average intervals

A GREAT NORTHERN SADDLETANK LOCOMOTIVE.

being 3·143 and 3·095 minutes respectively, and that more time than this was really required, seeing that there were three double junctions to be passed, and that the ingress and egress at the Moorgate Street terminus was by single line. It was impossible for any impartial person to dispute the need for new accommodation.

The great difficulty, of course, was its huge cost. Thus, as long before as 1882, the Great Northern directors had supported the incorporation of the "North Metropolitan Railway and Canal Company," to purchase the Regent's Canal and construct a line along its course from Paddington to King's Cross, and thence, partly on the Canal Company's lands but mainly through houses, to a City station at the Barbican; indeed, they had gone so far as to offer a guarantee upon a portion of its capital. Yet, notwithstanding this, the scheme, owing to its costliness, had found no favour with investors, and its promoters were now anxious to abandon it as far as the City line was concerned. London suburban travellers, it seemed, could grumble heartily, but there appeared to be no public spirit amongst them to do what we have seen done repeatedly by Yorkshiremen—to share, as investors, in the risk of improving the railway facilities.

Nevertheless, if only for the sake of keeping a fair field for their long-distance traffic, the Great Northern authorities could not treat the matter with indifference, and so they had several surveys made for a City extension of their own to leave the main line at Holloway or Finsbury Park. But they found, in Mr. Oakley's words, that "with a reasonably good station in the City, nothing under three millions," *i.e.*, a million a mile, "would look at it," and that therefore an extension of the ordinary kind was "commercially impossible." However, when in December, 1890, the first of London's deep-soil railways was successfully opened on the other side of the Metropolis—a kind of line much cheaper in construction than any London had yet seen—hope of a solution of their difficulty revived at King's Cross.

For the present, however, Mr. Oakley and his colleagues had plenty of Parliamentary work in hand in connection with the Manchester, Sheffield, and Lincolnshire (Extension to London) Bill, and the Provisional Order to confirm the Board of Trade's obnoxious schedule of new rates. The fight over the former came first, beginning on 17 April, 1891, before a House of Commons Committee, presided over by Mr. Woodall. Mr. Littler, as usual, led for the Sheffield; Mr. Pope, Mr. Balfour Browne, and Mr. Cripps were for the Great Northern; Mr. Pope also represented the London and North Western, and Mr. Bidder the Midland. All three of the great north-and-south powers were, it is needless to say, against the Bill.

Nevertheless the Sheffield authorities professed themselves confident of success, and they had no difficulty in making out a strong case for public interest. They could point to the fact that the Great Northern, Midland, and Great Eastern had each in turn established themselves as trunk lines in the teeth of vested interests, and that, while the trade of the country and its population were continually increasing, the last of the new routes to the North—that of the Great Eastern—was already ten years old. Against the Great Northern particularly, Mr. Littler could direct some telling quotations from Lord Colville's speeches as to its urgent need for more accommodation near London, and make effective play with a catch-phrase of Sir Edward Watkin's that there had been too much "poulticing" of the old lines already—that a new line was what the public must have. As to the Fifty Years

Agreement with the Great Northern, the Sheffield counsel said: "We say that, now that Article 14 is gone from it—*i.e.* the article expunged at the instance of the Huddersfield people—this Bill which we are promoting has nothing to do with that agreement. We shall continue to carry the traffic under that agreement as we have done hitherto. The only difference will be that we shall have a route of our own by which we shall also send it."

The case for the Bill lasted until the end of May, Mr. Pollitt, *not* Sir Edward Watkin, being chief witness, and then the landowners' opposition was taken, to be followed by that of the London and North Western and Midland companies. Under the influence, perhaps, of Mr. Bidder's impassioned speech for the latter Company, in which he characterized the case for the Sheffield Company as "acres of rubbish and flummery," the *Times* of 12 June confidently predicted the failure of the Bill, with the result that its editor was threatened in the Committee-room with "committal for contempt"; but the Sheffield authorities maintained their confidence. On this same day, Friday, 12 June, 1891, "Sir Henry Oakley" was called.

Having been knighted but a few weeks since, Sir Henry entered

Sir Henry Oakley.

the box "with all his blushing honours fresh upon him." Under the guidance of Mr. Pope, he plunged at once into the question of the agreement of 1860. "The effect of the construction of this line," said he, "must be the absolute disruption of that agreement, because the existence of a competing interest on the part of the Sheffield Company would be absolutely contrary to its very soul and spirit, which was that the two companies were to unite to do their best in every respect to promote the joint interest." The agreement had been made, he went on to explain, at a time when the Sheffield Company had been in very great difficulties,* so that the Great Northern had had "to put

* "We picked the Sheffield up out of the dirt," the reader may remember Mr. Denison, Q.C., had said in 1873.

its best leg forward" to make the new service with Manchester remunerative. The Great Northern had then taken "the labouring oar" as regards speed, and supplied the rolling stock, until the Sheffield had turned the corner on the road to improvement; and since then the traffic *via* Retford had been worked to all intents and purposes as a partnership without any discord between the officers or any complaint from one Board to the other, until this "bolt from the blue" had appeared. The intervention of Mr. Underdown in the Huddersfield case had been an error in the Sheffield view, seeing that Mr. Pollitt now said that Huddersfield was not in the agreement, "and it does seem to our limited vision," said Sir Henry, "especially hard that advantage should now be taken of the excision of Clause 14 from the agreement owing to the error of their own manager, to justify the Sheffield in departing from what was its original object and intention."

"It is altogether an illusion," he continued, "to attribute to the possession of arbitrary running powers by the Great Northern any adequate means of repairing the loss that must inevitably ensue from the transfer of the goodwill of the Sheffield Company to another route." Such running powers could be made use over so great a distance only as a last resource to get some traffic, and they were provided for in the agreement as a remedy against slackness of energy on the part of either of the companies, and not with any idea of separation of interests. Even on the improved terms offered by Mr. Pollitt in 1889 there would not be any appreciable recompense for the injury the Great Northern would suffer. "Your argument, I take it," interposed the Chairman, "is that the construction of this new line to London will convert a co-partnership into a fierce competition"; and Sir Henry assented, glad to find that his points were going home in the right quarter.

Then Mr. Balfour Browne took up the examination, and in answer to him Sir Henry explained the injury which the new line would inflict on the Great Northern in regard to the Cheshire lines and the South Yorkshire coalfield. "I have utterly failed to persuade myself," he said in answer to another interposition from the Chairman, "that Mr. Pollitt or any other manager with a burden of six millions of new capital on his back, will not send all the traffic he possibly can over the new line on which he has spent the money. But if he does what he has promised, and continues to send by our line for the sake of the bonus, his traffic case for the Bill has largely gone." Then, after a few more questions and answers the hearing was adjourned to the following Monday, and so the Great Northern manager was left an interval before him in which to prepare a few more shafts for the renewal of his evidence on that day.

In his vigorous speech for the Midland company, Mr. Bidder had drawn pointed attention to the financial position of the Sheffield Company. "They have got nearly seven millions of unexecuted capital powers at the present moment," said he, "and I should have thought that with a reasonable appetite in the way of aggression and competition six millions and three-quarters was about enough to deal with at once, without coming for a further six millions to carry out further aggressions." Upon this the Chairman had suggested to the Sheffield counsel that it would be convenient if a statement were furnished showing the extent to which the Company had uncompleted liabilities on hand, and this statement had accordingly been put in just before the commencement of Sir Henry Oakley's evidence on the Friday. Now it occurred to him that he and his assistant, Mr. W. J. Grinling, could not employ the interval till the Monday better than in elaborating this a little for the further enlightenment of the Committee.

The result was the preparation of a statement that came in as a dramatic finish to the Great Northern manager's examination-in-chief on that day. It showed that the Sheffield Company was already committed to raise capital to the extent of £5,000,394 for new lines and £2,109,264 for general purposes, and that during the previous ten years it had raised £4,002,264 only. "How has that £4,002,264 been raised?" asked Mr. Balfour Browne. "It has been raised by debenture stock, guaranteed stock, and preference stock." "Has any of it been raised by ordinary stock?" "None."

That the thrust had gone home was proved by an immediate interruption from Mr. Littler. "It is an extraordinary thing," said he, "that the Great Northern should start such evidence as this now without having based a syllable of cross-examination upon it, and I shall ask to recall Mr. Pollitt." "If there is anything that you want to explain you are entitled to recall Mr. Pollitt," retorted Mr. Pope. But when a few minutes later the Sheffield counsel rose to cross-examine, he could find nothing better to suggest about the figures than that they were "rather the business of the shareholders"; and in his speech in reply upon the whole case on the following day, his detailed criticism of them, carefully prepared overnight, amounted to little more than that their production had been "a little bit of malice on the Great Northern's part." Mr. Pollitt had *not* been recalled.

At the conclusion of Mr. Littler's speech, which lasted well on into the afternoon of this day—16 June, 1891—the hearing ended, but the Chairman then announced that the Committee wished to have a little time to deliberate. Accordingly they adjourned until five o'clock. At that hour in a crowded room, and amid much pent-up excitement,

Mr. Woodall gave their decision. "It is not necessary," he said, "to assure all those who are interested in the case how careful, how conscientious an amount of attention has been given to all that has been presented to the Committee during this very long hearing, and after deliberating very fully upon all the material points, the Committee find the preamble *not* proved." The Bill was rejected.

Meanwhile the hearing of the Provisional Orders to enforce the new Board of Trade classification and schedules of rates had been commenced before a Joint Committee of the two Houses, presided over by the Duke of Richmond. The London and North Western Company's Order had been taken first; but, as it had been agreed that its provisions, when settled, should be taken as models for the other companies, it had been necessary for the Great Northern's counsel and its officers—Sir Henry Oakley, Mr. Twelvetrees, and Mr. Barrs—to be in attendance from the first. They had to continue their exertions until 17 July, when, after a hearing which added forty-eight days to the eighty-five days already consumed by the preliminary Board of Trade inquiry, the first batch of Orders passed through Committee. These, which applied to the nine companies having termini in London, were issued on 5 August, 1891, but they were not to come into force until 1 August, 1892. It was impossible as yet to gauge their effect upon railway revenue.

Though quite overshadowed by the other business just recorded, the Bill which the Great Northern Company itself promoted in 1891 was of some importance. It sought powers for the extension of the Leen Valley line from Annesley northwards about twelve miles to Langwith, the extension to more than double its existing size of the City goods depôt at Farringdon Street—a very costly work—and various widenings and improvements of the main line and branches. As a result of the rejection of the Sheffield Bill the Leen Valley project was withdrawn, but, nevertheless, in its Act as passed the Great Northern took powers to raise a million of new capital. Following upon the new million authorized so recently as the preceding session, this indicated an accelerated rate of capital expenditure—a tendency, in short, to return to the policy so long followed prior to 1884 of adding to capital account at the rate of a million a year. Two elements in this have not yet been alluded to. These were a heavy current expense for new waggons (partly as the result of the Midland's latest *coup d'état*, the purchase of the whole stocks of the colliery owners trading on its lines) and the cost of oil-gas works for the lighting of carriages, which were being erected at Holloway, at Doncaster, and at Leeds. An experiment with electric lighting had proved unsuccessful except for trains *en bloc*, and so the directors had decided to adopt "Pope's system" of oil-gas lighting in place of the oil lamps used up to this date.

Meantime, immediately upon the rejection of their Bill, Sir Edward Watkin and his colleagues had announced their determination to revive their extension scheme in the following session, and they had repeated their invitation to the Great Northern to join them in its promotion and construction. "The obvious reply," said Lord Colville at the Great Northern meeting on 10 August, 1891, "is a refusal to join in, and spend our capital upon, a scheme which can only be successful by diverting traffic which comes within the agreement existing between the two companies. But if the Sheffield Company desires to modify the existing agreement, we are quite willing to listen to any fair and reasonable proposition."

The outcome was that in the autumn of the year negotiations were formally opened between the two companies through Sir Henry Oakley and Mr. Pollitt. Sir Henry had already said in his evidence, that "the price of the new line" to London must be the abolition of the old agreement and the loss of its "bonus mileage" to the Sheffield Company, and this, with full access for the Great Northern to its joint property in Manchester, Liverpool, and Cheshire by running powers over all the Manchester, Sheffield, and Lincoln lines west of Sheffield and north of Nottingham, was the irreducible minimum on which he now insisted as the condition of the withdrawal of his Company's opposition to the re-deposited Sheffield Bill. Mr. Pollitt, on his part, asked and obtained for his Company, in return, running powers over all the Great Northern lines north of Doncaster, *i.e.*, in the West Riding. It was further arranged that a "living wage," namely, 33⅓ per cent. of the gross receipts, should be allowed by the owning to the running company in either case. The Great Northern, moreover, obtained an important advantage by securing a half-share in the "central station" projected by the Sheffield Company in Nottingham. This, together with the running powers over the new line northwards from that town, promised to secure for it what had long been an object of its ambition, a route through Nottingham to Sheffield and Manchester, alternative to the existing route *via* Retford. Nevertheless, the agreement was admittedly a *pis aller* so far as the Great Northern was concerned.

In this same autumn of 1891 a project was set on foot which gave good promise of relieving the Great Northern Company from the worst weight of its "suburban incubus." In October of the year Mr. J. H. Greathead, the pioneer of deep-soil tunnelling, and Mr. Francis Fox submitted a scheme to the directors at King's Cross for a line, similar in construction to the City and South London Railway, to run from Finsbury Park by Drayton Park and Essex Road to a City terminus at Finsbury Pavement, the traffic to be worked by electricity. To this the Great Northern authorities objected that it meant a "break of gauge" at Finsbury Park, whereupon Messrs. Greathead and Fox replied that it would be quite feasible, not only to make the tunnels big enough for the standard gauge, but to haul the ordinary Great Northern carriages through them by electric motors. A week or two later they came again to King's Cross with a positive assurance on this latter point from Mr. Siemens, the electrician. So confident, indeed, were they and their backers of the merits of this amended plan that, to be in time for the session of 1892, they deposited without further delay a Bill under the title of the "Great Northern and City Railway." Thereupon the Great Northern directors declared their intention to support the scheme by every fair and legitimate means in their power.

This, however, aroused the strong opposition of the Metropolitan Company, who contended that it was a breach of the agreement of 1869 under which the Great Northern was running its suburban trains over "the widened lines" between King's Cross and Moorgate Street. So when Sir Henry Oakley appeared to give evidence in favour of the Great Northern and City Bill in June, 1892, he found himself cross-examined on behalf of the Metropolitan by his opponent of the previous year, Mr. Littler, who, of course, attempted to turn the tables in the matter of agreement-keeping. But there could be no doubt about there being "a little bit of malice" this time, for when the case for the opponents began, Sir Edward Watkin, as chairman of the Metropolitan, himself came into the box, and described the action of the Great Northern as "simply a repudiation" of the agreement of 1869. "I know," he said, "that it has been stated in this room that there is no specific clause saying that the 'widened lines' shall be used; but I have always understood that honesty always interprets these agreements that where two companies have agreed and where one has performed his part of the agreement, the other should do so without any denial of it." Nevertheless, the Committee passed the Great Northern and City Bill.

The Manchester, Sheffield, and Lincoln Extension to London Bill also passed this session, and, besides getting powers under this to make a junction line in Nottingham to connect with the proposed joint "central station" there, the Great Northern, by an Act of its own, obtained the powers from which it had withdrawn in the previous session, to extend its Leen Valley line to Langwith. It also obtained authority to raise yet another million of capital—the third million in successive years, exclusive of borrowing powers. This suggested that such "rest" as had been given to the capital account between 1884 and 1887 had been artificial and was now being paid for.

Early in June, 1892, the new Maiden Lane tunnel at King's Cross, and at the close of the same month the "down" single-line tunnel between Southgate and Barnet, were opened for traffic—works which completed the duplicate tracks, both "up" and "down," all the way between King's Cross and Barnet. But by this time two new important improvements had been put in hand within the suburban area. These were the construction of a viaduct over the main lines at Haringay, to form a return road for engines bringing trains to the sidings there— a very difficult work, because it had to be built "on the skew" with spans of unequal length, and, of course, a sharp rise and fall in gradient—and a further widening at Holloway, to provide a separate track for "down" goods traffic.

This latter work necessitated the placing of a new large plate-girder bridge across the Holloway Road, and great interest was excited in the locality when the news spread that the crucial part of this work—the moving of the girders into position overhead—was to be carried out as one operation in the small hours of the morning of Sunday, 2 October, 1892. The two girders, each 110 feet long and 10 feet high, were first built up on the south abutment of the bridge on a series of four steel rollers. Then, alongside the abutment, projecting about one foot above its top, two piles were driven some eight feet into the ground. To the bridge itself and to the top of these piles pulley blocks were then fixed, and to these strong steel wire was attached in connection with a powerful steam winch placed in a siding some distance away. On the Thursday, the Stockton Forge Company's engineers built alongside the southern abutment two large trestles, each fitted with twelve wheels capable of running on ordinary rails, and on the Friday morning the bridge was moved forward by means of the wire and the winch, until it overhung the abutments by about twenty feet, and slightly projected over the trestles. Then operations were suspended until the last tram-car should have passed at Saturday midnight. Then, despite the hour, a crowd of many thousand persons collected, and these were with difficulty kept back by policemen, while the tram rails and pavement were taken up and replaced by the rails for the trestles which the engineers had ready to hand in sections laid on a strong timber framework. About 3.30 a.m. these preparations were completed, and then, just as the first streaks of dawn were beginning to light up the faces of the undiminished crowd, the steam winch was set to work. Motion was at once imparted to the trestles, and soon the huge mass of the bridge was moving slowly and steadily forward amid the hearty cheers of the onlookers. Every now and then a short stoppage had to be made to ascertain that the tackle had kept in order and that the strains were equally distributed, but with this exception no hitch occurred, and the girders were got into exact position and the roadway replaced in time for the passage underneath of the first Sunday tram.

Meantime, work of a very different character was engrossing the attention, and entrenching also upon the Sundays, of Mr. Twelvetrees, the goods manager, and a large staff of regular and supple-

BRIDGE OVER HOLLOWAY ROAD WHEN IN COURSE OF DUPLICATION.

mentary clerks at King's Cross. This was the preparation of the new rates in accordance with the Provisional Order of 1891. Already the time originally fixed for these to come into force had gone by, and even the five months' grace—till 1 January, 1893—which the companies had subsequently obtained, was proving quite inadequate for the enormous amount of clerical work entailed upon them. For comparing the new "cast-iron" Board of Trade classification with the more elastic "Clearing House" classification under which the companies had worked up to this time, it had been found that of 3000 items contained in the latter, 341 had been raised in class, 192 had been reduced, and about 900 omitted altogether, and with regard to every one of these separate advices had to be sent to every station. The number of separate rates affected was 13,000,000 on the Great

Northern alone. Moreover, seeing that the Provisional Orders for the non-London companies had not been issued until 20 June, 1892—nearly a year after the others—the fixing of the through rates—by far the most difficult part of the work—had had to be left to the last. The result was that the officials found it impossible to do more than to insert the ordinary "class-rates" in the rate-books by the date fixed for their publication—16 December, 1892. The "special rates," under which the bulk of the traffic was nominally carried, were all left to be dealt with afterwards.

But if by the tactics thus forced upon them the railway authorities thought to "score off" the traders, they very soon found out their mistake. The charging of the new maximum class rates as the actual rates evoked at once a storm of indignation throughout the country; the newspapers were flooded with complaints; meetings were held, and deputations demanding redress waited upon the Board of Trade. Worse than this, traders generally refused to pay the new charges, and the whole system of traffic accounting was in danger of becoming disorganized. Coming on the top of all the new and strenuous work which had been entailed upon them since the passing of the Act of 1888, this agitation drove the goods managers and their clerks well-nigh to despair. The only practical remedy was temporarily to restore the old "Clearing House classification" until the new maxima could be adapted to the new one, and on the Great Northern this latter work was taken so energetically in hand that at the half-yearly meeting on 14 February, 1893, Lord Colville was able to announce that upwards of 100,000 of its rates had already been amended in the new books. "It is somewhat remarkable," he added, "that during the whole of the outcry not a word has been uttered by traders as to the reductions that have been made."

In the session of 1893 the Great Northern and Midland companies obtained powers to acquire jointly the eastern section of the Eastern and Midlands Company's system—lines, 113 miles in length, extending from Lynn to Cromer, Yarmouth, and Norwich. The consideration agreed upon was £1,200,000 of Midland and Great Northern rent-charge stock, entitled to a fixed dividend of 3 per cent. per annum, but the liability of £36,000 per annum thus involved was not to fall immediately upon the purchasing companies. The stock was to be divided into £748,000 of A stock, and £452,000 of B stock, and while the former was to receive 3 per cent. after the first year, the latter was to get no dividend until June, 1897, and thereafter a progressive dividend not reaching the full 3 per cent. until 1901. Thus it will be seen that the two companies acquired these

2 E

113 miles of agricultural railway at a decidedly low price, and when the seaside traffic between London and Cromer, Sheringham, etc., is more fully developed, the bargain is likely to prove to have been a very good one for the Great Northern.

This new acquisition was vested with what had been the western section of the Eastern and Midlands in the Midland and Great Northern Joint Committee from 1 July, 1893; and it increased the Great Northern's mileage total to 879, of which no less than 228 miles represented shares in joint undertakings. From 1 December, 1893, the new junction line, about two miles in length, between Dudley Hill and Low Moor, Bradford, was opened, and in 1894 the Company took over by perpetual lease, under an Act of that year, the twelve miles of the Stamford and Essendine Railway which it had worked ever since its opening in 1856. Under the same Act powers were obtained to enable the Company to purchase jointly with the Lancashire and Yorkshire the Halifax High Level line, three and a quarter miles. These operations raised the Company's mileage, at 30 June, 1895, to 894 miles, and its capital to just about £46,000,000—over £50,000 per mile. Evidently the cheap price at which the new agricultural lines had been acquired had been more than balanced by the expenditure on existing mileage in London and Yorkshire. It should be added that the Company was working, in addition, forty-four miles of lines owned by other companies, and running trains over 121 "foreign" miles more.

Meantime, thanks to the "great coal strike," which had lasted over no less than sixteen weeks of the second half of 1893, the Company's dividend had suffered most severely, having sunk for that year so low as 3 per cent.; and the same and other adverse influences continuing throughout 1894, it rose in that year to £3 10s. per cent. only. Under these circumstances it could not be surprising that at the half-yearly meeting on 13 February, 1895, shareholders complained rather strongly. However, the Right Hon. W. L. Jackson, M.P.—who was in a few weeks to succeed Lord Colville as chairman of the Company—was felt to strike the right note when he said, "Do not let us decry our own position too much. We have difficulties enough to meet; but we are going to face them, and we think we shall get through them." Already this prophecy has, to a large extent, been fulfilled.*

In the summer of 1893 the rivalry between the East Coast, West Coast, and Midland-Scotch routes had resulted in the simultaneous putting-on of a new midday service by each of the three, in all of which dining-car accommodation had been given for the first time to

* September, 1897.

third-class, penny-a-mile passengers. But since "the race to Edinburgh" no speed-cutting worthy the name had been attempted, and eight and a half hours still remained the best time alike between King's Cross and Waverley and Euston and Prince's Street. North of Edinburgh, however, the North British, having by this time put its house into

better order, had, in 1894, quickened the twelve and a quarter hours service from London to Aberdeen, initiated in 1890, to eleven hours thirty-five minutes, and had thus beaten the West Coast's best time by fifteen minutes. This was the state of things at the beginning of the summer season of 1895.

Late in June of that year the West Coast companies announced *inter alia* that, to make sure of a connection with the Great North of Scotland, their best train, the 8 p.m. from Euston, would be accelerated from 1 July to reach Aberdeen at 7.40 a.m., five minutes only behind the East Coast. The East Coast replied *inter alia* by accelerating their best, the 8 p.m.

THE RIGHT HON. W. L. JACKSON, M.P.

from King's Cross, to arrive at 7.20. This latter was a very important step, because it meant that for the first time since August, 1888, a train was to be booked to run between London and Edinburgh in less than eight and a half hours, the precise time now allowed for the East Coast night express being eight hours thirteen minutes.

Of course the West Coast remonstrated, whereupon the East Coast authorities replied that "the informal understanding" of 1888 had never been meant to apply to the night trains. And indeed, whether it was meant so to apply or not, it did not seem reasonable to attempt to tie the shorter route down indefinitely to a time which was quite easy going for the day train, even with its twenty minutes stop for luncheon at York. On the other hand, the West Coast could not be expected to submit to take second place not only for Edinburgh, but for Perth and Aberdeen—places which had long been regarded as its strongholds. Needless to say, the authorities of the North Western and

Caledonian companies had no such intention, and to prove conclusively that they had not, they announced on 15 July, 1895, by huge blue posters on the portals of Euston and elsewhere, that from that very evening their time from London to Aberdeen would be eleven hours, *i.e.* twenty minutes better than their rivals'. The same night they did this feat with fourteen minutes to spare, and on the morning of the 17th their train ran into Aberdeen at 6.21, no less than thirty-nine minutes before time.

An East Coast Third-Class Dining Car.

The East Coast reply did not come until 22 July, and then it was not very effective in light of the actual times which the West Coast was making. All it did was to cap the latter's booked time by fifteen minutes by making its own booked time ten hours forty-five minutes. To do this the Great Northern booked London to York in three hours thirty-five minutes, the same time as its first "racing" allowance in 1888. The West Coast put out no answering advertisement, but simply settled down quietly to do its sixteen miles longer journey in five minutes less than its rival, *i.e.* ten hours thirty-five minutes. As in 1888 the East Coast ran the heavier trains, but the loads by both were larger than in 1888. A more important difference was that on the

East Coast booked times of departure were punctiliously observed at every stopping station, the train being often kept back thereby, while the West Coast observed no booked times at all. The result was that, though by spurting north of Arbroath the East Coast drivers managed

AN EAST COAST DINING-CAR TRAIN.

all through the week to be in at Aberdeen five minutes (once seven minutes) before time, every morning they found the West Coast "racer" already there.

Though perplexed by the silence of the other side, who still made no announcement of an earlier arrival than 7 a.m., the East Coast proclaimed a further quickening of twenty minutes for the following Monday, 29 July. To this the Great Northern contributed seven minutes, making its time to York two minutes better than the best booked time in 1888, though five minutes under its actual best performance then. The train on the Monday consisted of eleven vehicles weighing 179 tons, and the engine employed to Grantham was not, for once in a way, one of the "8 ft. singles," but a "7 ft. 7 in.," with inside cylinders (18 × 26) and no bogie. Nevertheless it drew the heavy load over the first 105 miles in the remarkable time of one hour fifty-three minutes. Then an "8 ft. single" came on, and York was reached in three hours twenty-four minutes—just two minutes behind the "record" of 1888, but with nearly double the load. However, when Aberdeen was reached at 6.20, the West Coast with a load of about 160 tons had been there fifteen minutes already. Moreover on the following morning, 31 July, the West Coast train arrived at 5.59, one minute within ten hours. Yet at Euston Square and on every North Western parcels cart the blue posters still read: "Aberdeen arr. 7.0 a.m."

Throughout the "grouse" fortnight the West Coast continued to be in invariably first at Aberdeen, the East Coast runs being usually spoiled by signal stops or by undue delays at stations caused by the greater number of its passengers. But on the morning of Thursday, the 15th, there was almost a tie at Kinnaber Junction, the West Coast getting the road (which thence to Aberdeen, it will be remembered, is the same by both routes) by about a minute only. On the following Monday morning, 19 August, the "be-ready" bells, it is said, rang together in the junction signal-box, and the Caledonian signalman magnanimously gave the road to the "foreign" train. However this may be, on that morning the East Coast train for the first time in the "race" ran in ahead at 6.17.

Meantime Mr. Cockshott and his colleagues had put out a new notice, dated 16 August, and this time it *was* an effective reply. It announced that from the following Monday, 19 August, the East Coast time would be 9 hours 40 minutes—nineteen minutes better than the best run of its rivals up to date. As far as the Great Northern was concerned, this meant that London to York was to be booked in 3 hours 18 minutes—four minutes better than its "record" of 1888. The train on the eventful Monday night consisted of an eight-wheeled sleeping car and five six-wheeled coaches, weighing in all 105 tons. The engine was Mr. Stirling's No. 668, an "8 ft. single" of the older class. Grantham, 105 miles, was reached in the quite unprecedented time of 105 minutes 52 seconds; and thence, with another "8 ft. single," No. 775, the phenomenal run of 82¾ miles in 79 minutes 9 seconds was accomplished, making the arrival time at York 11.9, and beating the 1888 "record" by thirteen minutes, with a train of about the same weight. Despite several signal checks Edinburgh was reached in 6¾ hours, but the North British authorities would not allow a "before time" departure, either there or at Dundee, and so the race was lost. For though Aberdeen was reached at 5.31—nine minutes before time—the unconquerable West Coast, with as heavy a load, had been there fifteen minutes already, having done its 540 miles in 555 minutes.

On the following night, 20–21 August, there was another superb race. The Great Northern arrived at York at 11.7, two minutes better than the night before, and as the North Eastern got a clear road this time, and the North British threw aside punctiliousness, victory seemed assured. But as the racer passed Montrose, and the enthusiasts on board, stiff with excitement, glued their eyes on the west, the steam of the rival train came clearly into view; and fairly and squarely, though by less than a minute, the West Coast got the "line clear" at Kinnaber, bringing their train into Aberdeen at 4.58, while the East Coast, checked at the junction and beyond, did not arrive till 5.11.

On Wednesday, 21 August, the East Coast authorities made a final, and what they thought must be a conclusive effort. With a load of 101 tons behind it, "No. 668"—the same engine as on the Monday and Tuesday nights—passed Peterborough, 76¼ miles, in 72 minutes, and in 101 minutes Grantham, 105¼, was reached—63·3 miles per hour throughout so far. But with the better gradients, there came even a better rate than this. Between Grantham and York, 82¾ miles —with "No. 775" again on, as on the two previous nights, a speed of 65·5 miles per hour was maintained throughout, and the train drew up at York platform at 11.1, 188 miles in 181 minutes inclusive, or 179 minutes "running time." At the time of "the race to Edinburgh" Mr. Stirling had said that London to York in three hours was quite possible, and now it had been done. A "record" to Edinburgh of 6 hours 19 minutes followed, and Aberdeen was reached at 4.40, 14½ minutes ahead of the rival train, though it too had done its best time up to date. The East Coast run had been at 60 miles an hour throughout, with 3½ minutes to spare.

After this there was no more racing, for the East Coast companies thought they had done enough for honour; but on the following night, 22–23 August, the West Coast, with the field to itself, gave an "exhibition run," which beat all records. The whole journey was done in 8 hours 32 minutes, a speed of 63⅓ miles per hour throughout.

The East Coast had to be content with gaining an advantage of thirty-five minutes in booked time under the truce thereafter patched up.*

Fifty years before, in 1845, when the Great Northern had been a "monster infant" not yet christened, the best daily time between London and York had been 7 hours 40 minutes, and the "racing" time exclusive of stops, as performed in that "feat unparalleled in the annals of railway travelling in the kingdom," Hudson's "special" to Gateshead on 18 June, 1844, 5 hours 38 minutes. Now, in 1895, the racing time was 2 hours 59 minutes, and the best daily time as fixed after the race to Aberdeen, 3 hours 28 minutes. With this concrete example of what it had done in the first fifty years of its career, we will leave for the present the history of the Company which was first known to the world as "the London and York."

* For facts cited in the above account of the "race to the north," I must acknowledge my indebtedness to Rev. W. J. Scott's pamphlet *Kinnaber*, Mr. Rous-Marten's articles in *The Engineer*, Mr. Acworth's articles in *The Times*, and Mr. Norman Macdonald's articles in *The Scotsman*.

GREAT NORTHERN EXPRESS PASSENGER LOCOMOTIVE. "8-feet Single."

INDEX

A

Aberdeen, first G. N. bookings to, 146.
  time to in 1876, 317.
  ,, in 1889, 396.
  ,, in 1890, 403.
  Race to, 419,
Accidents on G. N., 136, 228, 298, 306, 321, 349, 350, 353, 373.
Act, cost of passing original G. N., 62.
  Cardwell, 141, 151, 183.
Agreement, Fifty Years, with M. S. & L., 161, 191, 253, 288, 341, 344, 347, 393, 395, 409, 413.
Alexandra Palace, 232, 280, 293, 294, 304.
Alliance of existing companies against G. N. project, 19.
  with M. S. & L. Company, 161.
  Triple, 182.
  policy of Triple reversed, 191.
  East Coast, 221.
  between G.N. and L. & N.W., 283.
  between Midland and M. S. & L., 283.
Allport, James, 8, 93, 95, 142, 155, 157, 165, 184, 192, 241, 246-255, 272, 274, 288, 290.
Amalgamation proposed with Eastern Counties, 49.
  with Direct Northern, 52.
  proposed, of South Yorkshire, 116.
  proposed, of Ambergate, 116.
  proposed, with Midland, 122.
  Attitude of Parliament to, 133, 141.
  of Ambergate, 145.
  various from 1860 to 1866, 235.
  proposed, of Great Eastern, 319, 325.
  proposed, of M. S. & L. jointly with L. & N. W., 327.
Ambergate line (Grantham to Nottingham), 117, 121, 145.
Amsinck, Major, 10, 25, 26, 298.
Arbitration, *re* pooling of passenger traffic, 99, 105, 155, 160.
  re coal traffic rates, 241, 244, 245.

Astell, William, 15, 16, 23, 36, 54, 64.
Astell, J. H., 15, 16, 298, 378.

B

Ballard, Stephen, 80.
Barriers to G. N. Service, 93, 95, 96, 134, 145, 151, 152.
Battle of the Railways, 157.
Baxter, Robert, 2, 26, 32, 62, 70, 72, 101, 116, 119, 129, 164, 207, 211, 240, 249-255, 287, 328-331.
Beckett, Sir E., see Denison, E. B.
Bills, G. N., original, passed, 55.
  Deviation, rejected, 67, 77.
  for Church, 147.
  G. N. and M. S. & L. arrangement, 164.
  to legalize fraudulent Stock, 172.
  Three Companies', 182.
  Midland extension to London, 195.
  Derbyshire extensions, 264.
  Newark and Leicester, 266, 270.
  Melton and Leicester, 292.
  Bradford and Thornton, 292.
  Cheshire Lines, 298.
  G. N. further powers, 298.
  Spalding and Lincoln, 332.
  Various powers, 345.
  M. S. & L. extension to London, 408-412.
  G. N. and City, 414.
Block System of Signalling, 140, 193, 230, 231, 262, 297, 306, 314, 323, 357, 374.
Board of Trade, adverse report on original G. N. scheme, 30, 35.
  inquiry into Railway Rates, 404.
Brake-power, 322, 348, 381.
Brassey, Thomas, 63, 80, 90.
Bridges, G. N., 79, 113, 115, 281, 336, 347, 357, 397, 398, 415.
Bruce, Henry, 42, 45.
Bury, Edward, 72, 88.

INDEX

C

Calls upon original G. N. Shareholders, 65, 67, 68, 71.
Cardwell Act, 141, 151, 183.
Carriages, passenger, G. N., 72, 163, 343, 365, 420.
Cawkwell, William, 185.
Chairmen, G. N. Board—
  William Astell, 54.
  Edmund Denison, 64.
  Colonel Packe, 212.
  Hon. O. Duncombe, 298.
  Lord Colville of Culross, 338.
  Rt. Hon. W. L. Jackson, 418.
Chaplin, Charles, 11, 16, 36.
Church, at Doncaster, for employees, 138, 147, 149.
Clarke, Seymour, 88, 98, 153, 155, 161, 194, 239, 245.
Coal Traffic, defects of, in Lincolnshire, 11.
  case for G. N. Bill, 36, 37.
  early importance of to G. N., 101.
  opening of, to London, 103.
  difficulties of S. Yorks, 115.
  trains stopped in South Yorkshire, 131.
  increase of, 143.
  complaints about, 144.
  effect of Ambergate line on, 145.
  stunted development of, 187.
  agreement with Midland as to, 196.
  fighting with Great Eastern for, 207.
  outcome of Midland agreement as to, 236.
  arbitration on, 244.
  rate war, 250.
  Mr. Baxter's new line for, 254.
  G. N. position as to Derbyshire, 263.
  effect of "coal famine" on, 286, 299.
  re-opening of, from Derbyshire, 304.
  effect of a "great coal strike" on, 418.
Cockshott, Francis P., 231, 277, 309, 321, 343, 385, 422.
Colville of Culross, Lord, 338, 355, 418.
Committee of Inquiry, 176.
Competition, great, for passenger traffic in 1851, 103.
  in 1856, 157.
  result of, 159.
  in 1857, 164.
  in 1862, 193.
  for coal traffic, in 1870-1, 252.
  effect of Midland on G. N., 314.
  cause of decline in G. N. prosperity, 357.

Confederacy, Euston Square, 93, 98 143, 151, 159.
Courtenay, Lord, 34, 40, 46.
Cubitt, William, 23, 25, 28, 37, 114.
Cubitt, Joseph, 71, 80, 84, 140.
Cubitt, Benjamin, 72.
Cubitt, Lewis, 114.

D

Denison, Edmund—frontispiece, 2, 12, 16, 20, 30, 36, 54, 64, 78, 81, 82, 99, 100, 102, 107, 108, 110, 120, 122, 129, 131, 138, 144, 148, 153, 158, 166-178, 185-190, 197, 211, 298.
Denison, E. B. (afterwards Sir Edmund Beckett and Lord Grimthorpe), 35, 130, 148, 175, 186, 219, 254-5, 272, 289, 292, 298, 330, 356, 374, 375.
Denison, Christopher, 212, 358, 369.
Derbyshire coalfield, 117, 145, 187, 195, 205, 236-255, 263, 273, 287, 304, 312, 347, 360.
Direct Northern Scheme, 10, 15, 24, 26, 30, 33, 50, 52.
Dividends, G. N., 106, 115, 127, 147, 172, 212, 235, 280, 298, 310, 366, 397, 418.
Doncaster, 32, 86, 137, 138, 148, 149.
Duncombe, Hon. O., 15, 16, 298, 336, 338.

E

Eastern Counties Railway Company, 4, 9, 13, 19, 47, 49, 51, 69, 97, 108-9, 145, 205.
East Coast Route, 6, 74, 220-223, 243, 317, 358, 385-8, 396, 419-424.
Edinburgh, first through service to, by G. N., 96.
  first service beyond, 145.
  race to, 379, 385-8.
  (See also East Coast Route.)
Engineers, G. N., Cubitt, William, 23.
  Cubitt, Joseph, 71.
  Fraser, John, 260.
  Johnson, Richard, 263.
  Fowler, John, 340.
  Beswick, William, 348
Engines, see Locomotives.
English and Scotch Alliance, 154, 183, 192, 223, 242, 244.
Euston Square Confederacy, 93, 98, 110, 142-3, 151, 159, 165.

INDEX

Extensions, G. N., from 1860 to 1866, 234.
  in the West Riding, 260.
  in Derbyshire, 263.
  in Leicestershire, 266.
  from 1871 to 1876, 311.
  from 1876 to 1884, 366.
  from 1884 to 1888, 389.
  from 1888 to 1895, 418.

F

Fens or "towns," 20.
  laying G. N. line over, 80.
Fifty Years Agreement with M. S. and L., 161, 191, 253, 288, 341, 344, 347, 393, 395, 409, 413.
Finsbury Park Station, 203, 257, 373, 376.
Firth, William, 111, 266-7.
Fowler, Sir John, 73, 77, 202, 208, 211, 282, 340, 358.
Fraser, John, 260, 267-8, 285, 299, 304, 348.
Frauds, Redpath, 166-178.

G

Gibbs, Joseph, 3, 5, 13, 16.
Gladstone, W. E., 20, 36.
  arbitration by, 99, 100, 105, 106, 150, 165, 244.
Goods Traffic, 17, 87, 97, 135, 295-6, 301-2, 304, 314-5, 329, 388.
Great Northern Railway Company—
  first Bill rejected, 4.
  scheme revived, 13.
  united with London and York, 16.
  Act obtained, 55.
  first general meeting, 56.
  first contracts let, 63.
  first alliance with M. S. & L., 77.
  opening of, to London, 90.
  begins coal traffic to London, 103.
  fierce competition with, 103.
  original cost of, 127.
  locomotive head-quarters, 137.
  Fifty Years Agreement with M. S. & L., 161.
  huge frauds on, 178.
  position established, 179.
  coal traffic agreement with Midland, 196.
  position of, in the West Riding, 198.
  attitude on City extension, 201.
  difficulties with Great Eastern, 204 *et seq.*
  position with regard to East Coast Route, 220.
  battle with Midland *re* coal rates, 244-255.

G. N. Railway Co.—*continued.*
  extensions in the West Riding, 260.
  scheme for tapping Derbyshire coalfields, 263.
  extensions in Leicestershire, 266.
  speed on in 1871, 277.
  alliance with L. & N. W., 283.
  review of financial condition of, 311.
  negotiations and fight with Great Eastern, 315-332.
  position of, in 1878, 336.
  speed on, in 1883, 364.
  position of, in 1884, 356.
    ,, ,, in 1886, 373.
  speed on, in 1888, 387.
  fight with M. S. & L., 408.
  position of, in 1893, 418.
Great Eastern Railway Company, 205-211, 216, 219, 224-7, 233, 242, 251, 254-5, 315-6, 318-320, 324, 326, 328-332 (see also Eastern Counties Railway Company).
Grimthorpe, Lord, see Denison, E. B.
Grinling, W., 168, 370, 400-1.
Grinling, James, 237.
Grinling, W. J., 411.

H

Hudson, George, 2, 8, 9, 17, 27, 29, 38, 47, 49, 58, 60, 82, 91.
Huish, Capt., 92, 94, 142, 151, 155, 160, 165.

J

Johnson, Richard, 229, 230-1, 263-4, 266, 304, 309, 370, 398.

K

Karslake, Sir John, 244-5.
King's Cross, description of original passenger terminus, 114.
  opening of, 124.
  opening of connection with Metropolitan at, 202.
  congestion of traffic near, 233.
  alteration of roof of, 258, 377.
  congestion in goods station, 295.

L

Lancashire and Yorkshire Railway Company, 76, 81, 93, 95-6, 111-2, 146, 184, 199, 214-6, 219, 259, 269, 356-7.
Land, cost of, for G. N., 70.
Laws, Captain, 11, 21, 60, 81, 125.
Leech, Joseph, 130, 320.
Leith, Walter, 196, 277.
Locke, Joseph, 16, 21, 22.

INDEX

Locomotives, G. N., 72-3, 87, 89, 104, 136, 137, 277, 279, 343, 362, 380-1, 388, 407, 424.
London and York Railway, see Great Northern.
London and North Western Railway Company, 58, 75, 92-5, 98, 110, 133, 142-3, 151, 159, 165, 179, 182, 190, 269, 283, 289, 298, 302, 338, 385, 419.
Loop-line, G. N., 25, 69, 77, 79, 207, 233.

M

Managers, General, G. N.—
  Captain Laws, 60.
  Seymour Clarke, 88.
  Henry Oakley, 245.
Manchester, opening of G. N. route to, 163.
  speed to, 176, 362, 380.
  Central Station at, 327.
Manchester, Sheffield, and Lincolnshire Railway Company, 56, 72, 77, 94, 112, 142, 161-3, 191, 253, 288, 341, 344, 347, 393, 395, 409, 413.
Maps, G. N. system in Lincolnshire, &c., 209.
  G. N. system in Yorkshire, 215.
  Cheshire Lines system, 218.
  G. N. system near London, 232.
  G. N. system west of Nottingham, 265.
  G. N. & Midland Joint system, 383.
Meetings, G. N. Half-yearly, 62, 68, 70, 81, 83, 100, 115, 127, 129, 138, 147, 166, 172, 174, 294, 310, 336, 338, 348, 359, 364, 368, 392, 405, 417.
Metropolitan Railway Company, 126, 201-2, 257, 296, 391, 407, 414.
Midland Railway Company, 9, 17, 29, 59, 93, 117, 121, 133, 145, 151, 159, 165, 180-4, 188, 194-7, 217, 223, 231, 239, 241-255, 263-275, 277, 282-292, 299, 300, 317, 329, 343, 357, 383, 409, 417.

N

Nelson, Henry, 320.
Newark, 32, 306.
North British Railway Company, 18, 59, 74, 95, 96, 221-2, 224, 278, 317, 357, 404, 419.
North Eastern Railway Company, 141, 221-2, 224, 278, 317, 357, 386-8, 422-4.

Nottingham, 117, 121, 134, 145, 375, 413.

O

Oakley, Sir Henry, 168, 245, 247-254, 286, 307, 309, 316, 330, 339, 340, 357, 393, 409-411, 413, 414.
Octuple Agreement, 99, 150, 153.
Opening of G. N. lines Louth to New Holland, 72.
  Peterboro' to Lincoln, 79.
  Lincoln to Gainsboro', 83.
  Retford to Doncaster, 86.
  London to Peterboro', 90.
  Royston to Hitchin, 86.
  Peterboro' to Retford towns line, 120.
  Doncaster to Wakefield, 227.
  March to Spalding, 233.
  Honington to Lincoln, 233.
  Gainsboro' to Doncaster, 233.
  Finsbury Park to Edgware, 234.
  Bourn to Sleaford, 280.
  Finchley to Barnet, 280.
  Highgate to Muswell Hill, 293.
  extension to Skegness, 294.
  Laister Dyke to Shipley, 299.
  Ossett to Batley, 299.
  Halifax to Ovenden, 299.
  Derbyshire extension to Pinxton, 311.
  Bradford to Thornton, 325.
  Stanningley to Pudsey, 325.
  duplicate Copenhagen Tunnel, 325.
  Manchester Central Station, 326.
  Newark to Bottesford, 333.
  extension to Derby and Egginton, 333.
  duplicate Maiden Lane tunnel, 334.
  Bottesford to Melton and Market Harborough, 338.
  Queensbury to Ovenden, 338.
  Spalding to Lincoln, 359.
  Tilton to Leicester, 361.
  Thornton to Denholme, 364.
  triplicate Copenhagen tunnel, 376.
  Beeston to Batley, 381.
  triplicate Maiden Lane tunnel, 415.

P

Packe, Col., 12, 16, 36, 212, 298.
Parliamentary charges for G. N., 72.
Pearson, Charles, scheme of, for Central London Station, 125.
Pease, Joseph, on prospects of G. N. coal traffic, 36.
Plimsoll, Samuel, 144.
"Pooling" of traffic, 92, 98, 99, 103, 151, 244.

INDEX

R

Race to Edinburgh, 386.
— to Aberdeen, 419.
"Railway Times" newspaper, 6, 13-15, 19, 31.
Redpath, Leopold, frauds committed on G. N. by, 166–178.
Running powers granted to G. N., 69, 77, 82, 95, 134, 140, 283, 299, 357, 395, 413.
Running powers granted by G. N., 181, 224, 357, 413.
Running powers, threat to withdraw, 112.

S

Schools, G. N., at Doncaster, 138, 148.
Signalling, Block system of, 140, 193, 230, 231, 262, 297, 306, 314, 323, 357, 374.
Solicitors to G. N.—
Baxter, Rose, and Norton, 70.
Johnson, Farquhar, and Leech, 130.
Nelson, Barr, and Nelson, 320.
William Barrs, 404.
Speed on G. N., 276, 364, 380, 387, 424.
Stirling, Patrick, 277, 279, 322, 343, 348, 381, 385, 422.
Stock, G. N.—
splitting of, 77-8.
conversion of, 400.
Stock, rolling, G. N., see locomotives or carriages.
Sturrock, Archibald, 88, 137, 163, 202, 277.

T

Telegraphic communication on G. N., 140, 231.
Time-table, first G. N., 73.
"Times" newspaper, 43, 49, 158, 370.
Triple Alliance, 182, 191.

W

Warfare, Railway, at Nottingham, 121.
— at Manchester, 163.
Watkin, Sir Edward, 142, 155, 161, 185, 186, 191, 213, 216, 240, 242, 244–255, 268, 283, 391, 405, 409, 414.
Welwyn Tunnel accident, 228.
West Riding of Yorkshire, 198, 260.
Wharncliffe, Lord, 102.
Wrangham, Serjeant, 35, 40, 164.

PLYMOUTH
WILLIAM BRENDON AND SON
PRINTERS

A CATALOGUE OF BOOKS AND ANNOUNCEMENTS OF METHUEN AND COMPANY PUBLISHERS : LONDON 36 ESSEX STREET W.C.

CONTENTS

	PAGE
FORTHCOMING BOOKS,	2
POETRY,	8
BELLES LETTRES,	9
ILLUSTRATED BOOKS,	11
HISTORY,	12
BIOGRAPHY,	14
TRAVEL, ADVENTURE AND TOPOGRAPHY,	15
NAVAL AND MILITARY,	17
GENERAL LITERATURE,	18
SCIENCE,	19
TECHNOLOGY,	20
PHILOSOPHY,	20
THEOLOGY,	21
FICTION,	23
BOOKS FOR BOYS AND GIRLS,	34
THE PEACOCK LIBRARY,	34
UNIVERSITY EXTENSION SERIES,	35
SOCIAL QUESTIONS OF TO-DAY,	36
CLASSICAL TRANSLATIONS	37
EDUCATIONAL BOOKS,	37

FEBRUARY 1898

February 1898.

Messrs. Methuen's
Announcements

Poetry

THE POEMS OF WILLIAM SHAKESPEARE. Edited with an Introduction and Notes by GEORGE WYNDHAM, M.P. *Demy 8vo. Buckram, gilt top.* 10s. 6d.

This edition contains the 'Venus,' 'Lucrece' and Sonnets, and is prefaced with an elaborate introduction of over 140 pp. The text is founded on the first quartos, with an endeavour to retain the original reading. A set of notes deals with the problems of Date, The Rival Poets, Typography, and Punctuation; and the editor has commented on obscure passages in the light of contemporary works. The publishers believe that no such complete edition has ever been published.

Travel and Adventure

THREE YEARS IN SAVAGE AFRICA. By LIONEL DECLE. With an Introduction by H. M. STANLEY, M.P. With 100 Illustrations and 5 Maps. *Demy 8vo.* 21s.

Few Europeans have had the same opportunity of studying the barbarous parts of Africa as Mr. Decle. Starting from the Cape, he visited in succession Bechuanaland, the Zamhesi, Matabeleland and Mashonaland, the Portuguese settlement on the Zamhesi, Nyasaland, Ujiji, the headquarters of the Arabs, German East Africa, Uganda (where he saw fighting in company with the late Major 'Roddy' Owen), and British East Africa. In his book he relates his experiences, his minute observations of native habits and customs, and his views as to the work done in Africa by the various European Governments, whose operations he was able to study. The whole journey extended over 7000 miles, and occupied exactly three years.

EXPLORATION AND HUNTING IN CENTRAL AFRICA. By Major A. ST. H. GIBBONS, F.R.G.S. With 8 full-page Illustrations by C. WHYMPER, photographs and Map. *Demy 8vo.* 15s.

This is an account of travel and adventure among the Marotse and contiguous tribes, with a description of their customs, characteristics, and history, together with the author's experiences in hunting big game. The illustrations are by Mr. Charles Whymper, and from photographs. There is a map by the author of the hitherto unexplored regions lying between the Zamhezi and Kafukwi rivers and from 18° to 15° S. lat.

WITH THE MASHONALAND FIELD FORCE, 1896. By Lieut.-Colonel ALDERSON. With numerous Illustrations and Plans. *Demy 8vo.* 12s. 6d.

This is an account of the military operations in Mashonaland by the officer who commanded the troops in that district during the late rebellion. Besides its interest as a story of warfare, it will have a peculiar value as an account of the services of mounted infantry by one of the chief authorities on the subject.

MESSRS. METHUEN'S ANNOUNCEMENTS 3

CAMPAIGNING ON THE UPPER NILE AND NIGER.
By Lieut. SEYMOUR VANDELEUR. With an Introduction by Sir G. GOLDIE. With two Maps, Illustrations and Plans. *Large Cr. 8vo.* 10s. 6d.

A narrative of service (1) in the Equatorial Lakes and on the Upper Nile in 1895 and 1896; and (2) under Sir George Goldie in the Niger campaign of January 1897, describing the capture of Bida and Ilorin, and the French occupation of Boussa. The book thus deals with the two districts of Africa where now the French and English stand face to face.

THE NIGER SOURCES. By Colonel J. TROTTER, R.A. With a Map and Illustrations. *Crown 8vo.* 5s.

A book which at the present time should be of considerable interest, being an account of a Commission appointed for frontier delimitation.

LIFE AND PROGRESS IN AUSTRALASIA. By MICHAEL DAVITT, M.P. With two Maps. *Crown 8vo.* 6s. 500 pp.

This book, the outcome of a recent journey through the seven Australasian colonies, is an attempt to give to English readers a more intimate knowledge of a continent colonised by their own race. The author sketches the general life, resources, politics, parties, progress, prospects, and scenery of each colony. He made a careful examination of the West Australian goldfields, and he has paid special attention to the development of practical politics in the colonies. The book is full of anecdotes and picturesque description.

History and Biography

A HISTORY OF THE ART OF WAR. By C. W. OMAN, M.A., Fellow of All Souls', Oxford. Vol. II. MEDIÆVAL WARFARE. *Demy 8vo Illustrated.* 21s.

Mr. Oman is engaged on a History of the Art of War, of which the above, though covering the middle period from the fall of the Roman Empire to the general use of gunpowder in Western Europe, is the first instalment. The first battle dealt with will be Adrianople (378) and the last Navarette (1367). There will appear later a volume dealing with the Art of War among the Ancients, and another covering the 15th, 16th, and 17th centuries.
The book will deal mainly with tactics and strategy, fortifications and siegecraft, but subsidiary chapters will give some account of the development of arms and armour, and of the various forms of military organization known to the Middle Ages.

RELIGION AND CONSCIENCE IN ANCIENT EGYPT. By W. M. FLINDERS PETRIE, D.C.L., LL.D. *Fully Illustrated. Crown 8vo.* 2s. 6d.

This volume deals mainly with the historical growth of the Egyptian religion, and the arrangement of all the moral sayings into something like a handbook. But far larger interests are also discussed as the origin of intolerance, the fusion of religions, the nature of conscience, and the experimental illustration of British conscience.

SYRIA AND EGYPT FROM THE TELL EL AMARNA TABLETS. By W. M. FLINDERS PETRIE, D.C.L., LL.D. *Crown 8vo.* 2s. 6d.

This book describes the results of recent researches and discoveries and the light thereby thrown on Egyptian history.

THE DECLINE AND FALL OF THE ROMAN EMPIRE.
By EDWARD GIBBON. A New Edition, edited with Notes, Appendices, and Maps by J. B. BURY, M.A., Fellow of Trinity College, Dublin. *In Seven Volumes. Demy 8vo, gilt top.* 8s. 6d. *each. Crown 8vo.* 6s. *each. Vol. V.*

THE EASTERN QUESTION IN THE EIGHTEENTH CENTURY. By ALBERT SOREL of the French Academy. Translated by F. C. BRAMWELL, M.A., with an Introduction by R. C. L. FLETCHER, Fellow of Magdalen College, Oxford. With a Map. *Crown 8vo.* 4s. 6d.

This book is a study of the political conditions which led up to and governed the first partition of Poland, and the Russo-Turkish war of 1768-1774. It is probably the best existing examination of Eastern European politics in the eighteenth century, and is an early work of one of the ablest of living historians.

THE LETTERS OF VICTOR HUGO. Translated from the French by F. CLARKE, M.A. *In Two Volumes. Demy 8vo.* 10s. 6d. *each. Vol. II.* 1815-35.

A HISTORY OF THE GREAT NORTHERN RAILWAY, 1845-95. By C. H. GRINLING. With Maps and many Illustrations. *Demy 8vo.* 10s. 6d.

A record of Railway enterprise and development in Northern England, containing much matter hitherto unpublished. It appeals both to the general reader and to those specially interested in railway construction and management.

ANARCHISM. By E. V. ZENKER. *Demy 8vo.* 7s. 6d.

A critical study and history, as well as trenchant criticism of the Anarchist movement in Europe. The book has aroused considerable attention on the Continent.

THOMAS CRANMER. By A. J. MASON, D.D., Canon of Canterbury. With a Portrait. *Crown 8vo.* 3s. 6d.

[*Leaders of Religion.*

Theology

THE MINISTRY OF DEACONESSES. By CECILIA ROBINSON, Deaconess. With an Introduction by the LORD BISHOP OF WINCHESTER, and an Appendix by Professor ARMITAGE ROBINSON. *Crown 8vo.* 3s. 6d.

This book is a review of the history and theory of the office and work of a Deaconess and it may be regarded as authoritative.

DISCIPLINE AND LAW. By H. HENSLEY HENSON, B.D., Fellow of All Soul's, Oxford; Incumbent of St. Mary's Hospital, Ilford; Chaplain to the Bishop of St. Albans. *Fcap. 8vo.* 2s. 6d.

This volume of devotional addresses, suitable for Lent, is concerned with the value, method, and reward of Discipline; and with Law—family, social and individual.

REASONABLE CHRISTIANITY. By HASTINGS RASHDALL, M.A., Fellow and Tutor of New College, Oxford. *Crown 8vo.* 6s

This volume consists of twenty sermons, preached chiefly before the University of Oxford. They are an attempt to translate into the language of modern thought some of the leading ideas of Christian theology and ethics.

MESSRS. METHUEN'S ANNOUNCEMENTS

THE HOLY SACRIFICE. By F. WESTON, M.A., Curate of St. Matthew's, Westminster. *Pott 8vo.* 1s.

A small volume of devotions at the Holy Communion, especially adapted to the needs of servers and of those who do not communicate.

The Churchman's Library.

Edited by J. H. BURN, B.D.

A series of books by competent scholars on Church History, Institutions, and Doctrine, for the use of clerical and lay readers.

THE BEGINNINGS OF ENGLISH CHRISTIANITY. By W. E. COLLINS, M.A., Professor of Ecclesiastical History at King's College, London. With Map. *Crown 8vo.* 3s. 6d.

An investigation in detail, based upon original authorities, of the beginnings of the English Church, with a careful account of earlier Celtic Christianity. The larger aspects of the continental movement are described, and some very full appendices treat of a number of special subjects.

SOME NEW TESTAMENT PROBLEMS. By ARTHUR WRIGHT, Fellow and Tutor of Queen's College, Cambridge. *Crown 8vo.* 6s.

This book deals with a number of important problems from the standpoint of the 'Higher Criticism,' and is written in the hope of advancing the historico-critical study of the Synoptic Gospels and of the Acts.

The Library of Devotion.

Messrs. METHUEN have arranged to publish under the above title a number of the older masterpieces of devotional literature. It is their intention to entrust each volume of the series to an editor who will not only attempt to bring out the spiritual importance of the book, but who will lavish such scholarly care upon it as is generally expended only on editions of the ancient classics.

The books will be furnished with such Introductions and Notes as may be necessary to explain the standpoint of the author, and to comment on such difficulties as the ordinary reader may find, without unnecessary intrusion between the author and reader.

Mr. Laurence Housman has designed a title-page and a cover design. *Pott 8vo.* 2s.; *leather* 3s.

THE CONFESSIONS OF ST. AUGUSTINE. Newly Translated, with an Introduction and Notes, by C. BIGG, D.D., late Student of Christ Church.

This volume contains the nine books of the 'Confessions' which are suitable for devotional purposes.

THE CHRISTIAN YEAR. By JOHN KEBLE. With Introduction and Notes, by WALTER LOCK, D.D., Warden of Keble College, Ireland Professor at Oxford.

6   MESSRS. METHUEN'S ANNOUNCEMENTS

THE IMITATION OF CHRIST. A Revised Translation with an Introduction, by C. BIGG, D.D., late Student of Christ Church.

Dr. Bigg has made a practically new translation of this book, which the reader will have, almost for the first time, exactly in the shape in which it left the hands of the author.

A BOOK OF DEVOTIONS. By J. W. STANBRIDGE, M.A., Rector of Bainton, Canon of York, and sometime Fellow of St. John's College, Oxford. *Pott 8vo.*

This book contains devotions, Eucharistic, daily and occasional, for the use of members of the English Church, sufficiently diversified for those who possess other works of the kind. It is intended to be a companion in private and public worship, and is in harmony with the thoughts of the best Devotional writers.

General Literature

THE GOLFING PILGRIM. By HORACE G. HUTCHINSON. *Crown 8vo.* 6s.

This book, by a famous golfer, contains the following sketches lightly and humorously written :—The Prologue—The Pilgrim at the Shrine—Mecca out of Season—The Pilgrim at Home—The Pilgrim Abroad—The Life of the Links—A Tragedy by the Way—Scraps from the Scrip—The Golfer in Art—Early Pilgrims in the West—An Interesting Relic.

WORKHOUSES AND PAUPERISM. By LOUISA TWINING. *Crown 8vo.* 2s. 6d.   [*Social Questions Series.*

Educational

THE ODES AND EPODES OF HORACE. Translated by A. D. GODLEY, M.A., Fellow of Magdalen College, Oxford. *Crown 8vo.* 2s.   [*Classical Translations.*

PASSAGES FOR UNSEEN TRANSLATION. By E. C. MARCHANT, M.A., Fellow of Peterhouse, Cambridge ; and A. M. COOK, M.A., late Scholar of Wadham College, Oxford : Assistant Masters at St. Paul's School. *Crown 8vo.* 3s. 6d.

This book contains Two Hundred Latin and Two Hundred Greek Passages, and has been very carefully compiled to meet the wants of V. and VI. Form Boys at Public Schools. It is also well adapted for the use of Honour men at the Universities.

EASY LATIN EXERCISES ON THE SYNTAX OF THE SHORTER AND REVISED LATIN PRIMER. By A. M. M. STEDMAN, M.A. With Vocabulary. *Seventh and Cheaper Edition. Crown 8vo.* 1s. 6d. Issued with the consent of Dr. Kennedy.

A new and cheaper edition, thoroughly revised by Mr. C. G. Botting, of St. Paul's School.

TEST CARDS IN EUCLID AND ALGEBRA. By D. S. CALDERWOOD, Headmaster of the Normal School, Edinburgh. In a Packet of 40, with Answers. 1s.

A set of cards for advanced pupils in elementary schools.

Byzantine Texts

Edited by J. B. BURY, M.A., Professor of Modern History at Trinity College, Dublin.

EVAGRIUS. Edited by PROFESSOR LÉON PARMENTIER of Liége and M. BIDEZ of Gand. *Demy 8vo.*

PSELLUS (HISTORIA). Edited by C. SATHAS. *Demy 8vo.*

Fiction

SIMON DALE. By ANTHONY HOPE. Illustrated by W. ST. J. HARPER. *Crown 8vo. 6s.*
A romance of the reign of Charles II., and Mr. Anthony Hope's first historical novel.

TRAITS AND CONFIDENCES. By The Hon. EMILY LAWLESS, Author of 'Hurrish,' 'Maelcho,' etc. *Crown 8vo. 6s.*

THE VINTAGE. By E. F. BENSON, Author of 'Dodo.' Illustrated by G. P. JACOMB-HOOD. *Crown 8vo. 6s.*
A romance of the Greek War of Independence.

A VOYAGE OF CONSOLATION. By SARA JEANETTE DUNCAN. Author of 'An American Girl in London.' *Crown 8vo. 6s.*
The adventures of an American girl in Europe.

A NEW NOVEL. By B. M. CROKER, Author of 'Proper Pride.' *Crown 8vo. 6s.*

ACROSS THE SALT SEAS. By J. BLOUNDELLE-BURTON. *Crown 8vo. 6s.*

MISS ERIN. By M. E. FRANCIS, Author of 'In a Northern Village.' *Crown 8vo. 6s.*

WILLOWBRAKE. By R. MURRAY GILCHRIST. *Crown 8vo. 6s.*

THE KLOOF BRIDE. By ERNEST GLANVILLE, Author of 'The Fossicker.' Illustrated. *Crown 8vo. 3s. 6d.*
A story of South African Adventure.

BIJLI, THE DANCER. By JAMES BLYTHE PATTON. Illustrated. *Crown 8vo. 6s.*
A Romance of India.

JOSIAH'S WIFE. By NORMA LORIMER. *Crown 8vo. 6s.*

BETWEEN SUN AND SAND. By W. C. SCULLY, Author of 'The White Hecatomb.' *Crown 8vo. 6s.*

CROSS TRAILS. By VICTOR WAITE. Illustrated. *Crown 8vo. 6s.*
A romance of adventure in America and Australia.

THE PHILANTHROPIST. By LUCY MAYNARD. *Crown 8vo. 6s.*

VAUSSORE. By FRANCIS BRUNE. *Crown 8vo. 6s.*

A LIST OF

Messrs. Methuen's
PUBLICATIONS

Poetry

RUDYARD KIPLING'S NEW POEMS

Rudyard Kipling. THE SEVEN SEAS. By RUDYARD KIPLING. *Third Edition. Crown 8vo. Buckram, gilt top.* 6s.

'The new poems of Mr. Rudyard Kipling have all the spirit and swing of their predecessors. Patriotism is the solid concrete foundation on which Mr. Kipling has built the whole of his work.'—*Times.*

'The Empire has found a singer; it is no depreciation of the songs to say that statesmen may have, one way or other, to take account of them.'—*Manchester Guardian.*

'Animated through and through with indubitable genius.'—*Daily Telegraph.*

'Packed with inspiration, with humour, with pathos.'—*Daily Chronicle.*

'All the pride of empire, all the intoxication of power, all the ardour, the energy, the masterly strength and the wonderful endurance and death-scorning pluck which are the very bone and fibre and marrow of the British character are here.' —*Daily Mail.*

Rudyard Kipling. BARRACK-ROOM BALLADS. By RUDYARD KIPLING. *Twelfth Edition. Crown 8vo.* 6s.

'Mr. Kipling's verse is strong, vivid, full of character. . . . Unmistakable genius rings in every line.'—*Times.*

'The ballads teem with imagination, they palpitate with emotion. We read them with laughter and tears; the metres throb in our pulses, the cunningly ordered words tingle with life; and if this be not poetry, what is?'—*Pall Mall Gazette.*

"Q." POEMS AND BALLADS. By "Q." *Crown 8vo.* 3s. 6d.

'This work has just the faint, ineffable touch and glow that make poetry.'—*Speaker.*

"Q." GREEN BAYS: Verses and Parodies. By "Q.," Author of 'Dead Man's Rock,' etc. *Second Edition. Crown 8vo.* 3s. 6d.

E. Mackay. A SONG OF THE SEA. By ERIC MACKAY. *Second Edition. Fcap. 8vo.* 5s.

'Everywhere Mr. Mackay displays himself the master of a style marked by all the characteristics of the best rhetoric.'—*Globe.*

Ibsen. BRAND. A Drama by HENRIK IBSEN. Translated by WILLIAM WILSON. *Second Edition. Crown 8vo.* 3s. 6d.

'The greatest world-poem of the nineteenth century next to "Faust." It is in the same set with "Agamemnon," with "Lear," with the literature that we now instinctively regard as high and holy.'—*Daily Chronicle.*

"A. G." VERSES TO ORDER. By "A. G." *Cr. 8vo. 2s. 6d. net.*

'A capital specimen of light academic poetry. These verses are very bright and engaging, easy and sufficiently witty.'—*St. James's Gazette.*

Cordery. THE ODYSSEY OF HOMER. A Translation by J. G. CORDERY. *Crown 8vo. 7s. 6d.*

'This new version of the Odyssey fairly deserves a place of honour among its many rivals. Perhaps there is none from which a more accurate knowledge of the original can be gathered with greater pleasure, at least of those that are in metre.'—*Manchester Guardian.*

Belles Lettres, Anthologies, etc.

R. L. Stevenson. VAILIMA LETTERS. By ROBERT LOUIS STEVENSON. With an Etched Portrait by WILLIAM STRANG, and other Illustrations. *Second Edition. Crown 8vo. Buckram. 7s. 6d.*

'Few publications have in our time been more eagerly awaited than these "Vailima Letters," giving the first fruits of the correspondence of Robert Louis Stevenson. But, high as the tide of expectation has run, no reader can possibly be disappointed in the result.'—*St. James's Gazette.*

Henley. ENGLISH LYRICS. Selected and Edited by W. E. HENLEY. *Crown 8vo. Buckram gilt top. 6s.*

'It is a body of choice and lovely poetry.'—*Birmingham Gazette.*
'Mr. Henley's notes, in their brevity and their fulness, their information and their suggestiveness, seem to us a model of what notes should be.'—*Manchester Guardian.*

Henley and Whibley. A BOOK OF ENGLISH PROSE. Collected by W. E. HENLEY and CHARLES WHIBLEY. *Crown 8vo. Buckram gilt top. 6s.*

'A unique volume of extracts—an art gallery of early prose.'—*Birmingham Post.*
'An admirable companion to Mr. Henley's "Lyra Heroica."'—*Saturday Review.*
'Quite delightful. A greater treat for those not well acquainted with pre-Restoration prose could not be imagined.'—*Athenæum.*

H. C. Beeching. LYRA SACRA : An Anthology of Sacred Verse. Edited by H. C. BEECHING, M.A. *Crown 8vo. Buckram. 6s.*

'A charming selection, which maintains a lofty standard of excellence.'—*Times.*

"Q." THE GOLDEN POMP : A Procession of English Lyrics from Surrey to Shirley, arranged by A. T. QUILLER COUCH. *Crown 8vo. Buckram. 6s.*

'A delightful volume : a really golden "Pomp."'—*Spectator.*

W. B. Yeats. AN ANTHOLOGY OF IRISH VERSE. Edited by W. B. YEATS. *Crown 8vo. 3s. 6d.*

'An attractive and catholic selection.'—*Times.*

G. W. Steevens. MONOLOGUES OF THE DEAD. By G. W. STEEVENS. *Foolscap 8vo.* 3s. 6d.

A series of Soliloquies in which famous men of antiquity—Julius Cæsar, Nero, Alcibiades, etc., attempt to express themselves in the modes of thought and language of to-day.

'The effect is sometimes splendid, sometimes bizarre, but always amazingly clever.' —*Pall Mall Gazette.*

Victor Hugo. THE LETTERS OF VICTOR HUGO. Translated from the French by F. CLARKE, M.A. *In Two Volumes. Demy 8vo.* 10s. 6d. *each. Vol. I.* 1815-35.

C. H. Pearson. ESSAYS AND CRITICAL REVIEWS. By C. H. PEARSON, M.A., Author of 'National Life and Character.' With a Portrait. *Demy 8vo.* 10s. 6d.

W. M. Dixon. A PRIMER OF TENNYSON. By W. M. DIXON, M.A., Professor of English Literature at Mason College. *Crown 8vo.* 2s. 6d.

'Much sound and well-expressed criticism and acute literary judgments. The bibliography is a boon.'—*Speaker.*

W. A. Craigie. A PRIMER OF BURNS. By W. A. CRAIGIE. *Crown 8vo.* 2s. 6d.

'A valuable addition to the literature of the poet.'—*Times.*
'An admirable introduction.'—*Globe.*

Magnus. A PRIMER OF WORDSWORTH. By LAURIE MAGNUS. *Crown 8vo.* 2s. 6d.

'A valuable contribution to Wordsworthian literature.'—*Literature.*
'A well-made primer, thoughtful and informing.'—*Manchester Guardian.*

Sterne. THE LIFE AND OPINIONS OF TRISTRAM SHANDY. By LAWRENCE STERNE. With an Introduction by CHARLES WHIBLEY, and a Portrait. 2 *vols.* 7s.

'Very dainty volumes are these; the paper, type, and light-green binding are all very agreeable to the eye. *Simplex munditiis* is the phrase that might be applied to them.'—*Globe.*

Congreve. THE COMEDIES OF WILLIAM CONGREVE. With an Introduction by G. S. STREET, and a Portrait. 2 *vols.* 7s.

Morier. THE ADVENTURES OF HAJJI BABA OF ISPAHAN. By JAMES MORIER. With an Introduction by E. G. BROWNE, M.A., and a Portrait. 2 *vols.* 7s.

Walton. THE LIVES OF DONNE, WOTTON, HOOKER, HERBERT, AND SANDERSON. By IZAAK WALTON. With an Introduction by VERNON BLACKBURN, and a Portrait. 3s. 6d.

Johnson. THE LIVES OF THE ENGLISH POETS. By SAMUEL JOHNSON, LL.D. With an Introduction by J. H. MILLAR, and a Portrait. 3 *vols.* 10s. 6d.

Burns. THE POEMS OF ROBERT BURNS. Edited by ANDREW LANG and W. A. CRAIGIE. With Portrait. *Demy 8vo, gilt top.* 6s.

This edition contains a carefully collated Text, numerous Notes, critical and textual, a critical and biographical Introduction, and a Glossary.

'Among the editions in one volume, Mr. Andrew Lang's will take the place of authority.'—*Times.*

F. Langbridge. BALLADS OF THE BRAVE: Poems of Chivalry, Enterprise, Courage, and Constancy. Edited by Rev. F. LANGBRIDGE. *Crown 8vo.* 3s. 6d. *School Edition.* 2s. 6d.

'A very happy conception happily carried out. These "Ballads of the Brave" are intended to suit the real tastes of boys, and will suit the taste of the great majority.'—*Spectator.* 'The book is full of splendid things.'—*World.*

Illustrated Books

Bedford. NURSERY RHYMES. With many Coloured Pictures. By F. D. BEDFORD. *Super Royal 8vo.* 5s.

'An excellent selection of the best known rhymes, with beautifully coloured pictures exquisitely printed.'—*Pall Mall Gazette.*
'The art is of the newest, with well harmonised colouring.'—*Spectator.*

S. Baring Gould. A BOOK OF FAIRY TALES retold by S. BARING GOULD. With numerous illustrations and initial letters by ARTHUR J. GASKIN. *Second Edition. Crown 8vo. Buckram.* 6s.

'Mr. Baring Gould is deserving of gratitude, in re-writing in honest, simple style the old stories that delighted the childhood of "our fathers and grandfathers."'—*Saturday Review.*

S. Baring Gould. OLD ENGLISH FAIRY TALES. Collected and edited by S. BARING GOULD. With Numerous Illustrations by F. D. BEDFORD. *Second Edition. Crown 8vo. Buckram.* 6s.

'A charming volume. The stories have been selected with great ingenuity from various old ballads and folk-tales, and now stand forth, clothed in Mr. Baring Gould's delightful English, to enchant youthful readers.'—*Guardian.*

S. Baring Gould. A BOOK OF NURSERY SONGS AND RHYMES. Edited by S. BARING GOULD, and Illustrated by the Birmingham Art School. *Buckram, gilt top. Crown 8vo.* 6s.

'The volume is very complete in its way, as it contains nursery songs to the number of 77, game-rhymes, and jingles. To the student we commend the sensible introduction, and the explanatory notes.'—*Birmingham Gazette.*

H. C. Beeching. A BOOK OF CHRISTMAS VERSE. Edited by H. C. BEECHING, M.A., and Illustrated by WALTER CRANE. *Crown 8vo, gilt top.* 5s.

A collection of the best verse inspired by the birth of Christ from the Middle Ages to the present day.

'An anthology which, from its unity of aim and high poetic excellence, has a better right to exist than most of its fellows.'—*Guardian.*

History

Gibbon. THE DECLINE AND FALL OF THE ROMAN EMPIRE. By EDWARD GIBBON. A New Edition, Edited with Notes, Appendices, and Maps, by J. B. BURY, M.A., Fellow of Trinity College, Dublin. *In Seven Volumes. Demy 8vo. Gilt top. 8s. 6d. each. Also crown 8vo. 6s. each. Vols. I., II., III., and IV.*

'The time has certainly arrived for a new edition of Gibbon's great work. . . . Professor Bury is the right man to undertake this task. His learning is amazing, both in extent and accuracy. The book is issued in a handy form, and at a moderate price, and it is admirably printed.'—*Times.*

'This edition, so far as one may judge from the first instalment, is a marvel of erudition and critical skill, and it is the very minimum of praise to predict that the seven volumes of it will supersede Dean Milman's as the standard edition of our great historical classic.'—*Glasgow Herald.*

'The beau-ideal Gibbon has arrived at last.'—*Sketch.*

'At last there is an adequate modern edition of Gibbon. . . . The best edition the nineteenth century could produce.'—*Manchester Guardian.*

Flinders Petrie. A HISTORY OF EGYPT, FROM THE EARLIEST TIMES TO THE PRESENT DAY. Edited by W. M. FLINDERS PETRIE, D.C.L., LL.D., Professor of Egyptology at University College. *Fully Illustrated. In Six Volumes. Crown 8vo. 6s. each.*

    Vol. I. PREHISTORIC TIMES TO XVITH. DYNASTY. W. F. M. Petrie. *Third Edition.*

    Vol. II. THE XVIITH AND XVIIITH DYNASTIES. W. M. F. Petrie. *Second Edition.*

'A history written in the spirit of scientific precision so worthily represented by Dr. Petrie and his school cannot but promote sound and accurate study, and supply a vacant place in the English literature of Egyptology.'—*Times.*

Flinders Petrie. EGYPTIAN TALES. Edited by W. M. FLINDERS PETRIE. Illustrated by TRISTRAM ELLIS. *In Two Volumes. Crown 8vo. 3s. 6d. each.*

'A valuable addition to the literature of comparative folk-lore. The drawings are really illustrations in the literal sense of the word.'—*Globe.*

'It has a scientific value to the student of history and archæology.'—*Scotsman.*

'Invaluable as a picture of life in Palestine and Egypt.'—*Daily News.*

Flinders Petrie. EGYPTIAN DECORATIVE ART. By W. M. FLINDERS PETRIE. With 120 Illustrations. *Cr. 8vo. 3s. 6d.*

'Professor Flinders Petrie is not only a profound Egyptologist, but an accomplished student of comparative archæology. In these lectures he displays both qualifications with rare skill in elucidating the development of decorative art in Egypt, and in tracing its influence on the art of other countries.'—*Times.*

S. Baring Gould. THE TRAGEDY OF THE CÆSARS. With numerous Illustrations from Busts, Gems, Cameos, etc. By S. BARING GOULD. *Fourth Edition. Royal 8vo. 15s.*

'A most splendid and fascinating book on a subject of undying interest. The great feature of the book is the use the author has made of the existing portraits of the Caesars, and the admirable critical subtlety he has exhibited in dealing with this line of research. It is brilliantly written, and the illustrations are supplied on a scale of profuse magnificence.'—*Daily Chronicle.*

H. de B. Gibbins. INDUSTRY IN ENGLAND: HISTORICAL OUTLINES. By H. DE B. GIBBINS, M.A., D.Litt. With 5 Maps. *Second Edition. Demy 8vo.* 10s. 6d.

This book is written with the view of affording a clear view of the main facts of English Social and Industrial History placed in due perspective.

H. E. Egerton. A HISTORY OF BRITISH COLONIAL POLICY. By H. E. EGERTON, M.A. *Demy 8vo.* 12s. 6d.

This book deals with British Colonial policy historically from the beginnings of English colonisation down to the present day. The subject has been treated by itself, and it has thus been possible within a reasonable compass to deal with a mass of authority which must otherwise be sought in the State papers. The volume is divided into five parts:—(1) The Period of Beginnings, 1497-1650; (2) Trade Ascendancy, 1651-1830; (3) The Granting of Responsible Government, 1831-1860; (4) *Laissez Aller*, 1861-1885; (5) Greater Britain.

'The whole story of the growth and administration of our colonial empire is comprehensive and well arranged, and is set forth with marked ability.'—*Daily Mail.*
'It is a good book, distinguished by accuracy in detail, clear arrangement of facts, and a broad grasp of principles.'—*Manchester Guardian.*
'Able, impartial, clear. . . . A most valuable volume.'—*Athenæum.*

A. Clark. THE COLLEGES OF OXFORD: Their History and their Traditions. By Members of the University. Edited by A. CLARK, M.A., Fellow and Tutor of Lincoln College. *8vo.* 12s. 6d.

'A work which will certainly be appealed to for many years as the standard book on the Colleges of Oxford.'—*Athenæum.*

Perrens. THE HISTORY OF FLORENCE FROM 1434 TO 1492. By F. T. PERRENS. *8vo.* 12s. 6d.

A history of Florence under the domination of Cosimo, Piero, and Lorenzo de Medicis.

J. Wells. A SHORT HISTORY OF ROME. By J. WELLS, M.A., Fellow and Tutor of Wadham Coll., Oxford. With 4 Maps. *Crown 8vo.* 3s. 6d.

This book is intended for the Middle and Upper Forms of Public Schools and for Pass Students at the Universities. It contains copious Tables, etc.
'An original work written on an original plan, and with uncommon freshness and vigour.'—*Speaker.*

O. Browning. A SHORT HISTORY OF MEDIÆVAL ITALY, A.D. 1250-1530. By OSCAR BROWNING, Fellow and Tutor of King's College, Cambridge. *Second Edition. In Two Volumes. Crown 8vo.* 5s. each.

    VOL. I. 1250-1409.—Guelphs and Ghibellines.
    VOL. II. 1409-1530.—The Age of the Condottieri.

'Mr. Browning is to be congratulated on the production of a work of immense labour and learning.'—*Westminster Gazette.*

O'Grady. THE STORY OF IRELAND. By STANDISH O'GRADY, Author of 'Finn and his Companions.' *Cr. 8vo.* 2s. 6d.

'Most delightful, most stimulating. Its racy humour, its original imaginings, make it one of the freshest, breeziest volumes.'—*Methodist Times.*

Biography

S. Baring Gould. THE LIFE OF NAPOLEON BONAPARTE. By S. Baring Gould. With over 450 Illustrations in the Text and 12 Photogravure Plates. *Large quarto. Gilt top.* 36s.

'The best biography of Napole in our tongue, nor have the French as good a biographer of their hero. A book very nearly as good as Southey's "Life of Nelson."'—*Manchester Guardian.*

'The main feature of this gorgeous volume is its great wealth of beautiful photogravures and finely-executed wood engravings, constituting a complete pictorial chronicle of Napoleon I.'s personal history from the days of his early childhood at Ajaccio to the date of his second interment under the dome of the Invalides in Paris.'—*Daily Telegraph.*

'Particular notice is due to the vast collection of contemporary illustrations.'—*Guardian.*

'Nearly all the illustrations are real contributions to history.'—*Westminster Gazette.*

Morris Fuller. THE LIFE AND WRITINGS OF JOHN DAVENANT, D.D. (1571-1641), Bishop of Salisbury. By Morris Fuller, B.D. *Demy 8vo.* 10s. 6d.

'A valuable contribution to ecclesiastical history.'—*Birmingham Gazette.*

J. M. Rigg. ST. ANSELM OF CANTERBURY: A Chapter in the History of Religion. By J. M. Rigg. *Demy 8vo.* 7s. 6d.

'Mr. Rigg has told the story of the great Primate's life with scholarly ability, and has thereby contributed an interesting chapter to the history of the Norman period.'—*Daily Chronicle.*

F. W. Joyce. THE LIFE OF SIR FREDERICK GORE OUSELEY. By F. W. Joyce, M.A. With Portraits and Illustrations. *Crown 8vo.* 7s. 6d.

'This book has been undertaken in quite the right spirit, and written with sympathy, insight, and considerable literary skill.'—*Times.*

W. G. Collingwood. THE LIFE OF JOHN RUSKIN. By W. G. Collingwood, M.A. With Portraits, and 13 Drawings by Mr. Ruskin. *Second Edition.* 2 *vols.* 8vo. 32s.

'No more magnificent volumes have been published for a long time.'—*Times.*
'It is long since we had a biography with such delights of substance and of form. Such a book is a pleasure for the day, and a joy for ever.'—*Daily Chronicle.*

C. Waldstein. JOHN RUSKIN: a Study. By Charles Waldstein, M.A., Fellow of King's College, Cambridge. With a Photogravure Portrait after Professor Herkomer. *Post 8vo.* 5s.

'A thoughtful, impartial, well-written criticism of Ruskin's teaching, intended to separate what the author regards as valuable and permanent from what is transient and erroneous in the great master's writing.'—*Daily Chronicle.*

MESSRS. METHUEN'S LIST 15

Darmesteter. THE LIFE OF ERNEST RENAN. By MADAME DARMESTETER. With Portrait. *Second Edition. Cr. 8vo. 6s.*
A biography of Renan by one of his most intimate friends.
'A polished gem of biography, superior in its kind to any attempt that has been made of recent years in England. Madame Darmesteter has indeed written for English readers "*The* Life of Ernest Renan."'—*Athenæum.*
'It is a fascinating and biographical and critical study, and an admirably finished work of literary art.'—*Scotsman.*
'It is interpenetrated with the dignity and charm, the mild, bright, classical grace of form and treatment that Renan himself so loved; and it fulfils to the uttermost the delicate and difficult achievement it sets out to accomplish.'—*Academy.*

W. H. Hutton. THE LIFE OF SIR THOMAS MORE. By W. H. HUTTON, M.A. *With Portraits. Crown 8vo. 5s.*
'The book lays good claim to high rank among our biographies. It is excellently, even lovingly, written.'—*Scotsman.* 'An excellent monograph.'—*Times.*

Travel, Adventure and Topography

Johnston. BRITISH CENTRAL AFRICA. By Sir H. H. JOHNSTON, K.C.B. With nearly Two Hundred Illustrations, and Six Maps. *Second Edition. Crown 4to. 30s. net.*
'A fascinating book, written with equal skill and charm—the work at once of a literary artist and of a man of action who is singularly wise, brave, and experienced. It abounds in admirable sketches from pencil.'—*Westminster Gazette.*
'A delightful book . . . collecting within the covers of a single volume all that is known of this part of our African domains. The voluminous appendices are of extreme value.'—*Manchester Guardian.*
'The book takes front rank as a standard work by the one man competent to write it.'—*Daily Chronicle.*
'The book is crowded with important information, and written in a most attractive style; it is worthy, in short, of the author's established reputation.'—*Standard.*

Prince Henri of Orleans. FROM TONKIN TO INDIA. By PRINCE HENRI OF ORLEANS. Translated by HAMLEY BENT, M.A. With 100 Illustrations and a Map. *Second Edition. Crown 4to, gilt top. 25s.*
The travels of Prince Henri in 1895 from China to the valley of the Bramaputra covered a distance of 2100 miles, of which 1600 was through absolutely unexplored country. No fewer than seventeen ranges of mountains were crossed at altitudes of from 11,000 to 13,000 feet. The journey was made memorable by the discovery of the sources of the Irrawaddy.
'A welcome contribution to our knowledge. The narrative is full and interesting, and the appendices give the work a substantial value.'—*Times.*
'The Prince's travels are of real importance . . . his services to geography have been considerable. The volume is beautifully illustrated.'—*Athenæum.*
'The story is instructive and fascinating, and will certainly make one of the books of 1898. The book attracts by its delightful print and fine illustrations. A nearly model book of travel.'—*Pall Mall Gazette.*
'An entertaining record of pluck and travel in important regions.'—*Daily Chronicle.*
'The illustrations are admirable and quite beyond praise.'—*Glasgow Herald.*
'The Prince's story is charmingly told, and presented with an attractiveness which will make it, in more than one sense, an outstanding book of the season.'—*Birmingham Post.*
'An attractive book which will prove of considerable interest and no little value. A narrative of a remarkable journey.'—*Literature.*
'China is the country of the hour. All eyes are turned towards her, and Messrs. Methuen have opportunely selected the moment to launch Prince Henri's work.'—*Liverpool Daily Post.*

R. S. S. Baden-Powell. THE DOWNFALL OF PREMPEH. A Diary of Life in Ashanti, 1895. By Colonel BADEN-POWELL. With 21 Illustrations and a Map. *Demy 8vo.* 10s. 6d.

'A compact, faithful, most readable record of the campaign.'—*Daily News.*

R. S. S. Baden-Powell. THE MATEBELE CAMPAIGN 1896. By Colonel BADEN-POWELL. With nearly 100 Illustrations. *Second Edition. Demy 8vo.* 15s.

'As a straightforward account of a great deal of plucky work unpretentiously done, this book is well worth reading. The simplicity of the narrative is all in its favour, and accords in a peculiarly English fashion with the nature of the subject.'—*Times.*

Captain Hinde. THE FALL OF THE CONGO ARABS. By L. HINDE. With Plans, etc. *Demy 8vo.* 12s. 6d.

'The book is full of good things, and of sustained interest.'—*St. James's Gazette.*
'A graphic sketch of one of the most exciting and important episodes in the struggle for supremacy in Central Africa between the Arabs and their European rivals. Apart from the story of the campaign, Captain Hinde's book is mainly remarkable for the fulness with which he discusses the question of cannibalism. It is, indeed, the only connected narrative—in English, at any rate—which has been published of this particular episode in African history.'—*Times.*

W. Crooke. THE NORTH-WESTERN PROVINCES OF INDIA: THEIR ETHNOLOGY AND ADMINISTRATION. By W. CROOKE. With Maps and Illustrations. *Demy 8vo.* 10s. 6d.

'A carefully and well-written account of one of the most important provinces of the Empire. In seven chapters Mr. Crooke deals successively with the land in its physical aspect, the province under Hindoo and Mussulman rule, the province under British rule, the ethnology and sociology of the province, the religious and social life of the people, the land and its settlement, and the native peasant in his relation to the land. The illustrations are good and well selected, and the map is excellent.'—*Manchester Guardian.*

A. Boisragon. THE BENIN MASSACRE. By CAPTAIN BOISRAGON. With Portrait and Map. *Second Edition. Crown 8vo.* 3s. 6d.

'If the story had been written four hundred years ago it would be read to-day as an English classic.'—*Scotsman.*
'If anything could enhance the horror and the pathos of this remarkable book it is the simple style of the author, who writes as he would talk, unconscious of his own heroism, with an artlessness which is the highest art.'—*Pall Mall Gazette.*

H. S. Cowper. THE HILL OF THE GRACES: OR, THE GREAT STONE TEMPLES OF TRIPOLI. By H. S. COWPER, F.S.A. With Maps, Plans, and 75 Illustrations. *Demy 8vo.* 10s. 6d.

'The book has the interest of all first-hand work, directed by an intelligent man towards a worthy object, and it forms a valuable chapter of what has now become quite a large and important branch of antiquarian research.'—*Times.*

Kinnaird Rose. WITH THE GREEKS IN THESSALY. By W. KINNAIRD ROSE, Reuter's Correspondent. With Plans and 23 Illustrations. *Crown 8vo.* 6s.

W. B. Worsfold. SOUTH AFRICA. By W. B. WORSFOLD, M.A. With a Map. *Second Edition. Crown 8vo.* 6s.

'A monumental work compressed into a very moderate compass.'—*World.*

Naval and Military

G. W. Steevens. NAVAL POLICY: By. G. W. STEEVENS. *Demy 8vo.* 6s.

This book is a description of the British and other more important navies of the world, with a sketch of the lines on which our naval policy might possibly be developed.
'An extremely able and interesting work.'—*Daily Chronicle.*

D. Hannay. A SHORT HISTORY OF THE ROYAL NAVY, FROM EARLY TIMES TO THE PRESENT DAY. By DAVID HANNAY. Illustrated. 2 *Vols. Demy 8vo.* 7s. 6d. each. Vol. I., 1200-1688.

'We read it from cover to cover at a sitting, and those who go to it for a lively and brisk picture of the past, with all its faults and its grandeur, will not be disappointed. The historian is competent, and he is endowed with literary skill and style.'—*Standard.*
'We can warmly recommend Mr. Hannay's volume to any intelligent student of naval history. Great as is the merit of Mr. Hannay's historical narrative, the merit of his strategic exposition is even greater.'—*Times.*
'His book is brisk and pleasant reading, for he is gifted with a most agreeable style. His reflections are philosophical, and he has seized and emphasised just those points which are of interest.'—*Graphic.*

Cooper King. THE STORY OF THE BRITISH ARMY. By Lieut.-Colonel COOPER KING, of the Staff College, Camberley. Illustrated. *Demy 8vo.* 7s. 6d.

'An authoritative and accurate story of England's military progress.'—*Daily Mail.*
'This handy volume contains, in a compendious form, a brief but adequate sketch of the story of the British army.'—*Daily News.*

R. Southey. ENGLISH SEAMEN (Howard, Clifford, Hawkins, Drake, Cavendish). By ROBERT SOUTHEY. Edited, with an Introduction, by DAVID HANNAY. *Second Edition. Crown 8vo.* 6s.

'Admirable and well-told stories of our naval history.'—*Army and Navy Gazette.*
'A brave, inspiriting book.'—*Black and White.*

W. Clark Russell. THE LIFE OF ADMIRAL LORD COLLINGWOOD. By W. CLARK RUSSELL, With Illustrations by F. BRANGWYN. *Third Edition. Crown 8vo.* 6s.

'A book which we should like to see in the hands of every boy in the country.'—*St. James's Gazette.* 'A really good book.'—*Saturday Review.*

E. L. S. Horsburgh. THE CAMPAIGN OF WATERLOO. By E. L. S. HORSBURGH, B.A. *With Plans. Crown 8vo.* 5s.

'A brilliant essay—simple, sound, and thorough.'—*Daily Chronicle.*

H. B. George. BATTLES OF ENGLISH HISTORY. By H. B. GEORGE, M.A., Fellow of New College, Oxford. *With numerous Plans. Third Edition. Crown 8vo.* 6s.

'Mr. George has undertaken a very useful task—that of making military affairs intelligible and instructive to non-military readers—and has executed it with laudable intelligence and industry, and with a large measure of success.'—*Times.*

General Literature

S. Baring Gould. OLD COUNTRY LIFE. By S. BARING GOULD. With Sixty-seven Illustrations. *Large Crown 8vo. Fifth Edition.* 6s.

'"Old Country Life," as healthy wholesome reading, full of breezy life and movement, full of quaint stories vigorously told, will not be excelled by any book to be published throughout the year. Sound, hearty, and English to the core.'—*World.*

S. Baring Gould. HISTORIC ODDITIES AND STRANGE EVENTS. By S. BARING GOULD. *Fourth Edition. Crown 8vo.* 6s.

'A collection of exciting and entertaining chapters. The whole volume is delightful reading.'—*Times.*

S. Baring Gould. FREAKS OF FANATICISM. By S. BARING GOULD. *Third Edition. Crown 8vo.* 6s.

'Mr. Baring Gould has a keen eye for colour and effect, and the subjects he has chosen give ample scope to his descriptive and analytic faculties. A perfectly fascinating book.'—*Scottish Leader.*

S. Baring Gould. A GARLAND OF COUNTRY SONG: English Folk Songs with their Traditional Melodies. Collected and arranged by S. BARING GOULD and H. F. SHEPPARD. *Demy 4to.* 6s.

S. Baring Gould. SONGS OF THE WEST: Traditional Ballads and Songs of the West of England, with their Traditional Melodies. Collected by S. BARING GOULD, M.A., and H. F. SHEPPARD, M.A. Arranged for Voice and Piano. In 4 Parts. *Parts I., II., III.,* 3s. each. *Part IV.,* 5s. *In one Vol., French morocco,* 15s.

'A rich collection of humour, pathos, grace, and poetic fancy.'—*Saturday Review.*

S. Baring Gould. YORKSHIRE ODDITIES AND STRANGE EVENTS. *Fourth Edition. Crown 8vo.* 6s.

S. Baring Gould. STRANGE SURVIVALS AND SUPERSTITIONS. With Illustrations. By S. BARING GOULD. *Crown 8vo. Second Edition.* 6s.

S. Baring Gould. THE DESERTS OF SOUTHERN FRANCE. By S. BARING GOULD. *2 vols. Demy 8vo.* 32s.

Cotton Minchin. OLD HARROW DAYS. By J. G. COTTON MINCHIN. *Crown 8vo. Second Edition.* 5s.

'This book is an admirable record.'—*Daily Chronicle.*

'Mr. Cotton Minchin's bright and breezy reminiscences of 'Old Harrow Days' will delight all Harrovians, old and young, and may go far to explain the abiding enthusiasm of old Harrovians for their school to readers who have not been privileged to be their schoolfellows.'—*Times.*

W. E. Gladstone. THE SPEECHES OF THE RT. HON. W. E. GLADSTONE, M.P. Edited by A. W. HUTTON, M.A., and H. J. COHEN, M.A. With Portraits. *8vo. Vols. IX. and X.* 12s. 6d. each.

MESSRS. METHUEN'S LIST 19

J. Wells. OXFORD AND OXFORD LIFE. By Members of the University. Edited by J. WELLS, M.A., Fellow and Tutor of Wadham College. *Crown 8vo. 3s. 6d.*
'We congratulate Mr. Wells on the production of a readable and intelligent account of Oxford as it is at the present time, written by persons who are possessed of a close acquaintance with the system and life of the University.'—*Athenæum.*

J. Wells. OXFORD AND ITS COLLEGES. By J. WELLS, M.A., Fellow and Tutor of Wadham College. Illustrated by E. H. NEW. *Second Edition. Fcap. 8vo. 3s. Leather. 4s.*
This is a guide—chiefly historical—to the Colleges of Oxford. It contains numerous illustrations.
'An admirable and accurate little treatise, attractively illustrated.'—*World.*
'A luminous and tasteful little volume.'—*Daily Chronicle.*
'Exactly what the intelligent visitor wants.'—*Glasgow Herald.*

C. G. Robertson. VOCES ACADEMICÆ. By C. GRANT ROBERTSON, M.A., Fellow of All Souls', Oxford. *With a Frontispiece. Pott. 8vo. 3s. 6d.*
'Decidedly clever and amusing.'—*Athenæum.*
'The dialogues are abundantly smart and amusing.'—*Glasgow Herald.*
'A clever and entertaining little book.'—*Pall Mall Gazette.*

L. Whibley. GREEK OLIGARCHIES : THEIR ORGANISATION AND CHARACTER. By L. WHIBLEY, M.A., Fellow of Pembroke College, Cambridge. *Crown 8vo. 6s.*
'An exceedingly useful handbook : a careful and well-arranged study.'—*Times.*

L. L. Price. ECONOMIC SCIENCE AND PRACTICE. By L. L. PRICE, M.A., Fellow of Oriel College, Oxford. *Crown 8vo. 6s.*
'The book is well written, giving evidence of considerable literary ability, and clear mental grasp of the subject under consideration.'—*Western Morning News.*

J. S. Shedlock. THE PIANOFORTE SONATA : Its Origin and Development. By J. S. SHEDLOCK. *Crown 8vo. 5s.*
'This work should be in the possession of every musician and amateur. A concise and lucid history of the origin of one of the most important forms of musical composition. A very valuable work for reference.'—*Athenæum.*

E. M. Bowden. THE EXAMPLE OF BUDDHA : Being Quotations from Buddhist Literature for each Day in the Year. Compiled by E. M. BOWDEN. *Third Edition. 16mo. 2s. 6d.*

Morgan-Browne. SPORTING AND ATHLETIC RECORDS. By H. MORGAN-BROWNE. *Crown 8vo. 1s. paper ; 1s. 6d. cloth.*
'Should meet a very wide demand.'—*Daily Mail.*
'A very careful collection, and the first one of its kind.'—*Manchester Guardian.*
'Certainly the most valuable of all books of its kind.'—*Birmingham Gazette.*

Science

Freudenreich. DAIRY BACTERIOLOGY. A Short Manual for the Use of Students. By Dr. ED. VON FREUDENREICH. Translated by J. R. AINSWORTH DAVIS, B.A. *Crown 8vo. 2s. 6d.*

MESSRS. METHUEN'S LIST

Chalmers Mitchell. OUTLINES OF BIOLOGY. By P. CHALMERS MITCHELL, M.A., *Illustrated. Crown 8vo. 6s.*

A text-book designed to cover the new Schedule issued by the Royal College of Physicians and Surgeons.

G. Massee. A MONOGRAPH OF THE MYXOGASTRES. By GEORGE MASSEE. With 12 Coloured Plates. *Royal 8vo.* 18s. *net.*

'A work much in advance of any book in the language treating of this group of organisms. Indispensable to every student of the Myxogastres.'—*Nature.*

Technology

Stephenson and Suddards. ORNAMENTAL DESIGN FOR WOVEN FABRICS. By C. STEPHENSON, of The Technical College, Bradford, and F. SUDDARDS, of The Yorkshire College, Leeds. With 65 full-page plates, and numerous designs and diagrams in the text. *Demy 8vo.* 7s. 6d.

'The book is very ably done, displaying an intimate knowledge of principles, good taste, and the faculty of clear exposition.'—*Yorkshire Post.*

HANDBOOKS OF TECHNOLOGY.
Edited by PROFESSORS GARNETT and WERTHEIMER.

HOW TO MAKE A DRESS. By J. A. E. WOOD. *Illustrated. Crown 8vo.* 1s. 6d.

A text-book for students preparing for the City and Guilds examination, based on the syllabus. The diagrams are numerous.

'Though primarily intended for students, Miss Wood's dainty little manual may be consulted with advantage by any girls who want to make their own frocks. The directions are simple and clear, and the diagrams very helpful.'—*Literature.*
'A splendid little book.'—*Evening News.*

Philosophy

L. T. Hobhouse. THE THEORY OF KNOWLEDGE. By L. T. HOBHOUSE, Fellow of C.C.C, Oxford. *Demy 8vo.* 21s.

'The most important contribution to English philosophy since the publication of Mr. Bradley's "Appearance and Reality." Full of brilliant criticism and of positive theories which are models of lucid statement.'—*Glasgow Herald.*
'A brilliantly written volume.'—*Times.*

W. H. Fairbrother. THE PHILOSOPHY OF T. H. GREEN. By W. H. FAIRBROTHER, M.A. *Crown 8vo.* 3s. 6d.

'In every way an admirable book.'—*Glasgow Herald.*

F. W. Bussell. THE SCHOOL OF PLATO: its Origin and its Revival under the Roman Empire. By F. W. BUSSELL, D.D., Fellow and Tutor of Brasenose College, Oxford. *Demy 8vo.* 10s. 6d.

'A highly valuable contribution to the history of ancient thought.'—*Glasgow Herald.*
'A clever and stimulating book, provocative of thought and deserving careful reading.'—*Manchester Guardian.*

F. S. Granger. THE WORSHIP OF THE ROMANS. By F. S. GRANGER, M.A., Litt.D., Professor of Philosophy at University College, Nottingham. *Crown 8vo.* 6s.

'A scholarly analysis of the religious ceremonies, beliefs, and superstitions of ancient Rome, conducted in the new light of comparative anthropology.'—*Times.*

Theology

HANDBOOKS OF THEOLOGY.

General Editor, A. ROBERTSON, D.D., Principal of King's College, London.

THE XXXIX. ARTICLES OF THE CHURCH OF ENGLAND. Edited with an Introduction by E. C. S. GIBSON, D.D., Vicar of Leeds, late Principal of Wells Theological College. *Second and Cheaper Edition in One Volume. Demy 8vo.* 12s. 6d.

'Dr. Gibson is a master of clear and orderly exposition, and he has enlisted in his service all the mechanism of variety of type which so greatly helps to elucidate a complicated subject. And he has in a high degree a quality very necessary, but rarely found, in commentators on this topic, that of absolute fairness. His book is pre-eminently honest.'—*Times.*

'After a survey of the whole book, we can bear witness to the transparent honesty of purpose, evident industry, and clearness of style which mark its contents. They maintain throughout a very high level of doctrine and tone.'—*Guardian.*

'An elaborate and learned book, excellently adapted to its purpose.'—*Speaker.*

'The most convenient and most acceptable commentary.'—*Expository Times.*

AN INTRODUCTION TO THE HISTORY OF RELIGION. By F. B. JEVONS, M.A., Litt.D., Principal of Bishop Hatfield's Hall. *Demy 8vo.* 10s. 6d.

'Dr. Jevons has written a notable work, which we can strongly recommend to the serious attention of theologians and anthropologists.'—*Manchester Guardian.*

'The merit of this book lies in the penetration, the singular acuteness and force of the author's judgment. He is at once critical and luminous, at once just and suggestive. A comprehensive and thorough book.'—*Birmingham Post.*

THE DOCTRINE OF THE INCARNATION. By R. L. OTTLEY, M.A., late fellow of Magdalen College, Oxon., and Principal of Pusey House. *In Two Volumes. Demy 8vo.* 15s.

'Learned and reverent: lucid and well arranged.'—*Record.*

'Accurate, well ordered, and judicious.'—*National Observer.*

'A clear and remarkably full account of the main currents of speculation. Scholarly precision . . . genuine tolerance . . . intense interest in his subject—are Mr. Ottley's merits.'—*Guardian.*

C. F. Andrews. CHRISTIANITY AND THE LABOUR QUESTION. By C. F. ANDREWS, B.A. *Crown 8vo.* 2s. 6d.

S. R. Driver. SERMONS ON SUBJECTS CONNECTED WITH THE OLD TESTAMENT. By S. R. DRIVER, D.D., Canon of Christ Church, Regius Professor of Hebrew in the University of Oxford. *Crown 8vo.* 6s.

'A welcome companion to the author's famous 'Introduction.' No man can read these discourses without feeling that Dr. Driver is fully alive to the deeper teaching of the Old Testament.'—*Guardian.*

T. K. Cheyne. FOUNDERS OF OLD TESTAMENT CRITICISM. By T. K. CHEYNE, D.D., Oriel Professor at Oxford. *Large crown 8vo.* 7s. 6d.

This book is a historical sketch of O. T. Criticism in the form of biographical studies from the days of Eichhorn to those of Driver and Robertson Smith.

'A very learned and instructive work.'—*Times.*

H. H. Henson. LIGHT AND LEAVEN: HISTORICAL AND SOCIAL SERMONS. By the Rev. H. HENSLEY HENSON, M.A., Fellow of All Souls', Incumbent of St. Mary's Hospital, Ilford. *Crown 8vo.* 6s.

'They are always reasonable as well as vigorous, and they are none the less impressive because they regard the needs of a life on this side of a hereafter.'—*Scotsman.*

W. H. Bennett. A PRIMER OF THE BIBLE. By Prof. W. H. BENNETT. *Second Edition. Crown 8vo.* 2s. 6d.

'The work of an honest, fearless, and sound critic, and an excellent guide in a small compass to the books of the Bible.'—*Manchester Guardian.*

'A unique primer. Mr. Bennett has collected and condensed a very extensive and diversified amount of material, and no one can consult his pages and fail to acknowledge indebtedness to his undertaking.'—*English Churchman.*

C. H. Prior. CAMBRIDGE SERMONS. Edited by C. H. PRIOR, M.A., Fellow and Tutor of Pembroke College. *Crown 8vo.* 6s.

A volume of sermons preached before the University of Cambridge by various preachers, including the late Archbishop of Canterbury and Bishop Westcott.

E. B. Layard. RELIGION IN BOYHOOD. Notes on the Religious Training of Boys. By E. B. LAYARD, M.A. *18mo.* 1s.

W. Yorke Faussett. THE *DE CATECHIZANDIS RUDIBUS* OF ST. AUGUSTINE. Edited, with Introduction, Notes, etc., by W. YORKE FAUSSETT, M.A., late Scholar of Balliol Coll. *Crown 8vo.* 3s. 6d.

An edition of a Treatise on the Essentials of Christian Doctrine, and the best methods of impressing them on candidates for baptism.

A Kempis. THE IMITATION OF CHRIST. By THOMAS À KEMPIS. With an Introduction by DEAN FARRAR. Illustrated by C. M. GERE, and printed in black and red. *Second Edition. Fcap. 8vo. Buckram.* 3s. 6d. *Padded morocco,* 5s.

'Amongst all the innumerable English editions of the "Imitation," there can have been few which were prettier than this one, printed in strong and handsome type, with all the glory of red initials.'—*Glasgow Herald.*

J. Keble. THE CHRISTIAN YEAR. By JOHN KEBLE. With an Introduction and Notes by W. LOCK, D.D., Warden of Keble College, Ireland Professor at Oxford. Illustrated by R. ANNING BELL. *Second Edition. Fcap. 8vo. Buckram.* 3s. 6d. *Padded morocco,* 5s.

'The present edition is annotated with all the care and insight to be expected from Mr. Lock. The progress and circumstances of its composition are detailed in the Introduction. There is an interesting Appendix on the MSS. of the "Christian Year," and another giving the order in which the poems were written. A "Short Analysis of the Thought" is prefixed to each, and any difficulty in the text is explained in a note.'—*Guardian.*

Leaders of Religion

Edited by H. C. BEECHING, M.A. *With Portraits, crown 8vo.*

A series of short biographies of the most prominent leaders of religious life and thought of all ages and countries.

The following are ready—

CARDINAL NEWMAN. By R. H. HUTTON.
JOHN WESLEY. By J. H. OVERTON, M.A.
BISHOP WILBERFORCE. By G. W. DANIEL, M.A.
CARDINAL MANNING. By A. W. HUTTON, M.A.
CHARLES SIMEON. By H. C. G. MOULE, M.A.
JOHN KEBLE. By WALTER LOCK, D.D.
THOMAS CHALMERS. By Mrs. OLIPHANT.
LANCELOT ANDREWES. By R. L. OTTLEY, M.A.
AUGUSTINE OF CANTERBURY. By E. L. CUTTS, D.D.
WILLIAM LAUD. By W. H. HUTTON, B.D.
JOHN KNOX. By F. M'CUNN.
JOHN HOWE. By R. F. HORTON, D.D.
BISHOP KEN. By F. A. CLARKE, M.A.
GEORGE FOX, THE QUAKER. By T. HODGKIN, D.C.L.
JOHN DONNE. By AUGUSTUS JESSOPP, D.D.

Other volumes will be announced in due course.

Fiction

SIX SHILLING NOVELS

Marie Corelli's Novels

Crown 8vo. 6s. each.

A ROMANCE OF TWO WORLDS. *Seventeenth Edition.*
VENDETTA. *Thirteenth Edition.*
THELMA. *Seventeenth Edition.*
ARDATH. *Eleventh Edition.*
THE SOUL OF LILITH. *Ninth Edition.*
WORMWOOD. *Eighth Edition.*
BARABBAS: A DREAM OF THE WORLD'S TRAGEDY. *Thirty-first Edition.*

'The tender reverence of the treatment and the imaginative beauty of the writing have reconciled us to the daring of the conception, and the conviction is forced on us that even so exalted a subject cannot be made too familiar to us, provided it be presented in the true spirit of Christian faith. The amplifications of the Scripture narrative are often conceived with high poetic insight, and this "Dream of the World's Tragedy" is, despite some trifling incongruities, a lofty and not inadequate paraphrase of the supreme climax of the inspired narrative.'—*Dublin Review.*

THE SORROWS OF SATAN. *Thirty-sixth Edition.*

'A very powerful piece of work.... The conception is magnificent, and is likely to win an abiding place within the memory of man.... The author has immense command of language, and a limitless audacity.... This interesting and remarkable romance will live long after much of the ephemeral literature of the day is forgotten.... A literary phenomenon ... novel, and even sublime.'—W. T. STEAD in the *Review of Reviews.*

Anthony Hope's Novels
Crown 8vo. 6s. each.

THE GOD IN THE CAR. *Seventh Edition.*

'A very remarkable book, deserving of critical analysis impossible within our limit; brilliant, but not superficial; well considered, but not elaborated; constructed with the proverbial art that conceals, but yet allows itself to be enjoyed by readers to whom fine literary method is a keen pleasure.'—*The World.*

A CHANGE OF AIR. *Fourth Edition.*

'A graceful, vivacious comedy, true to human nature. The characters are traced with a masterly hand.'—*Times.*

A MAN OF MARK. *Fourth Edition.*

'Of all Mr. Hope's books, "A Man of Mark" is the one which best compares with "The Prisoner of Zenda."'—*National Observer.*

THE CHRONICLES OF COUNT ANTONIO. *Third Edition.*

'It is a perfectly enchanting story of love and chivalry, and pure romance. The Count is the most constant, desperate, and modest and tender of lovers, a peerless gentleman, an intrepid fighter, a faithful friend, and a magnanimous foe.'—*Guardian.*

PHROSO. Illustrated by H. R. MILLAR. *Third Edition.*

'The tale is thoroughly fresh, quick with vitality, stirring the blood, and humorously, dashingly told.'—*St. James's Gazette.*
'A story of adventure, every page of which is palpitating with action.'—*Speaker.*
'From cover to cover "Phroso" not only engages the attention, but carries the reader in little whirls of delight from adventure to adventure.'—*Academy.*

S. Baring Gould's Novels
Crown 8vo. 6s. each.

'To say that a book is by the author of "Mehalah" is to imply that it contains a story cast on strong lines, containing dramatic possibilities, vivid and sympathetic descriptions of Nature, and a wealth of ingenious imagery.'—*Speaker.*
'That whatever Mr. Baring Gould writes is well worth reading, is a conclusion that may be very generally accepted. His views of life are fresh and vigorous, his language pointed and characteristic, the incidents of which he makes use are striking and original, his characters are life-like, and though somewhat exceptional people, are drawn and coloured with artistic force. Add to this that his descriptions of scenes and scenery are painted with the loving eyes and skilled hands of a master of his art, that he is always fresh and never dull, and under such conditions it is no wonder that readers have gained confidence both in his power of amusing and satisfying them, and that year by year his popularity widens.'—*Court Circular.*

ARMINELL : A Social Romance. *Fourth Edition.*

URITH : A Story of Dartmoor. *Fifth Edition.*
'The author is at his best.'—*Times.*

MESSRS. METHUEN'S LIST

IN THE ROAR OF THE SEA. *Sixth Edition.*
'One of the best imagined and most enthralling stories the author has produced.'
—*Saturday Review.*

MRS. CURGENVEN OF CURGENVEN. *Fourth Edition.*
'The swing of the narrative is splendid.'—*Sussex Daily News.*

CHEAP JACK ZITA. *Fourth Edition.*
'A powerful drama of human passion.'—*Westminster Gazette.*
'A story worthy the author.'—*National Observer.*

THE QUEEN OF LOVE. *Fourth Edition.*
'Can be heartily recommended to all who care for cleanly, energetic, and interesting fiction.'—*Sussex Daily News.*

KITTY ALONE. *Fourth Edition.*
'A strong and original story, teeming with graphic description, stirring incident, and, above all, with vivid and enthralling human interest.'—*Daily Telegraph.*

NOÉMI: A Romance of the Cave-Dwellers. Illustrated by R. CATON WOODVILLE. *Third Edition.*
'A powerful story, full of strong lights and shadows.'—*Standard.*

THE BROOM-SQUIRE. Illustrated by FRANK DADD. *Fourth Edition.*
'A strain of tenderness is woven through the web of his tragic tale, and its atmosphere is sweetened by the nobility and sweetness of the heroine's character.'—*Daily News.*

THE PENNYCOMEQUICKS. *Third Edition.*

DARTMOOR IDYLLS.
'A book to read, and keep and read again; for the genuine fun and pathos of it will not early lose their effect.'—*Vanity Fair.*

GUAVAS THE TINNER. Illustrated by FRANK DADD. *Second Edition.*
'There is a kind of flavour about this book which alone elevates it above the ordinary novel. The story itself has a grandeur in harmony with the wild and rugged scenery which is its setting.'—*Athenæum.*

BLADYS. *Second Edition.*
'A story of thrilling interest.'—*Scotsman.*
'A sombre but powerful story.'—*Daily Mail.*

Gilbert Parker's Novels
Crown 8vo. 6s. each.

PIERRE AND HIS PEOPLE. *Fourth Edition.*
'Stories happily conceived and finely executed. There is strength and genius in Mr. Parker's style.'—*Daily Telegraph.*

MRS. FALCHION. *Fourth Edition.*
'A splendid study of character.'—*Athenæum.*
'But little behind anything that has been done by any writer of our time.'—*Pall Mall Gazette.*   'A very striking and admirable novel.'—*St. James's Gazette.*

THE TRANSLATION OF A SAVAGE.
'The plot is original and one difficult to work out; but Mr. Parker has done it with great skill and delicacy. The reader who is not interested in this original, fresh, and well-told tale must be a dull person indeed.'—*Daily Chronicle.*

MESSRS. METHUEN'S LIST

THE TRAIL OF THE SWORD. *Fifth Edition.*

'A rousing and dramatic tale. A book like this, in which swords flash, great surprises are undertaken, and daring deeds done, in which men and women live and love in the old passionate way, is a joy inexpressible.'—*Daily Chronicle.*

WHEN VALMOND CAME TO PONTIAC: The Story of a Lost Napoleon. *Fourth Edition.*

'Here we find romance—real, breathing, living romance. The character of Valmond is drawn unerringly. The book must be read, we may say re-read, for any one thoroughly to appreciate Mr. Parker's delicate touch and innate sympathy with humanity.'—*Pall Mall Gazette.*

AN ADVENTURER OF THE NORTH: The Last Adventures of 'Pretty Pierre.' *Second Edition.*

'The present book is full of fine and moving stories of the great North, and it will add to Mr. Parker's already high reputation.'—*Glasgow Herald.*

THE SEATS OF THE MIGHTY. *Illustrated. Ninth Edition.*

'The best thing he has done; one of the best things that any one has done lately.'—*St. James's Gazette.*

'Mr. Parker seems to become stronger and easier with every serious novel that he attempts. He shows the matured power which his former novels have led us to expect, and has produced a really fine historical novel. The finest novel he has yet written.'—*Athenæum.*

'A great book.'—*Black and White.*

'One of the strongest stories of historical interest and adventure that we have read for many a day. . . . A notable and successful book.'—*Speaker.*

THE POMP OF THE LAVILETTES. *Second Edition.* 3s. 6d.

'Living, breathing romance, genuine and unforced pathos, and a deeper and more subtle knowledge of human nature than Mr. Parker has ever displayed before. It is, in a word, the work of a true artist.'—*Pall Mall Gazette.*

Conan Doyle. ROUND THE RED LAMP. By A. CONAN DOYLE, Author of 'The White Company,' 'The Adventures of Sherlock Holmes,' etc. *Fifth Edition. Crown 8vo. 6s.*

'The book is, indeed, composed of leaves from life, and is far and away the best view that has been vouchsafed us behind the scenes of the consulting-room. It is very superior to "The Diary of a late Physician."'—*Illustrated London News.*

Stanley Weyman. UNDER THE RED ROBE. By STANLEY WEYMAN, Author of 'A Gentleman of France.' With Twelve Illustrations by R. Caton Woodville. *Twelfth Edition. Crown 8vo. 6s.*

'A book of which we have read every word for the sheer pleasure of reading, and which we put down with a pang that we cannot forget it all and start again.'—*Westminster Gazette.*

'Every one who reads books at all must read this thrilling romance, from the first page of which to the last the breathless reader is haled along. An inspiration of manliness and courage.'—*Daily Chronicle.*

Lucas Malet. THE WAGES OF SIN. By LUCAS MALET. *Thirteenth Edition. Crown 8vo. 6s.*

Lucas Malet. THE CARISSIMA. By LUCAS MALET, Author of 'The Wages of Sin,' etc. *Third Edition. Crown 8vo. 6s.*

MESSRS. METHUEN'S LIST 27

S. R. Crockett. LOCHINVAR. By S. R. CROCKETT, Author of 'The Raiders,' etc. Illustrated. *Second Edition. Crown 8vo. 6s.*

'Full of gallantry and pathos, of the clash of arms, and brightened by episodes of humour and love. . . . Mr. Crockett has never written a stronger or better book. An engrossing and fascinating story. The love story alone is enough to make the book delightful.'—*Westminster Gazette.*

Arthur Morrison. TALES OF MEAN STREETS. By ARTHUR MORRISON. *Fourth Edition. Crown 8vo. 6s.*

'Told with consummate art and extraordinary detail. In the true humanity of the book lies its justification, the permanence of its interest, and its indubitable triumph.'—*Athenæum.*

'A great book. The author's method is amazingly effective, and produces a thrilling sense of reality. The writer lays upon us a master hand. The book is simply appalling and irresistible in its interest. It is humorous also; without humour it would not make the mark it is certain to make.'—*World.*

Arthur Morrison. A CHILD OF THE JAGO. By ARTHUR MORRISON. *Third Edition. Crown 8vo. 6s.*

'The book is a masterpiece.'—*Pall Mall Gazette.*
'Told with great vigour and powerful simplicity.'—*Athenæum.*

Mrs. Clifford. A FLASH OF SUMMER. By Mrs. W. K. CLIFFORD, Author of 'Aunt Anne,' etc. *Second Edition. Crown 8vo. 6s.*

'The story is a very sad and a very beautiful one, exquisitely told, and enriched with many subtle touches of wise and tender insight.'—*Speaker.*

Emily Lawless. HURRISH. By the Honble. EMILY LAWLESS, Author of 'Maelcho,' etc. *Fifth Edition. Crown 8vo. 6s.*

A reissue of Miss Lawless' most popular novel, uniform with 'Maelcho.'

Emily Lawless. MAELCHO: a Sixteenth Century Romance. By the Honble. EMILY LAWLESS. *Second Edition. Crown 8vo. 6s.*

'A really great book.'—*Spectator.*
'There is no keener pleasure in life than the recognition of genius. A piece of work of the first order, which we do not hesitate to describe as one of the most remarkable literary achievements of this generation.'—*Manchester Guardian.*

Jane Barlow. A CREEL OF IRISH STORIES. By JANE BARLOW, Author of 'Irish Idylls.' *Second Edition. Crown 8vo. 6s.*

'Vivid and singularly real.'—*Scotsman.*
'Genuinely and naturally Irish.'—*Scotsman.*
'The sincerity of her sentiments, the distinction of her style, and the freshness of her themes, combine to lift her work far above the average level of contemporary fiction.'—*Manchester Guardian.*

J. H. Findlater. THE GREEN GRAVES OF BALGOWRIE. By JANE H. FINDLATER. *Fourth Edition. Crown 8vo. 6s.*

'A powerful and vivid story.'—*Standard.*
'A beautiful story, sad and strange as truth itself.'—*Vanity Fair.*
'A work of remarkable interest and originality.'—*National Observer.*
'A very charming and pathetic tale.'—*Pall Mall Gazette.*
'A singularly original, clever, and beautiful story.'—*Guardian.*
'Reveals to us a new writer of undoubted faculty and reserve force.'—*Spectator.*
'An exquisite idyll, delicate, affecting, and beautiful.'—*Black and White.*

Messrs. Methuen's List

J. H. Findlater. A DAUGHTER OF STRIFE. By Jane Helen Findlater, Author of 'The Green Graves of Balgowrie.' *Crown 8vo.* 6s.

'A story of strong human interest.'—*Scotsman.*
'It has a sweet flavour of olden days delicately conveyed.'—*Manchester Guardian.*
'Her thought has solidity and maturity.'—*Daily Mail.*

Mary Findlater. OVER THE HILLS. By Mary Findlater. *Crown 8vo.* 6s.

'A strong and fascinating piece of work.'—*Scotsman.*
'A charming romance, and full of incident. The book is fresh and strong.'—*Speaker.*
'There is quiet force and beautiful simplicity in this book which will make the author's name loved in many a household.'—*Literary World.*
'Admirably fresh and broad in treatment. The novel is markedly original and excellently written.'—*Daily Chronicle.*
'A strong and wise book of deep insight and unflinching truth.'—*Birmingham Post.*
'Miss Mary Findlater combines originality with strength.'—*Daily Mail.*

H. G. Wells. THE STOLEN BACILLUS, and other Stories. By H. G. Wells. *Second Edition. Crown 8vo.* 6s.

'The ordinary reader of fiction may be glad to know that these stories are eminently readable from one cover to the other, but they are more than that; they are the impressions of a very striking imagination, which, it would seem, has a great deal within its reach.'—*Saturday Review.*

H. G. Wells. THE PLATTNER STORY AND OTHERS. By H. G. Wells. *Second Edition. Crown 8vo.* 6s.

'Weird and mysterious, they seem to hold the reader as by a magic spell.'—*Scotsman.*
'No volume has appeared for a long time so likely to give equal pleasure to the simplest reader and to the most fastidious critic.'—*Academy.*

E. F. Benson. DODO: A DETAIL OF THE DAY. By E. F. Benson. *Sixteenth Edition. Crown 8vo.* 6s.

'A delightfully witty sketch of society.'—*Spectator.*
'A perpetual feast of epigram and paradox.'—*Speaker.*

E. F. Benson. THE RUBICON. By E. F. Benson, Author of 'Dodo.' *Fifth Edition. Crown 8vo.* 6s.

Mrs. Oliphant. SIR ROBERT'S FORTUNE. By Mrs. Oliphant. *Crown 8vo.* 6s.

'Full of her own peculiar charm of style and simple, subtle character-painting comes her new gift, the delightful story.'—*Pall Mall Gazette.*

Mrs. Oliphant. THE TWO MARYS. By Mrs. Oliphant. *Second Edition. Crown 8vo.* 6s.

Mrs. Oliphant. THE LADY'S WALK. By Mrs. Oliphant. *Second Edition. Crown 8vo.* 6s.

'A story of exquisite tenderness, of most delicate fancy.'—*Pall Mall Gazette.*
'It contains many of the finer characteristics of her best work.'—*Scotsman.*
'It is little short of sacrilege on the part of a reviewer to attempt to sketch its outlines or analyse its peculiar charm.'—*Spectator.*

W. E. Norris. MATTHEW AUSTIN. By W. E. NORRIS, Author of 'Mademoiselle de Mersac,' etc. *Fourth Edition. Crown 8vo.* 6s.

"An intellectually satisfactory and morally bracing novel.'—*Daily Telegraph.*

W. E. Norris. HIS GRACE. By W. E. NORRIS. *Third Edition. Crown 8vo.* 6s.

'Mr. Norris has drawn a really fine character in the Duke of Hurstbourne, at once unconventional and very true to the conventionalities of life.'—*Athenæum.*

W. E. Norris. THE DESPOTIC LADY AND OTHERS. By W. E. NORRIS. *Crown 8vo.* 6s.

'A budget of good fiction of which no one will tire.'—*Scotsman.*

W. E. Norris. CLARISSA FURIOSA. By W. E. NORRIS, *Crown 8vo.* 6s.

'As a story it is admirable, as a *jeu d'esprit* it is capital, as a lay sermon studded with gems of wit and wisdom it is a model.'—*The World.*

W. Clark Russell. MY DANISH SWEETHEART. By W. CLARK RUSSELL, Author of 'The Wreck of the Grosvenor,' etc. *Illustrated. Fourth Edition. Crown 8vo.* 6s.

Robert Barr. THE MUTABLE MANY. By ROBERT BARR, Author of 'In the Midst of Alarms,' 'A Woman Intervenes,' etc. *Second Edition. Crown 8vo.* 6s.

'Very much the best novel that Mr. Barr has yet given us. There is much insight in it, much acute and delicate appreciation of the finer shades of character and much excellent humour.'—*Daily Chronicle.*
'An excellent story. It contains several excellently studied characters, and is filled with lifelike pictures of modern life.'—*Glasgow Herald.*

Robert Barr. IN THE MIDST OF ALARMS. By ROBERT BARR. *Third Edition. Crown 8vo.* 6s.

'A book which has abundantly satisfied us by its capital humour.'—*Daily Chronicle.*
'Mr. Barr has achieved a triumph whereof he has every reason to be proud.'—*Pall Mall Gazette.*

J. Maclaren Cobban. THE KING OF ANDAMAN: A Saviour of Society. By J. MACLAREN COBBAN. *Crown 8vo.* 6s.

'An unquestionably interesting book. It contains one character, at least, who has in him the root of immortality, and the book itself is ever exhaling the sweet savour of the unexpected.'—*Pall Mall Gazette.*

J. Maclaren Cobban. WILT THOU HAVE THIS WOMAN? By J. M. COBBAN, Author of 'The King of Andaman.' *Crown 8vo.* 6s.

Robert Hichens. BYEWAYS. By ROBERT HICHENS. Author of 'Flames,' etc. *Crown 8vo.* 6s.

'A very high artistic instinct and striking command of language raise Mr. Hichens' work far above the ruck.'—*Pall Mall Gazette.*
'The work is undeniably that of a man of striking imagination and no less striking powers of expression.'—*Daily News.*

Percy White. A PASSIONATE PILGRIM. By PERCY WHITE, Author of 'Mr. Bailey-Martin.' *Crown 8vo.* 6s.

'A work which it is not hyperbole to describe as of rare excellence.'—*Pall Mall Gazette.*
'The clever book of a shrewd and clever author.'—*Athenæum.*
'Mr. Percy White's strong point is analysis, and he has shown himself, before now, capable of building up a good book upon that foundation.'—*Standard.*

W. Pett Ridge. SECRETARY TO BAYNE, M.P. By W. PETT RIDGE. *Crown 8vo.* 6s.

'Sparkling, vivacious, adventurous.—*St. James's Gazette.*
'Ingenious, amusing, and especially smart.'—*World.*
'The dialogue is invariably alert and highly diverting.'—*Spectator.*

J. S. Fletcher. THE BUILDERS. By J. S. FLETCHER, Author of 'When Charles I. was King.' *Second Edition. Crown 8vo.* 6s.

'Replete with delightful descriptions.'—*Vanity Fair.*
'The background of country life has never, perhaps, been sketched more realistically.'—*World.*

Andrew Balfour. BY STROKE OF SWORD. By ANDREW BALFOUR. Illustrated by W. CUBITT COOKE. *Fourth Edition. Crown 8vo.* 6s.

'A banquet of good things.'—*Academy.*
'A recital of thrilling interest, told with unflagging vigour.'—*Globe*
'An unusually excellent example of a semi-historic romance.'—*World.*
'Manly, healthy, and patriotic.'—*Glasgow Herald.*

I. Hooper. THE SINGER OF MARLY. By I. HOOPER. Illustrated by W. CUBITT COOKE. *Crown 8vo.* 6s.

'Its scenes are drawn in vivid colours, and the characters are all picturesque.'—*Scotsman.*
'A novel as vigorous as it is charming.'—*Literary World.*

M. C. Balfour. THE FALL OF THE SPARROW. By M. C. BALFOUR. *Crown 8vo.* 6s.

'A powerful novel.'—*Daily Telegraph.*
'It is unusually powerful, and the characterization is uncommonly good.'—*World.*
'It is a well-knit, carefully-wrought story.'—*Academy.*

H. Morrah. A SERIOUS COMEDY. By HERBERT MORRAH. *Crown 8vo.* 6s.

H. Morrah. THE FAITHFUL CITY. By HERBERT MORRAH, Author of 'A Serious Comedy.' *Crown 8vo.* 6s.

L. B. Walford. SUCCESSORS TO THE TITLE. By Mrs. WALFORD, Author of 'Mr. Smith,' etc. *Second Edition. Crown 8vo.* 6s.

Mary Gaunt. KIRKHAM'S FIND. By MARY GAUNT, Author of 'The Moving Finger.' *Crown 8vo.* 6s.

'A really charming novel.'—*Standard.*
'A capital book, in which will be found lively humour, penetrating insight, and the sweet savour of a thoroughly healthy moral.'—*Speaker.*

M. M. Dowie. GALLIA. By MÉNIE MURIEL DOWIE, Author of 'A Girl in the Carpathians.' *Third Edition. Crown 8vo.* 6s.

'The style is generally admirable, the dialogue not seldom brilliant, the situations surprising in their freshness and originality, while the characters live and move, and the story itself is readable from title-page to colophon.'—*Saturday Review.*

J. A. Barry. IN THE GREAT DEEP. By J. A. BARRY. Author of 'Steve Brown's Bunyip.' *Crown 8vo.* 6s.

'A collection of really admirable short stories of the sea, very simply told, and placed before the reader in pithy and telling English.'—*Westminster Gazette.*

J. B. Burton. IN THE DAY OF ADVERSITY. By J. BLOUNDELLE-BURTON.' *Second Edition. Crown 8vo.* 6s.

'Unusually interesting and full of highly dramatic situations.—*Guardian.*

J. B. Burton. DENOUNCED. By J. BLOUNDELLE-BURTON. *Second Edition. Crown 8vo.* 6s.

'The plot is an original one, and the local colouring is laid on with a delicacy and an accuracy of detail which denote the true artist.'—*Broad Arrow.*

J. B. Burton. THE CLASH OF ARMS. By J. BLOUNDELLE-BURTON, Author of 'In the Day of Adversity.' *Second Edition. Crown 8vo.* 6s.

'A brave story—brave in deed, brave in word, brave in thought.'—*St. James's Gazette.*
'A fine, manly, spirited piece of work.'—*World.*

W. C. Scully. THE WHITE HECATOMB. By W. C. SCULLY, Author of 'Kafir Stories.' *Crown 8vo.* 6s.

'It reveals a marvellously intimate understanding of the Kaffir mind, allied with literary gifts of no mean order.'—*African Critic.*

Julian Corbett. A BUSINESS IN GREAT WATERS. By JULIAN CORBETT. *Second Edition. Crown 8vo.* 6s.

'Mr. Corbett writes with immense spirit. The salt of the ocean is in it, and the right heroic ring resounds through its gallant adventures.'—*Speaker.*

L. Cope Cornford. CAPTAIN JACOBUS: A ROMANCE OF THE ROAD. By L. COPE CORNFORD. Illustrated. *Crown 8vo.* 6s.

'An exceptionally good story of adventure and character.'—*World.*

L. Daintrey. THE KING OF ALBERIA. A Romance of the Balkans. By LAURA DAINTREY. *Crown 8vo.* 6s.

M. A. Owen. THE DAUGHTER OF ALOUETTE. By MARY A. OWEN. *Crown 8vo.* 6s.

MESSRS. METHUEN'S LIST

Mrs. Pinsent. CHILDREN OF THIS WORLD. By ELLEN F. PINSENT, Author of 'Jenny's Case.' *Crown 8vo. 6s.*

G. Manville Fenn. AN ELECTRIC SPARK. By G. MANVILLE FENN, Author of 'The Vicar's Wife,' 'A Double Knot,' etc. *Second Edition. Crown 8vo. 6s.*

L. S. McChesney. UNDER SHADOW OF THE MISSION. By L. S. MCCHESNEY. *Crown 8vo. 6s.*

'Those whose minds are open to the finer issues of life, who can appreciate graceful thought and refined expression of it, from them this volume will receive a welcome as enthusiastic as it will be based on critical knowledge.'—*Church Times.*

J. F. Brewer. THE SPECULATORS. By J. F. BREWER. *Second Edition. Crown 8vo. 6s.*

Ronald Ross. THE SPIRIT OF STORM. By RONALD ROSS, Author of 'The Child of Ocean.' *Crown 8vo. 6s.*

C. P. Wolley. THE QUEENSBERRY CUP. A Tale of Adventure. By CLIVE P. L LEY. *Illustrated. Crown 8vo. 6s.*

T. L. Paton. A HOME IN INVERESK. By T. L. PATON. *Crown 8vo. 6s.*

John Davidson. MISS ARMSTRONG'S AND OTHER CIRCUMSTANCES. By JOHN DAVIDSON. *Crown 8vo. 6s.*

H. Johnston. DR. CONGALTON'S LEGACY. By HENRY JOHNSTON. *Crown 8vo. 6s.*

R. Pryce. TIME AND THE WOMAN. By RICHARD PRYCE. *Second Edition. Crown 8vo. 6s.*

Mrs. Watson. THIS MAN'S DOMINION. By the Author of 'A High Little World.' *Second Edition. Crown 8vo. 6s.*

Marriott Watson. DIOGENES OF LONDON. By H. B. MARRIOTT WATSON. *Crown 8vo. Buckram. 6s.*

M. Gilchrist. THE STONE DRAGON. By MURRAY GILCHRIST. *Crown 8vo. Buckram. 6s.*

E. Dickinson. A VICAR'S WIFE. By EVELYN DICKINSON. *Crown 8vo. 6s.*

E. M. Gray. ELSA. By E. M'QUEEN GRAY. *Crown 8vo. 6s.*

THREE-AND-SIXPENNY NOVELS
Crown 8vo.

DERRICK VAUGHAN, NOVELIST. By EDNA LYALL.
MARGERY OF QUETHER. By S. BARING GOULD.
JACQUETTA. By S. BARING GOULD.
SUBJECT TO VANITY. By MARGARET BENSON.
THE SIGN OF THE SPIDER. By BERTRAM MITFORD.
THE MOVING FINGER. By MARY GAUNT.
JACO TRELOAR. By J. H. PEARCE.
THE DANCE OF THE HOURS. By 'VERA.'
A WOMAN OF FORTY. By ESMÉ STUART.
A CUMBERER OF THE GROUND. By CONSTANCE SMITH.
THE SIN OF ANGELS. By EVELYN DICKINSON.
AUT DIABOLUS AUT NIHIL. By X. L.
THE COMING OF CUCULAIN. By STANDISH O'GRADY.
THE GODS GIVE MY DONKEY WINGS. By ANGUS EVAN ABBOTT.
THE STAR GAZERS. By G. MANVILLE FENN.
THE POISON OF ASPS. By R. ORTON PROWSE.
THE QUIET MRS. FLEMING. By R. PRYCE.
DISENCHANTMENT. By F. MABEL ROBINSON.
THE SQUIRE OF WANDALES. By A. SHIELD.
A REVEREND GENTLEMAN. By J. M. COBBAN.
A DEPLORABLE AFFAIR. By W. E. NORRIS.
A CAVALIER'S LADYE. By Mrs. DICKER.
THE PRODIGALS. By Mrs. OLIPHANT.
THE SUPPLANTER. By P. NEUMANN.
A MAN WITH BLACK EYELASHES. By H. A. KENNEDY.
A HANDFUL OF EXOTICS. By S. GORDON.
AN ODD EXPERIMENT. By HANNAH LYNCH.
SCOTTISH BORDER LIFE. By JAMES C. DIBDIN.

HALF-CROWN NOVELS
A Series of Novels by popular Authors.

HOVENDEN, V.C. By F. MABEL ROBINSON.
THE PLAN OF CAMPAIGN. By F. MABEL ROBINSON.
MR. BUTLER'S WARD. By F. MABEL ROBINSON.
ELI'S CHILDREN. By G. MANVILLE FENN.
A DOUBLE KNOT. By G. MANVILLE FENN.
DISARMED. By M. BETHAM EDWARDS.
A MARRIAGE AT SEA. By W. CLARK RUSSELL.
IN TENT AND BUNGALOW. By the Author of 'Indian Idylls.'

MY STEWARDSHIP. By E. M'QUEEN GRAY.
JACK'S FATHER. By W. E. NORRIS.
JIM B.
A LOST ILLUSION. By LESLIE KEITH.

Lynn Linton. THE TRUE HISTORY OF JOSHUA DAVIDSON, Christian and Communist. By E. LYNN LINTON. *Eleventh Edition. Post 8vo.* 1s.

Books for Boys and Girls

A Series of Books by well-known Authors, well illustrated.

THREE-AND-SIXPENCE EACH

THE ICELANDER'S SWORD. By S. BARING GOULD.
TWO LITTLE CHILDREN AND CHING. By EDITH E. CUTHELL.
TODDLEBEN'S HERO. By M. M. BLAKE.
ONLY A GUARD-ROOM DOG. By EDITH E. CUTHELL.
THE DOCTOR OF THE JULIET. By HARRY COLLINGWOOD.
MASTER ROCKAFELLAR'S VOYAGE. By W. CLARK RUSSELL.
SYD BELTON: Or, The Boy who would not go to Sea. By G. MANVILLE FENN.
THE WALLYPUG IN LONDON. By G. E. FARROW.

The Peacock Library

A Series of Books for Girls by well-known Authors, handsomely bound in blue and silver, and well illustrated.

THREE-AND-SIXPENCE EACH

A PINCH OF EXPERIENCE. By L. B. WALFORD.
THE RED GRANGE. By Mrs. MOLESWORTH.
THE SECRET OF MADAME DE MONLUC. By the Author of 'Mdle Mori.'
DUMPS. By Mrs. PARR, Author of 'Adam and Eve.'
OUT OF THE FASHION. By L. T. MEADE.
A GIRL OF THE PEOPLE. By L. T. MEADE.
HEPSY GIPSY. By L. T. MEADE. 2s. 6d.
THE HONOURABLE MISS. By L. T. MEADE.
MY LAND OF BEULAH. By Mrs. LEITH ADAMS.

University Extension Series

A series of books on historical, literary, and scientific subjects, suitable for extension students and home-reading circles. Each volume is complete in itself, and the subjects are treated by competent writers in a broad and philosophic spirit.

Edited by J. E. SYMES, M.A.,
Principal of University College, Nottingham.

Crown 8vo. Price (with some exceptions) 2s. 6d.

The following volumes are ready:—

THE INDUSTRIAL HISTORY OF ENGLAND. By H. DE B. GIBBINS, D.Litt., M.A., late Scholar of Wadham College, Oxon., Cobden Prizeman. *Fifth Edition, Revised. With Maps and Plans.* 3s.

'A compact and clear story of our industrial development. A study of this concise but luminous book cannot fail to give the reader a clear insight into the principal phenomena of our industrial history. The editor and publishers are to be congratulated on this first volume of their venture, and we shall look with expectant interest for the succeeding volumes of the series.'—*University Extension Journal.*

A HISTORY OF ENGLISH POLITICAL ECONOMY. By L. L. PRICE, M.A., Fellow of Oriel College, Oxon. *Second Edition.*

PROBLEMS OF POVERTY: An Inquiry into the Industrial Conditions of the Poor. By J. A. HOBSON, M.A. *Third Edition.*

VICTORIAN POETS. By A. SHARP.

THE FRENCH REVOLUTION. By J. E. SYMES, M.A.

PSYCHOLOGY. By F. S. GRANGER, M.A. *Second Edition.*

THE EVOLUTION OF PLANT LIFE: Lower Forms. By G. MASSEE. *With Illustrations.*

AIR AND WATER. By V. B. LEWES, M.A. *Illustrated.*

THE CHEMISTRY OF LIFE AND HEALTH. By C. W. KIMMINS, M.A. *Illustrated.*

THE MECHANICS OF DAILY LIFE. By V. P. SELLS, M.A. *Illustrated.*

ENGLISH SOCIAL REFORMERS. By H. DE B. GIBBINS, D.Litt., M.A.

ENGLISH TRADE AND FINANCE IN THE SEVENTEENTH CENTURY. By W. A. S. HEWINS, B.A.

THE CHEMISTRY OF FIRE. The Elementary Principles of Chemistry. By M. M. PATTISON MUIR, M.A. *Illustrated.*

A TEXT-BOOK OF AGRICULTURAL BOTANY. By M. C. POTTER, M.A., F.L.S. *Illustrated.* 3s. 6d.

THE VAULT OF HEAVEN. A Popular Introduction to Astronomy. By R. A. GREGORY. *With numerous Illustrations.*

METEOROLOGY. The Elements of Weather and Climate. By H. N. DICKSON, F.R.S.E., F.R. Met. Soc. *Illustrated.*

A MANUAL OF ELECTRICAL SCIENCE. By GEORGE J. BURCH, M.A. *With numerous Illustrations.* 3s.

THE EARTH. An Introduction to Physiography. By EVAN SMALL, M.A. *Illustrated.*

INSECT LIFE. By F. W. THEOBALD, M.A. *Illustrated.*

ENGLISH POETRY FROM BLAKE TO BROWNING. By W. M. DIXON, M.A.

ENGLISH LOCAL GOVERNMENT. By E. JENKS, M.A., Professor of Law at University College, Liverpool.

THE GREEK VIEW OF LIFE. By G. L. DICKINSON, Fellow of King's College, Cambridge. *Second Edition.*

Social Questions of To-day

Edited by H. DE B. GIBBINS, D. Litt., M.A.

Crown 8vo. 2s. 6d.

A series of volumes upon those topics of social, economic, and industrial interest that are at the present moment foremost in the public mind. Each volume of the series is written by an author who is an acknowledged authority upon the subject with which he deals.

The following Volumes of the Series are ready:—

TRADE UNIONISM—NEW AND OLD. By G. HOWELL. *Second Edition.*

THE CO-OPERATIVE MOVEMENT TO-DAY. By G. J. HOLYOAKE, *Second Edition.*

MUTUAL THRIFT. By Rev. J. FROME WILKINSON, M.A.

PROBLEMS OF POVERTY. By J. A. HOBSON, M.A. *Third Edition.*

THE COMMERCE OF NATIONS. By C. F. BASTABLE, M.A., Professor of Economics at Trinity College, Dublin.

THE ALIEN INVASION. By W. H. WILKINS, B.A.

THE RURAL EXODUS. By P. ANDERSON GRAHAM.

LAND NATIONALIZATION. By HAROLD COX, B.A.

A SHORTER WORKING DAY. By H. DE B. GIBBINS, D.Litt., M.A., and R. A. HADFIELD, of the Hecla Works, Sheffield.

BACK TO THE LAND: An Inquiry into the Cure for Rural Depopulation By H. E. MOORE.

TRUSTS, POOLS AND CORNERS. By J. STEPHEN JEANS.

THE FACTORY SYSTEM. By R. W. COOKE-TAYLOR.

THE STATE AND ITS CHILDREN. By GERTRUDE TUCKWELL.

MESSRS. METHUEN'S LIST 37

WOMEN'S WORK. By LADY DILKE, Miss BULLEY, and Miss WHITLEY.
MUNICIPALITIES AT WORK. The Municipal Policy of Six Great Towns, and its Influence on their Social Welfare. By FREDERICK DOLMAN.
SOCIALISM AND MODERN THOUGHT. By M. KAUFMANN.
THE HOUSING OF THE WORKING CLASSES. By E. BOWMAKER.
MODERN CIVILIZATION IN SOME OF ITS ECONOMIC ASPECTS. By W. CUNNINGHAM, D.D., Fellow of Trinity College, Cambridge.
THE PROBLEM OF THE UNEMPLOYED. By J. A. HOBSON, B.A.,
LIFE IN WEST LONDON. By ARTHUR SHERWELL, M.A. *Second Edition.*
RAILWAY NATIONALIZATION. By CLEMENT EDWARDS.

Classical Translations

Edited by H. F. FOX, M.A., Fellow and Tutor of Brasenose College, Oxford.

ÆSCHYLUS—Agamemnon, Chöephoroe, Eumenides. Translated by LEWIS CAMPBELL, LL.D., late Professor of Greek at St. Andrews. 5*s.*

CICERO—De Oratore I. Translated by E. N. P. MOOR, M.A. 3*s.* 6*d.*

CICERO—Select Orations (Pro Milone, Pro Murena, Philippic II., In Catilinam). Translated by H. E. D. BLAKISTON, M.A., Fellow and Tutor of Trinity College, Oxford. 5*s.*

CICERO—De Natura Deorum. Translated by F. BROOKS, M.A., late Scholar of Balliol College, Oxford. 3*s.* 6*d.*

LUCIAN—Six Dialogues (Nigrinus, Icaro-Menippus, The Cock, The Ship, The Parasite, The Lover of Falsehood). Translated by S. T. IRWIN, M.A., Assistant Master at Clifton; late Scholar of Exeter College, Oxford. 3*s.* 6*d.*

SOPHOCLES—Electra and Ajax. Translated by E. D. A. MORSHEAD, M.A., Assistant Master at Winchester. 2*s.* 6*d.*

TACITUS—Agricola and Germania. Translated by R. B. TOWNSHEND, late Scholar of Trinity College, Cambridge. 2*s.* 6*d.*

Educational Books

CLASSICAL

PLAUTI BACCHIDES. Edited with Introduction, Commentary, and Critical Notes by J. M'COSH, M.A. *Fcap.* 4*to.* 12*s.* 6*d.*
'The notes are copious, and contain a great deal of information that is good and useful.'—*Classical Review.*

TACITI AGRICOLI. With Introduction, Notes, Map, etc. By R. F. DAVIS, M.A., Assistant Master at Weymouth College. *Crown 8vo.* 2*s.*

TACITI GERMANIA. By the same Editor. *Crown 8vo.* 2*s.*

HERODOTUS: EASY SELECTIONS. With Vocabulary. By A. C. LIDDELL, M.A. *Fcap. 8vo.* 1*s.* 6*d.*

SELECTIONS FROM THE ODYSSEY. By E. D. STONE, M.A., late Assistant Master at Eton. *Fcap. 8vo.* 1s. 6d.

PLAUTUS: THE CAPTIVI. Adapted for Lower Forms by J. H. FRESSE, M.A., late Fellow of St. John's, Cambridge. 1s. 6d.

DEMOSTHENES AGAINST CONON AND CALLICLES. Edited with Notes and Vocabulary, by F. DARWIN SWIFT, M.A., formerly Scholar of Queen's College, Oxford. *Fcap. 8vo.* 2s.

EXERCISES ON LATIN ACCIDENCE. By S. E. WINBOLT, Assistant Master at Christ's Hospital. *Crown 8vo.* 1s. 6d.

An elementary book adapted for Lower Forms to accompany the shorter Latin primer.
'Skilfully arranged.'—*Glasgow Herald.*
'Accurate and well arranged.'—*Athenæum.*

NOTES ON GREEK AND LATIN SYNTAX. By G. BUCKLAND GREEN, M.A., Assistant Master at Edinburgh Academy, late Fellow of St. John's College, Oxon. *Crown 8vo.* 2s. 6d.

Notes and explanations on the chief difficulties of Greek and Latin Syntax, with numerous passages for exercise.
'Supplies a gap in educational literature.'—*Glasgow Herald.*

GERMAN

A COMPANION GERMAN GRAMMAR. By H. DE B. GIBBINS, D. Litt., M.A., Assistant Master at Nottingham High School. *Crown 8vo.* 1s. 6d.

GERMAN PASSAGES FOR UNSEEN TRANSLATION. By E. M'QUEEN GRAY. *Crown 8vo.* 2s. 6d.

SCIENCE

THE WORLD OF SCIENCE. Including Chemistry, Heat, Light, Sound, Magnetism, Electricity, Botany, Zoology, Physiology, Astronomy, and Geology. By R. ELLIOTT STEEL, M.A., F.C.S. 147 Illustrations. *Second Edition. Crown 8vo.* 2s. 6d.

ELEMENTARY LIGHT. By R. E. STEEL. With numerous Illustrations. *Crown 8vo.* 4s. 6d.

ENGLISH

ENGLISH RECORDS. A Companion to the History of England. By H. E. MALDEN, M.A. *Crown 8vo.* 3s. 6d.

A book which aims at concentrating information upon dates, genealogy, officials, constitutional documents, etc., which is usually found scattered in different volumes.

THE ENGLISH CITIZEN: HIS RIGHTS AND DUTIES. By H. E. MALDEN, M.A. 1s. 6d.

A DIGEST OF DEDUCTIVE LOGIC. By JOHNSON BARKER, B.A. *Crown 8vo.* 2s. 6d.

MESSRS. METHUEN'S LIST 39

METHUEN'S COMMERCIAL SERIES
Edited by H. DE B. GIBBINS, D.Litt., M.A.

BRITISH COMMERCE AND COLONIES FROM ELIZABETH TO VICTORIA. By H. DE B. GIBBINS, D.Litt., M.A. 2s. *Second Edition.*

COMMERCIAL EXAMINATION PAPERS. By H. DE B. GIBBINS, D.Litt., M.A., 1s. 6d.

THE ECONOMICS OF COMMERCE. By H. DE B. GIBBINS, D.Litt., M.A. 1s. 6d.

FRENCH COMMERCIAL CORRESPONDENCE. By S. E. BALLY, Modern Language Master at the Manchester Grammar School. 2s. *Second Edition.*

GERMAN COMMERCIAL CORRESPONDENCE. By S. E. BALLY. 2s. 6d.

A FRENCH COMMERCIAL READER. By S. E. BALLY. 2s.

COMMERCIAL GEOGRAPHY, with special reference to Trade Routes, New Markets, and Manufacturing Districts. By L. W. LYDE, M.A., of the Academy, Glasgow. 2s. *Second Edition.*

A PRIMER OF BUSINESS. By S. JACKSON, M.A. 1s. 6d.

COMMERCIAL ARITHMETIC. By F. G. TAYLOR, M.A. 1s. 6d.

PRÉCIS WRITING AND OFFICE CORRESPONDENCE. By E. E. WHITFIELD, M.A. 2s.

WORKS BY A. M. M. STEDMAN, M.A.

INITIA LATINA: Easy Lessons on Elementary Accidence. *Second Edition.* *Fcap. 8vo.* 1s.

FIRST LATIN LESSONS. *Fourth Edition. Crown 8vo.* 2s.

FIRST LATIN READER. With Notes adapted to the Shorter Latin Primer and Vocabulary. *Fourth Edition revised.* 18mo. 1s. 6d.

EASY SELECTIONS FROM CAESAR. Part I. The Helvetian War. 18mo. 1s.

EASY SELECTIONS FROM LIVY. Part I. The Kings of Rome. 18mo. 1s. 6d.

EASY LATIN PASSAGES FOR UNSEEN TRANSLATION. *Fifth Edition. Fcap. 8vo.* 1s. 6d.

EXEMPLA LATINA. First Lessons in Latin Accidence. With Vocabulary. *Crown 8vo.* 1s.

EASY LATIN EXERCISES ON THE SYNTAX OF THE SHORTER AND REVISED LATIN PRIMER. With Vocabulary. *Seventh and cheaper Edition re-written. Crown 8vo.* 1s. 6d. Issued with the consent of Dr. Kennedy.

THE LATIN COMPOUND SENTENCE: Rules and Exercises. *Crown 8vo.* 1s. 6d. With Vocabulary. 2s.

NOTANDA QUAEDAM: Miscellaneous Latin Exercises on Common Rules and Idioms. *Third Edition. Fcap. 8vo.* 1s. 6d. With Vocabulary. 2s.

LATIN VOCABULARIES FOR REPETITION: Arranged according to Subjects. *Sixth Edition. Fcap. 8vo.* 1s. 6d.

A VOCABULARY OF LATIN IDIOMS AND PHRASES. 18mo. Second Edition. 1s.
STEPS TO GREEK. 18mo. 1s.
EASY GREEK PASSAGES FOR UNSEEN TRANSLATION. Third Edition revised. Fcap. 8vo. 1s. 6d.
GREEK VOCABULARIES FOR REPETITION. Arranged according to Subjects. Second Edition. Fcap. 8vo. 1s. 6d.
GREEK TESTAMENT SELECTIONS. For the use of Schools. Third Edition. With Introduction, Notes, and Vocabulary. Fcap. 8vo. 2s. 6d.
STEPS TO FRENCH. Second Edition. 18mo. 8d.
FIRST FRENCH LESSONS. Second Edition. Crown 8vo. 1s.
EASY FRENCH PASSAGES FOR UNSEEN TRANSLATION. Third Edition revised. Fcap. 8vo. 1s. 6d.
EASY FRENCH EXERCISES ON ELEMENTARY SYNTAX. With Vocabulary. Crown 8vo. 2s. 6d.
FRENCH VOCABULARIES FOR REPETITION: Arranged according to Subjects. Fifth Edition. Fcap. 8vo. 1s.

SCHOOL EXAMINATION SERIES

EDITED BY A. M. M. STEDMAN, M.A. *Crown 8vo. 2s. 6d.*

FRENCH EXAMINATION PAPERS IN MISCELLANEOUS GRAMMAR AND IDIOMS. By A. M. M. STEDMAN, M.A. *Ninth Edition.*
A KEY, issued to Tutors and Private Students only, to be had on application to the Publishers. *Fourth Edition. Crown 8vo. 6s. net.*
LATIN EXAMINATION PAPERS IN MISCELLANEOUS GRAMMAR AND IDIOMS. By A. M. M. STEDMAN, M.A. *Eighth Edition.*
KEY (*Third Edition*) issued as above. 6s. net.
GREEK EXAMINATION PAPERS IN MISCELLANEOUS GRAMMAR AND IDIOMS. By A. M. M. STEDMAN, M.A. *Fifth Edition.*
KEY (*Second Edition*) issued as above. 6s. net.
GERMAN EXAMINATION PAPERS IN MISCELLANEOUS GRAMMAR AND IDIOMS. By R. J. MORICH, Manchester. *Fifth Edition.*
KEY (*Second Edition*) issued as above. 6s. net.
HISTORY AND GEOGRAPHY EXAMINATION PAPERS. By C. H. SPENCE, M.A., Clifton College.
SCIENCE EXAMINATION PAPERS. By R. E. STEEL, M.A., F.C.S., Chief Natural Science Master, Bradford Grammar School. *In two vols.* Part I. Chemistry; Part II. Physics.
GENERAL KNOWLEDGE EXAMINATION PAPERS. By A. M. M. STEDMAN, M.A. *Third Edition.*
KEY (*Second Edition*) issued as above. 7s. net.

Printed by T. and A. CONSTABLE, Printers to Her Majesty
at the Edinburgh University Press

www.ingramcontent.com/pod-product-compliance
Lightning Source LLC
Chambersburg PA
CBHW051240300426
44114CB00011B/822